RUNNING Microsoft® Internet Explorer 5

Bryan Pfaffenberger

PUBLISHED BY
Microsoft Press
A Division of Microsoft Corporation
One Microsoft Way
Redmond, Washington 98052-6399

Library of Congress Cataloging-in-Publication Data
Pfaffenberger, Bryan, 1949-
Running Microsoft Internet Explorer 5 / Bryan Pfaffenberger.
p. cm.
Includes index.
ISBN 1-57231-949-6
1. Microsoft Internet Explorer. 2. Internet (Computer network)
3. World Wide Web (information retrieval system) I. Title.
TK5105.883.M53P46 1999
005.7'13769--dc21 98-43580
CIP

Printed and bound in the United States of America.

1 2 3 4 5 6 7 8 9 QMQM 4 3 2 1 0 9

Distributed in Canada by ITP Nelson, a division of Thomson Canada Limited.

A CIP catalogue record for this book is available from the British Library.

Microsoft Press books are available through booksellers and distributors worldwide. For further information about international editions, contact your local Microsoft Corporation office or contact Microsoft Press International directly at fax (425) 936-7329. Visit our Web site at mspress.microsoft.com.

Acquisitions Editor: Christey Bahn
Project Editor: Anne Taussig
Editorial Assistant: Kristen Weatherby

For Suzanne

Chapters at a Glance

Table of Contents

Acknowledgments

Books of this length aren't produced by solitary writers; it's a team effort involving many talented people. I'd like to thank my agent, Carole McClendon, for hooking me up with contacts that eventually led to my relationship with Microsoft Press. Special thanks are due to Christey Bahn (acquisitions editor) and Anne Taussig (project editor) at Microsoft Press, and to all the great folks at Technical Publishing, which handled this book's production, including Bob Kern (production supervisor), Allen Wyke (technical editor), Ellen Fussell (copy editor), Lorraine Elder (compositor), Jessica Ryan (proofreader), and Tim Griffin (indexer). They've burned the midnight oil and cut vacations short to get this book to you—thanks to all.

Bryan Pfaffenberger

Introduction

Welcome to the inside scoop on Microsoft Internet Explorer version 5—the latest version of the leading Web browser. Version 5 builds on the achievements of version 4, which established Internet Explorer's ascendancy among browser packages. You'll find awesome new features that enable you to take full advantage of new Internet media, including Internet radio stations, which are accessible by the new Radio toolbar. And of course, with Internet Explorer version 5, you get a full set of tools for accessing every type of content that's out there, including e-mail, Usenet newsgroups, Web multimedia, VRML (virtual reality) worlds, Internet videoconferencing, and much more. Each of these tools (including version 5 of Outlook Express, the best e-mail program available) has new features—and they're easier to use than ever before. This book shows you how to extract the maximum performance from the best available browser and from all the programs that work with it.

I'm glad you've chosen this book to get the most out of Internet Explorer. You'll find that it's organized to get you up and running quickly, and then build on your skills to take your enjoyment of the Internet to new heights. Internet Explorer, Outlook Express, NetMeeting, and all the rest of the tools discussed in this book are "best of class" programs, one and all; learning them will give you a decisive advantage when it comes to harnessing the information and contacts that the Internet offers. As you gain experience with Internet Explorer, you can use this book as a reference to the many advanced features and capabilities of these programs. To help you find your way, a detailed table of contents, a comprehensive index, and a cross-referencing system will help you find the solutions you need.

Who This Book Is For

This book is for anyone who wants to extract the maximum advantage out of the Internet—and that includes beginners. With easy-to-follow, step-by-step instructions, beginners and experienced Web surfers alike can begin at the level that's most appropriate. And as your knowledge increases, this book takes you to full mastery of Internet Explorer and its associated suite of tools—and that means full mastery of the Internet since there's no better software you can use.

You can use this book either as a tutorial or a reference. If you're new to the Internet, or to any of the Internet resources this book discusses, you can use the step-by-step tutorials to get up to speed quickly. Once you've mastered the essentials, you can return to this book as a handy reference for the many advanced features you'll find in all of the programs discussed.

Why not read a shorter book on Internet Explorer? You can, but you'll miss out on the extensive reference material concerning the advanced features of Internet Explorer version 5 and the additional programs provided with the Internet Explorer software suite. Many of these features hold the key to a pleasant and productive Internet experience; for instance, if you plan to use e-mail, you'll sooner or later want to learn how to write rules that route low-priority incoming mail to named folders, where you can browse these messages at your leisure. Doing so leaves your Inbox uncluttered, so you can see your important messages.

How This Book Is Organized

Internet Explorer version 5 comes with a suite of powerful Internet applications, including Microsoft Media Player for Web-based multimedia, Outlook Express for e-mail and newsgroups, Microsoft Chat for online text chatting, Microsoft NetMeeting for online videoconferencing, and FrontPage Express for do-it-yourself Web publishing. Because all these tools are designed to be used together, you'll be glad to know that a single set of skills will suffice to get you started with all of these applications. Often, this book shows how to use these tools together to enable you to take full advantage of the Internet.

Part I introduces Internet Explorer version 5 and all the rest of the tools included in the Internet Explorer software suite. If you're a newcomer to Microsoft Windows, you'll find a complete introduction to Windows application use, including windows, menu bars, toolbars, scroll bars, and more. You'll learn all the basics you need to use Internet Explorer comfortably and productively.

Part II shows you how to connect your computer to the Internet using the Internet Connection Wizard, an easy-to-use utility that comes with Internet Explorer version 5. If you don't already have an Internet service provider (ISP), you can use the Connection Wizard to find an ISP in your area, and you can sign up online. You'll be online in minutes! If you already have an ISP, you can use the Connection Wizard to establish your existing connection, whether you use a modem or a network connection.

Part III focuses on Internet Explorer version 5 and the World Wide Web—and takes you from the beginning all the way to mastery. You'll learn how to take full advantage of Internet Explorer version 5's new features, including the new Search Assistant, which enables you to peruse a variety of search services until you find just what you're looking for. You'll learn how to transform Internet Explorer version 5 into a personal information appliance of incredible power; you'll store favorite sites, create shortcuts to the information that's most valuable to you, and download content so that you can view all of it—including graphics—when you're offline. To take full advantage of the booming new world of electronic commerce, you'll learn how to make sure that your Web shopping is done with industrial-strength security on your side.

Part IV turns to Internet messaging, and fully explores the incredibly rich features of Outlook Express version 5. You'll go from the basics of e-mail to the most advanced features, including rules for filtering low-priority messages, junk-mail detection for eliminating unwanted commercial advertising, and secure e-mail for ultra-confidential communications. You'll also learn how to participate in online newsgroups. With Microsoft Chat, you'll learn how to join real-time (live) Internet chat groups, and you'll also learn how to get into the exciting world of Internet telephony and videoconferencing with the best software available, Microsoft NetMeeting.

Part V enables you to have your say on the Web. Using FrontPage Express, you can quickly create Web pages that will look as though they were professionally designed. With the tools packaged with FrontPage Express, you can send your page to your Web publishing provider—and before long, other Internet users will be browsing your pages!

Conventions Used in This Book

Throughout this book, you'll find handy, step-by-step instructions for accomplishing tasks, and you'll often find illustrations that show how windows look on screen when you're doing these tasks. In the instructions, you'll find lots of mouse actions, including "click," "double-click," "drag," and "right-click." If you're not familiar with these basic mouse maneuvers, you may wish to read the introductory booklet that came with your copy of Microsoft Windows.

Sometimes, you'll see keyboard shortcuts, such as Ctrl + V. This means, "hold down the Ctrl key and press the V key."

Look for tips throughout this book. Located in shaded boxes, tips provide helpful information that can save you time and make your Internet Explorer experience more rewarding.

Check the margins for See Also cross-references. These tell you when a subject receives additional attention elsewhere in the book.

Installing and Maintaining the Software

This book's CD-ROM contains Internet Explorer version 5 and all the tools discussed in this book, including Outlook Express version 5, Windows Media Player, Microsoft Chat, Microsoft NetMeeting, and Microsoft FrontPage Express. Before you begin Chapter 1, you should install this software by following the instructions in Appendix A.

After you've installed the software, you can quickly check for new versions and accessories by clicking Tools on the Internet Explorer menu bar, and choosing Windows Update from the menu. You'll learn whether any new versions of the software are available, and you'll also have an opportunity to obtain new accessories should they become available.

TIP

> Be sure to choose Windows Update frequently—at least once a month. Despite Microsoft's best efforts, sometimes quality assurance personnel or users discover bugs (errors) in the program code. Usually these are minor, but sometimes they pose some security risks. You'll be wise to obtain the latest versions of the software to make sure you're using the most stable and safest programs available.

PART I

Introducing Internet Explorer 5

CHAPTER 1

A Quick Tour of Internet Explorer 5

Microsoft Internet Explorer 5 is the consummate tool for full use of the Internet and everything that it offers. Included in the Internet Explorer software suite is the best available browser, Internet Explorer, and an armada of accessory programs for almost everything you can do on the Internet, including e-mail, newsgroups, videoconferencing, multimedia, the use of the Internet as a free long-distance telephone, and more. In this chapter, you'll learn what Internet Explorer and the rest of these tools do and how you can use them to place Internet information and entertainment at your fingertips. Once you've understood what's included in the Internet Explorer suite, you'll be ready to get started with Internet Explorer interface basics, the subject of the next chapter.

Introducing Internet Explorer

Welcome to Internet Explorer version 5, Microsoft's Web browser (and application suite) for Internet use. The version 5 release builds on the pioneering achievements of version 4, which established Internet Explorer's reputation as the best available Internet software. The complete Internet Explorer suite contains the following programs and accessories:

- Internet Connection Wizard, for connecting to the Internet effortlessly—this is true whether you're using a dial-up (modem) connection, a local area network (LAN) connection, or cutting-edge connection technologies such as ISDN, a new standard for digital telephone service.
- Microsoft Internet Explorer, the best available Web browser. With Internet Explorer, you can browse the Web, search for information on the Internet, go shopping with excellent security, and save links to your favorite Web sites.
- Microsoft Wallet, a utility that electronically shows your identification and supplies your credit card information when you're shopping online, saving you the trouble of entering this information manually every time you purchase something.
- Microsoft Media Player, an outstanding utility for playing virtually any type of sound or video that you can find on the Internet, including streaming audio and video presentations that begin playing without a lengthy download.
- Microsoft Outlook Express, the best available Internet e-mail and news program, with an impressive list of cutting-edge features such as secure (encrypted) e-mail, junk-mail (spam) filters, HTML (rich formatting) capability, and much more.
- Microsoft NetMeeting, the best available program for placing voice calls via the Internet and collaborating with co-workers—even if they're located on another continent.
- Microsoft Chat, a fun utility for exploring the wackiness of Internet text chatting.
- Microsoft FrontPage Express, the page-editing portion of Microsoft's FrontPage 2000 Web publishing program. With FrontPage Express, you can explore FrontPage's impressive capabilities for editing and formatting Web pages. If you upgrade to FrontPage 2000, part of the Microsoft Office 2000 software suite, you get

the rest of the FrontPage software, which includes the site management software needed to maintain professional Web sites.

- Microsoft Web Publishing Wizard, an easy-to-use utility that enables you to upload your FrontPage Express creations to your Internet service provider's Web publishing directories.

All of these applications are covered in this book and in detail. Later in this chapter, you'll learn what each of them does.

CAUTION

> Internet Explorer version 5 is available for distribution and downloading in a "small footprint" (minimal) version, which does not include many of the above applications. If you've obtained the minimum version, you can obtain additional applications by choosing Tools on the menu bar and selecting Windows Updates. In addition, Internet Explorer version 5 introduces Install-On-Demand technology, which automatically begins downloading any needed components that aren't already installed on your system.

What's the benefit of the Internet Explorer software suite? In a word, *integration*. The Internet Explorer suite of applications uses the same, familiar user interface, so you don't have to learn new concepts and procedures unnecessarily. What's more, the Internet Explorer applications are designed to work smoothly and integrate with Microsoft Windows, as well as with Microsoft's flagship productivity software suite, Microsoft Office 2000.

As you'll learn in this book, Internet Explorer holds the key to transforming the way you use your computer. With Internet Explorer working to pull all your software components together, Microsoft Windows is able to present all the resources available to you in a unified way, whether they're on your local drives, a corporate network, or the Internet. If that's not sufficient incentive, it's worth mentioning that the individual Internet Explorer applications—including the Internet Explorer Web browser, Outlook Express e-mail and news, Windows Media Player, NetMeeting, and more—are consistently winning the "best in class" sweepstakes in independent, critical reviews. The Internet Explorer suite contains the finest software you can use to reap the full benefits of your Internet connection.

TIP

> If you're upgrading to Internet Explorer from Netscape, you can make use of several features designed to make the transition easier. For example, click Internet Explorer's Help menu; you'll find an option called "For Netscape Users." You can import your Netscape bookmarks (favorite sites), and your Netscape Messenger mail messages too.

Introducing the Internet

To understand what the various components of the Internet Explorer software suite do, it's a good idea to begin with a solid understanding of the Internet, including what the Internet is, a little about how it works, and the various services that are available on the Internet. You don't need a lot of technical information to use Internet Explorer, but you'll find that the following concepts will help you understand what Internet Explorer can do.

SEE ALSO
To import your Netscape bookmarks into Internet Explorer, see "Sharing Favorites," page 291. To import your mail from Netscape or Eudora, see "Importing Mail from Another Program," page 327.

Basic Internet Concepts

In brief, the Internet is a public *wide area network* (WAN) that enables any two Internet-connected computers to establish contact and exchange data. Unlike a *local area network* (LAN), a WAN such as the Internet is designed to operate over all geographic distances, large and small. Other WANs exist, but the Internet is remarkable for its enormous size and rapid growth. Current growth forecasts indicate that the Internet will have roughly 200 million users worldwide by the year 2000. It's apparent that the Internet is well on its way to becoming a new public medium, perhaps someday becoming as popular as radio and television.

The same technology that underlies the Internet can also be used to create non-public networks designed for use within an organization. Called *intranets*, these networks work just like the Internet does, and you can use all the Internet Explorer tools to access information on an intranet. Some intranets permit users to access the Internet; check with your network administrator to find out what type of access is permitted. (You may also hear the term *extranet*, which refers to the use of the Internet to connect various intranets that have been made available selectively to outsiders, such as research labs, branch offices, corporate allies, or key customers.) Although this book focuses on Internet use, much of what you'll learn is relevant to intranets, and you'll find notes and special sections devoted to the use of Internet Explorer in an internal corporate network.

Clients and Servers

Local or long distance, computer networks connect computers, and enable them to share data. But the data sharing doesn't happen automatically. To make networks usable, programmers create two kinds of network programs, *servers* and *clients*.

- **Servers** are programs that make information available on a computer network. They are designed so that many other computers

SEE ALSO
Learn more about fundamental Web-server concepts in Chapter 21, "Publishing Your Pages on the Internet."

can access this information simultaneously. Some of the most capable Web servers can make information available to tens or even hundreds of thousands of users. Microsoft Internet Information Server (IIS) is a server program designed to make Web documents available to network users.

- **Clients** are programs that run on users' computers. A client is designed to communicate with a certain type of server. For example, an e-mail client such as Outlook Express communicates with e-mail servers, which receive your incoming messages and send your outgoing messages.

Now you know much of what's needed to understand the Internet Explorer software suite. Basically, Internet Explorer is largely a collection of client programs, each of which is designed to access a certain type of server that's available on the Internet. The suite also contains some utilities and a server.

You also know enough to understand another fundamental Internet concept. The standards-based pairing of a certain type of server and clients is called an *Internet service*. An example of an Internet service is the World Wide Web, which is based on the HyperText Transfer Protocol (HTTP) and enables Web browsers to retrieve information from Web servers. Other popular services include e-mail, newsgroups (Usenet), and file transfer (FTP). You'll explore the various services in a subsequent section; for now, you'll find it helpful to examine Internet standards, called *protocols,* without which Internet services wouldn't exist.

Internet Protocols

Internet services require standards, called *protocols*. In brief, a protocol defines how clients and servers should communicate. What's made the Internet so phenomenally successful is the fact that these protocols are *open protocols*, which are published and freely available for use by anyone without paying a licensing fee. Experience and history show that open protocols benefit everyone. They create a larger market for information products and services. The opposite of an open protocol is a *proprietary protocol*, a trade secret that is created by a company and available only in its products (or those under license from that company).

To understand the benefit of an open protocol, consider the world telephone system. In its early years, telephone systems used proprietary protocols. They served a few customers in urban markets. Using one company's telephone, you could not connect with someone who used another company's telephone. Subsequently, the telephone industry adopted open protocols for telephone services. These protocols are governed by an international agency now called the International Telecommunication Union (ITU), a branch of the United Nations. When these open protocols were adopted, telephones greatly increased in value because users could call more people. Telephone use exploded, and everyone benefited.

Hundreds of protocols govern the various Internet services, and most are maintained by independent standards organizations. These nonprofit organizations, such as the World Wide Web Consortium (W3C), bring together industry practitioners as well as experts drawn from academia and research institutes. Standardized Web protocols include HyperText Transfer Protocol (HTTP), the protocol that defines World Wide Web services, and HyperText Markup Language (HTML), the markup language that underlies the appearance of Web pages.

Microsoft is strongly committed to supporting Internet and Web standards. For example, at this writing, Internet Explorer is the only available Web browser that supports the latest and most sophisticated Web standards, Cascading Style Sheets (CSS) Level 2, eXtensible Markup Language (XML), and the Document Object Model (DOM). You'll learn more about these new protocols in this book, and they will take the Web to a new level of visual appeal, interactivity, and usefulness (see Figure 1-1).

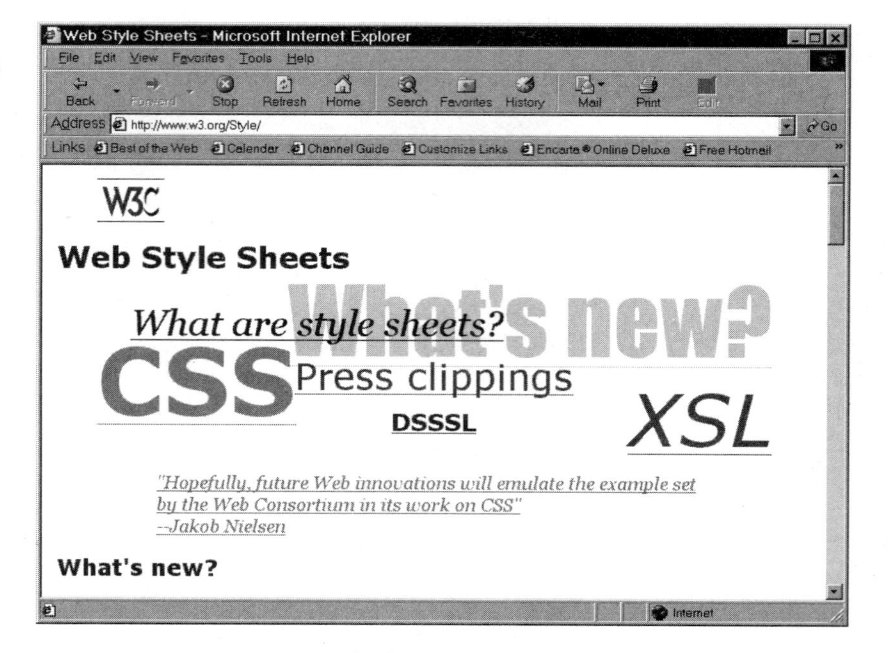

FIGURE 1-1. Cascading Style Sheets (CSS) bring fonts and sophisticated document layouts to the Web, and Internet Explorer provides the best CSS support.

Not all Internet standards are regulated by standards bodies, and some are proprietary, despite the advantages of open protocols. For example, a variety of streaming audio and video formats are competing for dominance of the market for Internet multimedia software. (In streaming audio and video, the multimedia program starts playing before the file has finished downloading.)

Other non-standard protocols are simply too new to have been addressed by standards bodies. When several competing protocols exist, you may have to use several different programs to access the information you want—and that's a hassle that drives users away. Until the standards process finally produces a clear set of protocols that all software follows, there's an advantage to using a market-leading browser such as Internet Explorer, which can deal with all the latest Web standards (including the new CSS and XML standards), as well as a wide variety of proprietary standards.

Internet Services

As you've just learned, a Web service consists of a server program, a client program, and protocols that define how clients and servers interact via the Internet. Here's a list of the most popular Internet services, including an assessment of each service's plusses and minuses. In the next section, you'll learn how Internet Explorer version 5 enables you to access all of these services, and solves many of the problems users are experiencing when they access the Internet.

SEE ALSO
For information on connecting to the Internet, see Part II of this book, entitled "Getting Happily Connected."

- **Internet dialup connections.** Most people access the Internet by means of a *modem*, a telephone line, and a subscription with an Internet service provider (ISP). A modem is a device that enables your computer to exchange information with other computers via telephone connections. By means of Internet protocols such as the Point-to-Point Protocol (PPP), you can connect to an ISP, which gives you a gateway to the entire Internet.

SEE ALSO
For the basics of browser use, see Chapter 5, "Mastering Browser Essentials."

- **World Wide Web.** To use the Web, you need a program called a *browser*, which displays Web pages. On most pages, you see underlined and colored text (called *hyperlinks*) that you can click to go to a different page. What's amazing about the Web is that the new page you see might be stored on the same computer as the original page, or it might be coming from halfway around the world. But the Web's best feature, hypertext navigation, is also its down side. It's easy to get lost as you click link after link. In addition, it's difficult to find information on the Web. Search services such as AltaVista or Hotbot can be used to locate information, but it isn't easy to get good results from these services. Important Web standards include HyperText Transfer Protocol (HTTP), HyperText Markup Language (HTML), Cascading Style Sheets (CSS), Document Object Model (DOM), and eXtensible Markup Language (XML).

SEE ALSO

To learn how Internet Explorer protects your security while you're shopping online, see "Introducing Public-Key Cryptography," page 226. For information on online shopping, see "Shopping Safely on the Internet," page 233.

- **Electronic commerce.** After a slow start due to security concerns, electronic commerce is now growing at an estimated 200 percent annual clip. A recent survey disclosed that one out of every eight U.S. citizens has already made an online purchase. Electronic commerce is poised to transform the consumer market and will play an even greater role in business-to-business transactions. Thanks to security protocols such as Secure Sockets Layer (SSL), you can safely upload your credit card information to secure commerce sites such as market leader Amazon.com, which offers more than 2.5 million books and music for online ordering. Although millions of consumers are ordering online, problems remain. For example, merchants would like to have a way of determining the identity of somebody ordering online in the same way that some stores ask you to show your driver's license when you use a credit card. This would help to cut down losses due to credit card fraud. One proposed solution is the Secure Electronic Transactions (SET) standard, jointly developed by MasterCard, Visa, Microsoft, and other firms. SET employs an electronic ID that cannot be falsified. Other electronic commerce standards include Secure Sockets Layer security for secure transmission of credit card information via the Internet.

Learn how to use Microsoft Media Player in Chapter 8, "Grooving on Multimedia."

- **Internet multimedia.** It's possible to listen to music and watch videos over the Internet, but slow modem connections ensure that your home stereo and TV systems aren't about to become obsolete. Still, the Internet is an ideal medium for distributing short audio and video programs. What's held back the development of Internet audio and video is the profusion of conflicting standards. Microsoft Media Player deals with this situation by supporting nearly all of them, enabling you to enjoy Internet multimedia without worrying about which program you're going to run.

- **FTP.** Short for File Transfer Protocol, FTP enables Internet users to receive (download) as well as send (upload) computer files via the Internet, including graphics, audio, video, and software. The FTP standard ensures that the files are transferred without error. Some FTP sites offer anonymous FTP, which enables you to access public FTP file archives and download software. In the past, you had to use a separate FTP program if you wanted to upload (send) files to FTP servers. Thanks to Internet Explorer version 5, that's no longer true. Internet Explorer can now access private FTP sites, and enables you to log on using your user name and password. In addition, you can upload files just as easily as if you were working with the files on your computer. You just drag them from their current location and drop them into the remote FTP directory, and it's all done with Internet Explorer.

SEE ALSO
Learn the fundamentals of Internet e-mail in Chapter 11,"Introducing Outlook Express."

- **Electronic mail.** Generally known as e-mail, electronic mail is fast becoming indispensable for personal and professional communication. With e-mail, you can type and send a message to somebody, and it's received almost immediately. You can also attach documents, images, voice recordings, and videos to your message. However, e-mail isn't secure; your messages could be intercepted and read while they're en route, and many users complain of information overload due to too many incoming mail messages and *spam* (unsolicited commercial mail). Outlook Express offers excellent tools for coping with information overload, including rules that automatically filter incoming mail to named folders. Important e-mail protocols include Simple Mail Transfer Protocol (SMTP) for receiving mail, version 3 of the Post Office Protocol (POP3), version 4 of the Internet Message Access Protocol (IMAP) for receiving mail, and Secure Multipurpose Internet Mail Extensions (S/MIME) for secure e-mail.

SEE ALSO
Explore the riches (and weirdness) of Usenet in Chapter 16,"Joining Newsgroups."

- **Usenet.** Something like a letters-to-the-editor column on a global scale, Usenet enables an Internet user to post a message that can be accessed by many people. But there's not just one newspaper. Usenet includes more than 25,000 topically named discussion groups, called *newsgroups*, which contain messages from people all over the world. You'll also see replies to these messages, and your Usenet software, called a *newsreader*, groups these messages so you can see the flow of debate on a topic. Although there's a great deal of nonsense on Usenet, you'll also find thousands of serious newsgroups devoted to practical and technical subjects. You can use Outlook Express to read Usenet and to post your own messages. Like e-mail, Usenet presents problems of information overload. You'll need a way to organize and search messages for content of interest to you. Outlook Express solves this problem by enabling you to write rules that filter out unwanted messages, highlight the content that's most valuable to you, and organize messages for quick, productive reading. Usenet is supported by the Network News Transport Protocol (NNTP).

SEE ALSO
Get into IRC in Chapter 17, "Talking It Up with Microsoft Chat."

- **Internet Relay Chat (IRC).** Can you socialize on the Internet? You bet. IRC enables you to join real-time chat groups with other Internet users. This interchange is strictly text-based; you type a message, and everyone in the chat group sees it. You get replies, and soon you're in the middle of a conversation. If you'd like to talk privately to somebody, you can "whisper" so that just that one person hears, or the two of you can go to a private room. IRC is fun, but it isn't always a friendly or safe environment. For example, you'll need a way to find out who's in a chat room before entering. Microsoft Chat, the full-featured IRC client included within the Internet Explorer software suite, enables you to scan a chat room before entering, and offers many additional ways to make sure your IRC experience is a happy one. IRC is defined by the Internet Relay Chat protocol.

SEE ALSO
Explore Internet telephony and conferencing in Chapter 18, "Collaborating Online with Microsoft NetMeeting."

- **Internet telephony/videoconferencing.** You can use the Internet like a telephone. And what's more, it's free, even for long distance. (You place your "call" to somebody's computer, though, so this option is limited to exchanges between people who both have Internet connections and suitably equipped computers.) Advances in compression technology enable you to send and receive video, too. Those "picture telephones" you see in science fiction movies are close to becoming a reality! Microsoft NetMeeting, part of the Internet Explorer suite of software, is the most advanced program available for Internet telephony and videoconferencing. Although these applications are fun, they're not very useful if the people you're calling aren't online. You'll need a way to find out whether the users you're calling are on the Internet. Microsoft NetMeeting, the videoconferencing and Internet telephony program that's included with the Internet Explorer software suite, solves this problem by means of Internet-based locator services, which enable you to find out who's online. Audio and video conferencing via the Internet is regulated by the H.323 standard.

- **Web publishing.** One of the best things about the Internet is that you can create your own Web pages. Millions of people have created home pages, and so can you. In the past, you had to learn HyperText Markup Language (HTML) to do this, and it's time-consuming. You need a way to create good-looking Web pages without learning HTML. Thanks to FrontPage Express, the Web authoring program included with the Internet Explorer software suite, you can create fantastic-looking Web pages without having to write a line of HTML code.

Internet Explorer and Year 2000 (Y2K)

When the clock strikes midnight on December 31, 1999, many computers and computer programs will stop functioning correctly. The reason? Designers and programmers did not allow sufficient room for recording and tracking years with four digits. Instead, they used two digits. The result? In the year 2000, some systems will indicate "00" in the area used to store information about the year. Some programs may interpret this to mean "1900," which could have disastrous results if not corrected. For example, a payment-tracking system may conclude that your bill is 100 years overdue, and hit you with a bill for the accumulated interest!

Year 2000 (Y2K) problems are serious, and may cost the world economy hundreds of billions of dollars to resolve. In view of the gravity of this problem, it's essential that you make sure that every program you run can handle dates such as 2000 or 2001 without introducing errors.

If you're still using an old version of Internet Explorer (version 4.0 or earlier), you should know that this older software does not fully implement year 2000 safeguards. There's no danger of wiping out your bank account, but you'll be wise to upgrade to Internet Explorer version 5.

What's New in the Software?

If you've used a previous version of the Internet Explorer applications, you'll notice some subtle on-screen improvements right away. For example, the toolbars look more like Microsoft Office toolbars, and they work the way Office toolbars do. As you explore version 5, you'll find many thoughtful improvements, all of which are designed to make the use of Internet Explorer more enjoyable and less confusing. For those readers who have used previous versions of the software, this section briefly examines the new features of Internet Explorer version 5. All of these features are discussed in detail later in this book.

TIP

If you're new to Internet Explorer, you can skip this section. All the information that's mentioned here is introduced and explained in subsequent chapters of this book.

Version 5: What's Under the Hood?

The most important version 5 changes involve underlying program changes that aren't obvious in Internet Explorer's menus and toolbars. But they're *very* obvious when you access Web sites that take full advantage of Internet Explorer's new support for Web programming standards. These standards include Cascading Style Sheets (CSS) for magazine-quality page layouts, the Document Object Model (DOM) for scripts that bring action and interactivity to Web pages, and eXtensible Markup Language (XML) for interpreting rich, structured data. Just what all this means in practice will become apparent as developers take full advantage of version 5's new capabilities. For example, you'll see better-looking Web pages with reliable, on-screen fonts. And because version 5's DOM support enables developers to create scripts much more easily, you'll see more Web pages with dynamic features, such as lists that automatically expand when you move the pointer over an item. Unless you're a developer, you don't need to learn anything new to take full advantages of version 5's improved capabilities. Just browse the Web and enjoy!

Internet Explorer 5 *looks* very much like version 4. As you delve more deeply into the program, though, you'll see that the Internet Explorer development team has worked hard to make the program—and the Internet—easier to use. But ease of use isn't the only feature with which developers were concerned. The version 5 team wanted to make Internet Explorer more useful for users of notebook computers and Microsoft Office.

New Features in Internet Explorer

You'll find many usability improvements throughout Internet Explorer. Compared to previous versions, version 5 is easier and less confusing to use. Highlights include Explorer-like support for FTP, improved integration with Microsoft Office, and support for new, advanced Web standards.

Address Bar

Internet Explorer's Address Bar shows the current Internet location of the Web page you're viewing. To access Web addresses, you often directly type URLs (Uniform Resource Locators) in the Address Bar. But it's easy to make mistakes. In version 5, the program automatically corrects common typing errors (such as "www," or "http;"). You'll find improvements in AutoComplete, the utility that guesses the URLs you're typing. For example, you can choose alternative completions from a pop-up menu. You can even type page titles (or portions of page titles) in the Address Bar.

Channels

Introduced in version 4, channels provide a way to subscribe to Web sites, so that you can receive regularly scheduled updates. You can display the subscribed sites in your screen saver or on your desktop if you wish. Although channels are nifty, version 4's interface made them somewhat confusing to use. For example, what's the difference between a channel and a favorite? Like channels, Favorites enabled you to specify subscriptions and other channel-like options.

Version 5 eliminates the confusion by presenting channels separately. Gone from Internet Explorer's toolbar is the Channels button. You can still subscribe to a channel by clicking a subscription link at any Web site that offers channel subscriptions.

Just as channels have been separated from Favorites and simplified, Favorites have also been simplified. The process of "subscribing" to favorite Web sites is now linked to Internet Explorer version 5's nifty new offline browsing features, which enable you to download *all* of a site's content—including graphics, scripts, applets, the works—and browse this content when you're not connected to the computer.

Explorer Bar

In version 5, the Explorer bar is much easier to use, and works more smoothly. All the Explorer bars work the same way, reducing confusion.

Explorer bars now have title bars, which include helpful buttons. When you're viewing items in the History Explorer bar, for example, you can click Add to add the selected item to your Favorites list. Trying to get back to that cool site you visited a few days ago? You can search the history list, and sort it by date or the order in which you accessed sites.

FTP Support

Internet Explorer has always been able to access FTP sites for file downloading. Version 5 adds a new dimension of FTP support by presenting FTP file directories in a Windows Explorer view (see Figure 1-2), just the way you see files on your own computer. What's more, you can download and upload files by dragging and dropping—again, just as you would on your own computer system.

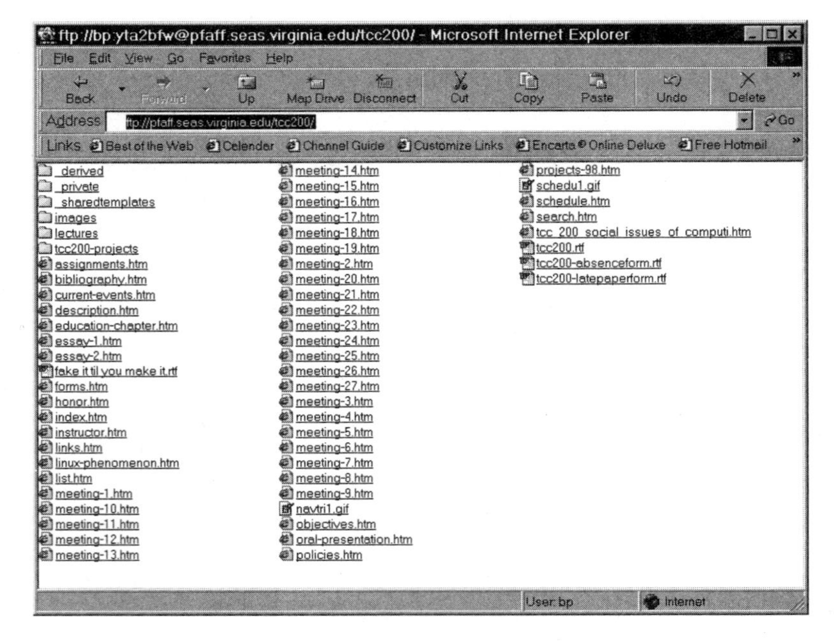

FIGURE 1-2.
Internet Explorer gives you drag-and-drop file capabilities when you access FTP sites. You can work with FTP files just like you work with files on your own system.

Favorites

If you like to save your preferred Web sites to the Favorites list, you'll be glad to know that version 5 makes it much easier to organize your favorite sites. You can also import Netscape bookmarks and export your favorites to an HTML file, which you can mail to other Internet users (or publish on the Web).

Offline Browsing

Imagine this scenario. You need to look at some documents on the Web, or on a corporate intranet. Trouble is, you're traveling. You can log on briefly using the hotel's Internet connection, but you can't stay online for hours. With Internet Explorer version 5, this isn't a problem, thanks to the program's new support for offline browsing. Integrated with the Favorites options, offline browsing enables you to download *all* of the content at a site, including graphics, scripts, and multimedia. When you're traveling or otherwise unable to stay logged on for a long period, you can download the sites you want, log off, and browse them later, at your convenience—even if you're not connected to the Internet.

You can also optimize Outlook Express for offline use. If you're traveling or can't stay online for a prolonged period, you can download newsgroup messages in full, and then read them while you're not connected to your computer. For information on using offline Usenet, see "Reading the News," page 519.

The Office Connection

Over the last 15 years, personal computers have taken the enterprise by storm, and wound up on the desktops of millions of employees. Companies have equipped these computers with productivity software, such as the Microsoft Office suite, currently the best-selling software suite on the market. Personal computers and productivity software have brought many benefits, but they also create a problem. The documents employees create are locked up in their computers. However, much of the work people do now involves collaboration. In large corporations, for example, an estimated 80 percent of all documents are collaboratively written. Employees can exchange documents by e-mailing them as attachments, or by making them available on FTP servers, but these solutions are cumbersome and require some technical savvy. The Web hasn't offered a solution, either. You can't simply place these documents on the Internet, because they're saved in proprietary file formats that the Web doesn't support. And if you translate them to HTML, the markup language used to code Web documents, they lose the refined appearance, page numbers, revision marks, and other features that have made productivity software so useful.

Working with Microsoft Internet Explorer version 5, Microsoft Office 2000 solves these problems. The solution, called *round-tripping*, works in two different ways. First, Internet Explorer version 5 can open any Office document, and make this document available for editing. (You must have Office 2000 installed on your system in order to take advantage of this feature.) To work on a document you're creating collaboratively, you use Internet Explorer to access and edit the document. Once you've completed your editing, you can save the document to the server (as long as it supports Microsoft's FrontPage extensions), and the whole process is just as easy as saving the document to your own system. In this solution, you're working with the native Office file formats.

The second approach is the most exciting. Using cutting-edge Web standards, Microsoft engineers have developed a way to encode Office files using open Web protocols: Cascading Style Sheets (CSS) Level 2, eXtensible Markup Language (XML), and the latest version of HTML, version 4.0. With this solution, authors will be able to publish richly formatted documents on the Web, and these documents will be accessible to any Internet user who has a CSS- and XML-compliant browser. These documents will retain all or most of the Office documents' formats, and will look visually appealing on any Web-capable system. If the user's system is equipped with Office 2000, the user will also be able to print the document with page numbering, headers, and footers—a level of functionality that the Web currently lacks.

Want to know when somebody has altered a document you're collaborating on? Use Internet Explorer version 5 to subscribe to the document. You'll receive automatic e-mail notification when the document has been altered.

The Office Connection ***continued***

Internet Explorer 5's support for Microsoft Office extends to all the Office applications, including PowerPoint, Excel, and Access. This support is so well integrated with the browser that it's necessary to think of Internet Explorer in a new way. In addition to offering great Web browsing, Internet Explorer is now the best way to access and share Office documents in a networked environment.

Performance Improvements

Internet Explorer version 5 will display some Web pages much more quickly, thanks to a bevy of under-the-hood technical improvements. Version 5 executes scripts much more quickly, thanks to complete revision of the program's script interpreting engine. If you access tables with fixed column widths, the program can start displaying the table right away, even if the page hasn't finished downloading, thanks to version 5's support for HTML progressive table rendering.

Search Assistant

Many Internet users find that it's difficult to find information on the Web. Key problems: users don't realize that search services have differing database coverage, and that a successful search often requires conducting the same search at two or more search services.

Version 5's new Search Assistant breaks new ground by focusing on the search task you're trying to accomplish rather than encouraging you to limit your search to one search service such as AltaVista or Yahoo. To initiate your search, you select a database category (such as Web pages, people, or software), and you enter search terms. You see the results in the Search explorer (see Figure 1-3). Here's the cool part: with a click of the mouse, you can repeat your search with additional search engines. You get much better results overall, and what's more, you can customize the Search Assistant so that it works with your favorite search services.

Toolbars

Version 5 introduces a cool new feature: a customizable toolbar. You can decide just which tools you want on your toolbar, and you can change the order in which they appear. If you're using Microsoft Office, you may wish to customize Internet Explorer version 5's toolbars so that they look like Office toolbars. For example, if some tools aren't visible because the window isn't wide enough, you see an arrow that you can click to display a drop-down menu. This menu contains the hidden toolbar icons.

Click here to repeat the same search in the next search engine.

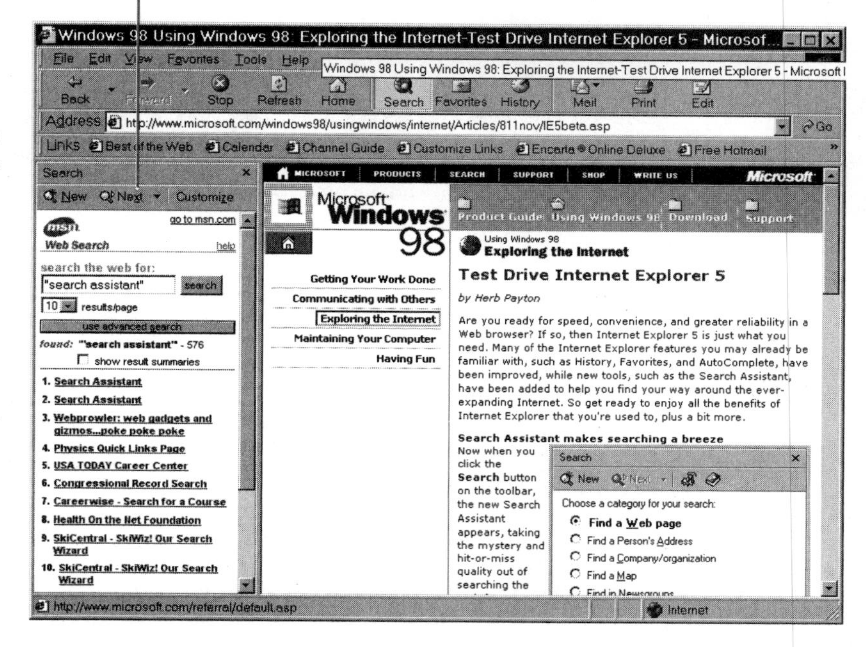

FIGURE 1-3.
The Search Assistant enables you to repeat a search in several search engines, increasing your chances of actually finding what you're looking for.

Radio Toolbar

A cool new feature of Internet Explorer version 5 is the Radio toolbar, which enables you to "tune in" to any one of tens of thousands of Internet "radio stations." These sites broadcast live or recorded audio content in every conceivable listening category, ranging from the broadcast options you hear on ordinary radios (news, sports, weather, rock, jazz, and classical) all the way to the far-out fringes of musical taste. You'll need a sound card and speakers to listen to Internet radio.

XML Support

Perhaps the most important news about version 5 is the program's support for tags written in XML, short for eXtensible Markup Language. In brief, XML enables Web authors to invent their own tags to describe their sites' unique content. For example, a Web page could contain XML tags for storing bibliographic information (HTML doesn't provide tags for this purpose). Using Cascading Style Sheets (CSS), Web authors can assign distinctive formats to these tags. XML enables a host of exciting new Web applications, including improved searching and new ways to navigate documents. You don't need to understand the technical details of CSS and XML to benefit from them. With Internet Explorer version 5, the Web will come alive with beautiful, magazine-quality document layouts and rich, interactive data.

New Features in Additional Internet Explorer Applications

You'll find additional new features in all the applications included within the Internet Explorer suite.

Chat

A new version of Microsoft Chat brings welcome new features, including the ability to search for the first available server and discover who's in a chat room prior to entering. As always, you can choose text chat, or take advantage of Comic Chat, in which you, and others in the chat room, appear in graphical form as comic characters.

FrontPage Express

In Internet Explorer version 5, FrontPage Express is essentially the Editor component of Microsoft's FrontPage 2000, the leading software for professional Web publishing. With FrontPage Express, you can create and edit Web pages using most of the tools available to FrontPage 2000 users. You can publish your pages on your Internet service provider's computer using Web Publishing Wizard. If you're lucky enough to be working on a computer with a fixed Internet address, you can use Personal Web Server to transform your computer into a fully functional Web server.

Can you publish your own Web pages from your computer? To do so, you need a permanent Internet address (also called an IP address). Most dial-up (modem) users do not have a permanent Internet address, because their Internet service provider assigns a temporary address when they log on. If you're using a computer that's connected to a corporate or university network, you may have a permanent Internet address. Check with your network administrator to find out whether you can publish Web pages from your computer, and if so, how you can get permission to do so. Be sure to check your organization's acceptable use policies to find out what type of pages you can publish.

Media Player

The new Microsoft Media Player replaces a variety of helper applications found in previous versions of Internet Explorer, including Active Movie and NetShow. Media Player can play a variety of audio and video formats, including RealAudio, RealVideo, and NetShow streaming formats.

NetMeeting

The newest version of NetMeeting takes Internet audio and video conferencing to a new level, offering acceptable video images even over a 28.8 Kbps modem connection. You can view video even if your computer doesn't have a video capture card, an accessory needed to create video images for video conferencing. In addition, NetMeeting fully supports the Intel MMX multimedia extensions, resulting in faster video and less demand on your processor.

Outlook Express

The latest version of Outlook Express improves on an already strong product. You'll find a more attractive user interface, better integration with the Windows Address Book, enhancements to incoming message filter rules, more stationery templates, and a new, customizable toolbar.

Wallet

SEE ALSO
Explore Wallet's nifty new capabilities in "Using Microsoft Wallet," page 240.

A new and welcome feature of Microsoft Wallet is support for the new Secure Electronic Transactions (SET) standard for secure electronic transactions, which was jointly developed by leading credit card companies, banks, and computer firms. This standard will help to assure a bright future for electronic commerce by greatly reducing the risk of credit card fraud.

Starting and Quitting Internet Explorer

In applications in the Internet Explorer suite of applications, all applications are Windows applications, and have the same overall appearance as any Windows application. In the next chapter, you'll review basics about using application windows and other fundamentals. Here, you'll learn how to start Internet Explorer, get help within the browser, and quit an application.

Starting Internet Explorer or Outlook Express

You can start Internet Explorer or Outlook Express in any of the following three ways (see Figure 1-4):

- Click the Start button, point to Programs and select the Internet Explorer or Outlook Express application.

- Click the Internet Explorer or Outlook Express icon on the taskbar.
- Click the Internet Explorer or Outlook Express icon on the desktop.

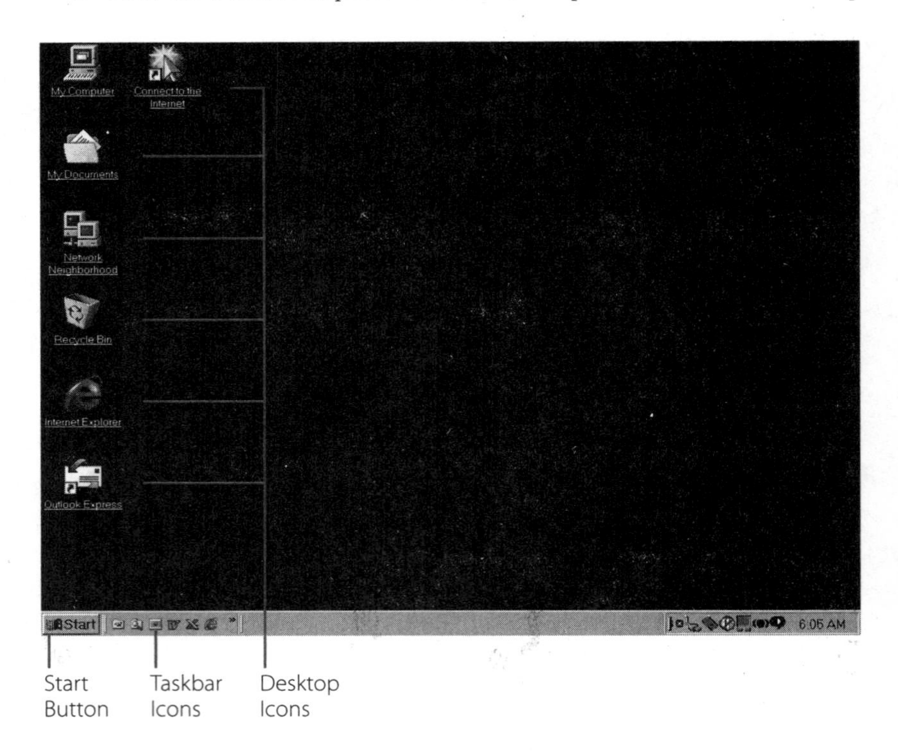

FIGURE 1-4. You can start Internet Explorer or Outlook Express in any of the indicated ways.

Starting Other Internet Explorer Applications

To start other Internet Explorer applications directly, use the Start menu, point to Programs, point to Internet Explorer, and select the application you want from the menu. If you don't see the application you're looking for, you may need to install it. In Internet Explorer, click Tools on the menu bar, and choose Windows Updates.

> **SEE ALSO**
> If you're new to Microsoft Windows, learn the basics of what's on-screen in Chapter 2, "Learning Internet Explorer Basics."

Switching between Internet Explorer Applications

Once you've started Internet Explorer, you can read your e-mail or news messages easily. Just click the Mail icon on the toolbar, and choose Read Mail or Read News. If you've hidden the toolbar, you can click Tools on the menu bar, and then choose Mail And News. Choose Read Mail or Read News from the submenu.

Once you have started more than one Internet Explorer application, you can use the Windows taskbar to switch between these applications. The *current* or *foreground* application, the one that's running and displayed on the screen, has a highlighted button, as shown in the following:

The *background* applications (running programs that aren't in the foreground) aren't highlighted. To make one of these applications active and place it in the foreground, just click the button on the taskbar.

Using the Help System

Need help with Internet Explorer or any of the applications in the software suite? You can obtain assistance by using the Help menu included with every Internet Explorer application. Each application's Help window includes a toolbar and tabs, which are explained in the following sections.

Use ScreenTips to get information about items you see on-screen. To view a ScreenTip, move the mouse pointer over the item, and let it "hover" there for a couple of seconds. You'll see a ScreenTip in a yellow box.

Help Window Toolbar

When you choose Contents and Index from the Help menu, you'll see a window with the following tools:

Here's what these tools do:

- **Hide.** This button hides the left portion of the window, enabling you to concentrate on the Help document displayed on the right portion of the Help window. When you've hidden the left portion of this window, the button's name changes to Show. To re-display the left portion of the window, click Show.
- **Back** and **Forward.** These buttons work just like the Back and Forward buttons in your browser. They enable you to go back to previously viewed Help windows (Back button), or to return to more recently viewed ones if you've gone back (Forward but-

ton). If a button is dimmed, it's unavailable.

- **Options.** This button displays a menu. On this menu, you'll find options for all the toolbar functions, as well as a Print command that enables you to print the help topic you're currently viewing. Also available is a list of recently viewed Help windows.
- **Web Help.** This button provides links to relevant Microsoft Web sites.

Tabs in the Help Window

In the Help window, you'll see the following tabs:

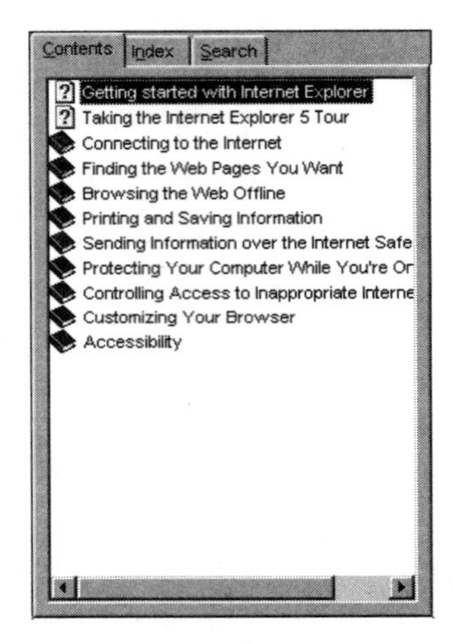

If you're switching from Netscape Navigator to Internet Explorer, click Help on the menu bar, and choose For Netscape Users. (You need to be connected to the Internet to use this feature.) You'll see a Microsoft Web site that's loaded with information that will make this switch as painless as possible.

Here's how to use these tabs to find the information you need:

- **Contents.** This tab contains an overview of Help contents, arranged by broad, general topics, such as "Getting Started with Internet Explorer" or "Connecting to the Internet." Start here to locate the subject on which you need help. If you can't find the subject here, go on to the next tab, Index.
- **Index.** This tab contains a lengthy, alphabetical list of help top-

ics, such as "accelerator keys" or "docking toolbars." To select a topic, you can scroll through the list or type the first few letters of the topic in the text box. To view a topic, select the topic's name and click Display. If you still can't find what you're looking for, go on to the next tab, Search.

- **Search.** This tab enables you to search for a word appearing anywhere within the Help documents. Type the word in the text box, and click List Topics to see all the help topics that contain this word. If you see a topic that's related to your needs, select it, and click Display.

Using Online Support

If you're having trouble solving a problem with any of the Internet Explorer applications, you can use Microsoft's Online Support. You must be connected to the Internet to use this feature.

To use Online Support, open Internet Explorer, click Help on the menu bar, and choose Online Support. You'll see the Support Online page, as shown in Figure 1-5. In other Internet Explorer applications, you can access Online Support by clicking Help on the menu bar, choosing Microsoft on the Web, and clicking Online Support or Frequently Asked Questions.

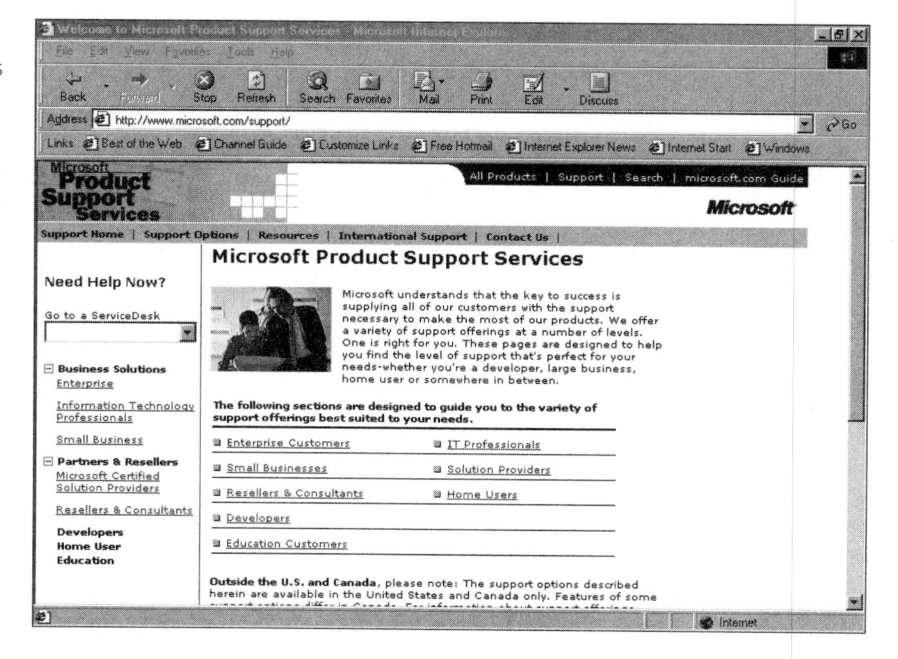

FIGURE 1-5.
Support Online enables you to search the Microsoft Knowledge Base for detailed technical information.

SEE ALSO
For information about search concepts and techniques, see Chapter 6, "Finding the Best Content."

Support Online offers two views, Basic and Advanced. You can try Basic View, but you'll get the best results from Advanced View—particularly if you know a few basics about searching for information on the Internet.

Once you've displayed Support Online as discussed above, follow these steps:

1 If you don't see the Advanced Search options, find the link that displays these options.

2 In the box labeled "My search is about," choose your application's name.

3 In the option button list titled "I want to search by," choose one of the following search options:

   - **Keywords.** Type one or more words that describe the concept you're looking for. To describe a phrase, enclose the phrase in quotation marks (for example, "accelerator keys"). You can use Boolean operators too (including AND, OR, NOT, and NEAR).

   - **Specific article ID number.** Use this option if you're trying to locate a document for which you have the exact article ID number. Each of the documents in Support Online has such a number.

   - **Specific driver or downloadable file.** Use this option if you know the specific file name of the driver or file you want help for.

   - **Specific troubleshooting tool.** To find a troubleshooting wizard for the problem you're having, choose this option and type a keyword that describes your problem.

   - **Natural language search.** Use this option to ask a question, such as "How do I save a favorite site?" Be sure to type a question and place a question mark at the end.

   - **What's new.** To see all the new documents for a subject, choose this option, and select the number of days.

4 Type your keywords or question in the My Question Is box. You can also use a built-in option, such as "Err or Error" or "Er Msg" (searches for information about error messages), or "My last 10 searches" (re-displays information you've previously accessed).

5 Click Find. Unless your search retrieved no results, you'll see a list of documents. Click a document's title to view the text.

Getting Product News and Updates

It's important to keep up with new Internet Explorer developments. If a flaw or security hole is discovered, you may need to download a *patch* (a program that updates your software to correct the problem). New versions of your software may become available too. Stay informed by visiting the following Web sites.

NOTE

> Please bear in mind that Microsoft is constantly improving its Web pages, so the Web page you access may look different (and have more features) than the ones discussed here. That's true of every Web site discussed in this book. On the Web, the only certainty is change!

Internet Explorer Home

Internet Explorer's home page, located at www.microsoft.com/ie (see Figure 1-6), has the latest news about the Internet Explorer software suite. You can access the Internet Explorer home page by clicking Internet Explorer News on the Links toolbar, or by typing the page's address in the Address Bar. On this page, you'll find information about product upgrades, including notices of *critical upgrades* that may affect Internet Explorer's reliability or security.

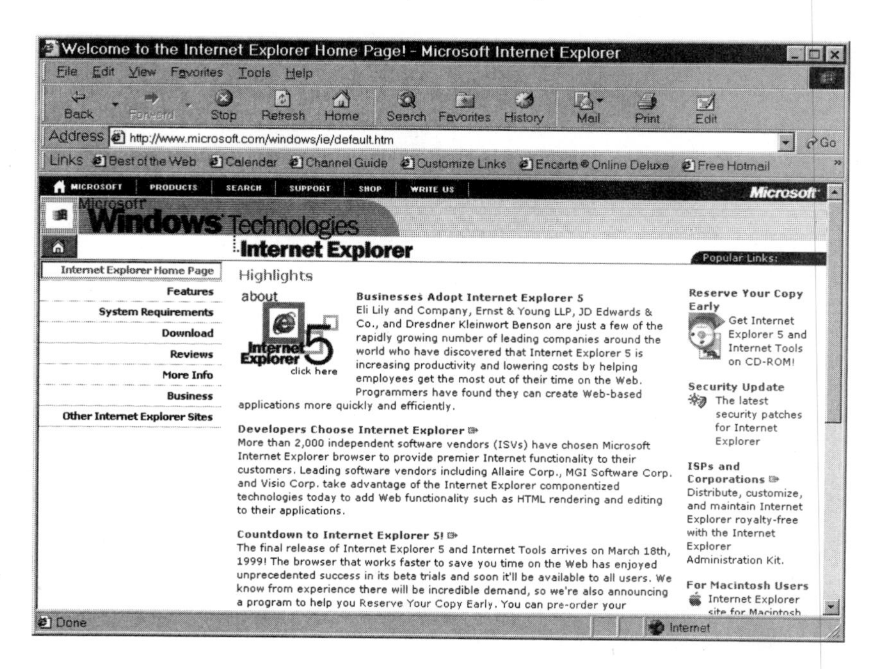

FIGURE 1-6. Internet Explorer's home page may look different when you visit it, but it's sure to have the latest news about Internet Explorer (including program updates).

Windows Updates

To find out whether you're running the latest version of the Internet Explorer applications and utilities, click Tools on the Internet Explorer menu bar, and choose Windows Updates. You'll be asked whether it's OK to check your system for installed software; click Yes, or just press Enter. You'll see a list of the latest Internet Explorer applications. This list indicates whether you've installed these applications. If you see an application or update that you'd like to have, just click the check box, and click Next. Follow the on-screen instructions to download and install your new software.

Quitting Internet Explorer

When you're finished using Internet Explorer, you should quit the browser properly—and the same goes when you're finished using your computer. Follow these instructions to quit Internet Explorer correctly:

To quit an Internet Explorer application, do one of the following:

- From the File menu, choose Close.
- Click the Close button in the title bar (it's the "X" in the upper right-hand corner).
- Press Alt + F4.
- On the taskbar, click the application's taskbar button with the right mouse button, and choose Close from the pop-up menu.

To quit Microsoft Windows, click Start, choose Shut Down, and select Shut Down from the dialog box.

CHAPTER 2

Learning Internet Explorer Basics

Internet Explorer and the rest of the programs in the Internet Explorer software suite share consistent user-interface features. (A *user interface* is the part of the program that interacts with you, the user.) If you spend a little time learning about these features, you'll find that working with these applications goes more smoothly.

The Internet Explorer applications are well-designed Microsoft Windows applications, and their user interfaces closely resemble other Windows programs, such as those in Microsoft Office. If you're already familiar with Microsoft Windows and Windows applications, you already know much of the material that's covered in this chapter. Still, it's worth skimming this chapter because the Internet Explorer applications offer some unique features that you'll want to learn. This chapter also details Internet Explorer's accessibility features for people with disabilities.

Understanding Mouse Terminology

If you're new to Windows, you'll find it helpful to learn a few essential terms related to mouse usage:

- **Point.** Move the mouse so that the *tip* of the arrow is over an item. You use this action frequently to *select* an on-screen item. When you've selected an item, it appears in reverse video (or sometimes with a dotted rectangle around it). If you subsequently request an action, this action will be performed on the selected item.
- **Hover.** Leave the mouse pointer over an item for a couple of seconds. If a *tooltip* is associated with this item, you'll see a small rectangle containing the tip.
- **Click.** While pointing to something on-screen, press and quickly release the left mouse button. Clicking is often used to choose an item.
- **Right-click.** While pointing to something on-screen, click the right mouse button. Right-clicking brings up a context-related pop-up menu, which shows available options for the area in which you clicked.
- **Double-click.** Click the left mouse button two times, in rapid succession.
- **Drag.** Point to something on the screen, hold down the left mouse button, and move the mouse (while you're still holding the button down).

TIP

To adjust mouse settings, including double-clicking speed, click Start on the taskbar, point to Settings, and choose Control Panel. Choose Mouse, and use the tabs to view your mouse control options.

While you're learning Internet Explorer applications, take some time to explore right-clicking. Point at various portions of the window, and click the right mouse button. You'll find that the pop-up menus contain options relevant to the area you've clicked. Right-clicking often provides the fastest and most convenient way to choose these options.

Microsoft's IntelliMouse: The Ideal Mouse for Web Browsing

When you're browsing the Web, you'll do a lot of scrolling, because most Web pages are larger than Internet Explorer's window. But it's a hassle to scroll windows using the scroll bar and scroll arrows. Microsoft's IntelliMouse solves this problem by adding a much-needed mouse feature: a scrolling wheel. Your index finger rests naturally on the wheel when you grip the mouse. To scroll the window, simply rotate the wheel. AutoScroll enables you to scroll through any lengthy document at an automatic scrolling speed; when you've found the scrolling speed you like, you can sit back and read the document without manipulating window controls.

Using Application Windows

For detailed information about Internet Explorer's window, see "Understanding What's on the Screen," page 96.

Internet Explorer's application windows provide the tools you need to access all the popular Internet services, including the World Wide Web, FTP, e-mail, Usenet, IRC, and more. In this section, you'll learn about the features that all Internet Explorer applications share, and you'll learn how to size and position these windows like a Windows pro.

Common Features in Application Windows

All of the Internet Explorer applications have the features discussed in this section (see Figure 2-1).

Title Bar

This rectangular bar appears at the top of every Internet Explorer application. It tells you what you're looking at, such as the title of a Web page, followed by the name of the application, as in the following illustration:

Excite - Microsoft Internet Explorer 

On the title bar, you'll see controls that are used to move, size, minimize, and maximize windows. You'll learn what these controls do in subsequent sections of this chapter.

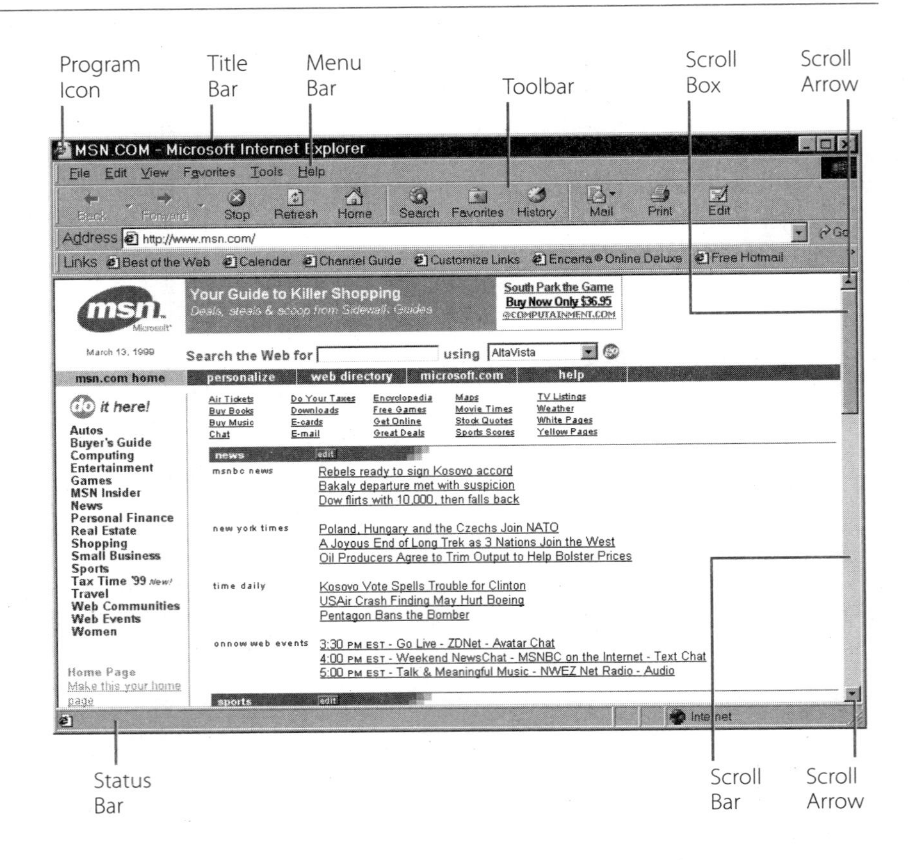

FIGURE 2-1. These user interface features appear in all Internet Explorer applications.

Menu Bar

The menu bar, such as the one shown in the following illustration, gives you full access to all the available commands and menu items (options).

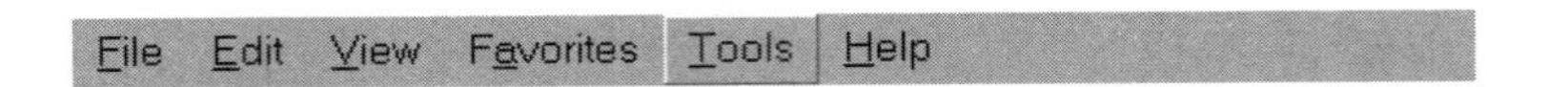

To open a menu, point to the menu name, and click the left mouse button.

> To access a menu with the keyboard, hold down the Alt key and press the underlined letter (for example, Alt + F opens the File menu).

Menus

Menus contain named items, and these items work in differing ways. Some items are commands that go to work right away when you choose them; others have symbols indicating that they work differently. The following illustration shows a typical menu; Table 2-1 explains what these menu items and symbols mean.

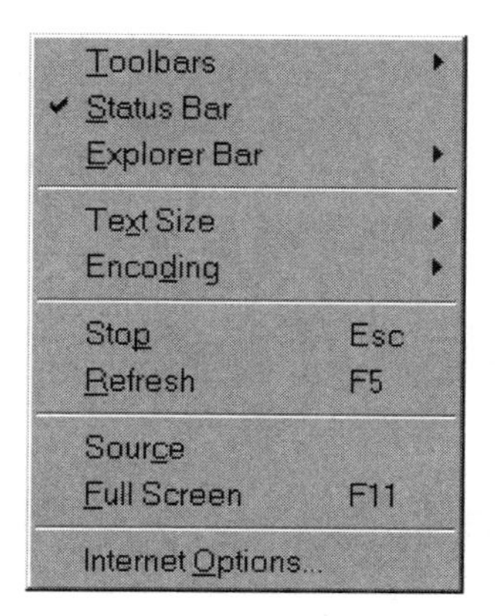

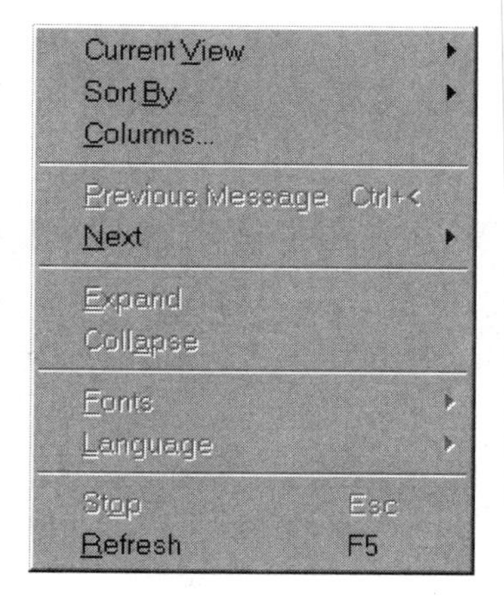

TABLE 2-1. Understanding Menu Options.

Menu item symbol	What it means	Example
Check mark	This item is currently switched on (selected). To turn the option off, choose it again.	✔ Status Bar
Right arrow (triangle)	This item displays a submenu. To see the submenu, point to the item's name.	Explorer Bar ▸
Three dots (ellipsis)	This item displays a dialog box, giving you additional choices.	Internet Options...
Underlined character	To choose this item with the keyboard, hold down the Alt key and press this letter (uppercase or lowercase).	Source
Dimmed item	This means that this item isn't accessible now.	Expand
Keyboard shortcut	You can press any of the indicated keys to the right of an item as a shortcut instead of choosing the item from the menu.	Refresh F5

TIP

You can use the keyboard to navigate menus. After opening a menu, you can use the down and up arrow keys to select items. Use the left and right arrow keys to navigate submenus.

Dialog Boxes

Some menu options display dialog boxes (for an example, see Figure 2-2). Table 2-2 explains what the various components of a dialog box do.

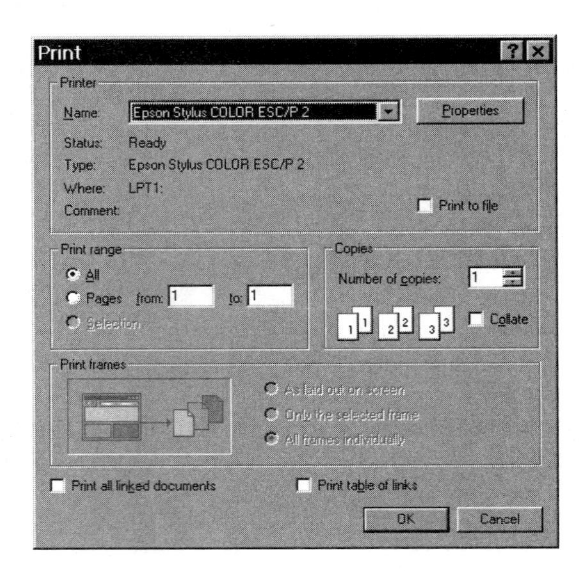

FIGURE 2-2. Dialog boxes enable you to choose many options. This dialog box provides printing options for the Internet Explorer browser.

If you prefer using the keyboard, you can press Tab to move through the areas of a dialog box (press Shift + Tab to move back). As you press Tab, notice that the selected area is highlighted with a dotted rectangle or reverse video. To activate or deactivate a selected radio button or check box, press the spacebar. To view and select the items in a selected list box, press the left or right arrow keys.

Some dialog boxes have tabbed pages that enable you to work with many options in the same dialog box. To see a hidden page, click its tab.

Program Icon

You'll see a program icon in most Internet Explorer applications. When this icon is moving, the application is busy downloading information you've requested. (*Downloading* means transferring data to your computer.) The download is complete when the animation stops.

TABLE 2-2. Understanding Dialog Box Options.

Dialog box item	What it does	Example
Dimmed item	This item isn't available in this situation.	All frames individually
Drop-down list box	Displays a list of items from which you can choose. To see the list, click the down arrow.	Name: Epson Stylus COLOR ESC/P 2
Text box	Accepts text you type. To add text, click within the box, edit the current text (if necessary), and type the text.	from: 1
Spinner control	Enables you to increase or decrease a number. Click the up arrow to increase the number, or click the down arrow to decrease it. In most boxes containing spinner controls, you can also type a number.	Number of copies: 1
Radio button (also called option button)	Enables you to choose one of several options in a boxed area. The currently selected option is shown with a dot. To select another option, click it.	All
Check box	Enables you to choose as many options as you like in an area. Selected options are shown with a check mark. To select an option, click it. To clear a selected option, click it so that the check mark disappears.	Print all linked documents
Command button	This button carries out an action. To choose the selected button, you can press Enter instead of clicking it.	OK
Cancel button	This button cancels all your choices in this dialog box, as if you had never made them, and returns to the application. You can press Esc instead of clicking Cancel.	Cancel

SEE ALSO

For the specifics about Internet Explorer's toolbars, see "Introducing the Toolbars," page 98.

Toolbars

Toolbars, such as the one shown in the following illustration, give you quick access to frequently used commands and options. Table 2-3 explains how to understand the toolbar's components.

TIP

If you'd like Internet Explorer's toolbars to look like Microsoft Office toolbars (small icons instead of large ones), click View on Internet Explorer's menu bar, select Toolbars, and click Customize. Click the Icon Options down arrow, and select Small icons. Click Close to resize the toolbar icons in all the Internet Explorer applications that have customizable toolbars.

SEE ALSO

For information on Outlook Express toolbars, see "Using the Toolbar," page 337, and "Customizing the Outlook Express Toolbars," page 457.

In most Internet Explorer applications, you'll find more than one toolbar. You can selectively display or hide each toolbar, and you can also add or remove tools. Later in this book, you'll find more information on each application's toolbars and toolbar customization.

NOTE

For information on the Outlook Express toolbar, see Chapter 11, "Introducing Outlook Express," as well as Chapter 13, "Personalizing and Maintaining Outlook Express."

Scroll Bars, Boxes, and Arrows

In applications with a scrollable workspace, you'll see tools that enable you to bring hidden parts of the workspace into view. These tools are scroll arrows and scroll boxes, which you'll find in scroll bars. Scroll bars may not appear if the entire document is visible. Often you'll see only a vertical scroll bar; at other times you'll see a horizontal scroll bar, and sometimes you'll see both. Table 2-4 shows how to use scroll arrows and scroll boxes.

TIP

If you're having trouble bringing a particular line or graphic into view by using the scroll arrows, try using the scroll box instead. The scroll box gives you more fine-grained control.

Status Bar

At the bottom of the application window, you'll find the status bar. The status bar displays information about the program, including low-priority messages. (High-priority messages appear in alert boxes.) Just what you see on the status bar depends on which application you're using, and also on what the application is doing. You'll learn more about status bar features later in this book, where specific applications are discussed.

Minimizing and Maximizing Windows

With Microsoft Windows, you can run more than one program at a time. And with Internet Explorer, you can place active Web content right on your desktop, beneath all the application windows. For these reasons, you'll often want to reduce the size of running windows, or hide them altogether. You use the window controls on the title bar for these purposes. These tools are summarized in Table 2-5.

TABLE 2-3. Understanding Toolbar Components.

Toolbar item	What it does	Example
Dimmed button	This button isn't available in this situation.	Forward
Down arrow	Click to display additional options.	Search
Highlighted button	This is the selected button; click it or press Enter to initiate the button's action.	Stop
Gray right arrow	Shows hidden buttons that the program could not display with the current window width.	
Vertical bar	Drag here to resize or reposition the toolbar.	

TABLE 2-4. Scrolling Controls.

Scrolling control	What it does	Example
Scroll arrow	Enables scrolling by a fraction of the length of the page. Click the arrow to scroll in the indicated direction. Click and hold to scroll continuously.	
Scroll box	Drag the box on the bar to scroll the screen in the direction in which you move the box.	

TABLE 2-5. Window Controls.

Window control	What it does	Example
Control menu	Displays the control menu, from which you can choose keyboard options for moving, sizing, minimizing, and maximizing the current window.	
Minimize icon	Hides the current window. You can redisplay the window by clicking the window's icon on the taskbar.	
Maximize icon	Zooms the window to full size. Does not appear if the window is already maximized.	
Restore icon	Restores a maximized window to its former (smaller) size. Appears only if the window is maximized.	

To minimize all windows, point to the taskbar, and click the right mouse button. From the pop-up menu, choose Minimize All Windows.

To maximize a window, double-click the title bar. To restore the window to its previous size, double-click the title bar again.

Controlling Window Size and Location

You can reposition any non-maximized window by dragging the window's title bar. To resize a window with the mouse, point to the window border that you want to move until the mouse pointer changes to a double-headed arrow shape. Then drag the border, and release the mouse button when you've sized the window to your tastes.

To size two borders at once, move the pointer to a window corner. When you see a diagonal double-headed arrow appear, drag the window corner.

If you prefer to use the keyboard, press Alt + Spacebar to display the Control menu. From this menu, you can maximize a window, or restore a maximized window; you can also minimize a window. To move a window, choose Move, and use the arrow keys to move the window. When you've finished moving the window, press Enter. To size a window, choose Size, and use the arrow keys to size the window; press Enter when you're done.

How to Adjust Your Display for Web Browsing

Your computer's display requires two hardware components, a video adapter and a monitor. With most of today's monitors, the video adapter plays the greatest role in determining the characteristics of the image shown on the monitor. To get the most out of Web browsing with Internet Explorer, you may need to adjust these characteristics, called *resolution* and *color depth.*

The term *resolution* refers to the number of distinct picture elements (called *pixels*) that the adapter generates. Resolutions are stated by indicating the number of lines of dots horizontally and the number of lines of dots vertically, as in 640 x 480 (pronounced 640 by 480), the lowest resolution for most adapters. You may need to use 640 x 480 for some older notebook computers with very small screens, but this resolution is too low to display most Web pages. You'll see only a portion of many Web pages and you'll have to scroll frequently to bring the hidden parts into view. For Web browsing, you should use a minimum resolution of 800 x 600; it's better to use 1024 x 768 (called Super VGA). If you have a 17-inch or larger monitor, you can try higher resolutions (such as 1280 x 1024 or 1600 x 1200), but you may have to sacrifice color depth, as explained in the next paragraph.

The term *color depth* refers to the number of colors that the monitor can display at one time. Color depth is generally stated by indicating the number of bits (basic units of information) used to store color information, as well as the number of colors that can be displayed. For example, an 8-bit color depth generates a total of 256 possible colors. Displaying more colors requires a greater bit length—and consequently, more memory. A 16-bit color depth (called *high color*) generates more than 64,000 colors, while a 24-bit color depth (called *true color*) generates 16.7 million colors. For each resolution you can choose, your adapter's video memory (VRAM) determines the maximum number of colors you can display. An older video adapter with only 1MB of memory may be able to generate high color at 800 x 600, but can only display 256 colors at 1024 x 768. To get the most out of the graphics you'll see on the Web, you should use a 16-bit (high color) color depth.

If your adapter can't display high color at a minimum resolution of 800 x 600, you may wish to consider upgrading or replacing your video adapter. You can upgrade many adapters by adding additional video memory (VRAM). In a desktop system, you may find it more convenient (and only slightly more costly) to replace the video adapter with a newer one that has 4MB (megabytes) or more of VRAM. The Web browsing experience is at its best with a 17-inch monitor, 1280 x 1024 resolution, and true color (24-bit) color depth.

 TIP

To redisplay a minimized window with the keyboard, press Alt + Tab to display the icons of available windows. To keep the list on-screen, keep holding down the Alt key, and press Tab to move the highlight through the icons. Below the icons, you'll see the window's title. When you've highlighted the window you want to display, release the keys.

CAUTION

The number of windows you can work with at one time is limited by the amount of RAM memory installed in your computer. If you open too many windows, performance degrades, because some of the on-screen information must be stored temporarily on your hard disk. When you're close to using up all the available memory, you'll see an on-screen warning advising you to close some windows. If you see this message, you can improve your system's performance by adding additional memory.

Working with Two or More Windows

Often, you'll work with two or more windows at once. For example, you can keep Outlook Express running while you're using other applications, such as Internet Explorer or Microsoft Word. You can use the window controls just discussed to manage multiple windows on-screen.

To arrange windows automatically, you can use the following commands:

- **Cascade.** When you cascade on-screen windows, they're stacked with a slight offset so you can see each window's title bar.
- **Tile.** When you tile windows, they're each apportioned a rectangular space on-screen.

To cascade or tile all the windows you've opened, point to the taskbar, and click the right mouse button. From the pop-up menu, choose Cascade Windows or the Tile option of your choice.

 TIP

If you're not happy with the results of cascading or tiling, point to the taskbar, click the right mouse button, and choose Undo Cascade or Undo Tile from the pop-up menu.

Using Accessibility Features

Internet Explorer contains many features for people with disabilities. These include keyboard access and control over the visual appearance of Web pages.

 TIP

Windows 98 includes a new Accessibility control panel, which you can access by clicking Start, pointing to Settings, choosing Control Panel, and clicking Accessibility. For the latest information on Microsoft disability initiatives, including accessibility support in Microsoft Windows and Internet Explorer, see the Accessibility Home Page (http://www.microsoft.com/enable).

SEE ALSO
For more information on keyboard access, see "Navigating with the Keyboard," page 115.

Keyboard Access

All Internet Explorer features are accessible by means of the keyboard as well as the mouse. You'll find keyboard shortcuts for commands and options. In the Internet Explorer Web browser, for example, you can press Tab and Shift + Tab to cycle through the on-screen items, including hyperlinks, links within images, the Address Bar, and frames. You can also use keyboard shortcuts for all the other actions you perform while Web browsing.

Colors and Fonts

Many Web authors unthinkingly choose color schemes, fonts, and font sizes that make their pages difficult to read for anyone, let alone people with limited vision. Often, you'll encounter pages with visually confusing background graphics that make the text all but illegible.

If you have limited vision, you'll be glad to know that you can override a page author's color, font, and font-size options for *every* page you view on the Web. You can then choose color, font, and font-size defaults suited to your needs.

To override the page author's color, font, or font-size choices, open the browser, click Tools on the menu bar, and choose Internet Options. In the Internet Options dialog box, click the General tab, if necessary, and click Accessibility. You'll see the Accessibility dialog box, shown in Figure 2-3.

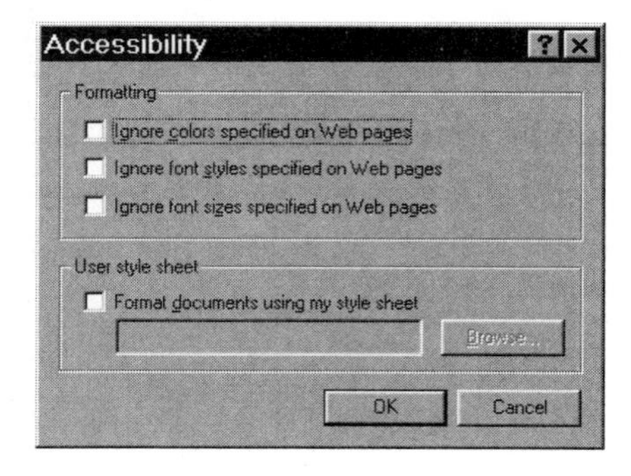

FIGURE 2-3.
In this dialog box, you can specify colors and fonts for Web pages.

SEE ALSO
For more information on the Internet Explorer browser options for people with limited vision, see "Adjusting Text Size," page 117.

In the Formatting area, you can override Web authors' choices for colors (including backgrounds), font styles, and font sizes. You can then choose your own color scheme and fonts by clicking the Colors and Fonts buttons in the General page of Internet Options. Figure 2-4 shows a Web page that includes the author's color, font, and font-size choices;

Figure 2-5 shows the same page with these choices overridden and replaced by the viewer's preferences.

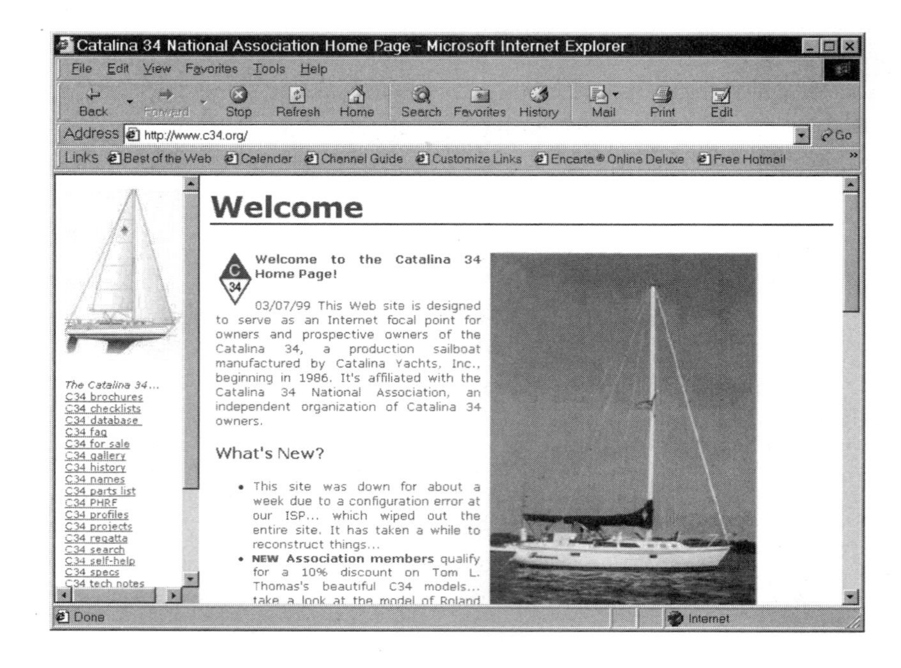

FIGURE 2-4. Here's a Web page that's shown with the page author's color, font, and font-size choices.

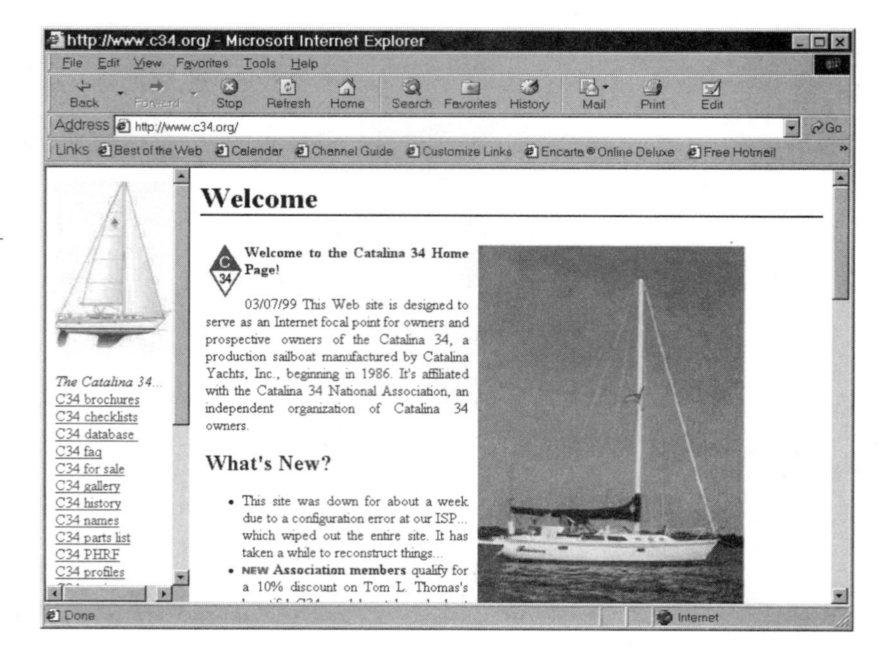

FIGURE 2-5. Here's what the same page looks like after overriding the author's choices, and substituting the viewer's font and font-size preferences.

In the Accessibility dialog box, you'll find an option that enables you to format documents according to a *style sheet*. A style sheet is a text file that redefines the format of common Web-page components, such as titles, headings, hyperlinks, and text. To create a style sheet, you need to know how to define styles using Cascading Style Sheets (CSS). Style sheets are easy to create. For an introduction to style sheets, see Microsoft's tutorial at http://www.microsoft.com/typography/web/designer/css01.htm.

PART II

Getting Happily Connected

CHAPTER 3

Understanding What You'll Need

To access the Internet with Microsoft Internet Explorer, you'll need an Internet connection and a system that's capable of running the Internet Explorer software. In this chapter, you'll explore your Internet connection options, and examine Internet Explorer's system requirements.

Connecting with a Modem

Most Internet users connect to the Internet by means of a modem, but that's about to change. According to a recent study conducted by Forrester Research, by 2002 up to 16 million U.S. households will have Internet connections at speeds of greater than 1 million bits per second (1 Mbps). If you're still at the stage where you're shopping for equipment, find out whether services such as ISDN, cable modems, or Digital Subscriber Line (DSL) are available in your area. They're all superior, and in some cases far superior, to modem-based connections.

Understanding Why Modems Are Needed

Derogatorily known these days as Plain Old Telephone Service (POTS), ordinary telephone lines are designed to carry the human voice. They handle voice calls well enough. But POTS lines can't handle computer data without *modulation*. In modulation, the computer's signals are translated into audio beeps, whistles, and warbling tones that the phone lines can carry. At the other end of the transmission, another modem *demodulates* these tones by translating them back into computer signals. To modulate and demodulate computer signals, you use a device called a *modem*—which is short for *mo*dulator/*dem*odulator.

Comparing Internal and External Modems

Modems fall into two categories, *internal modems* and *external modems*. An internal modem is designed to fit within one of your computer's expansion slots, located inside the system unit. An external modem has its own case and power supply, and plugs into your computer's serial port. (If you're using a notebook computer, you can get an external modem that fits into your computer's PC card slot.)

Which is best? Each has its boosters. Internal modems don't require any desk space, and they're cheaper because they don't require a case and power supply. But external modems don't require an expansion slot, and that's a plus if you don't have any available!

Modulation Protocols

What matters in a modem is *data transfer rate*, measured in *bits per second (bps)*. A modem's maximum data transfer rate is determined by the type of modulation protocol it uses. Today's fastest modems can communicate at a theoretical rate of approximately 56,000 bits per second (abbreviated 56 Kbps). (In practice, you'll get something more like

40,000 to 42,000 bits per second.) But 56 Kbps modems use three different protocols to achieve this data transfer rate, and it's important to understand the difference.

What's a modulation protocol? In brief, it's a communication standard, one that enables two modems to "speak the same language." Two kinds of modem standards exist. *Non-proprietary standards,* the best kind, are set by an international standards body—specifically, the International Telecommunications Union (ITU), a unit of the United Nations. ITU standards are numbered and prefaced with the letter *V,* as in V.90. *Proprietary standards* appear when modem makers have new technology that hasn't yet been worked into a new standard. Using a modem with a proprietary standard poses some risk, because your modem won't be able to communicate at maximum speed unless it can hook up with another modem made or licensed by the same manufacturer.

So here's the important point about modulation protocols. The ITU has recently released its 56 Kbps standard, called V.90. However, two proprietary 56 Kbps standards were developed prior to the ITU's action, and lots of modems use these proprietary protocols, which are called X.2 and K56Flex. And here's what all this means:

- Above all else, find out which protocols your Internet service provider (ISP) supports. (You'll learn about ISPs in a subsequent section.) If you already have an X.2 modem, you need to look for a service provider that supports X.2. Ask!
- If you're buying a modem, be sure to get one that conforms to the V.90 standard set by the ITU. This is the best way to ensure that you'll be able to communicate at 56 Kbps in the future.

What happens if your modem tries to link with another modem that doesn't use the same 56 Kbps protocol? When modems begin to communicate, they perform a social ritual (called *handshaking*) that enables them to determine the highest possible speed at which they can communicate. If they can't communicate at 56 Kbps, the modems "fall back" to a lower data transfer rate using an older, slower standard (33 Kbps).

Connecting Two Modems with Multilink

If one modem is good, two are better. That's the philosophy underlying a new Windows 98 feature called Multilink. With Multilink, you can install *two* modems. Windows 98 governs the modems' operations so that they work together, providing you with a data transfer rate of up to 128 Kbps (about 80 Kbps to 90 Kbps in practice). To get the best results, it's a good idea to use two identical modems—with the same manufacturer and made at the same time (so that they have the same internal programming). Although Multilink is a nifty feature, it has a major drawback: you'll need two phone lines and two Internet subscriptions. (Some ISPs offer a special Multilink connection that costs more than one subscription but less than two.) If ISDN is available in your area, you may find that it's a more attractive option than using Multilink with two ordinary phone lines. ISDN is discussed in the next section.

Connecting with ISDN

Increasingly available is Integrated Services Digital Network (ISDN). ISDN is an ITU-defined digital telephone standard that can be used to provide noise-free phone service and Internet access. What's neat about ISDN is its ability to work with ordinary phone wiring, called *twisted pair,* that's found in most homes and offices. Unlike ordinary telephone service, ISDN is fully digital, so you don't need a modem. (You will need some special equipment, though, as this section describes.) Another welcome ISDN feature is near-instantaneous connection; there's no tedious dial-up or logon process to go through before you're connected to the Internet.

In order to obtain ISDN service for Internet access, you need a local telephone company that offers ISDN at a reasonable price. (In some areas, ISDN service isn't available.) You also need an Internet service provider that offers an ISDN connection that's accessible by means of a local telephone call. Don't sign up for ISDN telephone service without first making sure that your local ISP supports ISDN connections.

CAUTION

Be aware that some telephone companies assess per-minute charges for ISDN connections, even if you're placing a local call. These charges add up. For Internet access, look for free unlimited local telephone calls. Also, be sure you're comfortable with your local service provider's ISDN charges. You may experience difficulty finding a service provider that will quote a reasonable rate for unlimited ISDN access.

Examining ISDN Connection Options

An ISDN connection consists of two different channels: a 16 Kbps channel used for control signals, and a 56 Kbps or 64 Kbps channel (called a *B channel*) for voice or data. With most telephone companies, you can choose from two types of ISDN services:

- **Basic Rate ISDN (BRI) at 56 Kbps or 64 Kbps.** This type of connection uses just one B channel. It's the least expensive, but doesn't offer much more speed than a 56 Kbps modem.
- **Basic Rate ISDN (BRI) at 112 or 128 Kbps.** This type of connection uses *two* B channels. Although it's more expensive, it comes with a plus. You can use one of the lines for a telephone

or fax machine. Even if you're connected at 128 Kbps (using both B channels), you can still place or receive incoming calls; the equipment automatically clears one of the lines without interrupting service on the other one. Windows 98 uses Multilink so that both of the B lines can work together.

ISDN Adapters

To connect your computer to an ISDN line, you'll need an *ISDN adapter*. Like modems, some ISDN adapters are internal, while others are external. External ISDN adapters often include a couple of POTS connectors, which is a genuine plus. You can connect an ordinary phone and fax machine, thus transforming your ISDN connection into a complete communications system for a home or small business office.

If you'd like to connect more than one computer to the Internet, consider connecting these computers via an Ethernet local area network (LAN) and connecting the network to an *ISDN router*. It isn't difficult to connect several computers in a simple network; you'll need network interface cards (Ethernet cards) for each computer, an Ethernet hub, and cables to connect the computers to the hub. All the software you need comes with Windows 95, Windows 98, and Windows NT. Once you've got the network functioning, you install the ISDN router between the Ethernet hub and the ISDN line. The result? The ISDN router handles the Internet connection, splitting a single subscription among all the computers you've connected to the LAN. Everyone using the LAN will have Internet access. Although the technical details of this type of connection are beyond the scope of this book, be assured that it's not as difficult as it sounds. Increasing numbers of homeowners are installing LANs and ISDN routers so that every member of the family can enjoy Internet access (without having to pay for multiple Internet subscriptions).

Connecting with Digital Subscriber Line (DSL)

Before you sign up for ISDN, find out whether *Digital Subscriber Line* (DSL), and also known as *xDSL* is available in your area. It's a new technology, but it's expected to supplant ISDN quickly wherever it's available. As with ISDN, you'll need a local telephone company that offers DSL, as well as a local service provider that provides Internet access via DSL. Among the regional Bell telephone companies, Pacific Bell (West coast) and Bell Atlantic (Northeast U.S.) have announced DSL services in selected communities.

DSL is a blanket term for a group of related technologies, including *Asymmetric Digital Subscriber Line* (ADSL). Already available in major metropolitan markets, ADSL is akin to ISDN in that it uses existing copper wiring. But ADSL is much faster than ISDN: typically, up to 1.5 Mbps when you're downloading data, and up to 256 Kbps when you're uploading data. In ADSL, the downloading speeds are much faster than uploading speeds; the discrepancy explains why the service is called "asymmetric." It's assumed that you'll be consuming information more often than publishing it.

How fast is DSL? With a 56 Kbps modem, you'll need about 2.5 minutes to download a 1 MB video clip. With DSL, you can download the same video in less than 5 seconds.

To connect to a DSL line, your computer will need a DSL modem, as well as a DSL phone line and an Internet service subscription that includes DSL service. A problem: DSL service isn't standardized, so you'll need a DSL modem that's compatible with your telephone company's particular type of DSL service. (Generally, you get the ADSL modem from the telephone company when you sign up for the service.) Standardization efforts are underway, however, and these efforts will reduce the cost and complexity of DSL installations.

Don't expect DSL service if you're located in an out-of-the-way area; DSL service is available only within a distance of 2 or 3 miles from a local telephone office.

Connecting with a Cable Modem

In growing numbers of areas served by cable TV companies, you've another option for connecting to the Internet: a *cable modem.* A cable modem isn't really a modem, because the connection offered by cable TV companies is a digital one, like ISDN.

Cable TV Internet services fall into two categories:

- **Single-path symmetric** (cable only). This is the best type of cable connection. It enables two-way connections, so that you can upload as well as download data. Most cable companies must upgrade their wiring and equipment before they can offer this type of connection.

- **Dual-path asymmetric** (requires a modem and phone line). Much less convenient is this type of connection, which requires a modem and phone line in order to send signals back to the Internet. The cable provides one-way data transfer (downloading) only. Cable TV companies are busily upgrading their systems to enable single-path symmetric connections, so you may wish to wait for a bit if your local cable company doesn't yet offer the two-way service.

Most cable modems require you to install an Ethernet card in your computer. An Ethernet card is a local area network (LAN) adapter card. You don't have to have a LAN to connect with a cable modem, though; the card is used to connect your computer to the cable modem.

How fast are cable modem connections? From your computer, you link to the cable TV's computers via an Ethernet connection, operating at 10 Mbps (10 million bits per second). But the cable TV company may have a "pipe" of much less capacity to the wider Internet, and all subscribers must share this "pipe's" total *bandwidth* (data transfer capacity). In practice, you'll experience data transfer rates of 250 Kbps (more than five times the rate of a 56 Kbps modem) to 1 Mbps (more than twenty times the rate of a 56 Kbps modem). If your cable TV company *caches* popular Web pages on its local computers, you'll be able to access these pages at Ethernet speeds (10 Mbps). When a service provider caches pages, the company stores copies of frequently accessed Web pages so that these pages can be retrieved without having to obtain them from the wider Internet.

Connecting with a Direct Broadcast Satellite (DBS)

Yet another connection option is provided by satellite TV companies. Digital satellite systems, called *Direct Broadcast Satellite* (DBS), use an 18- or 21-inch reception disk to receive digital TV signals. Increasingly, DBS operators offer Internet access as well as digital TV service. For example, Hughes Network Systems offers satellite Internet access at 400 Kbps. There's a drawback to connecting to the Internet via satellite: the satellite signal is strictly a one-way connection used for downloading only. You'll still need a modem and telephone line to send requests to the server as well as to upload files.

Connecting via a Local Area Network (LAN)

If you're accessing the Internet at work, chances are that you're doing so by means of a local area network (LAN). A local area network consists of a group of computers located within a maximum distance of about one mile of each other. Directly connected by cables or wireless radio signals, these computers can exchange data at high speeds (up to 100 Mbps). By connecting LANs to the Internet, organizations can provide Internet access to all or selected employees.

Connecting a LAN to the Internet poses security risks. For this reason, organizations create barriers called *firewalls* that shield the organization against external intrusions. Firewalls consist of special programs that are installed in a computer that's directly connected to the Internet. One function of the firewall is to hide the actual Internet addresses of computers inside the corporate network. Intruders can't attack internal computers if they can't find them!

One drawback to such security measures lies in their making it harder for internal users to access the external Internet. In order to access the Web from inside your organization, you may need to configure Internet Explorer to use a *proxy server*, discussed in Chapter 4. Proxy servers enable internal users to access the external Internet without giving away the internal computer's exact location.

Choosing a Service Provider

Be aware that an ISP's "unlimited access" offer does not mean that you can access the Internet continuously 24 hours per day, 7 days per week. If you read the fine print in your service contract, you'll probably find that this contract expressly prohibits such use. Should you remain on the Internet for more than 10 or 12 hours at a time, you may receive a message from the ISP warning you against excessive use.

Once you've decided what type of connection you want, it's time to consider how you'll subscribe to the Internet. As this section shows, you can choose from local and national Internet service providers (ISPs), as well as online services.

Introducing Internet Service Providers (ISP)

An *Internet service provider* (ISP) provides Internet subscriptions for a monthly fee. In general, you can subscribe for a low monthly fee that specifies a maximum number of connect hours per month (as low as $8 per month for 5 hours), or a higher fee ($25 or less) for "unlimited access." If you choose the lower rate with a fixed number of usage hours per month, be aware that additional hours may be charged at a hefty rate ($2.50 or more), and you can quickly run up a bill in excess of the unlimited access rate. Most experienced Internet users sign up for the unlimited access rate. In addition to the monthly fees, you may have to pay a setup fee.

Understanding Call-Failure Rates

ISPs have a fixed number of access ports, mostly analog (POTS) modems, through which subscribers can connect. However, they typically sell many times more subscriptions than the number of ports they have. They can do this because most subscribers use the Internet for only an hour or two per day. If the ISP sells 10 to 12 subscriptions per port, chances are that most users will be able to obtain a connection on the first phone call. But ISPs can make more money if they sell more subscriptions per port. The result is a higher *call-failure rate*, the percentage of access attempts that result in a busy signal. The best ISPs have call-failure rates of 5 percent or lower. With the worst ISPs, only two out of every five access attempts gets through.

TIP

Looking for current information on call-failure rates? Check out Inverse Corporation's Web site (www.inversenet.com), and follow the links to the News page. Inverse does marketing research, including studies of ISP call-failure rates, and the results are published in Internet-accessible magazines such as *PC World*. The News page contains links to articles in these magazines about ISP performance.

Examining the Types of ISPs

ISPs fall into the following categories:

- **Local ISPs.** Local ISPs are small businesses that make Internet service available in a community. Some of these are undercapitalized ventures that may go out of business, leaving you with a dead connection; others are professionally run companies that provide excellent service.
- **National ISPs.** These service providers maintain regional or national networks with local points of presence (POPs) in dozens or hundreds of areas. Some provide sub-par service and aren't rated highly; others provide the best Internet service available anywhere.

As you've just seen, there are good ISPs—and not-so-good ISPs—at both levels, locally and nationally. Before signing up with *any* ISP, try to talk to as many local Internet users as you can. Ask them which service they're using, and ask for a frank evaluation. Do they have trouble connecting? Is technical support available when it's needed?

To find local ISPs, check the Computers—On-Line Services section of your local Yellow Pages. If you have access to the Web, check out The List (thelist.internet.com), which lists nearly 5,000 Internet service providers. You can type in your local zip code (or a country code, outside the United States), and see a list of the ISPs available in your area.

Services Provided by ISPs

Most Internet service providers offer some or all of the following services:

- **Software.** Most ISPs provide software such as a Web browser and an e-mail program. You may not need this software if you're running Microsoft Internet Explorer, which comes with most of the Internet software you need.
- **E-mail account.** Included in the price of your subscription, generally, is one e-mail account, which enables you to send and receive e-mail.
- **Additional e-mail mailboxes.** If your computer and Internet subscription will be used by more than one person, and you want additional e-mail boxes for all users, find out whether this service is available.
- **Spam filters.** Unsolicited commercial e-mail, called *spam*, is increasingly common, and it's a major irritation to many Internet users. Some spam contains information about pornographic Web sites, so it's of special concern to parents who are obtaining Internet accounts for kids. Some ISPs have spam-filtering services that catch as much as 90 percent of unsolicited e-mail before it reaches subscribers' mailboxes.
- **Usenet newsgroups.** Most ISPs offer Usenet newsgroups, but some offer far more newsgroups than others. The total number of newsgroups now exceeds 50,000, and the flow of messages is close to one million per day. Because Usenet generates so much disk-filling data, ISPs may limit the number of newsgroups they carry, or keep messages current for only a few days or less. If you've some special interest in a particular Usenet newsgroup, ask prospective ISPs whether they carry it, and if so, how long they retain articles.
- **Free Web publishing space.** Some ISPs offer free Web publishing space, where you can make your Web-page creations available to other Internet users. The space is limited in size; for example,

most ISPs give you only one or two megabytes of storage, and there are restrictions on the number of monthly access or "hits." Should your usage exceed the storage or access limits, you may have to pay fees.

- **Web hosting.** Most ISPs offer Web-hosting services. This fee-based service includes some or all of the following services: Web page creation, scripting, and access monitoring and statistics.
- **Roaming access.** If you frequently travel and would like to access Internet services without paying long-distance telephone charges, ask whether your ISP offers a toll-free 800 access number. Some ISPs contract with national networks to offer free local telephone access from hundreds of points of presence (POPs).
- **Technical support.** The best ISPs offer 24-hour technical support as well as voluminous online information, including frequently asked questions (FAQs) concerning various aspects of Internet services.

Considering Online Services

Online services such as America Online and MSN offer most or all of the same services local and national ISPs offer, and more: rich proprietary content, chat rooms, and forums on a wide variety of topics. What many people find appealing about these services is the superior support they provide for socializing, which isn't as well supported or supervised on the Internet. If you want a good Internet connection and you're interested in schmoozing with others while you're online, an online service is a good bet.

Understanding Internet Explorer's System Requirements

To run Microsoft Internet Explorer version 5, you need at least the following:

- **Processor.** An Intel 486DX-2 running at 66 MHz
- **Operating System.** Windows 95, Windows 98, or Windows NT 4.0
- **Memory (RAM).** 16 MB
- **Free Disk Space.** 56 MB for a minimal installation; you'll need 72 MB to install the standard version. In addition, you'll need another 50 MB of free space to run Microsoft Internet Explorer.

These are the *minimum* requirements. In practice, you'll find that Microsoft Internet Explorer runs best on a system that's been optimized for Internet use:

- You'll need a reasonably high-powered Pentium system (at least a "classic" Pentium running at a clock speed of 166 MHz)—and the more memory, the better. The software runs with 16 MB of RAM, but performance degrades if you try to run more than one application besides Internet Explorer. If you often run two or more programs at once, you'll find that performance improves with 32 MB or 64 MB of RAM.
- Internet Explorer version 5 enables you to save entire Web sites for offline browsing. To take full advantage of this feature, you'll need a lot of hard disk space. Today, drives with 8 gigabytes (GB) of storage space or more aren't very expensive. If you're buying a new system, go for one with the biggest hard drive you can afford. If you're using an older system, consider upgrading the drive.
- To get the most out of the graphics you'll encounter on the Web, you may wish to upgrade your video adapter so that you can display 16.7 million colors at a resolution of 1024 by 768. If your existing video adapter can't display that many colors at this resolution, you may be able to upgrade the adapter by adding video memory.
- To take full advantage of Internet multimedia and telephony, you should equip your system with a sound card, speakers, and a microphone.

CHAPTER 4

Running the Connection Wizard

The Internet Connection Wizard provides all the help you need to get connected to the Internet. With the wizard, you can configure your computer to access the Internet with the information given to you by your Internet service provider (ISP). You can also configure a local area network (LAN) connection. If you haven't already found an ISP, you can use the wizard to access the Microsoft Referral Service, which lists ISPs available in your local calling area. Should you choose to subscribe to the Internet using one of these ISPs, you can sign up online, and you'll be browsing within minutes.

This chapter explores the Internet Connection Wizard, guiding you through the various connection options. Because most Internet users connect by means of an analog modem, this chapter begins by explaining the modem installation process and focuses on dial-up modem connections. You'll also learn how to connect your computer to an existing LAN.

If you haven't already installed Microsoft Internet Explorer 5, do so now. For information on obtaining and installing the program, see Appendix A.

Installing the Hardware You Need

To connect to the Internet by means of a dial-up connection (analog phone line or ISDN) or your cable TV service, you'll need to install the hardware that's needed to make the connection. You'll also need to arrange with the telephone or cable company to provide the needed service. If you've already installed the hardware you need, skip this section.

SEE ALSO
For information on your connection options, see Chapter 3, "Understanding What You'll Need." To learn more about service provider options, see "Choosing a Service Provider," page 54.

Installing an Analog Modem

If your new modem is plug-and-play compatible, the installation should be easy. (Plug-and-play is a standard that enables Windows to detect and install new hardware automatically.) If you're installing a modem that doesn't support Plug-and-Play, you may need to install the modem using the Modem icon in the Control Panel. The following sections detail these techniques.

Installing a Plug-and-Play Modem

Thanks to Windows 98's plug-and-play capabilities, this task is easy. Just follow the instructions that came with your hardware. In general, you install new hardware by turning off your PC and installing the new hardware device, following the manufacturer's instructions. When you restart your system, Windows 98 will detect the new hardware. Just follow the on-screen instructions to complete the installation.

SEE ALSO
For information on configuring your modem after running the Connection Wizard, see "Maintaining Connection Information," page 78.

Installing a Modem That Doesn't Support Plug-and-Play

If you're installing a modem that doesn't support plug-and-play, or if Windows couldn't detect the modem after you installed it, you need to install the modem using the Modems icon in the Control Panel. Begin by turning off your PC and installing your new modem. Use the following instructions only if Windows doesn't detect the new hardware.

To install a modem using the Modems icon in the Control Panel:

1. Click Start, choose Settings, and choose Control Panel. You'll see the Control Panel window.
2. Choose Modems. If you haven't previously installed a modem on your system, you'll see the New Modem Wizard.
3. Click Add to configure a new modem. You'll see the Install New Modem dialog box.
4. Do one of the following by following the directions on the dialog boxes:
   - If the modem manufacturer gave you a disk with the most up-to-date driver for this device, click the option that skips detection. You'll see a list of modem drivers. Click Have Disk, insert the disk that came with your new hardware, and click Finish to complete the installation.
   - If Windows detected your modem properly, click Finish to complete the installation.
5. Restart your system.

After you restart your system, your new modem should be installed and correctly configured.

Installing ISDN Adapters and Cable Modems

ISDN adapters and cable modems install in various ways. Some ISDN adapters install as if they were modems; other ISDN adapters, and most cable modems, have their own installation techniques that require you to run the manufacturer's installation software. Follow the manufacturer's instructions to install your new hardware.

TIP

If you're installing an ISDN adapter, you'll need an important code from your telephone company: the Service Profile Identifier (SPID). You'll need to supply this code for each ISDN telephone line you configure (a 128-Kbps ISDN line has two B lines, and therefore two telephone numbers).

Connecting to Online Services

If you would like to sign up with an online service such as Microsoft Network (MSN) or America Online (AOL), you don't need to run the Connection Wizard. To connect to the Microsoft Network, just click the MSN icon on the desktop. To connect with other online services, open the Online Services icon on the Windows desktop. To connect to one of these services, just click the service's icon.

Introducing the Connection Wizard

For information on modifying your Internet connection after you've created it, see "Maintaining Connection Information," page 78.

The Internet Connection Wizard lets you create a dial-up or LAN connection easily (see Figure 4-1). Using the wizard, you can do any of the following:

- Using the Microsoft Referral Service, search for Internet service providers (ISPs) that are accessible in your location with a local telephone call, and subscribe to the Internet using your credit card. If you don't already have an Internet connection, you can be connected—and browsing—in a matter of minutes.
- Configure your computer to access an Internet account, using the information your ISP gave you. This is the option to use if you've already signed up for Internet service from a local or national ISP.
- Set up your connection manually.
- Connect through a local area network (LAN). This is the option to use if you are able to connect to the Internet at work.

The following sections discuss each of these connection options in detail, beginning with using the Connection Wizard to obtain an Internet account.

If you don't have strong reasons to prefer an ISP other than the ones made available by the Microsoft Referral Service, consider using this service to obtain an Internet account. It's the easiest way to get connected. When you use the Referral Service, the ISP you select downloads information that configures your computer automatically. Within minutes, you'll be connected to the Internet and browsing the Web. For information on connecting with the Referral Service, see the next section.

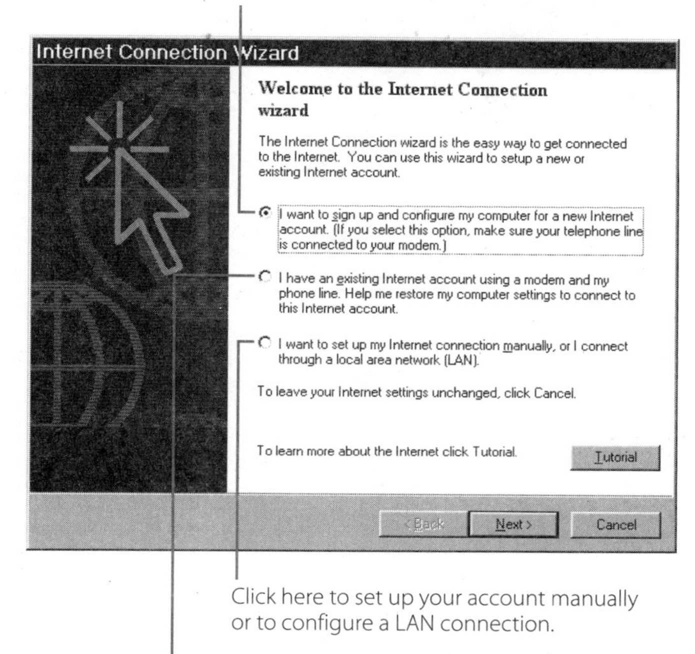

FIGURE 4-1.
Using the Connection Wizard, you can create a new Internet account, configure an existing one, or connect via a LAN.

Adjusting Telephony Settings

Configure your telephony settings before you run the Connection Wizard. To configure these settings, use the Telephony icon in the Control Panel.

> If your telephone line has Call Waiting, you should disable it during your Internet connections. Otherwise, your modem will probably lose your connection should somebody try to call your number while your Internet connection is in progress. Call your telephone company to find out what to dial in order to disable call waiting. You can type this code into the Dialing Properties dialog box, as explained here, and Windows will dial this code prior to dialing your Internet connection number.

To adjust your telephony settings:

1 Click Start, and choose Settings. Click Control Panel, and click the Telephony icon. You'll see the following Dialing Properties dialog box.

If you have Call Waiting, activate this option.

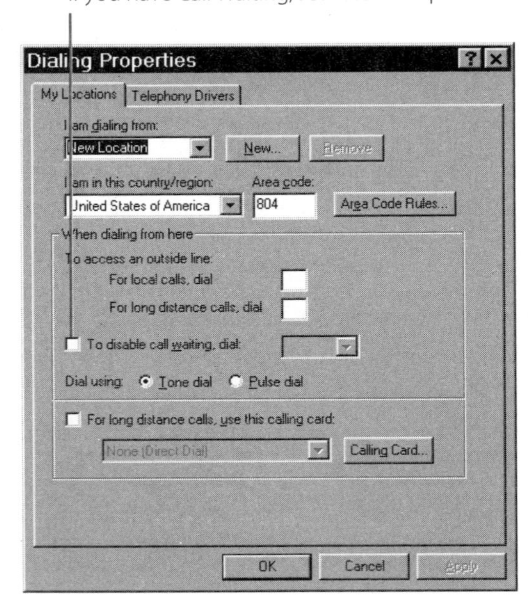

2 Click the My Locations tab, if necessary, and locate the area called How I Dial From This Location. In the text boxes, enter the codes you must dial to access local and long-distance lines.

3 If you must always dial an area code, even when placing a local call (10-digit dialing), click Area Code Rules, and activate the option called Always Dial The Area Code.

4 If you must dial "1" in order to access your service provider's computer, click Area Code Rules. Click the New button, type the prefix, and click OK.

5 If your telephone line has Call Waiting, click the check box next to To Disable Call Waiting, Dial, and type the code in the text box, or select it from the pull-down menu.

6 If your telephone service requires pulse dialing (instead of tones), activate Pulse Dial.

7 If you use a calling card for long-distance calls, check the Dial Using Calling Card check box, and then click the Change button to select your card type. Enter your phone card number and click OK.

If your card isn't listed, create one and then click the Rules button to set up rules for your card.

8 Click OK until you see the Control Panel again.

> If you're configuring a notebook computer and plan to access the Internet from more than one location, you can configure each dialing location separately. For more information, see "Creating Additional Calling Connections," page 87.

Obtaining a New Internet Account

You can use the Connection Wizard to obtain a new Internet account if you don't already have one. In order to use the Connection Wizard for this purpose, you must have the following:

- An installed modem
- A telephone line

The Connection Wizard will contact Microsoft's Referral Service via a toll-free phone call. Note that the Referral Service doesn't necessarily list all the ISPs in your area; the ISPs listed have made arrangements with Microsoft to be included in this list.

> Keep your Windows 98 CD-ROM handy when you run the Connection Wizard. The wizard may detect that you haven't installed some software that's needed for your Internet connection. If so, you'll be prompted to insert your Windows 98 CD-ROM.

To use the Connection Wizard to obtain a new Internet account:

1. From the Start menu, click Programs, Accessories, and Internet Tools. Then choose Connection Wizard from the submenu. You'll see the Connection Wizard, shown in Figure 4-1.
2. Click the first option, I Want To Sign Up And Configure My Computer For A New Internet Account, and click Next.
3. The Connection Wizard calls the Referral Service and obtains a list of the Internet service providers available in your area (see Figure 4-2). To select an ISP, choose an item in the Internet Service Providers list. You'll find information about the ISP in the Provider Information window, to the right.

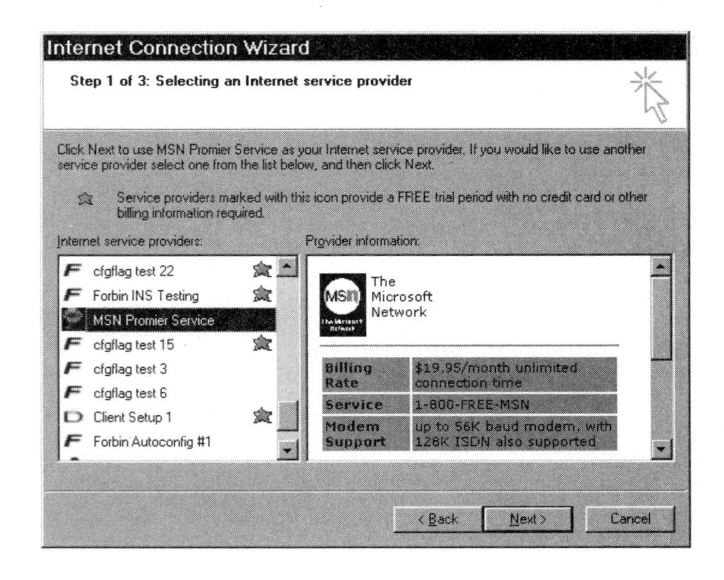

FIGURE 4-2.
Selecting an ISP from the Microsoft Referral Service.

4. Once you've selected an ISP, click Next. Enter your personal and billing information and click Next again. Keep following the on-screen instructions.

   When you click Finish, you're ready to browse the Web. The entire installation and configuration process is automatic. With most ISPs, this includes e-mail and Usenet configuration.

Transferring an Existing Internet Account to Another Computer

If you have already used the Microsoft Referral Service to obtain an Internet account, you can copy this account information to a second computer without having to perform any manual configuration. For example, suppose you have a computer in your home office. You created your Internet connection by using the Referral Service. You've just purchased a new notebook computer, and you want to configure this new computer to access the same Internet account.

To transfer Internet account information obtained from the Microsoft Referral Service to a second computer, do the following:

1. From the Start menu, click Programs, Accessories, and Internet Tools. Then choose Connection Wizard from the submenu. You'll see the Connection Wizard, shown in Figure 4-1.

2 Click the second option, I Have An Existing Internet Account Using A Modem And My Phone Line, and click Next.

3 The Connection Wizard calls the Referral Service and obtains a list of the Internet service providers available in your area (see Figure 4-2). Choose your ISP, click Next, and follow the on-screen instructions to transfer your existing account information to this computer.

Configuring a Dial-Up Account Manually

Follow the instructions in this section if you have obtained an Internet subscription from an Internet service provider without using the Microsoft Referral Service. You'll need an installed modem or an ISDN adapter, as well as a telephone line. You also need configuration information given to you by your ISP, as explained in the following section.

NOTE

If your ISP gave you a disk containing a setup program, use your ISP's setup program instead of configuring your connection manually. This program contains information that will automatically set up your Internet connection. Most ISPs provide a setup disk or CD-ROM. Most of the people who manually configure their connections are using accounts at a small business or an educational institution that doesn't have the resources to create a setup disk.

Getting the Information You'll Need for a Dial-Up Account

Before you run the Connection Wizard, make sure you have all the configuration information you need:

- **Phone number.** The number you call to access your ISP's computer. This should be a local call, but be sure to note the area code and country code if you need to dial these in addition to the phone number.
- **User name.** Also called login name or account name, this is the name you supply to identify yourself to your service provider.
- **Password.** This is the secret authorization code that confirms your identity. Don't give your password to any other person!
- **Connection type.** Ask your service provider whether your connection will be made by means of Point-to-Point Protocol (PPP) or Serial Line Interface Protocol (SLIP).

- **Logon procedure.** Ask whether you need to type something manually when you connect, or whether you can log on automatically after you supply Windows with your user name and password. If you need to type something, find out exactly what to type. You may need to use a *logon script*, a file containing commands that are automatically entered when you log on. Ask whether such a script is needed, and if so, whether the ISP can give you one to use.
- **Internet address.** Ask whether you need to configure your computer with a permanent IP address. Most ISPs assign an address when you connect.
- **E-mail address.** You'll need your e-mail address so you can configure Internet mail.
- **E-mail service type.** Outlook Express can work with POP3 servers, which store your mail temporarily until you download it to your computer. It can also work with IMAP servers, which store your mail on the server.
- **Address of mail servers.** You'll need the Internet address of both the incoming (POP3 or IMAP) and outgoing (SMTP) mail servers. Sometimes these are the same.
- **E-mail user name or account name.** Often, this is the same as your Internet account user name.
- **E-mail password.** This may differ from the password you use to access the Internet.
- **Authentication method.** Ask whether you need to confirm your e-mail program to use Secure Password Authentication (SPA).
- **Address of news server.** You'll need the Internet address of the news server available from your ISP.

TIP

When you run the Connection Wizard, keep your ISP's technical support number handy. If you neglected to obtain some of the above information, or noted it down incorrectly, you may need to call them. Run the wizard when the technical support office is open!

Using the Connection Wizard to Configure an Account Manually

SEE ALSO
To configure additional Internet connections to use on the same computer, see "Creating Additional Connections," page 86.

To configure an account using information given to you by your ISP, follow these steps:

1. From the Start menu, click Programs, Accessories, and Internet Tools. Then choose Connection Wizard from the submenu. You'll see the Connection Wizard.
2. Click the third option, I Want To Set Up My Internet Connection Manually, Or I Connect Through A Local Area Network (LAN). Click Next to go to the next page.
3. Activate the option called Connect Using My Phone Line, and click Next. You'll see the page titled Step 1 of 3: Internet account connection information, shown here:

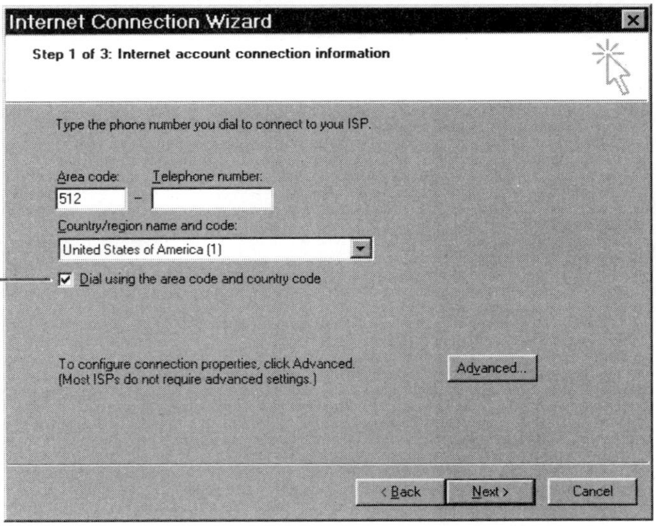

Click here if you must dial an area code to access the ISP's telephone number.

4. In the Telephone Number box, type your ISP's telephone access number. If you must dial an area code to access this number, click the check box next to Dial Using The Area Code And Country Code.
5. To continue, click the Advanced button on the Step 1 page. You'll see the Connection page of the Advanced Connection Properties dialog box, shown on the next page.

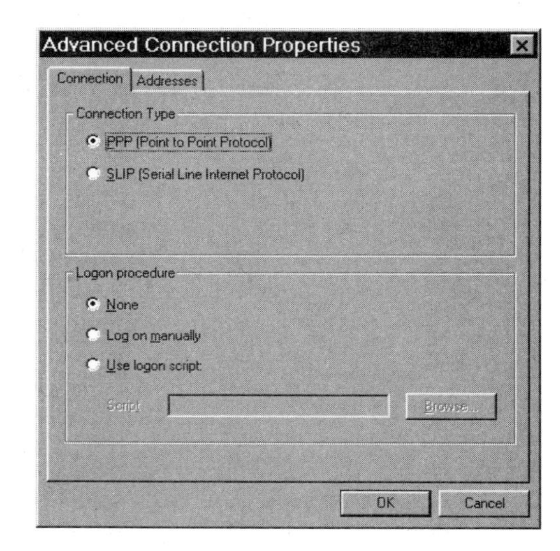

6 In the Connection Type area, choose the type of connection you will be making (PPP, SLIP, or C-SLIP).

For more information on logon scripts, see "Using a Logon Script," page 75.

7 In the Logon Procedure area, choose one of the three options. If you're connecting via PPP, the first option, None, is the most likely choice. If you're connecting via SLIP, you can log on manually, or you can connect via a logon script (a text file containing a stored logon procedure). If your ISP gave you a logon script file to use, click Use Logon Script, and click Browse to locate the file.

8 Click the Addresses tab. You'll see the Addresses page of the Advanced Connection Properties dialog box, shown on the next page:

If your ISP requires DNS numbers, type them carefully here (no spaces).

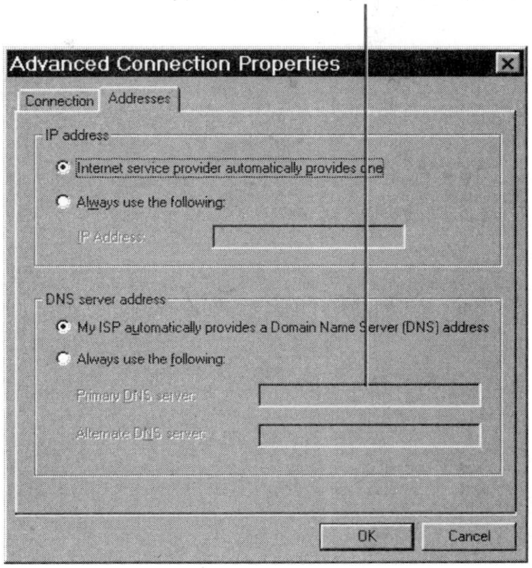

9 In the IP Address area, specify an IP address only if your ISP specifically told you to do so. Otherwise, use the default option (Internet Service Provider Automatically Provides One).

10 If your ISP told you that you had to type in DNS server addresses, click Always Use The Following, and type the primary and alternate DNS server addresses. Otherwise, click My ISP automatically provides a domain name server (DNS) address.

11 Click OK to return to the wizard's Step 1 of 3 page, and click Next. You'll see the Step 2 page, shown on the next page:

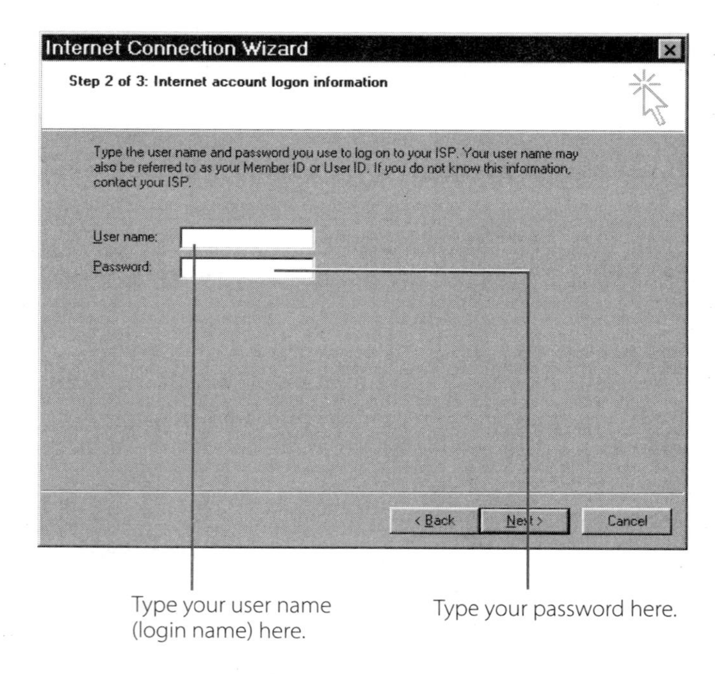

12 In the User Name box, type the user name or login name that your ISP gave you.

13 In the Password box, carefully type the password that your ISP gave you.

14 Click Next. You'll see the Step 3 of 3 page, shown here.

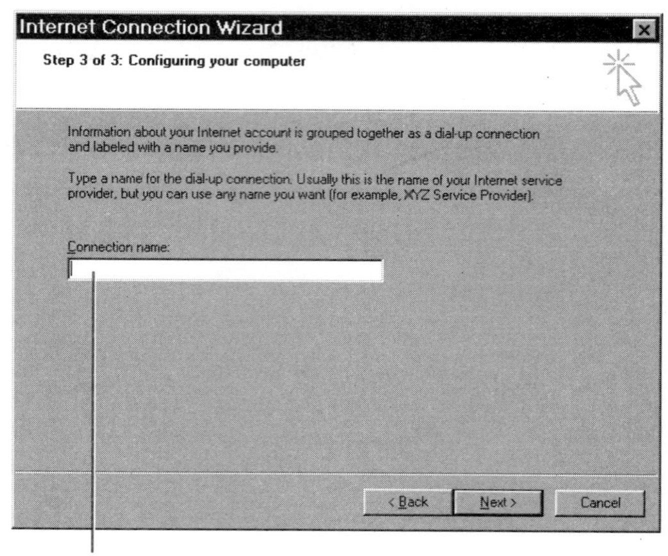

15 In the Connection Name box, type a descriptive name for this connection, such as your ISP's name.

16 Click Next. To set up your e-mail account, click Yes, and click Next.

If an e-mail account has already been set up on this computer, you'll see a page asking whether you'd like to use the existing connection. To use this connection, click Use An Existing Internet Mail Account, and select the account in the list box. To create a new connection, click Create A New Internet Mail Account. The next section shows you how to set up your Internet e-mail connection.

If you don't want to set up your e-mail connection now, click No, and click Next to complete the connection. You can set up your connection later by using Outlook Express, as explained in "Adding a New Account," in Chapter 13.

Setting Up Your E-Mail Connection

When you configure your Internet connection manually using the Connection Wizard, you can choose to set up your e-mail account. If you chose to do so, follow these steps to complete your connection.

1 In the Connection Wizard, you'll see the Your Name page after you choose to create a new e-mail account. In the Display name box, type your name.

TIP

The display name you type will appear in the From column of your correspondent's e-mail programs. To enable your correspondents to sort message lists more easily, consider supplying your last name first ("Smith, John"). You can use a nickname, but please think twice, particularly if you're thinking of something slightly off-color. Do you think a prospective employer will appreciate receiving a message from "Avenger" or "The Dark Lord"?

2 Click Next to continue. You'll see the Internet E-Mail Address page. In the E-Mail Address box, type your e-mail address.

3 Click Next to continue. You'll see the E-mail Server Names page, shown on the next page:

Choose POP3 or IMAP.

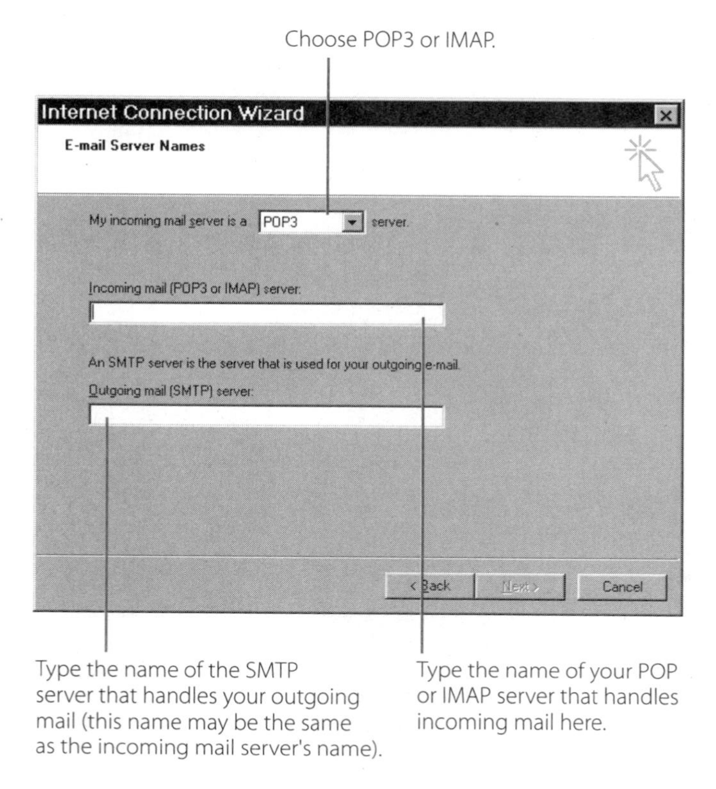

Type the name of the SMTP server that handles your outgoing mail (this name may be the same as the incoming mail server's name).

Type the name of your POP or IMAP server that handles incoming mail here.

4 In the drop-down list box, choose the type of server (POP3 or IMAP).

5 In the Incoming Mail (POP3 or IMAP) Server box, type the Internet address of the computer that handles your incoming mail.

6 In the Outgoing Mail (SMTP) Server box, type the Internet address of the computer that handles your outgoing mail. This address might be the same as the one for incoming mail, but type it here anyway. Sometimes this address is different.

7 Click Next to continue. You'll see the Internet Mail Logon page, shown on the next page.

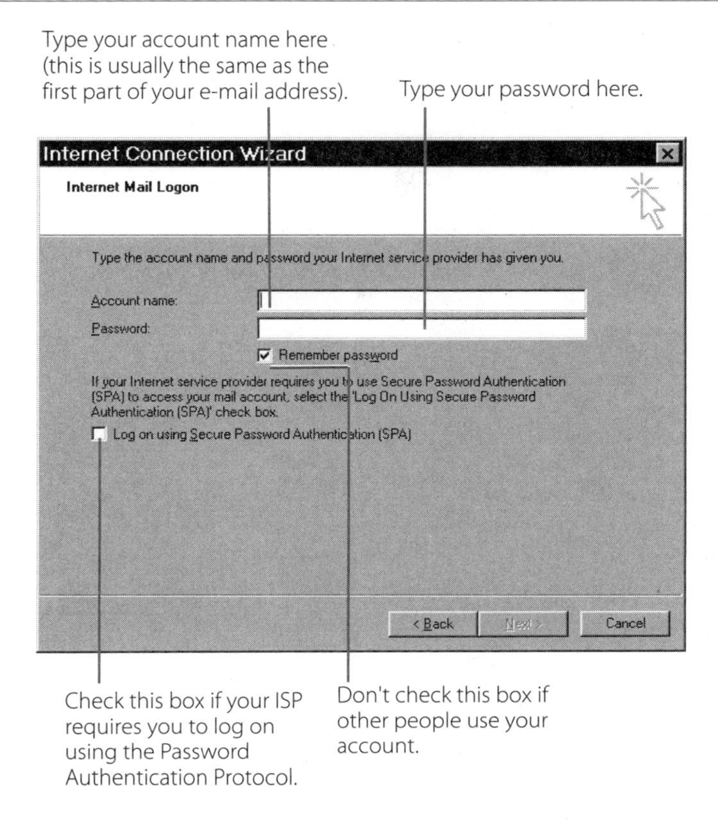

8 In the Account Name box, type the e-mail account name or logon name you were given by your ISP. This name may differ from the one you use to connect to the Internet.

9 In the Password box, type the e-mail password you were given by your ISP. This password may differ from the one you use to connect to the Internet. If you would like Outlook Express to remember your e-mail password, click Remember Password. If your service provider requires you to use Secure Password Authentication to access your e-mail, click Log On Using Secure Password Authentication (SPA).

TIP

Don't click Remember Password if you're using a computer that's accessible to people you don't completely trust. Someone could play a prank on you by sending mail from your computer, and the mail will look as though it came from you!

10 Click Next, and click Finish to complete your connection.

Creating a Multilink PPP Connection

To create a Multilink PPP connection using two analog modems or internal ISDN adapters, you must have two modems or two ISDN adapters installed in your system, as well as two free telephone lines and an account that supports Multilink PPP. To configure your Multilink PPP connection, follow these steps:

1. Follow the steps in the previous section to configure your connection using the first modem or ISDN adapter.
2. From the Start menu, click Programs, choose Accessories, and click Dial-Up Networking. In the Dial-Up Networking window (Windows 95 and 98 only), right-click the icon for the connection you want to make. From the pop-up menu, choose Properties. For Windows NT, select the connection from the drop-down list.
3. Click the Multilink tab. You'll see the Multilink page.
4. Activate the option called Use Additional Devices.
5. Click the Add button, and choose the modem or ISDN adapter that you want to use. If you need to dial a second number to access the Multilink service, enter the phone number.
6. Click OK to confirm your changes.

Using a Logon Script

Most ISPs do not require a logon script, but you may need to use one if you're connecting to a free network service or an ISP that's using out-of-date technology. You may be able to obtain a sample script from the ISP, but chances are you'll need to modify it prior to using it; ask for instructions.

If your ISP requires a script but can't supply you with a sample, you can open and edit one of several sample scripts that you can modify. You'll find sample scripts (the file names end in .scp) for menu-based SLIP and PPP connections. The sample scripts contain information that explains how the scripts work and how you can modify them.

To associate a logon script with an Internet connection:

1. In the Dial-Up Networking window (Windows 95 and 98 only), right-click the connection icon.
2. Click the Scripting tab. You'll see the Scripting page.
3. Click the Browse button to locate the script you want to use.
4. To edit the script, click the Edit button. You'll see the script in a Notepad window. Choose Save from the File menu to save your changes before exiting.
5. To test your script the next time you log on, activate Step Through Script. The script will execute one line at a time. To go to the next step, press Enter. This option lets you determine where errors are located. When you're certain your script is working properly, re-display the Scripting page and deactivate this option.
6. When you use a logon script, you see a terminal window while the connection is being made. The first few times you run the script, you should leave this window on-screen so you can read any error messages should your script contain an error. If your script works perfectly, you can hide the terminal window by activating Start Terminal Screen Minimized.
7. Click OK to confirm your choices.

Connecting to the Internet

You can start an Internet connection in any of the following ways:

- On the desktop, click the Internet Explorer icon.
- Start Outlook Express, NetMeeting, Microsoft Chat, or any other program that requires an Internet connection.
- From the Start menu, click Programs, choose Accessories, and click Dial-Up Networking. In the Dial-Up Networking window, click the icon for the connection you want to make.

  You'll see the Connect To dialog box (Windows 95 and 98 only), shown on the next page:

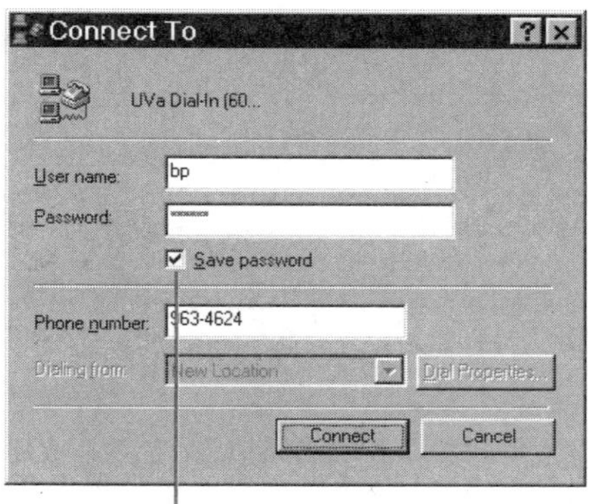

Don't check this option if other people use your computer.

Check the phone number to make sure it's correct, and click Connect.

If you activate Save Password, you won't have to type your password every time you connect. Despite the convenience of not having to type your password, you should not activate this option if other people use your computer or you sometimes leave it unattended. Your actions while online leave a trail for which you're responsible; make sure it's your trail and not someone else's.

Couldn't get through? If you're having trouble connecting to your ISP due to busy signals, you can configure Windows to dial the number repeatedly. Choose Internet Options from the Control Panel, click the Connections tab, select your connection, and click Settings. Click the Advanced button. Adjust the number of times to try to connect, and click OK.

Once you're connected, you'll see a connection icon on the taskbar (see Figure 4-3).

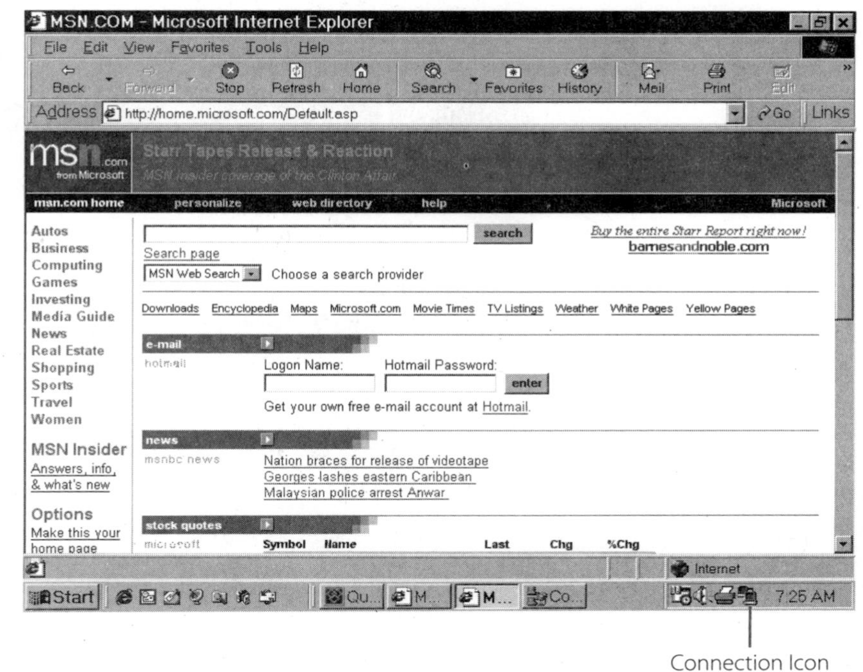

FIGURE 4-3.
When you're connected to the Internet via a dial-up connection, you see a connection icon on the taskbar.

Disconnecting from the Internet

To disconnect from the Internet, right-click the connection icon, and choose Disconnect from the pop-up menu.

Maintaining Connection Information

CAUTION
Don't change settings if your connection is working perfectly! You should adjust settings manually only if your connection information has changed, or if you'd like to select an option (such as reducing modem volume) that won't affect your connection.

After connecting successfully, you may want to change some of the connection settings—or you may need to. For example, your ISP may start using a new phone number, or require you to use a different password. In this section, you learn how to change connection information for an existing Internet connection. You'll learn how to edit connection information, should the need arise, and you'll also learn how to choose connection options.

To edit your telephone connection information, modem properties, or DNS (name server) addresses, do the following:

1 From the desktop, choose My Computer (Windows 95 and 98 only).

2 In the My Computer window, choose Dial-Up Networking. You'll see the Dial-Up Networking window, shown on the next page:

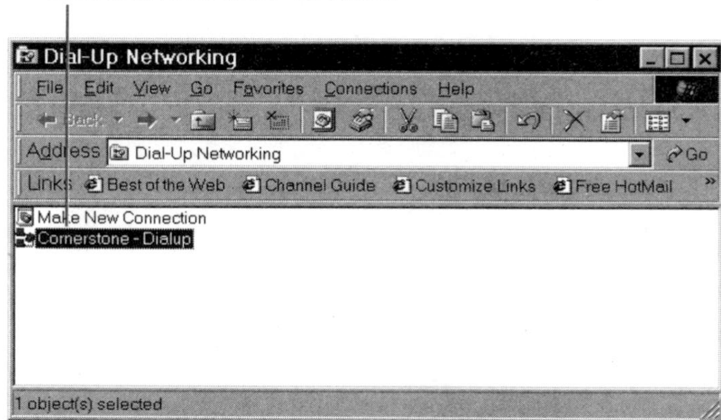

3 Right-click your connection, and choose Properties from the pop-up menu. You'll see a dialog box like the one shown here:

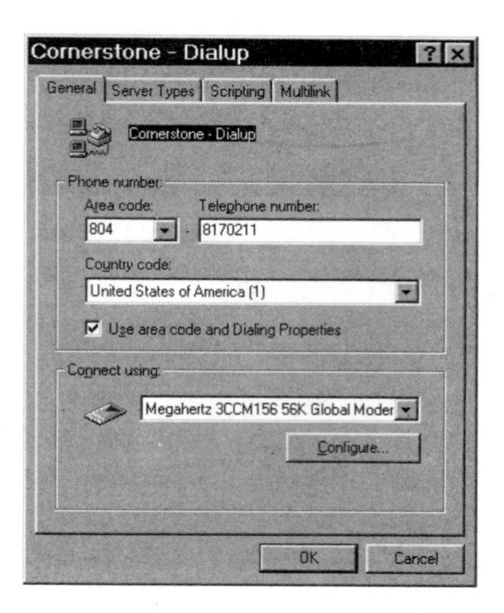

4 In the Phone Number area, you can correct the telephone number and area code. If you need to use the area code and dialing properties you've defined in the Telephony Settings dialog box (Control Panel), activate Use Area Code And Dialing Properties.

5 To change modem properties, click Configure. You'll see the properties dialog box for your modem, shown on the next page:

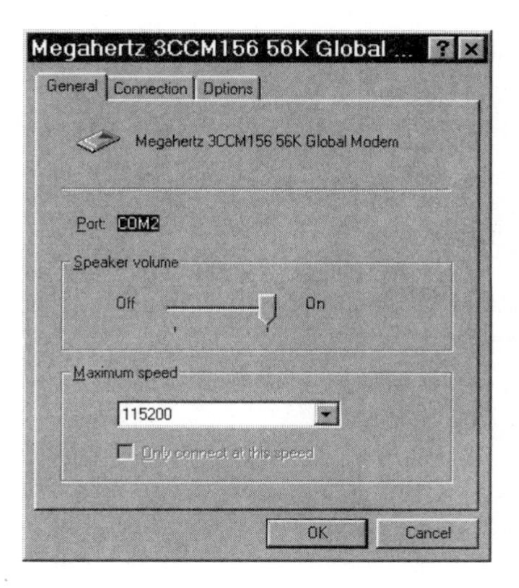

6 In the General page, you can set the speaker volume. The port and other settings should be correct; don't modify them unless you have specific reasons for doing so.

7 Click Connection to see the connection options, shown in the following illustration. Don't change the options in the Connection Preferences area unless you've been instructed to do so by a technical support expert. In the Call Preferences area, you can choose options concerning waiting for dial tones, canceling the call if a connection doesn't occur within a specified number of minutes, and disconnecting calls after a specified idle time.

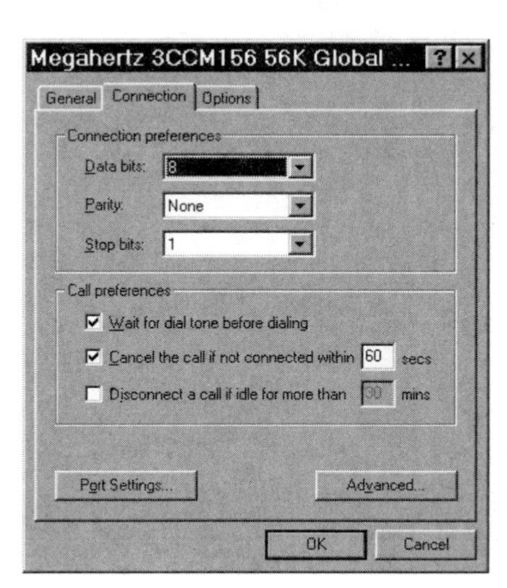

CAUTION

If you signed up for an Internet account with time-based billing, be aware that quitting Internet Explorer doesn't necessarily hang up the connection. To configure your connection to disconnect automatically, choose Internet Options from the Control Panel, click the Connections tab, select your connection, and click Settings. Click the Advanced button. In the Advanced Dial-Up dialog box, you can specify an idle period before automatic disconnect, and you can also activate an option that disconnects when all Internet applications exit.

8 Click OK to return to the Properties dialog box.

9 Click Server Types. You'll see the Server Types page, shown here:

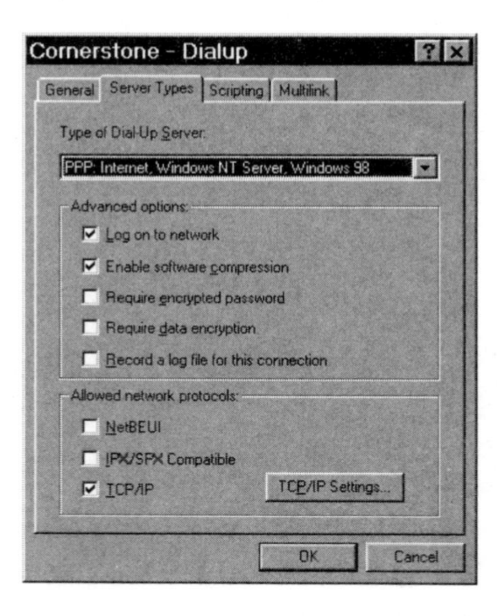

You shouldn't make any changes here unless you've been directed to do so by your Internet service provider.

10 Click TCP/IP. You'll see the TCP/IP settings for this Internet connection, shown here:

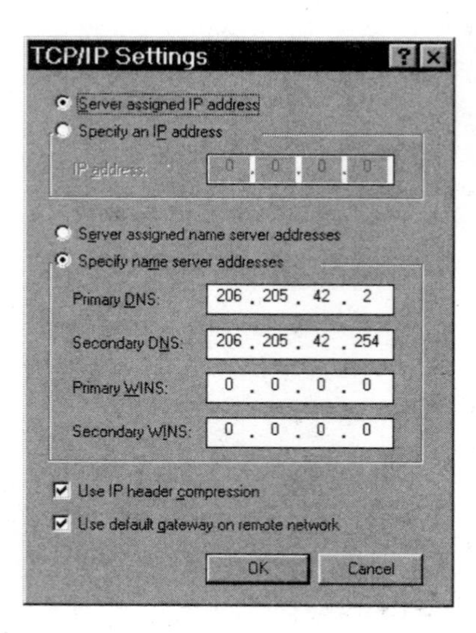

Here's where you can change the IP address or name server addresses if necessary.

11 Click OK until you see Microsoft Windows again.

SEE ALSO
To edit e-mail account information, see "Managing Accounts," page 451.

To change your user name or password, or to select a number of connection options, follow these instructions:

1 In the Control Panel, choose Internet Options. You'll see the Internet Properties dialog box, shown here.

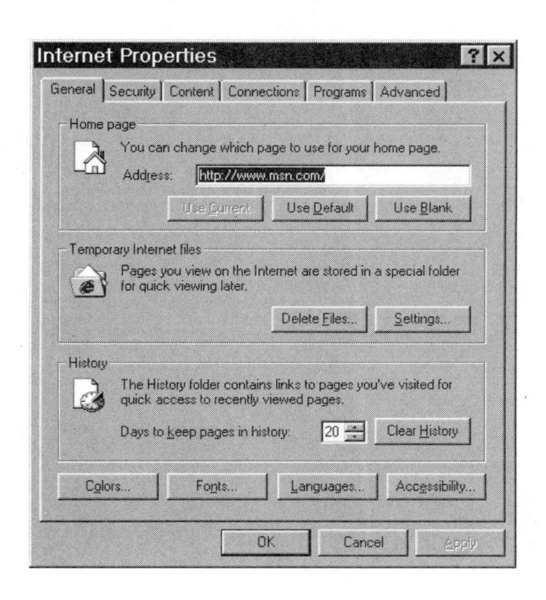

2 Click the Connections tab. You'll see the Connections page, shown on the next page:

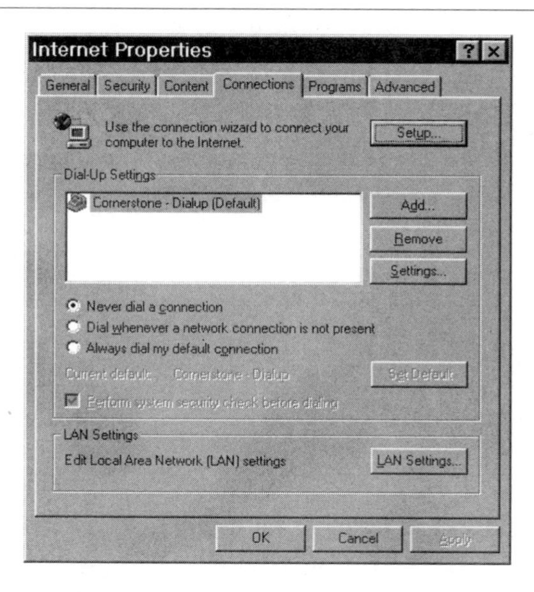

3 Select the connection you're using.

4 Click Settings. You'll see the Dialup Settings for the selected connection, shown here:

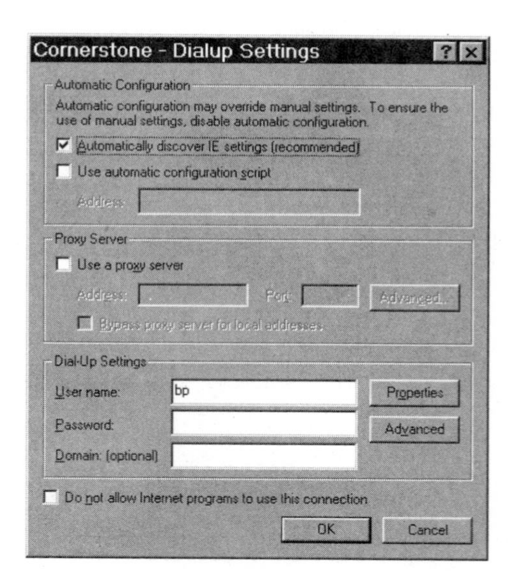

SEE ALSO
For a list of the information needed to sign up for a dial-up account, see "Getting the Information You'll Need for a Dial-Up Account," page 67.

5 In the Dial-Up Settings area, edit your user name or password.

6 Click Advanced. You'll see the Advanced Dial-Up dialog box, shown on the next page:

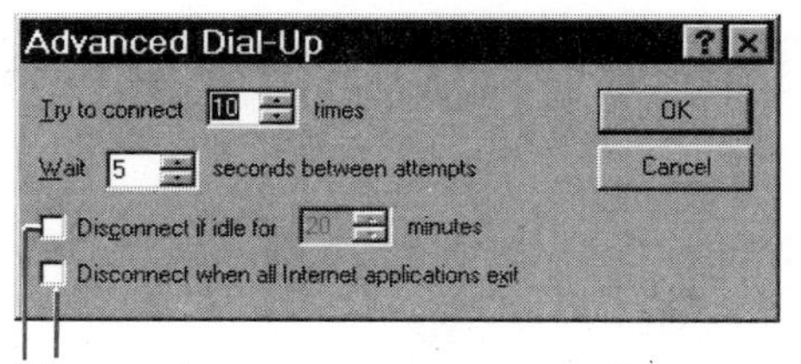

These options can save you money if you must pay per-minute charges for your connection.

In this dialog box, you can choose a number of connection options, including the number of times to attempt a connection, the amount of time to wait before re-trying, and the amount of idle time to wait before disconnecting. Choose connection options, and click OK.

7. Click OK until you see Microsoft Windows again.

Configuring a LAN Connection

If your computer is already connected to a local area network (LAN), and the LAN is connected to the Internet, you can easily configure your computer to access the Internet via the LAN. The following assumes that you or your network administrator have already installed your network adapter and successfully connected your computer to the LAN.

Obtaining the Information You Need for a LAN Connection

To prevent unauthorized intrusions into internal networks, most organizations use *proxy servers*, which disguise the location of computers on the LAN. Proxy servers stand between your computer and the external Internet, receiving your requests for information and then relaying them to external servers. So far as anyone on the Internet knows, the request is coming from the proxy server, not your machine. As a result, would-be intruders cannot determine the location of your computer.

Ask your network administrator whether you will access the Internet by means of a proxy server. If so, you'll need the following information:

- **Proxy server address.** Usually, the same proxy server is used for all available Internet services, such as the Web (HTTP), FTP, and Gopher. If so, you'll need the Internet address of the proxy server, as well as the port number to use. If a different proxy server is used for each service, you'll need all the proxy server addresses and port numbers.

- **Addresses that do not require a proxy server.** To access intranet resources, you can specify one or more internal domains for direct access (not mediated through a proxy server). Ask your network administrator which domain addresses to use.

- **Automatic configuration.** Organizations can use the Internet Explorer Administration Kit (IEAK) to configure the browser automatically. Ask your network administrator whether automatic configuration has been enabled, and how to activate it once you've connected to the network.

You'll also need much of the information required to sign up for a dial-up account, including your e-mail address, e-mail service type, address of the mail servers, e-mail user name, e-mail password, and authentication method.

Running the Connection Wizard

To configure a LAN connection using information given to you by your network administrator, follow these steps:

1. From the Start menu, click Programs, Accessories, and Internet Tools. Then choose Connection Wizard from the submenu.

2. Activate the option called I Want To Set Up My Internet Connection Manually, Or I Connect Through A Local Area Network (LAN). Click Next.

3. Activate the option called I Connect Through A Local Area Network (LAN), and click Next.

   You see the local area network Internet configuration page.

4. If you're using a LAN in an organization, you may need to configure proxy server settings. A proxy server hides internal Internet addresses from outside intruders. Just leave this page blank if your LAN does not use a proxy server.

   Do one of the following:

   - To enable Internet Explorer to detect the proxy server automatically, click Automatic Discovery Of Proxy Server. This is the recommended option.

     or

   - If your network administrator gave you the address of an automatic configuration script for the proxy server, click Use Automatic Configuration Script, and type the script's address in the Address box.

or

- If your network administrator gave you proxy server information and told you to configure your connection manually, click Manual Proxy Server, and click Next. Type the proxy addresses and port numbers of the proxy servers in the fields provided.

SEE ALSO

To configure your e-mail account from within Outlook Express, see "Adding a New Account," page 452.

5 Click Next. To set up your Internet mail account, click Yes. Turn to the section titled "Setting Up Your E-mail Connection," page 73, to complete your connection. If you click No, click Next to finish your connection.

TIP

Should you need to change the proxy server settings after running the Connection Wizard, start Internet Explorer, click Tools on the menu bar, and choose Internet Options. In the Internet Options dialog box, click the Connections tab, click LAN settings, and then click the Settings button. Click the Advanced button to display the Proxy Settings dialog box. Here, you can enter proxy server addresses and port numbers. You can also enter the domain names that do not require the proxy server.

Creating Additional Connections

When you create a connection using the Connection Wizard, Windows creates a connection icon and places this icon in the Dial-Up Networking window. It also makes this connection the default connection for Internet access. As you'll learn in this section, you can create connections for additional Internet accounts.

Adding an Internet Account

To add a second Internet account, just run the Connection Wizard again. After you've finished creating the connection, you'll see the new connection icon in the Dial-Up Networking window.

Choosing the Default Account

Once you've created two or more accounts, you can specify which of them is the default account for Internet use. Remember that the Connection Wizard automatically assigns default status to the most recently created connection. To change the default connection, do the following:

1. Choose Internet Options from the Control Panel, and click the Connections tab.
2. Click the connection that you want to set as the default.
3. Click Set Default.
4. Click OK.

Creating a Connection Shortcut

Once you've created more than one connection, you may find it convenient to create desktop shortcuts for these connections. With these shortcuts (Windows 95 and 98 only), you won't have to navigate to the Dial-Up Networking window in order to start these connections.

To create a desktop shortcut for a connection icon, open the Dial-Up Networking window, and right-click the connection icon. From the pop-up menu, click Create Shortcut. Answer Yes to the question about placing the shortcut on the desktop.

Creating Additional Calling Locations

If you're using a portable computer and want to access the Internet from different calling locations, you can create as many additional calling locations as you like. You can configure each location's dialing properties so that you can log on effortlessly. For example, in your office, you may need to use an outside-line code in order to access the Internet, but this code isn't needed when you dial from home.

To create additional calling locations:

1. Click Start, and choose Settings. Click Control Panel, and click the Telephony icon. You'll see the Dialing Properties dialog box.
2. To create a new dialing location, click New, and click OK. In the box under I Am Dialing From, give this connection a descriptive name (such as "Home" or "Office").
3. Configure the dialing properties for the new location.
4. Click OK.

After you create new locations, you can choose a location when you connect to the Internet. In the Connect To dialog box, click the list box next to Dialing From, and choose the location you want.

PART III

Browsing the Web

CHAPTER 5

Mastering Browser Essentials

Before you drive an unfamiliar car, you need to figure out some basic but very important things, such as how to adjust the stereo so you can tell which Beatle is singing—John, Paul, or George. The same principle applies to Microsoft Internet Explorer. This chapter introduces the basics of using Internet Explorer, including understanding what's on the screen and getting a grip on the fundamentals of navigation. In this chapter, you'll learn all the fundamentals of Web navigation with the best available browser.

Learning Web Terminology

You'll hear people talking about Web servers, Web sites, URLs, Web pages, and home pages. Let's clarify these basic terms:

- **Web server.** A program that listens for requests from browsers for a particular Web page (or the computer that's running the program). The server dishes out the page and then listens for more requests. If the server can't find the page, it sends an error message that says "not found" or something similarly vague and unhelpful.
- **Web site.** A collection of Web pages. A Web site has a unique Internet address that unambiguously identifies its location. Most Web sites contain dozens, hundreds, or even thousands of Web pages.
- **Web page.** A Web page is a single Web document. In actual length, some are shorter than a page, while some are longer—much longer. Most Web pages average about two screens full of text and graphics.
- **Home page.** People use this phrase in different ways. It basically means "home base." In Internet Explorer, you click Home (on the toolbar) to go to the msn.com home page. This phrase also refers to the welcome page of a Web site that includes many linked pages, so you might see a Home icon on somebody's pages. If you click this icon, you see the welcome page, not the MSN Internet Start page. When people say, "I can't wait to put my home page on the Web," what they're talking about is a personal page, which is likely to contain their resume, picture, favorite hobbies and pets, and a few favorite links.
- **URL.** Short for Uniform Resource Locator, a URL indicates the Internet address of the page you're currently viewing. A complete URL includes the type of Internet protocol you're using (for Web addresses, this is indicated by means of *http://*), the Internet address of the Web site you're accessing (such as http://www.c34.org), and the exact location and file name of the current Web page. (When you're accessing the site's default home page, you don't see any information about the page's exact location and name.)

NOTE

As you'll quickly discover, people use the terms *site* and *page* more or less synonymously. Somebody who says, "Hey, check out this awesome site," is usually referring to a specific Web page or document, not an entire collection of documents. This isn't done just by *newbies*, people new to the Internet, but by seasoned vets, too. I suspect it's because *site* sounds more high tech than *page* or *document*. Still, you'll have a better grasp of the Web if you keep the distinction in mind.

Connecting to the Internet

SEE ALSO

For information on installing Internet Explorer, see Appendix A.

Assuming you've installed Internet Explorer and have access to the Internet, you're ready to browse the Web. In this section, you learn how to connect to the Internet using the dial-up connection you created in Chapter 4, "Running the Connection Wizard." If you're connecting by means of a local area network (LAN), there's no dial-up procedure; your Internet connection is permanently on. To connect, simply start Internet Explorer or any other Internet application.

TIP

If you would like Windows to dial your ISP automatically every time you start any Internet application, open the Control Panel, choose Internet Options, and click the Connections tab. Make sure the option called Always Dial My Default Connection is activated.

To start Internet Explorer for the first time, follow these steps:

1. Do one of the following to start Internet Explorer and connect to the Internet:
   - On the desktop, click the Internet Explorer icon.
   - On the Quick Launch Toolbar, click the little Internet Explorer icon.
   - From the Start menu, choose Programs, Internet Explorer, and the Internet Explorer browser.
2. You'll see a sign-in dialog box, such as the one shown in Figure 5-1. Carefully type your user name and password, just as your Internet service provider (ISP) gave them to you—including capitalization.

3 If you have a portable computer and you created more than one dialing location (see Chapter 4), select your dialing location.

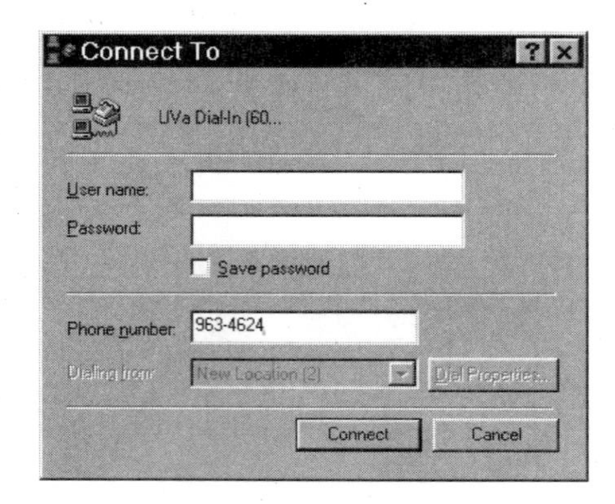

FIGURE 5-1.
To connect to the Internet, type the user name and password that your Internet service provider gave you.

4 When you're sure you've typed your user name and password correctly, click Connect, or just press Enter.

TIP

If you want to avoid typing your password every time you connect to the Internet, you can choose the Save Password option in the sign-in dialog box (or just press Alt + S). But think twice before you do this. Although your password will remain invisible, this option would enable anybody to sit down at your computer and get connected to the Internet.

Assuming all goes well with your connection, you'll see the msn.com home page (Figure 5-2). Because MSN constantly improves, this page will probably look different by the time you read this book, and it may work differently. At this writing, the MSN welcome page enables you to choose configuration options for Internet Explorer's *default-start page*, the Web page you'll see every time you start the program. Like other Web *portals,* this page provides a subject guide to interesting and useful Web pages, links to a free e-mail service (Microsoft's service is called Hotmail), current news, sports scores, stock quotes, weather, and more. The Welcome to the Web page enables you to customize your start page so that it reflects your interests. The initial customization currently asks for your time zone, zip code (U.S. users only), or region and city (international users only). Once you've made these choices and clicked Done, you see the MSN.com home page (see Figure 5-3). Because Internet Explorer has saved your time zone and location information, you'll see this page automatically every time you start Internet Explorer.

SEE ALSO
For information on HotMail, see Chapter 15, "Using Hotmail."

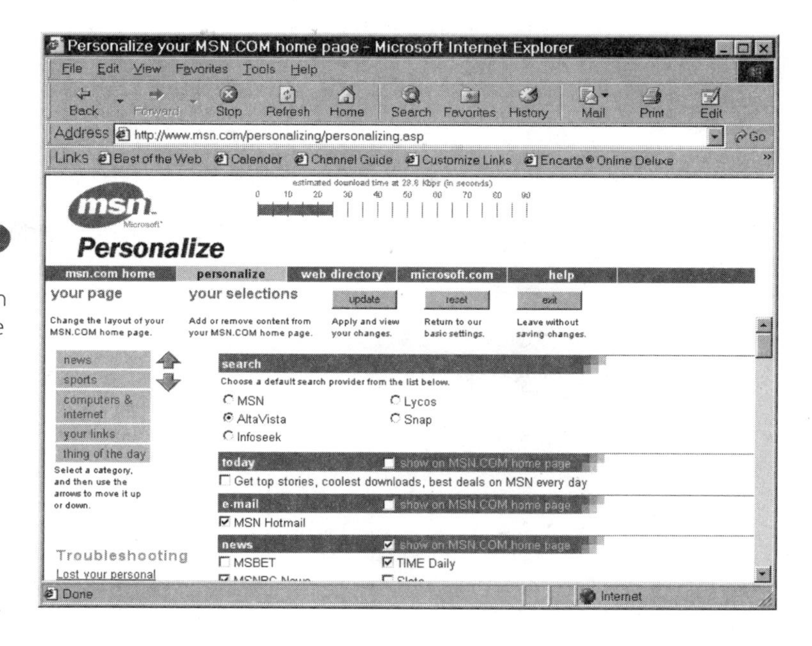

FIGURE 5-2.
The MSN.com home page enables you to choose your portal options.

CAUTION

To make sure you're using the safest version of Internet Explorer, be sure to click the Internet Explorer news link and visit the Internet Explorer home page periodically (http://www.microsoft.com/ie). You may see news about an Internet Explorer security flaw. Occasionally, researchers find security holes in Internet software that affects not only Internet Explorer but many other programs as well. Microsoft develops fixes for such holes very rapidly; you can download the fix, called a *patch*, from the Internet Explorer home page.

Troubleshooting Internet Connections

Here's what to do if you experienced difficulty connecting to the Internet.

- **Is your modem turned on?**
  If you have an external modem, be sure you've turned on the power.
- **Is the phone line plugged into the modem, and is it plugged into the right connector?**
  Some modems have different connectors for wall outlet and extension phone.
- **Are you getting a dial tone?**
  If not, there's something wrong with the way the phone line is hooked up.
- **Did you get a busy signal?**
  Try again later.
- **Did your ISP reject the logon attempt?**
  You might have typed your user name or password incorrectly. Try again.
- **Still doesn't work?**
  Call your Internet service provider and ask for help. They'll walk you through a status check of all your Internet settings to make sure everything's correct.

Understanding What's on the Screen

SEE ALSO
For information on sizing and moving the Internet Explorer toolbars, see "Displaying, Sizing, and Repositioning the Toolbars" page 102.

Take a seat and get oriented. Look at Internet Explorer's screen. Figure 5-3 shows what you'll see with all of the toolbars brought into view. You'll learn more about what the toolbars do in the next section.

If you don't see all the toolbars, right-click the menu bar. You'll see the following pop-up menu:

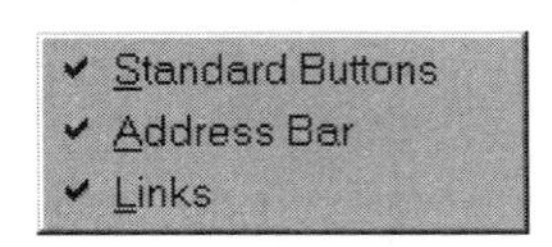

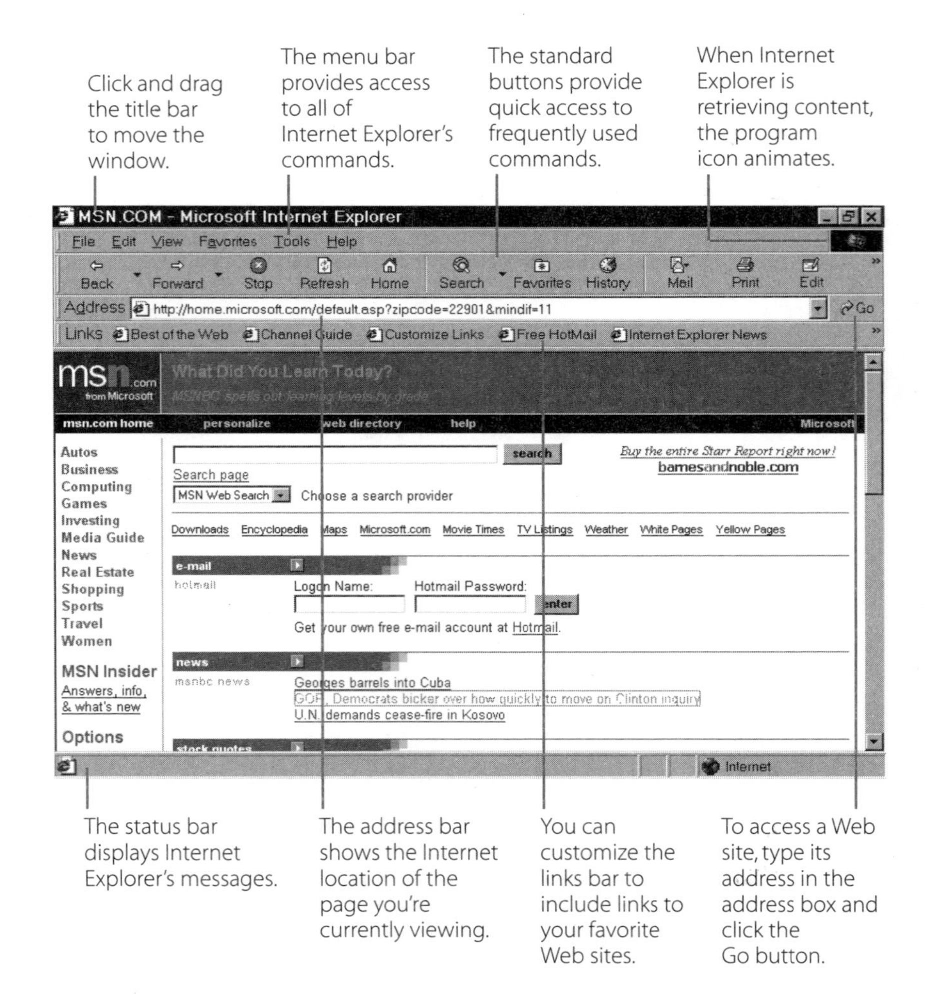

FIGURE 5-3.
The MSN.com home page shows you news, stock quotes, weather, and more every time you start Internet Explorer.

If a toolbar name doesn't have a check mark next to it, choose the name to activate the toolbar. Repeat this process until you've activated all three toolbars.

TIP

As you're learning Internet Explorer, display the Tip Of The Day. To display the tip, click View on the menu bar, choose Explorer Bar, and activate the Tip Of The Day option. You'll see the Tip Of The Day at the bottom of the screen. To close the Tip Of The Day, click the close button (the X on the left side of the Tip Of The Day panel).

Let's examine the screen from top to bottom.

SEE ALSO
For information on managing windows, see "Minimizing and Maximizing Windows," page 39.

- **Title bar.** Positioned at the top of the window, the title bar shows the title of the Web document you're currently accessing. You also see the standard Windows buttons for minimizing, restoring, or maximizing the window, and a close button, which enables you to quit the program. To move the window, click and drag the title bar.

- **Menu bar.** On the menu bar, you'll find the names of Internet Explorer's menus. If you select one of the menu names, a menu drops down, giving you additional options. The menus contain all of Internet Explorer's commands. However, the most frequently used commands appear on the toolbars. You probably won't use the menus much, and only for commands that aren't on the toolbars. This book will discuss these as they come up.

- **Program icon.** The program icon (a Windows symbol located at the right edge of the menu bar) becomes animated while Internet Explorer is retrieving a document for you. (Retrieving a document is sometimes called *downloading*.) The animation ceases when the whole document has been downloaded.

- **Standard buttons.** This toolbar contains the most frequently chosen commands.

TIP

If you see arrows at the right edge of a toolbar, at least one icon is hidden from view.

- **Address bar.** The address bar shows the current Web address of the page you're viewing. You'll learn more about Web addresses later in this chapter.

SEE ALSO
For information on the Search explorer, see Chapter 6, "Using the Search Assistant." For information on the Favorites explorer, see Chapter 7, "Creating Shortcuts to Favorite Pages." You'll learn about the History explorer later in this chapter (see "Using the History Explorer," page 106).

- **Links bar.** The links toolbar contains links that you can click to go to a specific Web page quickly. You'll find several predefined links, but you can customize this bar with your own favorite links.
- **Go button.** To go to a Web page, you can type the address in the Address bar and click this button to display the page. This is a new feature in Internet Explorer version 5.
- **Web page.** Within the Internet Explorer window, you see the Web document you're currently accessing. If the document is bigger than the window size, you'll see active scroll bars, which you can use to bring additional portions of the document into view.
- **Explorer Bar.** The Explorer Bar appears when you click Search, Favorites, or History on the standard toolbar. To hide the Explorer Bar, click the close button (the X mark) in the explorer's title bar.
- **Status bar.** In the status bar, Internet Explorer talks back. You'll learn more about Internet Explorer's messages as they come up.

Introducing the Toolbars

Internet Explorer has four toolbars:

To customize the Standard toolbar, see "Customizing the Toolbar," page 274

- **Standard Buttons.** The icons on this toolbar provide quick access to the commands and features you'll use most often, including navigation commands (Back, Forward, Stop, Refresh, and Home), the explorers (Search, Favorites, and History), printing, and access to other programs in the Internet Explorer suite (Mail and Edit).
- **Address Bar.** This toolbar displays the Web address (URL) of the Web page you are currently viewing. You can also access other Web pages by typing Web addresses in the Address text box, or by choosing a recently entered Web site from the drop-down menu.
- **Links.** This toolbar enables you to customize Internet Explorer so that it provides one-click access to your favorite sites. The Links toolbar contains some default sites, but you can customize the Links toolbar so that it contains the sites you use most often.
- **Radio.** This toolbar enables you to "tune in" to Internet radio stations. You can choose a station from the Radio Station guide and listen to Internet-based broadcasts. You'll find stations in all listening categories, including news, talk radio, classical, adult contemporary, and more.

If you don't see the Radio toolbar, you need to install Windows Media Player. For information on Windows Media Player, see Chapter 8.

The following sections briefly introduce the four toolbars. You'll learn more about the use of these toolbars in subsequent sections.

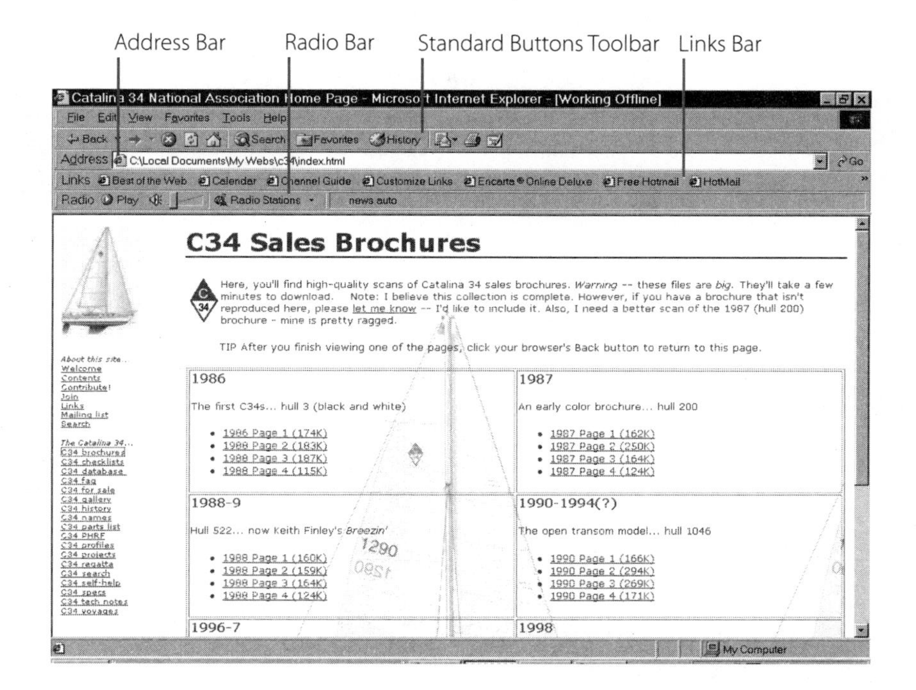

FIGURE 5-4.
Here's what Internet Explorer looks like with all four toolbars in view.

The Standard Buttons Toolbar

SEE ALSO
For more information about which icons appear on the standard buttons toolbar, see "Customizing the Toolbar," page 274.

Look closer now at the Standard toolbar, which you'll use often. The toolbar, shown below, provides quick access to many of Internet Explorer's most frequently accessed commands—especially Web navigation commands. Table 5-1 lists the icons on the toolbar and gives a brief description of what they do.

You can choose between small and large icons on the Standard Buttons toolbar. To change the icon size, click View on the menu bar, click Toolbars, and choose Customize from the submenu. In the Customize Toolbar dialog box, choose the icon size in the Icon Options list box.

TABLE 5-1. Browser Icon Functions.

Icon Name	What It Does
Back	Goes back one document in the list of documents you have retrieved in this session and displays the document in the workspace. (This tool is unavailable if you've just started Internet Explorer and haven't accessed anything but the start page.)
Forward	Goes forward one document in the list of documents you have retrieved in this session and displays the document in the workspace. (This tool is unavailable if you haven't clicked the Back button.)
Stop	Stops downloading the current document. This tool is handy if the document you're downloading seems to take forever or doesn't look very interesting.
Refresh	Downloads a new, fresh copy of the current document from the Internet. This tool is useful if you've clicked the Stop tool and then decide you'd still like to see the whole document.
Home	Re-displays the default start page, the one you see when you start Internet Explorer. You can change this page, as explained in Chapter 5.
Search	Displays the Search Explorer bar on the left side of the window. This Explorer bar enables you to search the Web for information.
Favorites	Displays the Favorites Explorer bar on the left of the window. This Explorer bar enables you to access your favorite sites quickly.
History	Displays the History Explorer bar on the left side of the window. This Explorer bar enables you to see all the sites you've recently visited. You'll learn how to use this cool, new feature later in this chapter.
Mail	Displays a menu of e-mail options. You can read your e-mail, send a new message, send a link to someone by e-mail, or send a Web page by e-mail. You can also access Usenet newsgroups.
Print	Prints the current page.
Edit	Displays a drop-down menu that lets you choose an HTML editor, if more than one is available on your system.

NOTE

If you have installed Microsoft Office 2000, you will see an additional button ("Discussions").

To use the Address toolbar to go to Web addresses, see "Going to a Web Page by Typing Its Address," page 108 and "Returning to Previously Viewed Sites," page 105.

The Address Toolbar

The Address toolbar, shown on the next page, is an invaluable navigation tool. It displays the address of the Web page you're currently viewing, and provides tools for accessing Web content quickly.

Address http://home.microsoft.com/

To the right of the Address toolbar, you'll see the Go button. You use this button after typing a Web address (URL) in the Address box. To access the URL you typed, click Go. (You can accomplish the same thing by pressing Enter.)

The Links Toolbar

SEE ALSO
For information on editing the Links toolbar and adding your own links, see "Adding Pages to the Links Toolbar," page 157.

The Links toolbar, shown here, gives you one-click access to the Web sites you access most often. When you begin using Internet Explorer, the program shows you the default links placed there by Microsoft or your system administrator. You can customize the Links toolbar by deleting existing links and adding your own.

Links Best of the Web Channel Guide Customize Links Free HotMail Internet Explorer News

Depending on how your copy of Internet Explorer was customized, you may see some or all of the following links:

- **Best of the Web.** This page displays a subject guide to excellent Web content. You'll find links to Web pages concerning business, computers, education, health, hobbies, lifestyles, news, sports, travel, and more.
- **Channel Guide.** Here, you'll find links to Windows media to which you can subscribe, so that new content is automatically downloaded to your computer.
- **Free Hotmail.** Click here to set up a free e-mail account with Hotmail, Microsoft's free Web-based e-mail service.
- **Internet Explorer News.** Click here to find out what's new with Internet Explorer.
- **Microsoft.** Click here to visit Microsoft's home page, where you can learn more about other Microsoft products.
- **Windows Update.** Click here to update your copy of Microsoft Windows.

SEE ALSO
For information on HotMail, see Chapter 15, "Using Hotmail."

The Radio Toolbar

The Radio toolbar, shown here, enables you to listen to Internet-based radio stations that broadcast live streams of news, talk, and music. Audio quality depends on the speed of your Internet connection, but it's at least as good as AM radio—and potentially as good as FM radio, if you have an ISDN, cable modem, or LAN connection.

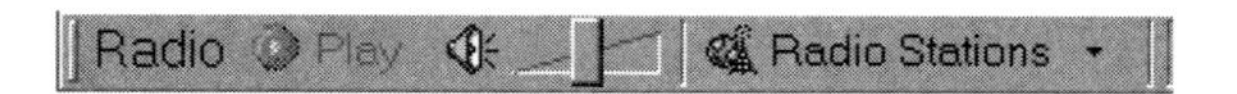

To choose a station, connect to the Internet, if necessary, and click Radio Stations. You'll see the Radio Station guide, a Web page at msn.com. Click a station to start playing; you'll see information on the station in the panel to the right of the Radio toolbar area. Note that the Start button changes to a Stop button while the radio's playing; you can pause playing by clicking the Stop button. To adjust the volume, drag the slider control.

If you find a station you like, add it to your radio station favorites by clicking Radio Stations on the Radio toolbar, and choose Add Station to Favorites. To start listening to your favorite in a subsequent session, click Radio Stations, and select your favorite station from the drop-down menu.

Displaying, Sizing, and Repositioning the Toolbars

Each of Internet Explorer's toolbars can be adjusted to suit your fancy.

To bring hidden toolbars into view, do one of the following:

- On the menu bar, click View, and choose Toolbars. To activate a toolbar, choose its name from the submenu.
- Right-click any toolbar. From the pop-up menu, choose the toolbar that you want to display.

What's the ideal toolbar setup? I like to see the Standard toolbar, the Address toolbar, and the Links toolbar in full width, with the standard toolbar on the top, the address bar in the middle, and the links bar at the bottom. I like the Standard toolbar on the top because it's near the menus, and I like to have all the commands grouped together. I like to have the links bar on the bottom because it can be customized. In Chapter 7, you'll learn how to add your own links to the link bar—links you'll use every day. They're easy to reach when they're on the bottom. You can show the Radio toolbar when you want to use it; when I'm not using it, I prefer to hide it so that there's more room for Web pages on the screen.

After the toolbar appears, you can adjust it by moving the *drag handle,* the vertical line on the toolbar's left edge. Try moving the drag handle left and right, and also up and down. As you can see, you can stack the toolbars any way you like. You can also combine toolbars.

While you're learning to use Internet Explorer, it's best to display all four toolbars in full width. Later, you can hide the ones you don't want to use. (To hide a toolbar, choose Toolbars from the View menu and then select the toolbar's name.)

Learning Navigation Fundamentals

Try a bit of Web navigation. In this mini-lesson, you'll learn about the all-important Back and Forward buttons, which are about as crucial as the gearshift lever in your car. It makes good sense to understand these features thoroughly.

Try the following:

1. On the start page, you'll see some text. (It changes every day, but there's always something.) In the text, some words may be underlined and displayed in a different color or change color when you place your mouse over them. Move the pointer to the underlined text, and note how the pointer changes shape. It becomes a hand, which indicates that the pointer is over a *hyperlink*. A hyperlink lets you select another Web document to display. Don't click yet.
2. Move the pointer over some of the graphics. As you can see, many of them are hyperlinks, too. Don't click yet.
3. Where will you wind up when you click a hyperlink? When the pointer changes to a hand shape, the status bar shows the link's destination. Look at the status bar as you're moving the pointer over links.
4. OK, now click a link. Internet Explorer displays the new page, and some other things happen, too. On the status bar, Internet Explorer tells you what it's doing: opening the page. If the page has a lot of graphics or other resources and is taking a while to download, the program tells you how many items remain to be downloaded. When the page is finished, you see the word *Done*.
5. On the page you just accessed, click another link. You'll see another new page.

Going Back

To practice going back to pages you previously viewed, use any of the following techniques:

- Click Home. You can also click View on the menu bar, choose Go To, and choose Home Page from the submenu.

  You'll see the start page again.

- Click Back. (You can also click the View menu, choose Go To, and choose Back from the submenu. You can also press Alt + Left Arrow.) This technique is best used for going back one or two pages.

  or

- Click the down arrow next to the Back button. You'll see a drop-down menu listing the pages you've displayed in this session, as shown below. This is the best option to use to go back more than two or three pages. You can see the same list by clicking View on the menu bar, choosing Go To, and choosing a recently visited site from the submenu.

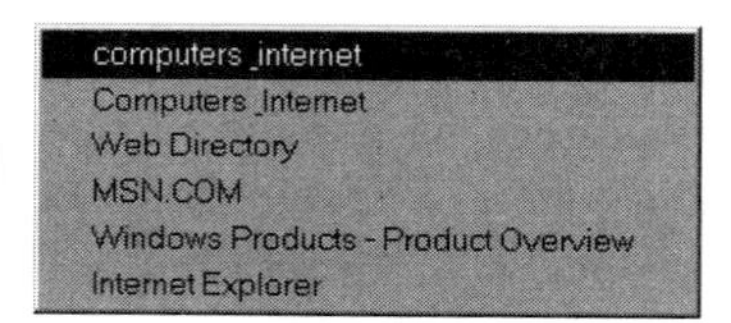

> If you're trying to find a site you visited previously and can't access it by using the Back button, use the History explorer. The History explorer keeps track of all the pages you visited in this and previous Internet Explorer sessions, up to a limit that you select (by default, this limit is three weeks).

Going Forward

One thing about Web browsers that's confusing for new users is the Forward button. In the previous section, you clicked a number of hyperlinks and then went back. If you did this, try clicking the Forward button. As you can see, this re-displays the sites you just went back from.

A little confusing? It is, at first. After a little practice though, the movements come naturally. Again, here's what the Back and Forward buttons do:

For ways to go back to pages you visited in previous sessions (or long ago in the current one), see "Returning to Previously Viewed Sites," page 106.

- **Back.** Click Back to see the document from which you just jumped via a hyperlink. If you keep clicking Back, you keep going back in the series of jumps you made in this session. When the Back button dims and becomes unavailable, you're looking at the first document you saw in this session. To go back to a particular site, it's easiest to display the Back button's drop-down menu, which enables you to choose the page you want to go back to.

- **Forward.** Click Forward to re-display documents you've gone back from. If you haven't clicked Back, Forward is dimmed.

> The Forward button has a drop-down menu just like the Back button does. You can click this button to display a list of the sites you can go forward to. This option is a real time-saver when you need to jump forward several pages.

SEE ALSO

To choose settings for the cache, see "Choosing Cache Options," page 281.

Did you notice that, when you click Back, pages re-display much more quickly than they did when you first accessed them? That's because Internet Explorer stores recently accessed Web documents in a *cache* (pronounced "cash"), which is a special folder on your hard disk. It's located by default in the Windows folder. When you return to a recently accessed document, Internet Explorer retrieves the document from the cache rather than downloading it from the Internet, which would take more time.

Refreshing a Page

When you go back to previously viewed pages, Internet Explorer retrieves the page from the cache, as you've just learned. But what if the page has changed? If you'd like to make sure you're viewing the most recent version of a page, do one of the following:

- Click Refresh.

  or

- From the View menu, choose Refresh.

  or

- Press F5.

Choosing Refresh forces Internet Explorer to retrieve a new copy of the page from the network.

Returning to Previously Viewed Sites

On the Address toolbar, you'll find a drop-down list, which you can display by clicking the down arrow. (You can also press F4.) If you display this list, you'll see a list of recently visited Web sites, such as the following:

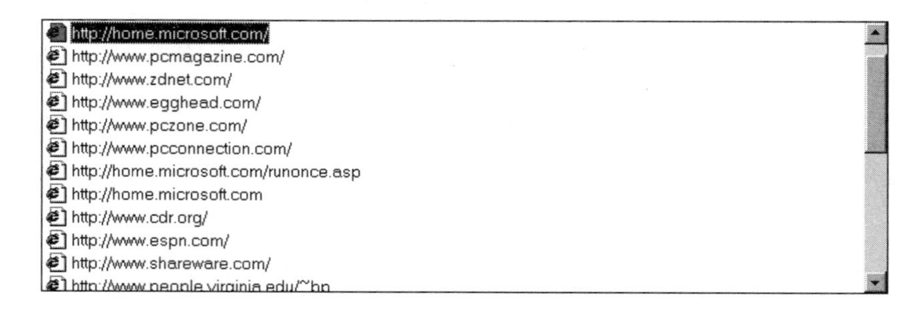

Note that this menu displays URLs that you have typed in rather than a list of the various Web pages you have visited. If you choose one of the URLs listed here, you'll see that page. To return to Web pages you previously viewed, use the History explorer, discussed in the next section.

Using the History Explorer

To save Web pages as favorites so you can return to them any time you wish, see "Creating Desktop Shortcuts to Favorites Pages," page 162. To add frequently visited sites to the Links toolbar, see "Customizing the Toolbar," page 274.

If you're trying to return to a recently viewed Web page and can't find it on the Back menu's drop-down list, the best place to look for the page is the History explorer. Internet Explorer version 5 includes a much-improved History explorer, which gives you several ways to organize previously viewed pages, and a search tool.

Displaying the History Explorer

To display the History explorer, do one of the following:

- On the Standard Buttons bar, click History.

  or

- From the View menu, click Explorer Bar, and choose History from the submenu.

  or

- Press Ctrl + H.

You'll see the Explorer bar, as shown in Figure 5-5. The History explorer title bar shows the name of the explorer (History), a close button (the letter *X* on the right edge of the explorer title bar), a View menu, and a Search button.

Navigating the History Explorer List

To browse for Web pages in the History explorer, click a calendar icon or folder to display its contents, if necessary. The pages within the folder are grouped within a box, as shown in the following illustration:

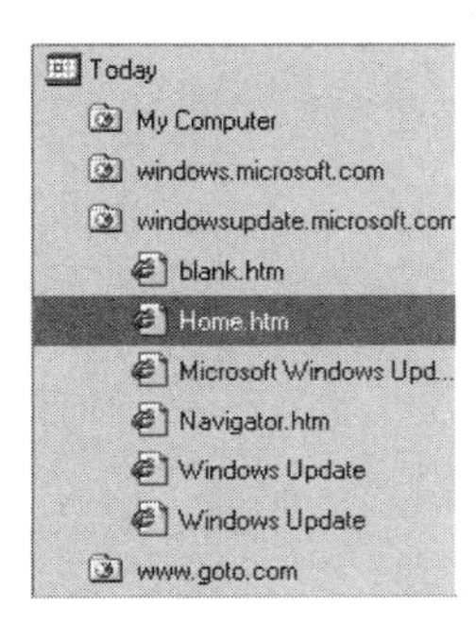

To go to one of the pages displayed in the list, just click the page title.

FIGURE 5-5.
The Explorer bar offers useful tools (including searching) for returning to Web pages that you've recently viewed.

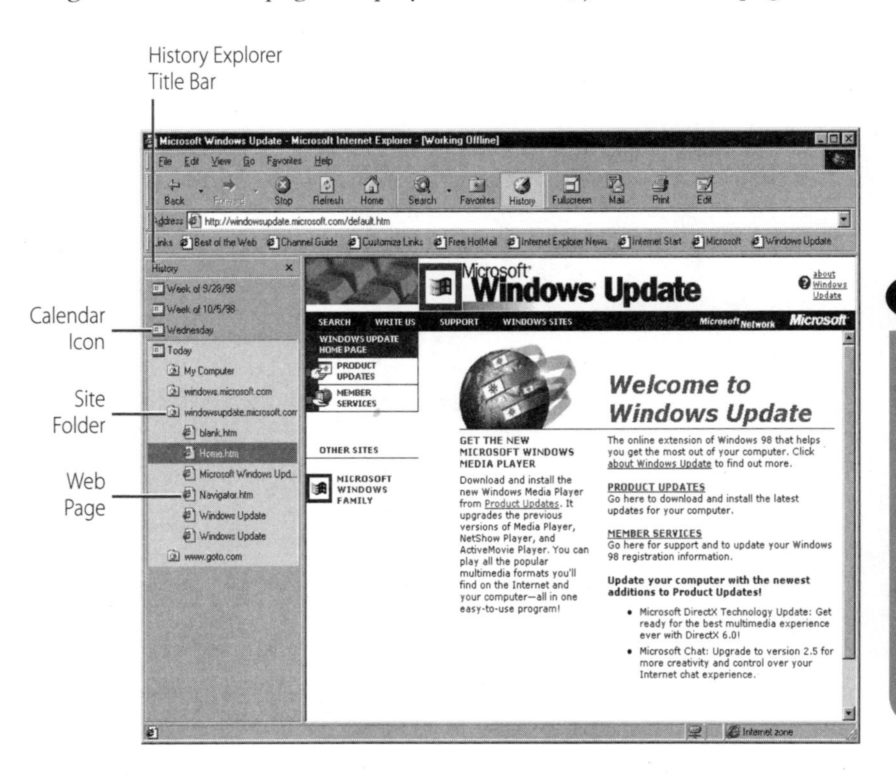

Choosing View Options

In the History explorer, you can choose the following options to display the list of recently visited sites:

- **By Date.** This is the default for displaying the list of Web pages in the History explorer. Recently visited pages are organized by calendar icons. Under the Today icon, you'll find folders that name the sites you've visited. Within the folders, you'll see the pages you visited today. If you used Internet Explorer in previous days and weeks, you'll see calendar icons for each previous day within the last week.
- **By Site.** This list-display option organizes recently visited Web pages by Web site. For example, suppose you visit Microsoft's site (http://www.microsoft.com), and visit several Web pages at Microsoft's site. All the pages you recently visited at this site will be listed within the Microsoft folder.
- **By Most Visited.** This list-display option organizes the pages you've recently visited by the number of visits you've made, with the most frequently visited pages shown at the top of the list.
- **By Order Visited Today.** In this display option, you see the list of pages you've visited today, shown in the order you visited them. This is a useful option if you're trying to return to a page you visited early in the current session, but can't remember the page's title or site name.

SEE ALSO
To determine how far back Internet Explorer keeps track of Web pages you've visited, see "Adjusting History Tracking," page 277.

Going to a Web Page by Typing Its Address

Once word gets around that you're using the Internet, somebody will rattle off a Web address and say, "You've *got* to see this!" Don't try to find the page by surfing. That would be like trying to find somebody in New York City by knocking on doors and asking around. You need to go to the page by typing its address.

Using the Address Bar

The best way to find a site you want is to use the Address bar. (If you don't see the Address bar, go to the View menu and select Toolbars. Then click Address Bar. If you can't see the address box, locate the toolbar's drag handle—it's a vertical line at the left edge of the bar—and drag until the box comes into view.) Click in the address box to select the current Web address, or press Alt + D.

To go to a Web page, type the address in the Address toolbar's text box. (Your typing will delete the current URL.) Click the Go button to go to the page.

You don't have to type the http:// part. For example, to access http://www.amazon.com, you just type www.amazon.com.

You can often find a company's home page just by typing *www* followed by a period, the company's name, another period, and *com*. Try some of these: www.pepsi.com, www.toyota.com, and www.washingtonpost.com.

Web addresses are also known as URLs, short for Uniform Resource Locator (URL). Some people pronounce this "Earl," while others spell it out ("you-are-ell").

What's in a URL?

URLs have three parts: the protocol, the domain name, and the resource location and name. In *http://www.microsoft.com/ie/default.asp*, for example, the *http://* part is the protocol, *www.microsoft.com* is the domain, and */ie/default.asp* is the resource location and name.

The first part of the URL indicates the *protocol* that's supposed to be used to access the data. A protocol is a communications standard that specifies how computers can exchange data over the network. Microsoft Internet Explorer is a Web browser, and it can work with the basic Web protocol, HTTP (the HyperText Transfer Protocol). But it can work with other protocols, too, such as FTP (the File Transfer Protocol), which enables you to copy files to your computer. Chapter 11 discusses FTP.

The second part of the URL gives the *domain name* of the computer that's running the server. A domain name is a user-friendly version of a numerical Internet address (which looks something like 228.137.190.15). An Internet service called the Domain Name Service (DNS) translates between these user-friendly alphabetical names (such as www.microsoft.com) and their numerical equivalents.

The third part of the URL gives the exact storage *location and name* of the specific resource you're after. This might include a directory path similar to the ones you use on your computer. Sometimes the third part of the URL is omitted. If so, you will go to the server's main welcome page. For example, if you type only *http://www.microsoft.com*, you will see Microsoft's home page.

Typing Web Addresses Correctly

Suppose you type the address and click the Go button, but nothing happens. The animation just runs and runs, and still nothing happens. Finally you see an page informing you that Internet Explorer couldn't open the site or the document. Chances are you didn't type the address correctly.

To avoid errors when you type Web addresses, note the following guidelines:

- URLs are case-sensitive, so be sure to copy the capitalization pattern exactly.
- Don't place any spaces within the address.
- Check to make sure you've put periods and slash marks (/) in the correct places.
- Most Web documents are named with an *extension* (the part of the file name that comes after the period). Most of the time this is *.html,* but sometimes it's *.htm,* or *.asp*. Make sure you type the extension correctly.
- If you're trying to visit somebody's home page, the URL might contain a tilde (~), which is often used to indicate the name of somebody's home directory on a Unix computer. It isn't a typo. Be sure to include the tilde.
- If you grew up with DOS, you poor thing, remember that these slash marks are forward slashes (/), not backward slashes (\).
- Check your typing. You have probably made some tiny, human, forgivable typing mistake that's hardly noticeable—except to computers.
- Maybe you didn't make a mistake. Sometimes Web pages disappear, leaving a *stale link* behind. (A stale link is a hyperlink that takes you to a "page not found" message.)

Using AutoComplete

Internet Explorer version 5 includes a much-improved AutoComplete feature, which helps you type the URLs of Web pages you've already visited. AutoComplete springs into play when you're typing addresses in the Address toolbar.

To use AutoComplete, just start typing the URL of a Web page you've already visited. As soon as Internet Explorer detects that you're typing the name of a Web page you previously visited, the program displays a drop-down list, like the one shown here:

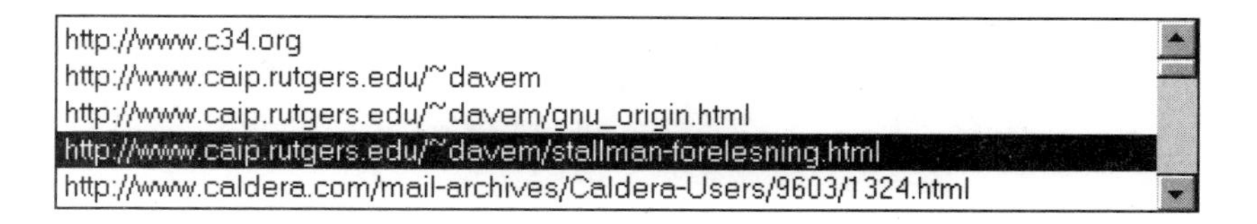

To narrow down the list of options, type additional characters if you remember what they are. If Internet Explorer finds several matches, you'll see scroll bars that enable you to scroll through the list. You can also size the list box by dragging the size icon in the lower right corner.

If you see the name of the Web page you want to access, choose it from the list. If not, you can choose Search to search the Web for a URL that contains the characters you've typed.

Stopping an Unwanted Download

Suppose you click the wrong hyperlink—and off Internet Explorer goes, obediently downloading some huge page with tons of graphics. It's taking forever, and you don't even want to see it. What to do? Simple: Click Stop (or press Esc). This button stops the download, enabling you to click Back so that you can try again.

Using Internal Navigation Aids

You've learned how to use the Back and Forward buttons. As you know, these buttons enable you to re-display pages you've previously viewed. Sometimes, though, they don't provide the best way to get around a site with multiple pages. If the site is well designed, you can use *internal navigation aids*. These are links, usually given in a list, that work like a table of contents. They show you the structure of the site and enable you to move around within it.

Web authors provide internal navigation aids in different ways. One of the best is shown in Figure 5-6: a row of navigation buttons running down the side of the page (or across the top or bottom). The best sites use this design consistently. No matter which page you're viewing, you still see the same list of links. This aid really helps to prevent disorientation.

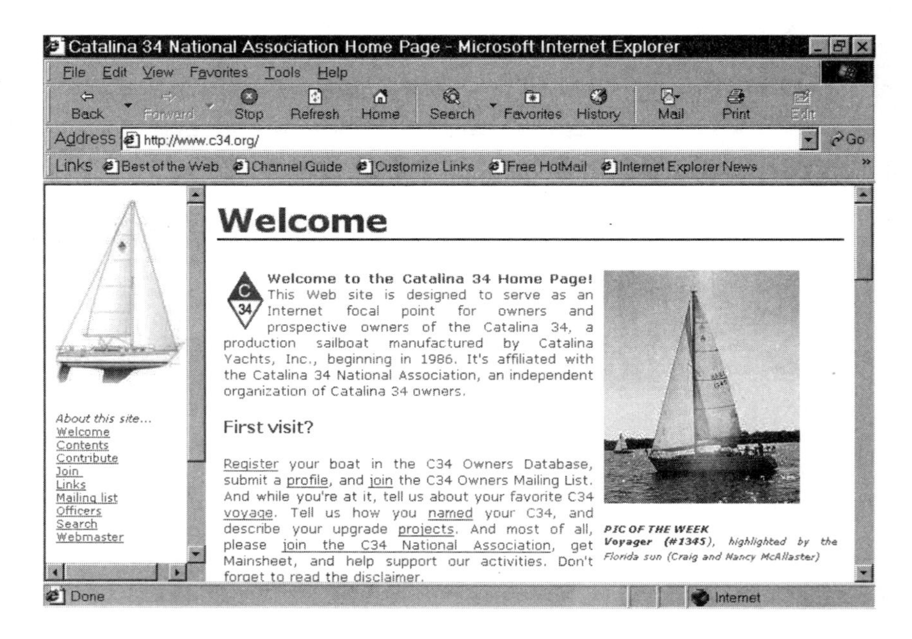

FIGURE 5-6.
Look for internal navigation aids, such as the hyperlinks on the left side of this page. They enable you to move around the site easily.

Navigating Framed Documents

SEE ALSO
Frames pose special challenges for printing. To learn how to print framed documents, see "Printing a Framed Document," page 190.

Framed documents (like in Figure 5-6) have two or more independent panels. Depending on how the page's author set them up, you might be able to scroll the frame and adjust its border; this can be prevented, though, if the author prefers. You know you can scroll a frame if you see a scroll bar. To find out whether you can adjust a border, move the pointer to it and see whether it changes to an arrow shape.

The page shown in Figure 5-6 uses one of the frames—the one on the left—to display internal navigation aids. These aids stay put, even if you scroll the other panel. That's a very good reason right there to like frames. You click one of the links in the navigation aid list, and you see a new page in the adjacent panel.

Some people don't like frames, though. They find them confusing to use. For example, when you click the Back button, you see the previous panel. But you don't actually leave the page until you've gone back to the first panel you saw and then clicked Back once more. It isn't so confusing once you understand what's happening.

- Many sites let you choose between a framed and a non-framed version. If you just don't like fussing with frames, choose the non-framed version.

- Some frames are scrollable, and others aren't. You can tell the difference by looking to see whether there's a scroll bar.
- Sometimes Web authors enable you to adjust the frame borders. You can tell whether a border is adjustable by moving the pointer to the border. If the pointer changes shape to become an arrow, you can adjust the border.
- Only one frame is active (selected) at a time. When you click Back or Forward, your action affects only that frame, not any others.
- If you've viewed many pages within the frame site and want to go back to the previous site you viewed, it's faster to choose the previous site from the history list than to click Back. You might have to click Back many times to exit the framed site.
- If you're at the beginning of the framed site (the welcome page), clicking Back takes you out of that site to the previously viewed site.
- Sometimes panels don't have borders. (Authors can hide the borders if they want to.) But you can tell that the page uses frames if scroll bars appear that don't run the length or width of the window.

TIP

Some authors of framed documents like to try to "trap" the entire Web within one of their frames. Here's how it works. Suppose you click a link within a framed document that supposedly takes you out of the framed site. You see a page at some other Web site, but it appears within one of the frames, rather than its own, independent window. As you keep navigating, you're still locked within the same framed document. Some Web authors like this because it keeps their page title and advertising on-screen even though you've left the site long ago. To escape the frame trap, point to a hyperlink that links to a site other than the framed site, and click the right mouse button. From the pop-up menu, choose Open in New Window. You'll see this page in its own, separate window, free from the frames. Close the original window, and keep surfing!

Using Pop-Up Menus

Microsoft Internet Explorer makes good use of the right mouse button. Try right-clicking various things within the program's window—a graphic, the page background, a link. As you'll see, a pop-up menu appears with options that are relevant to what you're pointing at. For example, when you point at a text link, you see the menu shown here:

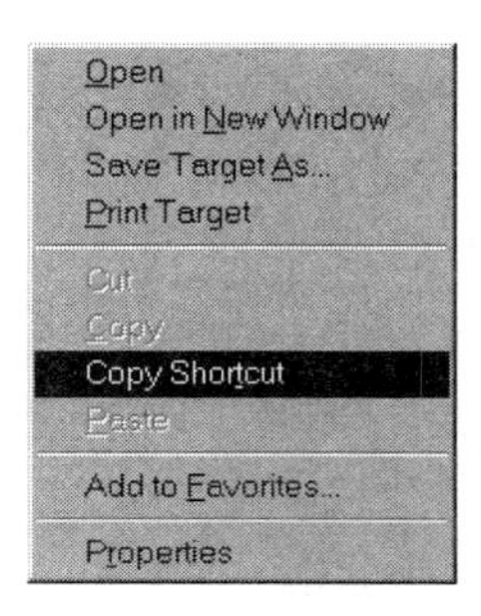

From this pop-up menu, you can choose from the following options: Open, Open In New Window, Save Target As (save the document referenced in the link), Print Target (print the document referenced in the link), Copy Shortcut (for pasting elsewhere), Add To Favorites, and Properties (information about the page).

Using the Full Screen View

When you click the Maximize button on the Internet Explorer title, Windows zooms the window to full size. But there's another way to get the big picture—the Full Screen view. Like Maximize, the Full Screen view zooms the screen to full size, but it also hides all the toolbars except the standard toolbar.

To see the Full Screen view, click View, and choose Full Screen. (You can also press F11.) In the Full Screen view, you see the Standard Buttons toolbar with reduced-size icons, but the rest of the screen is devoted to the Web page you're viewing. (This view hides the Start menu.)

To return to the normal view, press F11.

TIP

To see even more of a Web page, point to a toolbar in the Full Screen view, click the right mouse button, and select Auto Hide from the pop-up menu. This option hides the toolbar unless you move the pointer to the toolbar region.

The Full Screen view is the ideal environment for using the Explorer bars (Search, Favorites, and History). There's plenty of room to see the Web page you're viewing.

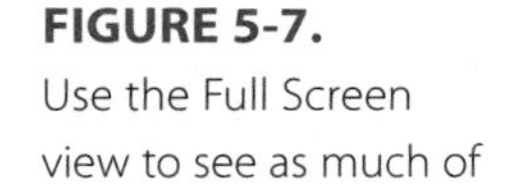

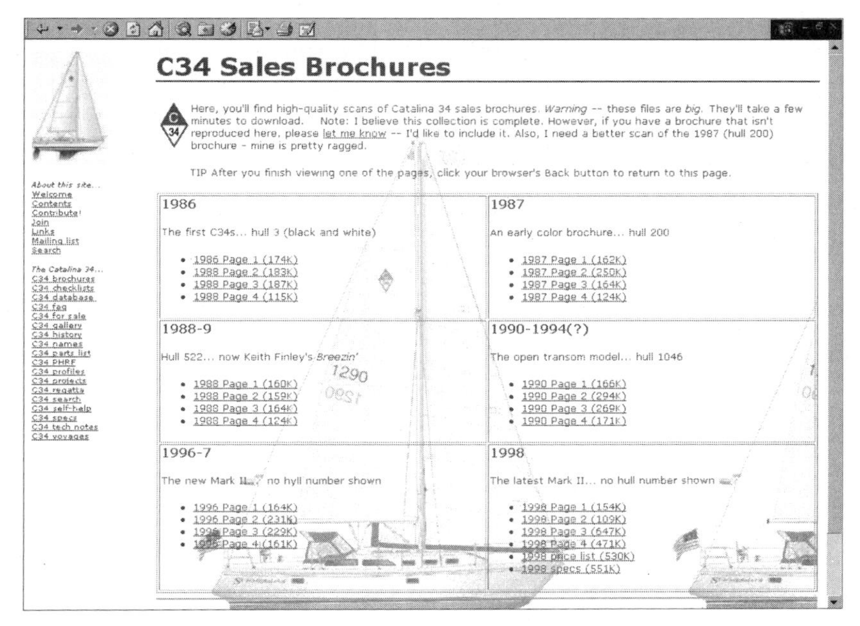

FIGURE 5-7.
Use the Full Screen view to see as much of a Web page as possible.

Navigating with the Keyboard

If you would prefer to use the keyboard instead of your mouse, you can use keyboard shortcuts (also called *hotkeys*). Table 5-2 lists hotkeys you can use for navigation and scrolling.

TABLE 5-2. Keyboard Shortcuts for Navigation and Scrolling.

To do this:	Press this:
Go back (same as clicking Back button).	Alt + Left arrow or Backspace
Go forward (same as clicking Forward button).	Alt + Right arrow
Move to next hyperlink.	Tab
Move to previous hyperlink.	Shift + Tab
Jump to the page referenced in currently selected hyperlink.	Enter
Refresh the current page.	F5

(continued)

TABLE 5-2 *continued*

To do this:	Press this:
Stop downloading.	Esc
Scroll down.	Down arrow
Scroll down in larger increments.	Page Down
Scroll to end of document.	End
Scroll up.	Up arrow
Scroll up in larger increments.	Page Up
Scroll to beginning of document.	Home

Finding Text within a Web Page

If you've downloaded a lengthy document, don't wear your eyes out looking for a specific passage of text. Let Internet Explorer do the searching for you. The following technique enables you to search for text *within* a Web page. (For information on searching the Web, see the next chapter.)

To search for text on a Web page, follow these steps:

1 Do one of the following:

- From the Edit menu, choose Find (On This Page).

  or

- Press Ctrl + F.

You'll see the Find dialog box, shown here:

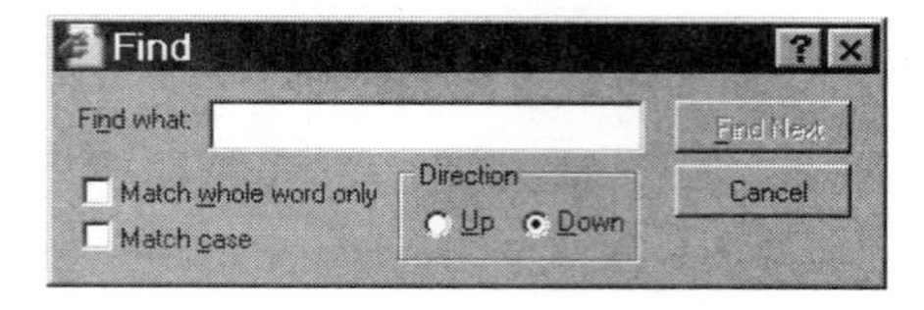

2 In the Find What box, type the text you're looking for.

- To avoid finding matches where the letters you typed are part of a larger word (such as *pie* in *piety*), check Match Whole Word Only.

- If you would like Internet Explorer to match the capitalization pattern you typed, place a check mark next to Match Case.

3 Choose a direction, if necessary.

- If the cursor is currently positioned at the top of the document, choose Down, if necessary (this is the default option).
- If you've positioned the cursor at the bottom of the document, click Up.

4 Click Find Next.

- If Internet Explorer finds a match, the Find dialog box stays on-screen. Click Find Next to continue the search, or click Cancel to close the Find dialog box and return to the Web page.
- If no matches are found (or no *more* matches are found), you see an alert box informing you that Internet Explorer has reached the end of the document. Click OK to return to the Find dialog box. You can search again by typing new search text, or closing the Find dialog box.

Adjusting Text Size

SEE ALSO

For information on choosing permanent overrides for fonts and font sizes in Web pages, see "Using Accessibility Features," page 42.

To make on-screen reading easier, you can adjust the text size. By default, text appears in medium size, but you can adjust the font size. Figure 5-8 shows a document with the smallest text size, while Figure 5-9 shows a document with the largest text size.

To change the text size, do the following: from the View menu, choose Text Size and select a size from the pop-up menu. (Note that the current text size is marked with a dot.) You can choose from Largest, Larger, Medium (the default size), Smaller, and Smallest.

Internet Explorer prints your document using the current text-size choice. For printing, you can use a smaller text size and still produce a readable printout. For information on printing the documents you find on the Web, see "Printing a Web Page" on page 186.

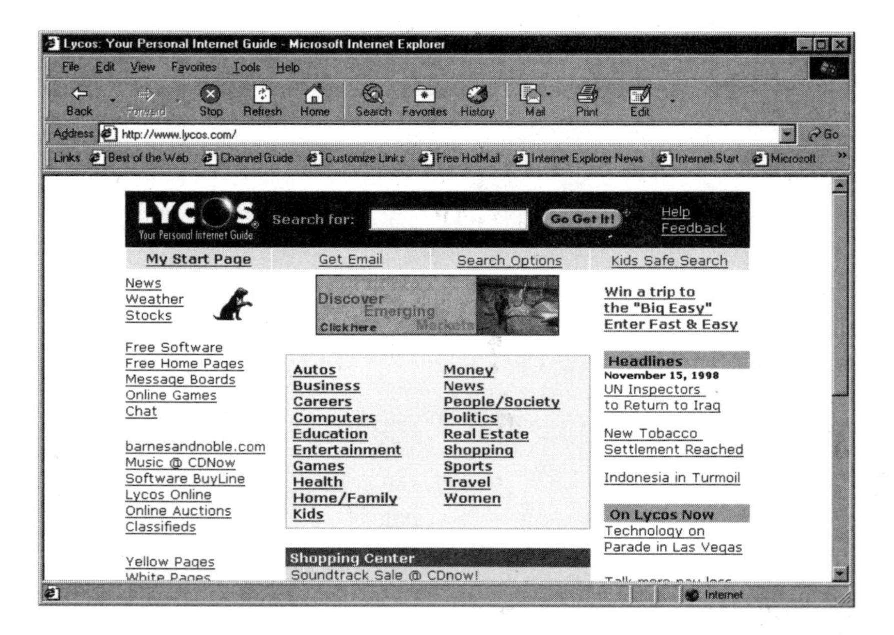

FIGURE 5-8.
If you choose the smallest text size, you see more text on-screen. This is a good option for printing.

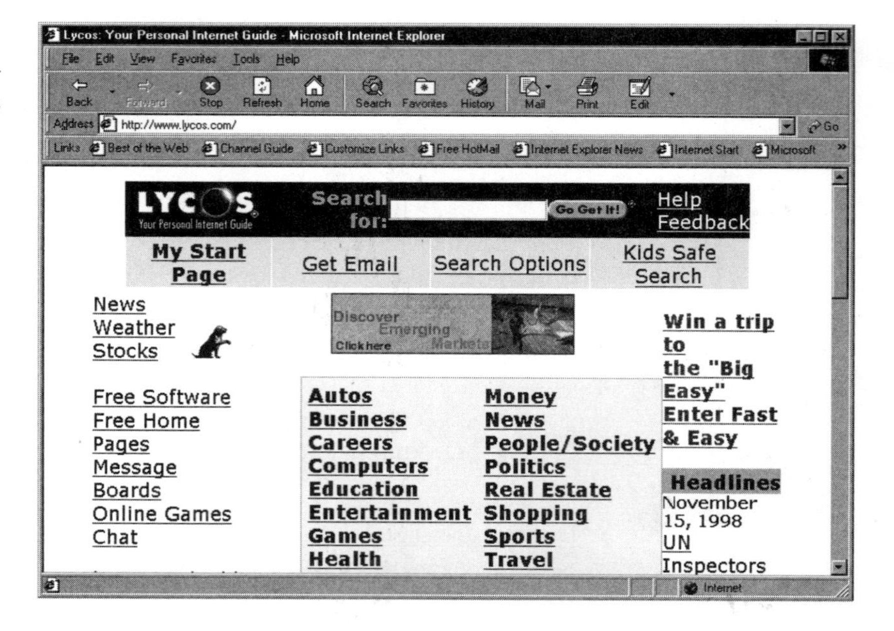

FIGURE 5-9.
If you choose the largest text size, the text is easier to read.

CHAPTER 6

Finding the Best Content

Some people have the impression that the Web is just a waste of time and that there isn't much quality content out there. But people who say this probably haven't seen the best of what the Web has to offer. It's a really good idea to start your surfing by visiting the best and most useful sites on the Web. Once you've seen the best of the Web, you won't waste your time on inferior Web pages, and you'll be on your way to transforming the Web (and Microsoft Internet Explorer) into a tool of genuine value to you, personally and professionally.

To locate useful content, you'll also need to learn how to search the Web. As you'll surely agree if you've tried searching, results are often unsatisfactory. Internet Explorer version 5 includes an outstanding new feature, the Search Assistant, which addresses some of the shortcomings of Web searching and helps you achieve better results.

Judging a Site's Quality

You'll have your own ideas about site quality after browsing for a while, but really great sites have several or all of these characteristics:

- **Rich content.** You want more than just a bunch of splashy graphics (which take forever to download) and a few words here and there. A great site offers entertaining and useful information. It takes a lot of work to make great sites—which is why they're so rare.
- **World-class design.** We're not talking about just good looks. A well-designed site is easy to navigate; just by looking at the page for a few seconds, you should be able to tell what's there and what you can do.
- **Interactivity.** A great site invites exploration and gives you ways to get involved. At Amazon.com (http://www.amazon.com), you can add your own book reviews. At the excellent Web site of Wine Spectator (http://www.winespectator.com), you can add your own tasting notes and join in wine tasting discussions.
- **Frequently updated, timely information.** The site's content changes frequently, and it's worth visiting again and again.
- **Free, useful goodies.** A really good site offers images and software to download, on-screen calculators, checklists, rich and searchable archives, and more.

Exploring the Microsoft Network

Some of the best sites on the Web are brought to you by the same company that makes your favorite browser. When you access MSN.com, Internet Explorer's default-start page, you can access the following Microsoft Network (MSN) sites by clicking the links on the start page.

CarPoint

CarPoint (http://carpoint.msn.com, shown in Figure 6-1) is Microsoft's answer to the most popular car-buying site on the Internet, Auto-by-Tel (http://www.autobytel.com). These sites offer car buyers an alternative to pushy showroom sales tactics; you can obtain a fixed-price quote for the car you're hoping to buy, and avoid the sales personnel entirely. At CarPoint, you can research used and new car prices, select options, get quotes, and even shop for car insurance.

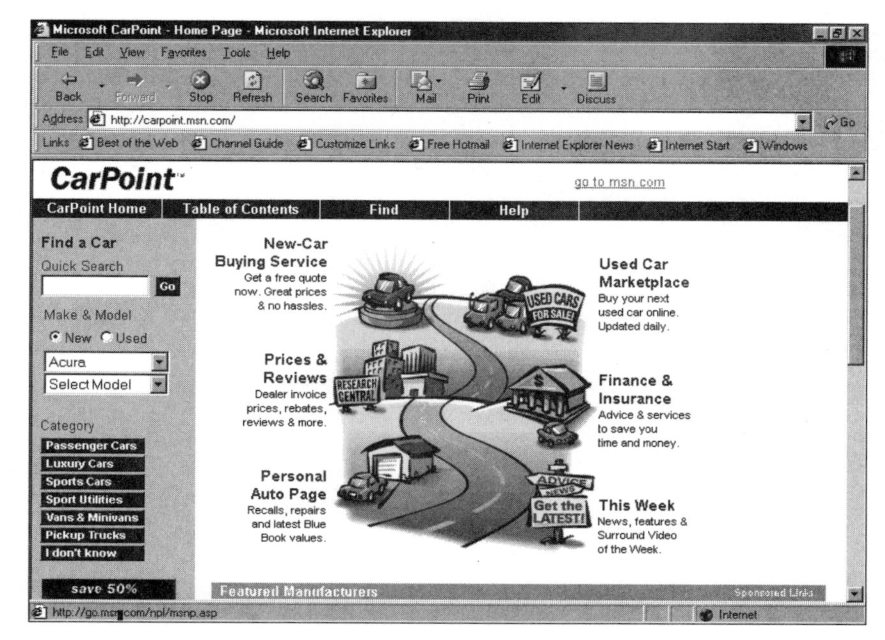

FIGURE 6-1.
CarPoint offers a complete car-buying service that enables you to bypass pushy showroom sales tactics.

Expedia

There's a travel agency on the Web? Yes, and it's free. At Microsoft Expedia (http://expedia.msn.com), you can learn about travel destinations, view maps, get travel tips, and even make air, hotel, and car reservations. As you can see from Figure 6-2, this site is beautifully done. You can search for the lowest current airfares for a trip you're planning to make. This feature lets you see the same data that travel agents see and lets you select the flight.

Microsoft Investor

If you're looking for help managing and tracking your investments, Microsoft Investor (investor.msn.com) is loaded with useful tools and information, including a portfolio tracker. You type in the ticker symbols of your stocks or mutual funds, and Microsoft Investor shows your portfolio's current value. There's more, too. You can search for information about companies, research new investment opportunities, view current market results, see an online stock ticker, and even buy and sell stocks online. You'll also find feature articles that show you how to explore the world of investments (Figure 6-3).

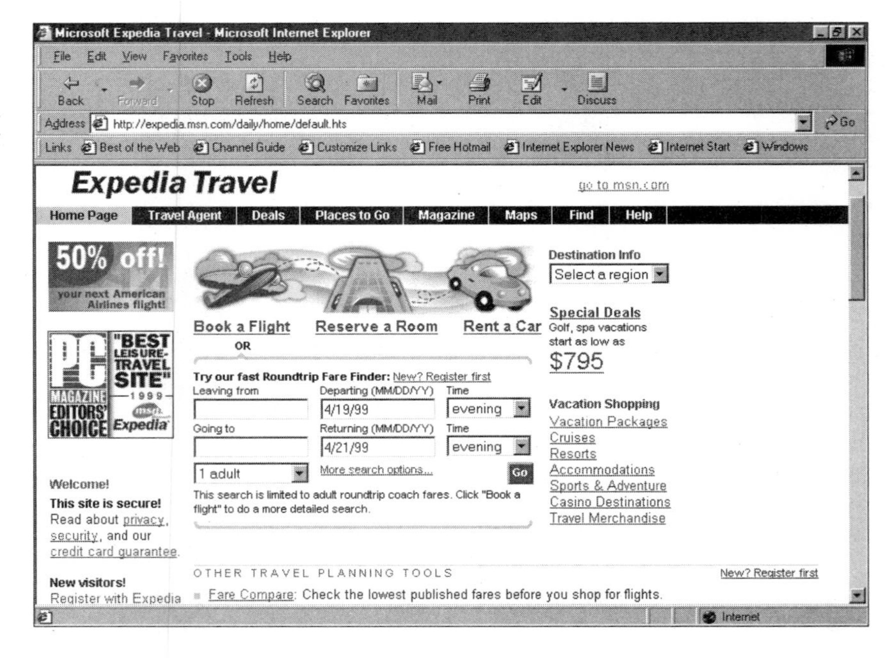

FIGURE 6-2.
Expedia is a complete online travel agency; you can even buy your tickets, make auto rental reservations, and choose a hotel.

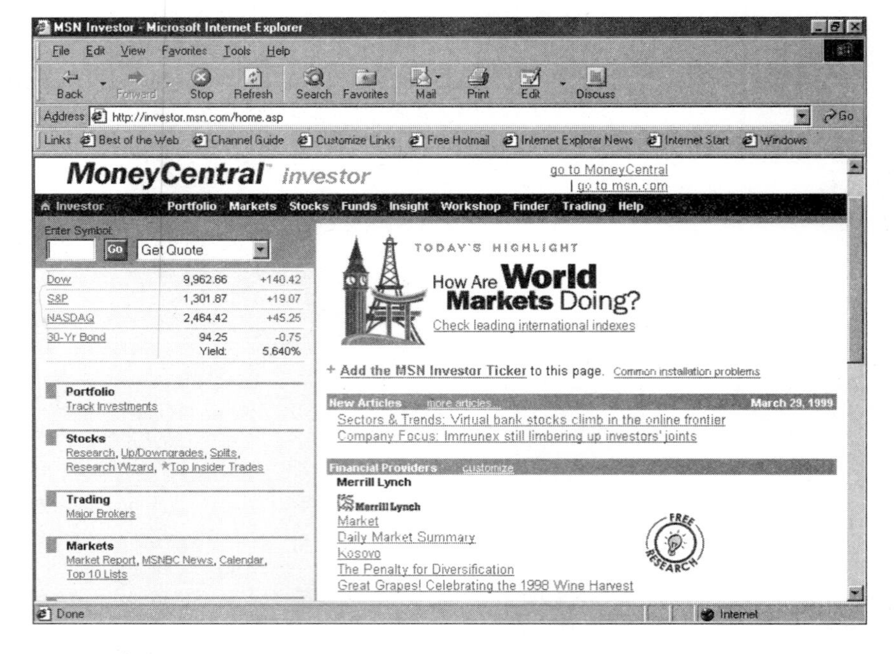

FIGURE 6-3.
Microsoft Investor provides in-depth investment analysis, research resources, market reports, and even a portfolio tracker.

MSNBC

And now for the news. MSNBC, a joint venture between Microsoft and NBC, brings you the latest news (http://www.msnbc.com). To navigate the site, you can use the internal navigation aids at the top of the screen (Figure 6-4), which enable you to select news categories (such as commerce, sports, or weather). Inside, you'll find in-depth news articles that are easy to read on-screen. Often, these articles include audio and video clips that you can view with Media Player (see Chapter 8).

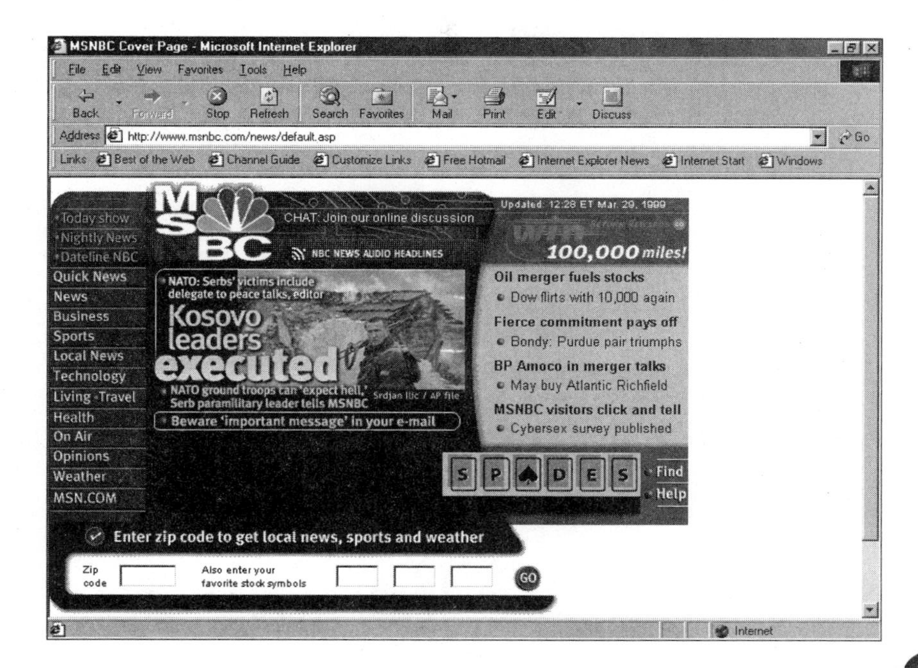

FIGURE 6-4.
Get the news from MSNBC.

Exploring the Best of the Web

Want to see the best of what's out there? You'll find several pages on the Web that list picks for the best pages on the Web. They vary based on the interests and expertise of the people who put them together. Hyperlinks take you directly to pages that look interesting.

Best of the Web

If you're looking for the best Web pages on a general subject, such as automobiles or tax preparation, begin by searching some of the following "best of the Web" services. This is a much better strategy than trying to find pages on such a subject by searching; a search may retrieve pages relevant to your interests, but they may not be of high quality.

- **EBLAST** (http://www.eblast.com). *Encyclopedia Britannica* experts pick the best of the Web in more than a dozen subject categories. Highly recommended.
- **Lycos Top 5% Of The Web** (http://point.lycos.com). Oriented to consumers and home Internet users, this service indexes sites that have been reviewed for quality content.
- **Microsoft's Best Of The Web.** This one's easy to get to. Just click Best Of The Web on the Links toolbar.
- **NetGuide** (http://www.netguide.com). This service enables you to perform a search for sites that merit NetGuide's "Best of the Web" award.
- **Netscape Netcenter** (http://home.netscape.com). This site offers a subject guide to Web pages; when you click a subject category, you see a list of recommended Web sites. This is an excellent place to begin your exploration of the Web.
- **Suite101.com** (http://www.suite101.com). High-quality site featuring subject pages that include in-depth essays on Internet resources. Highly recommended.
- **WWWomen** (http://www.wwwomen.com/feature/bestwww.shtml). This page contains a great list of women's sites, encompassing sports, labor issues, health, networking, family issues, and more.

Top 100 Sites

The following sites offer differing views on which sites are the top 100 on the Web.

- **PC Magazine's Top 100 Sites** (http://www.zdnet.com/pcmag/special/web100). This site offers great links to computer companies and computer resources on the Web, particularly Windows-based systems and Windows-compatible computers. You'll also find useful sections on entertainment, news, and reference.
- **The Web 100** (http://www.web100.com). User ratings determine the rankings on this list. So here's a great way to find out which pages Web users prefer. You can view them by rank, in groups of 10 at a time, or by topic (including arts and entertainment, business and commerce, education and reference, government and politics, health and medicine, news and information, sports and leisure, and science and technology). In the top 10 this week

are: SeniorCom, Healthfinder, CDnow, and—English teachers are going to love this—The Complete Works of William Shakespeare.

What's Cool

Apart from the best and most popular sites, there's the cool. And what does *cool* mean? Admittedly, *cool* is hard to define. At the Cool Site of the Day (http://cool.infi.net), you'll find a FAQ (short for "Frequently Asked Questions") that employs scientific research in an effort to pin down just what makes certain Web sites cool. According to the FAQ, a site's coolness can be attributed to a trace element called *coolium*. However, most of the sites that wind up on "what's cool" lists tend to have discovered one or more of the following secrets to success:

- **Awareness of the Internet's potential as a new medium.** One of the most popular sites on the Web, frequently named in What's Cool lists, is *Word,* an exclusively online magazine (http://www.word.com). A literary magazine stressing Generation X sensibilities, *Word* combines text with graphics, animations, and photographs in a full expression of the Web's multimedia possibilities (Figure 6-5).

FIGURE 6-5.
Word fully explores the Web's multimedia possibilities.

- **Savvy music stuff.** I wonder how many otherwise obscure bands have become major sellers because of the Internet? Word about music that's unusual, interesting, or hip gets around quickly on "the Net." Don't miss the Ultimate Band List (http://www.ubl.com), which tracks pages—both amateur pages and those sponsored by record companies—about bands of all kinds, ranging from the best-known acts to obscure but up-and-coming local ensembles.

- **Techno-zaniness.** At last count, there were more than 500 devices connected to the Web, including a talking machine (what you type is spoken out loud), a lava lamp, a CD player, hot tubs, and hundreds of live cameras. For a list, go to Yahoo! (http://www.yahoo.com) and search for the phrase "Interesting Devices."
- **Secret knowledge revealed.** As you'll see in the Hidden Mickeys of Disney site, Disney Imagineers embed Mickey Mouse shapes here and there throughout the Disney theme parks as a joke; find the scoop on how to locate them at http://www.oitc.com/Disney.
- **Hip graphics.** Some of the world's best graphic designers are working on the Web; it's an exciting new medium for them. There's currently a preference for 1950s nostalgia graphics. For an example, see the Internet Underground Music Archive (Figure 6-6) accessible from http://www.iuma.com.

FIGURE 6-6.
Internet Underground Music Archive (IUMA) is at or near the top of just about everybody's "What's Cool" list.

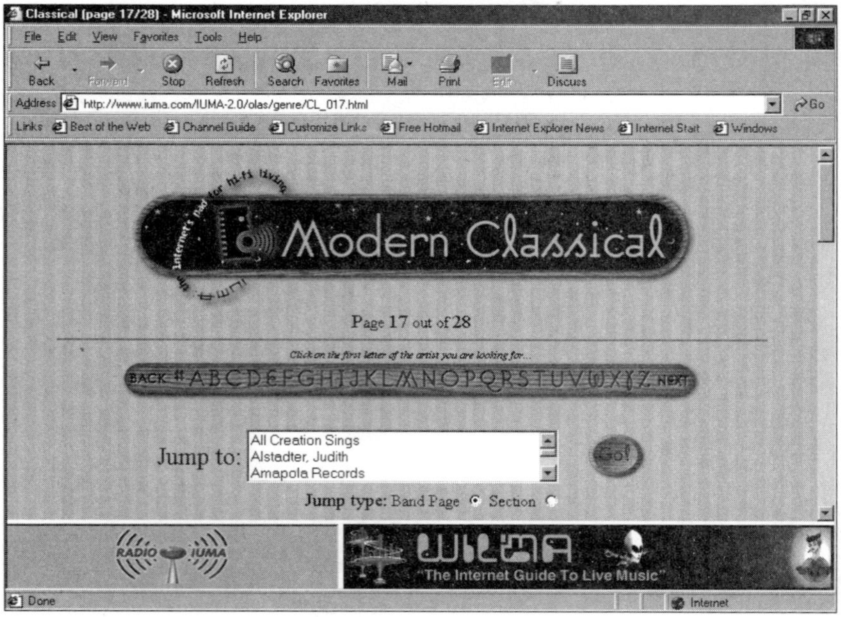

You'll find several sites that offer lists of what's cool.

- **Yahoo!'s Picks of the Week** (http://www.yahoo.com/picks). The yahoos at Yahoo! put together a weekly list of sites that are timely, informative, or just plain wigged out.
- **Cool Site of the Year** (http://cool.infi.net/csoty). From the folks who bring you the Cool Site of the Day, here's the Cool Site of the Year, along with some runners-up.
- **Netscape Communication's What's Cool** (http://home.netscape.com/netcenter/cool.html). This page should be titled "What's Cool in Corporate America," but it's well worth a visit.

What's Hot

What's hot isn't exactly the opposite of what's cool: hot sites are the most popular, and some of them are cool, too. You can find out what's hot by checking out the following sites:

- **100 Hot Games** (http://www.100hot.com/games). This page lists the hottest sites for games of all kinds (including computer games, video games, chess, cards, role-playing, and more) based on Web-traffic statistics.
- **100 Hot Web Sites** (http://www.100hot.com). This list is compiled objectively using Web-traffic statistics. The list doesn't include college sites or home pages. Categories include models and celebrities, the best of the WWW, games, show business, online services, sports, live audio, places, travel, technology, chat lines, kids, business, jobs, service providers, and shopping.

What's New

Hundreds, sometimes thousands, of new Web sites appear daily. There's no way to keep up with all of them, but the following Web services keep track of some of the most interesting and useful new sites:

- **Netscape Guide's What's New** (http://home.netscape.com/netcenter/new.html). This list of interesting new sites in Netscape Communications' Guide is well worth exploring, even if you're not using Netscape Navigator.
- **What's New On Yahoo!** (http://www.yahoo.com/new). Hundreds of new sites go online daily, and they'll appear in Yahoo!, the Web's best subject tree.

Daily Inspiration

Here are some great Web sites that change every day, bringing you new information that will make you learn and laugh:

- **Cool Jargon of the Day** (http://www.bitech.com/jargon/cool). Those ever-enterprising technobabblers are sure to come up with ever-more-confusing terms.
- **Cool Site of the Day** (http://cool.infi.net). Every day there's a new, cool site. Check it out!
- **David Letterman's Top Ten List** (http://www.cbs.com/lateshow). Did you miss the *Late Show?* Check out this site for Letterman's latest Top Ten List.
- **Those Were the Days** (http://www.440.com/twtd/today.html). You think today's news is bad?
- **Urgent News of the Day** (http://dailynews.yahoo.com/headlines/ts/). Skip the newspaper, skip Dan Rather—it's all here.

IntelliMouse: A Better Way to Surf

While you're browsing through all these interesting sites, your mouse—and your elbow—are going to get a workout. But there's a better way. Microsoft Internet Explorer is optimized to make full use of Microsoft's IntelliMouse, an innovative mouse that includes a scrolling-wheel button between the two mouse buttons. When you've installed IntelliMouse, you can:

- Scroll through a Web page by rotating the wheel button forward or back—no more fussing with scroll bars.
- Continuously scroll the page by holding down the wheel button while moving the mouse.
- Jump to a link by pointing to it and *datazooming* forward. (To datazoom, hold down the Shift key while you rotate the wheel.)

Making the Web Useful

Cool, intriguing, entertaining, zany, wild, fun—these are the adjectives that you'll use to describe the sites you've visited so far. But what about *useful?* Is the information *practical?*

You bet. Here's a sample of what Internet Explorer and the Web can help you do:

- **Get help with your kids' homework.** Looking for teaching resources, or for some help with homework? The Education Index (http://www.educationindex.com) lists hundreds of excellent education sites. It's organized both by subject and age level (lifestage).
- **Look for college scholarships.** Search for colleges and scholarships—and you can even apply online, thanks to CollegeNet (http://www.collegenet.com).
- **Find out how much your used car is worth.** You'll find this information, plus the dealer invoice cost of the new car you're considering, at Edmund's online site (http://www.edmunds.com). Don't miss the tips on negotiating with dealers; you could save thousands of dollars.

Yahoo! Internet Life's 25 Most Incredibly Useful Sites

Don't miss this useful page: http://www.zdnet.com/yil/content/depts/useful/25mostuse.html. It lists Yahoo! Internet Life's all-time favorite Incredibly Useful Sites. For example, you learn how to:

- avoid speed traps
- avoid tax audits
- estimate college costs
- find the closest ATM
- fix your own cable TV
- hear your newspaper
- track your packages
- unclog your drain

There's a new Incredibly Useful Site every day, so check back often.

Staying Informed

How much are you spending on magazine and newspaper subscriptions? You could possibly pay for your Internet access (and then some) by getting the news and magazine articles you want from the Web. The following *free* sites contain the *full text* of the most recent edition of newspapers and magazines. What's more, they offer search and navigation tools that help you find what you're looking for. At *TV Guide*'s Web site, for instance, you can set up a personal profile that enables you to list only those shows that conform to your interests, for up to a week in advance.

- *Atlantic Monthly* http://www.theatlantic.com/issues/current/contents.htm
- *Christian Science Monitor* http://www.csmonitor.com
- *Los Angeles Times* http://www.latimes.com
- *Money* http://www.pathfinder.com
- *New York Times* http://www.nytimes.com
- *Time* http://www.pathfinder.com
- *TV Guide* http://www.tvgen.com
- *US News and World Report* http://www.usnews.com
- *USA Today* http://www.usatoday.com
- *Washington Post* http://www.washingtonpost.com

Understanding the Web's Search Services

Among the Web's most popular sites are two kinds of search services: subject directories (also called *Web directories* or *subject trees*) and search engines. It's not surprising that they're so popular. These are the tools people *must* use to find what they're looking for. In this section, you'll learn the difference between the two, so you'll know which one is best to use for a particular search.

Many Web portals offer a subject guide that looks like Yahoo!'s, but portals generally index far fewer Web pages than a directory such as Yahoo!.

Subject Directories

A subject directory is like the subject catalog in a library: it groups Web sites by topic (such as art, entertainment, or chemistry). Unlike a library's subject catalog, though, subject directories contain only a small fraction of the total number of documents on the Web. All the indexing has to be done by a human being, and furiously working Yahoo! staffers are able to index only about 2000 sites per day.

So here's the important point: subject directories such as Yahoo! index only a tiny fraction of the total documents available on the Web. But this isn't necessarily a bad thing. For the most part, the pages indexed in Yahoo! are valuable pages. Yahoo! indexes only those pages that meet its criteria for high-quality content. What confuses most Internet users, however, is the fact that you can search subject directories. Many users think they're searching the entire Web, but they're not.

The welcome page for Yahoo! shows the top-level subjects (Figure 6-7). After you click a subject category, you see progressively more detailed subjects and lists of Web pages (Figure 6-8).

You can also search Yahoo!. Just bear in mind that this is not the same thing as searching the whole Web. You're just searching within Yahoo!, which contains far fewer documents than the whole Web does.

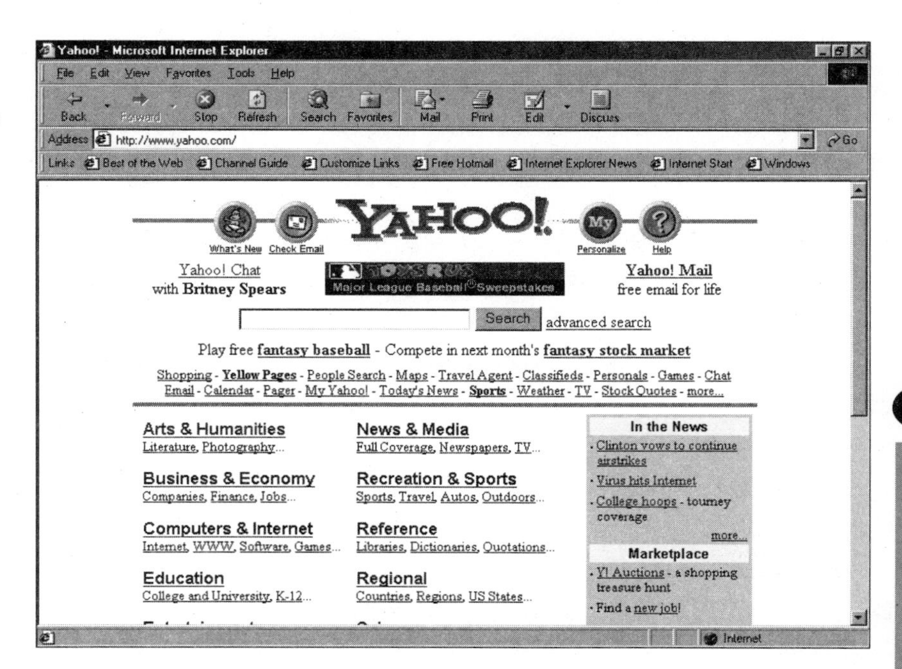

FIGURE 6-7.
Subject categories in Yahoo! are like a library's subject card catalog.

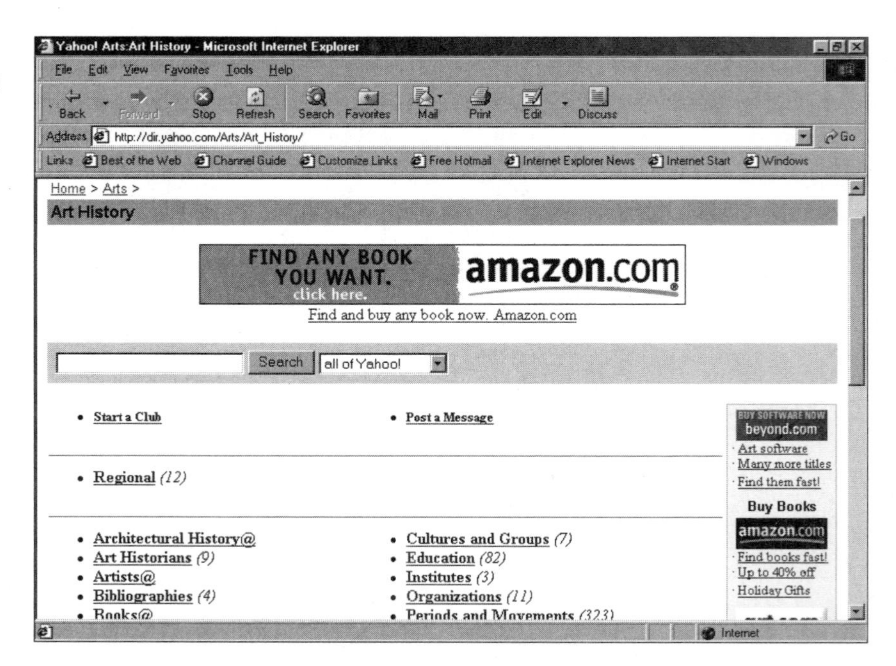

FIGURE 6-8. You can browse Yahoo! to find more detailed subjects and lists of Web pages.

A Quick Guide to the Web's Subject Directories

Subject directories contain only a tiny fraction of the documents available on the Web. However, these services try to feature the best content in a given subject. It's a good idea to start your search by browsing or searching one of these subject directories.

- **Argus Clearinghouse (http://www.clearinghouse.net).** This is a subject guide to subject directories maintained by independent individuals and organizations, and it's decidedly slanted toward serious academic subjects. Each item indexed is reviewed and ranked. An excellent place to start research on a college-level subject. Top-level categories include arts and humanities, business and employment, communication, computers, education, engineering, government and law, health and medicine, places and people, recreation, science and math, social sciences, and social issues.

- **Galaxy (http://galaxy.tradewave.com).** Described as a "professional's guide," Galaxy does not contain a great deal of content, and may not be as frequently updated as Clearinghouse and Virtual Library, its closest competitors; still, it's worth a look if you're hunting for serious information on college-level subjects. Top-level categories include business and commerce, engineering and technology, government, humanities, law, medicine, reference, science, and social science.

A Quick Guide to the Web's Subject Directories ***continued***

- **InfoMine (http://lib-www.ucr.edu).** Outstanding source of academic information, created by library staff at the University of California, Irvine. Top-level categories include biological, agricultural, and medical sciences; government information; instructional resources (K-12 and university level); Internet enabling tools; maps and geographical information systems; physical sciences, engineering, computing, and math; regional and general interest; social sciences and humanities; visual and performing arts.
- **LookSmart (http://www.looksmart.com).** An excellent subject guide to high-quality Web pages, with more than 20,000 subjects indexed. Oriented to consumers, home Internet users, and students. Top-level categories include automobiles, business and finance, computers and Internet, health and fitness, hobbies and interests, home and family, people and chat, reference and education, shopping and services, society and politics, sports and recreation, travel and vacations.
- **NewHoo (http://www.newhoo.com).** A Yahoo!-inspired subject directory that relies on volunteers to index high-quality content. Top-level categories include: Arts, Business, Computers, Games, Health, News, Recreation, Reference, Regional, Shopping, Society, Sports, and World.
- **WWW Virtual Library (http://vlib.org).** Like Argus Clearinghouse, this is a subject guide to subject directories. Unlike the Clearinghouse, the individuals responsible for each of the subject directories is affiliated with the Virtual Library. Generally, these individuals possess expertise in their subject fields, so this is an outstanding place to look for *reliable* information. Top-level subject categories include agriculture, computer science, communications and media, education, engineering, humanities, information management, international affairs, law, business and economics, recreation, regional studies, science, and society.
- **Yahoo! (http://www.yahoo.com).** The oldest and (some say) the best subject directory on the Web, Yahoo!, indexes tens of thousands of documents. Top-level subject headings include arts and humanities, business and economy, computers and Internet, education, entertainment, government, health, news and media, recreation and sports, reference, regional, science, social science, and society and culture.

Search Engines

Because subject directories index only a small fraction of the total number of available Web documents, you might not find what you're looking for in a subject directory. You might need to use a *search engine* such as AltaVista (Figure 6-9) or InfoSeek to find what you're looking for. Search engines provide "industrial-strength" database-search software that is capable of searching enormous databases containing all the words used in millions of Web documents.

Unlike subject directories, which are created by people, search services rely on automated programs to detect and index Web sites. These programs, called *robots* or *spiders,* roam the Web, hunting for new documents. When one of these programs finds a new document, it reports the document's address, retrieves all or part of the document's text, and adds the words to a huge database. For example, suppose you publish a page containing the word *Cleveland.* Sooner or later, a spider will detect your page and tuck it into the database so that your URL is listed (along with many thousands of others) as a Web document that mentions *Cleveland.* If users search for *Cleveland,* they'll get a list of Web documents that includes your personal Web site.

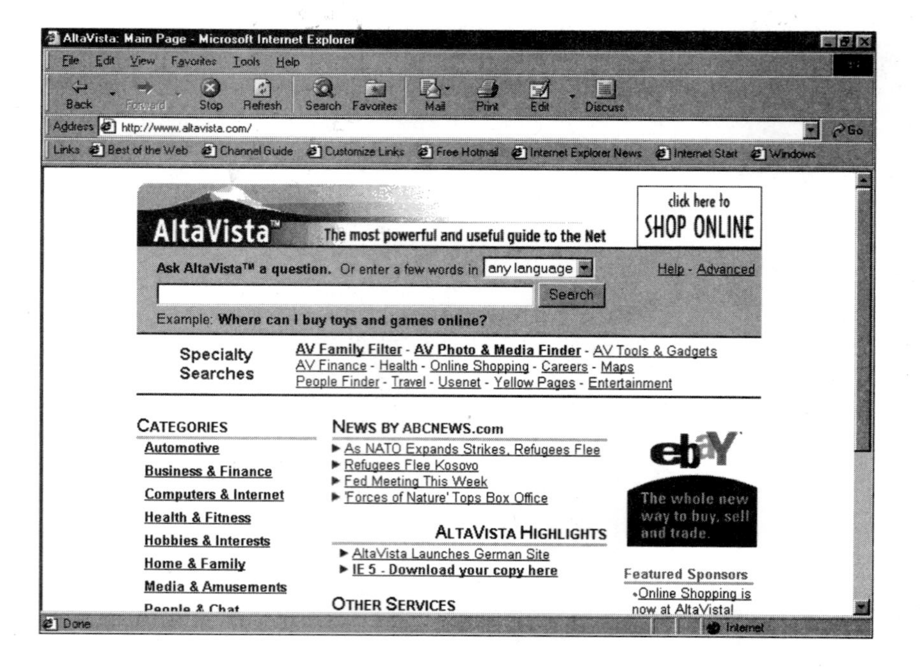

FIGURE 6-9.
AltaVista is one of the powerful search engines available to you on the Web.

Keep up with the fast-evolving search engine picture with Search Engine Watch (http://www.searchenginewatch.com), which features reviews, status reports, and links.

Remember that search engines vary in coverage. Each uses a different technique to collect and store Web-page references, and their databases are not identical. What's more, no search engine indexes the entire Web. To find the information you're looking for, you may need to use two or more search engines.

This example helps to explain both what's good about search services and what's bad about them. The good thing is that a competent searcher, armed with some of the tricks you'll learn later in this chapter, can zero in on pertinent Web pages with an amazing degree of precision. For example, you can combine search words to focus your search. But even competent searchers retrieve many pages that aren't relevant to their subject. For example, suppose a page is autobiographical, and it says something like, "I was born in Cleveland, but I really don't know anything about it because we moved away when I was six months old." For somebody searching for information about Cleveland, this fact isn't going to be particularly informative. Still, these services are invaluable, if you're willing to put up with their basic inaccuracy.

Use a search engine if you didn't find what you want in a subject directory. You'll need to learn some search techniques to avoid retrieving too many irrelevant documents.

My recommendations for search-engine selection:

- For a quick introductory search on a general or popular topic: InfoSeek.
- For a quick introductory search on a specialized topic: HotBot.
- If you can't find what you're looking for on InfoSeek or HotBot, try AltaVista.

A Quick Guide to the Web's Search Services

Most Web users don't realize that search engines differ. Here, you learn which search engines are most appropriate for a given search.

- **AltaVista (http://www.altavista.com/).** This search service indexes the full text of every document that its spider detects. What this means is that many of the pages you retrieve mention your search words in a

A Quick Guide to the Web's Search Services *continued*

peripheral way. You get a huge list of retrieved documents, but almost all of them are irrelevant to the research focus. Use this service when you want to make sure that you're not missing something that's out there.

- **Excite (http://www.excite.com).** This service offers a really big database, and it's easy to use. The retrieval list includes a percentage figure that indicates a guesstimate concerning the document's relevance to your interests. This search engine is a good place to start for any search.
- **GoTo (http://www.goto.com).** This search engine can search the whole Web, but you need to be aware that Web sites can contract with this service to have their links pop up in your retrieval list. That's not necessarily a bad thing if you're looking for commercial sites. If you're shopping for something on the Web, this is a good place to start hunting.
- **HotBot (http://www.hotbot.com).** Combining a big database with a sophisticated search method that seems to produce lots of relevant documents, HotBot is a good choice for an initial search.
- **InfoSeek (http://www.infoseek.com).** Although this search service has a small database, you'll find that InfoSeek searches generally produce a more useful retrieval list than most other search services. However, the small database means that there are surely more documents of interest out there. Use this service to search for a few good documents on a popular subject, but avoid it for more specialized subjects.
- **Lycos (http://www.lycos.com).** This service offers a medium-sized database of Web pages, but the database isn't as large as AltaVista's or HotBot's. In addition, Lycos doesn't index the full text of Web documents. Instead, it concentrates on important words in the first 20 lines or so of text and gives preference to titles. As a result, you may miss documents in which your subject is mentioned only peripherally. Lycos is a good choice if you would like to find pages in which your search terms are mentioned in the document's title or the first few lines of text. Top-level categories include arts and humanities, business and economy, computers and Internet, education, entertainment, government, health, news and media, recreation and sports, reference, regional, science, social science, and society and culture.
- **Northern Light (http://www.northernlight.com).** A good general-purpose search engine is combined with a fee-based special collection that enables you to search magazines, journals, and newspapers. If you opt for the special collections, you'll have to pay to see the full text of items in the special collection.

Using the Search Explorer

You can customize the Search assistant by adding your favorite Web search engines. For more information, see "Customizing the Search Assistant," page 287.

The Search explorer provides quick access to the Web's leading search engines. Version 5 of Internet Explorer includes a new Search Assistant, which not only makes searching easier, but helps you improve your search technique. The following sections introduce the Search explorer features.

Why the Search Explorer Is So Terrific

What's so cool about the Search Explorer? Searching by going to a search service directly is inconvenient. You type in one or more search terms and get a retrieval list. Something looks interesting, so you click it, but it turns out to be a dud. You have to click Back to return to the retrieval list. The whole procedure is time-consuming and tedious. With the Search Explorer bar, you see the results of the search in the Explorer bar itself; you can just click away at the retrieved sites until you find the one you're looking for (Figure 6-10).

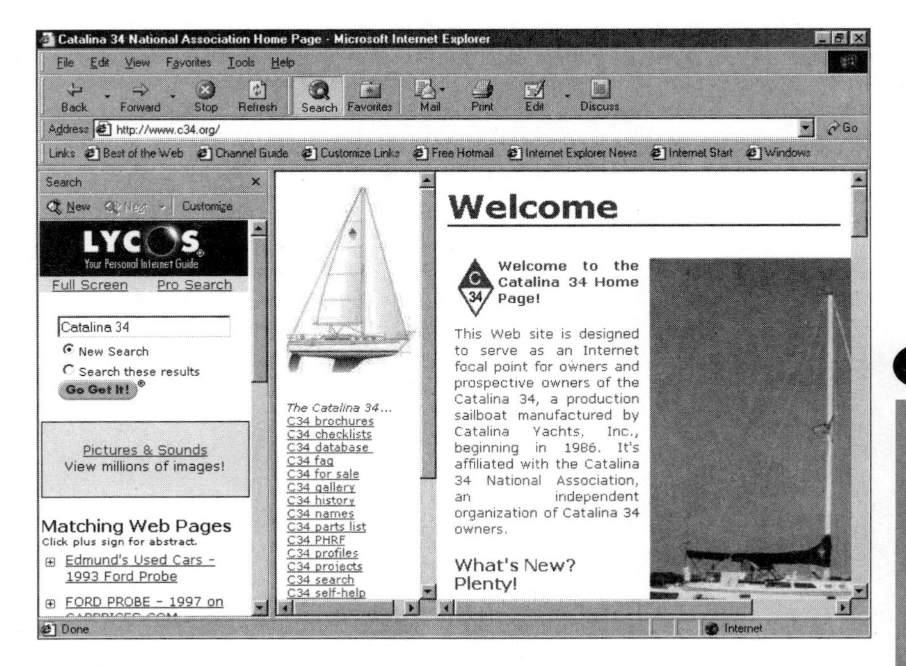

FIGURE 6-10.
The Search Explorer bar (the panel on the left) gives you a convenient way to search.

 TIP

> The first time you type something in a text box and upload this text to a Web site, you'll see a security alert warning you that someone might be able to read what you've typed. That's true, but there's little chance anyone would be interested in what you're searching for. This warning is designed to heighten your awareness about uploading sensitive or confidential information, such as your Social Security number for U.S. residents or your credit card number. If you don't want to see this message again, activate the option that hides the message—but remember to upload sensitive or confidential information only to secure sites. See Chapter 9, "Using the Internet Safely."

Using the Search Assistant

New to Internet Explorer version 5 is the Search Assistant, a well-designed utility that enables you to search more than one search engine. The Search Assistant helps you improve search results by making it easier to search more than one search engine. When you use the Search Assistant, Internet Explorer automatically uses the search words you type to search two or more search engines; you don't have to type the same search words over again.

To use the Search Assistant, follow these steps:

1. On the Standard Buttons toolbar, click Search. You'll see the Search explorer bar.
2. On the Search explorer toolbar, click New.
3. Choose a category for your search. You can search for a Web page, a person's address, a company or organization, or a map. You can also retrieve previous searches.

   If you click the More button, you can also search an encyclopedia or Usenet newsgroups.
4. In the search engine's text box, type at least two or three words describing your search subject.
5. Press Enter, or click the button that starts the search.

   You'll see the first page of the search results in the explorer.
6. If you see a page title that looks interesting, move the mouse pointer over the title.

You'll see a ToolTip that shows information about the page.

7. To view a page, click the page's title.

   You'll see the page in the browser window.

8. To view another page, click a different title. To see more page titles, scroll to the bottom of the explorer window and look for a link to additional pages of search results.

9. To see the results of the same search for another search engine, click Next. Internet Explorer uses the same search words that you supplied for the first search engine. Repeat steps 6 through 8 to browse the list of retrieved items.

10. Continue clicking Next to view the results from additional search engines if you wish.

11. When you've finished using the Search Assistant, click the explorer's close button.

Troubleshooting Your Search

If your search didn't work out well, consider the following possibilities:

- **Did you spell the search terms correctly?** A typo or misspelling can ruin your search.
- **Try a synonym.** If you're searching for a wine called Shiraz, you should also search for Syrah, a different name for the same wine.
- **Did you use the wrong capitalization pattern?** Use capital letters only when they're appropriate. Don't type your search terms in all capital letters.

Closing the Search Explorer Bar

When you're finished searching, you can close the Search Explorer bar in any of the following ways:

- Click the Search button again.

  or

- Click the close button on the Search explorer's title bar.

  or

- Go to the View menu; select Explorer Bar and None.

Looking for the Needle in the Haystack

Still haven't found what you're looking for? It's time for AltaVista. This search service is the least convenient to use for quick, easy searches because it retrieves too many documents. If you're willing to learn a bit more about AltaVista's advanced search syntax, though, you can use this service with an incredible degree of precision.

- **Phrase searching.** If you're looking for a phrase, surround the phrase in quotation marks. For example, search for *"Outer Banks"* rather than *Outer Banks,* so you won't get the page describing the new banking ventures in Outer Mongolia.
- **Wildcard characters.** Use a wildcard character to make sure you're getting all the documents relevant to your interests. Most Web search services don't enable you to do this, but AltaVista lets you type an asterisk to match one or more characters at the end of a word. For example, you can type *kayak** to match *kayak, kayaks,* and *kayaking.*
- **Requiring a certain word.** Put a plus sign right in front of your most important word. If you see lots of stuff on the Outer Banks but nothing on kayaks, for example, type:

  "Outer Banks" +kayak.*

  The plus sign brings documents containing this word to the top of the list.
- **Rejecting a certain word.** If the retrieval list is stuffed with documents pertaining to something you don't want, type a term that describes these documents and place a minus sign in front of it. For example, the Outer Banks kayak search nets many documents, for some reason, that mention Asheville, N.C. To demote these documents to the bottom of the list, type:

  -Asheville.

These nifty tricks enable you to perform a pinpointed search, one that works much better than just typing the terms without any special symbols. Suppose you're looking for Web pages concerning kayaking on North Carolina's Outer Banks. If you type in *outer banks kayaking,* you get over 80,000 documents—a few too many to go through! If you search for *+"Outer Banks" +kayak,* you only get 125—and they're mostly very good. See what I mean?

Can you use the same tricks at all the sites you visit? Unfortunately, each of the Web's search services uses its own search *syntax,* the rules for typing search terms and search commands properly. But there's some overlap. For example, you can use the plus and minus signs in Lycos and InfoSeek, and you can perform a phrase search in InfoSeek by surrounding the search term in quotation marks.

Using Specialized Search Services

The Web's search engines and directories are great tools, but they don't contain all the information that's out there. Often, using a specialized directory or search engine is much better than trying to search the whole Web. In this section, you'll find some great tips concerning searching for information on specific subjects. This section isn't meant to be comprehensive but only to give you an idea of the incredible richness that's out there and why it makes sense sometimes to focus on specialized search services rather than using Web search engines.

There are two wonderful collections of Web search services that I strongly recommend you visit: Internet Sleuth (http://www.isleuth.com), which offers keyword search access to more than 2000 Web-accessible databases in every conceivable field; and the University of California, Berkeley's Index to the Internet (http://sunsite.berkeley.edu/InternetIndex).

Specialized Search Indexes

Search.com (http://www.search.com) indexes more than 100 specialized search engines in the following subject areas: automotive, classifieds, computing, employment, entertainment, health, learning, living, local, money, news, shopping, sports, and travel.

The biggest specialized search service of them all, Internet Sleuth (http://www.isleuth.com), is a must-visit. A Web pioneer, the site first appeared in March, 1995, which is something like the Web's Lower Paleolithic. Now offering more than 3,000 searchable databases, the Internet Sleuth is well organized and enables you to perform searches without leaving the Sleuth's pages. Knowledgeable searchers will find useful clues about which search operators you can use with each of the indexed databases.

Exploring Specialized Search Services

Here's a sample of some of the specialized search services that you'll find on the Web, organized by subject. As you explore these sites, bear in mind that the resources they contain are generally *not* listed in Web search engines; that's because they're stored in specialized databases that aren't directly accessible to Web search engines' spiders. To repeat this chapter's theme: there's a ton of quality content out there—you just have to know where to find it!

Arts

To find out what's happening in the arts, you can check out CultureFinder (http://www.culturefinder.com), the online address for the performing arts. CultureFinder (Figure 6-11) includes a searchable calendar for more than 900 arts organizations in the United States and Canada. Like to explore the arts online? World Art Treasures (http://sgwww.epfl.ch/BERGER) offers a collection of 100,000 slides compiled by art historian Jacques-Edouard Berger.

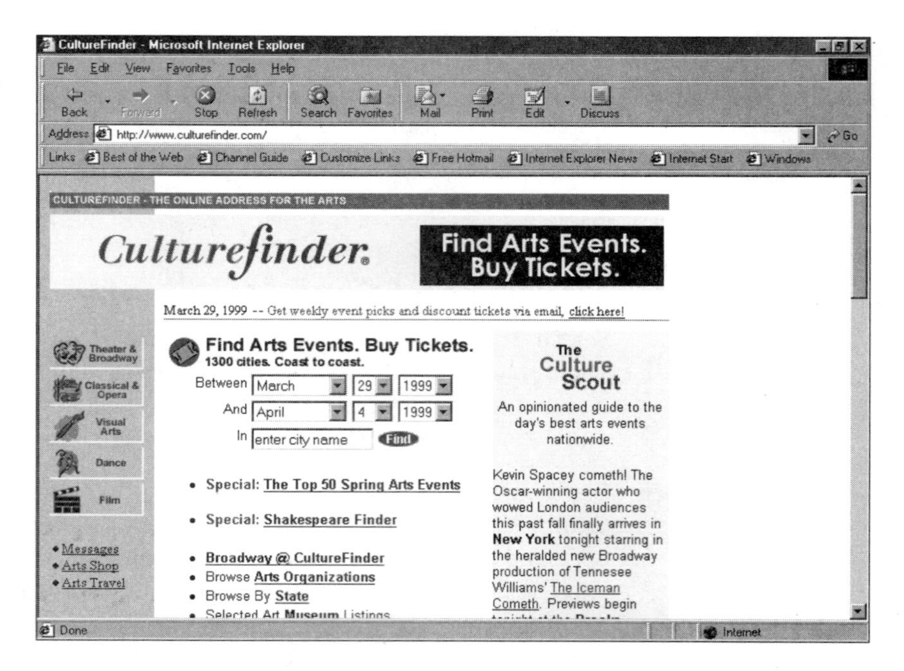

FIGURE 6-11.
CultureFinder enables Web users to search for information concerning more than 900 arts organizations in the United States and Canada.

Business

If you're trying to track down basic information about businesses, check out Hoover's Online (http://www.hoovers.com), which offers a free database of more than 10,000 of the largest public and private U.S. companies. Looking for Securities and Exchange Commission (SEC) data on stocks that are publicly traded? Look no farther than the EDGAR Database (http://www.sec.gov/edgarhp.htm). This is a fully searchable index to post 1994 SEC filings, including quarterly and annual financial reports. For a Web version of the Yellow Pages, try BigBook (http://www.bigbook.com), which is searchable and offers local listings for your area (Figure 6-12).

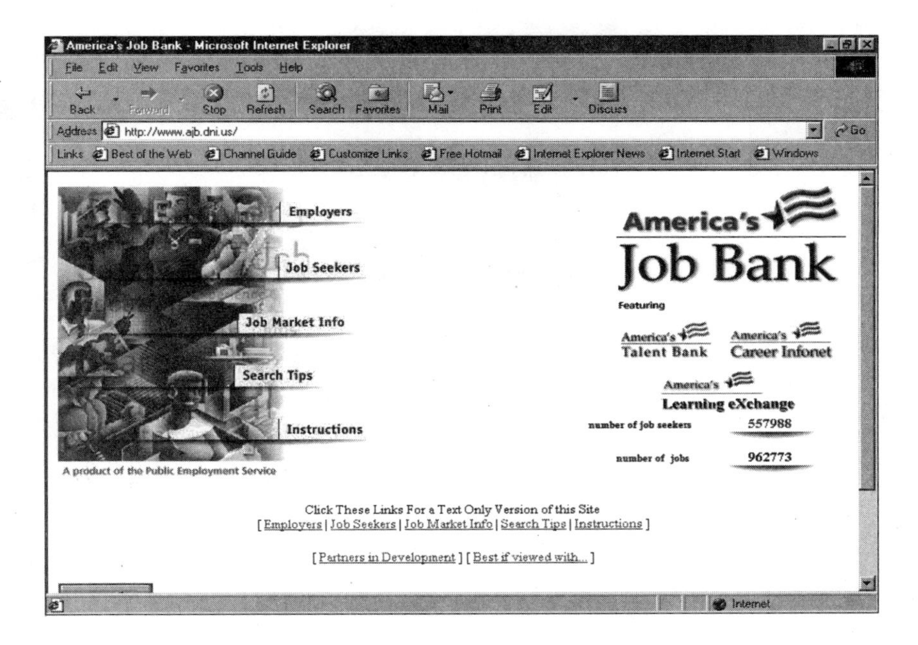

FIGURE 6-12.
BigBook offers a Web-based version of the Yellow Pages.

Government

Like to know what your elected representatives are up to? Vote Smart (http://www.vote-smart.org) tracks the voting records of more than 13,000 political leaders. You can use this service to find out the names and addresses of all the representatives in your zip code. THOMAS (http://thomas.loc.gov/home/thomas2.html) provides a searchable database of current bills as well as the *Congressional Record.*

Health

Healthfinder (http://www.healthfinder.gov) is an excellent place to start searching for medical information on the Web. If you'd like to search the scientific literature, HealthGate Medline Search (http://www.healthgate.com) offers free Web access to the largest database of medical research reports, Medline.

Jobs

Increasing numbers of people are finding jobs on the Internet. To find out why, check out America's Job Bank (http://www.ajb.dni.us), with a searchable database of more than 250,000 job openings (Figure 6-13). CareerMosaic (http://www.careermosaic.com) enables you to search for openings at specific companies.

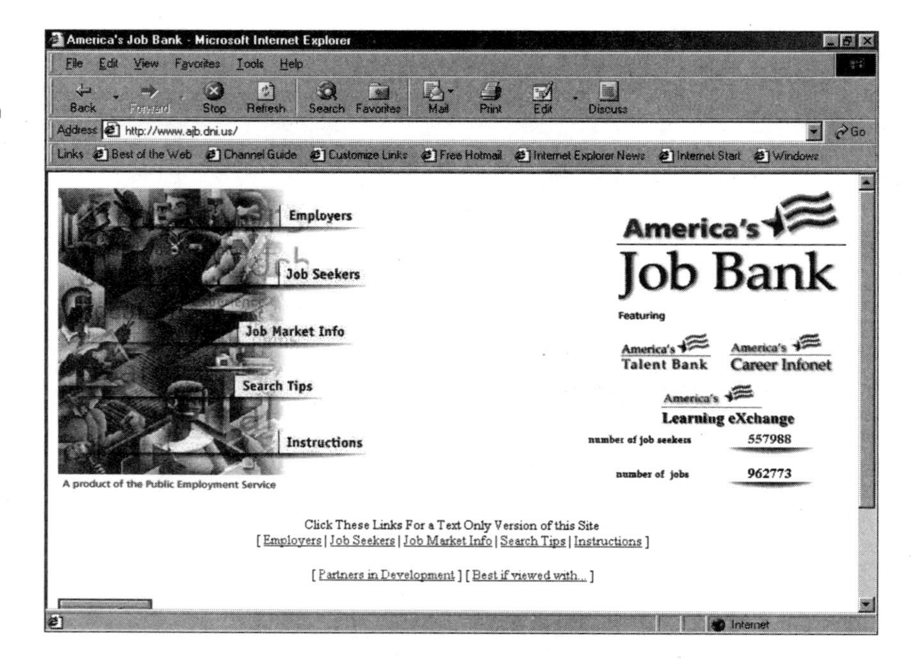

FIGURE 6-13. America's Job Bank enables you to search a database of more than 250,000 current job openings.

Maps

MapQuest (http://www.mapquest.com) is a free interactive atlas of the United States that enables you to plan driving itineraries, with outcomes that are sometimes slightly quirky. For a map locating any street address in the United States, see Yahoo! Maps (http://maps.yahoo.com), which enables you to search by address or zip code; the result is a detailed local map (see Figure 6-14). For general geographic and demographic information on the United States, see U.S. Gazetteer (http://www.census.gov/cgi-bin/gazetteer). You type in a zip code and out come maps and the latest census data.

MSN offers a free driving-direction service; you can access this by clicking the links on the Internet Explorer default start page.

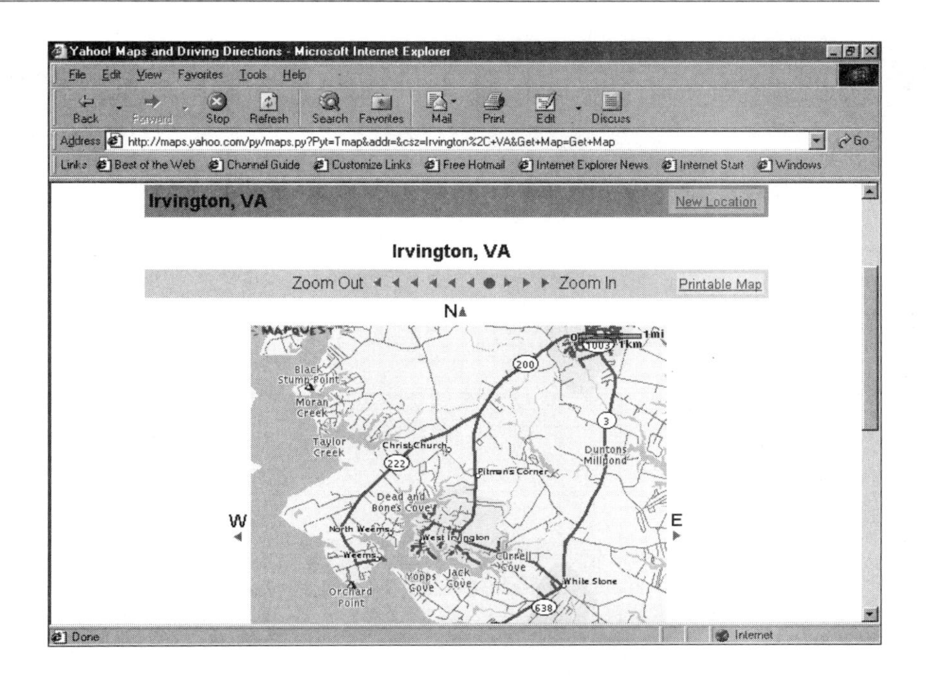

FIGURE 6-14.
The Yahoo! Maps site provides detailed local maps.

Multimedia

Scour.net (http://www.scour.net) is an amazing multimedia search engine that enables you to search for images, video clips, and sounds. You can search for more than one million multimedia resources on the Web.

People

InfoSpace (http://www.infospace.com) provides access to 112 million U.S. and Canadian telephone listings, including businesses as well as individuals. AT&T's Toll-Free Internet Directory (http://www.tollfree.att.net) enables you to search for toll-free (800 and 888) numbers, but you should also try Internet 800 Search (http://inter800.com), which includes non-AT&T toll-free numbers as well. Other convenient people-finding services include WhoWhere (http://www.whowhere.lycos.com/) and Bigfoot (http://www.bigfoot.com), which enable you to search for e-mail addresses.

Recipes

Epicurious (http://www.epicurious.com) is a beautiful site (Figure 6-15) that includes, among many other things, an incredible database of more than 6000 recipes. If that's not enough, try Internet Chef On-Line Magazine, with a searchable archive of almost 30,000 recipes (http://www.ichef.com).

Wine Spectator Online (http://www.winespectator.com) offers an amazing database of approximately 15,000 wines containing ratings and tasting notes. If you're confused about some of the terminology you encounter in these recipes or wine-tasting notes, don't miss Epicurious's dictionary of more than 4,200 food, wine, and culinary terms (http://www.epicurious.com/db/dictionary/terms/indexes/dictionary.html). If you're concerned about the nutritional value of the food you eat, check out the USDA Nutrient database (http://www.nal.usda.gov/fnic/foodcomp/Data/SR12/sr12.html).

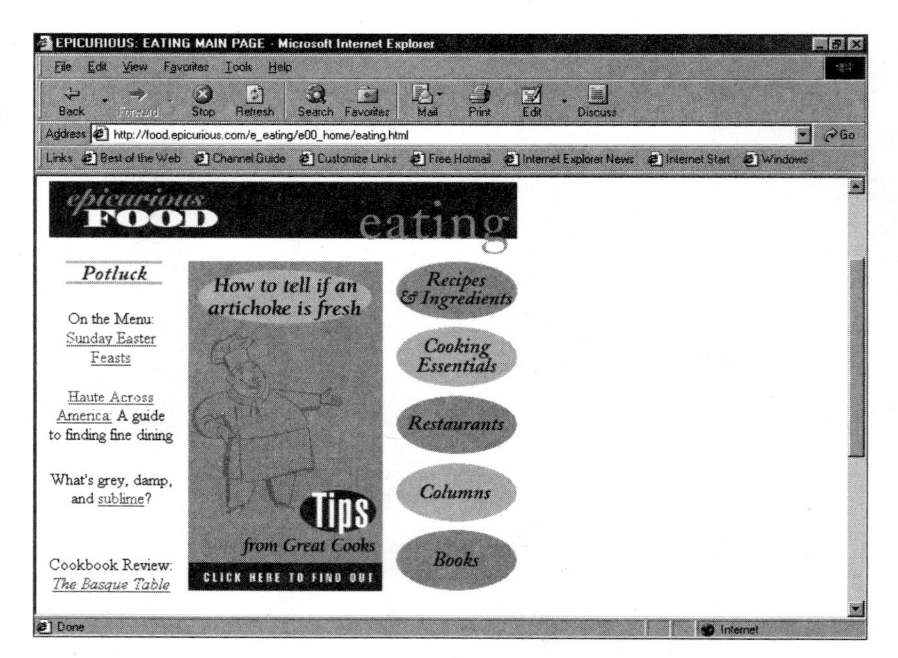

FIGURE 6-15. Epicurious offers a database of more than 6000 recipes.

Schools

The American School Directory (http://www.asd.com) is a searchable database of 106,000 schools at the K-12 level in the United States. There's a ton of information here about public and private schools. If you're a teacher, you'll love the Eisenhower National Clearinghouse (http://carson.enc.org), with a searchable database of more than 7000 K–12 curriculum resources.

Reference

The Web is loaded with reference resources; it's like having a library's reference room on your desktop. Just to whet your appetite, here's a sample: Merriam-Webster Online (http://www.m-w.com), shown in Figure 6-16. Here, you can search the WWWebster Dictionary and Thesaurus.

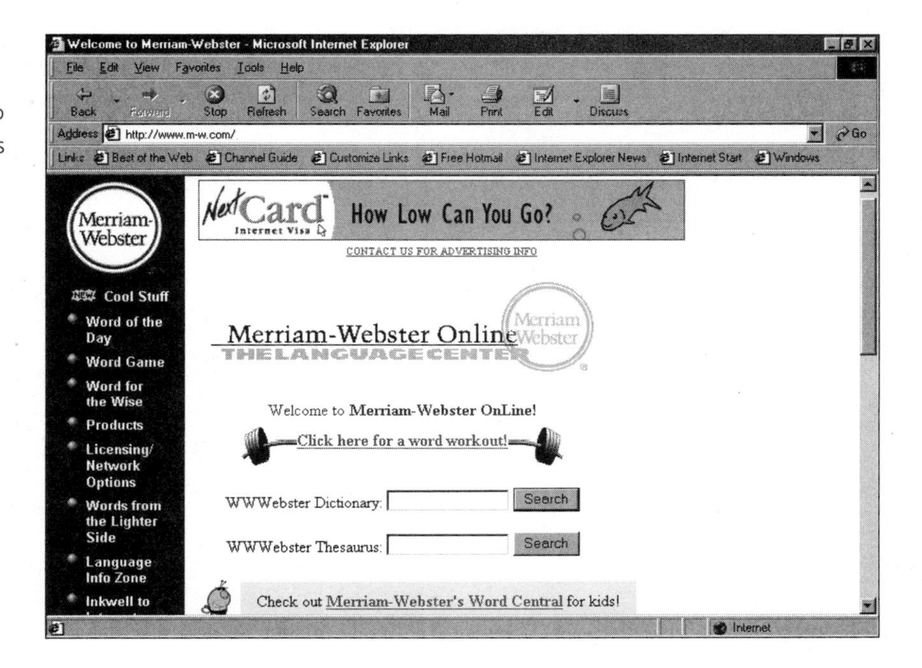

FIGURE 6-16. Merriam-Webster Online enables you to search online versions of a dictionary and thesaurus.

Weather

The Weather Channel has a great Web site (http://www.weather.com) that lets you see local forecasts. The U.S. National Weather Service (http://www.nws.noaa.gov) has a good site, too, with current weather and storm warnings.

Finding Related Pages

Is there a better way to search the Web? Alexa is a browser add-on program that enables you to search using a new approach. Instead of searching the Web directly, Alexa records the pathways that Alexa users travel as they move from a site to related sites, and uses this information to build a database of site relationships. When you're visiting a Web page, you can use Alexa to see the current list of related pages.

Like to try Alexa? There's a mini-version of Alexa built into Internet Explorer 5. Here's how to try it:

1. Visit one of your favorite Web pages.
2. From the Tools menu, choose Show Related Sites.
   You'll see the Alexa explorer bar, shown in Figure 6-18.

Take a look at the list of related sites. (If Alexa didn't find any related sites, visit another favorite and try again.) You'll probably find that the list differs somewhat from a search engine's results—you'll see some pages that appear to use the same key words as the Web page you're viewing, but you may also see some page titles that have different subjects. Some of these might be completely unrelated to the Web page you're viewing; still, Alexa users went to these pages from the one you're currently viewing, so it's possible—even likely—that there's some kind of relationship. It's an interesting approach, and well worth trying.

If you're pleased with the results of the mini-Alexa browser, you can download the full version by clicking the link within the Alexa explorer bar. The full Alexa service appears in its own window on the screen, replete with advertisements. (Alexa is an advertiser-supported service.)

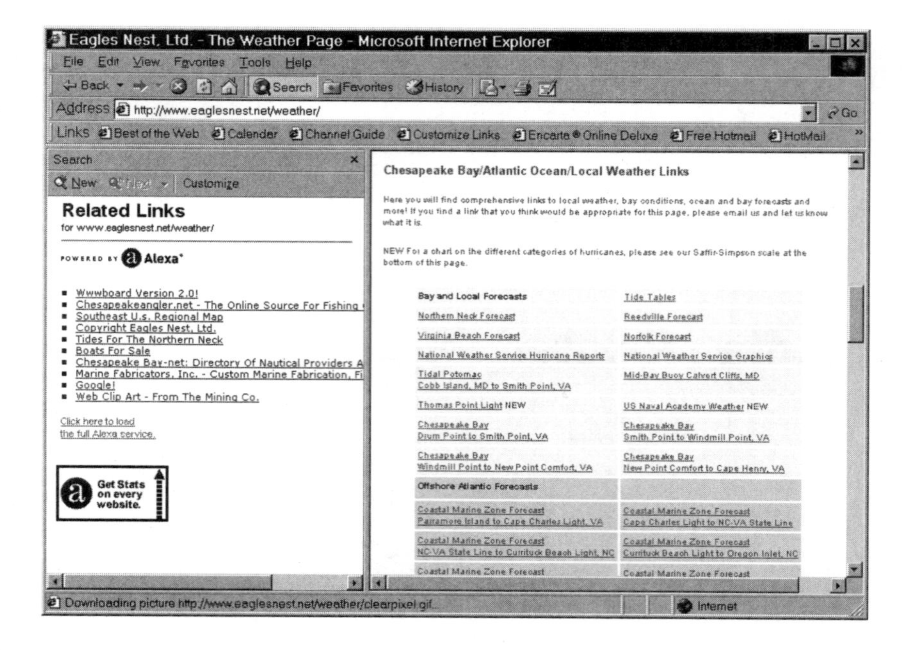

FIGURE 6-18.
To try the Alexa service, display a favorite Web page, click Tools on the menu bar, and choose Show Related Pages.

CHAPTER 7

Saving the Best Content

Thanks to the many ways Internet Explorer enables you to save links to Web content, or the content itself, you'll find that it's easy to retrace your steps. In this chapter, you'll learn how to change the default start page, add links to the Links toolbar, create shortcuts that enable you to start the program and go directly to a specified Web page, and create hundreds—even thousands—of links to favorite sites. You'll also learn how to print Web documents and save entire Web pages, graphics and all, for offline viewing.

Understanding Your Options for Saving Content

Before you modify Internet Explorer with links to the best Web content, take a moment to examine your options. Some of these make Web content directly accessible from the browser window and toolbars; others store links away in somewhat less-accessible menus. To decide which option to use for a given Web page, you'll need to consider which pages you'll return to time and again, and which ones will get an occasional repeat visit.

- **Changing the default start page.** Make this change if you would like Internet Explorer to display the start page of your choice every time the program starts. The page you choose should be one that you almost always display in order to begin your Internet Explorer sessions. If you're setting up your computer for kids, for example, you might want Internet Explorer to display Yahooligans every time the program starts. Yahooligans is a wonderful Web directory of content suitable for kids.
- **Adding pages to the Links toolbar.** You can modify the Links toolbar so that it contains the four or five Web pages that you consult most frequently. These pages should offer frequently updated content that you find indispensable for professional or personal reasons. For example, a professional writer could add links to online dictionaries, style guides, and writers' chat groups.
- **Creating desktop shortcuts to Web pages.** Create shortcuts if you would like to have two or more options for starting Internet Explorer and displaying a page other than the default start page.
- **Adding Web pages to the Favorites menu.** Use this technique to store pages to which you'd like to return, but not as frequently as those you save as Link toolbar items or desktop shortcuts. By creating folders and subfolders for your favorite items, you can save the pathway to many Web sites—thousands, if you wish. In time, your Favorites menu becomes a truly valuable, personal guide to Web content.
- **Saving pages for offline browsing.** You can save complete Web sites, including graphics and active content, for offline browsing. This is a good option for anyone who wants to minimize connection time, and it's especially useful for notebook computer

users. Once you've saved content for offline browsing, you don't need to be connected to the Internet in order to browse this content. What's more, you can set up automatic updates, called *synchronization*, that check these pages when you are online. If the content has changed, Internet Explorer automatically updates your saved copies.

- **Copying or saving page content.** You can save selected text or graphics from Web pages. For example, if you've found a Web graphic that you particularly like, you can make it your default Windows wallpaper.
- **Printing Web pages.** You can print any Web page that you can display with Internet Explorer. You can then read the page at your leisure or file the content for reference purposes.

As you use these features, Internet Explorer grows in value. The Web seems less like a maze, and more like an incredibly useful tool. And the more content you discover and save, the more useful it becomes. Soon, Internet Explorer becomes so useful that you'll wonder how you did without it. This program enables you to transform the Web into a personal information utility of immense usefulness.

Setting Up Windows for Multiple Users

Before you begin modifying Internet Explorer by following the suggestions in this chapter, consider whether your computer and Internet Explorer are used by more than one person. If so, you may wish to define user profiles for each person using the computer. Once you have defined user profiles, users are asked to supply their user names (and optionally a password) when Windows starts. After they log on, they see their own, customized version of Windows and Internet Explorer. It's as if your computer had two or more completely separate copies of Windows and Internet Explorer, each with its own, personalized settings. Internet Explorer features that can be customized for each user include the default start page, items on the Links toolbar, items in the Favorites folder, content downloaded for offline browsing, Outlook Express mailboxes and newsgroup subscriptions, and much more.

Table 7-1 lists the items that can be personalized for each user.

TABLE 7-1. Settings That Can Be Personalized.

Activate this:	To let users personalize this:
Desktop folder and Documents menu	Everything on the desktop, including shortcuts, background wallpaper, appearance choices, and active content (see Chapter 22 for a discussion of routing active content to the desktop). This option also ensures that the Documents menu will show the current user's recently accessed documents.
Start menu	Everything on the Start menu, including links to installed software.
Favorites folder	All aspects of the Favorites folder, including links to favorite pages, folders, and subfolders.
Downloaded Web pages	All offline Web content that's been saved for offline viewing, including subscription settings for automatic updating.
My Documents folder	This is the default storage location for documents created with application programs, such as the Microsoft Office applications.

TIP

Even if you're the only user of this computer, you may still want to create different user profiles. For example, suppose you have a notebook computer that you use at work, and you later use the same computer at home and weekends for hobby purposes. You could create two profiles, one called Work and the other called Home. On the same computer, you'll have what amounts to two completely different versions of Internet Explorer, the one customized for work purposes, and the other customized for your avocational interests. For example, the Work user profile displays your company's home page at the start of each browsing session, while the Home user profile displays MSN.com, with its news, sports, and weather.

TIP

When you define users, you can decide whether each user starts with a blank slate, as if Windows and Internet Explorer had just been installed, or with all the settings you've chosen up to now. For the Web-related options, you may wish to let each user start fresh, but consider giving each user the current Start menu. This menu now contains links to the applications you've installed. Unless you choose the option that copies existing settings to the new profiles, this menu will contain almost nothing, and the new user may not realize that the computer has many installed applications.

Adding a New User

To add the names of users, follow these steps:

1. In the Windows Control Panel, choose Users.
2. Click New User, if necessary, to open the Add User wizard.
3. Click Next.
4. In the User Name text box, type a name for the new user, up to 128 characters in length, and click Next.
5. If you would like to define a password that this user must type to access this user profile, type the password, and type it again to confirm that you've typed it correctly. Leave both boxes blank if you do not require this user to supply a password. Click Next to continue.
6. Choose the items you want to personalize (see Figure 7-1). If you select one of these options, users see their own customization choices for this option, but not those of other users. For example, if you activate the Favorites folder, this user will see a custom Favorites folder containing only those items that this user selects.
   - To create custom Internet Explorer profiles, I suggest that you activate Desktop Folder and Documents Menu, Favorites Folder, and Downloaded Web Pages.
   - To give the new user all the content that already exists for the items you have selected, activate the option called Create Copies Of The Current Items And Their Contents. To give the new user a clean slate, click Create New Items To Save Disk Space.

   Click Next when you're done choosing these options.
7. Click Finish to complete the user profile.

To change users without restarting your computer, click Start, and choose the option that begins with "Log off" followed by the user name. Windows will restart, and you can change the user profile by typing the user's name (and password, if you defined one).

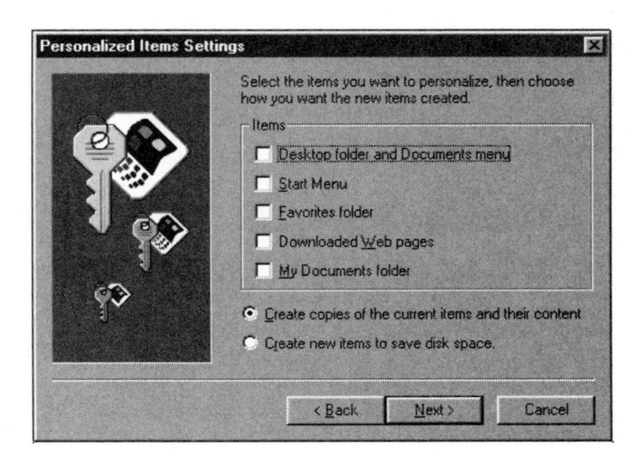

FIGURE 7-1.
You can choose which items you want the new user to be able to personalize.

Displaying a List of Users When Windows Starts

After you've created user profiles, you'll see a dialog box when you restart Windows. To log on using your user profile, type your user name, and your password if you defined one.

If you would rather choose the user name from a list, follow these steps:

1. On the desktop, right-click Network Neighborhood.
2. Choose Properties from the pop-up menu.

   You'll see the Network dialog box, with the Configuration page visible.
3. Click Add.

   You'll see the Select Network Component Type dialog box.
4. Select Client, and click Add.

   You'll see the Select Network Client dialog box.
5. In the list on the left, select Microsoft.
6. In the list on the right, click Microsoft Family Logon, and click OK.
7. In the Primary Network Logon box, choose Microsoft Family Logon.
8. Click OK to confirm your choice.

When you start your computer, you'll see a dialog box that enables you to choose your user profile from a list.

> To modify user settings, open the Control Panel, and choose Users. Select the user profile that you want to modify. In the User Settings dialog box, you can choose Set Password to modify the selected user's password, or Change Settings to change the features that this user can customize. You can also delete user profiles that are no longer needed. To delete a profile, select the profile and click Delete.

Changing User Settings

Once you've defined users, you can modify the user's profile. To do so, follow these steps:

1. In the Control Panel, choose Users.
2. In the User List, select the user profile you want to modify.
3. To change the password, click Set Password, and follow the on-screen instructions.
4. To change the settings that define which Windows and Internet Explorer features are customized for this user, click Change Settings, and activate or deactivate the features you want to change.
5. Click OK to confirm your changes.

Changing the Default Start Page

Unless your copy of Internet Explorer was modified by your service provider, you see MSN.com's home page when you start the program. This page is an excellent portal, offering news, weather, a subject guide, stock quotes, and more. However, you may wish to change the default start page, so that your preferred page is displayed every time you start the program.

For example, suppose you are using Internet Explorer on a corporate intranet (an internal network that enables you to use Internet tools, such as Internet Explorer). You may wish to start your browsing sessions with your company's home page.

In this section, you learn how to change the default start page. You also learn how to display a blank page when Internet Explorer starts, and how to restore the MSN.com start page, should you wish to restore the program default.

Specifying a New Start Page

To change the default start page, follow these steps:

1. Navigate to the Web page that you want to display.
2. From the Tools menu, choose Internet Options.

   You'll see the Internet Options dialog box, shown in Figure 7-2.
3. In the Home Page area, click Use Current.
4. Click OK.

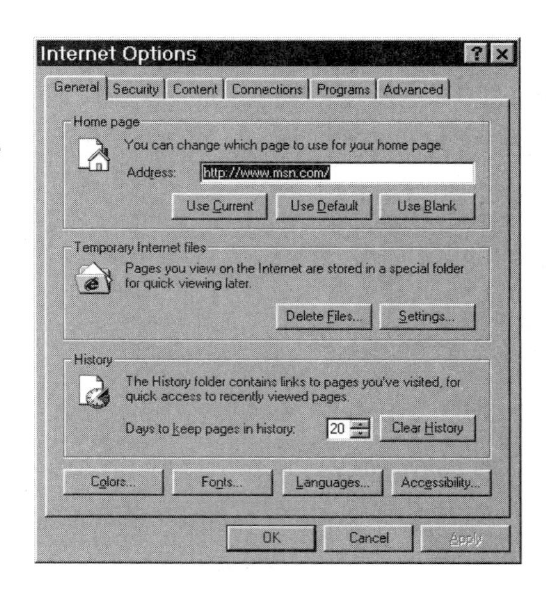

FIGURE 7-2.
You can change the default home page by navigating to the page you want to use, and clicking Use Current in the Home Page area.

To test your new default start page, click the Home button, or click View on the menu bar, point to Go To, and choose Home Page. These commands now take you to your new default start page, rather than MSN.com.

Starting with a Blank Page

You can start Internet Explorer with a blank page if you wish. You'll find that Internet Explorer starts faster, since the program doesn't have to access the Internet to get the latest copy of the start page.

To start with a blank page, follow these steps:

1. From the Tools menu, choose Internet Options.

   You'll see the Internet Options dialog box, shown in Figure 7-2.

2. In the Home page area, click Use Blank.

3. Click OK.

If you changed the default start page, you can visit MSN.com by choosing Internet Start from the Links toolbar.

Restoring the Original Default Start page

If you would like to restore the original default start page, follow these steps:

1. From the Tools menu, choose Internet Options.

   You'll see the Internet Options dialog box, shown in Figure 7-2.

2. In the Home Page area, click Use Default.

3. Click OK.

Adding Pages to the Links Toolbar

Of all the options available for returning to your favorite Web sites, the Links toolbar is the quickest. When you add a Web page to this toolbar, you can return to the page quickly by clicking the page's name.

Deciding Which Pages to Add

Which pages should you add to the Links toolbar? Here are some Web-page characteristics that make them good candidates:

- The page contains frequently updated content. You visit the page time and again to see what's new.
- The page contains reference resources that you frequently use. Perhaps it's the home page of a specialized search service (see Chapter 6, "Finding the Best Content") that contains information you need for your profession or hobby.
- You use the page almost every time you browse the Web. If you will return to the page less frequently, save it as a Favorite (see "Saving Web Pages as Favorites" on page 163).

The Links toolbar isn't the best place for links to search engines or subject directories (see Chapter 6, "Finding the Best Content"). You can access these easily by clicking the Search button's drop-down list. So including them on the Links menus takes up valuable space that you could use for other types of pages. If the Search list does not contain the services you prefer, you can customize it; see Chapter 10, "Personalizing Internet Explorer," for details.

If you don't see the Links toolbar, right-click the menu bar background, and choose Links from the pop-up menu.

Adding Web Pages to the Links Toolbar

You add links to the Links toolbar using drag and drop. As shown in Figure 7-3, you can add a link to Yahoo!'s home page (or any other page you're displaying) by dragging the page icon to the Links toolbar.

You can also add items to the Links toolbar by dragging a hyperlink on a Web page to the Links toolbar.

To add a link to the page you're currently viewing, do the following:

1. Make sure the Address toolbar and Links toolbar are visible. To display a hidden toolbar, right-click the menu bar background, and choose the toolbar name from the pop-up menu. If only the toolbar name is visible, drag the toolbar handle to bring the entire toolbar into view.
2. In the Address bar, point to the page icon (see Figure 7-3).
3. Hold down the left mouse button, and drag the page icon to the Links toolbar. Without releasing the button, drag the pointer back and forth on the toolbar until you see the I-pointer. (The I-pointer appears when you have positioned the mouse pointer between two existing links, or at the beginning or end of the Links toolbar.)
4. When you have positioned the I-pointer where you want the link to appear, release the mouse button.

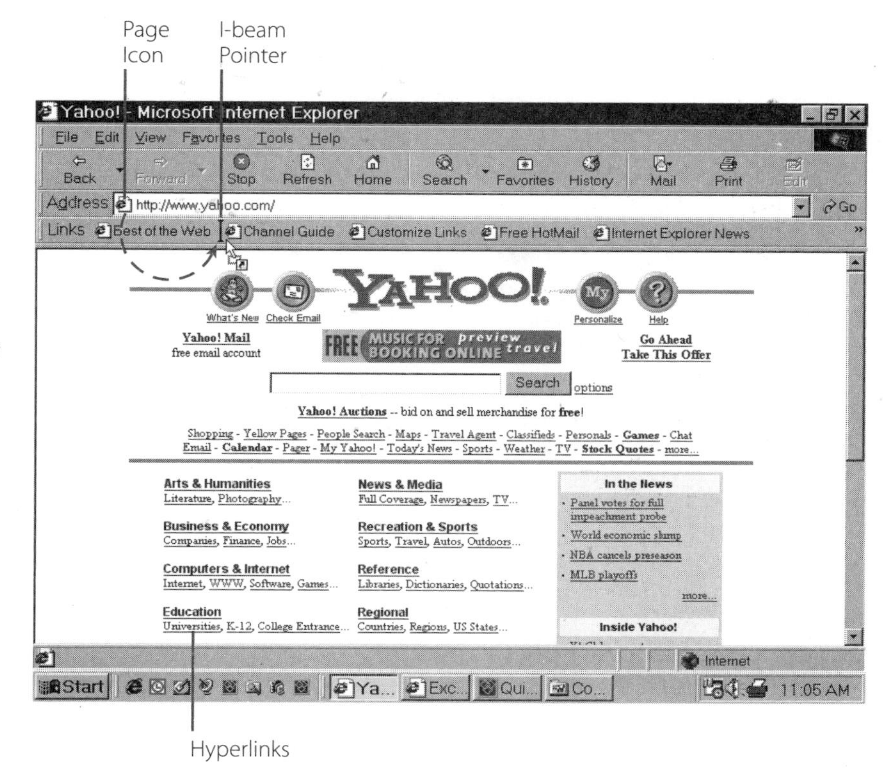

FIGURE 7-3.
To add items to the Links toolbar, drag a hyperlink or the page icon to the toolbar, move the I-pointer to the location you want, and release the mouse button.

TIP

> If the link title takes up too much room, you can shorten it. For more information, see "Renaming Links Toolbar Items" on the next page.

Rearranging Links Toolbar Items

It's easy to rearrange links on the Links toolbar. To do so, follow these instructions:

1. Point to the link you want to move, and hold down the left mouse button. Drag the link left or right until you see the I-pointer. (The I-pointer appears when you have positioned the mouse pointer between two existing links, or at the beginning or end of the Links toolbar.)

2. When you have positioned the I-pointer where you want the link to appear, release the mouse button.

Place the most frequently used items on the left of the toolbar. If the window isn't wide enough to display all the Links toolbar items, the ones on the right will be hidden from view. (You can view these items by clicking the double right arrow that appears on the right edge of the toolbar when some items are hidden.)

Renaming Links Toolbar Items

When you add a Web page to your Links toolbar, Internet Explorer names the link after the page title that the page author chose. Often, these names are too long. Few Web authors use one- or two-word page titles. Sometimes, they choose titles that aren't helpful guides to the page's actual content. Fortunately, you can rename your links.

To change the link name, follow these steps:

1 On the Links toolbar, point to the link you want to rename, and click the right mouse button.

   You'll see a pop-up menu.

2 Choose Rename.

   You'll see the Rename dialog box, shown here:

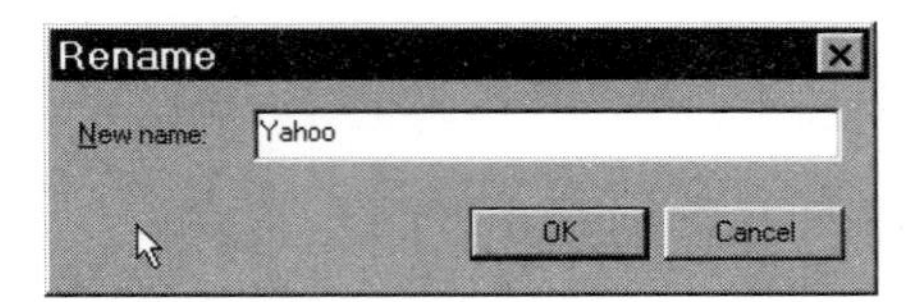

   Within the New Name text box, you see the page's existing name.

3 Edit the existing name, or delete it and type a new one. Keep it short!

4 Click OK to confirm the new link name.

Deleting Links Toolbar Items

In previous versions of Internet Explorer, the Links toolbar had room for only a few items. For this reason, you needed to delete seldom-used items in favor of those you used more frequently. In Internet Explorer version 5, you don't need to do this. All toolbars, including the Links toolbar, can contain more items than there's room to display. If some toolbar items are hidden from view, you can see a drop-down menu listing these items. To do so, click the double right arrow that appears on the right edge of the toolbar.

If there's an item on the Links toolbar that you would still prefer to delete, you can do so by following these instructions:

1. Point to the Links toolbar item that you want to delete, and click the right mouse button.
2. From the pop-up menu, choose Delete.

   You'll see the following alert box:

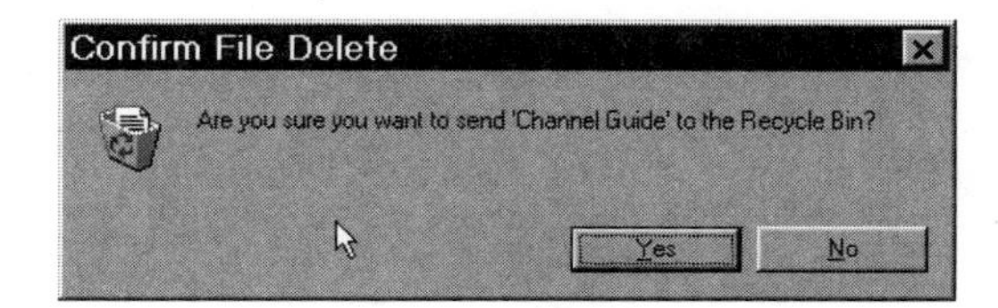

3. To confirm the deletion, click Yes.

Creating Keyboard Shortcuts to Items on the Links Toolbar

If you prefer to navigate using the keyboard, you can create keyboard shortcuts to the items on your Links toolbar. These shortcuts use the Ctrl + Alt keys, followed by a letter, such as Ctrl + Alt + B. Keyboard shortcuts aren't case-sensitive; you get the same result from typing Ctrl + Alt + b as you do by typing Ctrl + Alt + B.

> So that you'll remember your keyboard shortcuts, create shortcuts using the first letter of the names given to your Links toolbar items. To create a shortcut to InfoMine, for example, use the letter *I* (Ctrl + Alt + I). If you have two Links items that start with the same letter, consider renaming one of them so that its name begins with a different letter.

To create a keyboard shortcut, follow these instructions:

1. Point to the Links toolbar item, and click the right mouse button.

   You'll see a pop-up menu.

2. Choose Properties, and click the Web Document tab if necessary. You'll see the Properties dialog box for this item, shown in Figure 7-4.

3 Click in the Shortcut Key text box, and type the letter you want to use for the keyboard shortcut. Internet Explorer adds Ctrl + Alt automatically.

4 Click OK to confirm.

If you are running another Windows application that uses the same keyboard shortcuts, the shortcut might not work. However, few applications use the Ctrl + Alt key combination, so this shouldn't be a problem. Also, note that you can't use any of the following keys: Esc, Enter, Tab, Spacebar, Print Screen, or Backspace.

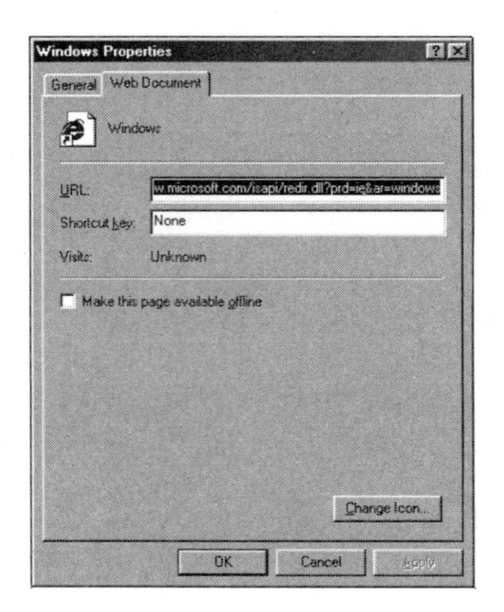

FIGURE 7-4.
In the Properties dialog box for Links toolbar items, you can create a keyboard shortcut to this item.

Creating Desktop Shortcuts to Web Pages

SEE ALSO
For ways to make desktop shortcuts more accessible, see "Adding Web Pages to the Links Toolbar" on page 158.

When you start Internet Explorer by clicking the program icon or choosing the program's name from the Start menu, the program displays the default start page. But there's another way to start Internet Explorer. If you create a desktop shortcut for a Web page, Internet Explorer will start and display the page linked to the shortcut instead of the default start page. In other words, creating a desktop shortcut gives you a way to start the program and go directly to a Web page that you want to use, without wasting the time needed to display the default start page.

Creating the Shortcut

To create a desktop shortcut for a Web page, follow these steps:

1 Display the page.

2 Do one of the following:

- Choose the File command; select Send and Shortcut To Desktop.

  or

- Point to the Web page's background, click the right mouse button, and choose Create Shortcut from the pop-up menu. Click OK to confirm.

After you've created the shortcut, you'll see the shortcut on your desktop. The shortcut uses the Internet Explorer icon, and indicates the page's title. You can now launch Internet Explorer and display this page by choosing this shortcut.

To bring your desktop into view quickly, point to the taskbar, click the right mouse button, and choose Minimize All Windows.

Renaming the Shortcut

Like Link toolbar items, desktop shortcut names may be too long or inaccurate. To change the name of a desktop shortcut, point to the shortcut, click the right mouse button, and choose Rename from the pop-up menu. Edit the page name, and click the desktop to confirm.

Assigning the Shortcut to a Key Combination

Once you've created a desktop shortcut, you can assign the shortcut to a key combination. Like the shortcut keys you can create for Links toolbar items, these shortcuts use the Ctrl + Alt key combination. To assign a shortcut to a key combination, right-click the shortcut icon, and choose Properties from the pop-up menu. In the Shortcut dialog box, click the Shortcut tab, if necessary. In the Shortcut Key box, type the key that you want to use with Ctrl + Alt, and click OK.

Saving Web Pages as Favorites

Imagine a copy of Internet Explorer customized with links that you've collected to hundreds or even thousands of Web resources, all neatly organized into topically named folders. Suppose you're an artist, and you've created folders called Galleries, Graphics, Marketing, Shows, and Technique. Stored within these folders are pages you've found on the Web that are helpful to you in your artistic work. And as you encounter new Web pages that fit within these categories, you can add them, further enriching your repertoire of online resources. To create new categories, you can create new folders. In time, Internet Explorer becomes an indispensable resource for your professional work.

SEE ALSO
For information on organizing your Favorites list, see "Organizing Your Favorites Folder," page 288.

The key to this valuable transformation of Internet Explorer lies in saving favorites, the subject of this section. Here, you'll learn how to save Web pages as favorites so that they're accessible on the Favorites menu, the Favorites explorer, and indeed throughout Windows. As you'll see, you can even access your favorites from the Start menu.

Deciding Which Pages to Save As Favorites

As you're considering what type of pages to save as favorites, consider that favorites aren't quite as accessible as Links toolbar items. However, you can save as many favorites as you like. By creating folders for your favorite pages, you can store hundreds or even thousands of pages. These facts suggest that you should save your most frequently accessed pages on the Links toolbar. They also suggest that you should create a new favorite for just about any Web page that you think you may wish to visit again.

TIP

You can return to previously visited pages using the History explorer, but bear in mind that this explorer keeps only your most recent history information. (By default, this is 20 days.) If a history item expires, Internet Explorer erases the history item, so you won't be able to return to the page using the History explorer. For this reason, be sure to save a Web page as a favorite if you believe it's of sufficient value that you'd like to visit it again; with the information saved as a favorite, you'll be able to revisit the page easily.

Planning Your Favorites Folders

When you create a favorite, you can choose between adding it to the top-most level of the Favorites menu and adding it to a folder—either one you've already created, or a new folder. Don't save too many pages at the top-most level of the Favorites menu, or this menu will quickly become unwieldy. If you save a favorite to a folder, you see the folder name on the menu. When you click the folder name, you see a submenu that shows all the items within this folder—and these items can include additional folders, as shown in Figure 7-5.

The ability to store favorites within folders and subfolders enables you to save many sites without creating an unwieldy Favorites menu. But it also requires you to devote some thought to how you'd like to organize these folders. You could name your folders according to any of the following:

- **Topic.** Name the folder after one of your interests, such as "Rock Collecting" or "Management."
- **Usefulness.** To differentiate between really useful pages and others, you could create a subfolder called "Best Pages" to contain the pages you'll visit time and again.
- **Page type.** To indicate what type of page you've stored, you could differentiate between, say, "Indexes" (pages that contain lots of links pertinent to a given subject) and "Content Pages" (pages that contain substantive material about the subject).

Here's a way to organize folders and subfolders that combines all three of the above folder-naming strategies:

Sailing
    Best Pages
    Charts
    Books
    Dictionary
    Indexes
    Supplies
    Tutorials
    Weather

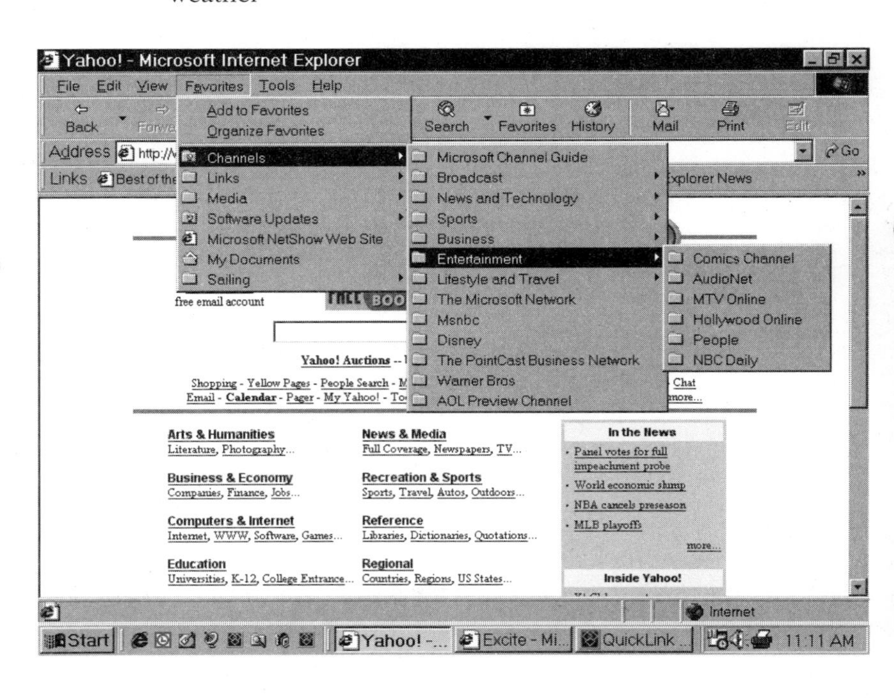

FIGURE 7-5.
The Favorites menu can contain folder names, which display submenus. These submenus can contain folder names, which in turn display additional submenus.

Don't worry about getting your folders organized just right. You can always go back and reorganize them, as shown in "Organizing Your Favorites Folder," page 288.

Saving a Favorite

As just explained, you can add a favorite to the top level of the Favorites menu, or you can add it to an existing folder or a new folder. If you save the page in a folder, it appears within a submenu on the Favorites menu.

Adding a Favorite to the Favorites Menu

When you add a favorite to the top level of the Favorites menu, you see the favorite's name right away (it isn't buried in a submenu). However, you can't add more than a dozen or so favorites to the Favorites menu without creating an unwieldy menu. Use these instructions for important sites that you'll frequently access.

To add a Web page to the Favorites menu, do the following:

1. Display the page.
2. Press Ctrl + D.

Internet Explorer adds the page to your Favorites menu at the topmost level.

Adding a Favorite to a Submenu

To avoid adding too many Web pages to the top level of the Favorites menu, you should save most pages in folders. When you save a page to a folder, you avoid cluttering your Favorites menu. You see the folder name on the menu; when you click the folder name, you see a submenu containing the pages you've saved within this folder.

To add a favorite to a folder so that it appears within a submenu on the Favorites menu, follow these steps:

1. Do one of the following:
   - From the Favorites menu, choose Add To Favorites.

     or

   - Right-click the page background, and choose Add To Favorites from the pop-up menu.

     or

- Click Favorites on the Standard Buttons toolbar, and click Add.

You'll see the Add Favorites dialog box, shown in Figure 7-6.

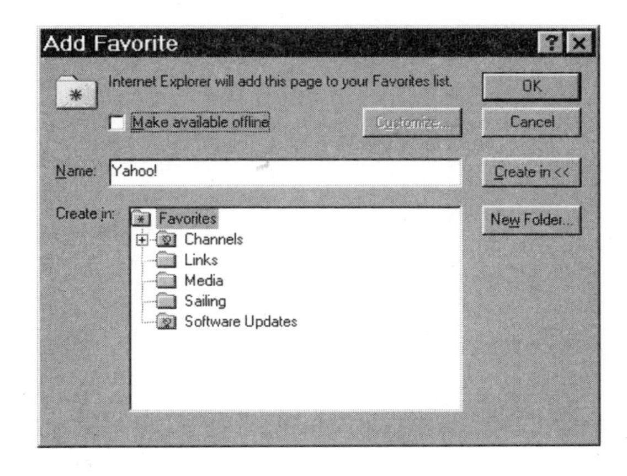

FIGURE 7-6.
In this dialog box, you can save a favorite to an existing folder or create a new one.

2 Do one of the following:

- To add the page to an existing folder, click Create In, if necessary, to display the list of available folders. In the folder list, select the folder, and click OK.
- To create a new folder, click New Folder. You'll see the Create New Folder dialog box shown here:

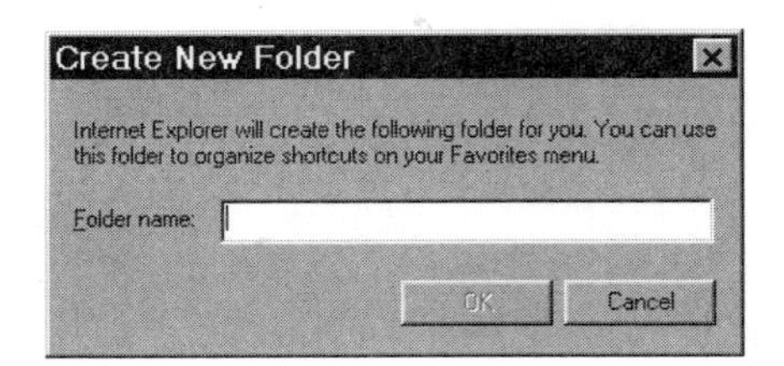

Type the name of the new folder, and click OK until you see Internet Explorer again.

Adding Favorites from the History Explorer

Suppose you visit a Web page, and you don't save it as a favorite. A few days later, you realize that you would like to save this page as a favorite. If so, you can use the History explorer to add the page to your Favorites list. Follow these instructions:

1 On the Standard Buttons toolbar, click History. You'll see the History explorer.

2 Locate the page you previously visited. If you can't find the page by browsing, click Search on the History Explorer bar.

3 When you've found and selected the page you previously viewed, right-click this item within the History explorer.

4 From the pop-up menu, choose Add To Favorites.

   You'll see the Add Favorite dialog box (see Figure 7-6). Add this page to a new or existing folder, as explained in the previous section. To add the page to the top level of the Favorites menu, just click OK.

Revisiting Favorite Web Pages

Once you've saved Web pages as favorites, you can revisit them easily. To revisit a favorite page, do one of the following:

- Click Favorites on the menu bar, and choose the page you want to visit.

  or

- Click Favorites on the Standard Buttons toolbar, and choose the page you want to visit from the Favorites explorer bar (see Figure 7-7).

  or

- Click Start on the taskbar, choose Favorites, and choose the page you want to visit.

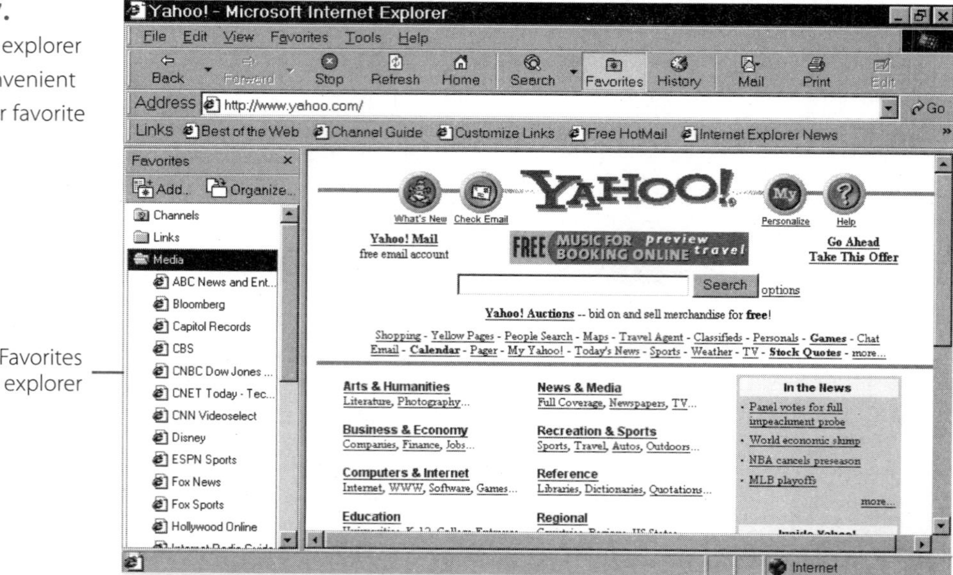

FIGURE 7-7.
The Favorites explorer gives you convenient access to your favorite sites.

Mailing a Page to Someone

For more information on sending mail with Outlook Express, see Chapter 12, "Reading and Composing Messages."

As you're browsing the Web, you'll run across pages that might interest friends or co-workers. You can mail the page to them, and they can see it for themselves. In order to receive the page, your correspondent must have an e-mail program (such as Microsoft Outlook Express or Netscape Messenger) that can display HTML.

Here's how to mail the Web page. Click File on the menu bar, choose Send, and then choose Page By E-mail from the pop-up menu. Internet Explorer starts Outlook Express and displays a New Message window that shows the Web page. Enter the recipient's e-mail address, and click the Send button.

If your recipient's e-mail program can't read HTML, you can send a link instead. Click File on the menu bar, choose Send, and click Link By E-mail.

Saving Content for Offline Browsing

SEE ALSO

To save a Web page without making the page a favorite, see "Saving a Document as a Complete Web Page," page 186.

If you're using a notebook computer or accessing the Internet via a phone line, you might want to save Web pages for offline browsing. Doing so enables you to browse Web content while you're not connected to the Internet. For example, while you're traveling or when somebody wants to use the phone line for a telephone call.

Saving content for offline browsing is an option available when you create a favorite. In the following pages, you learn how to create a new favorite and make the page available for offline browsing at the same time. You also learn how to make existing favorites available for offline browsing, and how to update offline content to make sure you're seeing the latest version.

NOTE

In version 4 of Internet Explorer, the process of saving a Web page for offline browsing was called "subscribing." This confused many users because they had trouble distinguishing offline browsing from channels, which are discussed in "Saving a Web Page and All the Content Linked to the Page" on the next page. In version 5, offline browsing and channels are clearly differentiated, making the program less confusing to use.

Saving a Web Page for Offline Browsing

To save a page for offline browsing, you save it as a favorite, and choose an option that makes the page available offline. Follow these instructions:

1. Display the page you want to make available for offline browsing.
2. Do one of the following:
   - From the Favorites menu, choose Add To Favorites.

     or
   - Right-click the page background, and choose Add To Favorites from the pop-up menu.

     or
   - Click Favorites on the Standard Buttons toolbar, and click Add.

     You'll see the Add Favorites dialog box, previously shown in Figure 7-6.
3. Activate the option Make Available Offline.
4. Do one of the following:
   - To add the page to the top level of the Favorites menu, just click OK.
   - To add the page to an existing folder, click Create In, if necessary, to display the list of available folders. In the folder list, select the folder, and click OK.
   - To create a new folder, click New Folder. You'll see the New Folder dialog box.
5. Type the name of the new folder, and click OK until you see Internet Explorer again.

Internet Explorer downloads the page along with all associated content, including graphics, sounds, scripts, applets, and text. To make sure you're viewing the latest content on this page, see "Synchronizing Offline Content," on page 174.

Saving a Web Page and All the Content Linked to the Page

If you wish, you can download all the pages linked to a favorite page. You can then view the pages offline. Follow these steps to select linked pages when you save a favorite for the first time:

1. Follow the steps given in the previous section to save a site as a favorite and enable offline browsing, but click Customize instead of clicking OK.

You'll see the Offline Synchronization Wizard.

2. Click Next. You'll see the wizard's first page.
3. If the page you're saving includes links, and you'd like these to be available when you're offline, click Yes. Click Next to continue.
4. Click Finish.

If you've already saved the page as a favorite, you can choose advanced downloading options for the page. See the section titled "Choosing Downloading Options" on the next page.

Making an Existing Favorite Available for Offline Browsing

If you have already saved the page as a favorite, you can make it available for offline browsing by following these steps:

1. On the Standard Buttons toolbar, click Favorites.

   You'll see the Favorites explorer.

2. In the Favorites list, right-click the Web page that you want to make available for offline browsing.
3. From the pop-up menu, choose Properties. You'll see the Properties dialog box for the page, shown in Figure 7-8.

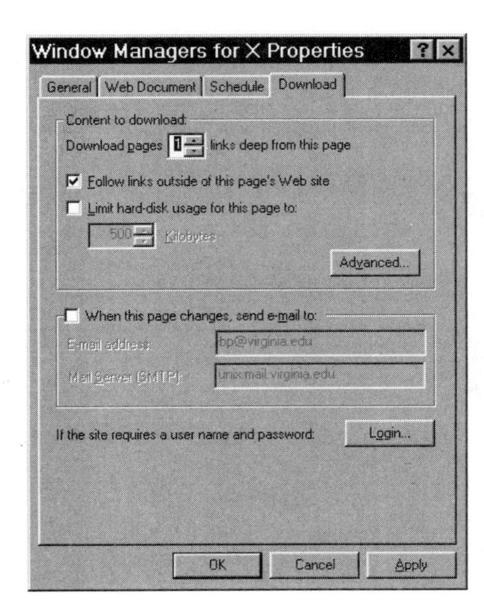

FIGURE 7-8.
In the Properties dialog box for a page you've saved for offline browsing, you can choose advanced downloading options.

4 In the Properties dialog box, click Web Document, if necessary, and click Make Page Available Offline.

5 Click OK.

Choosing Downloading Options

If you've already saved a favorite and would like to save content associated with that page, you can modify the downloading options so that Internet Explorer downloads the pages linked to the page you're modifying. You can also choose advanced downloading options, including downloading content up to three link depths away from the current page, and receiving e-mail notification of site changes.

Be aware that increasing the link depth can result in a great deal of content being downloaded to your computer.

- If you choose a link depth of 1, Internet Explorer downloads the current page plus all the Web pages that are linked to the current page—that is, all the pages that are one link depth away. If the current page contains four links, the program will download a total of five pages, including the current page.
- If you choose a link depth of 2, Internet Explorer downloads all the pages that are linked on the pages 2 link depths away from the current page. If the current page links to 4 pages, and each of these pages contains 4 links, the program will download 17 pages, including the current page.
- If you choose a link depth of 3 (the maximum), the program will download all the pages 3 link depths away. Assuming that all the linked pages each contain 4 links, you're asking the program to download 65 pages, including the current page.

If you choose a link depth of 2 or 3, consider disabling the options that follow links outside the current page's Web site, and enabling the option that limits the total amount of hard disk usage to an amount you specify.

To choose downloading options for a favorite you've already saved, and to choose advanced downloading options, follow these steps:

1 On the Standard Buttons toolbar, click Favorites.

You'll see the Favorites explorer.

2 In the Favorites list, right-click the Web page that you have already made available for offline browsing.

3. From the pop-up menu, choose Properties. You'll see the Properties dialog box for the page.
4. Click the Download tab. You'll see the Download options, shown in Figure 7-8.
5. In the Content To Download area, indicate the link depth you want.
6. To prevent the program from downloading content outside the current page's Web site, disable the option called Follow Links Outside Of This Page's Web Site.
7. To limit the amount of hard-disk space used to store offline content for this item, activate the option called Limit Hard-Disk Usage For This Page, and select the maximum amount of hard-disk space in the Kilobytes box.
8. To specify what type of content is downloaded, click the Advanced button. You'll see the Advanced Download Options dialog box, shown here:

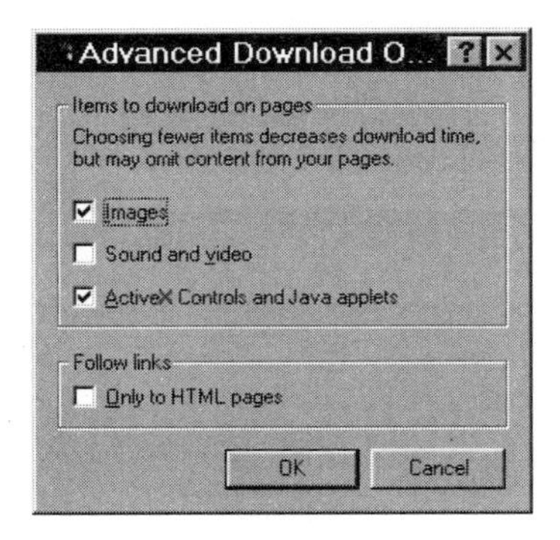

9. Choose the type of content that you want to download. You'll probably want to download images, ActiveX controls, and Java applets, but consider omitting sounds and videos, which require lengthy downloads.
10. To restrict downloading of linked content to HTML pages only, activate the option called Only To HTML Pages.
11. Click OK. You'll see the Properties dialog box again.
12. To receive e-mail notification when this page's content changes, activate the option called When This Page Changes, Send E-mail To, and type your e-mail address and mail server address if these are not already entered.

13 If this Web site requires a user name and password to access, click Login, type your user name and password, and click OK.

14 Click OK to confirm your downloading options.

Browsing Offline Content

Once you've saved content for offline viewing, you can view this content without being connected to the Internet. First, go offline by clicking File on the menu bar and clicking Work Offline if necessary. (If you see a check mark next to Work Offline, you're already offline.)

To access your offline content when you're in offline mode, choose an offline page from the Favorites menu (or the Favorites explorer). If you try to access content that requires an Internet connection, you'll see the dialog box shown in the following illustration:

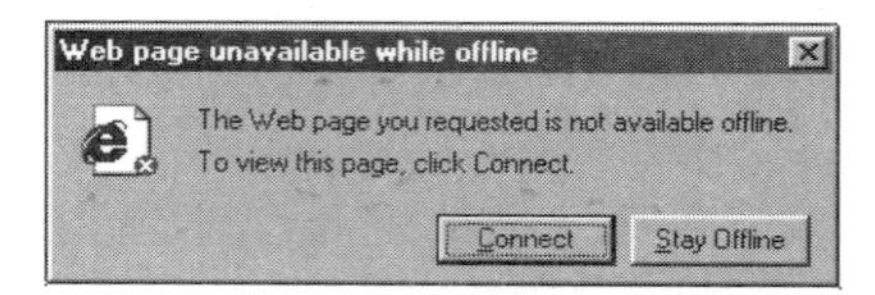

If a connection is available and you'd like to connect, click Connect. You'll see the page you requested. To keep working offline, click Stay Offline. You won't be able to see the page you requested.

Synchronizing Offline Content

Once you've saved content for offline viewing, you can synchronize the content. In synchronization, Internet Explorer accesses the Web site that makes your offline content available, and checks to see whether this content has changed. If so, Internet Explorer downloads a new copy of the pages that have changed. In this way, you can be sure that you are viewing up-to-date copies of the pages you've saved for offline browsing.

You can synchronize content in two ways:

- **Manual synchronization.** In manual synchronization, you synchronize when you prefer to do so. This is the best choice for notebook users or modem users who connect to the Internet irregularly.
- **Scheduled synchronization.** In scheduled synchronization, you choose a schedule for automatic synchronization.

Synchronizing Offline Content Manually

To synchronize content manually, do the following:

1. From the Tools menu, choose Synchronize. You'll see the Items To Synchronize dialog box, shown in Figure 7-9.
2. Select the items you want to synchronize.
3. Click Synchronize. You'll see the Synchronization Settings dialog box, shown in Figure 7-10. Internet Explorer begins synchronizing the items in the order they're listed. While synchronization is underway, you can choose from the following options:
   - To skip an item, click Skip.
   - To stop synchronizing, click Stop.
   - To see whether any errors occurred, click Results.

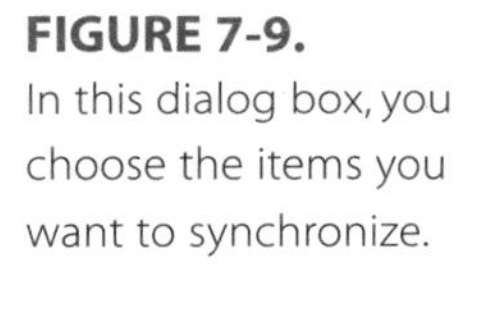

FIGURE 7-9.
In this dialog box, you choose the items you want to synchronize.

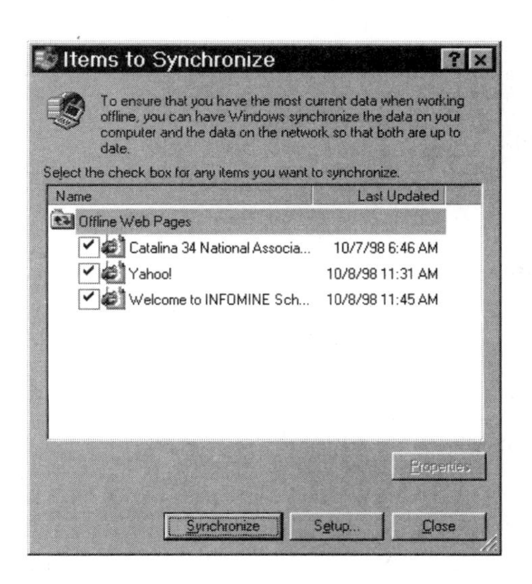

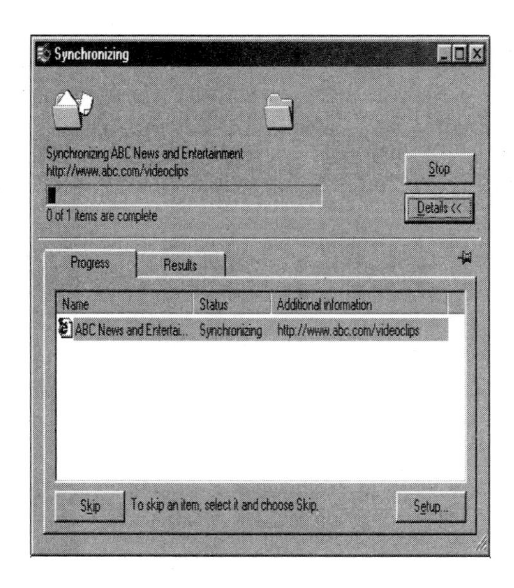

FIGURE 7-10. This dialog box tracks synchronization. To see more specific information, click the Details button.

Scheduling Synchronization

You can specify a schedule for automatic synchronization of offline content. First, you should understand which options are available for automatic synchronization.

Understanding Schedule Options

You can choose from the following options for scheduled synchronization:

- **Logon.** Internet Explorer synchronizes your content when you logon. This is a good option if you connect to the Internet by means of a modem.
- **On Idle.** You can specify synchronization when your computer has been idle for a specified period of time (by default, 15 minutes). This is a good option if you connect to the Internet by means of a local area network (LAN), ISDN, or ADSL, but it's not a good option for modem users.
- **Scheduled.** You can specify a synchronization schedule. This is a good option for users of any connection who know that they will be online at a certain time.

If you connect to the Internet in more than one way, you can choose synchronization options for each connection you create. For example, a notebook user may connect via a local area network (LAN) while at work, and via a modem while traveling.

You can also choose different synchronization options for differing items. For example, you could choose to synchronize important items every time you log on, while delaying synchronization for less important items by assigning them to a weekly scheduled update.

Synchronizing on Logon

Synchronization on Logon is a good choice for modem users. Rather than occurring at a preset time or when your computer has been idle, synchronization occurs when you make or terminate your Internet connection.

To enable synchronization on logon, follow these steps:

1. From the Tools menu, choose Synchronize. You'll see the Items to Synchronize dialog box, shown in Figure 7-9.
2. On the Items To Synchronize dialog box, click Setup. You'll see the Synchronization Settings dialog box, shown in Figure 7-11. Click the Logon tab if necessary.

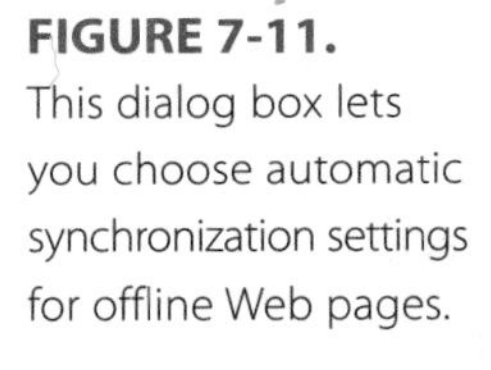

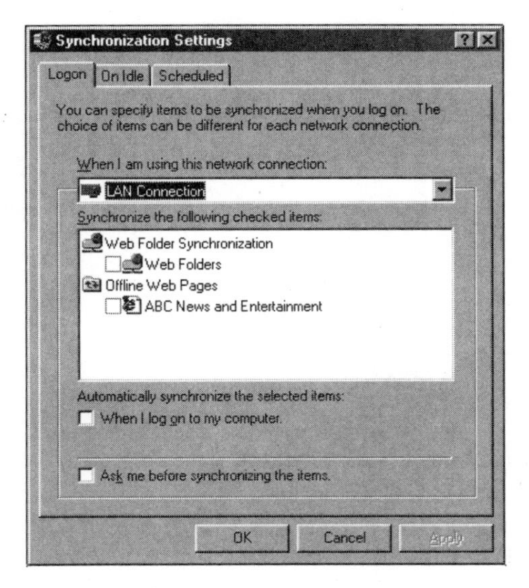

FIGURE 7-11.
This dialog box lets you choose automatic synchronization settings for offline Web pages.

3. If you created more than one network connection, choose the network connection you want to define.
4. In the list of offline items, check the items you want to synchronize.
5. To turn on Logon synchronization, enable one of the synchronization options. (Just which options appear depends on the type of network connection you've selected.)

6 If you would like to confirm synchronization, click Ask Me Before Synchronizing The Items.

7 Click OK until you see Internet Explorer again.

Synchronizing After Your Computer Has Been Idle

Synchronizing on idle is a good choice for users who connect via local area networks (LANs), ISDN, and ADSL, all of which offer on-demand connectivity. It's not a good idea for modem users because this setting will initiate a dial-up connection after an idle period, and this could interfere with your use of the phone line.

To synchronize content automatically, after your computer has been idle for a specified period (15 minutes, by default), follow these steps:

1 From the Tools menu, choose Synchronize. You'll see the Items To Synchronize dialog box, shown in Figure 7-9.

2 On the Items To Synchronize dialog box, click Setup. You'll see the Synchronization Settings dialog box, shown in Figure 7-11. Click the On Idle tab. You'll see the On Idle options, shown in Figure 7-12.

3 If you created more than one network connection, choose the network connection you want to define.

4 In the list of offline items, check the items you want to synchronize.

5 Click Synchronize The Selected Items While My Computer Is Idle.

6 To specify the idle time, click Advanced. You'll see the Idle Settings dialog box, shown in Figure 7-13.

7 In the first text box, increase or decrease the idle time.

8 In the second text box, increase or decrease the time to wait before repeating the synchronization.

9 If you're using a portable computer, you can save battery power by enabling the option that prevents synchronization when the computer is running on batteries.

10 Click OK until you see Internet Explorer again.

FIGURE 7-12.
On this page, you can choose options that synchronize downloaded content when your computer has been idle for a specified period.

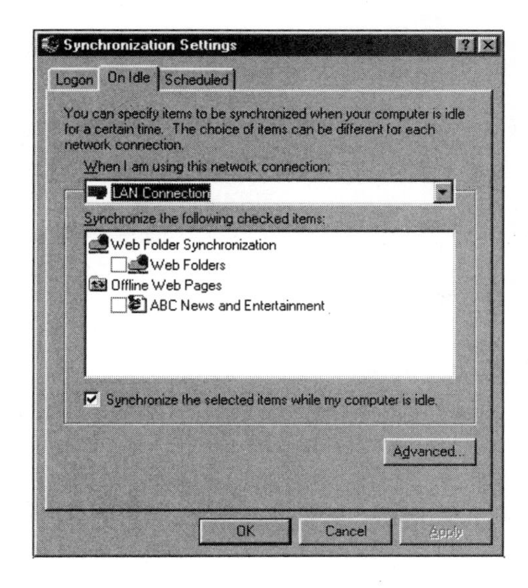

FIGURE 7-13.
Here, you can specify idle intervals and the time to wait before synchronization repeats.

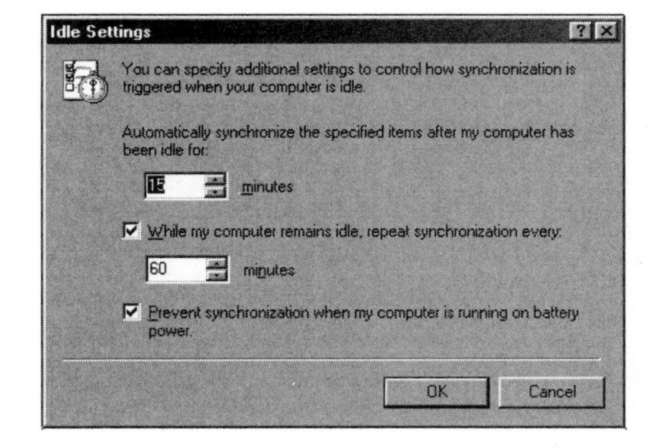

Scheduling Synchronization

This option is a good one if you know that you're going to be online at a certain time, such as 7 p.m. every weekday evening.

To create a synchronization schedule, do the following:

1. From the Tools menu, choose Synchronize. You'll see the Items To Synchronize dialog box, shown in Figure 7-9 on page 175.

2. On the Items To Synchronize dialog box, click Setup. You'll see the Synchronization Settings dialog box. Click the Scheduled tab.

   You'll see the Scheduled page.

3. Click Add. You'll see the Scheduled Synchronization Wizard. Click Next to see the first page.
4. Choose the network connection for this task. In the list of offline pages, check the pages that you want to synchronize using this task. If you would like the computer to log on if it's not connected, enable the item that connects automatically. Click Next to see the page where you can set the schedule (Figure 7-14).
5. In the Start Time box, choose a time for the synchronization to begin. In the Perform This Task area, choose a synchronization interval (Every Day, Weekdays, or a number of days that you specify). In the Start Date box, choose a start date. Click Next.
6. Choose a name for your synchronization, such as "Important Pages" or "Infrequently Updated Pages." Click Next to continue.
7. Click Finish.
8. To create additional schedules for other offline content, click Add, and repeat steps 1 through 7.
9. Click OK until you see Internet Explorer again.

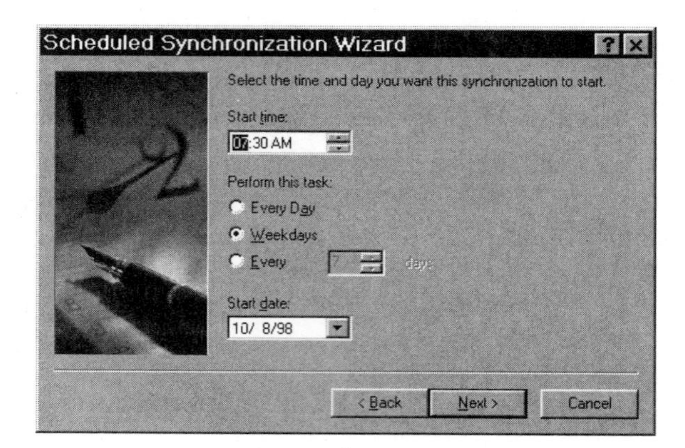

FIGURE 7-14.
In this dialog box, you can set up a synchronization schedule.

Editing Schedules

If you've created a synchronization schedule and would like to edit the schedule, follow these steps:

1. From the Tools menu, choose Synchronize. You'll see the Items To Synchronize dialog box.
2. On the Items To Synchronize dialog box, click Setup. You'll see the Synchronization Settings dialog box. Click the Scheduled tab.

3. Click the schedule you want to edit, and click Edit. You'll see the schedule properties for the schedule you selected.

4. Click the Synchronization Items tab. Choose the network connection for this synchronization task, and click the items you want to synchronize. If you would like your computer to connect automatically in order to synchronize these items, click the option that connects automatically to start synchronization.

5. Click the Schedule tab.

6. In the Schedule Task list box, choose the schedule interval (Daily, Weekly, Monthly, Once, At System Startup, At Logon, or When Idle). Once you've chosen a schedule interval, you can choose additional settings in the area below the list box. For example, if you choose Weekly, you can choose the day of the week on which you want the synchronization to occur.

7. In the Start Time box, choose the time that you want the synchronization to occur. If you click Advanced, you can choose additional schedule options including a start date, end date, and repetition intervals.

8. Click Settings. In the Settings page, you can choose the following options:

    - If you chose Once in Step 6, click Delete The Task If It Is Not Scheduled To Run Again when finished.

      The task will try to run until it is complete, but it may not be able to complete if one of the servers it's accessing has gone down. To set an upper time limit on the time the task can run, choose a maximum time for the task to run.

    - If you chose Idle in Step 6, you can specify idle settings in the Idle Time area.

    - If you're using a portable computer, choose the settings you prefer in the Power Management area.

9. Click OK.

Copying and Saving Graphics

You can copy or save any graphic that you see in a Web document. Once you've copied the graphic, you can paste it into a document that you're creating with another application. If you save the graphic, you can open it later with a graphics program, through which you can display, modify, copy, or print the image.

Copying a Graphic

If you see a graphic that you would like to use in one of your documents, you can copy it to the Clipboard. Simply right-click the graphic and choose Copy from the pop-up menu.

To paste the graphic into a document that you're creating with another application, position the cursor where you want the graphic to appear. Then choose the Paste command from the Edit menu, press Ctrl + V, or click Paste on the toolbar.

When you copy a graphic to the Clipboard, Windows automatically converts the graphic to the Windows bitmap format. If you want to preserve the original graphics-file format of the graphic, you must save the graphic to your hard disk.

Saving a Graphic

Internet Explorer enables you to save a graphic to a disk file so that you can reuse it anytime you want. When you save it, Windows will preserve the graphic's original file format.

To save a graphic, follow these steps:

1. Right-click the graphic.
2. From the pop-up menu, choose Save Picture As. You'll see the Save Picture dialog box. In the File Name box, Internet Explorer displays the document's name. In the Save As Type box, Internet Explorer displays the document's file format. There's no need to change either of these settings.
3. If you want, choose a different location for the saved graphic.
4. Click the Save button.

Copying and Saving a Background Graphic

Some of the documents you'll encounter on the Web have graphic backgrounds. If you'd like to copy or save the background graphic or save it as your default Windows wallpaper, Internet Explorer makes it simple.

Viewing the Source HTML

If you're an aspiring Web author and would like to see the HTML code producing the document you're viewing, you can display it using the Notepad utility. From there, you can save or print the HTML code. To view the source HTML, do one of the following:

- From the View menu, choose Source.

  or

- Right-click the document's background. From the pop-up menu, choose View Source. You'll see the HTML code in a Notepad window.

To print the HTML code, choose the Print command from the File menu in Notepad. To save the HTML code, choose File, click Save As, and specify a file name and location.

To exit Notepad, go to the File menu and choose the Exit command.

Copying a Background Graphic

To copy a background graphic to the Clipboard, right-click the background and choose Copy Background from the pop-up menu.

To paste the graphic into a document that you're creating with another application, position the insertion point where you want the graphic to appear. Choose the Edit menu's Paste command, press Ctrl + V, or click Paste on the toolbar.

Saving a Background Graphic

To save a background graphic, follow these steps:

1. Right-click the background.
2. From the pop-up menu, choose Save Background As. You'll see the Save As dialog box. In the File Name box, Internet Explorer displays the document's name. In the Save As Type box, Internet Explorer displays the document's file format. There's no need to change either of these settings.
3. If you want, choose a different location for the saved image.
4. Click the Save button.

Making a Graphic the Default Wallpaper

You can choose a graphic to serve as *wallpaper,* the image that's displayed on the desktop. If you run across a graphic on the Web that you think you can live with every day, you can quickly make the graphic the default wallpaper. Start by right-clicking the graphic. Then, choose Set As Wallpaper from the pop-up menu.

Copying and Saving Text

If you find some text on the Web that you'd like to reuse in a document you're creating, you can copy it to the Clipboard or save it on your hard disk.

Copying Text to the Clipboard

To copy text from a Web document to the Clipboard, follow these steps:

1. Position the mouse pointer at the beginning of the text you want to copy. The mouse pointer changes from an arrow to an I-beam shape.
2. Drag the mouse pointer to select the text.
3. Go to the Edit menu and select the Copy command. Other options are to right-click your selection and choose Copy from the pop-up menu or to press Ctrl + C.

To select all of the text in the document, choose Select All from the Edit menu or press Ctrl + A. You can also point to any of the document's text and right-click; from the pop-up menu, choose Select All.

Saving Text

You can save any document that Internet Explorer can display in four ways:

- **Text File.** Internet Explorer strips all the HTML code from the document, producing a plain-text document that you can later modify easily with a word processing program such as Notepad or WordPad.
- **Web Page, HTML Only.** Internet Explorer saves the HTML source code, just as you see it when you use the Source command from the View menu. However, Internet Explorer does not save any graphics in the document. If you want to save the graphics, you must use the right-clicking technique (described earlier in this chapter), and you must save each graphic individually. You might

decide it's not worthwhile to go to all of this trouble. If you merely want to make sure you can visit a particular site again later, save it as a favorite, as described in "Saving a Favorite," on page 166. Be aware, however, that the site could change, and a particular document may no longer be available.

- **Web Archive For Email.** This option saves all of the content needed to display the page in a single file.
- **Web Page, Complete.** This option is the same as making the page available offline. It saves the Web page with all associated content, including graphics, frames, and style sheets. All the files are saved in their original format.

Saving a Document as a Text File

This option is useful if you want to have a *plain-text* version of the document you're viewing on-screen, without the graphics and HTML codes. (Plain text is also known as ASCII text, which stands for American Standard Code for Information Interchange; it is a standardized coding method for letters, numbers, and other characters.)

To save a document as plain text, follow these steps:

1. Choose Save As from the File menu. You'll see the Save Web Page dialog box. In the File Name box, type a name for the document. In the Save As Type box, choose Text File.
2. Click the Save button. Internet Explorer saves the document in plain-text format.

Saving a Document as a Web Page (HTML Only)

This procedure isn't recommended unless you are an aspiring Web author and want to save the HTML code for later experimentation or inclusion in your own HTML documents. Save a site as a favorite, or make it a desktop shortcut if you just want to make sure you can get back to it.

To save a document as HTML, follow these steps:

1. Choose Save As from the File menu. You'll see the Save Web Page dialog box. In the File Name box, type a name for the document. In the Save As Type box, choose Web Page, HTML Only.
2. Click the Save button. Internet Explorer saves the document in HTML format.

Saving a Document as a Web Archive for E-Mail

This option saves the current Web page in a single document, using the same type of encoding (called MIME) that's used to save attachments to e-mail messages. You can't use this option unless you've installed Microsoft Outlook or Microsoft Outlook Express.

To save a document as HTML, follow these steps:

1. Choose Save As from the File menu. You'll see the Save Web Page dialog box. In the File Name box, type a name for the document. In the Save As Type box, choose Web Archive For Email.
2. Click the Save button. Internet Explorer saves the document in MIME format.

Saving a Document as a Complete Web Page

This option enables you to save complete Web documents, including associated graphics. However, this isn't a convenient choice if you would like Internet Explorer to update (synchronize) the saved content. To save a Web page so that you can synchronize the content manually or automatically, see "Saving Content for Offline Browsing," page 169. To save a document as HTML, follow these steps:

1. Choose Save As from the File menu. You'll see the Save Web Page dialog box. In the File Name box, type a name for the document. In the Save As Type box, choose Web Page, Complete.
2. Click the Save button. Internet Explorer saves the Web page and all associated content in their native file formats.

Printing a Web Page

When you run across a Web page with interesting text content, you may wish to print it so you can read it more comfortably or keep the text for future reference.

Printing documents with Internet Explorer is easy, and the results look great, especially if you have a color printer. You can print all or part of a document, and you can also make changes to the default page format.

Computer displays are hard on the eyes because it's difficult for the eye to focus on the pattern of tiny dots shown on-screen. As you're viewing the screen, your eyes tire quickly from focusing. In addition, people don't blink as often when they're viewing a computer display, so eyes become dehydrated. If your eyes often burn when you're using the computer, try to remember to blink often, or see your eye doctor for information about special eye washes that are designed for computer users.

If you've been viewing Web pages with larger-than-normal fonts for easy viewing, the printout will also have large fonts. You probably won't need such large fonts for reading on paper, and the large font size will consume more paper. To reduce font size for printing, click the View menu, choose Text Size, and choose Smaller or Smallest.

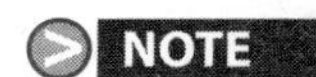

Before you can print with Internet Explorer, you must install a printer. If you have not yet done so, click Start, choose Settings, and choose Printers from the submenu. In the Printers window, choose Add New Printer, and follow the on-screen instructions.

Printing a Non-Framed Document

Most of the documents you'll see on the Web don't use frames, and for good reason: most Web users dislike frames. One reason for this dislike is the fact that frames make printing more difficult. This section shows you how to print a non-framed document. If you're printing a framed document, skip to the section called "Printing a Framed Document," page 190.

Does the document have frames or not? With some Web pages, it's close to impossible to tell. Those big ugly frame borders are a dead giveaway that the document uses frames, but many Web authors prefer to hide these borders precisely because they're so ugly! If you're not sure whether the Web page you're viewing has frames, here's a trick that should enable you to tell. Click the lower-right corner of the Internet Explorer window, and reduce the size of the window down to a small rectangle. If there are frames in the document, scroll bars will appear if you reduce the window size to the point that some content is hidden.

To change the default page layout options, see "Choosing Page Setup Options," page 192.

Performing a Quick Print

If you want only one copy of the page and don't want to select any other options, you can bypass the Print dialog box by initiating printing with the Print button, on the Standard Buttons toolbar. Just click the Print button to start printing the document with default printing and page layout options.

Printing with Print Options

You can choose the following options when you print a page:

- **Number of copies.** You can print more than one copy of a page—up to 9,999, if you're so inclined, and have ream upon ream of paper available.
- **Collation.** If you're printing more than one copy, you can print with collation. This allows you to print multiple-page documents as complete sets, rather than multiple copies of the first page, followed by multiple copies of the second page, and so on.
- **Linked documents.** You can print a copy of all the documents that are referenced in hyperlinks on the current page. Note that this could start a lengthy printing session if the page contains many links!
- **Table of links.** This is a nifty option if you'd like to have a printed record of all the hyperlinks contained on a page. The links are printed in a table at the end of the printout.

SEE ALSO
To save a page and all associated content for offline browsing, see "Saving Web Pages as Favorites," page 163.

- **Page range.** Because Web pages don't have page numbers, you can't predict how the document will be paginated for printing. Still, this option might be useful if you know that you want to print only the first two or three pages of a document.
- **Print to a file.** If you need to save the print output for later printing, you can save the output to a file rather than sending it to the printer. Later, you can open this file to start printing.

To print a document and choose printing options, follow these steps:

1 Do one of the following:

- Choose Print from the File menu.

  or

- Press Ctrl + P.

  or

- Right-click the page background, and choose Print from the pop-up menu.

You'll see the Print dialog box (Figure 7-15).

2 If you want to print more than one copy, type a number in the Number Of Copies box, or click the up and down buttons to specify the number of copies you want printed. Click the Collate check box if you want Internet Explorer to collate the copies.

3 If you would also like to print all the documents that are linked from the current page, click Print All Linked Documents. (Be aware, though, that you might go through several reams of paper if you choose this option!)

4 If you would like Internet Explorer to print a table containing all the Web addresses found in the document, click the Print Table Of Links option.

5 If you want to print a specific page range, click the Pages option in the Print Range area. Then type the beginning page in the From box, and type the ending page in the To box.

6 To print the document to a printer output file for later printing, activate the Print To File option.

7 Click OK to start printing with the options you've chosen.

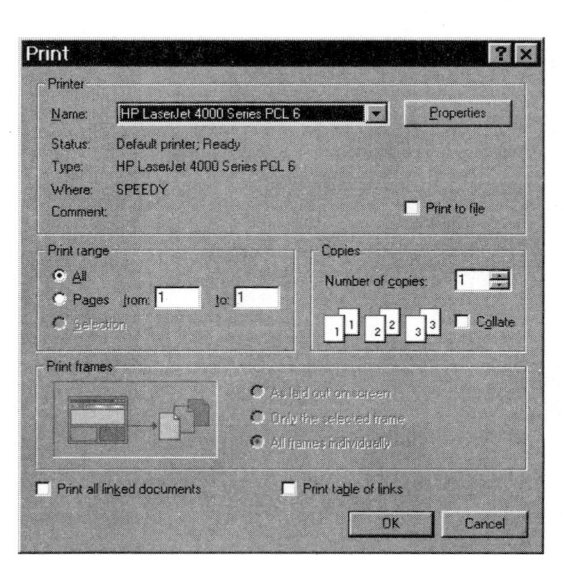

FIGURE 7-15.
The Print dialog box lists several options for printing Web documents.

Printing a Framed Document

Framed documents display content in independent panels. In reality, each panel contains a separate document (see Figure 7-16).

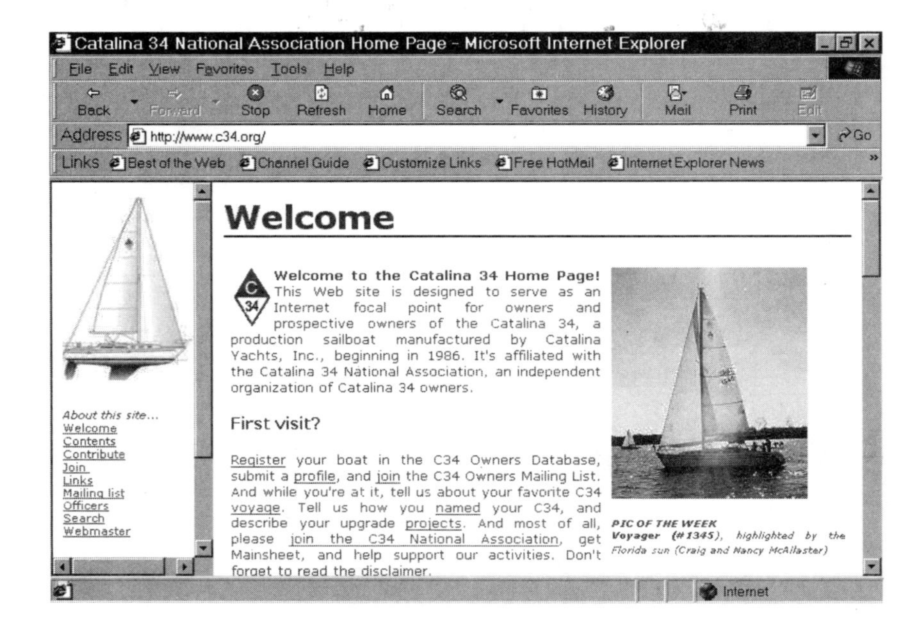

FIGURE 7-16.
A framed document consists of separate documents, each of which is placed in its own, independent panel.

Understanding Frame Printing Options

When you print a framed document, you can choose from the following options:

- **Only The Selected Frame.** This is the option you'll use most often. The program prints all of the frame's contents, even if there are portions that are hidden from view.
- **As Laid Out On The Screen.** Internet Explorer will try to print the page as it appears on the screen. This option isn't satisfactory if some of the content is hidden—the program prints only what's visible on-screen.
- **All Frames Individually.** This option prints all the content in each of the document's frames. However, you will probably use this option very rarely. Generally, framed pages use one frame for a document title, a second for navigation aids, and a third for the content. It's the content you're after, most likely.

Printing the Selected Frame

To print an individual frame, you must first select it. You can do so by clicking the frame. Avoid clicking a link or a linked graphic, which will display a different page.

To print one of the frames:

1. Select the frame by clicking the page's background.
2. Do one of the following:
    - To print one copy of the selected frame without choosing print options, click Print on the Standard Buttons toolbar.
    - To print with print options, choose Print from the File menu, press Ctrl + P, or right-click the page background and choose Print from the pop-up menu. Choose the print options you want, and click OK.

Printing All the Frames

To print the frames as they're laid out on-screen, or to print all the frames individually, follow these steps:

1. Do one of the following:
    - Choose Print from the File menu.

      or
    - Press Ctrl + P.

      or
    - Right-click the page background, and choose Print from the pop-up menu.
2. In the Print Frames area, choose one of the following:
    - All Frames Individually (prints all the frames, one after the other).

      or
    - As Laid Out On-Screen (prints the page the way it appears on-screen).
3. Choose additional print options, if you wish.
4. Click OK to initiate printing.

Printing a Selection

If you want to print selected text rather than the whole document, follow these steps:

1. Select the text you want to print.
2. Choose Print from the File menu, or press Ctrl + P. You'll see the Print dialog box.
3. In the Print Range area, click the Selection option.
4. Click the OK button to initiate printing.

Choosing Page Setup Options

By default, Internet Explorer formats your printout with 0.75-inch margins on all four sides of the page. In addition, the program prints a header with the document's title positioned flush left and the page number positioned flush right. It also prints a footer with the current date positioned flush left and the current time positioned flush right.

As the following sections explain, you can change the paper size, paper tray, print orientation, margins, and headers. To change these settings, choose Page Setup from the File menu. You'll see the Page Setup dialog box (Figure 7-17). From there, you can select and change the printing options described below.

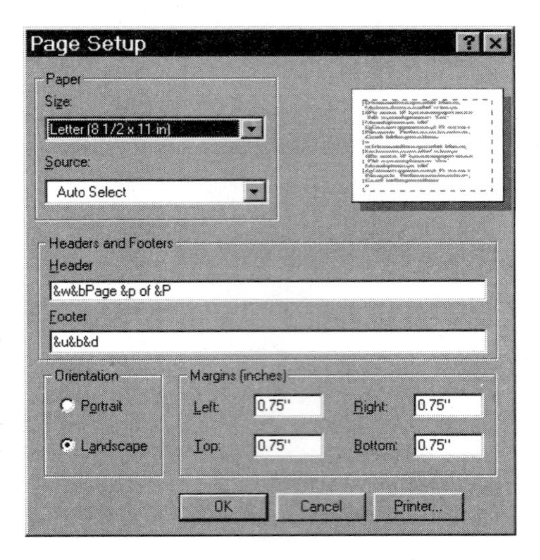

FIGURE 7-17.
From the Page Setup dialog box, you can format how your printed page will look.

Choosing paper size

If your printer can print with more than one size of paper, you can choose the paper size that you want Internet Explorer to use. From the Page Setup dialog box, select the Size list box and choose the paper size you want to use. (The options you see depend on your printer's capabilities.) Click OK.

Remember that the choices you make in the Page Setup dialog box remain in effect until you change them again. For example, if you choose Landscape printing, Internet Explorer will keep printing with this orientation until you choose Portrait.

Choosing the paper tray

If your printer has two or more paper trays, you can select the tray that you want your printer to use when it prints your Internet Explorer document. From the Page Setup dialog box, select the Source list box and choose the paper tray you want to use. (The options you see depend on your printer's capabilities.) Click OK.

Changing the printing orientation

Some Web pages look best when printed with a portrait orientation (the short side at the top), while others look best when printed with landscape orientation (the long side at the top). Internet Explorer can print Web pages either way. To choose the print orientation, you must first display the document you want to print. In the Orientation area of the Page Setup dialog box, click the orientation you prefer (Portrait or Landscape). Click OK.

Setting margins

By default, Internet Explorer formats your printout with 0.75-inch margins on all four sides of the page. You can change the margins if you wish. In the Margins area of the Page Setup dialog box, type the margins you want to use. Click OK.

Internet Explorer uses the current Windows settings for measurements. For example, copies of Windows that are sold in the United States display measurements in inches. If you would like to change the measurement format, click the Start menu, choose Settings, and click Control Panel. In the Control Panel window, double-click Regional Settings. In the Regional Settings Properties dialog box, select the Number tab if necessary. From the Measurement System list box, choose the number system you want to use, and click OK.

Defining headers and footers

Internet Explorer can print as many as six separate header and footer areas:

- **Left header.** The text is flush left at the top of the page. By default, this area contains the document's title.
- **Center header.** The text is centered at the top of the page. By default, this area is blank.
- **Right header.** The text is flush right at the top of the page. By default, this area contains the page number of the document.
- **Left footer.** The text is flush left at the bottom of the page. By default, this area contains the date the document was printed.
- **Center footer.** The text is centered at the bottom of the page. By default, this area is blank.
- **Right footer.** The text is flush right at the bottom of the page. By default, this area contains the time the document was printed.

You can enter any text in the Header and Footer fields. If you type *Web document* in the Header box of the Headers and Footers area, that's what you'll get on the printouts. If you want to turn off the header or the footer, simply clear the appropriate box.

You can also use special codes (see Table 7-2) to extract current information from the document (such as the page address) or from your computer system (such as the current date and time). Each of these codes begins with an ampersand (&) followed by a single letter. Note that the case of the letters is important. By using these codes, you can customize the headers and footers of the documents you print.

The code *&b* lets you specify where a given item should print in the header or the footer. Here's how it works:

- If you use the code only once, the text to the left of *&b* is printed flush left and the text to the right is printed flush right. For example, *&w&b&p* prints the document title flush left and the page number flush right.
- If you use the code twice, the text to the left of the first *&b* is printed flush left, the text between the two *&b* codes is centered, and the text to the right of the second *&b* is printed flush right. For example, *&d&b&p&b&t* prints the current date flush left, centers the page number, and prints the current time flush right. Got all that?

You can also combine text and codes. For example, if you type *Page &p of &P*, Internet Explorer prints the current page number and the total number of pages: page 7 of 10.

TABLE 7-2. Header and Footer Codes.

Type this:	To print this:
&w	Document title as it appears in the title bar.
&u	Page address (URL).
&d	Current date in the short format specified by the Regional Settings Control Panel.
&D	Current date in the long format specified by the Regional Settings Control Panel.
&t	Current time in the format specified by the Regional Settings Control Panel.
&T	Current time in 24-hour format.
&p	Page number.
&P	Total number of pages.
&&	A single ampersand.
&b	Position specifier (see text for explanation).

CHAPTER 8

Grooving on Multimedia

Internet Explorer version 5 is designed to work with the new Microsoft Windows Media Player, a universal media player that can play almost any audio or video content that's accessible on the Internet, including *streaming* audio and video programs that begin playing almost immediately. Media Player enables you to listen to recorded or live broadcasts (via the Internet) of musical events, lectures and presentations, sports events, news, and much more. If you're skeptical, you'll be interested to learn that there are more live radio stations accessible on the Internet than in any major metropolitan service area—thousands of radio stations, in fact. What's more, you can receive their broadcasts even though they're far out of range of normal radio broadcasting equipment. Imagine a day enriched by listening to Minnesota Public Radio's all-day classical music broadcast, or the BBC's World Service, and you'll begin to appreciate how much Media Player can enhance your computing experience.

Media Player makes multimedia easy by enabling you to use just one program for a wide variety of multimedia files. In the past, you had to install and use several different programs in order to play all the different types of multimedia files. Thanks to Media Player, that's no longer necessary. Media Player detects the multimedia file content and makes all the adjustments needed to play the file on your computer. For all the different types of content you access, you use the same, easy-to-understand controls. Even though Media Player is easy to use, it's flexible enough to enable you to customize it in many ways. It's even designed for automatic updating in case new versions appear that take advantage of new types of media content. This chapter explores Media Player, and shows you how to take full advantage of the Internet's multimedia resources. You'll also learn how to explore three-dimensional virtual reality worlds using Internet Explorer's virtual reality player.

Understanding Your Equipment Needs

To use Media Player, your computer needs a sound card and speakers. If your computer didn't come with these accessories, they're easy enough to add: just make sure you get a sound card with plug-and-play capabilities for hassle-free installation.

Examining Sound-Card Options

Any sound card reproduces the wave sounds that you'll encounter on the Web. A *wave sound* is an exact digital reproduction of an actual sound, such as music or a voice, that is made using recording techniques similar to those used in making audio CDs. However, if you want to download and listen to MIDI files, your sound card must be able to synthesize musical sounds. A MIDI file is a text file containing instructions to a synthesizer that tell it how to reproduce sounds.

You can get three types of sound cards that include the circuitry needed to synthesize sounds:

- **FM synthesis** sound cards provide the least expensive way to reproduce MIDI sounds, but music sounds as if it's coming out of a cheap electronic organ.
- **Wave table synthesis** sound cards base MIDI reproduction on stored recordings of actual musical instruments.
- **Wave guide** sound cards employ mathematical modeling techniques to reproduce all the aspects of a musical sound, including

non-musical sounds (like the pluck of a guitar pick) that are nevertheless what we recognize as part of an instrument's natural sound.

What's the best sound card choice? If you're planning to use your computer for musical composition, you may prefer a pricey wave-guide card, but most users will be happy with wave-synthesis cards. Avoid FM-synthesis-only cards unless you're on a very strict budget.

Exploring Speaker Options

Like high-fidelity speakers, computer speakers vary widely in quality. And you need good ones if you're interested in high-quality sound. As more than a few computer users have discovered, a PC makes a good sound system, particularly in cramped quarters like a dorm room. You can use your computer's CD-ROM drive to play CD-ROM discs, providing much of the functionality of a stereo system—and there's the added benefit of listening to Web multimedia. If your computer is equipped with a DVD drive, you can watch feature-length movies, too. But you won't enjoy the experience unless you've got decent speakers. A subwoofer provides the deep bass that's missing from most computer speakers, but please be considerate; remember that bass sounds can be heard over greater distances than higher-frequency sounds. A co-worker may not appreciate your taste for the beautiful rhythms and harmonies of African popular music—and that's because all she's hearing is "boom, boom, boom."

If you plan to put your speakers next to your monitor, be sure they are shielded speakers so that their electromagnetic fields don't distort the image on your monitor.

Understanding Multimedia File Formats

Multimedia resources, such as sounds or movies, are stored using a number of differing compression and storage methods called *file formats*. Each has its own identifying extension. For example, Windows movies are stored in .avi files. Over one dozen multimedia file formats are in common use on the Internet.

Before Media Player, you needed to know a lot about these file formats, and you needed to use several different players in order to play all of them. Thanks to Media Player, that's no longer true. Media Player takes much of the confusion out of multimedia by automatically playing almost any multimedia file, and enabling you to use the same, easy-to-understand controls for any of these files. Still, you may want to know what kinds of sounds and movies Media Player can handle. It's an impressive list.

- **Apple/Silicon Graphics sounds (.aiff).** Not frequently encountered, these are monaural sounds that have somewhat better quality than Sun/NeXT sounds.
- **MPEG audio (.mp2).** These sounds provide impressive near–CD-quality sound, including stereo. If you find one of these sounds, try downloading it. Compression is good, but these sounds still take lots of disk space.
- **MPEG movies (.mpg, .mpeg).** These movies conform to the MPEG standard. They offer good compression and quality on systems that have built-in MPEG support.
- **Musical Instruments Digital Interface (MIDI) (.mid).** These are compact text files that instruct a synthesizer how to play an instrumental musical composition.
- **QuickTime movies (.mov).** This is Apple's movie format, and it's a winner. QuickTime movies offer a good frame rate, relatively compact files, and optional sound.
- **RealNetworks RealAudio and RealVideo (.ra, .rm).** These are the most popular streaming audio and video formats on the Web.
- **Sun/NeXT sounds (.au, .snd).** Commonly found on the Web, these are low-quality monaural sounds, but they don't take up much disk space (which means they download faster). This format is suitable for music, but only to give you an idea of what something will sound like when it's played back properly. It's fine for voice. Often, you'll see two versions of a sound: an .au version, which enables you to see whether the sound is interesting to you, and a higher-quality .mpeg version, which takes up more disk space (and takes correspondingly longer to download).
- **Windows AVI movies (.avi).** These are native Windows movies. Like WAV sounds, they offer good quality, but they require lots of storage space and lengthy downloads.
- **Windows WAV sounds (.wav).** These are native Windows sounds. They offer excellent quality, and even stereo, but the WAV format requires lots of disk storage space.

Introducing Media Player

Media Player provides a single, customizable interface for all the popular media file formats that you'll encounter. To get started with Media Player, take a look at the Media Player window and understand its components, and then try playing a sound. You'll soon grow familiar with the easy-to-understand playback controls, which closely resemble those of a compact disc player.

Exploring the Media Player Window

Before you start using Media Player, take a few minutes to familiarize yourself with the basic components in the program's window. Here's what you'll see (Figure 8-1):

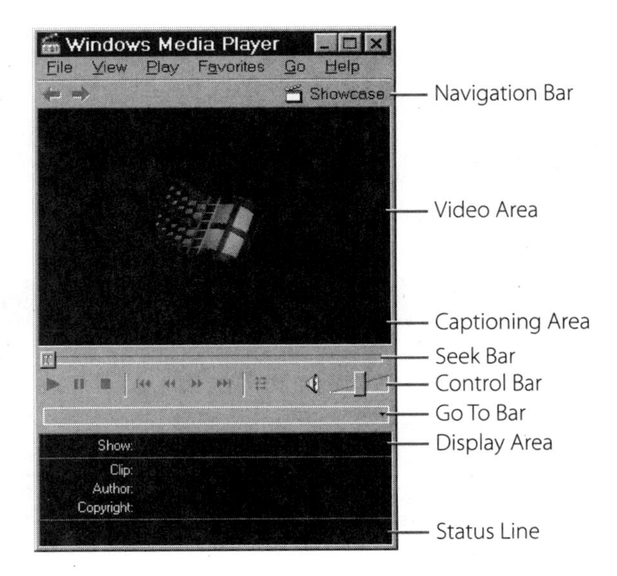

FIGURE 8-1.
The Media Player window provides tools for playing sounds and video.

- **Navigation Bar.** You can use the Forward and Back buttons to open media files you played earlier in the session. The Showcase button accesses Microsoft's Media Player Showcase site on the Web, helping you to sample a variety of media files.
- **Video Area.** If you're playing a video, this area shows the video. If you're playing a sound, Media Player hides this area.
- **Captioning Area.** This area displays closed captioning if the file contains it. You see this area only if you've chosen Captions on the View menu.

- **Seek Bar.** This bar shows how much of the current audio or video file has been played. With most files, you can drag the box on the seek bar to replay the file starting at the box's location.
- **Controls Bar.** Here you'll find VCR-like controls that enable you to control sound or video's playback.
- **Go To Bar.** In this area, you see markers, if any, that were created in the sound or video file. Markers enable you to begin playback at a certain location.
- **Display Area.** This area shows the file's title, author, and copyright information if that information is contained in the audio or video file.
- **Status Line.** This area displays messages concerning the downloading, playback, and quality of the audio or video file.

Understanding Status Line Symbols

While Media Player is working, you'll see symbols on the status line. The following table explains what these symbols mean.

TABLE 8-1. Media Player Status Line Symbols.

This symbol:	Means this:
	Media Player is opening the file.
	Media Player is connecting to the server.
	Media Player is storing some of the streaming content so that playback will be continuous.
	Media Player is receiving the best quality signal.
	Media Player is not receiving the best quality signal, but video quality will be acceptable.
	Media player is receiving a poor signal, and video quality will be poor.
	Media player is receiving such a poor signal that it can't display the video; only the audio portion will be played.
	Media player is receiving such a poor signal that it can't display the video or play the audio portions.

Getting into the stream of things (Streaming Audio and Video)

It's called *streaming multimedia*. Compared to the ordinary audio and video that you can download from the Internet, it's far superior in one very important way. The content begins playing almost immediately. Presentations arrive in data "streams." You don't have to wait for the whole thing to download before play begins.

Is there a downside to streaming multimedia? Yes, the quality isn't as good as in other audio and video files. In order to deliver streaming multimedia over slow modem connections, it's necessary to use extreme, state-of-the-art compression techniques. Although these techniques result in loss of quality, most users find this trade-off acceptable. Streaming audio is used mainly for delivering voice, which doesn't require CD-quality audio to be worthwhile and enjoyable. It's also used to provide full-length, sample versions of recorded music; since the quality's not that great, record companies figure that you'll run out and buy the CD rather than continue to listen to the sample (and they're right).

What about video? On a modem connection, streaming video isn't anything to write home about. You get jerky motion in a little window, and your first reaction is to laugh. But remember, you'd probably have felt that way looking at one of the first experimental televisions. Years from now, when millions of households have super-fast cable-modem connections, we might be watching streaming movies, chosen from a database of hundreds of thousands of films. For now, streaming video is best suited to corporate networks, which deliver data very quickly. But it's lots of fun on the Web, too, despite the often mediocre quality of the picture and sound.

Playing Sounds and Movies

There's nothing simpler than playing sounds and movies with Media Player: simply click the link that leads to the sound or movie. Internet Explorer downloads the multimedia content, and Media Player starts playing the sound or video.

SEE ALSO

For information on file downloading security, see Chapter 9, "Using the Internet Safely."

You might be concerned about file safety. If you're downloading a file from a trustworthy location, there's probably not too much to worry about. Also, multimedia files such as sounds and movies aren't dangerous at present; the only files that can contain viruses are executable files (those with the *.exe* extension) as well as documents created by applications (such as Microsoft Word) that can execute stored command files called *macros*. Still, virus authors are working overtime to try to figure out how to include harmful information in multimedia files, so it's best to be cautious. The bottom line: do *you* trust this site? If it's a well-known commercial site, it's probably OK.

Using the Media Player Controls

With most media, the content starts playing immediately. To pause playback, click the Pause button, or press the spacebar. To resume playback, click Play or press the spacebar.

Media Player's controls resemble those of a compact disc player. The following table explains what each of the controls does. Note that some of the controls aren't available with some types of media.

TABLE 8-2. Media Player Controls.

Use this control	To do this:
▶	Begin playing the file.
❚❚	Pause playing the file. Click Play to begin playing again.
■	Stops playing the current file.
⏮	Returns to the beginning of the current file. If you're at the beginning of the current file, skips back to the beginning of the previous file, if any.
◀◀	Rewinds the current file. When you release the button, playback resumes. (This option does not work with streaming media.)
▶▶	Fast-forwards the current file. When you release the button, playback resumes. (This option does not work with streaming media.)
⏭	Begins playback at the beginning of the next file, if any.
	Plays a short preview of the current file.
	Mutes the current file's audio output, if any.
	Controls the volume level. This control isn't available if your computer doesn't have a functioning sound card, or if the file doesn't have any sound.

Using Keyboard Controls

When playing a sound or a movie, you can also use keyboard controls, which are summarized in Table 8-3.

Using the Media Player Pop-Up Menu

You can also control movies and sounds by moving the mouse pointer within the movie or sound-control panel and clicking the right mouse button. Here's what the pop-up menu looks like:

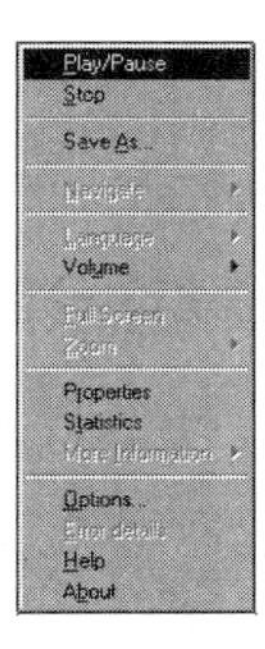

Adjusting Sound and Movie Properties

If you would like to gain more control over playback of sounds and movies, display the Media Player options. To display the options, click View on the menu bar and choose Options, or right-click the Media Player background and choose Options from the pop-up menu. The Playback page of the Options dialog box, shown in Figure 8-2, enables you to adjust the sound volume and balance, choose zoom levels, turn on auto repeat, and enable auto rewind. The following table sums up the options you can choose on the Playback page of the Options dialog box.

Media Player gives you easier ways to control most of the options accessible on the Playback page of the Options dialog box. But you'll need this page to enable *looping* (automatic repeat), a fun option that enables you to play a file repeatedly.

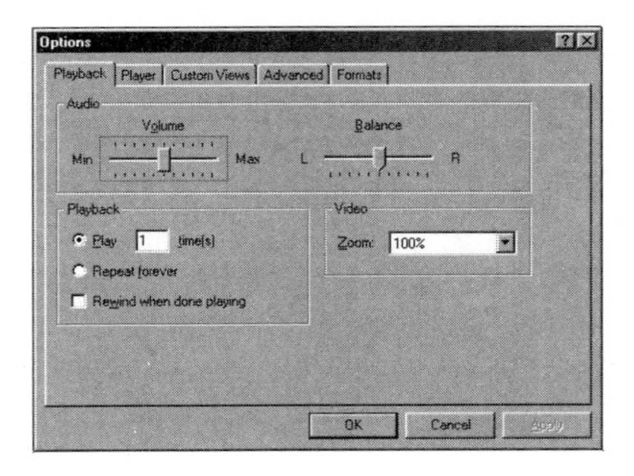

FIGURE 8-2.
Media Player's Options dialog box enables you to specify advanced settings for the sound or movie you're viewing.

TABLE 8-3. Media Player Keyboard Shortcuts.

Press this key:	To do this:
Spacebar	Play or pause the current file (same as clicking Pause and Play).
Period	Stop playback (same as clicking Stop).
Page up	Restart the current file or, if you're at the beginning of the current file, start playing the previous file from the beginning (same as clicking Skip Back).
Page down	Skip to the next file (same as clicking Skip Forward).
Left arrow	Rewind (works with stored files only). Playback resumes when you release the left-arrow key (same as clicking Rewind).
Ctrl + left arrow	Continuous rewind. Rewind continues until you choose another command.
Right arrow	Fast forward (works with stored files only). Playback resumes when you release the key (same as clicking Fast Forward).
Ctrl + right arrow	Continuous forward. Forward continues until you choose another command.
Alt + left arrow	Opens the previous file you played in this session.
Alt + right arrow	Opens the next media file in the list of files you played in this session.
M or Ctrl + M	Mute or unmute the sound.
Up arrow	Turn the volume up.
Down arrow	Turn the volume down.
Alt + Enter	Display the current video in full-screen mode, or return to original size if zoomed to full-screen mode.
Esc	Return to original size from full-screen mode.
Alt + S	Opens a Web site that provides access to media files.
Alt + 1	Size video to 50 percent of the original size.
Alt + 2	Size video to 100 percent of the original size.
Alt + 3	Size video to 200 percent of the original size.
Ctrl + 1	Use the Standard view.
Ctrl + 2	Use Compact view.
Ctrl + 3	Use Minimal view.
Ctrl + G	Select a marker for beginning playback, if the file has markers.
Ctrl + O	Open a file.
Ctrl + T	Keep Media Player on top of all other windows.
Ctrl + V	Preview the current media file.
Shift + F10	Display the same menu you see when you right-click within Media Player.

TABLE 8-4. Media Player Options (Playback page of the Options dialog box).

To accomplish this:	Do this:
Adjust the volume.	Adjust the volume slider.
Adjust the balance.	Adjust the balance slider.
Specify the number of times the sound plays.	Type a number in the Play Time(s) to box (default is 1).
Repeat the sound (looping).	Activate "Repeat Forever."
Rewind the sound when it finishes playing.	Activate "Rewind when done playing."

Troubleshooting Media Player Problems

If you're experiencing problems with Media Player, make sure you're using the most recent version. To upgrade your player, connect to the Internet, start Media Player, and click Help on the menu bar. Click Check for Player Upgrade. If there's a newer version, click Upgrade Now to install it.

You may run into problems playing media content. The following table helps you troubleshoot these problems. As you'll see, most of them can be solved, with the exception of Internet congestion. You can expect the worst congestion during the hours of 11 a.m. to 2 p.m. on weekdays; that's when people are online from both U.S. coasts, and a lot of people use their lunch breaks to use the Internet.

TABLE 8-5. Troubleshooting Media Player Problems.

Problem	Solution
The video area is green, or flashing green or pink bands or blocks.	You need to change one of the Windows Direct Draw settings. To do so, run the media file that's causing the problem. In Media Player, click File on the menu bar, choose Properties, and click the Advanced Tab. In the Filters In Use area, click Video Renderer, and click Properties. Click the Direct Draw tab, and clear the YUV Flipping check box. Click OK until you see Media Player again. You'll need to quit and restart Media Player in order to view the video.

(continued)

TABLE 8-5. *continued*

Problem	Solution
The streaming video plays, but with frequent interruptions.	This problem can be caused by many factors, and some are beyond your control, such as network traffic congestion. However, your connection speed may be too low to support the media file you are trying to play. For example, you will experience problems if you're using a 28.8 Kbps modem while you're trying to play a media file that requires a faster modem. Make sure your bandwidth setting is correct; for example, you will run into problems if you set Media Player for a 56 Kbps modem when your modem is actually capable of connecting only at 28.8 Kbps. To check your bandwidth setting, click View on the menu bar, and choose Options. Click the Advanced tab. Click Streaming Media (RealVideo), and click Change. Click the General tab, and choose the correct bandwidth. Click OK until you see Media Player again. If your connection is fast enough, try increasing the buffering time (the amount of time that the content is stored temporarily before playback begins. To do so, on the View menu, choose Options. On the Advanced Tab, click Streaming Media (Windows Media), and click Change. Increase the buffering time by clicking Buffer and typing the number of seconds you want to buffer data. The default is 5; try 10. Click OK until you see Media Player again. Note that after making this change, streaming audio and video files won't begin playing as quickly.
There's no sound.	Check the following: Does this presentation include sound? Some include video but no audio. Did you mute the sound within Media Player? On the View menu, make sure the Standard view is selected; then look at the control bar and make sure the Mute button (the one that looks like a speaker) doesn't have a cross through it. If it does, click the button to unmute the sound. Also, adjust the volume control upward if necessary. Are your speakers or headphones plugged in and, if necessary, turned on? Check the plugs, switches, and wiring.

(continued)

TABLE 8-5. *continued*

Problem	Solution
There's no sound.	Is another program using the sound card? Quit other programs that have audio capabilities. Are your system sound settings properly set? Click Start, point to Programs, choose Accessories, click Multimedia (Entertainment in Windows 98), and click Volume Control. Make sure the Mute All check box is cleared, and adjust the volume controls. Click OK. Is the appropriate playback device selected? To find out, click Start, point to Settings, and click Control Panel. Choose Multimedia, and click the Audio tab. In the Playback area, adjust the volume by clicking the slider button; then increase the volume in the resulting dialog box. Also, make sure that your sound card has been selected in the Preferred Device area. Click OK to confirm.
I'm getting sound, but no video.	Check the following: The connection speed might be too low to support this media file, or there may be severe network congestion. See the solutions under "The video plays, but with frequent interruptions," above in this table.
The video is showing a frozen frame, but sound is playing.	This might not be a problem at all. Some media use a slide-show presentation with sound linked to one or more still graphics. If you're sure you're supposed to be seeing a movie, see "The streaming video plays, but with frequent interruptions," above.
Media Player can't connect to certain types of media.	Your advanced settings may be incorrect. On the menu bar, click View, and click the Advanced tab. Click Streaming Media (Windows Media), and click Change. Make sure all the protocol boxes are checked. If you're using Media Player on a local area network (LAN), ask your network administrator whether you need to configure Media Player to work with a proxy server, and how you should supply the needed information. You may have set the security settings too high. For more information on security settings, see Chapter 9, "Using the Internet Safely."

Exploring the World of Multimedia Content

Multimedia content is increasingly available on the Web. You can attend live Web events, and listen to a huge and growing variety of live audio and video broadcasts.

Attending Web Events

On Microsoft's Best of the Web page (Figure 8-3), you currently find a list of the day's Web events: live Media Player broadcasts. Today's lineup: Bloomberg financial news, and a live concert broadcast from the Los Angeles Palladium.

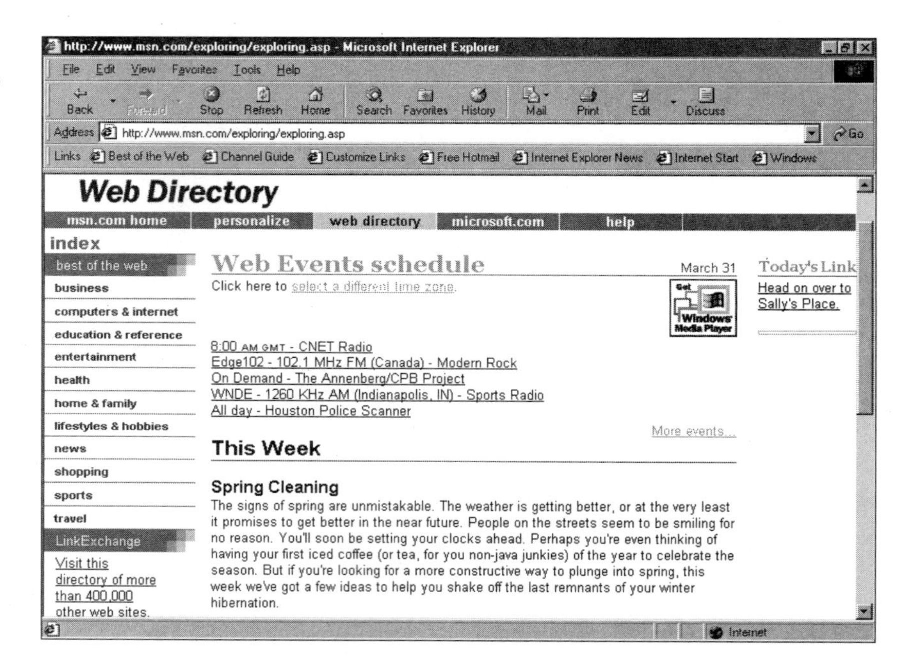

FIGURE 8-3.
Microsoft's Best of the Web page features today's lineup of live broadcasts.

Using the Windows Media Showcase

To access the Windows Media Showcase, click Showcase on the Navigation bar. You'll see the Media Showcase page, shown in Figure 8-4.

Finding Internet Radio Stations

Do you like to listen to the radio while you work? The Internet is fast becoming one of the best ways to listen to live radio broadcasts. Admittedly, the sound isn't consistently of FM quality, but this deficiency is more than compensated for by the amazing variety of content.

Here's a list of some of the sites on the Internet that index Internet radio broadcasts:

- **Audio Highway Network** (http://www.audiohighway.com) is a great place to find live news broadcasts, including stock quotes, NPR's Morning Edition, and sports news. You'll also find links to audio books, old-time radio rebroadcasts, and much more.
- **Broadcast.com** (http://www.radio.broadcast.com/radio) provides a guide to hundreds of Internet radio stations in every conceivable format. The home page lists today's featured stations.
- **BRS Radio Directory** (http://www.radio-directory.com/) bills itself as the Internet's first choice for radio. The listings are organized by state or format, with special categories for public and international stations.
- **InfoSearch Broadcasting Links** (http://www.broadcastinglinks.com/radio.html) features an alphabetized list of hundreds of radio broadcasts accessible over the Internet.
- **RadioTower** (http://www.radiotower.com) is another index to hundreds of Internet radio broadcasts, searchable by genre, name, and place.
- **World Radio Network** (http://www.wrn.org/audio.html) features live public radio programs from around the world, including Australia, the Netherlands, Denmark, Poland, and many more.

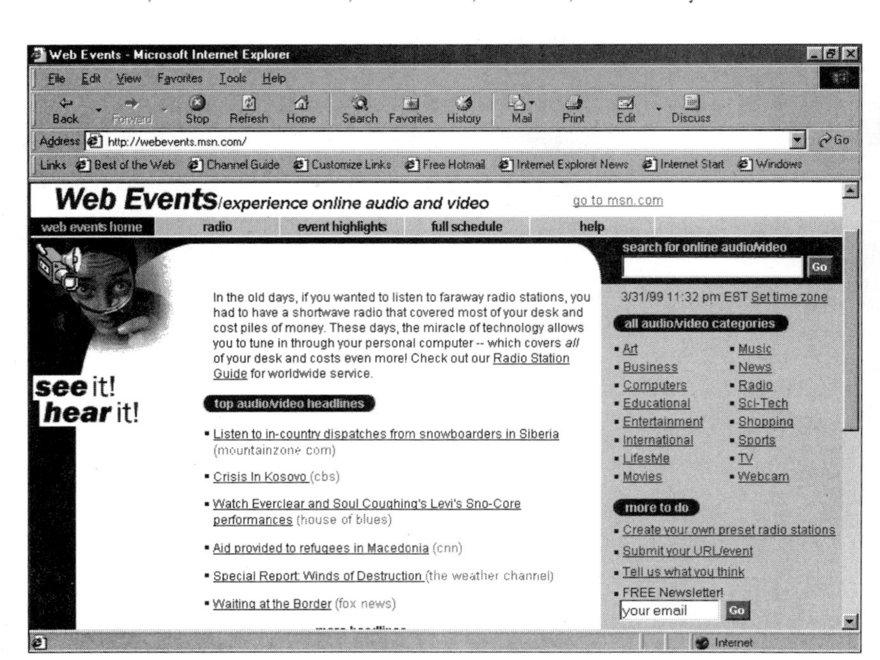

FIGURE 8-4.
Microsoft's Media Showcase page highlights cool content that you can access with Media Player.

Finding Live Video on the Internet

Internet TV broadcasting isn't as common as radio broadcasting, but you can still find some live content. There's a lot more content available in archived form.

- **Internet TV** (http://internettv.com) focuses on the arts (music videos, film trailers, and performing arts).
- **MediaCHANNEL** (http://www.mediachannel.com) provides a daily guide to Internet video. You can search the site listings, or browse by content in a variety of categories (including business, education, entertainment, health, interviews, kid's stuff, news, politics, spiritual, travel, weather, and Web cams).
- **Microsoft TV** (see http://www.broadcast.com/video/netshow/mstv) features live training videos. You can also access archived shows.

Creating and Using Favorites

Most of the media you'll play will be accessed by clicking links on Web sites. However, you can use Media Player to access media content directly. Media Player's Favorites menu contains preset links to Web pages with interesting media content. You can also add your own favorites to this list.

Your media favorites will appear within Internet Explorer's Favorites menu or Favorites explorer under the Media folder.

Adding Media to Your Favorites List

If you've found a media file that you'd like to play again, add it to your Favorites list by following these instructions:

1. Click Favorites on the menu bar, and choose Add To Favorites.
2. If you prefer, type a new name for the media file.
3. If you've created folders for your favorite media files, click Create In and select a folder.
4. Click OK.

You'll see your new favorite in the Favorites list.

Organizing Favorites

To begin to organize your favorites, click Favorites on the menu bar, and choose Organize Favorites. You'll see the Organize Favorites dialog box, shown in Figure 8-5.

- To create a new folder, click the Create Folder icon, and type a name for the new folder.
- To place a favorite in a folder, select the item you want to move. Then click the Move To Folder button, select the destination folder, and click OK.
- To rename favorites, select the favorite, and click Rename. Edit the text, and click away from the item.
- To delete a favorite, select the favorite, and click Delete. Click Yes to confirm.

Click Close once you're done organizing your favorites.

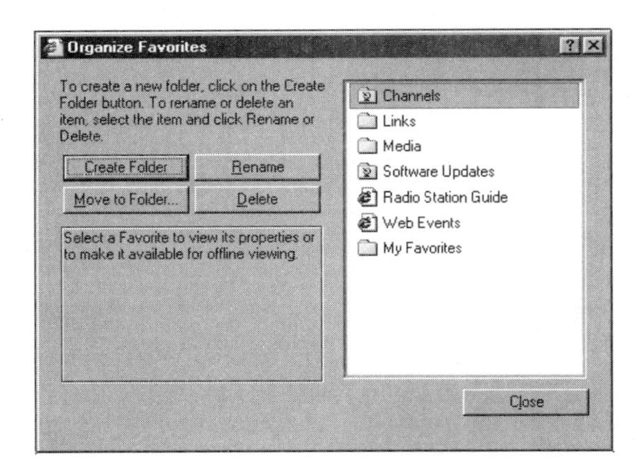

FIGURE 8-5.
In this dialog box, you can organize your favorite media sites.

Using Media Player Views

If you use Media Player frequently, you may wish to experiment with the program's view options. On the View menu, you can choose the Standard view (displays all of the window components available with the current file), Compact (reduces the window to the fewer components), and Minimal (displays the minimum components needed to control the current file). To keep Media Player on top of other applications, click View, and choose Always On Top (or press Ctrl + T).

You can create custom views if you wish. To do so, click View on the menu bar, choose Options, and click the Custom Views tab. In the Custom Views page (see Figure 8-6), you can define the components that appear when you choose Compact or Minimal.

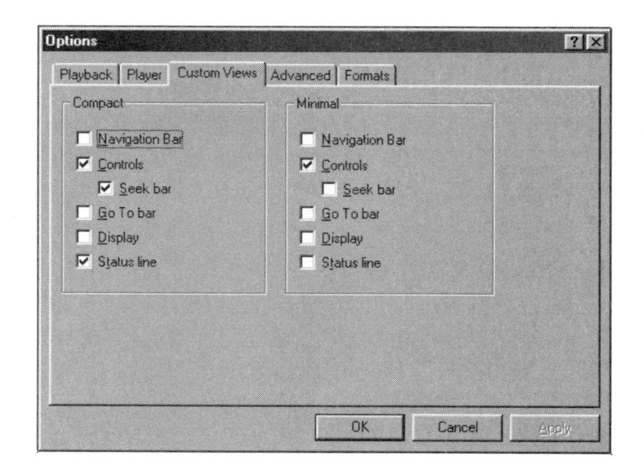

FIGURE 8-6.
The Custom Views page enables you to define which components appear in the compact or minimal views of the Media Player window.

On the Player page of the Options dialog box, you can choose preferences for Media Player's default operation, including the view (standard, compact, or minimal), whether the player is always on top of other windows, and whether the same player is used for each media file that you play (the alternative is to open a new player for each file). You can also choose whether the player will use Autozoom, a feature that selects the last zoom setting you chose, and whether controls are visible in full-screen view.

Exploring Three-Dimensional Worlds (Virtual Reality)

When you look at Web pages, you're seeing two dimensions. If you've ever played the computer game Doom or Descent (or any of the many imitators of these games), you'll know how interesting and exciting a three-dimensional computer display can be. Using your mouse or a joystick to navigate, you move *into* the screen, exploring rooms and passages as you please. The presentation of three-dimensional worlds in this way is often called *virtual reality,* because it seems as though you're entering a "real" world that exists entirely within the computer. It's great fun, and thanks to a new computer programming language called VRML, you can navigate three-dimensional worlds on the Web.

VRML stands for Virtual Reality Modeling Language. It's designed to enable Web authors to embed information about three-dimensional worlds in Web pages. If you're using a VRML-capable Web browser, the three-dimensional world appears *in-line* (that is, within the Web page you're viewing). You can enter this world and explore.

Internet Explorer can't view three-dimensional worlds without help; that help is Microsoft VRML Viewer. This add-on program is available on the CD that accompanies this book; it supports version 2.0 of VRML, which offers a number of advanced features, including audio. After installing VRML Viewer, your copy of Internet Explorer takes on new navigation capabilities, but these don't become evident until you access a page containing a VRML world. At that time, a new type of toolbar, called a navigation bar, appears on the left and bottom sides of the VRML window.

Accessing a VRML Site

To get started with the VRML Viewer, you need to access a Web site that includes a three-dimensional world. Connect to the Microsoft VRML site at http://www.microsoft.com/vrml, and choose the Offworld Exploits link. Click one of the worlds to enter three dimensions. You can start navigating this world right away. Just hold down the mouse button, and advance the mouse pointer in the direction in which you want to travel.

As you access this site, you'll notice that Internet Explorer takes a little longer to download the page than it would normally. That's because it's downloading the virtual-world file. When the downloading is complete, you'll see the VRML navigation bar on the left and bottom of the VRML world (Figure 8-7).

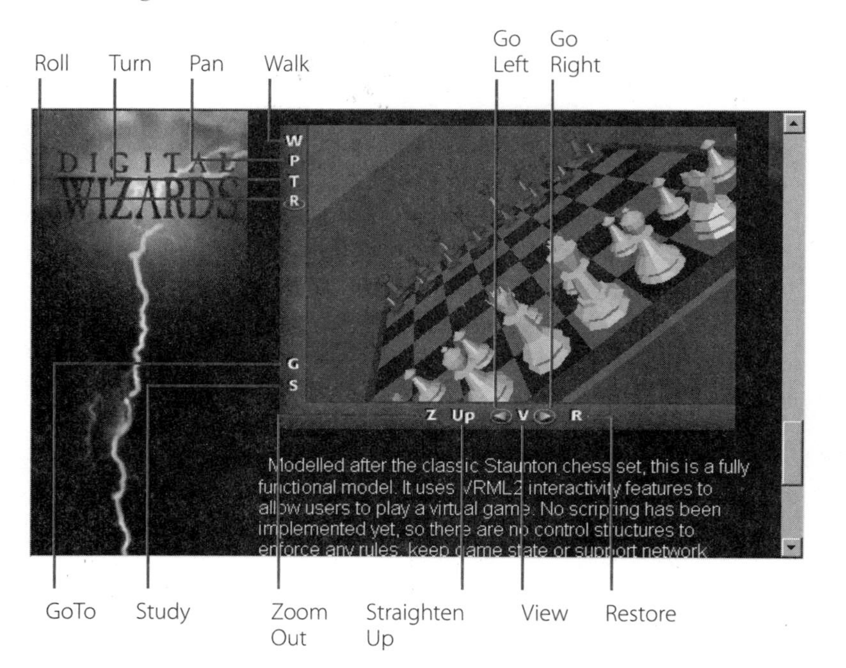

FIGURE 8-7.
VRML lets you to view a three-dimensional world in-line.

Using the VRML Navigation Bar

The VRML navigation bar appears when you access a page containing a virtual world. You'll see six buttons on the vertical portion. You'll see four additional buttons on the horizontal portion of the navigation bar.

HELP, I don't see a toolbar!
VRML authors can control whether the toolbars appear, so you might not see the toolbars if the author has chosen to switch them off. You can still choose navigation options by using the keyboard or pop-up menus.

Using Keyboard Shortcuts

You can also use keyboard shortcuts instead of selecting the toolbar items.

TABLE 8-6. VRML Navigation Bar.

Click this:	To do this:
Walk	Move forward or backward through the scene, turn to the left, or turn to the right.
Pan	Shift your viewpoint horizontally or vertically—without moving forward, backward, turning, or rolling.
Turn	Turn your viewpoint without moving.
Roll	Spin the virtual world around its center. If this produces unwanted effects, click Straighten Up.
Goto	Go to the place you click.
Study	Rotate objects automatically in front of you so you can see what they are.
Zoom Out	Go back to get perspective on the whole world.
Straighten Up	Cancel the roll and straighten your viewpoint with respect to the scene.
View	Go to named viewpoints (if any have been included in this world).
Restore	Go back to the beginning.

TABLE 8-7. VRML Keyboard Shortcuts.

To do this:	Press these keys:
Walk	Ctrl + Shift + W
Pan	Ctrl + Shift + P
Turn	Ctrl + Shift + T
Roll	Ctrl + Shift + R
Goto	Ctrl + Shift + G
Study	Ctrl + Shift + S
Zoom Out	Ctrl + Shift + Z
Straighten Up	Ctrl + Shift + U

Understanding the Cursors

When you've chosen a navigation mode, VRML Viewer displays a cursor showing the navigation option you're using. The following table shows these cursors and explains what they mean.

TABLE 8-8. VRML Cursors.

Cursor	Navigation option
Walk	Walk
Pan	Pan
Turn	Turn
Roll	Roll
Goto	Goto
Study	Study

 TIP

> If you see curved lines surrounding the cursor, it means you've encountered a special feature that's been built into this world. Click the left mouse button to find out what's up!

Starting Out with Viewpoints

The best way to start exploring a VRML world is to examine the author's predefined viewpoints if the world you're viewing has any. To see whether any viewpoints exist, click the View button, or click the right mouse button and choose Viewpoints from the pop-up menu. Select a viewpoint from the list.

If more than one viewpoint exists, you can move to the next or previous one by clicking the arrow buttons on either side of the View button. If no other viewpoints exist, these arrows are dimmed.

Maneuvering with the Mouse

The best way to learn how to navigate a virtual world is to try it. If you get lost, click the Restore button. As you maneuver, keep the following basic rules in mind:

- The direction in which you drag the mouse affects the direction in which you move.
- The distance you drag the mouse affects the speed with which you move. If you stop moving the mouse but continue pressing the button, you'll continue to move until you release the button.
- If the mouse pointer changes to a hand shape, you've found a hyperlink. Click it to go to the linked document.

Walk

Walking is the way you'll normally move through a virtual world. As you walk, the scene will rotate to accommodate your turns. To walk, click the Walk button, press and hold the left mouse button, and move the mouse in the direction in which you want to go. Drag straight up to go forward; drag straight down to go back.

Pan

When you pan the scene, it slides past you, as if you had just moved laterally or vertically without changing the way you're facing. To have the scene slide, click the Pan button, press and hold the left mouse button, and move the mouse in the direction in which you want to go.

Turn

You can turn around in place by clicking the Turn button and dragging left or right. Dragging up or down is similar to tilting your head up or down—except that in a virtual world *you* tilt up or down. Try dragging at an angle for a few moments, and then resume walking forward. Unless you're accustomed to zero gravity, you'll probably find the effect confusing (Figure 8-8). If so, click Straighten Up and the world will right itself.

Roll

You can tilt the virtual world any way you like. Click the Roll button and drag the mouse to the left or right to tilt the scene. Be aware, though, that if you're looking at a landscape—a scene that's meant to be navigated without a tilt—the effect might not be very pleasant. If you've tried a tilt and you're not too happy with the results, you can "de-tilt" the scene by clicking the Straighten Up button.

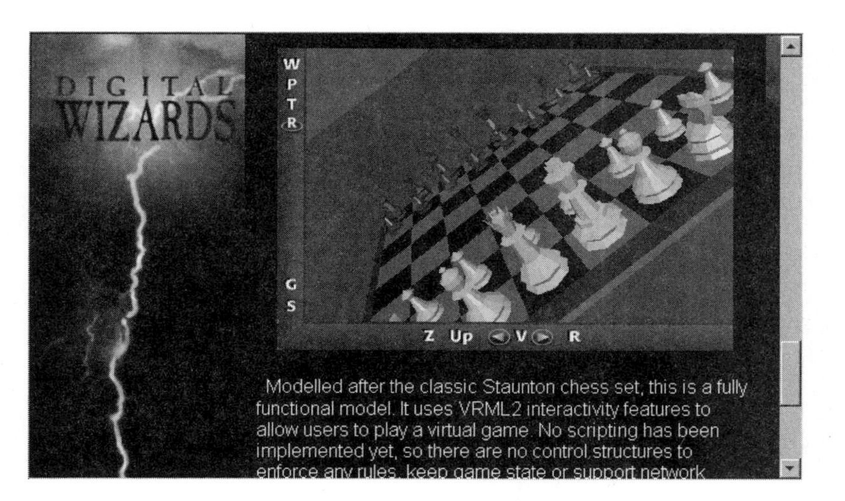

DIGITAL
WIZARDS
W
P
T
R
G
S
Z Up V R
Modelled after the classic Staunton chess set, this is a fully functional model. It uses VRML2 interactivity features to allow users to play a virtual game. No scripting has been implemented yet, so there are no control structures to

FIGURE 8-8.
This might be a good time to click the Straighten Up button.

Goto

To go to an object quickly, click Goto. The cursor changes to a cross-hair, and you can click the place to which you want to go. To cancel the Goto mode without clicking on an object, press Esc.

Study

To study an object, click Study and then click the object you want to study. Drag the mouse to rotate the object in front of you—or, more properly, to move your virtual self around the object.

Zoom Out

Clicking the Zoom Out button pulls you back from the virtual world until it all fits inside your screen. In some worlds, this feature can make objects extremely tiny, but it's a useful way to get a grasp of the layout of the entire world.

Maneuvering with the Keyboard

If you would prefer to use the keyboard to maneuver through virtual worlds, you can do so. Choose your navigation mode by using one of the keyboard shortcuts. Then use the arrow keys instead of the mouse to drag left, right, up, or down. To straighten up, press Ctrl + Shift + U. To zoom out, press Ctrl + Shift + Z. And to jump between viewpoints, press Page Down and Page Up.

In case you get lost or confused in the virtual world you've entered, VRML Viewer provides some survival tools:

- Is the scene tilted at a crazy angle? Straighten up and fly right by clicking the Straighten Up button.
- Can't see where you're going? Turn on the headlight. To do so, click the right mouse button, choose Graphics, and enable the Headlight option.
- Hopelessly lost? Return to the world's starting point by clicking the Restore button on the toolbar.

Improving Performance

If the world you're viewing seems to perform sluggishly, you can improve performance by choosing a flat or wireframe-image quality. By default, VRML Viewer displays the world with smooth shading, the best that's available. But you can change to flat shading, the medium quality setting, or wireframe, the lowest (Figure 8-9). To do so, click the right mouse button, select Graphics, and choose the image quality setting that you want.

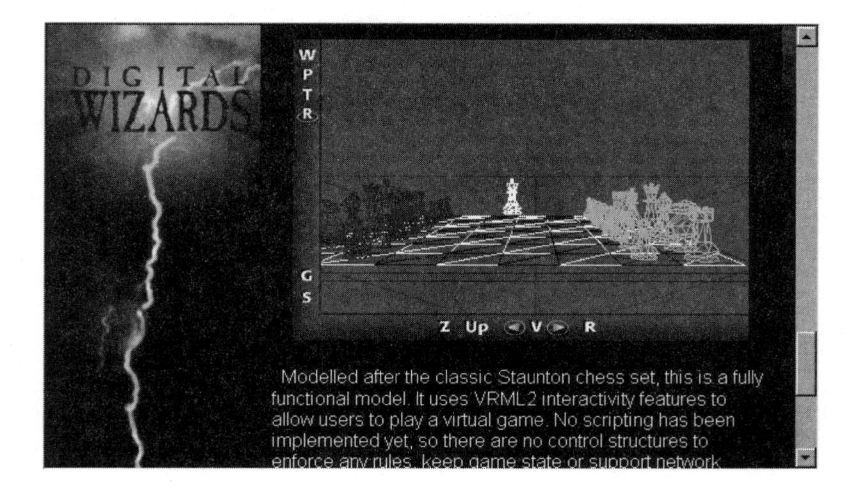
DIGITAL
WIZARDS
W
P
T
R
G
S
Z Up V R
Modelled after the classic Staunton chess set, this is a fully functional model. It uses VRML2 interactivity features to allow users to play a virtual game. No scripting has been implemented yet, so there are no control structures to enforce any rules, keep game state or support network

FIGURE 8-9.
This is the same view as in Figure 8-7 with wireframe graphics—ugly but fast.

You can also control the speed of apparent movement. By default, this speed is set to medium. To speed up or slow down movement, click the right mouse button, select Speed, and choose the speed you want.

Another way to improve performance is to disable the Full Color option. With Full Color on, you see the best possible color quality, but speed is sacrificed. To turn off Full Color, click the right mouse button, select Graphics, and click Full Color so that the check mark disappears.

You can get a slight improvement in performance by turning off *dithering,* which blends the shaded surface. With dithering turned off, you might see bands instead of smooth gradations in the images, but performance improves. To turn off dithering, click the right mouse button, select Graphics, and click Dithering so that the check mark disappears.

TIP

Does your graphics card have Direct3D graphics acceleration? Take full advantage of it by clicking the right mouse button, choosing Options, and enabling the Hardware Acceleration option.

CHAPTER 9

Using the Internet Safely

Thanks in part to many sensationalized articles in the press, some people overestimate the dangers of Internet use. At the same time, other people underestimate the dangers (particularly where kids are concerned). As with most things in life, the truth's somewhere in the middle. The Internet can be secure, safe, and incredibly rewarding—but you've got to inform and protect yourself. That's the goal of this chapter. Once you've read it, you'll be able to use the Internet with confidence.

Let's get started with some basic definitions and concepts, things that every Internet user really needs to understand. The chapter continues with a thorough exploration of all the great things Microsoft Internet Explorer version 5 can do to protect your security and privacy while you're online. You'll learn how to shop safely at secure sites, how to use Internet Explorer's security settings, how to use active Web content safely, and how to download and install software from the Internet.

Understanding Internet Security and Privacy

To begin, it's important to understand that security and privacy differ, and that sometimes people who are very interested in security aren't interested in privacy—and vice versa.

Differentiating between Security and Privacy

Security and privacy are two different things.

- **Security** refers to the protection of computer and networking systems against unauthorized intrusion or vandalism by pranksters and criminals. As a PC user, your main concern here is the possibility that you'll inadvertently download rogue content, which could damage your computer or even destroy data.

- **Privacy** refers to your ability to keep information about yourself hidden from prying eyes. You should be able to prevent anyone from obtaining information about you, your computer system, your Web-site viewing tastes, and other personal data.

Companies and individuals sometimes have common interests when it comes to security and privacy, and sometimes they don't. For example, you and everyone who tries to sell products on the Web would like to ensure the security and privacy of credit card information that you use to order on the Web. That's in everyone's interest. However, more than a few firms would love to invade your privacy while you're using the Web, compiling information about your browsing, searching, and shopping choices.

For criminals, the opposite is true. They want total privacy so that they can work out drug deals, terrorist attacks, and other illegal acts without government detection. You can see why governments have mixed feelings about safeguarding the privacy of Internet users. Unless something like a digital wiretapping scheme is worked out, which would enable investigators to obtain a warrant and unscramble encrypted messages, don't expect governments to show much enthusiasm for Internet privacy.

Assessing Security and Privacy Risks

It's paranoia time. The following is a rogue's gallery of the various guises that Internet predators can take.

- **Imposters.** Suppose you've decided to order something online. You've accessed a Web site that appears to be the official Web site of a famous West Coast winery. It's a glamorous production. However, you don't notice that the URL indicates that the site you've accessed is actually located outside the United States. You upload your credit card data and somebody goes on a shopping spree with it! This is called *spoofing*. Another variation: somebody logs on to a valid online ordering site with your credit card number, orders a bunch of stuff, has it delivered to a different shipping address, and you get the bill. While this isn't common, it has happened to a few people.

- **Criminals.** A *sniffer* is a program that runs on a computer connected to the Internet. The program scans all the messages that are routed through the network to which the computer is connected, looking for information that conforms to a certain pattern (such as a Visa card number). Because Internet messages are normally sent in plain text, this is easy to do, and a criminal computer hacker doesn't even need to monitor the program manually. When the pattern is found, the information is displayed on-screen, enabling the criminal to read it. Sniffers are frequently programmed to look for credit card numbers and passwords uploaded in plain, unencrypted text.
- **Saboteurs.** If you're not careful about where you obtain computer programs on the Internet, you could infect your system with a computer virus. The Internet is the greatest thing that ever happened to virus authors. It enables them to make trouble for many more people than they could prior to the Internet's explosive growth.
- **Snoops.** Some servers, mainly commercial ones, write data to your hard drive in files called *cookies*. In most cases, this practice is quite legitimate and in your own interest. The cookie files contain information about your preferences, customization choices, and previous page selections. Cookies make Web sites much more functional and easier to use. However, there is a major push underway to use cookies to collect marketing data. At some sites, cookies can be used to compile a dossier about the searching, browsing, and online ordering preferences associated with a particular computer. The companies that perform this tracking insist that they do not try to associate this information with a visitor's name. The tracking is done by tagging a particular computer with a unique, numerical identification number. But privacy advocates worry that this information might be linked to names by less scrupulous entrepreneurs.

- **Predators.** Are your kids using the Internet? You'd best be aware that there are adults out there who would love to hit on them, and they know that the Internet is a perfect way to do it. Before the Internet, there was always the danger of a parent intercepting a call or letter. Now, with lots of Internet-savvy kids and Internet-clueless parents, a whole new avenue of communication has opened up that allows sexual predators to get past parents. How common is this? Unfortunately, very common. Let me be perfectly clear: you're out of your mind if you let your kids use the Internet without protection and supervision. Kids might try to snoop around on porn sites, as well as porn-related newsgroups and chat rooms —and that's where the predators often find them.

Internet Explorer offers many solutions to security and privacy protection on the Internet. But as you'll see, there are some remaining problems, especially with respect to predators. The following sections indicate how the program gives you good protection against criminals, imposters, saboteurs, and snoops.

Introducing Public-Key Cryptography

The answer to these problems may not lie in more legislation but in technology. Most people do not realize that there has been a major technical revolution in cryptography, the science of encrypting or coding messages so that they cannot be read by anyone except the intended recipient. *Public-key cryptography* is a new method of sending super-secret messages between two parties *who have never communicated before.*

Why is public-key encryption such a major new discovery? The practice of scrambling a message so that nobody can read it except its intended recipient has been around since the time of Julius Caesar. But it's always had an Achilles' heel. Somehow you had to convey the *key*—which tells how to decode the message—to the recipient. This could be done by means of a courier, but as you can imagine, conveying the key this way is dangerous. What if the courier is disloyal?

Public-key cryptography solves this problem by using two keys, a *public key* and a *private key*. To engage in a secure transaction, you send your public key to somebody, and that person uses your public key to encrypt the message. Nobody can decode the message en route. Only you can decode it, using your private key. As long as the public key is carefully designed, it's practically impossible to break the code by deriving the private key from the public key.

When you use Internet Explorer to contact a secure server, the program and server exchange public keys, and a secure channel of communication is established. Both the data sent by you and by the server are transferred in encrypted form so that nobody—not even a criminal armed with a sniffer—can intercept it.

How will public-key encryption affect you? By making online commerce possible. (Although, as you'll learn elsewhere in this chapter, there's still a problem with protection against pilferers.) What's troubling about public-key encryption is the perfect cover it provides for illegal activity, such as drug dealing, money laundering, and terrorism. The U.S. Federal Bureau of Investigation (FBI) is deeply concerned that, in an encryption-driven future, the electronic equivalent of wiretapping will become impossible, creating unparalleled opportunities for organized crime. At this time, it's far from clear how these issues will develop and how they're going to be balanced against the legitimate privacy concerns of citizens and Internet users.

Examining How Public-Key Cryptography Works

In order to use public-key cryptography, users must have a program that enables them to generate two keys, the *public key* and the *private key*. Together, these are called a *key pair*. Microsoft Internet Explorer can create these for you. And here's what they do:

- You freely give the public key to anyone who wants to send you a message. (You don't have to worry about doing this; as you'll see, Internet Explorer does the job automatically.)
- You *never* give your private key to *anyone*.
- The *public key* encrypts a message. Once the message has been encrypted with the public key, the message cannot be decoded (decrypted) without the private key.
- When you receive a message encoded with your public key, Internet Explorer uses your private key to decode the message.
- Similarly, you send messages to others by encrypting with your correspondents' public keys. These messages can't be decoded without their corresponding private keys.

All that's needed to establish secure communication, then, is the exchange of public keys. When Internet Explorer contacts a *secure server* (a server that's running the software needed to work with encrypted messages), that's exactly what happens. Automatically, Internet Explorer and the server exchange their public keys, which they then use to encrypt the messages they send to each other. A secure channel of communication is established without the two parties ever having exchanged *any* information that could be intercepted and used to reveal the contents of the exchanged messages.

SEE ALSO
If you reside within the United States or Canada, you can obtain the 128-bit version of Internet Explorer by downloading the software from Microsoft's Web site. For more information, see "Obtaining the 128-bit version of Internet Explorer" in Appendix A.

Key-Bit Length and Security

How safe is public-key encryption? Any encrypted message can be decoded, eventually, by programming a computer to guess the decoding key. But "eventually" may mean a very, very long time. The most secure forms of encryption would require all the computers in the world to run for thousands of years.

What determines the security level of an encrypted message? It all depends on the *bit length* of the key used to encrypt your messages. The longer the bit length, the longer it takes for a computer to try to guess the key. An encoding bit length of 40 characters isn't very secure; by linking a few dozen computers together—an easy task, thanks to the Internet—it's possible to break 40-bit encryption in a day or two. Considerably more time and computational horsepower is required for 56-bit encryption, while 128-bit encryption is in the same league with the industrial-strength encryption used by financial institutions and intelligence organizations.

So why doesn't everyone use 128-bit encryption? In the United States and Canada, you can. And outside the United States and Canada, you can. You just can't *export* software containing strong encryption technology from the United States or Canada to a foreign country. That's because the U.S. Commerce Department defines strong encryption technology as ammunition—that's right, a weapon of war. This position isn't unreasonable considering the decisive role that encryption has played in most of the twentieth century's wars. But it flies in the face of the fact that strong encryption technology is *already* widely available outside North America. So U.S. companies, Microsoft included, are prohibited from exporting software that contains safe, 128-bit encryption.

Understanding the Need for Digital Certificates and Signatures

Public-key encryption enables Internet Explorer to contact secure servers and set up a secure channel of communication. You can upload credit card and other confidential information with a high degree of confidence that no one will be able to intercept and decode this information while it's en route. But this nifty new technology does nothing to prevent the most common types of credit card fraud. Suppose somebody steals your credit card, goes online, and orders a bunch of stuff. The online transaction will be encrypted, and the information is quite safe while it's on its way. But the information is coming from a stolen card! This sword cuts both ways. Suppose you're using your credit card to order something online, and you *think* you're ordering from a bona-fide online shopping site. Without realizing, though, you've been diverted to an imposter site, one that looks just like the real one but exists only to collect credit card numbers!

To prevent credit card fraud, more protection is needed. This protection is available in the form of *digital certificates* and *digital signatures*.

Digital Certificates

Digital certificates provide safeguards against imposters. A digital certificate is essentially a means of countersigning public keys with a "digital ID," the computer equivalent of your driver's license. Digital certificates are supplied by *certification authorities* (CA), which provide the certificates for free or for a small fee. When you send your public key, you include your certificate. By inspecting your certificate, people can see that the message is really from you. Similarly, the sites you contact also have certificates. When you inspect a certificate, you have an opportunity to judge whether you're doing business with the company you think you're doing business with.

Digital Signatures

What's to stop someone from forging a certificate by obtaining it and altering it? That's where digital signatures come in. Your computer creates the digital signature for each message you send by using a *hash*. A hash is a one-way mathematical function that reduces the content of your message to a short *message digest*. The cool thing about the message digest is that it's a sort of mathematical fingerprint of your message. Also, it's impossible to derive the message from the digest, even if the hash formula is known. All you can do with the hash function is make a new message digest.

Here's how the message digest works. When the receiving computer gets your message, it takes the message and runs the same hash function that you used. Then it compares the two message digests, the one you sent and the one it computed. If they don't agree, there's trouble. Something happened to the message—maybe just a data transmission error, or maybe somebody got hold of the message and altered it in some way. Either way, the message is rejected.

Exploring the Three Types of Certificates

Get started by understanding the types of certificates you can use and getting your own personal certificate. Internet Explorer uses three kinds of certificates:

- **Site certificates.** These certificates are issued and validated by an independent, third-party agency. When your browser accesses a secure Web site, your browser examines the site's security certificate. If the security certificate is valid, you know that the server you've accessed is really located at the company you want to do business with. If the security certificate isn't valid, it means that something in the certificate doesn't match up; for example, the site's name or e-mail address isn't what it's supposed to be. This problem might be due to sloppy record-keeping, or it might be due to criminal activity. In either case, you'd be well advised to skip ordering from this site.
- **Publisher certificates.** These certificates are presented by software publishers when you download software from the Internet. The certificate attests that the software really is from the software publisher (not some imposter) and that you can presume it's trustworthy. However, be aware that the certification authority does not personally inspect every program for viruses.
- **Personal certificates.** Companies selling goods on the Web have their own concerns about imposters. What if someone has stolen your credit card and is trying to use it to order goods illegally? Personal certificates identify you as the person you say you are. A personal certificate is like showing your identification when you write a check. It's in your interest as well as the merchants' and banks' interests to make sure that no one is using your card illegally. There are different levels of personal certificates. A Class 1 certificate reflects the lowest level of demanded identification; the only way the CA checks on your identity is to mail the identification to your e-mail account. Stronger identification is provided by Class 2 certificates, which are issued only after your identity has been verified by means of an online consumer database.

Getting a Personal Certificate

Get your own digital certificate now. At this writing, VeriSign, Inc., a leading certificate authority, was making trial certificates available

Internet Explorer users. As with everything on the Web, this offer is subject to change and might not be valid by the time you read this.

CAUTION

In order to obtain your digital ID, you need to set up your e-mail with Outlook Express. You probably did this when you installed Internet Explorer. If not, you need to install Outlook Express.

SEE ALSO

For information on setting up Outlook Express, see Chapter 11.

To get a Class 1 digital ID from VeriSign, follow this procedure:

1. Access VeriSign's Digital ID Center at http://digitalid.verisign.com.
2. Look for a button or for a link labeled Personal Ids, and click it. Look for a link labeled Try a Digital ID FREE for 60 days and click it.
3. You'll see a page explaining the difference between Class 1 and Class 2 digital IDs.
4. Click Class 1. You'll see a page asking you to supply information, including your name, e-mail address, and the password you want to use for your digital ID.
5. Type the requested information, and follow all the instructions to submit your request.
6. After a few minutes, check your e-mail. You'll find a message from VeriSign indicating your personal identification number (PIN).
7. Switch back to the VeriSign page in Internet Explorer, and click the link that takes you to the Web page at which you get your digital ID.
8. On this page, type your PIN and click Submit. Internet Explorer installs the certificate on your system.
9. To see your installed certificate, click Tools on the menu bar, choose Internet Options, and click the Content tab. Click Certificates, and click the Personal tab, if necessary. You'll see your certificate in the list (see Figure 9-1).

TIP

If you would like to use your certificate on more than one computer, don't go back to the certificate authority for another certificate. You can use Internet Explorer's Certificate Manager to export your certificate to other computers, and you use the same utility to import the certificate. For more information, see "Managing Certificates," page 303.

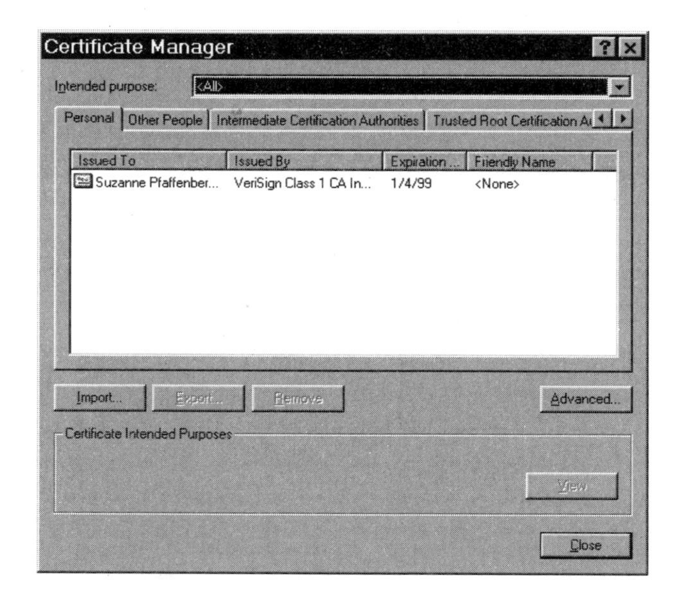

FIGURE 9-1.
After you've obtained your certificate, you can view it in the Certificate Manager.

SEE ALSO
For more information on Certificate Manager, see "Managing Certificates," page 303.

One drawback to current digital certificate technology is that you can't use your certificate unless you're sitting at the computer to which it was downloaded. In the future, computers will be accessed by means of *smart cards,* which are credit card-sized IDs that contain their own processing circuitry. They will contain your certificate, enabling you to establish your identity no matter which computer you're using.

Understanding Security Protocols

The key to safeguarding your data from criminals is to encrypt it, to scramble it so that it can't be read on any computer while en route. When the data arrives at its correct destination, the receiving computer decrypts it.

On the World Wide Web, encryption becomes possible with *secure browsers* and *secure servers.* A secure browser, such as Internet Explorer, can encrypt the data that you send, while a secure server can decrypt the data at the other end. All this is done automatically, almost instantly. And along the way, it is virtually impossible to decode and read the encrypted data.

For Internet browsers and servers to exchange encrypted data, both must be able to work with the same security protocol. A *security protocol* is a set of standards that specify how two computers can communicate by means of a secure (encrypted) channel. So that you can order safely from most of the secure sites on the Web, Internet Explorer recognizes and works with the security protocols listed below. You don't have to choose a protocol when you access a secure site; everything is automatic.

- **Secure Sockets Layer (SSL).** This protocol, originally developed by Netscape, is the one used in most secure Web sites. SSL version 3.0, supported by Internet Explorer 5, enables Web visitors and Web sites to exchange certificates for authenticating identity.
- **Private Communication Technology (PCT).** This Microsoft-developed protocol builds on SSL and introduces additional features that can help give a greater margin of security.

Shopping Safely on the Internet

Now that you understand the fundamentals of public-key encryption, digital certificates, and security protocols, you can shop with confidence. In this section, you'll explore shopping opportunities on the Internet, learn how to access a secure site and check out the site's credentials, and order online. You'll also learn how to use Microsoft Wallet, a utility that manages your personal information so that shopping is especially easy.

Introducing Web Commerce

A few decades ago, hardly anybody ordered things over the phone using a credit card. It was practically unheard of. "Give somebody my credit card number over the phone? Are you crazy?" My, how times have changed. Today credit card ordering is one of the cornerstones of the retail economy. Now people are saying, "Upload my credit card number over the Internet? Are you crazy?" Sounds like a repeat cycle, doesn't it?

A repeat cycle is what most business experts believe is happening. Internet commerce has been slow to develop mostly because it takes time for people to get used to the idea. But online commerce makes sense for many reasons: convenience and privacy for the customers, less expense and wider distribution for businesses. (Just think about the environmental effect of offering catalogs over the Web instead of mailing them by the millions.) And with the encryption technologies now available, ordering over the Internet is as safe as, and possibly even safer than, ordering by phone. The market is certainly there. By the year 2002, according to one recent projection, nearly 300 million people are expected to be using the Internet.

Already several thousand companies have opened up shop on the Web. It's a mixed bag, with people selling everything from hot sauce to lingerie, but some patterns seem to be emerging. In general, the businesses that succeed on the Web are those that offer products of particular interest to Web users, aren't as easily or readily available in "real-world" stores, or that take special advantage of the Internet's potential as a shopping medium. One example is Amazon.com (http://www.amazon.com), where database and Web technology are joined to offer something you can't get in just any neighborhood bookstore. Amazon.com offers more than 2.5 million book titles online, and has recently started selling audio CDs. The largest chain bookstores offer only about 170,000 titles, while the average mall bookstore stocks just 25,000.

After you've shopped around a bit, you'll see that certain types of products and services seem to be doing better online than others. Here's a snapshot of the current market:

- **Books and compact discs.** These are naturals for online ordering. A store can put its entire catalog (perhaps containing as many as 150,000 items) online with a searchable interface.
- **Cars.** Internet-based, automobile-buying services, such as Microsoft CarPoint, are making inroads into the traditional world of dealerships. You can understand why; it's so pleasant to order a car via the Internet, with no bargaining, hassles, or games with dealers.
- **Clothing.** You won't find just everyday items on the Web. The action here includes specialty items, such as exotic lingerie, bizarre T-shirts, funny ties and hats, and specialty shoes.
- **Computer equipment.** It makes sense that computer people would feel comfortable ordering computer equipment online. Several excellent online vendors offer great prices on selected equipment.
- **Gifts.** Flowers and specialty gift shops are prevalent on the Web, indicating that this is another popular area for online orders.
- **Specialty foods and wine.** You'll find hot sauces, Zinfandels, designer beers, spices, and sweets. All that surfing makes you hungry!
- **Sports and recreation gear.** There are plenty of online stores that sell specialty gear for golfers, sailors, backpackers, and other sports enthusiasts.

TIP

To keep on top of the Web's fast-breaking commercial developments, check out The All-Internet Shopping Directory (http://www.all-internet.com). This site lists Web vendors whose sites meet stringent guidelines for quality and service. You'll find lists of the Web's top shopping sites and plenty of links to the newest credit card burners on the Web. This very cool site is updated bi-weekly.

Accessing a Secure Site

Accessing a secure Web site is no different from accessing any other site on the Web: you click a hyperlink or type the URL directly. The site's welcome page often isn't secure. After all, many people are still using browsers that lack security features. Look for a link that enables you to access the secure version of the service.

When you access a secure site, you'll see a dialog box informing you that you're entering a secure zone. Similarly, when you exit a secure site, you'll see an alert box warning you that you're leaving the secure zone. If you do not wish to see these messages, check the option that hides them in the future.

After you've logged on to the secure service, look for a lock icon on the status bar, such as the one shown here:

The lock icon tells you that you have accessed a secure server and that the information you upload is safe from prying eyes.

Viewing Security Information

Once you've logged on to a secure Web page, you can view the security information, although it's not necessary unless you want to satisfy yourself that the transaction really is secure. To view security information, follow these steps:

1. Choose Properties from the File menu. You'll see the document Properties dialog box.
2. Click the Certificates button. You'll see another properties dialog box; this one shows the security certificate information (see Figure 9-2).
3. Click OK to exit the Certificate properties dialog box, and click OK to close the document Properties dialog box.

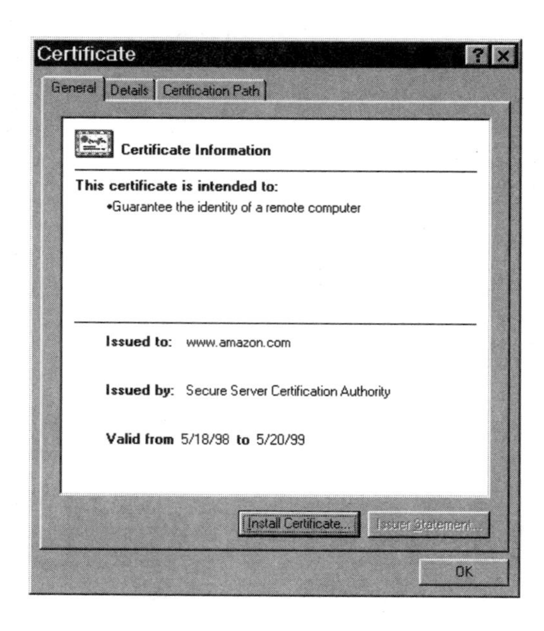

FIGURE 9-2. You can quickly look up certificate information about the Web page you are viewing.

Ordering Online

To see what online shopping is like, take a look at Amazon.com, which is worth exploring for another reason besides seeing what electronic commerce is all about. Far more than an online book-ordering site, Amazon.com is a community of authors, readers, publishers—anyone who loves books. You can submit your own reviews of any of the books listed in the voluminous catalog at Amazon.com. What's more, you'll find links to Internet-accessible book reviews, author biographies, and publisher sites. If you love books and reading, Amazon.com will quickly become one of your favorite sites on the Web. Recently, Amazon.com has added music (both popular and classical) and movies to its offerings.

Searching Amazon.com

To access Amazon.com, type *www.amazon.com* in the Address box. You'll see the latest version of Amazon.com's home page (Figure 9-3). The home page contains interesting news and offers, but let's search.

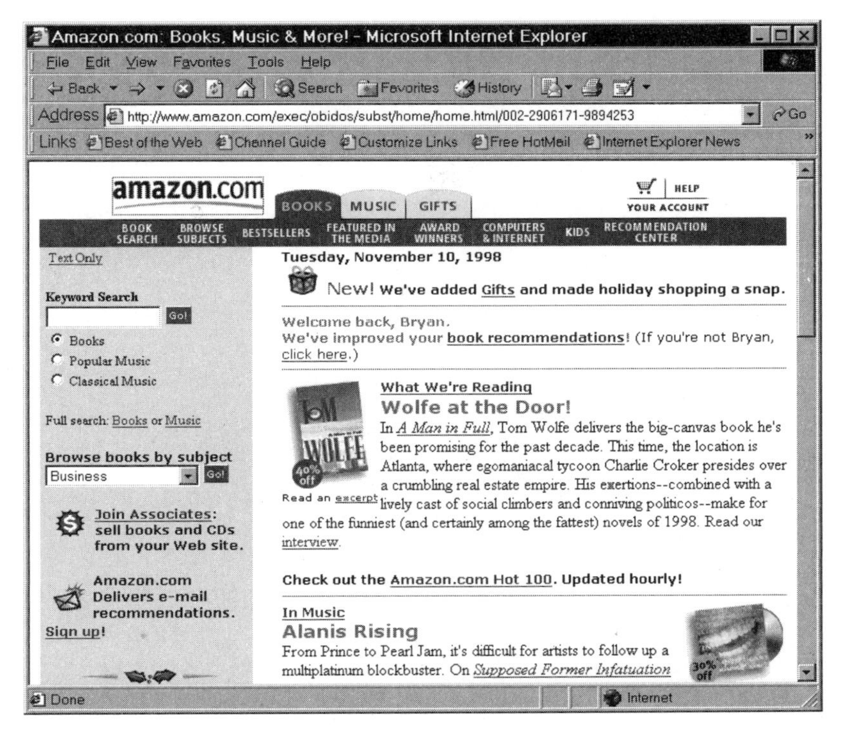

FIGURE 9-3.
You can search Amazon.com by author, ISBN, title, and combinations of these.

Suppose you're curious to see what one of the greatest science-fiction writers of all time, Robert Silverberg, has been up to lately. Let's try an author search. Find the search options, and click the option that enables you to search by author. Follow the search instructions, and you'll see a list. If you click one of the listed books (they're organized in reverse chronological order and also by availability), you'll see a page describing the book. You may also see a synopsis, links to published literary reviews, customer reviews, and even the author's own comments. You can even contribute your own review if you wish.

The first time you fill out a Web-based form and upload the data, you'll see a dialog box asking whether you'd like to turn on AutoComplete, a feature that can supply previously typed information in certain form fields. This is a genuine time-saver, but think twice about using it if other people often use your computer. Some other user could upload your personal information without your knowledge or consent.

Adding Items to Your Shopping Cart

If you find something you like, add it to your virtual shopping cart by clicking the button. (Adding items doesn't commit you; you can Adding remove them later.) If you'd like to find more books, click Continue Shopping. If you're ready to check out, click Proceed To Checkout.

Checking Out

When you proceed to checkout, you'll have the option of selecting the Amazon.com secure server. By all means, do so; it isn't safe to upload your credit card information in cleartext (non-encrypted text). When you're connected to the secure server, you'll see a lock icon in Internet Explorer's status line (lower-right corner in Figure 9-4).

You can tell you're connected to a secure server in other ways, too:

- **Look at the URL.** When you're connected to most secure servers, you see *https://* instead of *http://* in the Address bar.
- **Choose Properties from the File menu.** Click the Certificates button to see security information for this document. You'll see the site certificate.

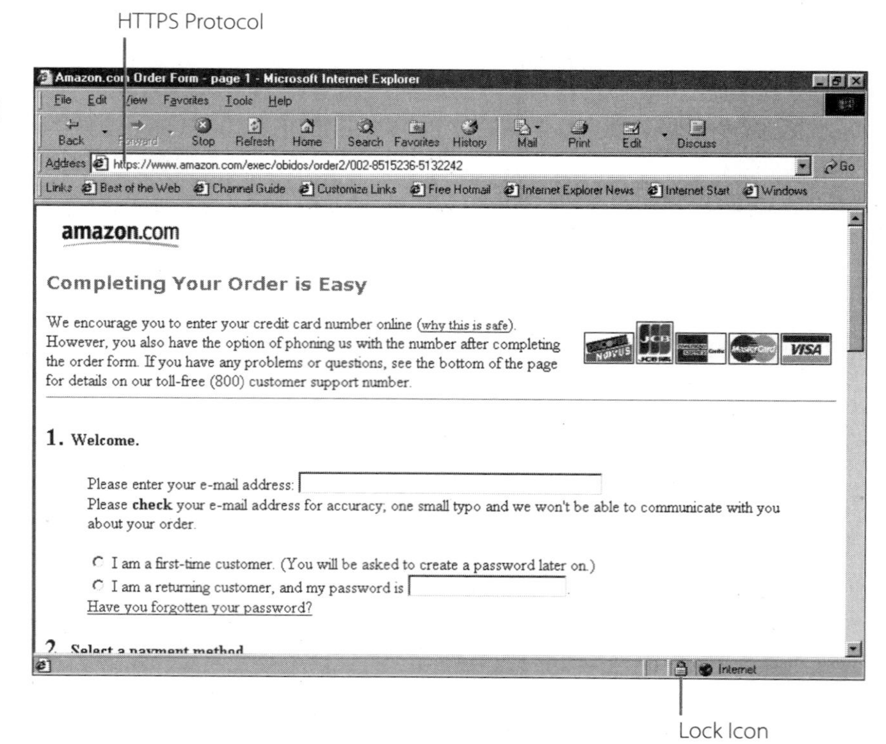

FIGURE 9-4.
When you're connected to a secure server, you see a lock icon in the program's status bar.

To complete your order, continue filling out the on-screen forms. You can choose gift-wrapping, payment methods, and delivery options. When you finish your order, you'll see a confirmation screen; you'll also receive notification by e-mail when your order is processed and again when it's shipped.

Using Microsoft Wallet

Microsoft Wallet safely stores address and credit card information, and makes this information available to online shopping sites that support Wallet. This information is protected by a password so that other users of your computer cannot view this sensitive data.

Before you use Wallet, you configure Wallet with your shipping address and credit card information, as described in the following sections. (You can define more than one credit card; when you shop, you can choose which one you want to use.)

Once you've configured Wallet, online shopping is much easier. When you're shopping at an online store that supports Wallet, your shipping address and credit card information are automatically supplied after you type your password—no more tedious typing. If you wish, the online store can place a copy of your sales receipt on your computer. Wallet enables you to view and manage these receipts, and even to track your order's progress online.

For secure online submission of your information, Microsoft Wallet uses SSL security. What's more, Wallet includes programming "hooks" that will enable Internet vendors to implement the industry-wide Secure Electronic Transaction (SET) standards, which will provide further safeguards against credit card fraud.

Configuring Microsoft Wallet

Microsoft Wallet is conveniently built into Internet Explorer. To store information in Microsoft Wallet, follow these steps:

1. From the Tools menu, choose Internet Options.
2. Click the Content tab.
3. In the Personal Information area of the Internet Options dialog box, click Wallet. You'll see the Microsoft Wallet dialog box.
4. In the Microsoft Wallet dialog box, click Addresses.

5 Click the Add button to display the Add A New Address dialog box, shown in Figure 9-5.

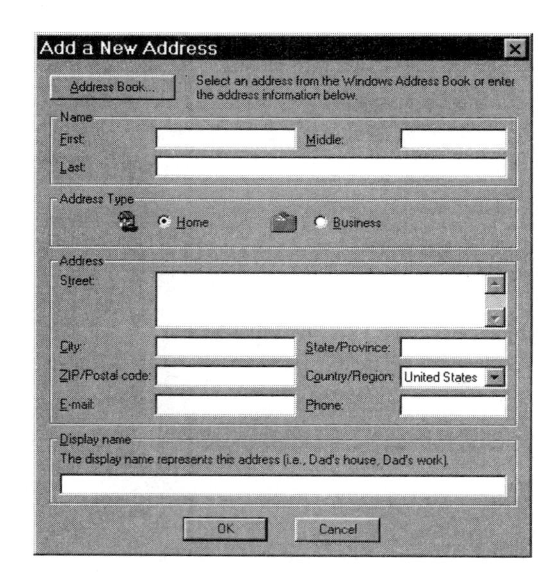

FIGURE 9-5. Adding a new address is simple.

6 Type your information in the Add A New Address dialog box. You can specify whether this is home or business information by selecting the Home or Business option.

7 When you're done, click OK. Leave the Microsoft Wallet dialog box on-screen, so you can configure your payment information (see the next section).

If you've already added your name and address to the Windows Address Book, just click Address Book to select this information instead of retyping it.

Now add your credit card information by following these steps:

1 In the Microsoft Wallet dialog box, left on-screen from the previous procedure, click Payments. You'll see the Payment Options dialog box.

2 Click Add and select the type of credit card you want to add. The Add A New Credit Card wizard appears. Read the introductory page and click Next.

3. Enter your credit card information and a display name (Figure 9-6). The display name lets you quickly identify your credit cards. Choose a name that is meaningful to you, such as Bryan's Corporate Card or Chelle's Debit Card. Click Next.

FIGURE 9-6.
Be sure to enter your credit card information exactly as it appears on your card.

4. You can choose the billing address for your credit card from the addresses you've already entered, or you can enter a new address. After you've specified the address, click Next.

5. The final page of the wizard requires you to select a password. This is important. The password is the key to your credit card information, so select it carefully and then enter it into both boxes.

   Click Finish, and you're done.

If you need to change any of this information, return to the Address Options or Payment Options dialog box, select the address or card to change, supply your password, and click Edit.

Where can you use Wallet? Find out at Microsoft's Wallet Directory (www.microsoft.com/wallet/directory/default.asp). Some examples: The Bombay Company (www.bombayco.com), Hudson's Bay (www.hudsonbay.com), and Universal Studios (store.universalstudios.com).

Selected Secure Shopping Sites

Here are some places to start your Internet shopping spree. Load up with the latest CDs, a brand new stereo, and some gourmet snacks before you hop on the plane to Hawaii.

- **CDWorld** (www.cdworld.com/). One of the best CD stores on the Internet, this site offers a convenient search engine that lets you scan more than 100,000 discs by artist's name, title, or recording label.
- **iMALL** (www.imall.com/). Here's an Internet shopping mall that's beautifully organized on a familiar plan—a real shopping mall! Among the goods you'll find for sale are housewares, arts and collectibles, specialty items, electronics, gourmet foods, computer gear, gifts, books, and more.
- **Internet Shopping Network** (www.internet.net/). If you're skeptical about Internet shopping, this is the place to start. You'll find very hot deals on computer and electronics equipment (some of the best deals around). You can see a picture of what you're buying and get full technical information; you generally get much more than you'd find in a print-based catalog.
- **Travel Now** (www.travelnow.com/). This secure site offers hotel and airline reservations, tours, cruises, and travel packages. An excellent feature is the hotel search page that enables you to search for the best rate.

Viewing and Managing Receipts

Wallet can automatically store digital copies of your sales receipts on your computer. You can then view and manage these receipts, and even track orders online.

TIP

If you do not want Web servers to store receipts on your computer, click the Receipts tab, click Advanced, and check Never Save A Receipt On My System From A Web Page.

Ready, Get SET, Shop!

With Microsoft Internet Explorer, you can send your credit card information through the Internet so securely that even the world's top spy agencies couldn't crack it. But once it gets to the vendor, what happens? It's decoded into cleartext (plain, readable text), and the vendor must manually process the information. Unfortunately, this means that your credit card information is visible to the firm's employees.

That visibility is the last remaining security hole in Internet commerce, and it's serious. Pilferage at the vendor level costs credit card holders and issuers millions of dollars annually. You take exactly the same risk when you order over the telephone. In fact, you take an even greater risk because you are telling people your number over an insecure phone line, which is easily intercepted by anyone with a modicum of knowledge and a few inexpensive snooping devices. If you use a portable phone, you might be broadcasting this information to your neighbors! So pilferage isn't a problem that's unique to Internet commerce. It's characteristic of mail-order/telephone-order (MOTO) transactions, too. In fact, with the Secure Electronic Transaction (SET) mechanisms, ordering over the Internet will soon become the most secure way you can do business.

Here's why. The SET standards create a three-way connection between you, the vendor, and the credit card issuer. That's great for the vendor because the authorization process becomes automatic; employees don't have to spend time obtaining the authorization manually. And it's even greater for you: no one from the vendor sees your credit card information. You submit your information via Microsoft Wallet, and it remains encrypted as it passes through the vendor's computer and on to the authorization process. All the vendor sees is an authorization code.

SET was jointly developed by a consortium of credit card issuers (including Visa and MasterCard) and industry practitioners (including Microsoft Corporation). Once the implications of this technology ripple through the economy, and people realize how safe Internet ordering will become, Internet commerce will gain momentum and grow very quickly. For now, SET is just being implemented, so don't expect many sites to give you this protection.

To use receipts, you need to choose a password. To choose a password, follow these steps:

1. In the Microsoft Wallet dialog box, click the Receipts tab. You'll see the Receipts Password dialog box.
2. In the Password box, type your password.
3. In the Confirm Password box, type your password again.
4. Click OK.

To change your password, click the Receipts tab, click Advanced, and click Change Password.

To view your receipts, just click the Receipts tab. You'll see the Receipts page, shown in Figure 9-7.

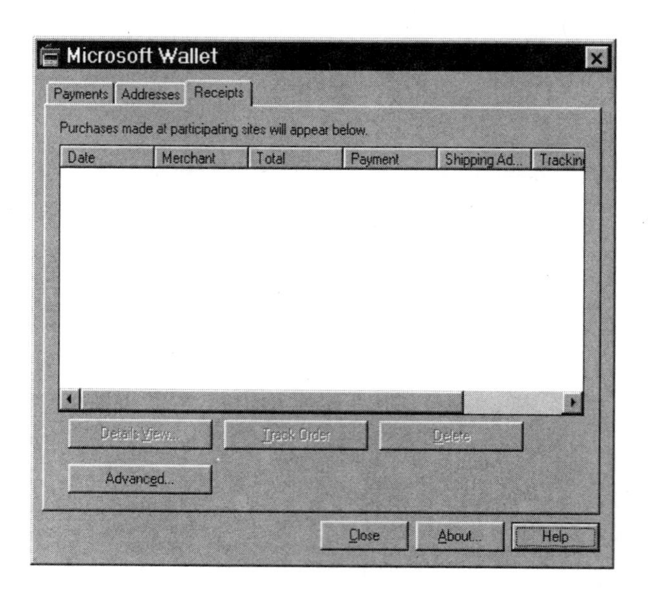

FIGURE 9-7. Wallet keeps digital copies of your sales receipts; in this dialog box, you can manage these receipts.

You can manage your receipts in the following ways:

- **Switching between views.** Click the Details View button to switch between the Details View and Reports View.
- **Tracking orders.** To track an order, select the receipt and click Track Order.
- **Deleting receipts.** Select the receipt you want to delete, and click Delete.

- **Changing view options.** Click Advanced, and choose a field in the Field Name dialog box. Choose a field width and sort order. Repeat these steps for additional fields. To change the field used to sort receipts, choose a field in the Sort Field list box. Click OK when you're done.

Using Microsoft Wallet

When you shop at an online vendor that supports Microsoft Wallet, you needn't do anything special.

Safeguarding Your Privacy

When asked why they don't shop on the Internet, many people say they're worried about privacy. They're probably worried about the confidentiality of their credit card information. As the previous section explains, Internet Explorer's security technology should give you confidence about shopping online. But people are also concerned about snooping—especially by marketers who collect information without their consent or knowledge, and then sell this information to marketing database companies. If you're concerned about privacy, this section shows you how Internet Explorer can help safeguard personal information while you're online.

Understanding How Web Sites Track Information About You

Many Web users are under the impression that you can browse the Internet in perfect anonymity, without anyone knowing which sites you've visited. This impression is false. Every time you visit a Web site, you risk leaving a great deal of information about yourself, including possibly the organization or company with which you're affiliated, your geographical location, the type of computer and operating system you're running, the browser you're using, the Internet address of the computer you're using, the exact time and date of your visit, and the pages you've looked at and how long you looked at them.

SEE ALSO
For information on downloading cookies selectively or turning off cookies altogether, see "Choosing Security Options," page 297.

The means to collect, store, and analyze this information is your own computer, used without your consent or knowledge. Many servers write files to your hard disk—called *cookies*—that compile additional information about you.

At many sites, the use of cookies is innocent enough; the goal is simply to tailor the site to your benefit. Cookies were introduced by Netscape

Communications to get around a problem in Web access—namely, that it's difficult for one page to pass information to another page without adding lots of incomprehensible codes to the URL. Cookies provide a way for one page to leave information for another page. At many sites, this information is used to record your preferences. For example, Microsoft uses cookies to record your start page and MSNBC preferences. That's why it's possible to customize these pages.

But not all cookies are used so innocently. Several marketing firms have figured out how to use cookies to track your movements through the several dozen commercial sites with which the company contracts. This advertising firm is building a database that tracks browsing behavior. This information helps Web advertisers to target their markets more effectively. If you've visited any of the sites that contract with this firm, there is a cookie on your hard drive that gives you a unique identification number. The more you visit these sites, the more likely it is that you'll start seeing advertising that reflects your interests.

Is this activity in your best interest? After all, you'll see ads tailored to your preferences. Privacy advocates worry that this monitoring activity goes far beyond the transaction monitoring common in the retail world; it amounts to surveillance concerning which store windows you've looked into. Worse, they say, it's done without the user's knowledge or consent. And to add insult to injury, it employs your own hard drive. However, Internet marketing companies insist that they do not try to associate individual names with this data. The cookies assign a unique numerical ID to your computer, and that's the only information that's used to match previous browsing preferences with advertising. What worries privacy advocates is the prospect that a marketing firm might start trying to associate this unique numerical ID with your actual identity. This information could then be sold to other companies, which might use it to send you junk snail mail (or even junk e-mail). It could also be stored in databases and sold to private investigators, prospective employers, or other interested parties.

TIP

> Like to see your cookies? Look for a directory named Cookies somewhere in your Windows directory. (Depending on your version of Windows, it might be buried a few levels down.) There they are! Don't think that you can prevent new ones from being written by deleting the entire Cookies directory; Internet Explorer will simply write a new directory.

Should you worry about cookies? There's no evidence yet that cookies are being used to associate Web activity with actual peoples' identities. And you can block them. With Internet Explorer, you can block cookies completely, or download them selectively—although, as you'll find, you lose a good deal of the Web's functionality if you choose not to use cookies. If you block cookies, you won't be able to use customization features at many sites—and at some sites, you won't even be able to get past the front door. If you choose to download cookies selectively, you'll be pelted with dialog boxes that ask you to confirm cookie downloading. And a single Web page might hit you with a half-dozen cookies or more.

CAUTION
If you're using a computer at work, please follow your company's rules for appropriate use of the Internet. Many companies use software that monitors the Web sites you access. Some people think that clearing the disk cache and history list, as described in this section, covers up their Web-browsing "trails," but this may not be true if your company is using Web-monitoring software. What's more, the deleted cache and history files could be recovered by a knowledgeable technician. The techniques discussed in this section give you some protection against casual snoopers, but they cannot completely disguise Web activities that breach company guidelines.

Personally, I worry about what an unscrupulous marketer might do with cookie tracking, but I leave cookies on. I'm just not willing to give up so much Web functionality just to safeguard my anonymity.

Looking for a Site's Privacy Policy

The best protection against snooping doesn't come from disabling cookies, but from cautious browsing. In particular, watch out for *site-registration* forms, which ask you to divulge personal information. Often, you must supply such information to get access to the "premium" levels of the site, which are free, but restricted to registered users. What's going on here? Possibly, it's perfectly valid; the site just wants to know who's accessing the information. But the site might be planning to sell the information to database marketing firms. So it turns out that the site isn't "free" after all. You're paying for it in the form of increased time spent dealing with unwanted telephone and "snail-mail" advertising.

Most reputable Web-site owners understand that Internet users are concerned about the sale of personal information, so they've established privacy policies (see Figure 9-8). The best sites explain their privacy policies up front, and enable you to choose whether you want the company to share your information with other firms. Companies that adopt these policies deserve your appreciation and your business.

Cleaning Up Your Browser's "Trails"

If you're concerned about privacy, you may wish to clear the trails Internet Explorer creates that enable you to return to previously accessed sites more quickly. You may also wish to clear your History list.

SEE ALSO
If you have plenty of hard disk space, you can improve Internet Explorer's performance by increasing the size of the cache. For more information, see "Choosing Cache Options," page 281.

Clearing the Cache

When you browse with Internet Explorer, the program makes a copy of recently accessed Web pages. These copies are stored in a *cache*, a portion of the disk that is set aside for storing this information. With Internet Explorer, the cache is a system folder called Temporary Internet Files.

Should you return to recently accessed pages in the same or a subsequent browsing section, the program examines the cache to see whether a copy of the page is stored there. It also checks the page you're accessing to see whether the page has been updated since you last accessed it. If there's a copy of the page in the cache, and the page hasn't been updated since you last accessed it, Internet Explorer retrieves the page from the cache rather than the network. Since the program can get the document from the cache much faster than it can retrieve the page from the network, Internet Explorer appears to run more quickly. For this reason, the cache is a benefit and it greatly improves Internet Explorer's apparent performance.

There's a down side to the cache; it leaves a "trail" that shows where you have been browsing recently. While you're away from your computer, or if your computer is often used by others, a snoop could inspect your Temporary Internet Files folder and find out just what you've been doing online. For this reason, you may wish to clear the cache periodically, or even choose a setting that deletes all the cache contents (except cookies) when you exit Internet Explorer.

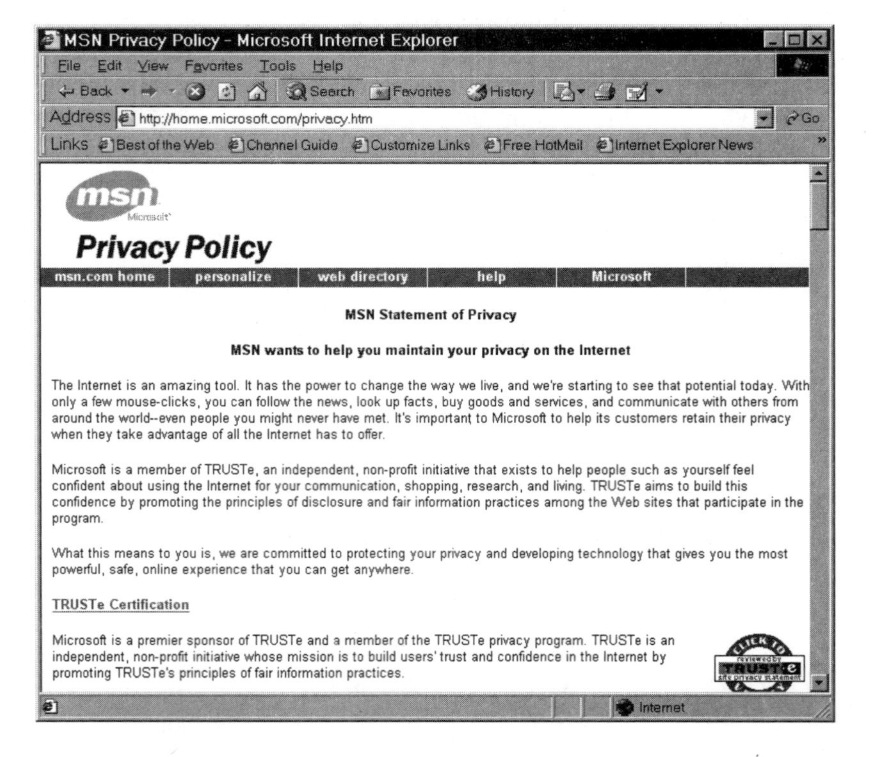

FIGURE 9-8.
At MSN.com, the privacy policy is made clear up front. To determine whether you're dealing with the best Internet businesses, look for a privacy statement such as this one.

To clear the cache contents, do the following:

1. From the Tools menu, choose Internet Options.
2. Click the General tab, if necessary.
3. In the Temporary Internet Files area, click Delete Files.
4. In the confirmation box, check Delete All Offline Content, if desired.
5. Click OK.

To clear the cache every time you quit Internet Explorer, do the following:

1. From the Tools menu, choose Internet Options.
2. Click the Advanced tab, if necessary.
3. In the Security area, check Empty Temporary Internet Files Folder When Browser Is Closed.
4. Click OK.

Clearing the History List

To clear the History list, follow these instructions:

1. From the Tools menu, choose Internet Options.
2. Click the General tab, if necessary.
3. In the History area, click Clear History.
4. Click Yes.

Disabling AutoComplete

By default, Internet Explorer version 5 uses AutoComplete. This feature makes typing easier by remembering what you type, and suggests word completions. Enabled by default, AutoComplete helps you type URLs in the Address box by listing possible matches from Web addresses you've visited before. AutoComplete also remembers what you've typed in forms, including personal information and passwords.

If your computer is used by more than one person, you can prevent your information from appearing when other people use the computer by defining multiple users, as explained in "Setting Up Microsoft Windows for Multiple Users" on page 151.

If you're concerned about snooping and wish to make sure that nobody can access AutoComplete information, you can disable the AutoComplete feature. To do so, follow these steps:

1. From the View menu, choose Internet Options. You'll see the Internet Options dialog box.
2. Click Content. You'll see the Content page.
3. In the Personal Information area, click AutoComplete. You'll see the AutoComplete Settings dialog box, shown here:

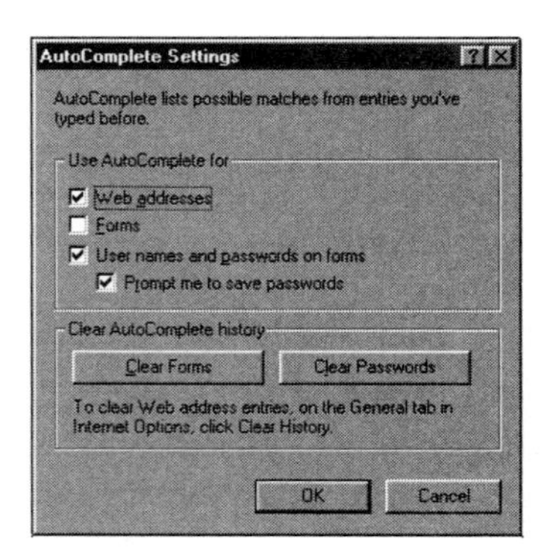

4. Uncheck the AutoComplete features that you don't want to use.
5. To clear all stored form entries, including passwords, click Clear Forms.
6. Click OK until you see Internet Explorer again.

Disabling Personal Information

For more information on the Address Book, see "Using the Address Book," page 394.

Microsoft Profile Assistant supplies your personal information when Web sites request it. It does so by supplying information from your personal entry in the Address Book. If you do not wish Internet Explorer to upload such information without your knowledge or consent, you must create an Address Book record with a dummy name, as described in the following:

1. From the Tools menu, choose Internet Options. You'll see the Internet Options dialog box.
2. Click the Content tab.
3. In the Personal information area, click My Profile. You'll see your personal information page from the Address Book.
4. Click Personal, and delete the information, if any appears. In the First Name box, type Anonymous, and in the Last Name box, type User.

5 Click the rest of the tabs, and delete any personal information that appears.

6 Click OK until you see Internet Explorer again.

Disabling Web-Site Hit Tracking

Internet Explorer contains a feature that enables Web authors to track your movements through their sites, including which pages you've viewed. This information is stored on your computer, and Web servers can read this information to learn about your browsing preferences on previous visits. Although this feature enables Web authors to tailor content to your preferences, you may wish to disable this feature. To do so, follow these instructions:

1 From the Tools menu, choose Internet Options. You'll see the Internet Options dialog box.

2 Click the Advanced tab.

3 In the Browsing area, disable the option called Enable Page Hit Counting.

4 Click OK.

Protecting Children

If children are using your computer, consider setting up the Microsoft Internet Explorer ratings system, which is based on the one created by the Recreational Software Advisory Council (RSAC). Thus far, RSAC has rated more than 35,500 Web sites.

You can set up Internet Explorer so that the program permits access to any Web site except those blocked by an RSAC rating that you select. For smaller kids, you can also set up the program so that it blocks any site that doesn't have an acceptable RSAC rating. (That's pretty inconvenient, though, since so few sites are rated.)

To use RSAC ratings with Internet Explorer, follow these steps:

1 Choose Internet Options from the Tools menu, and select the Content tab. You will see the Content options shown in Figure 9-9.

2 In the Content Advisor area, click Enable. Click the General tab. You'll see the the Content Advisor dialog box shown in Figure 9-10. Click Change Password. You'll see a password dialog box that asks you to type and confirm a password. Make sure this is something your kids won't figure out or find written down.

3 Click OK to confirm your password. (You'll type this password each subsequent time you access your ratings settings; nobody else will be able to get into them.) You'll see the Content Advisor dialog box again.

4 Click the Ratings tab to see the Ratings page (Figure 9-11). Consider whether you want to prohibit sites that have no rating—which is most of the Web—or to enable the supervisor to type the password to access sites that have no rating. The latter is the default setting, and it's the only realistic choice.

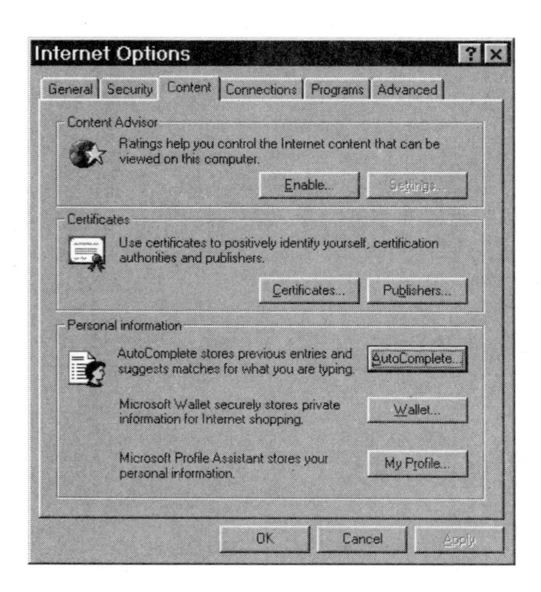

FIGURE 9-9.
From the Content tab, choose Settings to set ratings.

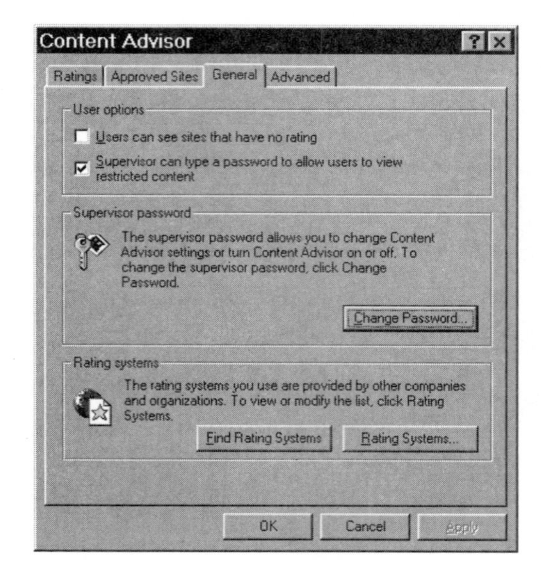

FIGURE 9-10.
You can choose to prohibit all sites that don't have ratings, but you will block most of the Web.

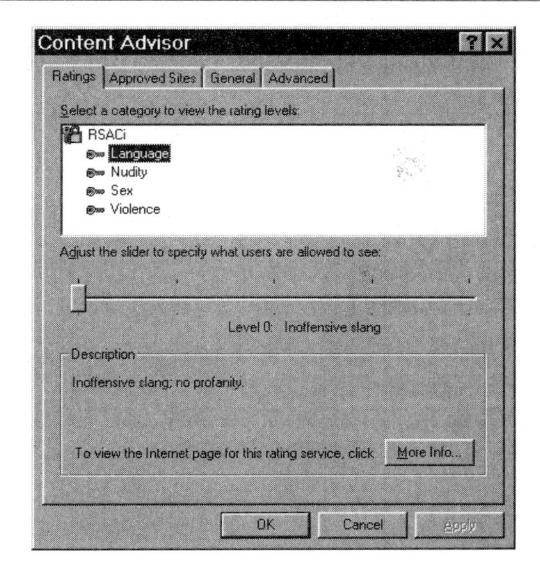

FIGURE 9-11.
In the Content Advisor, choose rating levels for language, nudity, sex, and violence.

5. Click a category, and move the slider to the level you're willing to permit.
6. Repeat step 5 until you've chosen levels for all the categories.
7. Click OK to confirm.

If you try to access a site that doesn't have a rating, you'll see the dialog box shown in Figure 9-12. This dialog box comes up often, since only a tiny fraction of the Web's sites are rated. You'll probably get tired of this pretty quick, so go to the Tools menu, select Internet Options again, click Content, and click Disable.

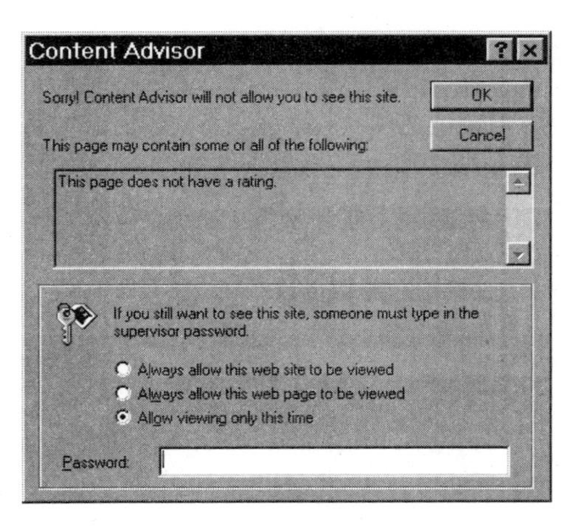

FIGURE 9-12.
A dialog box appears when you try to access a site with no rating.

The Recreational Software Advisory Council Ratings

RSAC uses the following numerical ratings to describe the violence, profanity, nudity, and sex in a rated Web site. To compare these to familiar movie ratings, 1 equals PG and 2 resembles PG-13. A rating of 3 is close to R, and 4 gets into the NC-17 area. In my opinion, the RSAC's system is more informative than movie ratings because it goes into detail about the exact nature of the offending content.

Violence

1 Creatures injured or killed, damage to realistic objects, fighting with no injuries

2 Humans or creatures injured or killed, rewards injuring non-threatening creatures

3 Blood and gore, rewards injuring non-threatening humans, rewards killing non-threatening creatures, accidental injury with blood and gore

4 Wanton and gratuitous violence, rape

Language

1 Mild expletives

2 Expletives, nonsexual anatomical references

3 Strong or vulgar language, obscene gestures

4 Extreme hate speech, crude language, explicit sexual references

Nudity

1 Revealing attire

2 Partial nudity

3 Nonsexual frontal nudity

4 Provocative frontal nudity

Sex

1 Passionate kissing

2 Clothed sexual touching

3 Non-explicit sexual activity, sexual touching

4 Explicit sexual activity

For more information on RSAC, see www.rsac.org/.

It's nice that this ratings feature is included. It can be so restrictive that you can enable it while you're out and feel pretty secure that your kids won't be able to access porn sites (or much of anything else, for that matter). But it's really not a complete solution. It doesn't provide much protection against the sexual predators who are trying to get to our children. I prefer "net nanny" programs, such as CyberPatrol, that block incoming and outgoing data at the network level. These put restrictions in place for every Internet application that your kids use, including newsgroups, e-mail, FTP, Internet Relay Chat (IRC), and other browsers. There's another great protection against predators: CyberPatrol can be configured to prevent kids from uploading personal data about themselves, such as their phone numbers and addresses.

Understanding Security Settings

Internet Explorer's *security settings* enable you to download software from the Internet with confidence. And that's all to the good. Used with caution, software downloaded from the Internet can greatly enhance your computer. Web sites can come alive with plug-ins, ActiveX controls, and Java applets. You can also download freeware, shareware, and commercial programs—more than one million of them—and install them on your computer. But there's a risk—specifically, a risk of *rogue content*, broadly defined as any downloaded content that's designed to cause trouble. It's not nice to think about, but more than a few miscreants spend much of their time figuring out how to trick unsuspecting Internet users into downloading rogue content. The consequences could amount to little more than an annoyance—but they could be worse. A virus designed to embarrass unsuspecting users attaches itself to Microsoft Word and posts copies of your documents to 23 newsgroups with titles such as, "Make Money Fast" or "Princess Diana's Secrets Revealed." At the worst, a virus could wipe out your entire hard drive.

Internet Explorer enables you to protect yourself from rogue content, as this section describes. Although the program's default settings are good for general use, you'll be wise to understand how Internet Explorer defines security zones and enables you to choose security settings for each zone. Once you've grasped the basic concepts, you can use active content and download software with confidence.

Recognizing the Dangers

Computer security involves a trade-off. If you want your computer to be *totally* secure from rogue content, you must be willing to give up on the goodies the Internet can offer. In this section, you explore the risks of using content that could make your Internet experience more engaging and productive.

- **ActiveX Controls.** These are mini-programs that are designed to enhance Internet Explorer's features, and they do this job very well. A lot of the cool functionality available on MSN.com, for example, stems from ActiveX controls that add functionality to Internet Explorer. But there is a risk. ActiveX controls have full access to your computer's file system, so it's quite possible for pranksters and vandals to create rogue ActiveX controls that could destroy data on your computer. For this reason, ActiveX controls are supposed to be *digitally signed*, thus attesting to their origins in reputable quarters (an established software company). *Unsigned* ActiveX controls could pose a threat. Most don't, but you don't want to open your computer to unsigned ActiveX controls when you're exploring the Internet away from the trustworthy sites.

- **Java applets.** Java is a programming language that enables Java code to run on many different computer systems. Java applets can add interesting functionality to Web pages, such as weather maps, mini-spreadsheets, and chat rooms. Unlike ActiveX controls, Java applets are designed to run in a "sandbox," kept at arm's length from your computer's file system. Still, some computer security experts worry that rogue programmers will figure out ways to create destructive Java applets.

- **Scripts.** Scripts are mini-programs written in a scripting language, such as JavaScript or VBScript. Many Web pages have scripts—indeed, *most* of the Web pages you'll visit at trustworthy sites, including MSN.com, use scripts. Although scripting languages are designed to prevent rogue programmers from harming your system, various unforeseen security holes have been discovered in these languages. The leading browser companies, Microsoft included, have quickly patched these holes, but security experts worry that vandals may discover new security flaws in the future.

- **Computer Viruses.** These scourges are mini-programs that are designed to copy themselves by attaching to useful programs, and then modifying these programs so that they spread the virus. Most viruses are nuisances, but a growing number of them are destructive, and sometimes viciously so. If you're worried about viruses, bear in mind that viruses require some kind of executable software to spread; typically, this means that viruses infect programs, but not data files. However, a new category of viruses, *macro viruses*, can infect the data files created by application programs that can run macros. A macro is a stored series of keystrokes that, when replayed, carries out a sequence of actions. In an infected data file, a rogue macro could instruct your computer to erase all your data files.

Here's the trade-off. You can use the Internet with complete peace of mind if you disable ActiveX controls, Java applets, and scripts, and never download *any* files. But you need to consider whether you've burned down the house to roast the turkey. Most of the active content and software you're rejecting helps make the Web much more fun. What's more, it's the key to interactivity at some of the Internet's best sites—including MSN.com, from which you have nothing to fear.

SEE ALSO

For information on creating custom security settings for your security zones, see "Customizing Security Settings," page 301.

Understanding Security Zones

Internet Explorer defines four different security zones, each of which can have a default security level. You can change the security level, or create custom security settings for each zone.

Which zone are you in? You see the current zone on the status line, as shown in Figure 9-13.

Internet

Current Security Zone

FIGURE 9-13. The status line indicates the current security zone.

- **Internet Zone.** This zone is the open, external Internet. The default security level is Medium, which enables you to access safe content without confirmation. To use potentially destructive content, you must approve the content by clicking OK in a confirmation dialog box.
- **Local Intranet Zone.** This zone is a local area network where you can be reasonably certain that you won't run into damaging content. The default security level is Medium Low.
- **Trusted Sites Zone.** You can set up a trusted sites zone for Low security, as long as you're sure you can really trust the sites. You need to set this up by adding sites to a list. This is an appropriate setting for a small office/home office network.

- **Restricted Sites Zone.** If you plan to visit sites that you're nervous about, you can assign these High security. You need to set this up by adding sites to a list. You won't be able to use the interactive features of these sites.

Adjusting Security Levels

Should you wish to adjust the default security levels, you can do so—but I don't recommend it. You should browse the Web with Medium security, and you should browse local area networks with Medium Low security. These settings are fine for most purposes. If you have compelling reasons to change these settings, you can do so by following these instructions:

1. From the Tools menu, choose Options. You'll see the Internet Options dialog box.
2. Click the Security tab. You'll see the Security options, shown in Figure 9-14.

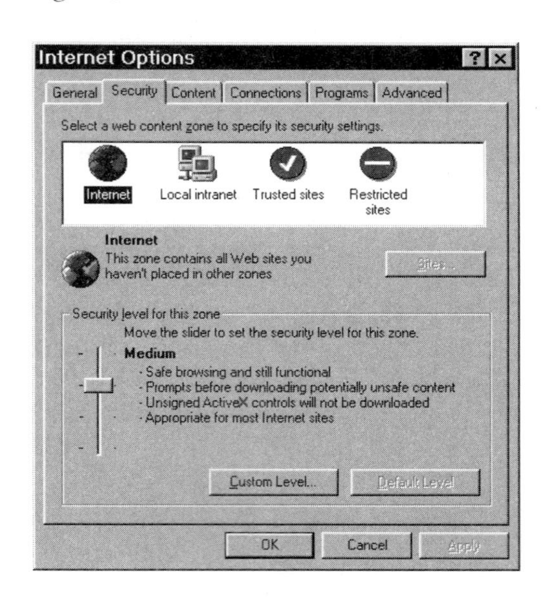

FIGURE 9-14.
In the Security options page, you can choose the security level you want for each of the four security zones.

3. Select the security zone you want to change. You can choose from Internet, local intranet, trusted sites, or restricted sites.
4. Drag the slider bar to select the security level you want.

   If you would like to restore the default security level, click Default Level. (This button is dimmed if the slider bar is positioned at the zone's default security level.)

5 Click OK.

Adding Web Sites to Security Zones

By default, Internet Explorer detects when you're connected to a local area network, and assigns the default security level (Medium Low). The program also detects when you're connected to the Internet, and assigns the default security level (Medium) for the Internet zone. For Trusted Sites and Restricted Sites, you must tell Internet Explorer which sites to include in these categories.

To assign a Web site to a security zone:

1. On the Tools menu, click Internet Options.
2. Click the Security tab.
3. In the Zone list, select Trusted Sites or Restricted Sites.
4. Click Sites. You'll see a dialog box that enables you to add sites to this zone.
5. In the text box titled Add This Web Site To The Zone, type the URL of the site you want to add (such as the fictitious http://www.malevolent_site.org).
6. Click Add.
7. Repeat steps 5 and 6 until you've added all the sites that you want to associate with your Trusted Sites or Restricted Sites profiles.
8. Click OK until you see Internet Explorer again.

Using Active Content

Now that you understand how Internet Explorer protects you from rogue content, you can examine the various types of active content that you'll encounter on the network. This section introduces plug-ins, Java applets, and ActiveX controls, and explains their benefits and security risks.

Using Plug-Ins

Before Java and ActiveX, the only way browsers could be made truly interesting was by means of *helper applications* (accessories, like Media Player, that jump in whenever an unusual file is encountered), or *plug-ins,* which give the browser new capabilities. The great thing about plug-ins is that they blend with the browser, sort of like a Vulcan mind meld. After installing the plug-in, the browser can cope with the data type of that plug-in without any help from an external application. When you visit a site that uses a plug-in, you'll see a dialog box that lets you know that a plug-in is needed (Figure 9-15).

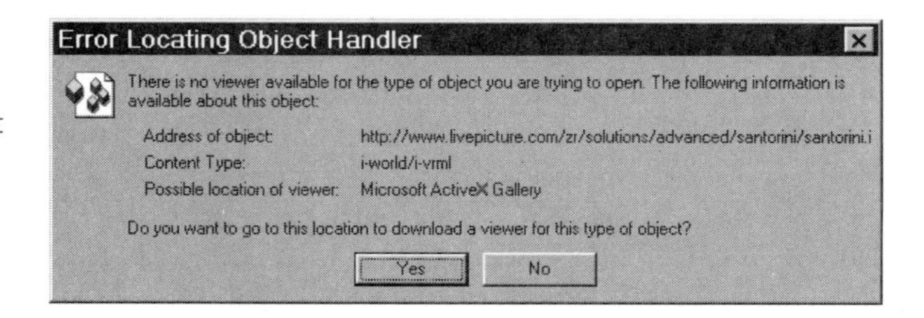

FIGURE 9-15. If a Web page calls for a plug-in that you don't have, you'll see this dialog box.

Plug-ins have their downside, though. Most of them are big—1 MB or more in size—and take a long time to download. Once they're downloaded, you must install them, and that often means you must restart your computer. This operational stuff really interrupts your surfing! For this reason, most people don't like plug-ins, and very few of them have become popular. Their functions are being replaced by Java applets and ActiveX controls (discussed later in this chapter).

If you encounter a Web site that uses a plug-in, click the link that enables you to download the file. You'll see the File Download dialog box. If you're confident that the file's source is reliable, click Run This Program From The Internet and then click OK. The File Download dialog box lets you know how much time will be needed for the download.

NOTE

HELP! It says the download will take 3 hours!

If the file's too big, skip it by clicking the Cancel button. You might want to return later and download it when you won't need to use your computer for a while or when your connection costs are lower.

Once you've finished downloading the file, Internet Explorer detects that you're about to run an executable (.exe) file and warns you that the security of this file can't be guaranteed (Figure 9-16). As you'll see, with ActiveX programs, you'll be able to view the software publisher's certificate of authenticity. But this precaution isn't possible with plug-ins.

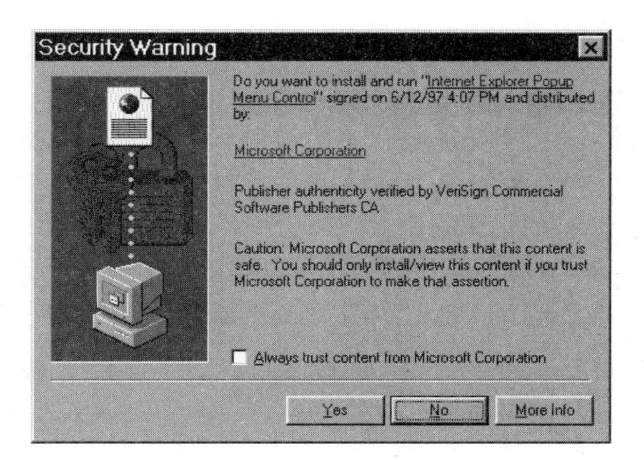

FIGURE 9-16.
A dialog box warns you that the file you're about to download might not be safe for your computer.

If you're sure you're downloading the plug-in from a reputable place, such as a major commercial site or an established organization, click Yes. Otherwise, click No to cancel.

After you click Yes, you'll see a Setup program for the plug-in. Follow the on-screen instructions to install the program on your computer.

Running Java Applets

A creation of Internet pioneer Sun Microsystems, the Java programming language enables professional programmers to prepare mini-programs called *applets* that download along with a Web page. After all the Java instructions are downloaded, the Web page you're viewing becomes much more interactive. For example, there are a number of Java-based mortgage calculators on the Web, and each of them enables you to type in numbers (such as the amount you want to finance) and immediately see the result of the computation. What's great about this is its immediacy: you don't have to wait for data to be uploaded to a distant server or for the server's results to be downloaded back to your computer. The software needed to process the data is right there on your computer, and the results display almost immediately. Another way to put this is that Java enables *client-side processing*; the processing occurs on your computer rather than on the server.

Trusted Java Sites

The following sites offer excellent examples of Java applets, and you can be reasonably certain that you won't run into a prank program if you visit them.

- **Gamelan** (www.gamelan.com). You'll discover over 3,000 applets at this well-organized site.
- **Java Center** (www.java.co.uk/javacentre.html). There are lots of applets to try, plus information and links.
- **Java Applet Rating Service** (www.jars.com). Here you'll find ratings of hundreds of popular applets. Check out the top 25.

Is it safe to download Java applets?

Good question. By design, Java applets run in a *virtual machine*, a simulated computer that doesn't have access to your computer's file system. Also called a *sandbox*, this virtual machine is supposed to prevent rogue Java applets from doing harmful things. However, some computer experts wonder whether there might be some hidden flaw in Java that would enable a clever prankster to get out of the sandbox and do some damage. Also, the word *sandbox* is well chosen because the limitations placed on Java applets mean that they aren't as useful for really serious work that involves storing data on disk. Still, Java is safe enough to use, as long as you're careful about where you download from.

Using ActiveX Controls

Microsoft's new ActiveX technology enables Web authors to prepare mini-programs, called ActiveX controls, which can be downloaded to run on your computer. These programs help bring Web pages to life, with effects such as live audio and scrolling banners. In this sense, ActiveX controls resemble Java applets, but there are at least two major differences. ActiveX offers the security protection that Java lacks, and ActiveX controls can be written in any popular programming language, including Java and Microsoft Visual Basic.

As an Internet Explorer user, you don't need to worry about the sophisticated technology that underlies ActiveX. You just need to devote some thought to whether you should download the control or not.

If you encounter a site that has an ActiveX control, Internet Explorer checks to see whether the control has been digitally signed. A digitally signed control has been independently certified to be free from computer viruses or destructive effects. If the control has been digitally signed, you'll see the certificate shown in Figure 9-17. It's safe to install this software, and you'll probably want to choose the options (below the certificate) that hide this message for additional controls made by the same company.

When the control doesn't have certification, you see an alert box. This notice doesn't mean you're about to download a destructive program;

it just means that the author hasn't obtained certification. If you're downloading the program from a trusted site, and you're sure you've backed up all your important work, click Yes. If you're rummaging around in college students' home pages, though, or if you have any reason to suspect that the site you're accessing isn't all that it says it is, click No.

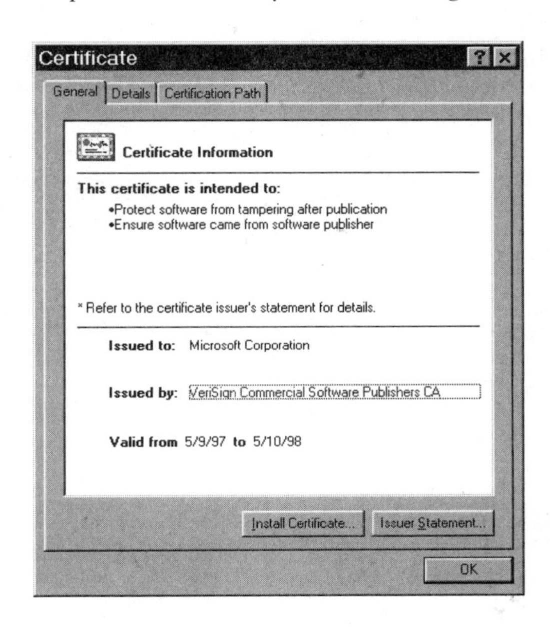

FIGURE 9-17.
An Authenticode certificate identifies controls that have been independently evaluated for safety.

Downloading Software

At last count, some 1,000,000 freeware or shareware programs were available on the Internet—that's right, a million! (The term *freeware* refers to programs that are copyrighted but can be freely redistributed, as long as distribution is not done for commercial gain. *Shareware* refers to programs that require payment of a registration fee if you want to keep using them.) These programs range from the not-very-impressive efforts of beginning programmers to highly professional, full-featured programs.

Searching for Software on the Internet

Looking for freeware or shareware? Here are two great places to start:

- **Microsoft Free Product Downloads** (www.microsoft.com/msdownload). For Microsoft Windows users, this is a computer playground from heaven (Figure 9-18). You'll find free TrueType fonts, games, accessories for Microsoft Internet Explorer and Microsoft Office products, monthly content updates for Cinemania and

Music Central, Windows 98 updates and upgrades, and tons more. When you visit, be sure you have lots of free disk space!

- **shareware.com** (www.shareware.com). This outstanding Web site (Figure 9-19) is a production of CNET; it enables you to search a database of more than 190,000 freeware and shareware programs by typing one or more key words. The search engine searches the product description database as well as the file name, so chances are good that you'll find what you're looking for, if it exists at all.

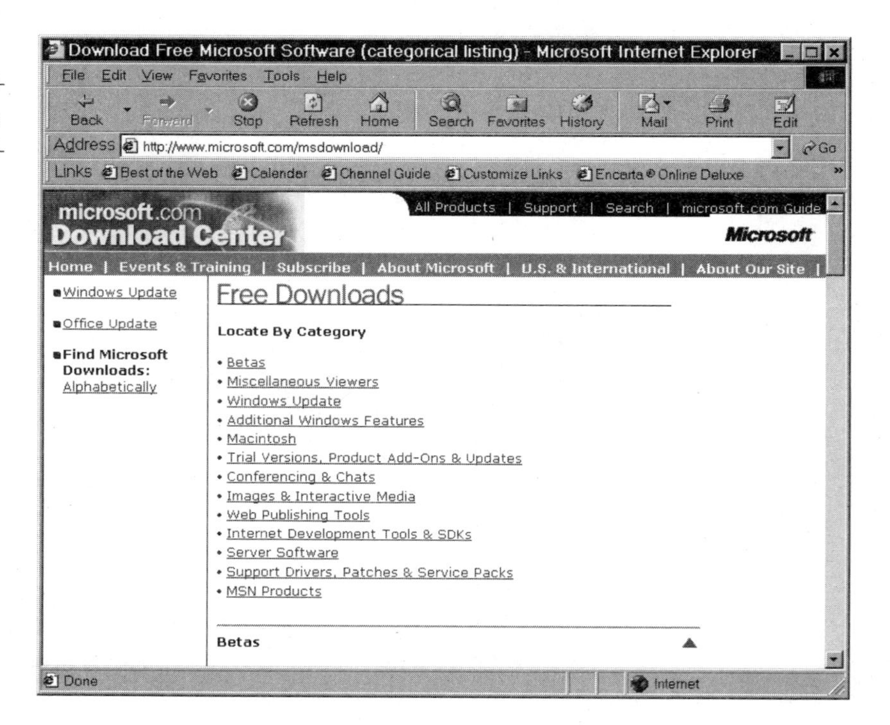

FIGURE 9-18.
The Microsoft Free Product Download site is a treasure chest of goodies for Windows users.

Deciding Whether to Download Software

If you click a link to a downloadable program, you might see the dialog box shown in Figure 9-20. Are you sure the file is from a trustworthy source, such as Microsoft's Free Product Download page? If so, choose one of the following options:

- **Open it.** If you choose this option, Internet Explorer will download the file and look for an application that can open it. If the file is an executable (.exe) file, Internet Explorer will tell Windows to run it. If it is a compressed (.zip) file, Internet Explorer will look for a decompression program, such as WinZip for Windows. If the file is a document (.doc), Internet Explorer will open the document with Word for Windows. As long as you have installed software that can deal with files with the same extension as the one you're downloading, this is the best option.

- **Save it.** If you choose this option, Internet Explorer will download the file to your hard disk. You'll see a Save As dialog box, enabling you to specify where the file should be stored. This is the best option if you don't have a program capable of opening the file. You can open it later after you obtain the necessary program.

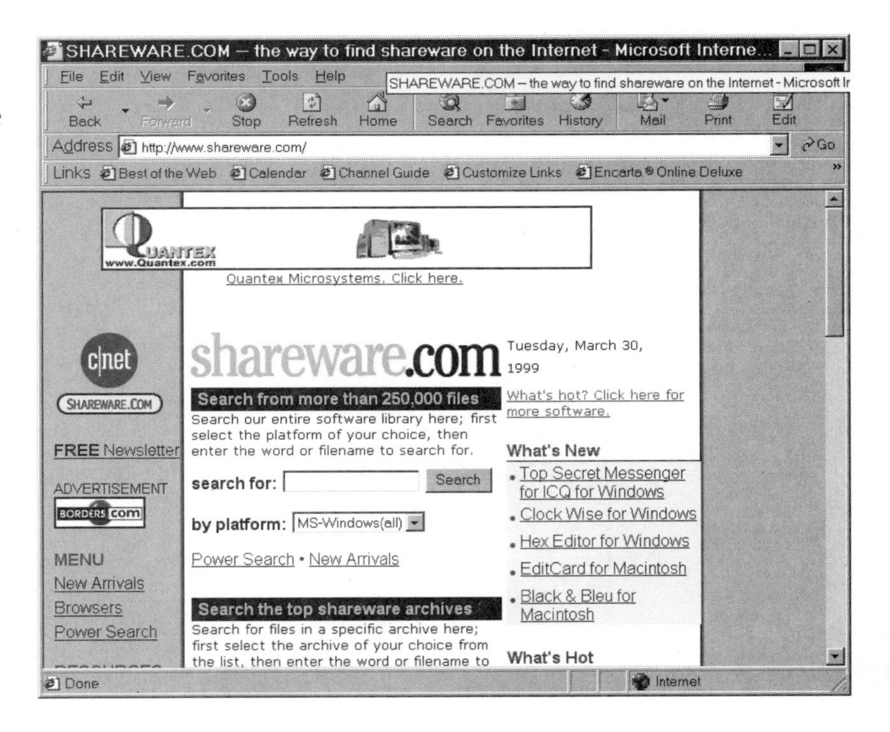

FIGURE 9-19.
At shareware.com, you can search an extensive collection of shareware and freeware.

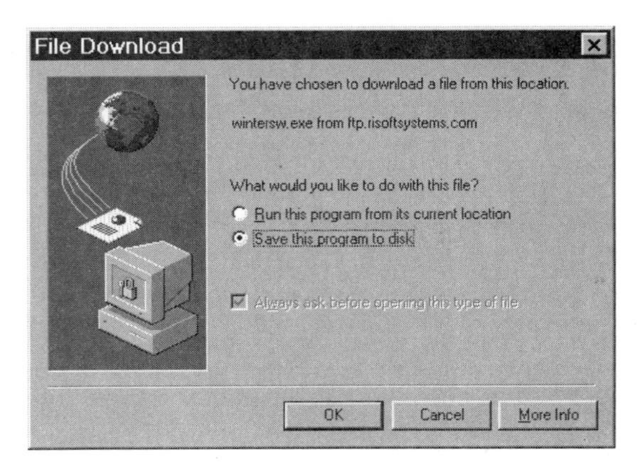

FIGURE 9-20.
When you download a file, you can either open it immediately or save it to a disk.

About Computer Viruses

It isn't much fun to think about, but hundreds—perhaps thousands—of programmers worldwide are busily trying to create rogue programs, called *viruses,* that are capable of harming computer systems and data. A computer virus replicates itself at will, infecting your computer and traveling outward by means of disk and Internet file exchanges. Why do virus authors create these vexing programs? Their motivations vary, but they stem from an inability or unwillingness to put technology in context, that is, to realize that there are people involved in computing. Virus authors focus narrowly on trying to outwit the software industry, which is doing all it can to prevent you-r computer from getting infected.

In the past, you could avoid computer viruses by using safe computing practices, but the rise of the Internet has created a new distribution medium for virus authors. In safe computing, you never run programs unless you've obtained them from a reputable source. With so many shareware and freeware programs on the Internet, though, how can you be sure your sources are reputable?

The safest course of action is to avoid downloading software altogether, but this takes away much of the Internet's fun and usefulness. A reasonable compromise is to download with caution. Begin by establishing a regular backup program so that your valuable data is protected if you should encounter a virus, despite all your precautions. If you're searching for a program, use a reputable search service to locate and download software from the Internet, such as CNET's shareware.com. If you know which program you're looking for, search for the software company's home page and download it directly from there. (You'll also be assured of getting the most recent version of the program.) Be careful that the page you're accessing really is the company's home page and not some imposter loaded with rogue programs. Don't ever download executable files from a Usenet newsgroup!

Above all, don't succumb to virus paranoia. I've seen too many users panic when something seems odd about their computer systems. The problem is often just a minor software glitch, which can be cured by a good, healthy restart. Also, remember that there are plenty of virus hoaxes on the Internet; they're all designed to make fools of novices. To avoid getting hoodwinked, bear in mind that viruses can propagate only by means of executable programs. They aren't present in graphics files or e-mail.

If you suspect that you've contracted a virus, check out the AntiVirus Research Center (www.symantec.com/avcenter/index.html). You'll learn about the latest virus and rogue program threats (the real ones, that is). Here's one to watch out for. There's a fake version of PKZIP (PKZIP300.EXE or PKZ300B.EXE), the popular file compression program, that reformats your hard drive. You should also consider purchasing an anti-virus program, which scans your computer's drives and memory for viruses.

TIP

It's a great tool for Windows computing, but a necessity once you've got your Internet connection: a program that can decompress .zip files. The standard in this area is WinZip for Windows 95, Windows 98, and Windows NT, available for downloading from Nico Mak Computing's home page (www.winzip.com/). The program is shareware and requires a registration fee of $29.

About Windows Software Security

If you chose the Open option when you began downloading an executable (.exe) file, you might see the alert box in Figure 9-21 when the download is complete. This alert box appears if you've downloaded an automatic software installation program, which is very common on the Web. The message informs you that the software has not been digitally signed by the publisher. Don't be alarmed; very few of the programs you'll download have been signed in this way. Digital signatures are used mostly for ActiveX controls, described in the previous section. As long as you're still sure that you downloaded the software from a reputable source, choose Yes to open the program and let it make changes to your system.

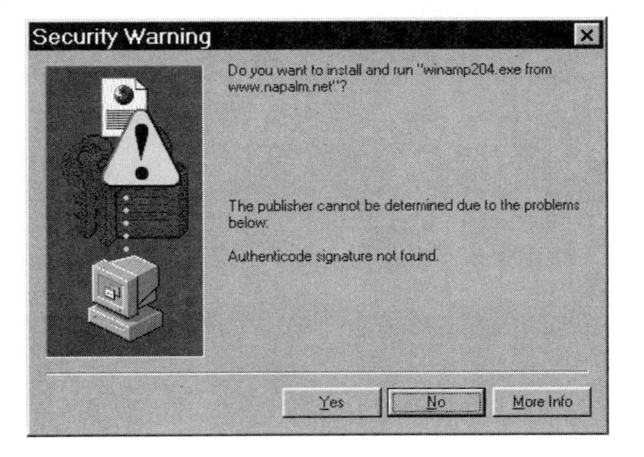

FIGURE 9-21.
When downloading an unsigned program, you might see a security warning.

Downloading the File

While the file is downloading, you'll see a message box that keeps you informed of the download's progress (Figure 9-22). If Internet Explorer is able to determine the size of the file, you'll see a progress indicator that shows visually how much of the file has been downloaded. In addition, you'll see an estimate of how much time is required to complete the download. While downloading is in progress, you can return to the Internet Explorer window and browse other sites.

If you're using Internet Explorer on a 14.4 or 28.8 Kbps modem, avoid downloading more than one file at a time. Internet Explorer doesn't prevent you from doing this; you can click file after file, and the program will keep downloading. But your Internet connection will bog down to the point that each of the downloads slows to a crawl. One at a time, please!

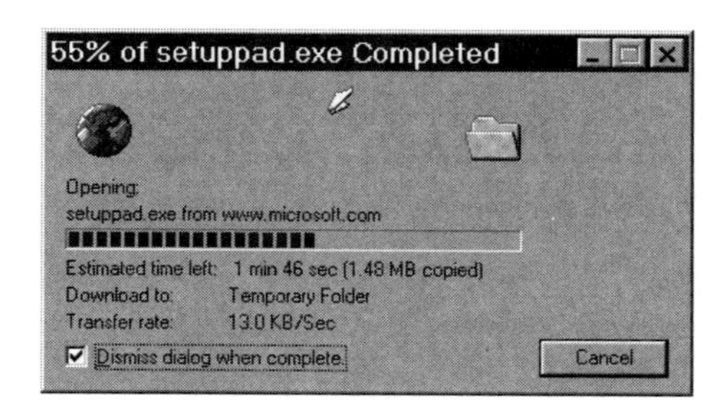

FIGURE 9-22. Watch your selected file travel through the Internet and into your computer.

Accessing FTP Sites Directly

You can download files, as just discussed, by clicking a downloading link on a Web page. But Internet Explorer can also directly access FTP sites. (Remember, FTP is short for File Transfer Protocol. It's a standard protocol for exchanging files on the Internet.)

Using FTP, you can access anything that's stored on the file system of an FTP-accessible computer. In fact, full FTP access lets you get into the file system of another computer and actually control the computer remotely. Yes, it's true. With full FTP access, you can delete files, overwrite them, open and modify them, and generally wreak havoc. I'm sure you can appreciate why most FTP-accessible computers demand a login name and password before such access is granted.

But there's another type of FTP service that isn't so persnickety about access. It's called *anonymous FTP*—"anonymous" because you don't need to supply a user name and password when you access the server. To be sure, the access you get is read-only. You can't erase or modify the files you find, but you can download them, and that's good enough to make anonymous FTP a valuable resource. Organizations make anonymous FTP services available to provide public access to shareware programs, public documents, and freebies of all kinds.

Accessing an Anonymous FTP Server

With Internet Explorer, you can access anonymous FTP sites in two ways:

- **Click an FTP hyperlink in a Web page.** Hyperlinks to FTP sites look the same on the screen as hyperlinks to other Web sites do. If you've enabled the full display of addresses by turning off the Show Friendly URLs option in the Internet Options dialog box, you can see what kind of site you're about to access by moving the pointer over the hyperlink and looking at the status line. If it's an FTP site, you'll see an address that begins with *ftp* instead of *http*.
- **Type the address to an FTP site directly.** You can choose the Open command from the File menu or, even better, type the address in the Address box.

Navigating FTP File Directories

The best thing about FTP is that it lets you directly navigate the file directories of a distant computer. That's also the worst thing. Navigating the directory structure will seem like a step backward into yesteryear's computer interfaces. It will help enormously if you're familiar with the concepts of directories and subdirectories—remember MS-DOS? Actually, most of the computers you'll access with anonymous FTP are Unix machines. Unix is a very powerful and not very user-friendly operating system. But don't let that throw you. The directory structure of Unix is much like that of MS-DOS for the simple reason that MS-DOS (beginning with version 2.0) incorporated Unix-like directories and subdirectories.

Here's a terminology refresher course, in case Windows has dimmed your recollection of MS-DOS terminology. A *directory* is a list of files (usually in alphabetical order). A *subdirectory* is a directory within a directory. If you select the subdirectory, you see a new directory—a new list of files. But you might want to get back to the *parent directory,* the directory that's one level "above" the subdirectory you're in right now. (With Windows, we now speak of *folders*, and *folders within folders*.)

When you first access an anonymous FTP server, you might find yourself at the upper level of the directory tree, at the *root directory* (Figure 9-23). If so, you will want to look for a directory named /pub (Figure 9-24). That's where the goodies usually are. A good FTP hyperlink will land you at the top of the /pub directory.

To open a subdirectory, just click it. It's much easier to navigate directories with Internet Explorer than it is with MS-DOS or Unix. Internet Explorer turns the items in directory lists into hyperlinks, so all you need to do is click the item you want. Presto! You see a new page with yet another directory—unless the item you clicked is a resource, such as a program, graphic, or sound. Clicking a hyperlink to a resource produces the appropriate action: programs download, graphics display, and sounds play (assuming you have the correct helper program installed).

To get back to a parent directory, scroll to the top of the page. You'll often find a hyperlink called something like "up to the parent directory" or perhaps "up to higher-level directory." (A link that's simply two periods is a Unixism that means the same thing.) Click this hyperlink to go up to the parent directory.

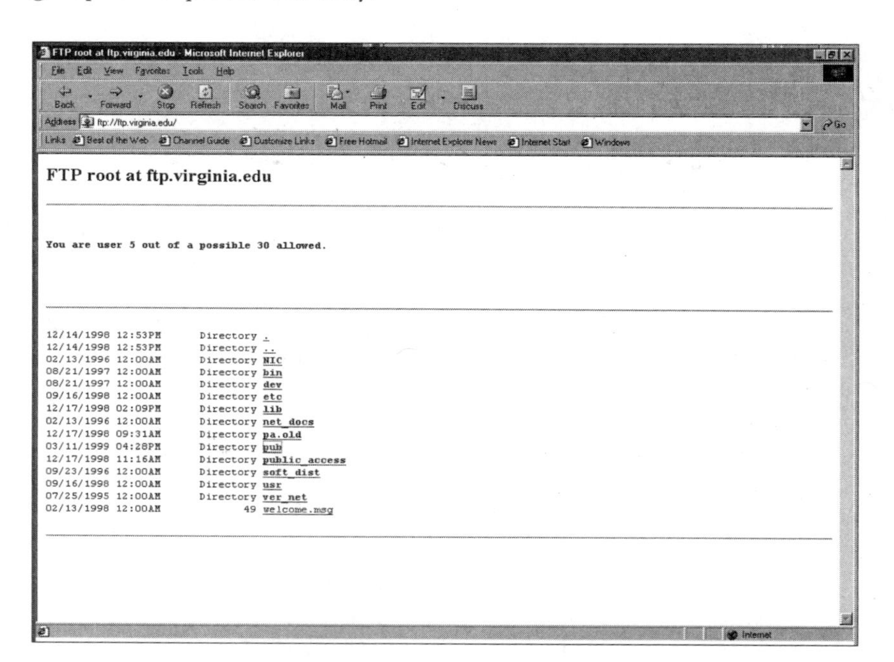

FIGURE 9-23.
The root directory is the upper level of the directory tree.

Downloading Files with Internet Explorer

If you've chosen to view your desktop in Web View, you can access anonymous FTP sites within Internet Explorer. To do this, you'll need the name of a public FTP site, such as ftp://ftp.microsoft.com or ftp://ftp.download.com. When you've successfully accessed the FTP site, you'll see the FTP directory. Navigate the FTP site's directories by clicking directory names; to go back up one level, simply click the Back button.

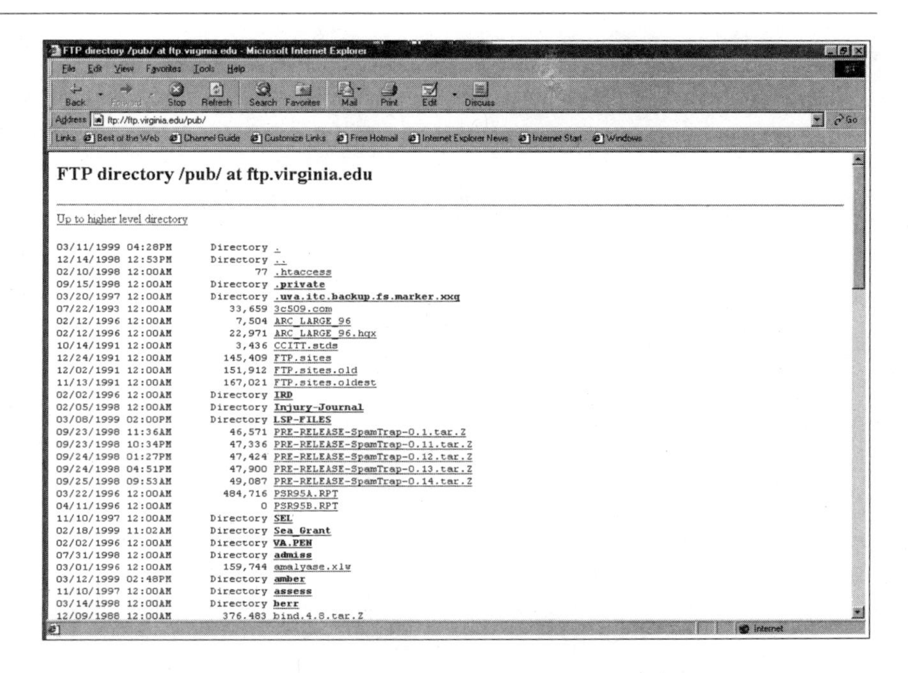

FIGURE 9-24.
The /pub directory of an anonymous FTP server shows the files you want to access.

When you see a file you'd like to download, click it. You'll see the File Download dialog box, discussed in the previous section. If you're confident the file is safe, click the Open option and continue just as if you'd clicked a download link on a Web page.

If you didn't choose Web View when you installed Internet Explorer, you can do so now. In any Windows Explorer or My Computer window, click View on the menu bar and choose As Web Page. (If you see a check mark next to As Web Page, the Web View is already selected.)

CHAPTER 10

Personalizing Internet Explorer

You can customize Microsoft Internet Explorer so that the program looks and works the way you prefer. Is customization worth the effort? Yes, emphatically. On the toolbar, for example, you can delete icons you don't use, reducing the screen's visual complexity. In addition, the time you spend organizing your favorite sites is very well spent. With a few minutes of dragging and dropping, you can transform the Favorites menu into a personalized tool for information access, one that will help convince you that the Web is definitely worth using.

In this chapter, you'll learn how to customize the toolbar, improve Internet Explorer's performance, customize the Search Assistant, organize your favorite sites, create custom security profiles, and much more.

Customizing the Toolbar

For information on displaying, moving, and sizing the toolbars, see "Introducing the Toolbars," page 98.

New to Internet Explorer version 5 is a completely customizable Standard Buttons toolbar. Just as you can customize the toolbar in Microsoft Office applications, you can decide which Internet Explorer buttons you want to display, how they're sized, and whether they contain explanatory text. In this section, you learn how to customize the Standard Buttons toolbar so that it looks just the way you want.

Deciding Which Buttons to Include

To customize the toolbar, right-click the toolbar background, and choose Customize from the pop-up menu. You can also click View on the menu bar, choose Toolbars, and choose Customize from the submenu. You'll see the Customize Toolbar dialog box, shown in Figure 10-1.

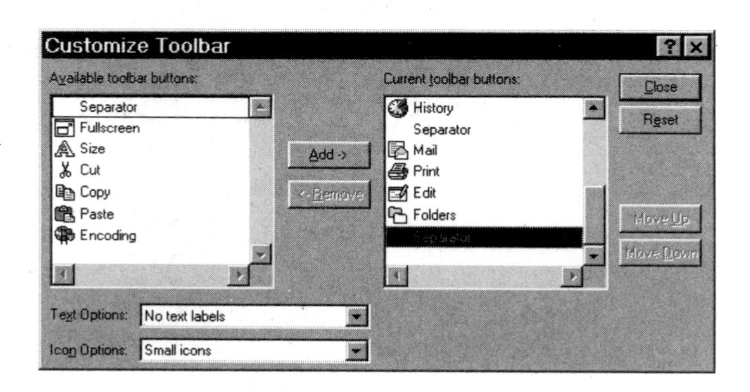

FIGURE 10-1.
In this dialog box, you can customize the Standard Buttons toolbar by adding or removing buttons. You can also select options for text display and button size.

In the Customize Toolbar dialog box, you can delete existing buttons, add buttons to the toolbar, organize buttons by placing separators between buttons, and change the button order. Table 10-1 explains which buttons are available, and what they do.

You may see more or fewer buttons, depending on which applications you've installed. For example, the Mail button does not appear if you didn't install Outlook Express. If you installed Microsoft Office 2000, you'll see a Discussion button, which enables you to access Web-based discussions that may be available in your organization.

TABLE 10-1. Available Toolbar Buttons.

Button name	Purpose
Default buttons	
Back	Display the previous Web page. Same as choosing Go Back from the View menu, or pressing the Alt + left arrow.
Forward	Display the next Web page. Same as choosing Go Forward from the View menu, or pressing the Alt + right arrow.
Stop	Stop downloading the current page. Same as choosing Stop from the View menu, or pressing Esc.
Refresh	Download a new copy of this page from the network. Same as choosing Refresh from the View menu, or pressing F5.
Home	Display the default start page. Same as choosing Go Home Page from the View menu.
Search	Displays the Search explorer.
Favorites	Displays the Favorites explorer.
History	Displays the History explorer.
Mail	Launches Outlook Express if you chose to install this program.
Print	Prints the current document.
Edit	Displays your default HTML editor (FrontPage Express) if you chose to install this program.
Discuss	Enables you to collaborate with other Office users in a Web discussion. Note: You see this button only if you have installed Office 2000.
Buttons you can add	
Folders	Displays a folder explorer, like the one you see in Windows Explorer. This is a neat option if you use Internet Explorer to access FTP sites; you can drag and drop between the remote and local file directories. Note: You see this button only if you have installed Office 2000.
Encoding	Enables you to choose language encodings, so it's a good choice if you do a lot of work with foreign languages. Same as choosing Encoding from the View menu.
Fullscreen	Same as choosing Fullscreen from the View menu, or pressing F11.
Size	Enables you to choose text-size options. This is a good choice if you have restricted vision and often need to adjust text size. Same as choosing Text Size from the View menu.
Cut	Same as choosing Cut from the Edit menu, or pressing Ctrl + X.
Copy	Same as choosing Copy from the Edit menu, or pressing Ctrl + C.
Paste	Same as choosing Paste from the Edit menu, or pressing Ctrl + V.
Messenger	Accesses MSN Messenger, Internet Explorer's buddy list software. You see this option only if you have installed MSN Messenger.

Choosing Button-Display Options

You can choose the following options for the buttons on the Standard Buttons toolbar:

- **Show Text Labels** displays text labels within the buttons.
- **Selective Text On Right** displays text labels on the Back, Search, Favorites, and History buttons, but not the standard navigation buttons.
- **No Text Labels** hides text labels on all buttons.

You can also choose the icon size:

- **Large icons.** The large buttons look like the ones used in previous versions of Internet Explorer.
- **Small icons.** The small icons are designed to look like the ones you see in Microsoft Office.

You can combine text display and button-size options; for example, you can display small icons with selective text.

To change button-display options, follow these steps:

1. In the Customize Toolbar dialog box, click the down arrow next to the Text Options list box, and choose the text option you want.
2. Click the down arrow next to the Icon Options list box, and choose the icon option you want.
3. Click Close to confirm your options.

Removing Unwanted Buttons

Chances are you're happy with most of the default buttons, but perhaps you could do without one or two that you never use. If you later decide you would like to have these buttons on the toolbar again, you can add them by following the procedure in the next section.

To remove unwanted buttons from the toolbar, follow these steps:

1. In the Customize Toolbar dialog box, locate and select the button from the Current toolbar buttons list.
2. Click Remove. Internet Explorer moves the button to the Available toolbar buttons list.
3. Click Close.

Adding Buttons

To add buttons to the toolbar, follow these steps:

1. In the Customize Toolbar dialog box, locate and select the button from the Available toolbar buttons list.
2. Click Add. Internet Explorer moves the button to the Current toolbar buttons list.
3. To change the location of the newly added button, select it, and click Move Up or Move Down.
4. To add a separator between buttons, click Separator in the Available toolbar buttons list, and click Add. Click Move Up or Move Down to move the separator to the location you want.
5. Click OK to confirm your toolbar choices.

Adjusting History Tracking

By default, Internet Explorer tracks your Web-browsing history for the last 20 days. During this period, you can revisit previously accessed sites by clicking History on the Standard Buttons toolbar, and locating the item in the History explorer. In this section, you learn how to increase or decrease the period during which Internet Explorer retains history items.

To adjust history tracking, follow these steps:

1. From the Tools menu, choose the Internet Options. You can also access the Internet Options dialog box by opening the Control Panel and choosing Internet.
2. Click the General tab if necessary. You see the options shown in Figure 10-2.
3. In the History area, click the arrows to increase or decrease the number of days to keep history items.
4. If you would like to clear the items in the history list, click Clear History.
5. Click OK to confirm your history-list choices.

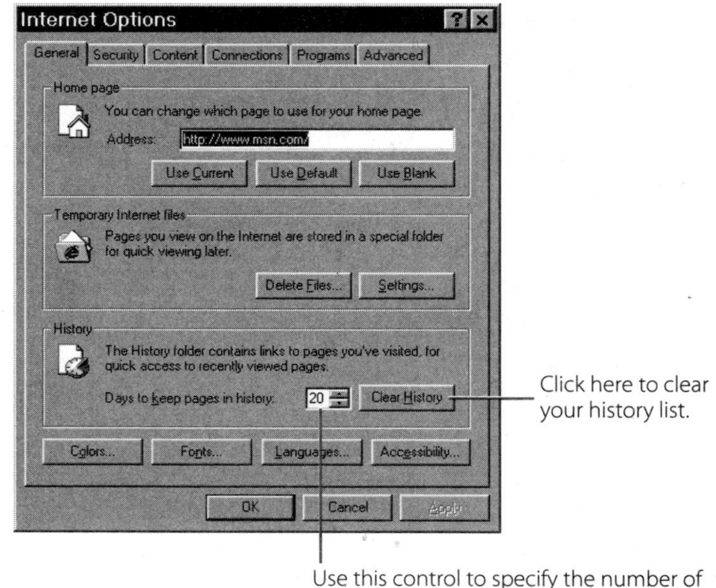

FIGURE 10-2.
In the History area, you can adjust the amount of time that Internet Explorer remembers the Web sites you've visited.

Choosing Multimedia Options

Multimedia files—pictures, animations, videos, and sounds—increase downloading time. If you're using Internet Explorer on a slow modem connection, you may wish to turn off automatic downloading of multimedia files. You can still view individual pictures if you wish.

Turning Off Multimedia

Here's what to do. Choose Internet Options from the Tools menu, and click the Advanced tab. In the Multimedia area of the Settings list (Figure 10-3), remove the check marks beside Show Pictures, Play Animations, Play Videos, Play Sounds, and Smart Image Dithering by clicking each one. Click OK.

After you turn off graphics, sounds, and video, the Web won't look or sound as nice, but it will download so much faster. In well-designed sites, you'll see *placeholders* (Figure 10-4) with text that describes what the pictures show.

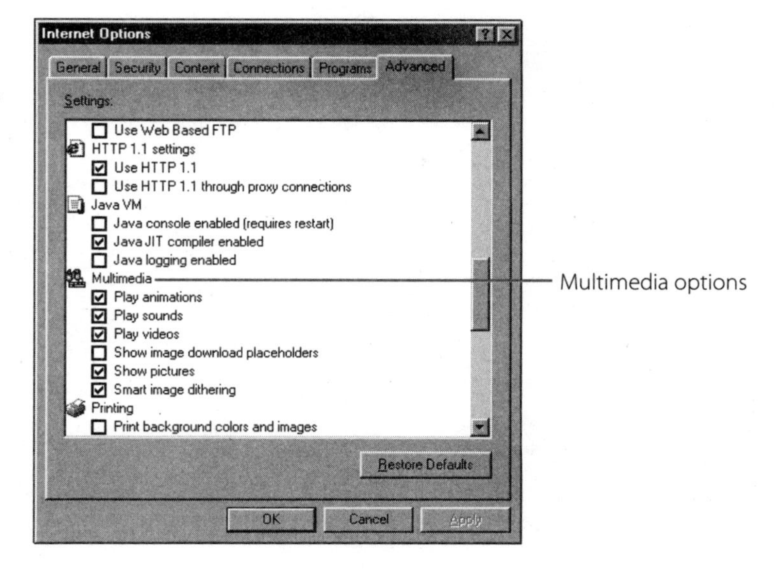

FIGURE 10-3.
You can turn off multimedia effects from the Internet Options dialog box.

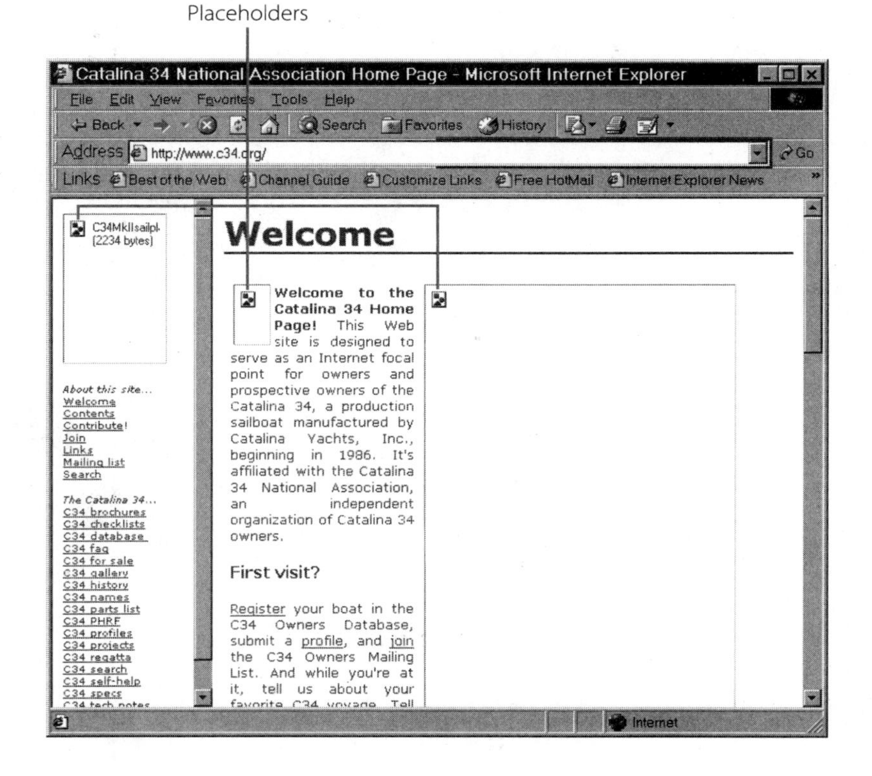

FIGURE 10-4.
Placeholders can appear instead of graphics after switching off multimedia.

If the page you are viewing contains pictures, you'll still see them after turning off multimedia. But don't worry; Internet Explorer is still working just fine. Your choices in the Internet Options dialog box affect only the new pages you download after turning multimedia off. To hide the pictures in the current page, click Refresh; this forces Internet Explorer to download a new copy of the page from the network.

Selectively Viewing Graphics

If you would like to see one of the pictures on a page, move the pointer to the placeholder, click the right mouse button, and choose Show Picture from the pop-up menu. You'll see just this one picture; the rest of the placeholders aren't affected (Figure 10-5).

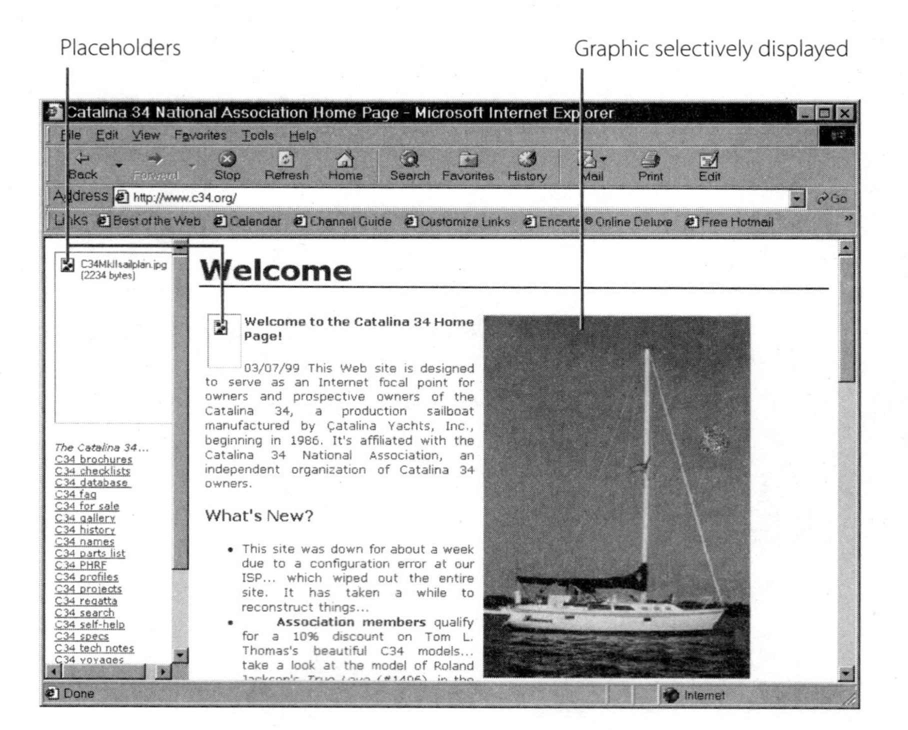

FIGURE 10-5.
This graphic has been displayed with the Show Picture command.

Restoring Multimedia

To view pictures and movies and hear sounds again, choose Internet Options from the Tools menu, click Advanced, and select all the multimedia options that you turned off earlier. This action won't affect the page you're viewing until you click Refresh on the Standard Buttons toolbar.

Choosing Cache Options

Like all good browsers, Internet Explorer keeps copies of previously accessed documents—including graphics, sounds, videos, and animations—in a cache. A *cache* is a special section of your hard disk that's set aside as an extension of a program's memory. In Internet Explorer, the cache is called Temporary Internet Files, and it's located in your hard disk's Windows folder.

You may be able to improve Internet Explorer's performance by adjusting cache options. You can change the frequency at which Internet Explorer checks for new versions of stored pages and increase the size of the disk cache. If you have more than one hard disk, you can move the cache to a disk that has more room.

To adjust cache options, display the Settings dialog box by following these instructions:

1. From the Tools menu, choose Internet Options. You'll see the Internet Options dialog box.
2. Click the General tab if necessary.
3. In the Temporary Internet Files area, click Settings. You'll see the Settings dialog box, shown in Figure 10-6.

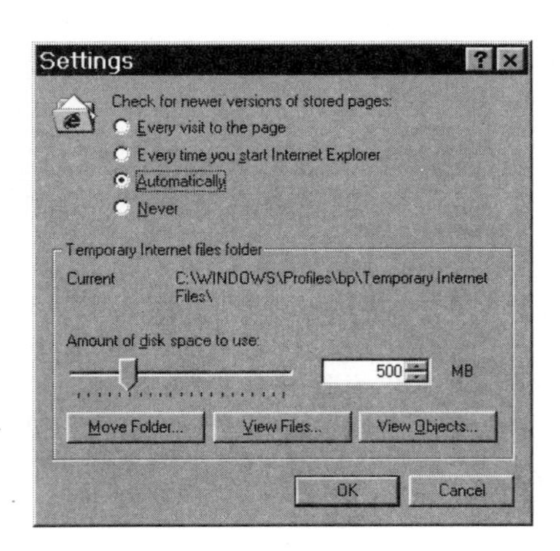

FIGURE 10-6.
In this dialog box, you can choose settings that affect how Internet Explorer stores temporary Internet files.

The following sections discuss the settings you can choose.

Adjusting the Cache Update Frequency

You can choose one of the following page update options:

- **Every Visit To The Page.** Internet Explorer will always check to see whether a page has changed before retrieving that page from the cache. Although this setting ensures that you will always view the latest version of a page, it slows down Internet Explorer's performance because every page (and every graphic on every page) must be retrieved from the Internet whenever you visit the site.

- **Every Time You Start Internet Explorer.** If you choose this option, Internet Explorer does not check for page changes if you revisit a page during the same browsing session. If you restart the program and revisit a previously visited page, the program checks to see whether the page has changed before retrieving that page from the cache.
- **Automatically.** This option works like the previous one (pages are not checked unless you restart the program), except the program performs a calculation to determine how often older pages appear to be updated. If a page does not appear to be updated often, the program does not check the page for changes, even after you restart the program.
- **Never.** This option never checks to see whether a previously accessed page has been updated. You must perform the check yourself by clicking Refresh.

CAUTION

You can greatly speed Internet Explorer's performance by choosing Never, but here's the risk: you might be looking at old or outdated copies of a page without realizing it.

Unless you choose the option that checks for updates every time you visit a page, there's a chance you're viewing content that has been updated since your last visit in the same Internet Explorer session. To make sure you're viewing the latest copy of a page, click Refresh on the toolbar. The Refresh command forces Internet Explorer to retrieve a fresh copy.

Increasing the Cache Size

The cache size directly affects your browsing speed. When Internet Explorer encounters a Web site, the program first checks to see whether there's a copy of the site and its various components, including graphics, in the cache. Next it checks to see whether anything on the page has changed since you last accessed it. If not, the program loads the page from your hard disk instead of the network.

Now you know why it's so much faster to go back (by clicking the Back button) than it is to access sites you've never visited. When you click Back, Internet Explorer restores the page by loading it from your computer's hard disk. When you access a site you've never visited before, the program must retrieve the page and its components from the network, which is much slower.

The cache speeds Internet Explorer's performance, but it fills up quickly. When it's full, the program erases previously visited pages to make room for copies of new ones. If you subsequently return to one of those previously visited pages, the program will not be able to find a copy on your disk, so it must retrieve a fresh copy from the network.

By increasing the size of the cache, you allow more room for storing copies of Web pages. You also increase the chance that the cache will contain a copy of a page that you previously visited. As a result, Internet Explorer will seem to perform more quickly, and that's definitely a good thing.

Where the Cache Is Stored

By default, Internet Explorer stores copies of the Web pages you access in a folder called Temporary Internet Files, within the Windows folder. This folder fills up very quickly with all the pages, graphics, sounds, videos, applets, and controls you're downloading.

TIP

How much disk space should you set aside for Internet Explorer's use? It depends on how much you have free. If you're using a 1.2-GB (gigabyte) drive and you've only used 220 MB (megabytes), you have lots of free space. You can set aside 15% of your drive (150 MB) and still have plenty of room for new programs and data.

How to Increase the Cache Size

To increase the size of Internet Explorer's cache, follow these instructions:

1. In the Settings dialog box, do one of the following:
   - Drag the slider to specify how much disk space to use.

     or

   - Type or select the number of megabytes (MB) to set aside for storage.
2. Click OK to confirm the new cache size.

NOTE

If you get low on disk space in the future, remember that you can free up lots of disk space—potentially dozens of megabytes—by reducing the size of the cache. You would return to the Internet Options dialog box and erase all the cache files by clicking Delete Files. Then, in the Settings dialog box, use the slider bar to reduce the amount of disk space set aside for cache files.

Moving the Cache

If you have more than one hard disk, consider moving the cache to a disk other than the one where you store Windows and your programs. Doing so will leave more space for new programs and enable you to choose a larger cache size.

Some hard disks have been divided into *partitions*, which appear as though they are physically separate drives. For example, some Dell notebook computers have only one hard disk, but the factory prepares the disk so that the computer apparently has two hard disks (drive C and D). On such computers, you can create more room for programs and more room for cache files by moving the temporary Internet files to drive D.

To move the cache to a different hard disk, do the following:

1. In the Settings dialog box, click Move Folder. You'll see the Browse For Folder dialog box, shown here:

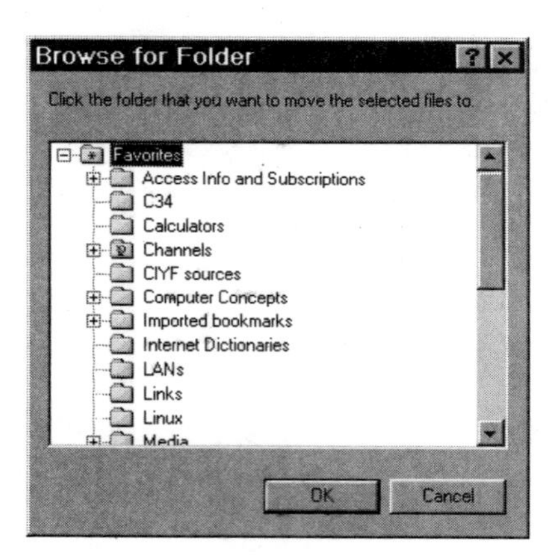

2. In the folder list, select the disk or folder in which you would like to store the temporary Internet files.
3. Click OK.

Viewing Cache Files

The Temporary Internet Files folder uses a special storage technique that prevents you from opening the stored files directly. However, you can use the View Files option to see information about each item in the cache, including the file's size, the date of last modification, the date on which you last accessed the file, and the date on which Internet Explorer last checked the file for an update.

> Although the View Files button enables you to view a list of files, this procedure does not enable you to view content offline. To view content offline, see Chapter 7, "Saving Content for Offline Browsing," page 169.

If you'd like to view the cache contents, follow these instructions:

1. In the Settings dialog box, click View Files. You'll see a Windows Explorer window that shows you a list of all the files stored in your computer's Temporary Internet Files folder (see Figure 10-7).

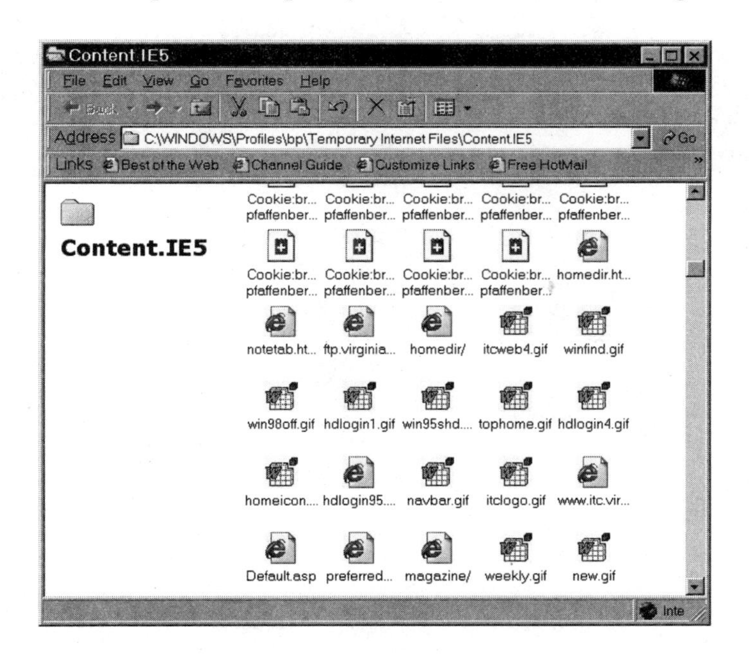

FIGURE 10-7.
The View Files button enables you to view a list of the files stored in the Temporary Internet Files folder.

2. To view information about a file, right-click the file name, and choose Properties. You'll see the information about the file in the properties dialog box, shown in Figure 10-8.

3. To return to Internet Explorer, close Windows Explorer.

Viewing Downloaded Objects

You can also view a list of the Java and ActiveX controls that you've downloaded and installed on your computer. To view a list of those controls, follow these steps:

1. In the Settings dialog box, click View Objects. You'll see a Windows Explorer window that shows you a list of all the files stored in the Downloaded Program Files folder.

2 To view information about an object, double-click the file name. You'll see the information about the file in the Properties dialog box, shown in Figure 10-9.

To see information about the files on which this object depends, click the Dependency tab.

To see version information, click the Version tab.

3 Click OK until you see Internet Explorer again.

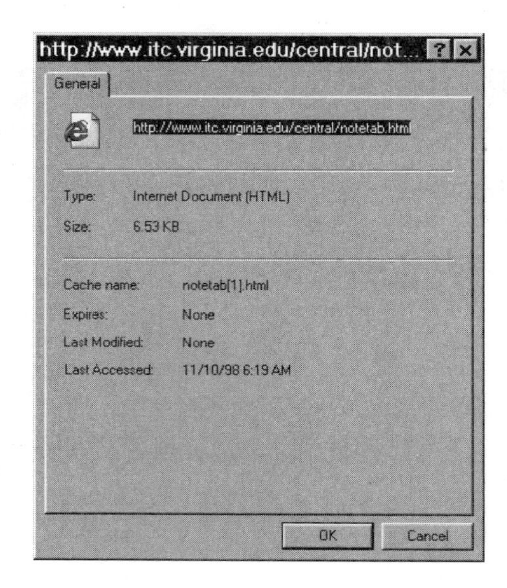

FIGURE 10-8.
The file's Properties dialog box shows information about the file that's stored in the cache.

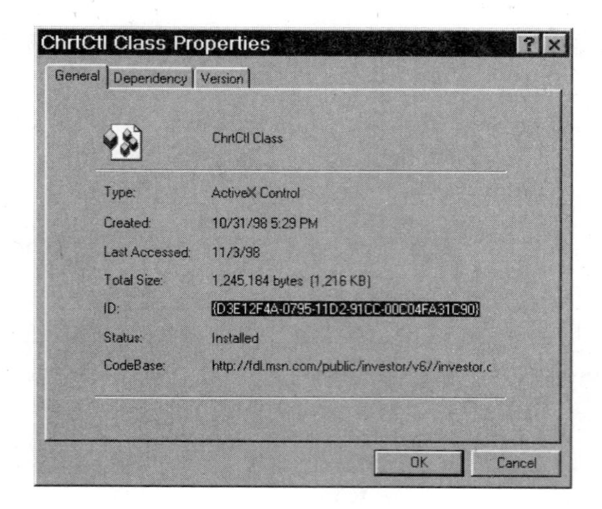

FIGURE 10-9.
An object's Properties dialog box provides information about the object, including version information and the files on which the object depends.

Customizing the Search Assistant

The Search Assistant, introduced in Chapter 6, helps you find the best Internet content. To make the Search assistant more useful, you can decide which search categories appear within the Search Explorer bar, and which search engines are available in each category.

It's always a good idea to select more than one search provider for each search category. Search services use differing databases, so you might need to search several of them if you wish to do the most comprehensive search possible.

To customize the Search Assistant, follow these steps:

1. On the Standard Buttons toolbar, click Search.
2. In the Search Explorer bar, click the Customize button.

   You'll see the Customize Search Settings dialog box, shown in Figure 10-10.

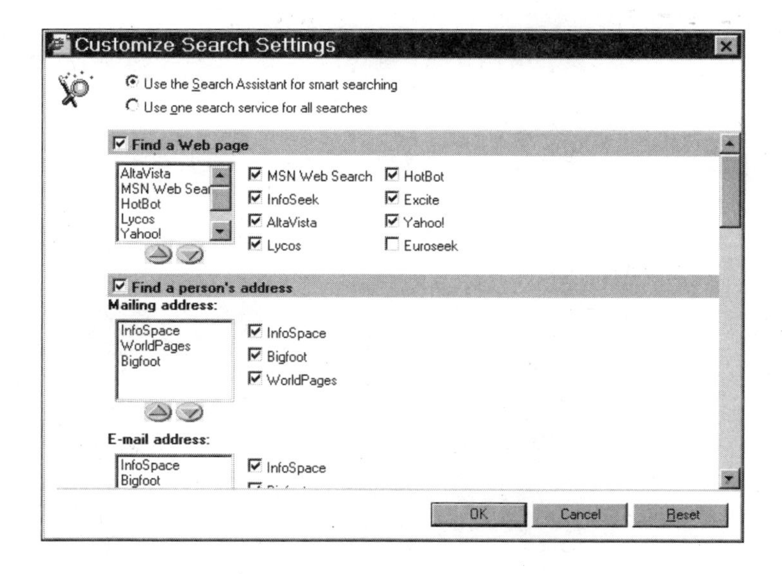

FIGURE 10-10.
In this page, you can choose Search assistant options.

3. To choose which categories are available in the Search explorer bar, select the check box for each category you want to display.
4. To change the order in which categories are displayed, select a category, and then click the Up or Down button.

5 To choose which search services are available within a category, click the check box so that a check mark appears next to each service you want.

6 If you would like Internet Explorer to save previous searches so that you can use them again, place a check mark next to Previous Searches.

7 Click Update to confirm your choices.

Organizing Your Favorites Folder

When you save favorite sites to your Favorites menu, it's wise to save them in folders, as suggested in Chapter 6. As your history list grows, however, you may decide that you need to reorganize your folders in a more logical way. Thanks to Internet Explorer version 5's redesigned Organize Favorites dialog box, it's easy to do so.

In the Organize Favorites dialog box, you can create new folders, rename or delete items in the Favorites list, and move items to folders. To display the Organize Favorites dialog box, do one of the following:

- From the Favorites menu, choose Organize Favorites.

  or

- If the Favorites explorer is on-screen, you can click the Organize button in the Favorite explorer's title bar.

You'll see the Organize Favorites window, shown in Figure 10-11.

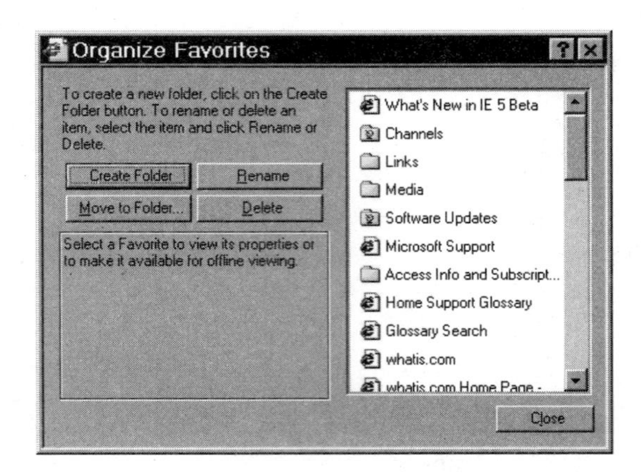

FIGURE 10-11. In this dialog box, you can organize your favorite sites by creating folders, moving items into folders, reorganizing folders, and removing unwanted items.

Using the Favorites List

In the Organize Favorites dialog box, you'll see a Favorites list that looks just like the Favorites explorer. That's no accident, and what's more, the list works the same way. To see the items stored within a folder, click the folder. To hide the items, click the folder again. When you click an item, you select the item, and you see information about the item in the panel to the left.

TIP

Give some thought to how you'd like to organize your folders. At the upper level, create folders with the most general names, such as "Shopping Sites" and "Research Sites." Create subfolders with more specific names. Within "Shopping Sites," for instance, you can create subfolders titled "Books," "CDs," and "Software."

Making a Favorite Available Offline

While you're organizing your favorites, you have an opportunity to make items available offline. To make an item available for offline browsing, follow these steps:

1. In the Organize Favorites dialog box, select the item you want to make available for offline browsing.
2. Place a check mark next to Make Available Offline.

TIP

To free hard-disk space for items you've made available offline, select the item, and uncheck Make Available Offline.

Changing Offline Properties

SEE ALSO

For more information on schedules and download options, see "Synchronizing Offline Content," page 174.

If you've made an item available for offline browsing, you can adjust the item's properties by following these steps:

1. In the Organize Favorites dialog box, select the item you've made available for offline browsing.
2. Click Properties. You'll see the properties dialog box for the item you selected. Click the Web Documents tab, if necessary.
3. In the Web document page, you see the current offline settings.
4. To change schedule settings, click the Schedule tab, select the schedule you want to change, and click Edit.
5. To change downloading options, click Download, and adjust the downloading settings.
6. Click OK to confirm.

Creating a New Folder

To create a new folder, follow these instructions:

1. In the Organize Favorites dialog box, click Create Folder. You'll see a new folder in the window.
2. Type a name for your new folder.

Adding Favorites to a Folder

Now that you've created a new folder, you can move existing favorites into it. To add an item to a folder, use these steps:

1. In the Organize Favorites dialog box, select the favorite that you want to move.
2. Click Move To Folder. You'll see a Browse For Folder dialog box, shown here:

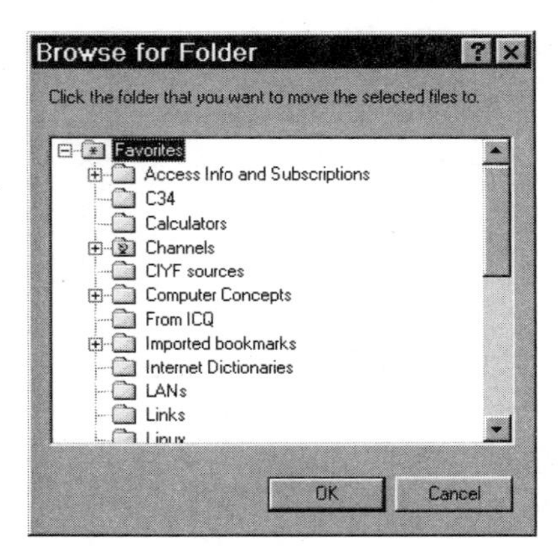

3. Click the folder to which you'd like to add the favorite.
4. Click OK. Internet Explorer moves the favorite into the folder.

Moving Folders

You can move folders as well as items. When you move a folder, you place the folder within another folder. In this way, you can create sub-folders. To move a folder, follow these steps:

1. In the Organize Favorites dialog box, select the folder that you want to move.
2. Click Move To Folder. You'll see the Browse For Folder dialog box.

3 Click the folder to which you'd like to add the folder.

4 Click OK. Internet Explorer moves the folder into the folder.

Renaming a Favorite

To rename a favorite or folder in the Organize Favorites window, select the favorite or folder and click Rename. Windows will highlight the current name. Just start typing to replace this name with the new one.

Deleting Favorites from a Folder

To keep your Favorites list well organized, you should periodically delete unwanted sites.

To remove unwanted sites from the Favorites list, follow these steps:

1 In the Organize Favorites dialog box, select the site you want to delete. To delete more than one, hold down the Ctrl key and click each site you want to delete.

2 Click Delete.

3 You'll see an alert box asking whether you're sure you want to move the deleted item to the Recycle Bin. If you're sure you're deleting the correct site, click the Yes button. (If you're not sure, click the No button and check what you've selected.)

> If you deleted the wrong site by accident, you can sometimes get it back. On the desktop, open the Recycle Bin. Select the site that you deleted accidentally. Choose the Restore command from the File menu. Windows will return the deleted item to the place from which you deleted it.

Sharing Favorites

In Netscape Navigator, favorites are called *bookmarks*. You can import Navigator bookmarks into your Favorites menu, and you can export your favorites as Navigator bookmarks.

This feature is useful for much more than exchanging your favorites with Navigator users. Because Internet Explorer uses the Navigator bookmark file format as a standard format for bookmark importing and exporting, you can also exchange your favorite items with other Internet Explorer users. If you use more than one computer, this feature also enables you to transfer your favorites from one computer to another.

If you used Netscape Navigator or Netscape Communicator prior to installing Internet Explorer, your bookmarks were automatically imported. In your Favorites folder, look for a folder called Imported Bookmarks.

Exporting Favorites

When you export favorites, Internet Explorer creates a Web page called bookmarks.htm, such as the one shown in Figure 10-12. Once you've created this page, you can do the following:

- Mail bookmarks.htm to someone.
- Place a copy of the file on the network, so that you can access it from other computers.
- Import the file into copies of Internet Explorer running on other computers.

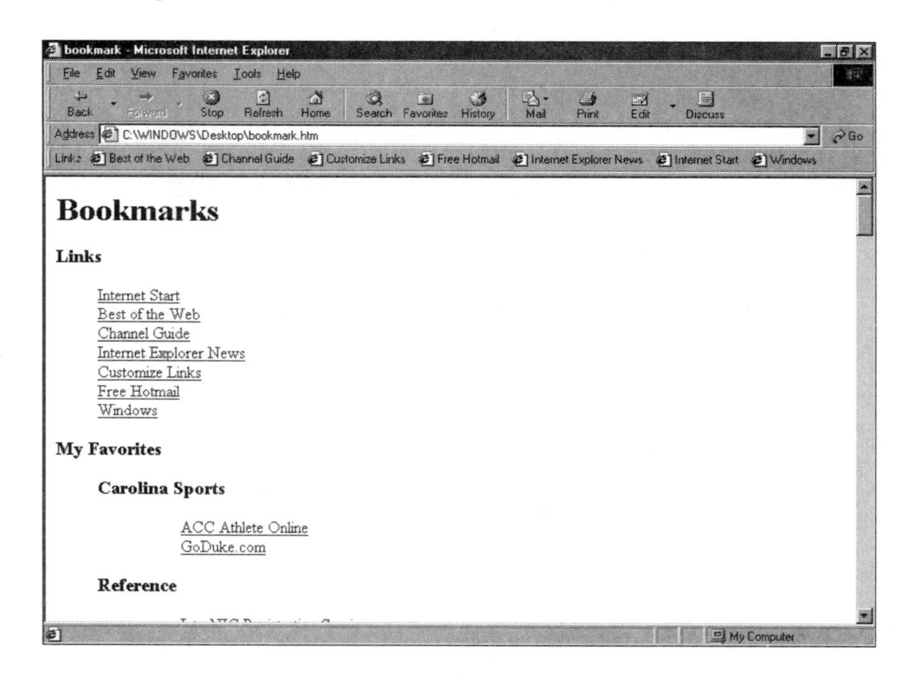

FIGURE 10-12.
When you export Favorites, Internet Explorer creates a Web page called bookmarks.htm. You can mail this page to others or import it into Internet Explorer on another computer.

To export your favorites into the file called bookmarks.htm, follow these steps:

1. From the File menu, choose Import and Export, and click Next. You'll see the Import/Export Selection page, shown here:

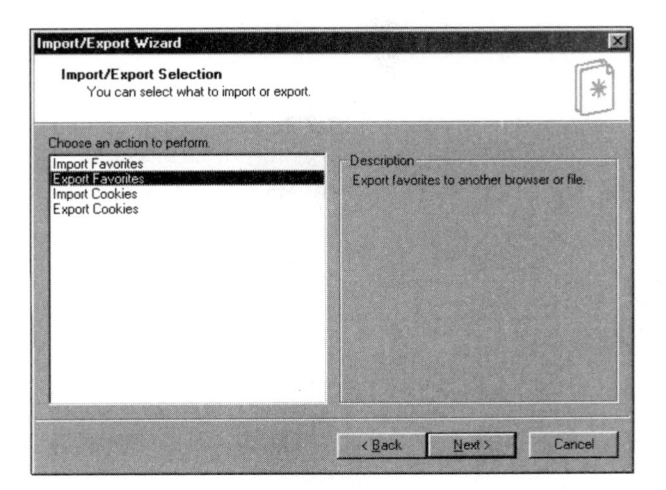

2. In the list box, select Export Favorites, and click Next. You'll see the Export Favorites Source Folder page, shown here:

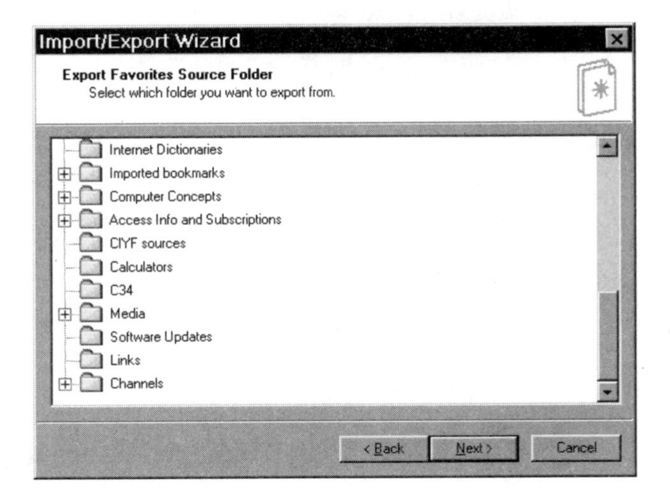

3. If you would like to export favorites from a folder within your Favorites list, rather than your entire list, select the folder from which you want to export, and click Next.

4. In the next page of the wizard, select the destination for the bookmark file.

If you have another browser installed on your computer, and you would like to export your favorites to that browser, click Export to an Application, and choose the browser's name in the list box. (This option is unavailable if Internet Explorer is the only browser installed on your system.)

If you would like to export your favorites to bookmarks.htm (a Web page containing your favorites), click Export to a File. To choose a destination other than the default, click Browse.

5. Click Next to continue, and click Finish to complete exporting your favorites.

To mail the exported favorites file to someone, open bookmarks.htm in the browser, click File on the menu bar, click Send, and choose Page By E-mail.

Importing Favorites

You can import favorites from a bookmarks.htm file or from an application (another browser installed on your computer). After you import the favorites, Internet Explorer adds them to your Favorites list. To import favorites, follow these steps:

1. From the File menu, choose Import and Export, and click Next. You'll see the Import/Export Selection page of the Import/Export Wizard.
2. In the Import/Export Selection page, select Import Favorites, and click Next.
3. In the Import Favorites Source page, do one of the following:
   - Click Import from an Application, and choose the application from which you would like to import favorites.

     or

   - Click Import from a File or Address, and type the file's location. You can type a Web address or a file location on your computer or another computer on your network.

4 Click Next to continue. You'll see the Import Favorites Destination page. If you would like to import favorites into a folder rather than at the upper level of your Favorites list, select the folder, and click OK.

5 Click Finish to complete importing favorites.

Exporting and Importing Cookies

As Chapter 9 explains (see "Understanding How Web Sites Track Information About You"), cookies are small files that Web servers store on your hard disk. Although cookies give privacy advocates qualms, most Internet users choose to accept them, if only because cookies provide so much functionality. (For example, cookies are required for most online shopping sites.)

Why would you want to export and import cookies? Suppose you've been using Internet Explorer on your home computer. Then you buy a new notebook computer, which comes with Internet Explorer installed. To get the most out of the Web sites you visit while using your notebook computer, you would like to have the cookies installed on your other system. You can do so by exporting the cookies from your old system, and then importing the cookies on the new one.

Exporting Cookies

When you export your cookies, Internet Explorer creates a file called cookies.txt. This text file can be imported into another copy of Internet Explorer. You can also import these cookies into Netscape Navigator if you wish.

To transfer the cookies.txt file from one computer to another, save the cookies.txt file to a floppy disk. (The file will be small enough to fit on a floppy.) You can then insert the floppy into the destination computer's floppy-disk drive, and import the file as described in the next section.

To export your cookies into the file called cookies.txt, follow these steps:

1 From the File menu, choose Import And Export, and click Next. You'll see the Import/Export Selection page of the wizard.

2 In the list box, click Export Cookies, and click Next. You'll see the Export Cookies Destination page, shown here:

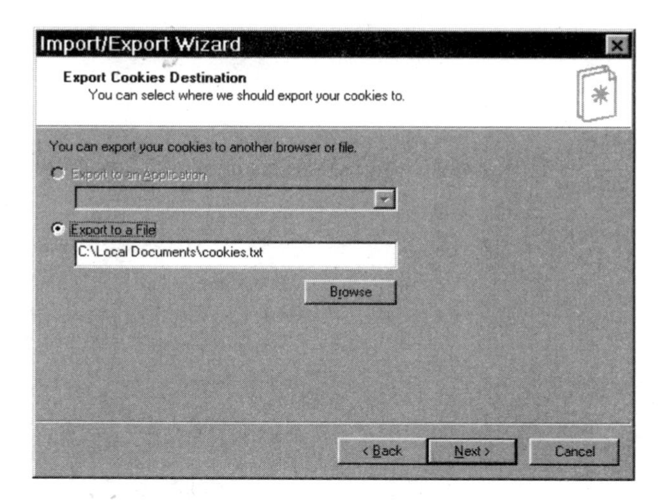

If you have another browser installed on your computer, and you would like to export your cookies to that browser, click Export to an Application, and choose the browser's name in the list box. (This option is unavailable if Internet Explorer is the only browser installed on your system.)

If you would like to export your cookies to cookies.txt (a text file containing your cookies), click Export To A File. To choose a destination other than the default, click Browse.

3 Click Next to continue, and click Finish to complete exporting your favorites.

To mail the exported favorites file to someone, open bookmarks.htm in the browser, click File on the menu bar, click Send, and choose Page By E-mail.

Importing Cookies

You can import an Internet Explorer or Navigator cookies file (cookies.txt). When you import the file, Internet Explorer adds the imported cookies to Internet Explorer's cookies list.

To import cookies from cookies.txt, follow these steps:

1 From the File menu, choose Import And Export and click Next. You'll see the Import And Export Favorites dialog box.

2 Click Import Cookies.

You'll see the Import Cookies Source page, shown here:

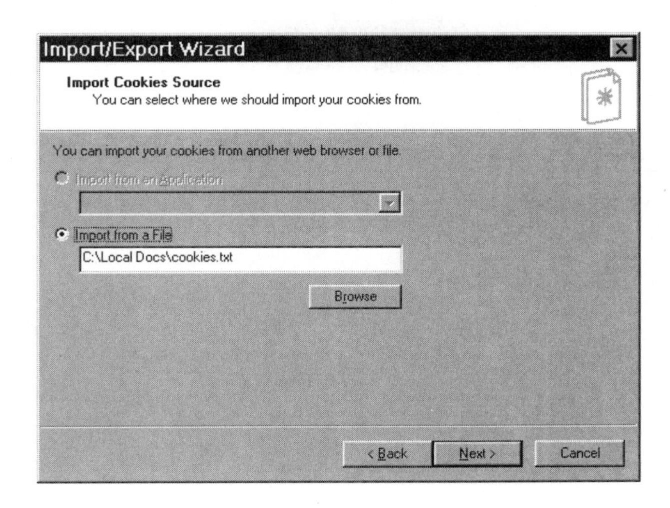

3 Do one of the following:

- To import cookies from another browser on the same computer, click Import From An Application, and select the browser from the list box.

  or

- To import cookies from the file cookies.txt, click Import From A File. To import the file from a location other than the default one, click Browse, and locate the file.

4 Click Next, and click Finish to import the cookies.

Choosing Security Options

If you would like to adjust Internet Explorer's privacy and security settings, go to the Tools menu and select Internet Options; then click the Advanced tab. Scroll down to see the Security options that affect online transactions (Figure 10-13). Table 10-2 on page 300 explains the function of each option; the default setting for each is given in parentheses.

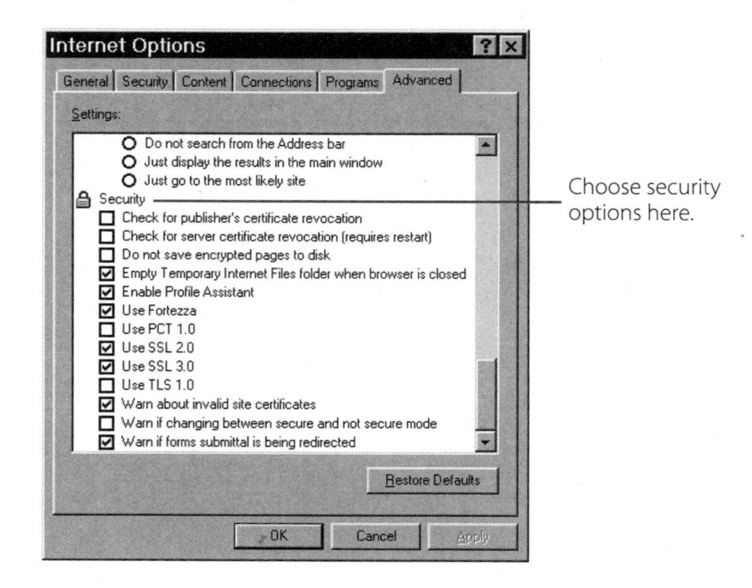

FIGURE 10-13.
You can choose security options in the Advanced page of the Internet Options dialog box.

Defining Custom Security Levels

Although the predefined security levels are appropriate for most users, you can choose custom security settings for each level. Table 10-3 on page 301 explains the various security settings, the risk they address, and the default security configuration for each of the four security levels. For most options, you can choose to enable the option (download without confirmation), prompt (ask for confirmation), or disable this type of content entirely.

To create a custom security profile, do the following:

1. From the Tools menu, choose Internet Options. You'll see the Internet Options dialog box.
2. Click the Security tab. You'll see the Security options dialog box, shown in Figure 10-14.
3. Select the security level you want to change. You can choose from Internet, Local Intranet, Trusted Sites, or Restricted Sites.
4. Click Custom Level. You'll see the Security Settings dialog box, shown in Figure 10-15.
5. In the Reset custom settings area, choose the security profile from which you would like to start, and click Reset.
6. Adjust the individual security settings.

- **Enable.** Allow this type of content to download without first asking for confirmation.
- **Prompt.** Before downloading this type of content, display a dialog box asking for confirmation.
- **Disable.** Do not download this type of content. Be aware that this option could disable functionality at many Web sites.

7 Click OK.

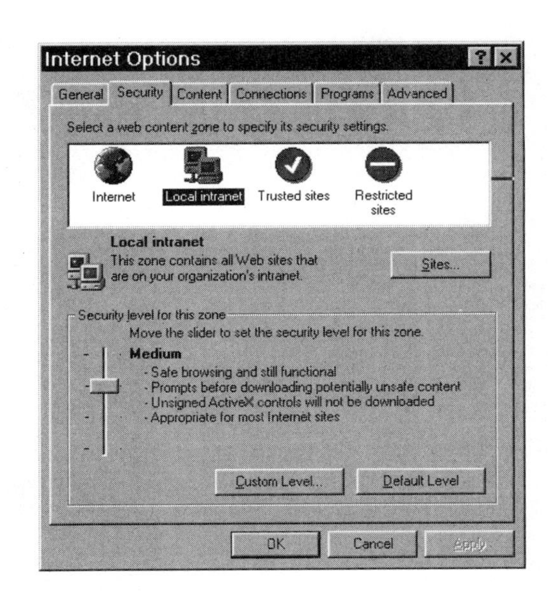

FIGURE 10-14.
To define security settings, you first select the security zone you want to change.

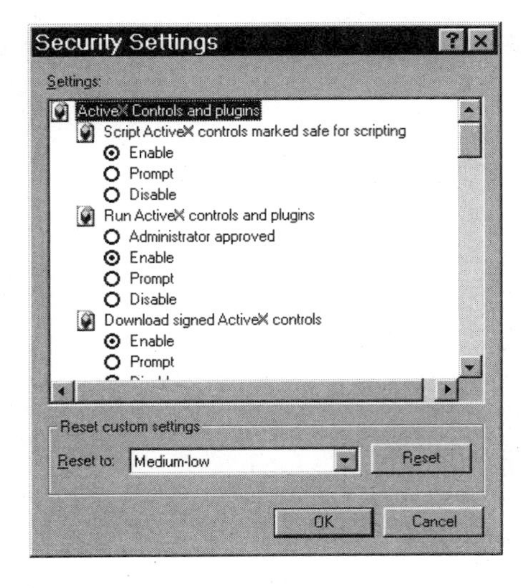

FIGURE 10-15.
The Security Settings dialog box enables you to choose custom security settings for each security zone.

TABLE 10-2. Advanced Security Options.

Setting	Default	Description
Check For Publisher's Certificate Revocation	Off	This service will enable you to check to see whether someone's certificate has been revoked.
Check For Server Certificate Revocation	Off	Checks to see whether the current secure server's certificate is valid.
Do Not Save Encrypted Pages To Disk	Off	If you're worried that somebody might snoop around in your computer to see secure pages you've visited, you can click this option.
Empty Temporary Internet Files Folder When Browser Is Closed	Off	Clears Internet Explorer's disk cache when you quit the program. This is a useful option if you're concerned that someone could snoop around in your computer to find out where you've been browsing.
Enable Profile Assistant	On	The Profile Assistant allows you to respond to a Web site's request for personal information with a click of the mouse. If you don't plan to use Profile Assistant, you can turn it off here.
Use Fortezza	On	Enable this option so that you can engage in secure transactions with Fortezza secure servers.
Use PCT 1.0	Off	Enable this option so that you can engage in secure transactions with PCT secure servers.
Use SSL 2.0	On	Enable this option so that you can engage in secure transactions with SSL 2.0 secure servers.
Use SSL 3.0	On	Enable this option so that you can engage in secure transactions with SSL 3.0 secure servers.
Use TLS 1.0	Off	Enable this option so that you can engage in secure transactions with TLS 1.0 secure servers.
Warn About Invalid Site Certificates	On	With this option, Internet Explorer will display a warning if the program detects a discrepancy between the security certificate and the particulars (such as the Internet address or e-mail address) of the site you've accessed. This could be a minor error on the server's part, but it could also mean that somebody has tried to set up a bogus site to collect credit card numbers. If you're sure the site is what it says it is, click OK. If you have any doubts or you're not sure, click Cancel. I recommend that you enable this option.
Warn If Changing Between Secure And Not Secure Mode	Off	This option shows a warning box when you move from an insecure to a secure connection, and vice versa. It's a pain—leave it off.
Warn If Forms Submittal Is Being Redirected	On	This option warns you if a Web form that you've filled out is about to be sent to a site other than the site you're currently viewing. This helps protect you against spoofing. Leave it on.

TABLE 10-3. Custom Security Settings.

Setting	Security Risk	Default Settings
ActiveX Controls and Plug-ins		
Download Signed ActiveX Controls	Signed ActiveX controls are generally safe, although it's wise to ask for a prompt before they download.	Prompt
Download Unsigned ActiveX Controls	This is a very risky operation. Unsigned ActiveX controls could do a great deal of damage to your computer. Don't download them unless you're doing so from a trusted site on your local intranet.	Disable
Initialize And Script ActiveX Controls Not Marked As Safe	This is also a very dangerous operation. There's little to worry about if you're downloading this content from a trustworthy Internet site (such as msn.com), but you should ask for confirmation.	Disable
Run ActiveX Controls And Plug-ins	This is an overall setting that determines whether ActiveX controls and plug-ins are allowed to run.	Enable
Script ActiveX Controls Marked Safe For Scripting	Although ActiveX controls don't pose much danger, a script could conceivably transform harmless scripts into something destructive.	Enable
Cookies		
Allow Cookies That Are Are Stored On Your Computer	Cookies that remain on your computer could contain identification information that could enable a Web server to track your use of the Web. You can disable it if you're concerned about the privacy implications, but you may impair functionality at valid Web sites.	Enable
Allow Per-Session Cookies (not stored)	Cookies are text files that enable a Web page to leave information on your computer. Such information could include your preferences concerning a Web page's options. This information is subsequently read by the server when another page is accessed. It's not very risky to enable this option.	Enable
Downloads		
File Download	You risk acquiring a computer virus if you download a program or data file. But the files you can obtain from trustworthy sites are usually quite safe.	Enable
Font Download	Some Web pages automatically download fonts.	Enable
Java		
Java Permissions	The various levels of Java permissions are associated with the four security levels, so this option enables you to set Java permissions higher or lower than the default level. Java does pose dangers, but they are not as great as unsigned ActiveX controls.	High Safety

(continued)

TABLE 10-3. *continued*

Setting	Security Risk	Default Settings
Miscellaneous		
Access Data Sources Across Domains	There's a trick that computer criminals can use that makes you think you're ordering from a valid commercial site, when in fact you're uploading your credit card data to a rogue site. If you disable this option, however, you may impair functionality at some bona fide sites.	Disable
Drag And Drop Or Copy And Paste Files	This is a helpful feature that could be exploited by rogue scripts.	Enable
Installation Of Desktop Items	This is a risky setting; you want to be able to take advantage of Microsoft's software updates, but you don't want to install rogue content on your desktop!	Prompt
Launching Applications And Files In An IFRAME	This is a trick that pranksters can exploit to display unwanted content on your computer. But it also has legitimate uses.	Prompt
Software Channel Permissions	This setting governs the downloading and installation of software from sites that can supply software automatically.	Medium Safety
Submit Non-Encrypted Form Data	When you submit information on a Web form, it's possible for somebody to read it en route. This isn't much of a risk unless you're uploading credit card or other sensitive personal information; you should do this only when you're connected to a secure Web site.	Prompt
Userdata Persistence	Stores information about your browsing actions that Web sites can track even after a session ends.	Enable
Scripting		
Active Scripting	Scripts are included in many Web pages and generally do not pose a serious security threat. If you turn them off, much of the Web's functionality will be lost. If you ask for confirmation, you will see too many confirmation dialog boxes.	Enable
Scripting Of Java Applets	Like scripted ActiveX applets, the risk here is greater than that for scripts or Java applets separately. Ask for confirmation if you're visiting untrustworthy sites.	Enable
User Authentication		
Logon	Internet Explorer can log you on to sites automatically, but this could enable an intruder to use your computer while you're away, and gain access to confidential information.	Automatic logon only in an intranet zone

Managing Certificates

When you make full use of Internet Explorer's security features for Web browsing and e-mail, you will acquire a collection of digital certificates, called a *certificate store*. If you wish, you can view and manage the various certificates you have accumulated. Here's a list of the types of certificates you'll work with:

- **Personal certificate.** This certificate identifies you for Web shopping and e-mail purposes.
- **Other people's certificates.** You receive these certificates when you establish secure e-mail communication with people.
- **Intermediate certificate authority (CA) certificate.** This certificate establishes the identity and validity of the certificate authorities that endorse personal and other certificates. Some of these certificates are used for advanced purposes, such as stamping the date on an e-mail message or downloaded file.
- **Trusted root certificate authority certificate.** CAs use this certificate to validate intermediate and personal certificates.
- **Publisher certificate.** This certificate identifies and validates the publishers of programs you can download.

With the Certificate Manager, you can view the certificates that are currently installed in the certificate store. You can also import and export certificates and remove unwanted certificates.

To view the Certificate Manager, do the following:

1. From the Tools menu, choose Internet Options. You'll see the Internet Options dialog box.
2. Click the Content tab. You'll see the Content page.
3. In the Certificates area, click Certificates. You'll see the Certificates Manager, shown in Figure 10-16.

TIP

Normally, you don't need to worry about certificates; they operate automatically. If you're using an intranet that uses certificates for internal purposes, your network administrator may direct you to use some of the Certificate Manager functions. For most readers, the only reason to use Certificate Manager is to export a personal certificate to another computer, as described below.

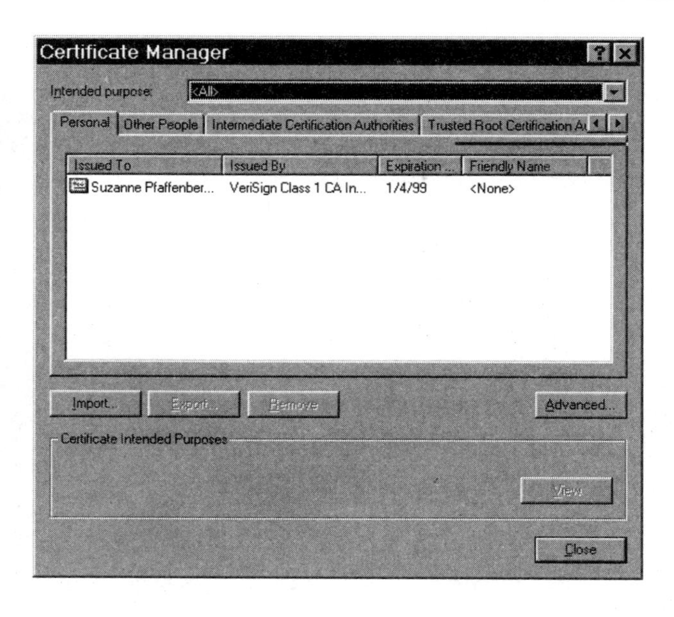

FIGURE 10-16. The Certificate Manager enables you to view, import, export, and remove certificates.

Viewing Certificates

You can view certificates to determine whether they are valid. For example, certificates expire on a certain date.

To view certificates, do the following:

1. In Certificate Manager, choose a certificate purpose in the Intended list box. You can choose from client authentication, secure e-mail, or advanced purposes.
2. Click a tab corresponding to the type of certificate you want to view.
3. Select the certificate you want to view.
4. Click View. You'll see the certificate's properties, shown in Figure 10-17.

   In the General page, you see summary information, including the certificate's purpose, the issuer, to whom the certificate was issued, and the validity dates.
5. To view detailed information about the certificate, click Details.
6. To view the *certification path* (the sequence by which the certificate received endorsements from CAs), click Certification path.
7. Click OK when you're finished viewing certificates.

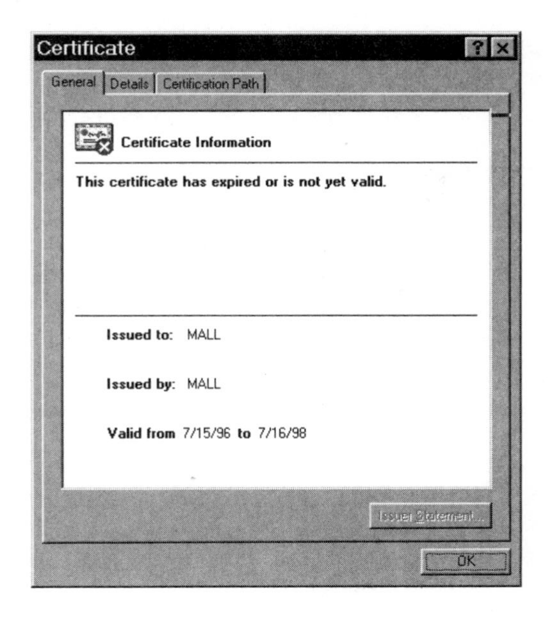

FIGURE 10-17.
You can view certificate properties. This certificate is no longer valid!

Exporting a Certificate

If you've obtained a personal certificate for your use in Web shopping and e-mail, you may wish to export this certificate so that you can use it on other computers. For example, suppose you have a notebook computer as well as a desktop computer. You may wish to export your certificate from your desktop computer for use on the notebook computer.

To export a certificate, do the following:

1. In Certificate Manager, click Export. You'll see the first page of the Certificate Manager Export Wizard.
2. Click Next. You'll see a list of certificate export file formats. If you're exporting to a copy of Internet Explorer running on another computer, the default format (DER encoded binary) is fine.
3. Click Next, and type a name for the export file you're creating.
4. Click Finish. Internet Explorer exports the certificate to the file you created.

TIP

Once you've exported the certificate to a file, you can transfer the file to another computer.

Importing a Certificate

If you've exported a certificate to a file, you can import the certificate to the certificate store. To import a certificate, follow these steps:

1. In Certificate Manager, click Import. You'll see the Certificate Manager Import Wizard.
2. Click Next, and select the file you want to import.
3. Click Next, and choose an option. Internet Explorer can automatically place the certificate based on its type, or you can save it into a store that you identify. The default option is fine if you're transferring a certificate to another computer.
4. Click Finish. Internet Explorer imports the certificate, and you see a message informing you that the certificate was imported successfully.
5. Click OK.

Removing Certificates

You may wish to remove a certificate if it has expired, or if you have some reason to think that it's not trustworthy. In general, though, you should not remove any certificate unless you have been directed to do so by a network administrator or a technical support person. If you remove a certificate that is needed for a security operation, you could prevent Internet Explorer from being able to access secure services.

To remove a certificate, do the following:

1. In Certificate Manager, select the certificate you want to remove.
2. Click Remove. You'll see an alert box warning you that you will not be able to use this certificate after removing it.
3. Click Yes if you're sure you want to continue.

Viewing Publisher Certificates

When you download software from the Internet, you have an opportunity to view the publisher's certificate. If you wish, you can check an option that defines this publisher as trustworthy. In the future, you won't have to approve the certificate again. You can see a list of the publishers that you've defined as trustworthy. You can also remove certificates from this list. Doing so doesn't prevent you from downloading software from this publisher; it just removes automatic approval.

To view publisher certificates:

1. From the Tools menu, choose Internet Options. You'll see the Internet Options dialog box.
2. In the Certificates area, click Publishers. You'll see the Authenticode Security Technology dialog box, shown in Figure 10-18.
3. To remove an unwanted certificate, click Remove. You'll see a confirmation box. Click OK to remove the certificate.
4. Click OK until you see Internet Explorer again.

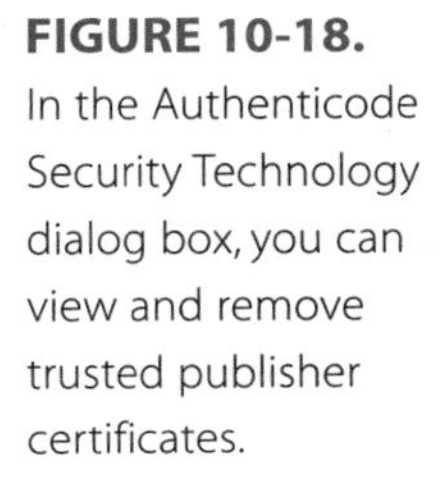

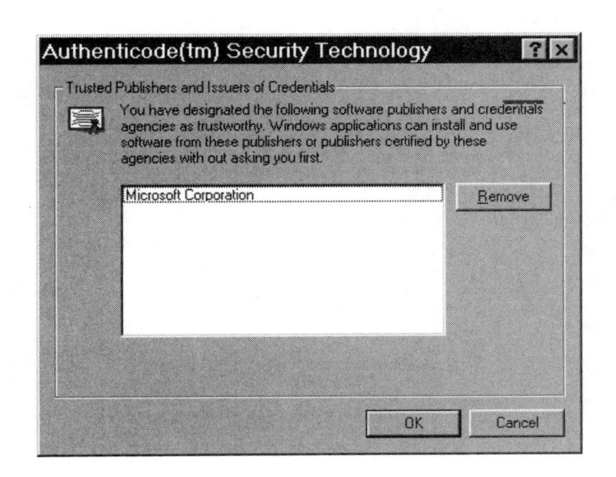

FIGURE 10-18.
In the Authenticode Security Technology dialog box, you can view and remove trusted publisher certificates.

Choosing Programs for Internet Services

While you're using Internet Explorer, you may come across a hyperlink to a type of data that the program can't handle by itself. For example, if you click a link to a newsgroup, Internet Explorer needs help from a program that knows how to read Usenet newsgroups. When you install the program, Internet Explorer is automatically configured to use other programs in the Internet Explorer suite, but you can change these settings, if you wish. Here are the programs you can specify:

- **HTML editor.** This program is used to edit Web pages. If you installed FrontPage Express when you installed Internet Explorer, this is the default setting.
- **E-mail program.** This program is used to send mail messages from within Internet Explorer. If you installed Outlook Express when you installed Internet Explorer, this is the default setting.
- **Newsgroups.** This program is used to access Usenet newsgroups from within Internet Explorer. If you installed Outlook Express when you installed Internet Explorer, this is the default setting.

- **Internet Call.** This program is used to place telephone calls via the Internet from within Internet Explorer. If you installed Net-Meeting when you installed Internet Explorer, this is the default setting.
- **Calendar.** This program is used to access scheduling services from within Internet Explorer. To use this option, you must install Microsoft Outlook.
- **Contact List.** By default, this option is set to use the Windows Address Book.

If you install another browser, such as Netscape Navigator, the newly installed browser will start when you open a Web page. By default, Internet Explorer is configured so that, when you start the program, it checks to see whether it is the default browser. If not, you have an opportunity to change the default-browser setting. If you do not wish Internet Explorer to make this check, uncheck the option called Internet Explorer Should Check To See Whether It Is The Default Browser, as explained in the following steps.

To change the default program settings, do the following:

1. From the Tools menu, choose Internet Options. You'll see the Internet Options dialog box.
2. Click the Programs tab. You'll see the Programs page, shown in Figure 10-19.

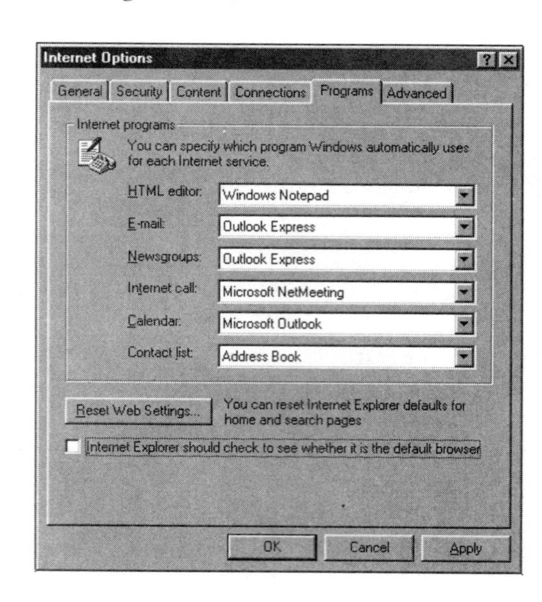

FIGURE 10-19. You can choose the programs Internet Explorer uses to supplement its capabilities.

3. Choose the programs you want to use.
4. If you want Internet Explorer to check to see whether it is the default browser, check this option. Uncheck this option if you wish to use another browser as the default browser.
5. Click OK.

Choosing Browser Options

To choose additional browser settings, go to the Tools menu and select Internet Options, and then click the Advanced tab. Scroll down to see the Browser options. Table 10-4 explains the function of each option; the default setting for each is given in parentheses.

Additional Options

You may also choose the customization options shown in Table 10-5. To do so, click Tools on the menu bar, choose Internet Options, and click Advanced. Scroll down to locate these options.

TABLE 10-4. Advanced Browser Options.

Setting	Default	Description
Always Send URLs As UTF-8	On	Enables you to send URLs in any language. This is a good option if you're using Internet Explorer in a non-English-speaking country, and some of the URLs you access are encoded in UTF-8.
Automatically Check For Internet Explorer Updates	On	Checks the Internet at the start of each browsing session to determine whether a new version of Internet Explorer exists.
Browse In A New Process	On	Specifies that Windows should start a new copy of Internet Explorer every time you start a new Internet Explorer-based function, such as Windows Explorer. This enables you to keep working should one of the Internet Explorer windows become disabled due to a software error.
Close Unused Folders In History And Favorites	On	In the History and Favorites explorers, this option collapses folder lists when you click a different folder. If you turn this option off, the folders stay open.
Disable Script Debugging	Off	Script debugging checks scripts for errors, and stops executing them if an error is found. Because script errors could cause problems for your system, such as crashing an application, it's wise to leave this option off (so that script debugging is enabled).

(continued)

TABLE 10-4. *continued*

Setting	Default	Description
Display A Notification About Every Script Error	Off	Many Web pages contain scripts that contain errors. Some of these errors are minor. If you turn this option off, you will receive no notification of the errors. The risk here lies in a major script error that ruins the page's functionality. If there's a major error, you may not realize the page is not working unless you leave this option on.
Enable Install On Demand	On	This option automatically downloads Internet Explorer features that you did not install when you set up the program.
Enable Offline Items To Be Synchronized On A Schedule	On	Enables you to create schedules to update offline content at specified times. Disable this option if you're using a modem connection and pay per-minute charges for your connection.
Enable Page Transitions	On	Enables a special transition effect in which one page fades out as another fades in. Turn this option off if your computer runs slowly when transitions occur.
Enable Page-Hit Counting	On	Enables Web sites to track your viewing preferences. Disable this option if you're concerned about privacy.
Notify When Downloads Complete	Off	This option displays a notification box when file downloads are complete. This is a good option to enable if you connect via a modem and need to know when to disconnect.
Show Channel Bar At Startup (if Active Desktop is off)	Off	Displays the Channel Bar on startup, even if the Web desktop isn't activated.
Show Friendly HTTP Error Messages	On	Displays helpful error messages when Internet Explorer has difficulty accessing a Web site.
Show Friendly URLs	Off	Shows simplified URLs by default in the Address bar and Status line.
Show Go Button In Address Bar	On	The Go button enables you to access a Web site after typing the address in the Address bar. However, you can do the same thing by typing the address and pressing Enter.
Show Internet Explorer On The Desktop	On	Displays an Internet Explorer icon on the desktop. To hide this icon, turn this option off.
Underline Links	Always	Choose Always to underline links at all times (recommended), Hover to underline links only when you move the mouse pointer over the link, or Never to eliminate link underlining.

(continued)

TABLE 10-4. *continued*

Setting	Default	Description
Use Inline AutoComplete For Web Addresses	Off	Places AutoComplete text into the Address bar, instead of just in the drop-down list box. Keep this option off if you find it confusing.
Use Inline AutoComplete In Integrated Shell	On	Enables you to use AutoComplete services in Windows Explorer.
Use Web-Based FTP	Off	Enable this option in order to access FTP sites as if they were Windows Explorer pages.
Use Smooth Scrolling	On	Enables continuous scrolling at a predefined speed.

TABLE 10-5. Additional Advanced Options.

Setting	Default	Description
HTTP 1.1 Settings		
Use HTTP 1.1	On	Some Web sites still use HTTP 1.0. If you're having difficulty connecting to a site, clear this check box.
Use HTTP 1.1 Through Proxy Connections	Off	Check with your network administrator to find out whether you can use HTTP 1.1 through proxy connections.
Java VM		
Java Console Enabled (requires restart)	Off	Turn this option on so that you can access all Java content (some Java applets require the Java console).
Java Logging Enabled	On	Keep this option enabled so that you can use all Java applets.
JIT Compiler For Virtual Machine Enabled (requires restart)	Off	Enable this option so that you can use Java applets that require the JIT (just-in-time) compiler.
Printing		
Print Background Colors And Images	Off	This setting isn't recommended because the background colors and images may make the text difficult to read.
Searching		
Autoscan Common Root Domains	On	You can choose the following options to search when the URL fails: Always Ask Before Searching, Always Search Without Asking, and Never Search.

PART IV

Mastering Internet Messaging

CHAPTER 11

Introducing Outlook Express

Microsoft Outlook Express, version 5, isn't a throw away add-on to supplement the best available browser, Internet Explorer. It's a great program in its own right, offering a winning combination of great features and ease of use. With an Internet connection and Outlook Express, you can exchange e-mail messages with anyone on the Internet. If your correspondent is also using Outlook Express, or another HTML-compatible browser, you can also format your messages with colors, fonts, and graphics. As you become more involved in Internet e-mail, you can customize Outlook Express to organize your stored messages. You can even write *filters* that route low-priority mail to folders so that you see only your important messages.

This brief list doesn't even scratch the surface of Outlook Express's impressive features, but don't worry about getting overwhelmed with the program's complexity. Feature-rich as it is, Outlook Express is also very easy to use. In this chapter, you'll learn the fundamentals of Outlook Express. In the next chapter, you'll learn how to send and receive e-mail messages via the Internet. Together, these chapters tell you all you need to know in order to use Internet e-mail. Should you wish to explore the program's intermediate and advanced features, you'll find what you're looking for in Chapters 13 and 14.

Introducing Internet E-Mail

When asked what they like best about the Internet, most people reply without hesitation, "Internet e-mail." In profession after profession, people soon conclude that they would be at a serious disadvantage if they couldn't communicate via e-mail.

Outlook Express isn't designed to work with online services, such as The Microsoft Network (MSN) or America Online (AOL). To send and receive Internet electronic mail from within these services, use the mail software that these services provide.

What's so great about e-mail? For one thing, it's faster than snail mail (a.k.a. the U.S. Postal Service), and for many people, that's justification enough for using it. In fact, you can send an e-mail message halfway around the world in less than a minute. (It's not instantaneous because the mail servers need a little time to retrieve and store messages.) It's also free, once you've paid for your Internet connection. This makes an unbeatable combination, and it helps to explain why an estimated 80 to 100 million people are now using it.

There's a downside to e-mail too, as you'll soon discover. Not everyone has e-mail, of course, so it's far from the universal messaging service that the postal service is. What's more, if your recipient doesn't log on to his or her e-mail account, your message isn't received. This makes it tough to stay in touch with people who are on vacation and forget to tell their correspondents that they'll be away from their computers. Still, once you begin using it, you'll soon have many dependable e-mail partners. Although e-mail doesn't replace conventional communications (phone, mail, fax, and express services), it supplements and complements them so nicely that you won't want to give it up.

Understanding How E-Mail Works

E-mail uses the Internet as its transmission medium, which means that the messages travel quickly. Often, messages arrive at their destination within as little as a minute or two. But you might not get your messages right away. When somebody sends you an e-mail message, it's received by an *e-mail server*, a program that's running on one of your Internet service provider's computers. The e-mail server stores your incoming mail in your *electronic mailbox*. This mailbox generally is part of the file storage system of an Internet service provider. You don't get your messages until you log on to the service provider's e-mail server and start your e-mail program. The program then checks your electronic mailbox and determines whether you've received any new messages.

You may then do any of the following:

- **Read your messages.** Outlook Express's preview pane enables you to view your messages without having to open a new window for each message.
- **Reply to a message.** Outlook Express can automatically *quote* (copy) the message to your reply, so that your correspondent can see the text to which you're replying.
- **Forward a message to someone else.** You can send all of the message, or you can edit the message to focus on the portions to which you want to call to someone's attention. You can also add your own text to explain why you're forwarding the message.
- **Create a new message.** If you have someone's e-mail address, you can create a new message and send it.

TIP

> E-mail is an excellent communication medium, but it isn't always appropriate. A phone call is a better choice if you need to make sure that your message gets through right away (remember, your recipients won't get their messages if they don't log on to their e-mail server).

Understanding E-Mail Protocols

Like other Internet services, e-mail relies on Internet *protocols* (communication standards). To understand your options for working with e-mail, you'll find it helpful to know the fundamentals concerning the e-mail protocols that are in widespread use on the Internet.

POP3

The Post Office Protocol (POP, also called POP3 or POP-3) is one of two (the other is called *IMAP*) that govern the way an e-mail server receives your mail and makes it available to you. It's the most widely used mail reception protocol; chances are good that your Internet service provider will give you a POP3 account.

With a POP3 account, your incoming messages are stored temporarily on your service provider's e-mail server. When you log on to your account, Outlook Express automatically starts downloading your messages to your computer. When the downloading is finished, Outlook

Express tells the e-mail server to erase the copies of the messages that are stored on the server. In this way, your service provider makes sure that the server's disk storage does not become overwhelmed with incoming messages.

POP3 accounts are ideal for dial-up users because you need not stay online in order to work with your messages. You can log on, download your mail, and log off. Subsequently, you can work offline, reading and replying to your messages as you please. You can then log on to send your replies and receive new messages.

POP3 accounts have one major disadvantage: once you've downloaded your mail to your computer, the downloaded messages are not available when you use other computers. If you travel frequently, or use more than one computer at work, you may prefer to use an IMAP account, discussed in the next section.

You can configure Outlook Express so that it leaves a copy of your messages on the POP server. However, the messages will pile up, and you will probably be notified by your ISP that you've exceeded the storage limits. To prevent this, you can choose options that delete messages after leaving them on the server for a certain number of days, or when you've deleted the messages on your local system. For more information, see "Choosing General Options," page 419.

IMAP

Like POP, the Internet Message Access Protocol (IMAP, also called IMAP4 or IMAP-4) governs mail reception and storage. With IMAP servers, your messages stay on the server—you don't have to download them, and they aren't automatically erased after you've accessed them.

Because an IMAP server keeps your messages in a central storage location, you can access your mail from any computer that's able to connect to this computer. If you're at work, you can read your mail from any computer that's connected to your company's network. If you're on the road, you can dial in to your IMAP server, and all your mail is available.

IMAP's disadvantage lies in the fact that you need to remain connected while you're working with your mail. For this reason, IMAP normally isn't a good choice for dial-up users who need to minimize their time online. However, Outlook Express enables you to synchronize your local and IMAP mail folders, so that you can work with your mail offline. When you connect with synchronization enabled, Outlook Express makes sure that any changes you've made to the messages stored on your computer are synchronized with the IMAP-based messages.

SMTP

Short for Simple Mail Transport Protocol, this is the standard used to send your mail. That's true whether you're using IMAP or POP to receive your mail.

MIME

Short for Multipurpose Internet Multimedia Extensions, this is the standard used to include files, graphics, sounds, and other non-text content within your e-mail messages. This content, called an *attachment*, enables you to exchange virtually any type of data with other Internet users. An updated version of the standard, called S/MIME, enables you to exchange secure, encrypted mail with other Internet users.

SEE ALSO
For more information on encrypted e-mail, see Chapter 14, "Using Secure E-Mail."

Understanding Internet E-Mail Addresses

To get your e-mail message across, you need to know how to use Internet e-mail addresses, which look like this: *frodo@bagend.shire.org*. Every address has three parts:

- **User name ("frodo").** This isn't a person's name; it's the name given to a person's electronic mailbox. The user name is often made up of components of the person's name (such as fbaggins or frodob).
- **At sign ("@").** This symbol is needed to separate the user name from the domain name.
- **Domain name ("bagend.shire.org").** This name is the Internet address of the computer that contains the person's electronic mailbox. Note that the various parts of the domain name are separated by periods; if you're telling someone your e-mail address, you pronounce the periods by saying "dot," as in "frodo at bagend-dot-shire-dot-org."

TIP

An Internet domain name can give you hints about where a person's mail is coming from. At the end of the name is the *top-level domain*, which is a general category. If the message originates outside the United States, the top-level domain usually indicates the country of origin. (For example, *uk* is the United Kingdom, and *fr* is France.) Within the United States, messages from universities and colleges use the top-level domain *edu*, government agencies use *gov*, corporations use *com*, and nonprofit organizations use *org*.

Configuring Your E-Mail Account

In order to use Internet Explorer for e-mail, you must configure the program to work with your account information. If you're using Internet Explorer on a network, this information is available from your network administrator. If you subscribe to the Internet through an independent Internet service provider (ISP), your ISP will give you this information.

Outlook Express uses Internet Explorer's connection to the Internet. If you haven't already configured Internet Explorer to access the Internet, go to Chapter 4, and run the Internet Connection Wizard to set up your Internet connection. You can also configure your e-mail information by following the steps in Chapter 4.

Chances are that you have already configured Outlook Express to work with your Internet e-mail account. If you installed Internet Explorer following the instructions in Chapter 4, "Running the Connection Wizard," you were asked for your e-mail information. If you supplied this information when you ran the Connection Wizard, you can skip the rest of this section.

TIP

Outlook Express enables you to work with more than one e-mail account at a time, so that all your messages from all your accounts are available in a single, integrated workspace. If you have more than one e-mail account, read this section and configure Outlook Express with the first e-mail account you use. For information on adding additional accounts, see "Managing Accounts," page 451.

Getting the Information You Need

To configure Outlook Express, you'll need to know the following information:

- **E-mail address.** Make sure you've written this down correctly. Your address should have three parts: a user name, an "at" sign (@), and a domain name. Within the user name or domain name, there might be one or more periods or other punctuation marks, such as an underscore. E-mail addresses do not have spaces.

- **Incoming mail-server name.** This is the server that stores your incoming mail. It's also called a POP3 server or IMAP server. The address will consist of two or more names separated by periods, without spaces (such as *mail.cstone.net*).

- **Outgoing mail-server name.** Also called the SMTP server, this server sends your outgoing mail. It's probably the same server that deals with your incoming mail, but sometimes it is different.
- **Account name (mailbox name).** This is the user name or account name that your Internet service provider gave you. Chances are, it's the same as the first part of your e-mail address, but this isn't always true.
- **Password.** This is the password that's used to access your e-mail server. It might be the same password that you use to access the Internet with Internet Explorer, but chances are it's different. Be sure to keep your password secret; never give it to anyone else.
- **Secure authentication.** Find out whether your mail server requires *Secure Password Authentication* (SPA).

Running the Internet Connection Wizard

If you didn't supply e-mail information when you ran the Connection Wizard to install Internet Explorer (see Chapter 4), Outlook Express will run the e-mail portion of this wizard when you start the program for the first time.

TIP

If you have already set up your Outlook Express e-mail account on another computer, you can import the account file and save yourself the trouble of running the Connection Wizard again. On the computer that has your account already set up, click Tools on the menu bar, choose Accounts, and select the Mail tab. Select your e-mail account, and click Export. Place a floppy disk in the disk drive, select the disk, and choose Save. Insert this disk into the computer where you want to import the connection information. Start Outlook Express, click Tools on the menu bar, click Accounts, and click Mail. Click Import, and open the connection file that's on the floppy disk.

SEE ALSO

If you have already run the Connection Wizard and wish to add a new e-mail account, see "Managing Accounts," page 451.

To configure your e-mail account with the Connection Wizard, follow these steps:

1 Start Outlook Express for the first time. The program detects that you haven't specified your e-mail information, and you see the Internet Connection Wizard.

If the Connection Wizard detects that you previously configured your e-mail information for a different e-mail program, you can use this information. You'll see a page titled Setting Up Internet Mail. Click the option that enables you to use the existing information, click Next, and follow the Wizard's instructions to complete the configuration. To configure Outlook Express with new information, instead of using the existing information, click the option that creates a new Internet mail account.

2 Click Next to display the Your Name page (Figure 11-1). In the Display Name box, type your name the way you want it to appear to other e-mail users. They'll see this name in the From column of their e-mail programs.

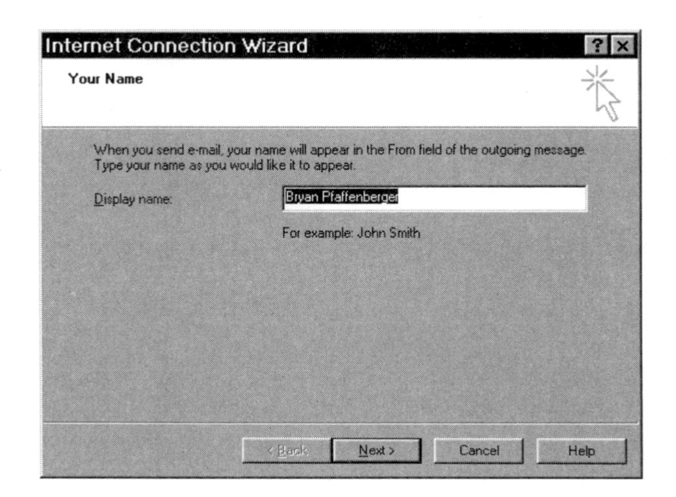

FIGURE 11-1.
In this page of the Internet Connection Wizard, you specify the name you want other people to see when they receive your e-mail.

3 Click Next to display the Internet E-mail Address page (Figure 11-2). In the E-mail Address box, carefully type your e-mail address, just the way it was given to you by your Internet service provider. Double-check your typing before proceeding.

4 Click Next to display the E-mail Server Names page (Figure 11-3). Select the type of server that's used to store your incoming mail (the options are POP3 and IMAP). Carefully type the Internet addresses of your incoming and outgoing mail servers.

5 Click Next to display the Internet Mail Logon page (Figure 11-4). Specify your account name and password, and double-check your typing.

If you would like Outlook Express to remember your password so that you do not have to supply it each time you log on, check

Remember Password. (If your computer is used by several people, consider un-checking this item so that no one can send Internet e-mail in your name.)

If your service provider requires you to log on using Secure Password Authentication (SPA), enable this option.

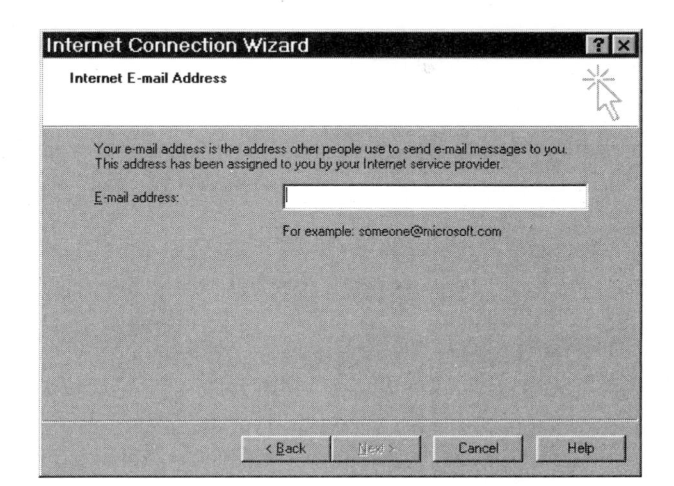

FIGURE 11-2.
Be sure to type your e-mail address carefully, and double-check your typing.

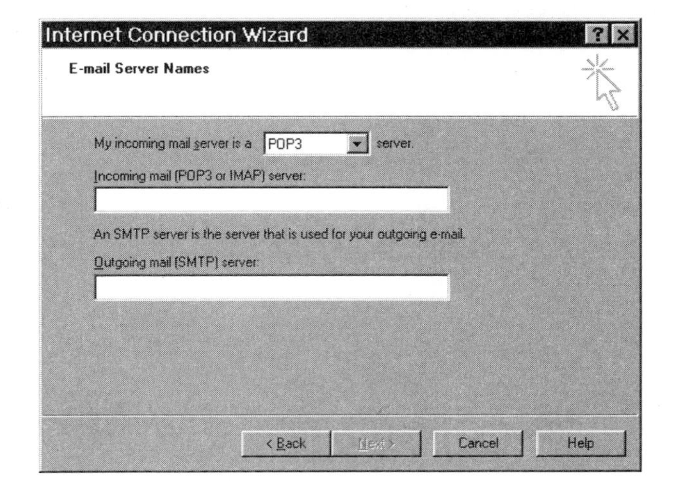

FIGURE 11-3.
Type the names of your incoming and outgoing mail servers. If the same server performs both tasks, type the name twice.

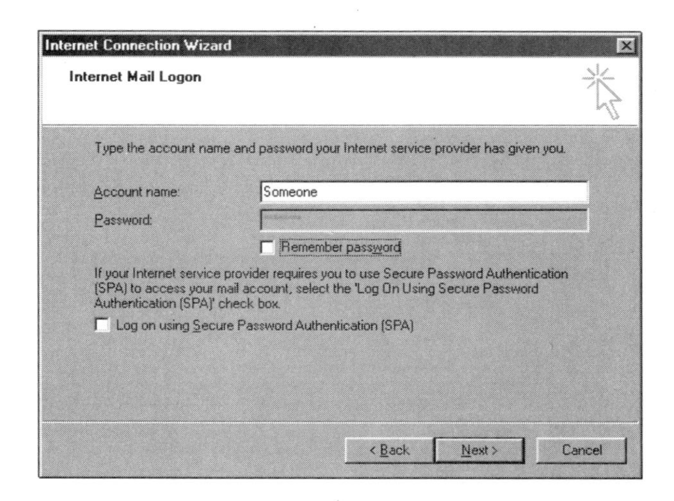

FIGURE 11-4. Type your account name and password carefully. If your computer is used by two or more people, consider unchecking the option that supplies your password automatically.

6 Click Next to complete the installation. You'll see the last page of the wizard (Figure 11-5); click Finish to close the wizard, and begin using your new account.

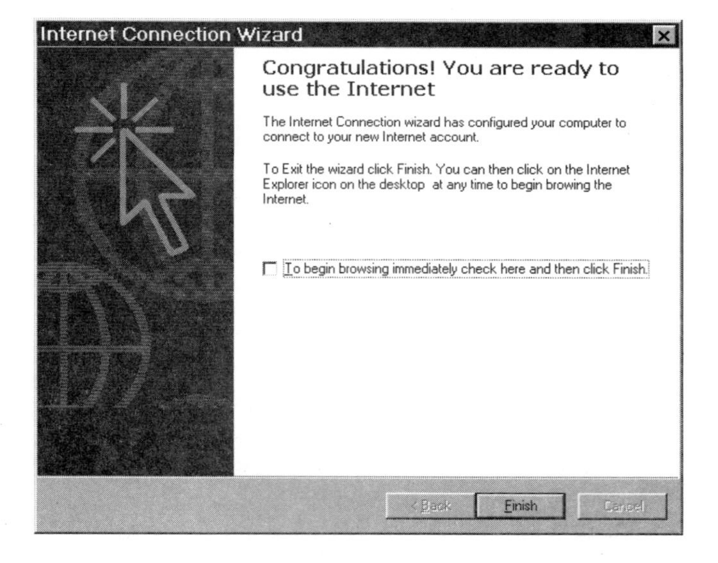

FIGURE 11-5. When you are finished running the wizard, click Finish to complete your account setup.

Troubleshooting Your Connection

If you experience problems connecting to your e-mail server with Outlook Express, try the following:

- Before trying to access your mail, establish your Internet connection. If you haven't set up your Internet connection yet, see Chapter 4, "Running the Connection Wizard."

- If you can connect to the Internet successfully, but you see an alert box informing you that there has been an error, find out the specifics. In the connection dialog box that appears when you click Send/Receive, click Details to see the details area, and click Errors to see the error messages. (If you don't see the dialog box that appears after you click Send/Receive, double-click the word "Error" on the status bar.)
- If the error involves a server timeout, increase the Server Timeouts setting. To do so, click Tools on the menu bar, click Accounts, and click the Mail tab. Select your account, and click Properties. Click Advanced, and drag the slider in the Server Timeouts area to the right.
- If adjusting the server timeouts doesn't solve the problem, call your service provider's technical support department. Click Tools on the menu bar, choose Accounts, and click the Mail tab. Click Properties. With the technical support person's help, review the information in the Servers, Connection, and Advanced pages.

Choosing Connection Options

Outlook Express shares Internet connection settings with Internet Explorer. However, you can choose some connection options that affect Outlook Express.

To choose connection options, do the following:

1. From the Outlook Express menu bar, click Tools, and choose Options.
2. In the Options dialog box, click the Connection tab. You'll see the Connection page of the Options dialog box (see Figure 11-6).
3. If you would like Outlook Express to connect when you start the program, remove the check mark next to At Start Up, Ask Me If I Would Like To Connect.

   Unchecking this option is recommended if you're using a network (LAN) connection, or if you're using a modem on its own, separate phone line. Keep this item checked if your modem and phone share the same line.
4. If you would like the program to hang up after checking your mail, place a check mark next to Hang Up After Sending And Receiving.

   Checking this option is recommended if your modem and phone share the same line, or if you pay per-minute long-distance or access charges. If you're using a network (LAN) connection or a separate phone line, and your account gives you unlimited access, uncheck this item.

5 Click OK to confirm your connection options.

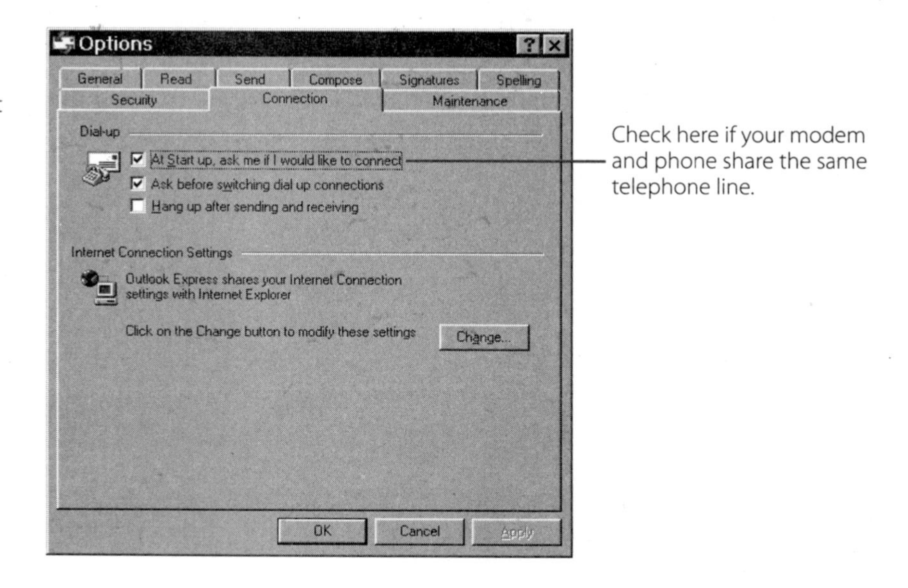

FIGURE 11-6. Choose the connection options that best suit your connection method.

Configuring an IMAP Account

If you're using an IMAP account, you may wish to choose some configuration options before using Outlook Express. Because IMAP servers vary, you should check with your mail administrator to find out how to configure these options; what follows is an overview of the options you can configure.

To configure IMAP options, do the following:

1 On the Outlook Express menu bar, click Tools, and choose Accounts.

2 Click the Mail tab.

3 Select your IMAP mail account.

4 Click Properties.

5 In the Root Folder Path area, type the path. This is the path name that identifies the location of your folders on the IMAP server. Check with your mail administrator to find out how to type the root-folder path.

If your IMAP server is a Cyrus server, your user folders must be contained within the Inbox folder. For Unix-based servers, your mail is usually stored within your home-user directory, which is named by using a tilde (~) followed by your account name, a slash, and Mail (as in ~fbaggins/Mail).

6. So that you can access sent items and drafts from other locations, be sure to check Store Special Folders On IMAP Server.
7. Click OK until you see Outlook Express again.

Importing Mail from Another Program

If you used a different e-mail program before you installed Outlook Express, you can import your messages into Outlook Express. You can import mail from the following programs:

- Eudora Pro or Light (through version 3.0)
- Microsoft Exchange
- Microsoft Internet Mail (32-bit version)
- Microsoft Internet Mail for Windows 3.1
- Microsoft Outlook
- Microsoft Outlook Express (version 4)
- Microsoft Windows Messaging
- Netscape Communicator
- Netscape Mail (version 2 or 3)

For information on importing an address book from other e-mail programs such as Netscape and Eudora, see "Importing Contact List Information," page 397.

To import your messages from another program, follow these steps:

1. In the Folders list, click Inbox.
2. From the File menu, click Import, and choose Messages from the submenu. You'll see the Outlook Express Import wizard.
3. Select the e-mail program from which you want to import messages, and click Next.
4. In the Location Of Messages page, you see the location in which your messages are currently stored. If you would like to import messages to a different location, click Browse, and select the location.
5. Click Finish to import your messages.

Setting Up Identities

If more than one person uses your copy of Outlook Express, you can set up more than one *identity*. For example, perhaps you use Outlook Express at home, and your spouse also uses Outlook Express. To keep your messages and contacts separate, you can create identities for each user of the program.

Do the people using your computer have more than one e-mail address or e-mail account? By setting up identities, you can configure Outlook Express so that each identity is associated with its own e-mail address and account information.

Creating a New Identity

To create identities for users of the program, do the following:

1. From the File menu, click Identities, and choose Add New Identity. You'll see the New Identity dialog box, shown here:

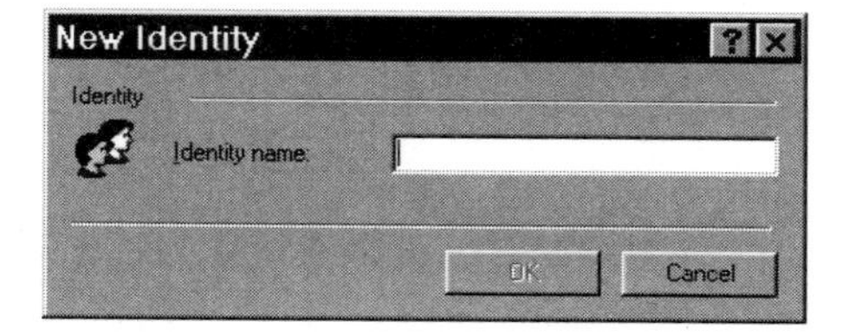

2. In the Identity Name box, type a name for this identity, and click OK. You'll see an alert box asking whether you would like to switch to this identity.
3. Click Yes to switch to the new identity you have created. You'll see the Internet Connection Wizard.
4. Do one of the following:
   - If the new identity uses the same e-mail account as the one you defined when you first configured Outlook Express, select the account, and click Use An Existing Internet Mail Account.

     or

   - To create a new account for this identity, click Create A New Internet Mail Account, and repeat the procedure you follow to create a new Internet mail account. (See "Running the Internet Connection Wizard," page 321.)

Identities enable you to switch from one user to another without interrupting your Internet connection or restarting Microsoft Windows. However, identities lack security. Any user can switch to your identity and read your mail. For better security, consider defining users and passwords at the Windows level. For more information, see "Setting Up Windows for Multiple Users," page 151. This approach enables you to define user passwords, and prevents users from browsing each other's settings (including Outlook Express messages and contacts). The disadvantage of the Windows approach lies in your having to stop your Internet connection and restart Windows when you switch users.

For information on sharing contact information with other identities, see "Sharing Address Book Information across Identities," page 416.

Switching Identities

While you're working with Outlook Express, you can switch identities without having to quit Outlook Express or restart Windows.

To tell which identity you're working with, just look at the title bar. You'll see the current identity's name.

To switch identities, follow these steps:

1. From the File menu, choose Switch Identities. You'll see the Switch Identities dialog box, shown here:

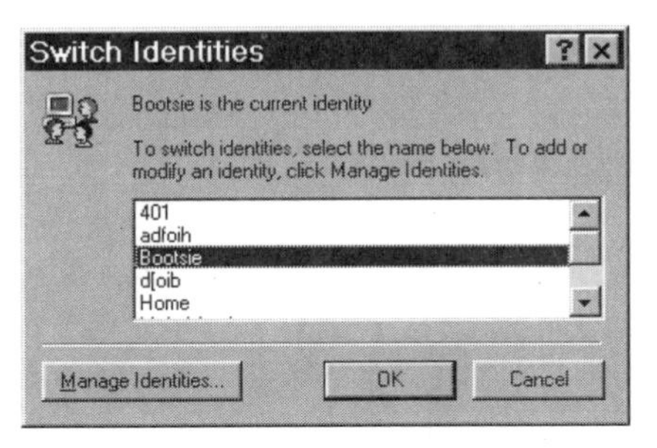

2. Choose the identity you want, and click OK.

   If the new identity requires a different connection, you'll see a dialog box asking whether you want to switch connections. Click Yes to proceed.

To switch connections automatically when you switch identities, click Tools on the menu bar, choose Options, and click the Connection tab. Remove the check mark next to Ask Before Switching Dial-Up Connections.

Logging Off from an Identity

When you quit Outlook Express, the program records the *current identity* (the identity you were using when you quit the program). When you start the program, Outlook Express will use this identity automatically, unless you log off from the identity. Logging off closes Outlook Express and tells the program to use the default startup settings the next time Outlook Express starts.

To log off from an identity that you're using, click File on the menu bar, click Identities, and Log Off.

Changing the Names of Identities

Once you've created identities, you can change the name you've assigned to an identity.

To change an identity name, follow these steps:

1 On the File menu, click Identities, and choose Manage Identities. You'll see the Manage Identities dialog box, shown in Figure 11-7.

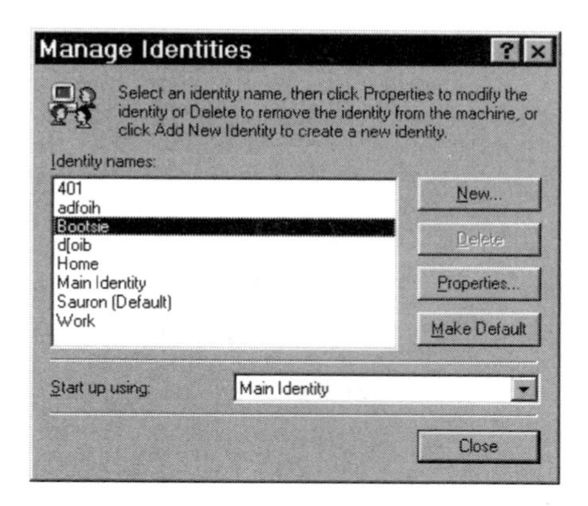

FIGURE 11-7.
The Manage Identities dialog box enables you to create, delete, and edit identities.

2 Select the identity you want to manage.

3. Click Properties. You'll see the Identity Properties dialog box for the identity you selected, as shown next:

4. Change the name of this identity, and click Close.

Choosing a Default Identity

When you quit Outlook Express, the program records the current identity. The next time you start the program, Outlook Express uses the current identity. If you log off the current identity, the program uses the default startup setting (Outlook Express asks which identity you'd like to use). If you wish, you can adjust these settings so that the program always starts with the same identity rather than asking you which one you prefer.

To choose a default identity and startup options, do the following:

1. In the Manage Identities dialog box, select the identity that you want to define as the default identity. (The current default is indicated in parentheses.)
2. Click Make Default.
3. In the list box, choose the identity to use when the program starts. By default, the program uses the Ask Me setting, which prompts you to choose an identity when the program starts.
4. Click Close.

TIP

You may wish to create more than one identity even if you're the only person who uses your copy of Outlook Express. For example, suppose you have two e-mail accounts, an account at work and an account for home use. You can create a Work identity for your work-related e-mail, and you can configure this identity to access your work e-mail account. You can also create a Home identity for your home-related e-mail, and you can configure this identity to access your home e-mail account. In this way, you can keep the two types of e-mail separate.

Setting Up Security Zones

As you'll learn in Chapter 12, Outlook Express can receive messages formatted in HTML. Such messages can include active content, such as scripts and Java applets. For this reason, you should be concerned about rogue content, just as you are when you're using Internet Explorer (see "Understanding Security Settings," page 255). Outlook Express uses Internet Explorer's current security-zone settings, but there's less risk of eliminating useful functionality by choosing more security. Unlike Web pages, most e-mail messages contain no HTML formatting at all, and very few contain scripts. The messages that do contain scripts are probably commercial messages—and more than likely, they're unsolicited.

To adjust security settings, do the following:

1. From the Tools menu, choose Options.
2. In the Options dialog box, click Security. You'll see the Security page (see Figure 11-8).
3. In the Security Zones, select Internet Zone to enable e-mail based scripts. For for better protection, select Restricted Sites Zone to prohibit most active content from executing.

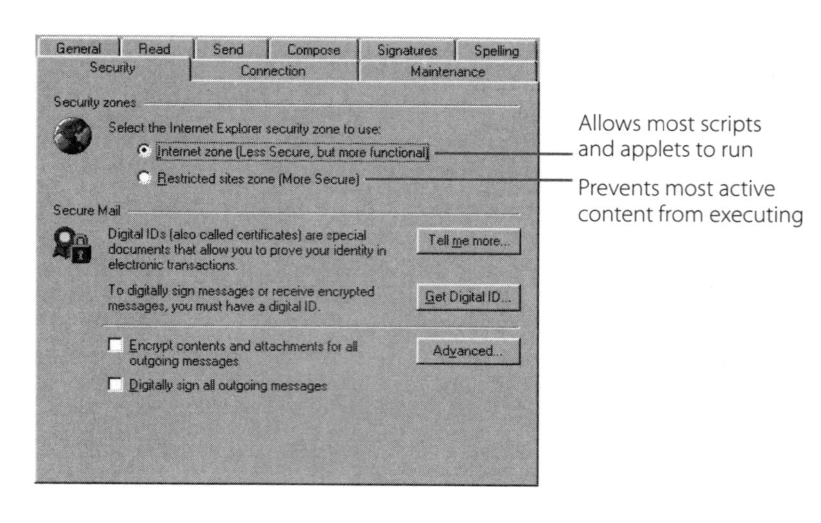

FIGURE 11-8.
To play it safe with active content in e-mail messages, you can choose Internet Explorer's Restricted sites zone security settings.

Understanding What's on the Screen

After you've finished adding your e-mail-account information and optionally configuring identities, take some time to explore Outlook Express's on-screen components (see Figure 11-9). The Outlook Express panel (the one on the right) gives you a quick overview of the three major tasks you can do with Outlook Express:

- **E-mail.** In this area, you can see how many unread messages you have. You can view these messages by clicking the underlined link. You can also create new mail messages or read your existing mail by clicking the links for these items.
- **Newsgroups.** If you haven't set up your newsgroup account, you can do so by clicking the link shown in this area. After you set up newsgroups, you can access subscribed newsgroups by clicking links here.
- **Contacts.** In this area, you can click links to open your Address Book, which enables you to store information about your contacts. You can also search the Internet for e-mail addresses, telephone numbers, and postal addresses.

SEE ALSO
For an introduction to newsgroups, see "Introducing Newsgroups," page 508.

SEE ALSO
For an introduction to the Address Book, see "Using the Address Book," page 394.

You'll also see a Tip Of The Day. You can click Previous or Next at the bottom of the Tip Of The Day pane to see additional tips. If you'd prefer to hide the tips, click the Close box at the top of the Tip Of The Day pane.

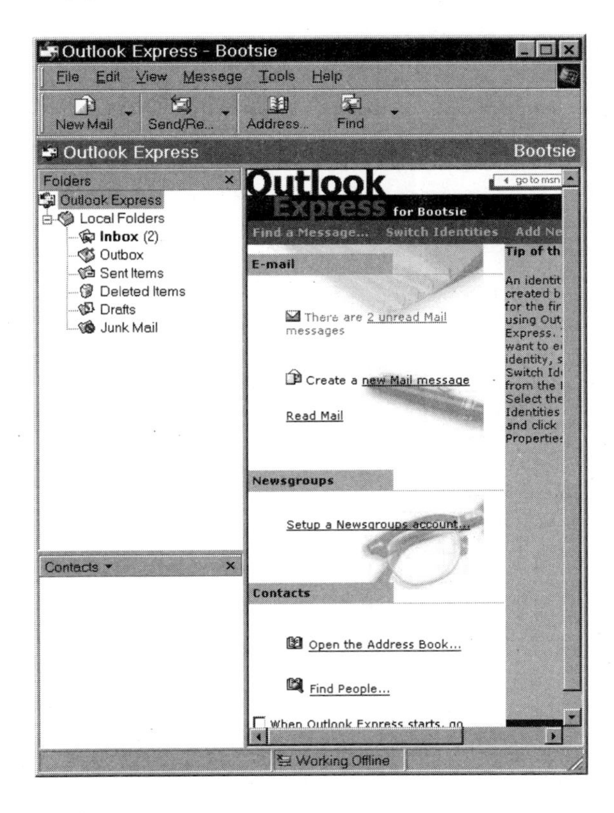

FIGURE 11-9.
The top-level view of Outlook Express offers a quick overview of its functions. The area on the right shows you what you can do with the program.

If you'd like Outlook Express to display your Inbox when the program starts, check the option at the bottom of the Outlook Express panel. This option is called When Outlook Express Starts, Go Directly To My Inbox. This option is a good one if you use Outlook Express for e-mail only.

Examining Outlook Express's On-Screen Components

Outlook Express is designed to look and work like Internet Explorer. There's much that's familiar, such as the program icon and the toolbars. You'll notice, though, that the toolbar buttons differ, and there are several panels within the workspace (Figure 11-10). Depending on how your copy of Outlook Express was configured (and which folder you're viewing), you may not see all of these features on-screen.

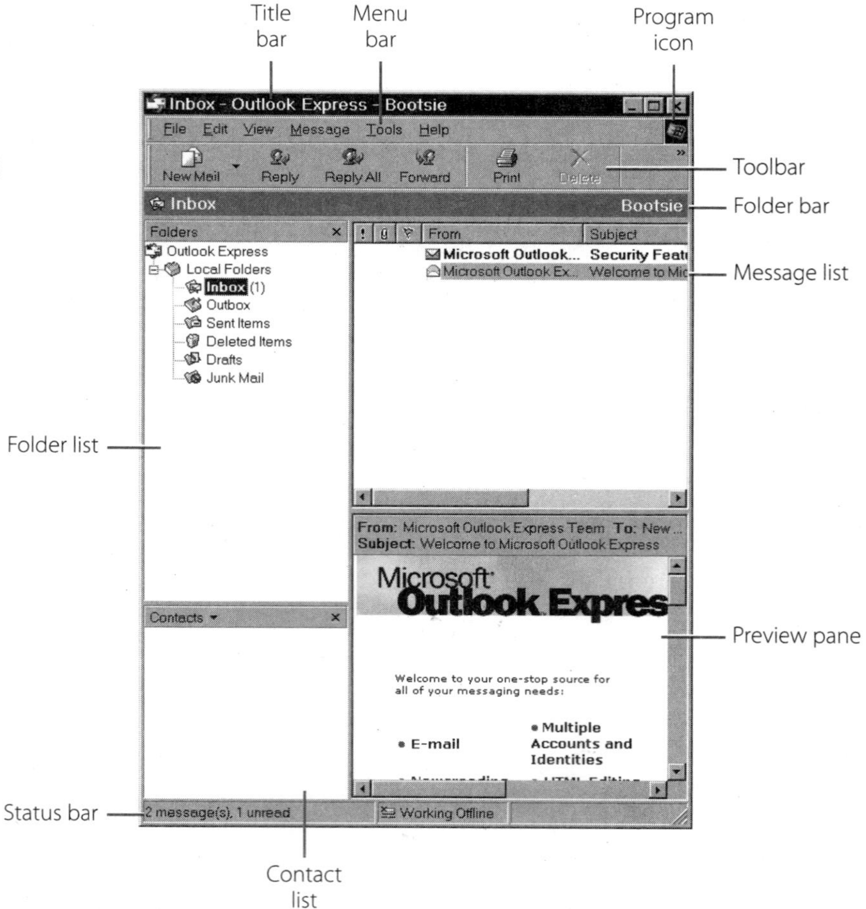

FIGURE 11-10.
Outlook Express's appearance changes when you select a mail folder. Here, you see the program's appearance after you choose the Inbox folder.

- **Title bar.** To reposition the Outlook Express window, drag the title bar. To maximize the window quickly, double-click the title bar. Double-click it again to restore it to the previous size.
- **Menu bar.** All the Outlook Express commands can be accessed from the menu bar, but the most frequently used commands are also found on the toolbar.
- **Program icon.** This icon shows an animation when Outlook Express is sending or receiving mail.
- **Toolbar.** Just what you see on the toolbar depends on what you're doing with Outlook Express. When you're viewing the main Outlook Express folder, you see just four buttons (New Mail, Send/Receive, Addresses, and Find). When you select one of the folders in the folder pane, you'll see additional buttons.
- **Outlook bar.** The Outlook Bar gives you access to various folders of mail, such as Inbox, Outbox, Deleted Items, and Drafts. You can also return to the main Outlook Express folder by clicking the Outlook Express icon. (The Outlook bar isn't displayed by default.)
- **Folder bar.** Outlook Express enables you to organize your mail into folders. The Folder bar displays the name of the current folder. If you created identities, the Folder bar also shows the name of the current identity.
- **Folder list.** In this list, you see the default folders (such as Inbox and Sent Items).
- **Message list.** Here, you see the selected folder's content.
- **Preview pane.** In the preview pane, you see the text of the message that's currently selected in the message list.
- **Status bar.** In this area, Outlook Express displays messages and information about its status and what it's doing. You can hide the status bar by choosing Layout and Status Bar from the View menu, but it's worth keeping it visible because some of the messages are useful or important.
- **Contact list.** Here, you see the contacts that you've created. If you created more than one identity, this list shows the current identity's contacts.

Understanding the Default Folders

Outlook Express is set up with the following local mail folders (Figure 11-11):

- **Inbox.** Here's where your new messages show up, and here they stay unless you move them elsewhere.
- **Outbox.** Here's where your messages are temporarily stored until you click Send And Receive; then they're electronically transported to your service provider.
- **Sent Items.** Here's where you'll find copies of messages you've sent.
- **Deleted Items.** If you delete an unwanted message from the Inbox, Outlook Express puts it here. Think of the Deleted Items folder as the Recycle Bin. To erase a message completely, you must open the Deleted Items folder and delete the message there. If you want to permanently delete all the messages in the Deleted Items folder, right-click the folder's icon and choose Empty Folder.
- **Drafts.** If you're composing a message and need to do something else before finishing the message, simply close the message and tell Outlook Express to save it. Outlook Express places the message in the Drafts folder to await your return.

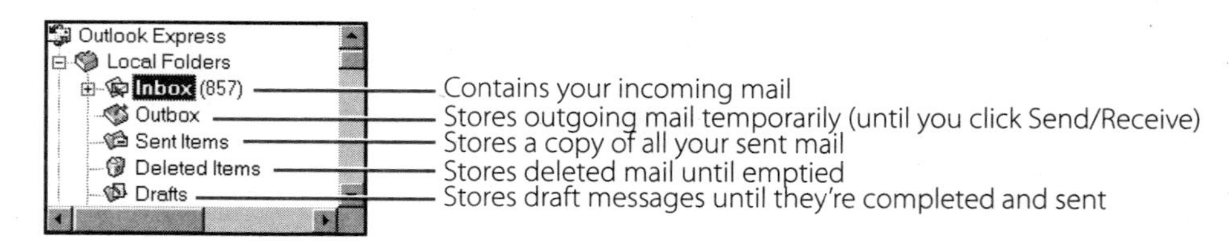
Outlook Express
Local Folders
Inbox (857)
Outbox
Sent Items
Deleted Items
Drafts
Contains your incoming mail
Stores outgoing mail temporarily (until you click Send/Receive)
Stores a copy of all your sent mail
Stores deleted mail until emptied
Stores draft messages until they're completed and sent

FIGURE 11-11. The default local folders provide the basics of mail organization. You can create your own folders, too.

To view the contents of a folder, click the folder's icon in the Outlook bar; you can also click the folder's title in the Folder list.

TIP

> To erase items in the Deleted Items folder when you exit Outlook Express, click Tools on the Menu bar, click Options, click the Maintenance tab, and place a check mark beside Empty Messages From The 'Deleted Items' Folder On Exit. If you're using an IMAP account, check Purge Deleted Messages When Leaving IMAP Folders.

Setting Up IMAP Folders

Skip this section if you're connecting via a POP e-mail account. If you're connecting to an IMAP server, you must specify the folders that you want to show in the Folder list.

To view mail folders on an IMAP server, follow these steps:

1. In the Folder list, select your IMAP account.
2. In the Synchronization Manager area, click IMAP Folders.
3. Select a folder that you want to view, and click Show. To select more than one folder, hold down the Ctrl key, click the folders you want to view, and click Show.

Using the Toolbar

The toolbar contains the commands you'll use most often. Table 11-1 on page 338 lists the buttons that appear when you've selected the Outlook Express folder. Table 11-2 lists the buttons that appear when you click a mail folder, such as Inbox or Sent Items.

Choosing Layout Options

Before you start working with Outlook Express, you may wish to choose layout options. With these options (see Figure 11-12), you can customize the main Outlook Express window to your liking.

To customize the main Outlook Express window, do the following:

1. From the View menu, choose Layout. You see the Window Layout Properties dialog box, shown in Figure 11-12.

Like Internet Explorer's Standard Buttons toolbar, the Outlook Express toolbar can be customized. See "Customizing the Outlook Express Toolbars," page 457.

TABLE 11-1. Toolbar Buttons (Outlook Express folder selected).

Button name	What it does
New Mail	Displays a blank New Message window, enabling you to write a new message to send to someone. If you click the down arrow, you can choose from a variety of templates, called *stationery*. To send a message with stationery to someone, your recipient must be using an e-mail program that can receive richly formatted (HTML) e-mail. For more information on stationery, see "Using Stationery," page 379.
Send/Receive	Connects with your mail server, automatically downloads any new mail, and sends any outgoing mail that you've written. If you click the down arrow, you can choose to receive mail only, or send mail only. If you set up Outlook Express to work with more than one e-mail account, you can also select the server you want to use. For more information on setting up multiple e-mail accounts, see "Adding a New Account," page 452.
Addresses	Displays the Address Book, and enables you to create or edit your contacts. For more information on the Address Book, see "Using the Address Book," page 394.
Find	Displays the Find Message dialog box, which enables you to search for a message. For more information on searching for messages, see "Finding a Message," page 361.

TABLE 11-2. Additional Toolbar Buttons (mail folder selected).

Button name	What it does
Reply	Enables you to reply to the selected message. For more information, see "Replying to a Message," page 385.
Reply All	Enables you to reply to the sender and all recipients of the selected message. For more information, see "Replying to a Message," page 385.
Forward	Forwards the selected message to a recipient that you specify. For more information, see "Forwarding a Message," page 387.
Print	Prints the selected message. For more information, see "Printing a Message," page 351.
Delete	Deletes the selected message. For more information, see "Keeping Your Inbox Tidy," page 355.

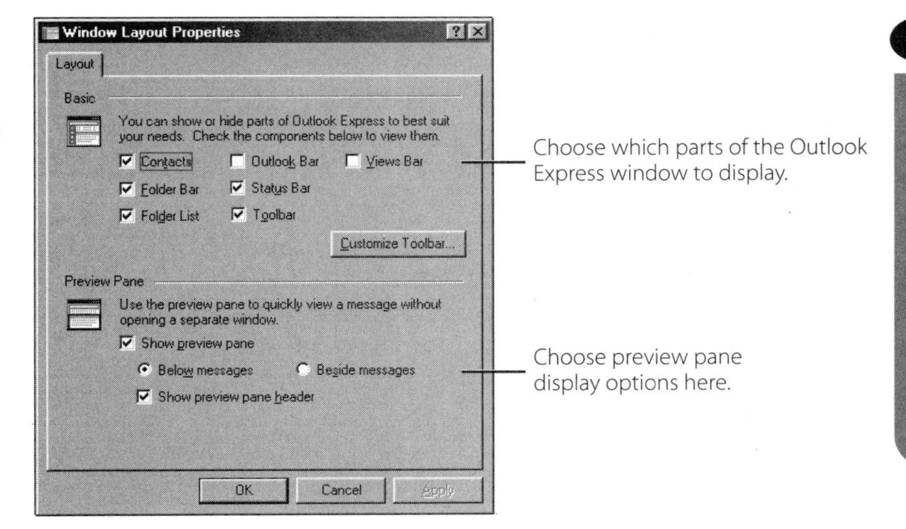

FIGURE 11-12.
In this dialog box you can specify the layout of the Outlook Express window.

2 In the Basic area, check the components that you want to display.

If you're working with a small screen, you may wish to hide the Folder list and the Outlook bar. When you hide the Folder list, the Folder bar gains a down arrow (see Figure 11-13). When you click this arrow, the Folder list appears temporarily, enabling you to choose a folder.

FIGURE 11-13.
If you hide the folder list, you can click the down arrow on the folder bar to see the folder list temporarily.

You can uncheck the Toolbar option to hide the toolbar if you wish. However, the toolbar is very useful, and you will probably want to keep it on-screen. If you need more room, uncheck Show Text On Toolbar Buttons. This option gives you small icons as well as removing the text.

3 In the Preview Pane area, you can uncheck Show Preview Pane if you wish, but you should try this feature (see Chapter 12) before doing so. (As you'll learn in the next chapter, you can read messages in a separate window, and this technique has some advantages. If you prefer reading messages in a separate window, you may wish to hide the preview pane so that you have more room to view the message list.)

If you're short on screen room, uncheck Show Preview Pane Header. This header displays information about the message, but it duplicates the information shown in the message list.

To choose the fonts to use when reading and composing messages, see "Choosing Read Options," page 421.

You can locate the preview pane beside messages (instead of below the messages, which is the default option), but this arrangement works well only if you're working with the Outlook Express window maximized (see Figure 11-14).

Choosing Text Size

Like Internet Explorer, Outlook Express enables you to choose a text size for comfortable viewing. The default is Medium; you can choose one of six sizes ranging from Smallest to Largest. To choose a text size, click View on the menu bar, click Text Size, and choose a text size from the submenu.

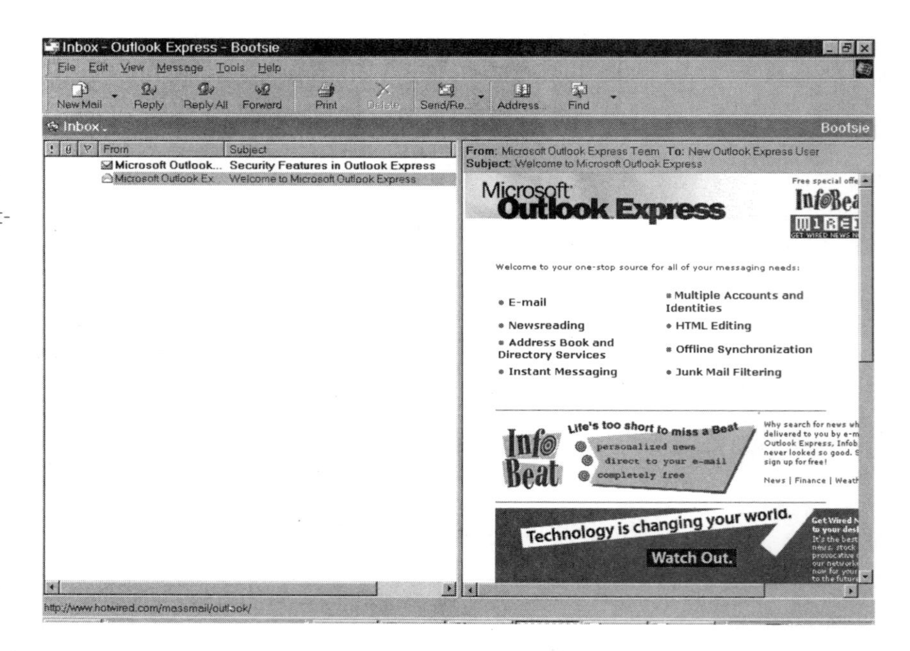

FIGURE 11-14.
You can position the preview pane next to the message list, but this works well only if you maximize the Outlook Express window.

Choosing an Encoding

By default, Outlook Express is configured appropriately for the country in which you're using the program. However, you may wish to choose a different character encoding in order to view messages in foreign languages. An *encoding* is a method of representing characters (letters and numbers) so that all the characters in one or more foreign languages can be shown on-screen.

To choose an encoding, click View on the menu bar, click Encoding, and choose an encoding from the submenu.

> If you don't see the encoding you want, you can download additional encodings. To do so, click Start on the Windows taskbar, and choose Windows Update. You'll see a list of available update items; scroll down to view available encodings.

Considering E-Mail Privacy

Before using e-mail, you need to understand clearly that employers generally believe that employees have no right to privacy when using the employer's computer system. In fact, in many companies, one or more full-time staff may be assigned to read employee e-mail. If you make fun of your boss, divulge confidential information to an outsider, or use company e-mail for personal purposes, you could find yourself packing your desk.

If you have your own e-mail account with an Internet service provider, you have somewhat more privacy, but it's far from absolute. In the United States, the Electronic Communications Privacy Act of 1986 requires U.S. government agencies to obtain search warrants to intercept and read electronic mail messages while they are en route. However, all mail servers maintain backup tapes, sometimes for years, of all the e-mail messages that pass through their systems. These backup copies are not protected. Any investigator can obtain access to these tapes and use them for any purpose whatsoever, even without obtaining a warrant.

You should also remember that any party to a lawsuit in which you or your company is involved can issue a subpoena to obtain copies of your e-mail, and Internet service providers must comply with valid subpoenas. For this reason, e-mail is not an appropriate medium for discussing confidential or sensitive matters that could become an issue in a legal proceeding. Remember that backup tapes may contain copies of your messages, even after you have deleted them from your computer.

TIP

> You'll be very wise to follow this advice: *Never, never, never write anything in e-mail that you wouldn't want to see the next morning on your boss's desk, your mother's coffee table, or the front page of your hometown newspaper.*

Learning E-Mail Etiquette

Experienced e-mail users appreciate working with correspondents who follow some simple rules of etiquette. The simplest of all of these rules is also the most fundamental: show consideration for others. Here's an overview of the e-mail etiquette you should know before you start sending messages.

Write Subject Lines

All e-mail messages should include a *subject line*, a short message title that appears in message lists. Many people receive dozens or even hundreds of messages per day. For this reason, be sure to use a subject line that concisely but accurately describes the subject of your message. Overly general subject lines such as "Request" or "Hello" don't convey very much information, and they may annoy the recipient to the point that they don't read your letter! A subject line such as "October acquisitions—order deadline?" helps your reader get oriented quickly. Don't make the subject line too long, because some e-mail programs display only the first 40 or 50 characters of the subject text. Put the important words first.

Orient Your Reader

Begin your e-mail message as you would a telephone call or a letter: state your purpose in writing the message, and provide background or orienting information if necessary.

Avoid Misinterpretation

Be aware that e-mail isn't a good medium for expressing sarcasm. A joke that might work over the water cooler could come across the wrong way in an e-mail message. Experienced e-mail users recognize this fact, and sometimes use text-based faces, called *smileys*, to indicate when they're just kidding. But remember that some recipients do not care for smileys; they believe that a good writer should be able to express humor or sarcasm without resorting to such visual cues. Play it safe—use other media for kidding around.

TABLE 12-4. Commonly Used Smileys.

Use this smiley:	To mean:
:-) or :)	I'm happy, or I'm just kidding.
:-(or :(	I'm sad, or I'm disappointed.
;-) or ;)	I'm kidding (wink).

Refrain from Anger

Many people do serious damage to their careers by firing off an e-mail message in a fit of anger. Such messages, called *flames,* will certainly antagonize their recipients, but bear in mind that it's very easy to forward messages to others. If you flame a co-worker, imagine what might happen if your co-worker forwards the message to your boss, with a note that says, "See?"

Don't ever send an e-mail message when you're hot under the collar. Sleep on it. Tomorrow, you'll probably wonder what you were so angry about.

Avoid "Shouting"

Experienced e-mail users do not like to read messages typed in all capital letters, which is called *shouting*. If you need to express emphasis, you can do so less offensively by placing asterisks before and after the word or phrase you want to emphasize (*like this*).

SEE ALSO
For more information on HTML and plain-text sending options, see "Choosing Mail Sending Options," page 423.

Choose the Right Format

With Outlook Express, you can send mail in one of two formats:

- **HTML.** This is Outlook Express's default mail-sending format. It enables you to send richly formatted e-mail, including stationery (backgrounds), fonts, and pictures. However, you can send HTML-enhanced mail only to people who are using HTML-capable e-mail clients, such as recent versions of Netscape Messenger, Eudora, Microsoft Outlook, and Outlook Express.
- **Plain Text.** This is the best format for most Internet users, many of whom are using e-mail programs that can't handle HTML. If you send them an HTML-formatted message, they'll see a lot of garbage characters and gibberish amidst your message, and they won't be very happy about it.

TIP

Play it safe by changing Outlook Express's default setting so that the program sends plain text e-mail. To choose this setting, click Tools on the menu bar, choose Options, and click the Send tab. In the Mail Sending format area, click Plain Text.

Using Keyboard Shortcuts

If you prefer to use keyboard shortcuts, you'll find plenty of them in Outlook Express. Table 11-3 lists the keyboard shortcuts that are available in the main Outlook Express window. As you'll learn in the next chapter, you can use additional keyboard shortcuts in the Message Viewing and Message Composition windows.

TABLE 11-3. Keyboard Shortcuts (main Outlook Express window).

To	Press
Go to your Inbox	Ctrl+I
Move between the message list, folder list, and preview pane	Tab
Show or hide the folder list	Ctrl+L
Send and receive mail	Ctrl+M

CHAPTER 12

Reading and Composing Messages

Without spending a great deal of time learning all the program's features, you can use Outlook Express to receive, send, and reply to e-mail messages. But this feature-packed program can do much more. To get the greatest benefit from e-mail, you should learn how to use the program's intermediate and advanced features, such as how to work with *attachments* (binary files, such as Word documents or pictures, that can be sent and received along with e-mail text). If you're corresponding with somebody who's using an HTML-capable e-mail program, such as Outlook Express or Netscape Messenger, you can exchange richly formatted messages that include fonts and font sizes, character emphasis (such as boldface), background colors, and pictures. It's easy to learn these and other features, which are fully discussed in this chapter.

This chapter is organized in the way that you're most likely to use Outlook Express: you begin by starting the program, and then you download and read your mail. Then you write new messages, or reply to existing ones. Perhaps you'll also forward a message to a third party.

Reading Your Mail

For information on storing contact information with Outlook Express, see "Using the Address Book," page 394

When you start Outlook Express, you can click the Send/Receive button to check for new mail. The program then displays your new messages. Depending on the type of connection you have, you may wish to change some of the default mail-checking options, as this section explains.

Starting Outlook Express

To start the program and check for new mail, do the following:

1 Start Outlook Express. Unless you connect by means of a local area network (LAN), you'll see the Dial-Up Connection dialog box, shown here:

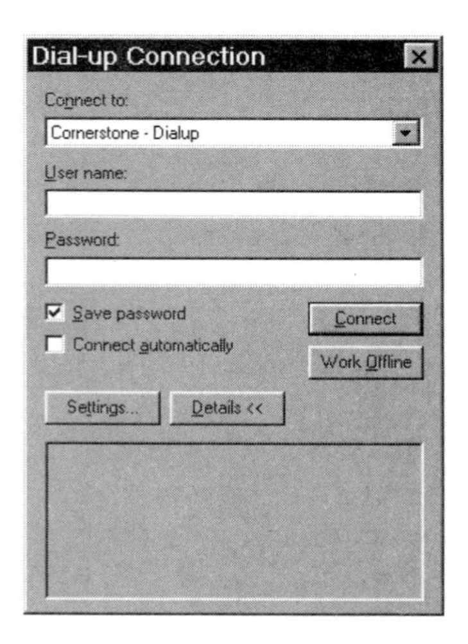

2 Specify your password, if necessary.

3 Click Connect.

To save your password so that you do not have to type it each time you log on, check Save Password in the Dial-Up Connection dialog box. If you have a separate phone line for your Internet connection and a subscription with unlimited connection time, click Connect Automatically; this bypasses the Dial-Up Connection dialog box and makes the connection without disturbing you.

Getting Your Mail

To get your mail from your mail server, click the Send/Receive button (or use one of its equivalents).

TIP

> If you have an IMAP account, you must activate an option before you can use the Send/Receive button to get your mail. First click Tools on the menu bar, and then choose Accounts. Select your IMAP account, and click Properties. Click the IMAP tab, and select Check For New Messages In All Folders.

SEE ALSO

If you're using a POP account, you can choose options that leave messages on the server instead of erasing them after you've downloaded the messages. For more information, see "Choosing Read Options," page 421.

To get your mail, do one of the following:

- On the toolbar, click Send/Receive.

  or

- Press Ctrl + M.

  or

- From the Tools menu, click Send and Receive, and choose Receive All from the submenu.

TIP

> The Send/Receive button (and its equivalents) do two tasks: they send outgoing messages as well as checking for new messages. If you want to check for new mail without sending outgoing messages, click the down arrow next to Send/Receive on the toolbar, and choose Receive All. You can also click Tools on the menu bar, click Send And Receive, and choose Receive All from the submenu.

TIP

> Did you see an error message when you tried to access your mail for the first time? The most likely cause is that you've typed some of your information incorrectly. (It's easy to do.) Click Tools on the menu bar, choose the Accounts command, and click the Mail tab. Select your mail account, and click Properties. Carefully check all the information to make sure it's correct. If you find a mistake, fix it and try clicking Send And Receive again. Still didn't work? Click the Details tab to see what's wrong. Perhaps your mail server is down. Call your ISP's technical support line for help.

After you receive your mail, look at the folder list. Folders containing new mail appear in bold. In the following illustration, note that the Inbox is shown in bold, and the number of unread messages is indicated:

Also, note that the Outlook Express top-level page (see Figure 12-1) indicates the number of unread messages in your Inbox.

Click here to read your new mail.

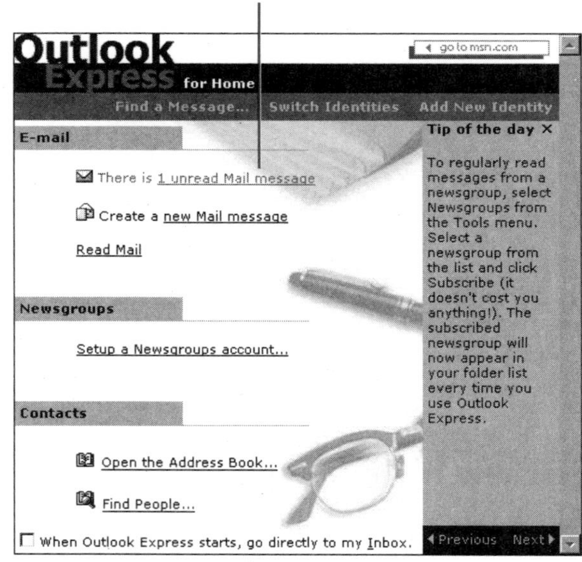

FIGURE 12-1.
After Outlook Express checks your mail, you see how many new messages you have received.

TIP

If you would like Outlook Express to display your Inbox when you start the program, click Outlook Express in the folder list, and scroll down until you see the option, When Outlook Express Starts, Go Directly To My Inbox. Check this option to display the Inbox on start-up.

Using the Inbox and Preview Pane

To read your mail, click Inbox in the folder list (if necessary) or click the Inbox icon on the Outlook Bar, if it's visible on the screen. (The Outlook Bar is hidden by default.) When you click a folder icon such as Inbox, the right portion of the Outlook Express window divides into the message list and the preview pane, as shown in Figure 12-2. Unread messages are shown in bold. Next to unread messages, you see an unopened letter icon.

When you select a message, you'll see the text of the message in the preview pane. At the top of the preview pane, you see basic information about the message (who it's from, who it's to, and the subject). This information stays put even if you scroll through the message.

After five seconds, the bold disappears, and the icon next to the message shows an opened letter, indicating that you've read the message.

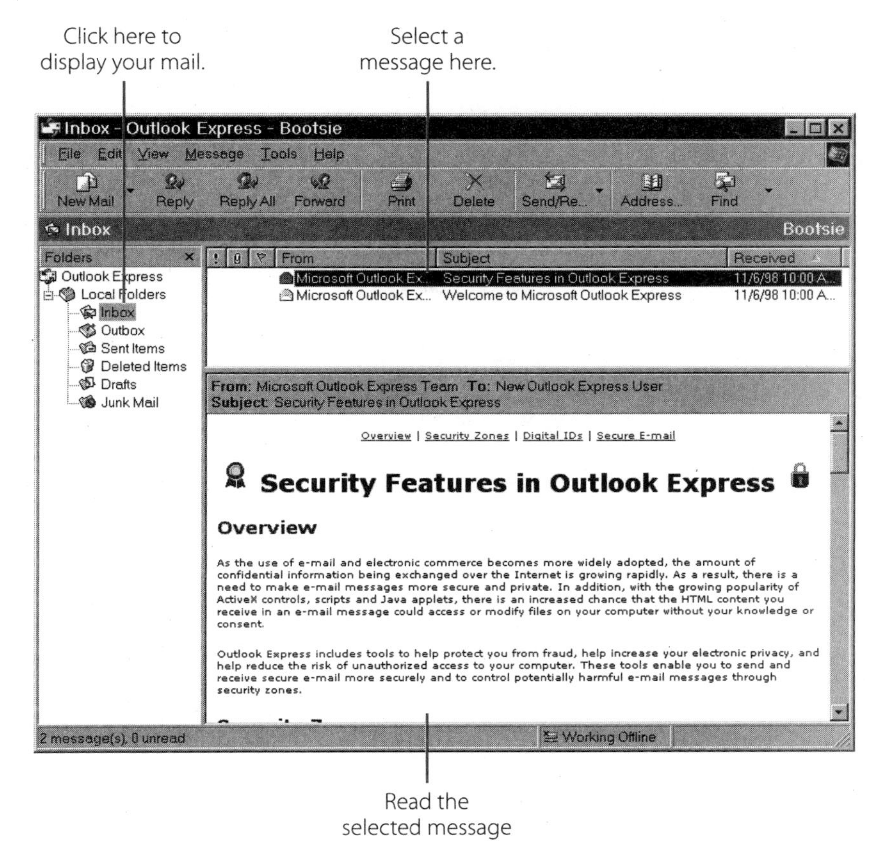

FIGURE 12-2.
When you select a folder to view, the right side of the screen divides into the message-list pane and the preview pane.

TIP

If you don't have time to read the whole message, and want to remind yourself to read it later, you can mark it as unread. This changes the icon back to an unopened letter and again displays the message's name in bold. To mark a message as unread, select it, click Edit on the menu bar, and choose Mark As Unread. You can also right-click the message in the message list, and choose Mark as Unread from the pop-up menu.

TIP

If you would like to increase the time it takes to mark a letter as read, go to the Tools menu, and select Options. Click Read, and increase the time in Mark Message Read After Displaying For *x* Seconds. Click OK to confirm.

Take a look at the sample message from Microsoft (which might be the only message you'll see at this point, unless there's an automatic message from your service provider). This message, shown in Figure 12-3, gives you a good hint of what you're in for with Outlook Express. Look at the formatting! With Outlook Express, you can send and receive messages formatted with HTML, the same markup language that underlies the appearance of Web documents. You don't even need to know any HTML to do this. As you'll see, formatting your messages is as simple as using a few basic commands that work just like the ones in a word processing program.

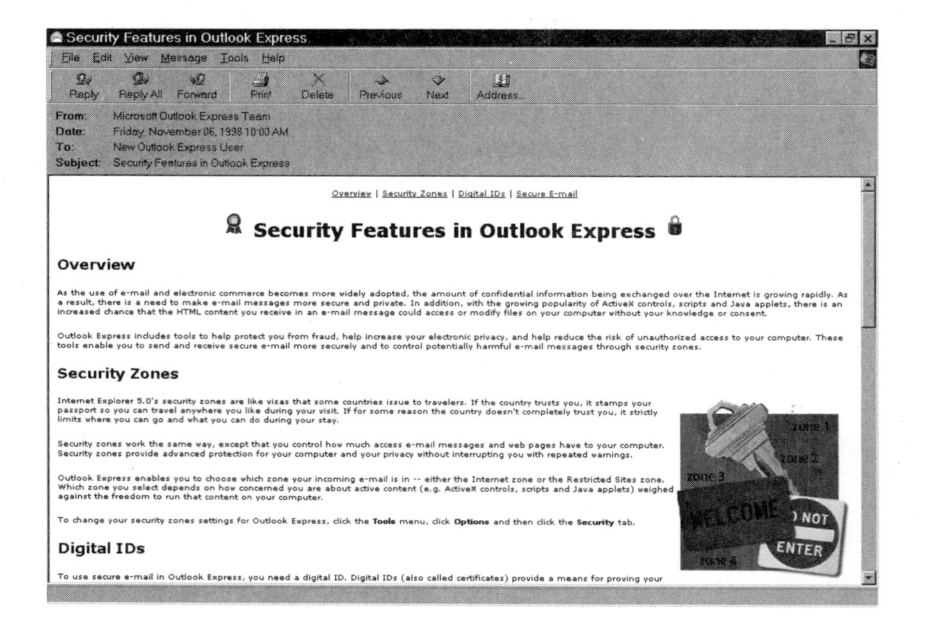

FIGURE 12-3.
This message uses HTML to provide rich formatting.

Understanding Message List Icons

You'll see icons in the message list, such as the closed and open envelopes that indicate (respectively) unread or read messages. Table 12-1 on page 352 shows the icons that can appear in the message list.

Sorting Messages

You'll notice that there's a row of buttons across the top of the message list. As Table 12-2 on page 353 explains, these buttons tell you what's in each column in the message list. They also enable you to sort the message list in a variety of ways.

By default, the message list is sorted by the date received, with the most recently received message at the top.

Outlook Express sorts in two ways: ascending (A to Z) or descending (Z to A). To change the sort order, click View on the menu bar, click Sort By, and choose Sort Ascending or Sort Descending from the submenu. Note that the current sort setting and sort order are shown by dots on the submenu, as in the following illustration:

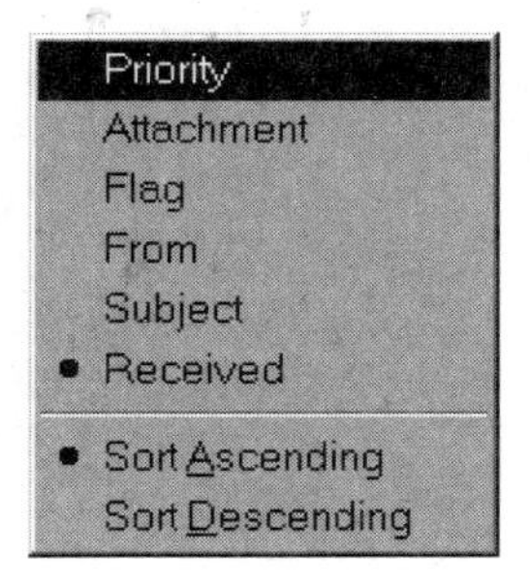

For most purposes, the best way to display your messages is to sort them by the date you received them and in descending order. You'll see your newest messages at the top of the window. The sort buttons become useful when you're looking for a message that has a high priority, flag, or attachment icon. For example, to see all the messages with flags, click the flag icon, and click it again, if necessary, to bring all the flagged messages to the top of the list. You can then quickly find the message you're looking for.

Printing a Message

To print a message that you've received, follow these steps:

1. In the message list, select the message you want to print.
2. Do one of the following:
   - On the toolbar, click Print.

     or
   - Press Ctrl + P.

     or
   - From the File menu, choose Print.

     or
   - Right-click the message title in the message list, and choose Print from the pop-up menu.

Some of these icons describe messages that have been digitally signed, encrypted, or both. For more information on these secure e-mail subjects, see "Secure E-Mail," page 464

TABLE 12-1. Icons in the Message List.

Icon	Description
	Attachment. The message has one or more files attached. For more information, see "Receiving an Attachment," page 359.
	High priority. This message's sender marked the message with high priority. It's urgent.
	Low priority. This message's sender marked the message with low priority. You can put off reading it until you've finished reading other new messages.
	Read message. To mark the message as unread again, right-click the message, and choose Mark As Unread.
	Unread message. This item appears in bold type.
	Draft message. You've saved a copy of this message in the Draft folder, but you haven't sent it yet. For more information on drafts, see "Saving a Draft," page 384.
	Marked for deletion on IMAP server. The message will be deleted the next time you connect. For information on deleting messages on an IMAP server, see "Keeping Your Inbox Tidy," page 355.
	Digitally signed and unopened. The unopened message is accompanied by a digital signature, which authenticates the sender's identity.
	Encrypted and unopened. The unopened message has been encrypted, and cannot be read without the decoding key.
	Digitally signed, encrypted, and unopened. The unopened message has been digitally signed and encrypted. It cannot be read without the decoding key.
	Digitally signed and opened. The opened message is accompanied by a digital signature, which authenticates the sender's identity.
	Encrypted and opened. This encrypted message has been decoded.
	Digitally signed, encrypted, and opened. This opened message has been digitally signed and encrypted, but it has been decoded.

You'll see the Print dialog box that appears when you print with Internet Explorer:

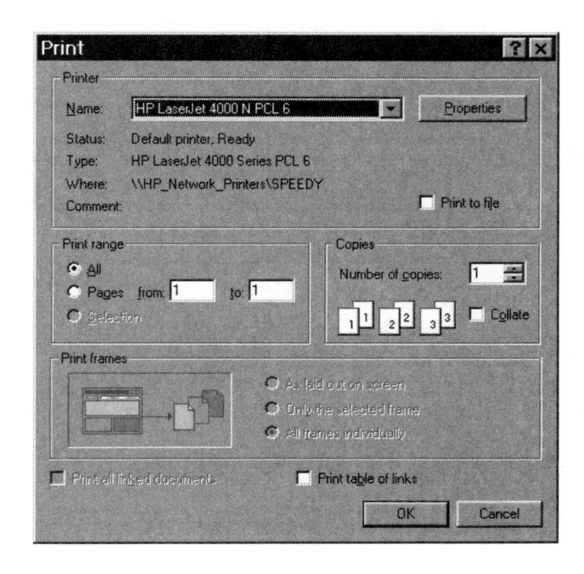

TABLE 12-2. Column Header Buttons.

Button name	What it does
Priority (exclamation point)	Sorts message according to priority, with urgent messages first. Same as clicking View, clicking Sort By, and choosing Priority from the submenu.
Attachment (paper clip icon)	Sorts messages by whether they contain an attached file; these files are shown first. Same as clicking View, clicking Sort By, and choosing Attachment from the submenu.
Flag	Sorts messages by whether they've been flagged. Same as clicking View, clicking Sort By, and choosing Flag from the submenu.
From	Sorts messages in alphabetical order by the sender's name. Same as clicking View, clicking Sort By, and choosing From from the submenu.
Subject	Sorts messages in alphabetical order by the message's subject. Same as clicking View, clicking Sort By, and choosing Subject from the submenu.
Received	Sorts messages by the date received. Same as clicking View, clicking Sort By, and choosing Received from the submenu.

3 Choose print options if you wish.

To specify the print range, click Pages, and choose the beginning and ending page by typing page numbers in the From and To boxes.

To specify the number of copies, click the down or up arrows in the Number Of Copies box, or type a number in the box. If you would like the pages collated so that all the pages of a copy print in sequence before the next copy starts printing, click Collate.

4 Click OK to start printing the message.

Flagging Messages

If you would like to remind yourself to return to an important message, you can attach a flag to it. To attach a flag to a message, follow these steps:

1 In the message list, select the message.

2 From the Message menu, choose Flag Message. You'll see a flag in the flag column, as shown in Figure 12-4.

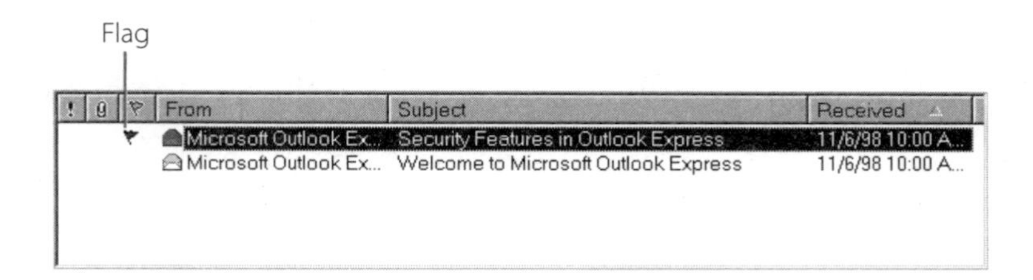

FIGURE 12-4.
You can flag important messages to make sure you review them later.

Adding an E-Mail Address to Your Address Book

As you will learn later in this chapter, the Address Book enables you to enter e-mail addresses quickly, and cuts down the chance that you'll make a typing mistake that could prevent your messages' delivery. The Address Book is also a very useful way to organize contact information so that it's available to Microsoft Office applications.

SEE ALSO
To learn how to add more information about a contact, see "Selectively Storing Contact Information," page 400.

When you receive a message from an important correspondent, take a moment to add this person's e-mail address to your Address Book. You can also add other contact information if you wish.

To add a person's e-mail address to your Address Book, follow these steps:

1. In the message list, select the message that contains the address you want to add.
2. Do one of the following:
   - From the Tools menu, choose Add Sender To Address Book.

     or

   - Right-click the message title, and choose Add Sender To Address Book from the pop-up menu. You'll see this person's name or e-mail address in the Contact list.

Outlook Express adds the sender's e-mail address to your Address Book.

If you don't see your contact list, click View on the menu bar, choose Layout, and activate Contacts.

Keeping Your Inbox Tidy

As you get involved with e-mail, you will find that your Inbox quickly becomes cluttered with messages—sometimes hundreds of them. A cluttered Inbox can cause stress due to information overload. You'll be wise to keep your Inbox tidy by doing the following:

- **Immediately delete any messages that you do not wish to keep.** To delete a message, select the message in the message list, and do one of the following: click Delete on the toolbar, press Ctrl + D, press the Delete key, or drag the message to the Deleted Messages folder. If you delete a message by mistake, you can recover it by dragging it from the Deleted Messages folder to the Inbox.
- **Move read messages to custom folders.** If you want to keep important messages that you've already read, you can store them in custom folders. For more information, see "Organizing Your Mail Into Folders," page 435.
- **Write rules that route unimportant mail into folders so that they do not appear in your Inbox.** If you subscribe to mailing lists or receive company mail on routine topics, this mail may not be so urgent that it needs to appear in your Inbox. You can write rules that route certain incoming messages to a custom folder. For example, suppose you subscribe to an e-mail newsletter. You can write a rule that routes this newsletter to a folder,

where you can read these messages at your convenience. For more information, see "Creating a Rule for Mail Messages," page 442.

When you delete a message, Outlook Express moves the deleted message to the Deleted Items folder. To finalize the deletion, do one of the following:

- From the Edit menu, choose Empty Deleted Items Folder.

  or

- In the folder list, point to the Deleted Items folder, click the right mouse button, and choose Empty Deleted Items Folder from the pop-up menu.

To finalize deletions from an IMAP server, click Edit on the menu bar, and click Purge Deleted Messages.

To finalize deletions automatically, click Tools on the menu bar, choose Options, and click the Maintenance tab. In the Cleaning Up Messages area, check Empty Messages From The 'Deleted Items' Folder On Exit. If you're using an IMAP server, also check Purge Deleted Messages When Leaving IMAP Folders.

Viewing Information About a Message

You can see a summary of all the information that Outlook Express has about a message, including hidden information about the route the message traveled, the originating e-mail address, the program used to create the message, and more. To view information about a message, do the following:

1. Select the message.
2. Click File on the menu bar, and choose Properties. You can also press Alt + Enter. You'll see the message's General properties, shown in Figure 12-5. Note that the message's title is shown on the title bar.
3. To see detailed information from the message's *header* (information automatically added to the message by the programs that sent it on its way to you), click Details. You'll see the message's header information (see Figure 12-6).
4. Click OK to return to Outlook Express.

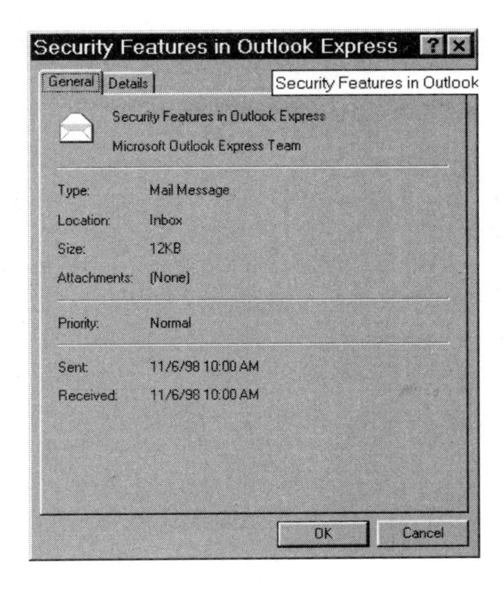

FIGURE 12-5.
A message's general properties summarize the information Outlook Express has detected about the message.

TIP

If you're having trouble displaying the text in a message, view the Details page and look for the Content-Type entry. This entry may tell you which character set was used to encode the message. Then click View on the menu bar, choose Encoding, and look for the encoding on the submenu. If the encoding doesn't appear, you may have to download the character set. To do so, click Start on the taskbar, choose Windows Update, and look for the character set in the list of downloadable Windows updates.

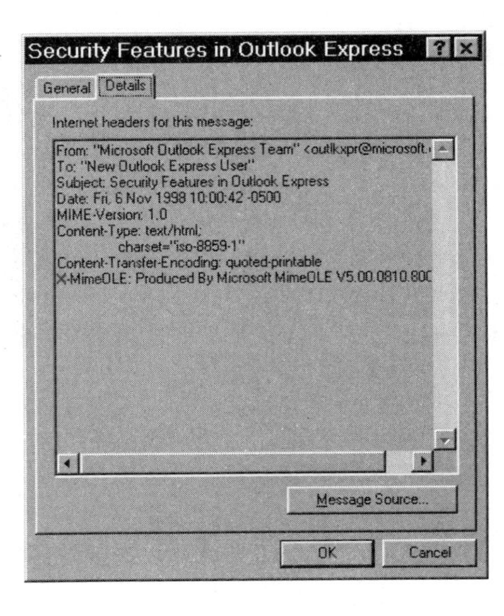

FIGURE 12-6.
The Details page enables you to see the hidden messages that various applications have added to the message along the way.

Navigating in the Message List

You can preview messages quickly by clicking them in the message list, but you may wish to learn some of the following navigation tricks.

Viewing the Next Message

To view the next message down in the list, do one of the following:

- Press Ctrl + > (same as the period key)

  or

- Click View on the menu bar, click Next, and choose Next Message from the submenu.

Viewing the Previous Message

To view the previous message (going up in the list), press Ctrl + < (same as the comma key).

Skipping to the Next Unread Message

To skip directly to the next unread message, do one of the following:

- Press Ctrl + U

  or

- Click View on the menu bar, click Next, and choose Next Unread Message from the submenu.

Skipping to the Next Folder with Unread Messages

In Chapter 13, you'll learn how to organize your mail into custom folders. You can also write rules that route incoming mail into folders, so that certain messages don't appear in your Inbox. After creating folders and rules, some of your custom folders may contain unread messages. If a folder contains at least one unread message, the folder list shows the folder name in bold. You could double-click the folder and select the unread message manually, but there's a better way. To go to the next unread message in the next folder containing unread messages, do one of the following:

- Press Ctrl + J

  or

- Click View on the menu bar, click Next, and choose Next Unread Folder.

Receiving an Attachment

An *attachment* is a file that's included with an e-mail message. Attachments are made possible by the MIME protocol, which Outlook Express and most other e-mail programs support. Any type of file can become an attachment, including graphics, text files, program files, sounds, movies, compressed files, and more.

If you receive a message that has an attachment, you'll see a paper-clip icon next to the envelope icon (see Figure 12-7). You also see the paper-clip icon in the preview pane's message header.

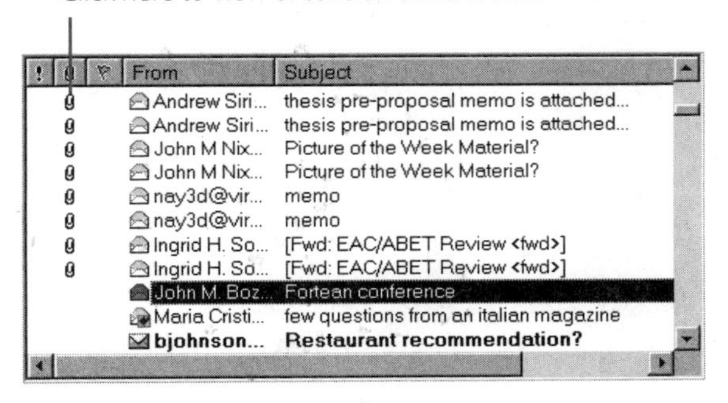

FIGURE 12-7.
If a message has an attachment, you can click the paper-clip icon to view or save the attachment.

To save the attachment, do one of the following:

- In the preview pane, click the paper-clip icon, and choose Save Attachments. Select a location in which to save the file, and click Save.

  or

- From the File menu, choose Save Attachments, choose a location, and click Save.

WARNING

> Be aware that attachments can contain computer viruses. Suspect files include any program file, as well as document files created by applications that have *macro* (automated keystroke) features. To play it safe, you can save attachments to a floppy disk; you can then run a virus checker on the file, or you can transfer the file to a machine that doesn't contain critical data.

Outlook Express displays the attachment as an icon. To view the attachment, double-click that icon. Windows will attempt to find an application that allows you to view the file. If no application exists that's capable of displaying the file, you'll see a dialog box asking you to associate this type of file with one of your applications.

If somebody wants to send you an attachment, ask that person to send a file that your application can read. For example, there are many different versions of the Microsoft Word file format. If you have an older version of Word and your correspondent has a newer one, ask your correspondent to save the file in an older Word format, or the Rich Text Format (.rtf), which any version of Word can read.

Using the Message Window

The main Outlook Express window, with its message list and preview pane, provides a convenient way to read your mail. The preview pane gives you a quick sense of what's in the selected message. You can scroll down to see more if you wish.

You can also read messages in the message window (see Figure 12-8). To view an entire message in this window, simply double-click the message header in the message list.

One good reason to read your messages in the message window rather than in the preview pane is that you can go through a whole bunch of mail quickly by clicking the Previous and Next buttons on the message window's toolbar. You'll see more of each one's content, too.

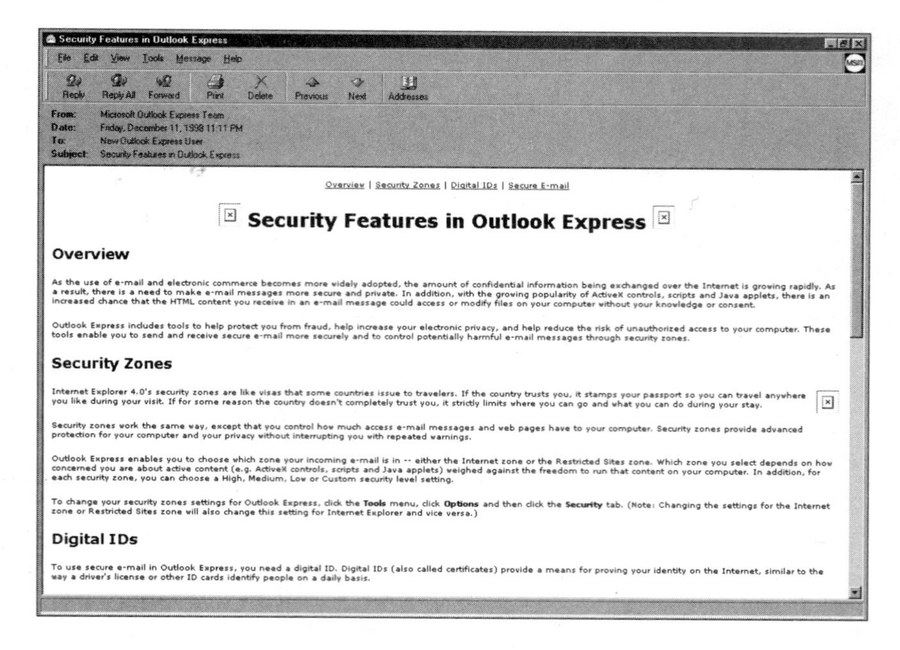

FIGURE 12-8.
The message window displays the message in an uncluttered window, and provides convenient message-list navigation tools.

The message window's toolbar includes convenient tools for your reading purposes. You'll learn more about these tools in the sections to come, but Table 12-3 on the next page explains what they do.

Finding a Message

Once you've received and sent many messages, you might find that manual search techniques are too much trouble. Save your eyes, and let Outlook Express search for you. As you'll learn in this section, you can search for messages in the current folder, or you can use the Advanced Find command to search for messages with many search options. If you're displaying a particularly lengthy message, you can also search for text within it.

Finding a Message in the Current Folder

You can use the Find dialog box to search for text in the current folder's messages. By default, this technique searches for text only in the message's From and Subject areas. You can also search all the text in downloaded messages.

To find a message in the current folder, follow these steps:

1. Do one of the following:
   - On the toolbar, click the arrow next to the Find button, and choose Message In This Folder.

     or
   - Press Shift + F3.

     or
   - From the Edit menu, click Find, and choose Message In This Folder from the submenu.

   You'll see the Find dialog box, shown here:

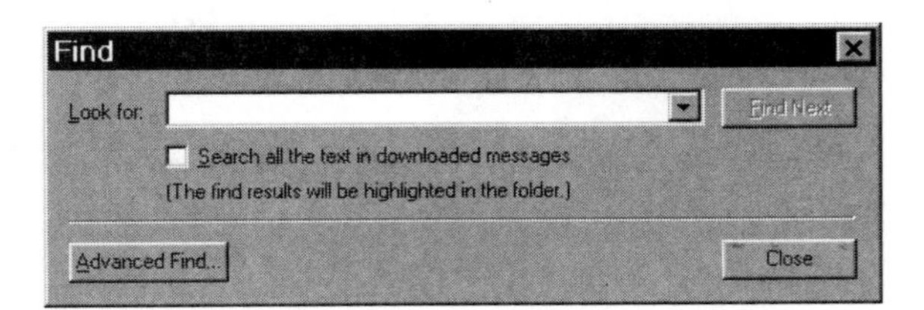

2. In the Look For box, type the text you're looking for.
3. If you would like to search for text anywhere in the downloaded

message (including the message body), check Search All The Text In Downloaded Messages.

4 Click Find Next to begin the search.

Outlook Express highlights the first message that contains the search text, if any is found. If the program can't find a match, you see a message informing you that the program has finished searching the folder.

5 Click Close.

Finding Messages with the Find Message Command

The Find Message dialog box provides an armada of search tools. You can:

- Search a folder and all the subfolders it contains.
- Specify text in specific message areas (From, To, Subject, and Message).

TABLE 12-3. Toolbar Buttons (Message Window).

Button name	What it does
Reply	Enables you to reply to the currently selected message. For more information, see "Replying to a Message," page 385.
Reply All	Enables you to send a reply to *all* of the addresses in the message that is currently selected. For more information, see "Replying to a Message," page 385.
Forward	Forwards the currently selected message to an e-mail address that you specify. For more information, see "Forwarding a Message," page 387.
Print	Prints the currently selected message. For more information, see "Printing a Message," page 351.
Delete	Deletes the currently selected message. For more information, see "Keeping Your Inbox Tidy," page 355.
Previous	Displays the previous message in the message list.
Next	Displays the next message in the message list.
Addresses	Displays the Address Book. For more information, see "Using the Address Book," page 394.

- Limit the search by reception time (before or after a date you specify).
- Limit the search to messages with an attachment or flag.

> Unlike the Find Message In This Folder command, the Find Message command groups retrieved messages in its own window. This enables you to group messages in various useful ways. For example, you can use this command to create a list of all the messages from a certain person, or all the messages received before a certain date.

To search for messages with Find Message, follow these steps:

1 Do one of the following:

- On the toolbar, click the arrow next to the Find button, and choose Message.

  or

- Press Ctrl + Shift + F.

  or

- From the Edit menu, click Find, and choose Message In This Folder from the submenu. Click the Advanced Find button.

You'll see the Find Message dialog box, shown in Figure 12-9.

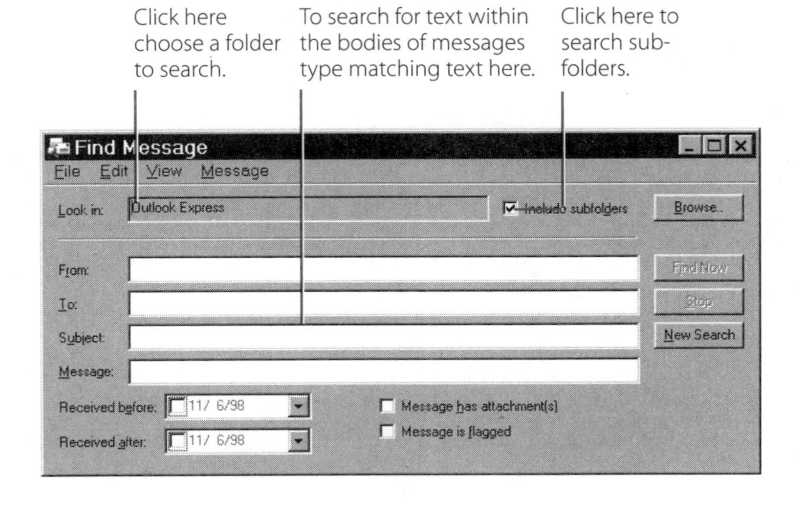

FIGURE 12-9.
In the Find Message dialog box, you can search for messages by typing text in one or more of the text boxes.

2 To choose the folder to search in, click Browse, choose a folder, and click OK. To search subfolders, check Include Subfolders.

3 Type search text in one or more of the text boxes. If you type text in more than one box, Outlook Express will retrieve only those messages that contain the search text in all the boxes you fill out. For example, if you're looking for the message from Barbara that mentions the Smith contract, type Barbara in the From box and Smith in the Message or Subject box.

4 To restrict the search to messages that arrived before or after a certain date, check either Received Before or Received After, and click the down arrow to choose a date. You'll see a drop-down calendar that enables you to choose the date easily.

5 To restrict the search to messages with attachments or flags, check one or both of these options.

6 Click Find Now to generate a list of files that match the criteria you specified (see Figure 12-10).

- To view one of the messages, double-click it.
- To start a new search, click New Search.
- To close the Find Message dialog box, click the close box.

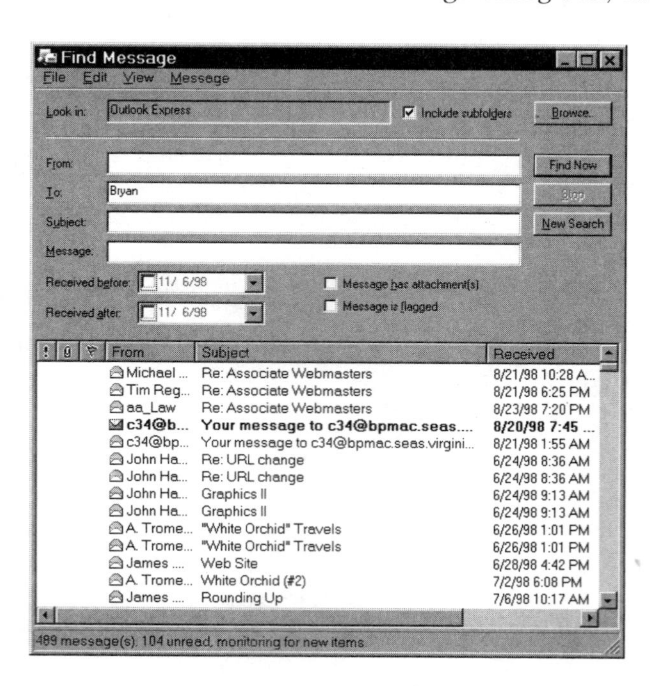

FIGURE 12-10.
The Find Message command generates a list of all the messages that conform to the criteria you specified.

Note that the list of retrieved items has column-header buttons, just like a folder's message list. You can use these buttons to sort the list of retrieved items.

Composing and Sending Messages

You can send messages in three ways: by composing a new message, by replying to a message you've received, and by forwarding a message you've received. In this section, you learn how to create new messages.

If you've never used an e-mail program before, remember that you don't need to save the messages you write. When you send a message, Outlook Express automatically saves a copy in the Sent Items folder. However, you may wish to save a draft of your message if you can't send it during the current session. For more information, see "Saving a Draft," page 384.

Understanding the New Message Window

You use the New Message window to address, write, and edit your message (Figure 12-11). To display the New Message window so you can start a new message, do one of the following:

- On the toolbar, click New Mail.

  or

- From the File menu, click New, and choose New Mail from the submenu.

You'll see the New Message window, shown in Figure 12-11. Note that this window has its own menu bar and two toolbars:

- **Standard Buttons toolbar.** This toolbar contains the most frequently used commands. You can customize this toolbar (see "Customizing the Outlook Express Toolbars," page 457).
- **Formatting toolbar.** This toolbar contains formatting options that you can use if you plan to send HTML-enhanced mail. If you choose plain-text formatting, this toolbar does not appear.

To show or hide the New Message window toolbars, right-click the toolbar background, or click View on the menu bar and choose Toolbar.

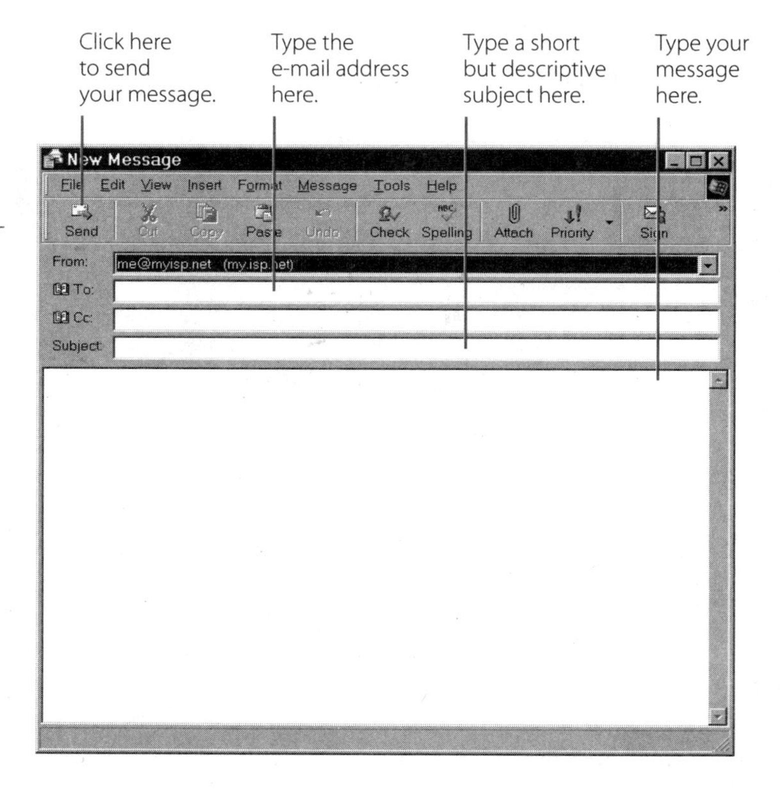

FIGURE 12-11.
In the New Message window, you can compose new messages.

The New Message window includes the following parts:

- **Title Bar.** To reposition the window, drag the title bar. To maximize the window quickly, double-click the title bar. Double-click again to restore the window to its previous size.
- **Menu Bar.** All the Outlook Express commands are on the menu bar, but the most frequently used commands are also found on the toolbar.
- **Toolbar.** The toolbar contains the following buttons, from left to right: Send, Cut, Copy, Paste, Undo, Check Names, Spelling, Attach, File, Set Priority, Digitally Sign Message, and Encrypt Message. You'll learn more about these tools later.
- **Header Information.** Here, you type the recipient's e-mail ad-

dress, the e-mail address for recipients of copies of the message (optional), and a brief subject line. If you have more than one e-mail account, you can also choose the account to send the message from.

- **Message Body.** Type your information in this area.

SEE ALSO

You can customize the New Message window toolbar by adding buttons or changing the toolbar's appearance. For more information, see "Customizing the Toolbar in the Main Outlook Express Window," page 457.

The New Message Window's Toolbar

The New Message window has its own toolbar. Table 12-4 provides a quick overview of each button's purpose.

TABLE 12-4. New Message Window Toolbar.

Button name	What it does
Send	Sends the message.
Cut	Cuts the selection to the Clipboard.
Copy	Copies the selection to the Clipboard.
Paste	Pastes the Clipboard contents at the cursor's location.
Undo	Undoes the last editing or formatting action.
Check	Checks the address aliases you've typed to make sure that the names are in your Address Book.
Spelling	Runs the spell checker on your message.
Attach	Attaches a file to the message.
Priority	Enables you to choose themessage priority (High, Normal, or Low).
Priority	Sets the message priority to Low, Normal, or High.
Sign	Signs the message with your digital signature. For more information on digital signatures, see Chapter 14.
Encrypt	Encrypts the message for secure transmission. For more information on encryption, see Chapter 14.
Online	Enables you to choose between online and offline mode.

Choosing the Mail-Sending Format

To choose the mail-sending format, click Format on the New Message window's menu bar, and choose Plain Text or Rich Text (HTML).

Unless you're sure that your correspondent's e-mail program can handle HTML, choose Plain Text.

SEE ALSO
To specify a default format (HTML or plain text), see "Choosing Mail-Composition Options," page 427.

Choosing the Sending Account

As you'll learn in Chapter 13, you can set up more than one e-mail account with Outlook Express. If you've defined more than one account, you can choose the account that you want to send the message from. You do this in the From box, which appears only if you've defined more than one account. To choose the mail-sending account, click the down arrow at the end of the From text box, and choose the account that you want to use. This will enable the recipient to automatically reply to the account from which you sent the message.

Understanding Sending Options

In the New Message window, you can type e-mail addresses in three areas: To, Cc, and Bcc. Here's what these options do:

- **To.** When you type an address in the To box of the New Message window, the message is sent with coding that identifies it as a message sent directly to the recipient. In the recipient's mail program, your message will be shown as a message to that person. For example, if you send a message to Candice Mowley, her mail program will show that a message has been sent to her.
- **Cc.** When you type an address in the Cc box, the message is sent with coding that identifies it as a "carbon copy" (a copy of a message sent to somebody else). As a result, the recipient's e-mail program will display the message as a message sent to the person named in the To line. For example, suppose you send Don Gray a copy of the message sent to Candice Mowley; Don's program will display the message as a message to Candice, not to Don. Note that Candice will know that you sent a "carbon

copy" to Don; Don's address shows up in Candice's copy.

- **Bcc.** When you type an address in the Bcc box, the recipient gets a "carbon copy," but the person named in the To line does not know this. Bcc stands for "blind carbon copy."

> You can type or insert more than one address in any of the three recipient boxes (To, Cc, and Bcc). If you type the address directly, be sure to separate each address by inserting a semicolon.

Specifying the Address

You can specify the recipient's e-mail address in two ways:

- **By typing it manually.** Be careful when you type the address; it's easy to make a mistake. Your message won't be delivered unless you type the address perfectly.
- **By choosing it from the Address Book.** This is the best way to enter an e-mail address because it reduces the chance of a typing error.

To add an address from your Address Book, do the following:

1 In the New Message window, click the Address Book icon next to the To or Cc box. Alternatively, click Tools on the menu bar, and choose Select Recipients.

You'll see the Select Recipients dialog box, shown in Figure 12-12.

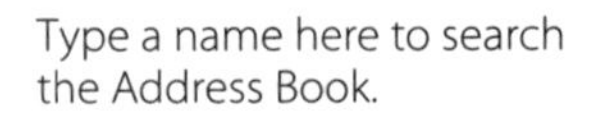

Type a name here to search the Address Book.

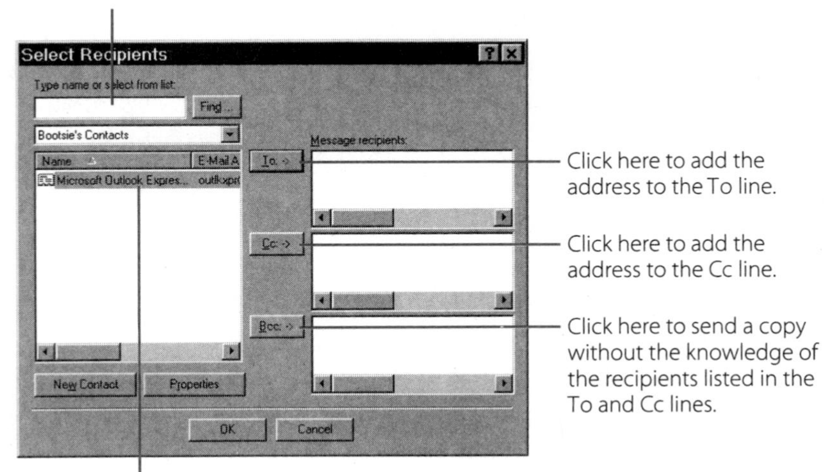

FIGURE 12-12. This dialog box enables you to choose mail recipients from your Address Book.

IV Mastering Internet Messaging

2 In the list on the left side of the dialog box, select the recipient's name. If the list is lengthy, start typing the recipient's name in the text box in the upper left corner; as you type, Outlook Express will search the list, trying to match what you're typing.

   To search for the recipient's name on Internet white-page services, click Find.

   If you don't see your recipient's name and address in the list, you can click New Contact to add this information to your Address Book. For more information, see "Adding an E-Mail Address to your Address Book," page 355.

3 When you've selected the recipient you want, do one or more of the following:

   - Click To to send the message to the selected recipient.
   - Click Cc to send the message as a "carbon copy" to the selected recipient.
   - Click Bcc if you would like the selected recipient to receive a copy of the message, but without the To or Cc recipients knowing.

4 Select additional recipients if you wish.

5 Click OK.

Typing a Subject

In the New Message window's Subject text box, type a short, but descriptive subject. Remember that many mail programs display no more than 30 characters of subject text in message lists, so keep it short. Put the most important words first.

Avoid subject lines such as "hi" or "a problem." These subject lines irritate some people because they do not say anything substantive about the message's content. Busy people may skip these messages or even delete them without reading them.

Typing the Text

In the text area, type the text of your message. Please remember to avoid typing in all capital letters, which comes across as "shouting" to many e-mail users. Also remember to start your message with a brief statement of purpose.

Inserting Text from a File

You can insert text from two types of files into your Outlook Express messages:

- **Text files (txt extension).** These are plain-text files that do not contain formatting.
- **HTML files (htm or html extension).** These are files containing Web pages.

If you want to insert an HTML file, you must choose the HTML mail-sending format.

If you would like to insert text from a file, do the following:

1. In the New Message window, position the cursor where you want the text to appear.
2. From the Insert menu, choose Text From File. You'll see a dialog box that enables you to locate the file you want to insert.
3. In the Files Of Type list box, select the type of file you want to insert.
4. Locate and select the file you want to insert.
5. Click Open to insert the file.

Formatting Your Message

If you would like to send your message with rich HTML formatting, click Format on the New Message window's menu bar, and choose Rich Text (HTML). You can add many formats to your messages, as this section explains, including fonts, font sizes, font colors, paragraph indentations and alignments, background graphics, background colors, and even background sounds that play while the reader is viewing your message.

TIP

If the formatting toolbar is dimmed, click Format on the menu bar, and choose Rich Text (HTML).

When you choose Rich Text formatting, Outlook Express activates the New Message window's formatting toolbar. Here's a guide to the various icons and tools on that toolbar:

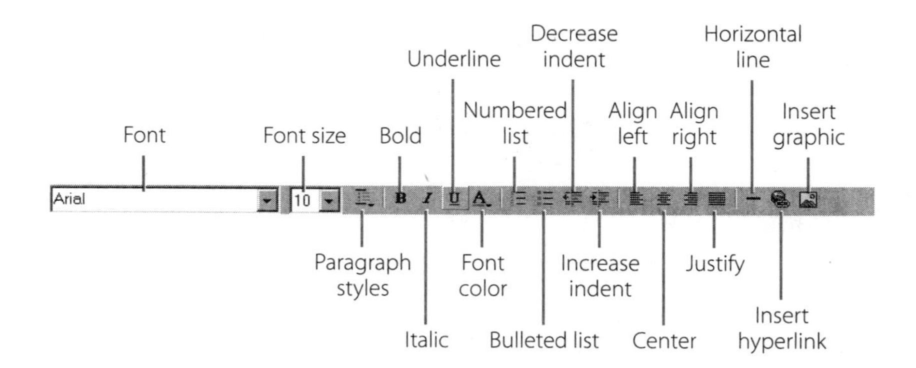

CAUTION
Be aware that your font choices may not show up on your recipient's computer screen, even if your recipient can receive richly formatted (HTML) messages. In order for the fonts to appear, they must be installed on the user's system. For this reason, you will be wise to restrict your font choices to commonly installed fonts such as Arial and Times New Roman. Anyone who has installed a full version of Internet Explorer will have the Microsoft-developed Web fonts, called Georgia, Trebuchet, and Verdana. Avoid specialty or symbol fonts.

Formatting Fonts and Emphases

You can choose fonts, font sizes, and character emphases (including bold, italic, and underlining), as in the following example:

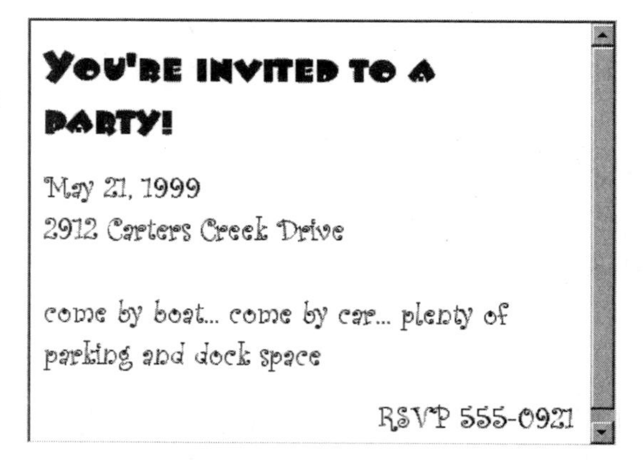

To format characters in your message, do the following:

1 Select the text you want to format.

2 Format one of the following:

- **Font.** On the formatting toolbar, select the font from the font list box.

- **Font size.** On the formatting toolbar, select the font size from the font size list box.

- **Emphases.** On the formatting toolbar, click the character emphasis you want (bold, italic, or underline).

- **Color.** On the formatting toolbar, click the Font Color button, and choose a font color from the list. If you don't see the color you want, click Format on the menu bar, choose Font, and click the color palette icon next to the Color box. Use the Color dialog box to select the color you want.

If you want to choose several font formats at once, click Format on the menu bar, choose Font, and choose font styles from the Font dialog box.

Formatting Paragraphs

You can choose from a variety of paragraph styles, as shown in the following example:

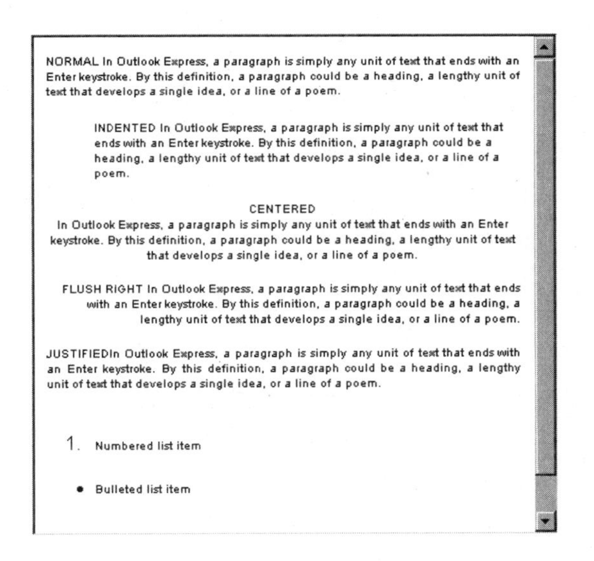

NORMAL In Outlook Express, a paragraph is simply any unit of text that ends with an Enter keystroke. By this definition, a paragraph could be a heading, a lengthy unit of text that develops a single idea, or a line of a poem.

INDENTED In Outlook Express, a paragraph is simply any unit of text that ends with an Enter keystroke. By this definition, a paragraph could be a heading, a lengthy unit of text that develops a single idea, or a line of a poem.

CENTERED
In Outlook Express, a paragraph is simply any unit of text that ends with an Enter keystroke. By this definition, a paragraph could be a heading, a lengthy unit of text that develops a single idea, or a line of a poem.

FLUSH RIGHT In Outlook Express, a paragraph is simply any unit of text that ends with an Enter keystroke. By this definition, a paragraph could be a heading, a lengthy unit of text that develops a single idea, or a line of a poem.

JUSTIFIEDIn Outlook Express, a paragraph is simply any unit of text that ends with an Enter keystroke. By this definition, a paragraph could be a heading, a lengthy unit of text that develops a single idea, or a line of a poem.

1. Numbered list item

- Bulleted list item

To format text paragraphs, do the following:

1 Place the cursor within the paragraph you want to format.

2 Do one of the following:

- **Create a numbered list.** Click the Formatting Numbers button, and type the list. When you press Enter, Outlook Express inserts the number and continues the format.

- **Create a bulleted list.** Click the Formatting Bullets button and type the list. When you press Enter, Outlook Express inserts a bullet and continues the format.

- **Increase indentation.** Click the Increase Indentation button.
- **Decrease indentation.** Click the Decrease Indentation button.
- **Specify alignment.** Click Align Left, Center, Align Right, or Justify.

To cancel a paragraph style, or switch back to normal formatting after pressing Enter, click Format on the menu bar, click Style, and choose Normal. If you're typing a numbered or bulleted list, just press Enter twice to restore the Normal style.

With the Paragraph Styles button on the formatting toollbar, you can also choose HTML paragraph styles, as shown in Table 12-5. Rather than use HTML paragraph styles, you'll find it easier to create paragraph styles by clicking the buttons on the formatting toolbar.

Notice that the directory, menu, and bulleted list styles are exactly the same? Don't blame Outlook Express. These styles are included so that Outlook Express can conform to version 3.2 of HTML. However, the directory and menu styles are very infrequently used and not distinguished from bulleted lists by most browsers. In the strict version of HTML 4, the directory and menu formats are discontinued. Just ignore them.

Inserting a Horizontal Line (Rule)

To insert a horizontal line (also called a rule) in your message, do the following:

1. Place the cursor where you want the rule to appear. To separate items, press Enter so that the rule will appear on a new line.
2. On the formatting toolbar, click the Insert Horizontal Line button. You can also click Insert on the menu bar, and choose Horizontal Line.

Inserting a Hyperlink

To include a hyperlink in your message, do the following:

1. Select the text that you want highlighted as a hyperlink.
2. On the formatting toolbar, click the Insert Hyperlink button.

You'll see the Hyperlink dialog box, shown here:

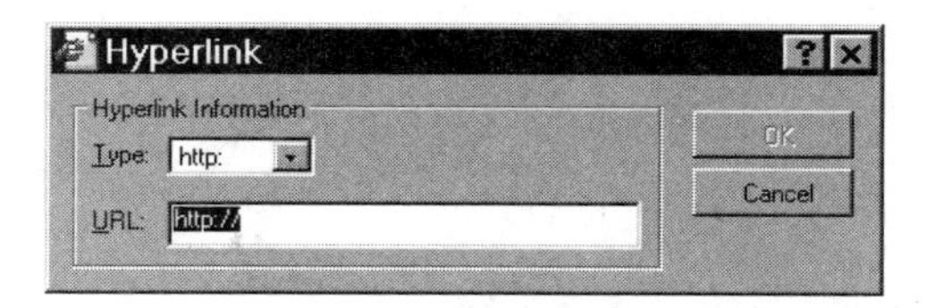

In the Type area, select the type of hyperlink you want to insert. For a Web hyperlink, choose http://. In the URL box, type the Internet address of the resource you're linking to.

3 Click OK.

TABLE 12-5. Paragraph Style Formatting Options.

Formatting option	What it does
Normal	Restores the normal text style for text paragraphs.
Formatted	Preserves your line breaks and spacing.
Address	Formats text with italics. Used to indicate an e-mail address within the body of your message.
Headings 1 through 6	Displays headings and subheadings with special emphasis denoting their importance.
Numbered List	Creates a numbered-list format and automatically numbers each paragraph.
Bulleted List	Creates a bulleted-list format and automatically enters a bullet before each paragraph.
Directory List	Creates a directory-list format, which is like a bulleted list.
Menu List	Creates a menu-list format, which is also like a bulleted list.
Definition	Creates a definition format, which is useful for typing glossaries. Use this format for typing the definition text.
Definition Term	Creates a definition-term format, which is useful for typing glossaries. Use this format for typing the definition term.
Paragraph	Creates a normal-text paragraph preceded by a blank line.

Inserting a Graphic

You can insert the following types of graphics into your message:

- **GIF or JPEG (.gif or .jpg extension).** These are the graphics files commonly used on the Web. Any HTML-capable mail program can display these graphics.
- **Windows bitmap (.bmp extension)** and **Windows metafiles (.wmf extension).** These are standard Windows graphics formats. It's OK to insert these if you are sending a message to another Windows user, but avoid this choice if you're sending a message to users of Unix or Macintosh computers.
- **X-Window Bitmap (XBM).** This is the default graphic format for Unix computers running the X Window system.
- **ART.** This is the default graphics format for America Online (AOL).

Bear in mind that graphic files are usually quite large, and your message may download slowly if your recipient is using a modem connection.

To insert a graphic into your message, do the following:

1. On the formatting toolbar, click Insert Picture. You can also click Insert on the menu bar, and choose Picture. You'll see the Picture dialog box, shown here:

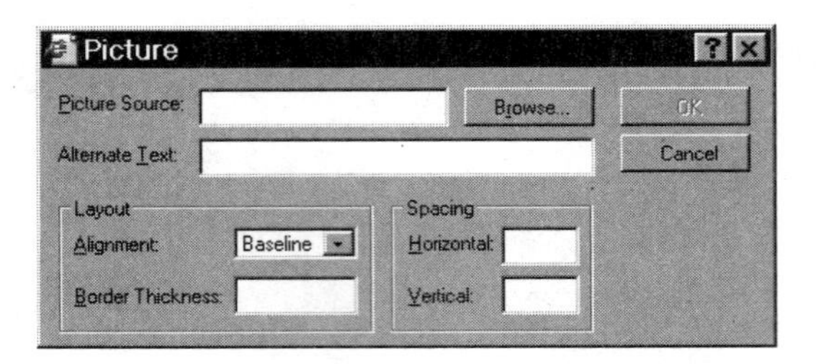

2. In the Picture Source area, type the picture's location, or click Browse to locate and select the picture.
3. In the Alternate Text area, type some text that appears in case your recipient's e-mail program can't display the graphic. The text should tell what the picture shows.
4. In the Layout area, specify an alignment by choosing one of the options from the list box. To position the graphic with text flowing past it on the right or left, choose Right or Left. The other

options align the picture with one line of text, and may have different results depending on which program your recipient is using. The best choice is either Right or Left.

5 In the Border Thickness box, type the width of the picture border in pixels, if you wish. If you leave this blank, the picture won't have a border.

6 In the Spacing area, type the number of pixels to leave blank between the picture and surrounding text. You can specify horizontal and vertical spacing.

7 Click OK to insert the picture.

Adding a Background Graphic

You can add a graphic to your message's background. Generally, background graphics are small graphics files, square or rectangular in shape. An HTML-capable e-mail program will automatically tile a background graphic so that it fills the entire background.

> Avoid busy background graphics that interfere with the text's readability. If you choose a dark color, consider choosing a light-colored (or white) font so that your text can be read.

To insert a background graphic into your message, do the following:

1 From the Format menu, click Background, and choose Picture from the submenu. You'll see the Background Picture dialog box, shown here:

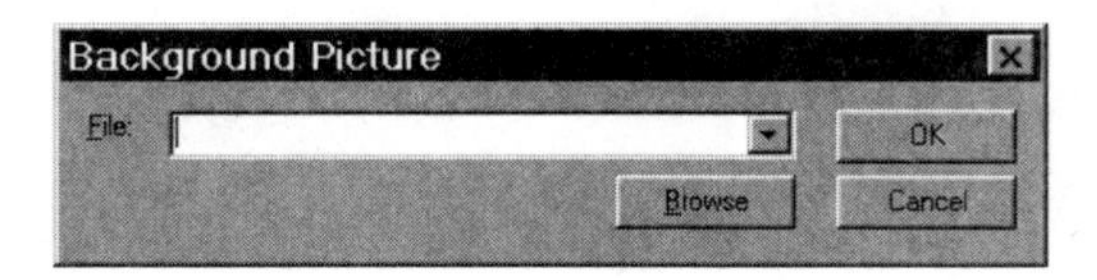

2 In the File box, type the picture's location, or click Browse to locate and select the file.

3 Click OK.

Choosing a Background Color

To choose a background color, follow these steps:

1 From the Format menu, click Background, and choose Color from the submenu.

2 From the pop-up menu, choose the color you want to use for your message's background.

Choosing a Background Sound

You can include a background sound in your message. Outlook Express can include any of the following sounds:

- **Audio files.** You can include files in the Windows WAV format, as well as any of the following sound formats that are used on the Internet: SND, AU, AIF, AFIC, and AIFF. Avoid sending lengthy audio files with your mail messages; your recipient may not appreciate your gesture if the file causes a lengthy download.
- **MIDI files.** You can include any MIDI file in your message. These are a good choice because they do not take very long to download.
- **Real Media files.** These are streaming audio and video file formats.

To insert a sound file into your message, do the following:

1 From the Format menu, click Background, and choose Sound. You'll see the Background Sound dialog box, shown here:

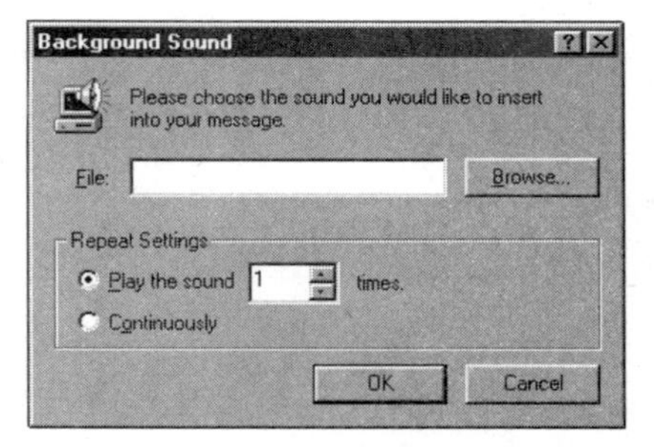

2 In the File box, type the picture's location, or click Browse to locate and select the file.

3 In the Repeat Settings area, you can specify the number of times the sound should play, or click Continuously to play the sound as long as the message is open.

4 Click OK.

Using Stationery

If you're thinking about composing rich messages, you can use templates called Stationery. These templates contain pre-configured formats such as backgrounds, colors, elaborate borders, and font choices. Available in the Stationery folder are a variety of Stationery templates, including Balloon, Party Invitation, New Baby Announcement, and Story Book (for an example, see Figure 12-13).

If you'd like to re-use the formatting you've done in other messages, you can save a message as Stationery (a template for creating new messages). To save a message as stationery, click File on the menu bar, and choose Save As Stationery. Type a name for the file, and click Save.

To compose a message with stationery, follow these steps:

1. In the main Outlook Express window, click Message on the menu bar, and click New Message Using.
2. From the submenu, choose the stationery you'd like to use.

To add stationery to an existing message, do the following:

1. In the New Message window, click Format on the menu bar, and choose Apply Stationery.
2. From the submenu, choose the stationery you'd like to use.

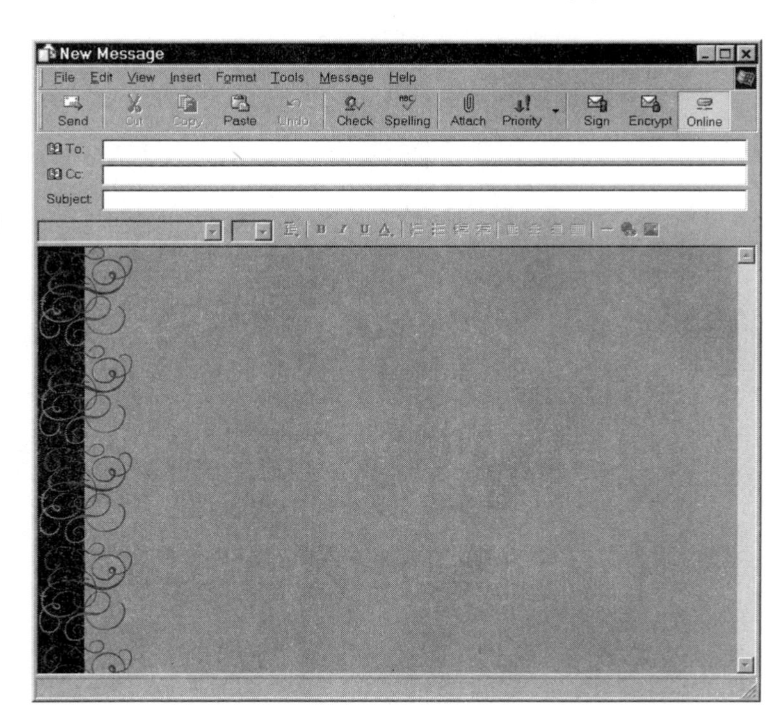

FIGURE 12-13.
With Outlook Express's stationery, you can send attractive messages with predefined styles and background graphics.

Setting the Priority

When you send your message, you can choose one of the following priorities:

- **High.** Your recipient's e-mail program will display the message with special formatting or an icon indicating that the message is urgent.
- **Normal.** Your recipient's e-mail program displays the message without any special formatting or icons. In Outlook Express, this is the default priority for all outgoing messages.
- **Low.** Your recipient's e-mail program displays the message with special formatting or an icon indicating that it is low priority and doesn't need to be read right away.

To change the message's priority, choose the Message menu, select Set Priority, and click High, Normal, or Low. You can also set the priority by clicking Priority on the toolbar, and choosing one of the priority options.

Adding Attachments (Files) to Your Messages

You can send formatted documents over the Internet, including Word, Excel, and Powerpoint files. This capability enables you to engage in collaborative work with people, even if you're separated by vast geographic distances.

Before you send an attachment to somebody, ask what type of attachment to include. For example, suppose you are sending a Microsoft Word file, created with Office 2000. But your recipient is still using the original version of Office, which uses an earlier file format. To make sure your recipient can read the file you send, you should save the file in Microsoft Word version 6, or the Rich Text Format (RTF) interchange format.

1 To include an attachment, do one of the following:

   - On the toolbar, click Attach.

   or

   - From the Insert menu, choose File Attachment.

You'll see the Insert Attachment dialog box, shown here:

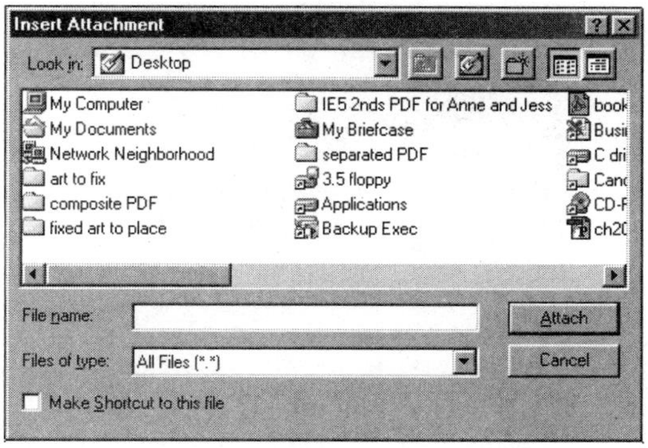

2 Locate and select the file you want to attach, and click Attach.

After you attach the file, you'll see the file's name—and an icon indicating the type of file you've attached—in the Attach area.

3 Compose and send your message. In your message, tell your recipient which version of the application you used to create the file, as well as which file format you used.

CAUTION

Be aware that you can spread computer viruses by sending data files as attachments. Some viruses, called macro viruses, attach themselves to document files. If you plan to exchange data files with other Internet users, make sure you have installed virus-checking software, and use this software frequently to make sure your system is free from virus infections. Also, be sure to equip your system with the latest versions of application software. This isn't a sales message; the latest versions incorporate safeguards against security flaws that have been discovered and documented.

Looking for E-Mail Addresses

If you don't know your correspondent's e-mail address, you can try searching for it in the following locations:

- **Address Book.** The Address Book is an Outlook Express accessory that you can use to store your recipient's e-mail addresses.
- **Commercial white-pages services.** These services maintain large databases of e-mail addresses. Like search engines, their coverage varies; you'll have a better chance of finding somebody's address if you search more than one service. (There's no single, comprehensive service that lists everyone's e-mail address.)

To search for somebody's e-mail address,

1 Do one of the following:

- From the Edit menu, click Find, and choose People from the submenu.

  or

  Press Ctrl + E.

You'll see the Find People dialog box, shown in Figure 12-14.

Choose where to search.

Carefully type the person's name.

FIGURE 12-14.
You can search for a person's e-mail address in your Address Book or in several online white-page services.

2. In the Look In list box, choose the service you want to search.
3. In the People area, type the person's name. Check your typing carefully.
4. If you're searching a white-pages service, you can see additional options by clicking the Advanced tab. You'll see the Advanced options, shown here:

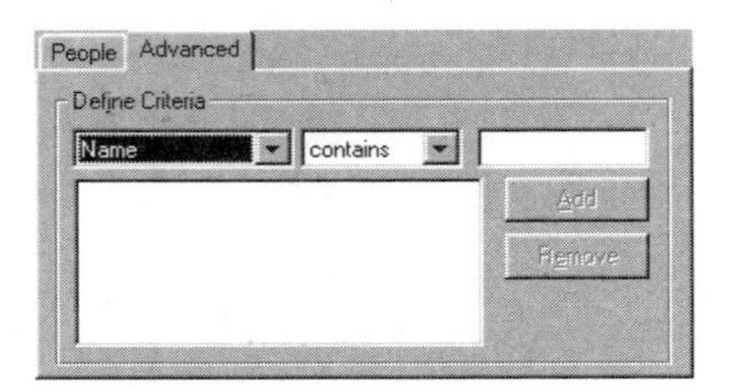

In the Define Criteria area, choose the item to search for (you can search for Name, E-mail, First Name, Last Name, or Organization) and a matching specification (you can choose Contains, Is, Starts With, Ends With, Or Sounds Like). Type the text you want to match in the blank text box, and click Add. You can repeat this process to add additional matching criteria if you wish.

5. Click Find Now. If matches are found, you'll see a list of names. If one of the names is correct, select it and click Add To Address Book. If the search didn't produce any results, try another white-pages service and repeat the search.

> If you're not sure how a person's last name is spelled, try an Advanced search with the "sounds like" matching specification. If you search for "Johnson," this search can find "Johnston," "Jonson," and other variations.

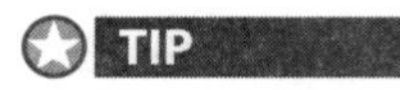

> To access one of the Internet white-page services directly, select the service, and click Web Site. On the search service's search page, you can use special features that aren't accessible from the Find People dialog box.

Checking Spelling

Be sure to check your spelling. A message with spelling errors creates a negative impression.

To check spelling, do the following:

1. Before you send the message, click Spelling. You'll see the Spelling dialog box, shown in Figure 12-15. If the document contains any words that aren't found in the spelling dictionary, you'll see the word in the Not In Dictionary box.
2. Do one of the following:
   - Click Ignore to ignore this instance of the word, or click Ignore All to ignore this word throughout the message.

     or
   - Correct the error manually in the Change To box, and click Change to change this instance of the word, or Change All to correct all instances of the word.

     or
   - Select a spelling in the Suggestions box, and click Change to change this instance of the word, or Change All to correct all instances of the word.

     or
   - If the word is correctly spelled, click Add to add the word to the dictionary.
3. Repeat step 2 until you've finished checking spelling throughout your document.

FIGURE 12-15.
Be sure to check your spelling before sending mail.

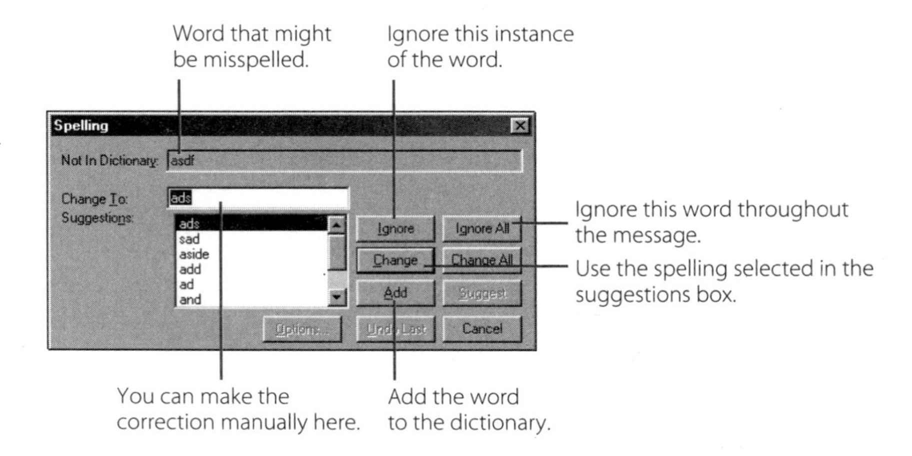

TIP

If you click the wrong button, click Undo Last to redo the last change.

Saving a Draft

If you can't finish a message during the current session, you can save it as a draft. Without sending the message, Outlook Express stores the message in the Drafts folder; you can then re-open the message, finish it, and send it.

TIP

Remember that you don't have to save a message if you plan to complete it during the current session.

To save a draft of a message:

1 Do one of the following:

- From the File menu, choose Save.

  or

- Press Ctrl + S.

2 Click the close box to close the message.

Replying to a Message

When you receive e-mail, you'll find that it's easy to reply: Outlook Express automatically adds the sender's e-mail address and subject line to your new message. However, you'll be wise to study your reply options so that you're sure you know what you're doing.

CAUTION

Be careful about clicking Reply To All by accident. You may think that you are replying to just one person, and say something private or personal, only to find that many people received the message—perhaps everyone in your entire organization! Many e-mail addresses are actually distribution lists. These look like e-mail addresses but actually refer to a lengthy list of e-mail addresses—potentially including everyone in an organization. If you don't notice such an address in the Cc: line and click Reply To All without thinking, you could be sending your message to hundreds or even thousands of people! Don't make yourself look stupid in front of hundreds of people. Please exercise caution when you click Reply To All. Examine the addresses carefully to make sure you understand who's getting the reply. If you aren't sure or don't feel quite comfortable for some reason, don't choose Reply To All!

Understanding Reply Options

To reply to a message, you have two options:

- **Reply To Author.** If you choose this option, your reply goes only to the e-mail addresses included in the From line in the header information. (Note that this might include more than one address.) No copies are sent to anyone on the courtesy copy (Cc:) list of the original message.
- **Reply To All.** If you choose this option, your message goes not only to the author but also to everyone on the Cc: list.

Replying to the Author

When you reply to the author, your message goes to the e-mail address listed in the From box of the author's message.

To reply to the message's author, follow these steps:

1. In the message list, select the message to which you want to reply.
2. Do one of the following:
   - On the toolbar, click Reply.

     or
   - Press Ctrl + R.

     or
   - From the Message menu, choose Reply To Sender.

   You'll see a New Message window (see Figure 12-16). Notice that Outlook Express has included the original text, added the recipient's e-mail addresses, and positioned the insertion point at the beginning of the letter, above the included text. In addition, the program has added *Re:* before the subject.
3. Type your message *above* the quoted text. (Most e-mail users do not like to scroll down past their message to see your reply.)
4. Check your spelling.
5. Click end.

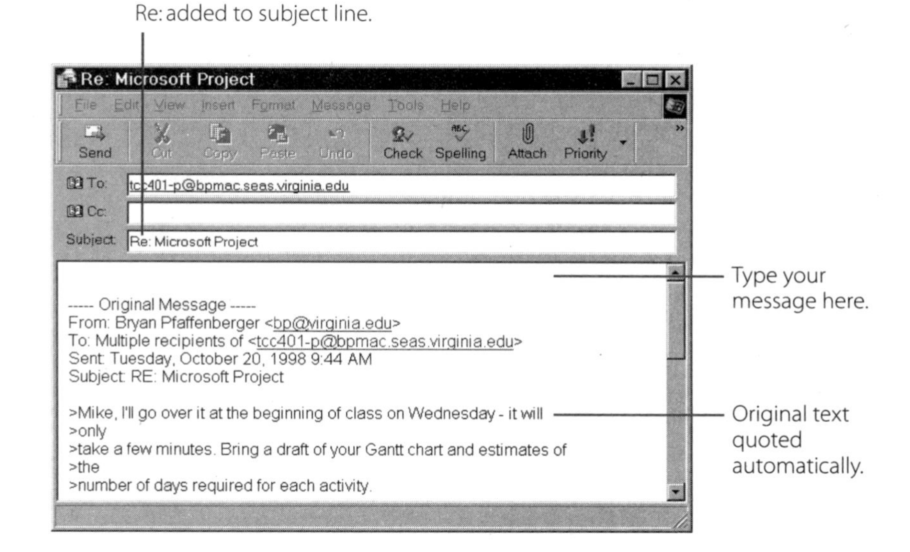

FIGURE 12-16. When you reply to a message, Outlook Express adds Re: to the subject line and quotes the original message.

TIP

If you're replying to a message that was sent to you with rich formatting (HTML), Outlook Express uses rich formatting for the reply. If you'd rather reply in plain text, click Format on the menu bar, and choose Plain Text.

Replying to All

When you reply to all, your reply goes to every e-mail address in the original message, including those who received carbon copies of the original message. Do not choose this option unless you really want to send mail to everyone involved in the original message.

CAUTION

Be aware that some messages contain more than one e-mail address in the From box. When you reply to the author, your reply goes to all the addresses in the From box. One of these might be a group mail address. Even if you choose Reply To Author, then, your reply might be sent not just to the author, but to other people as well—perhaps many people.

To reply to all addresses, follow these steps:

1. In the message list, select the message to which you want to reply.
2. Do one of the following:
   - On the toolbar, click Reply To All.

     or
   - Press Ctrl + Shift + R.

     or
   - From the Message menu, choose Reply To All.

To define the default format for replying to mail, see "Choosing Send Options," page 423.

You'll see a New Message window. Notice that Outlook Express has included the original text, added all the recipients' e-mail addresses, and positioned the insertion point at the beginning of the letter, above the included text. In addition, the program has added *Re:* before the subject.

3. Type your message *above* the quoted text.
4. Check your spelling.
5. Click Send.

Forwarding a Message

Forwarding works exactly like replying, except that Outlook Express doesn't supply the To address. To forward a message, follow these steps:

1. In the message list, select the message that you want to forward.
2. Do one of the following:
   - On the toolbar, click Forward.

     or
   - Press Ctrl + F.

     or
   - From the Message menu, choose Forward.

   You'll see a New Message window (see Figure 12-16). Notice that Outlook Express has included the original text, added the recipient, and positioned the insertion point at the beginning of the letter, above the included text. In addition, the program has added *Fw:*
3. Type your message *above* the quoted text.
4. Check your spelling.
5. Click Send.

Accessing Outlook Express from Internet Explorer

After you've installed and configured Outlook Express, you can explore some ways that you can send mail from within Internet Explorer. In order to do so, you need to make Outlook Express the default mail handler, as explained in the next section.

Making Outlook Express the Default Mail Handler

To make Outlook Express the default mail handler, do the following:

1. From the Tools menu, choose Options. You'll see the Options dialog box.
2. If necessary, click the General tab. You'll see the General page. In the Default Messaging Programs area, make sure Outlook Express is the default mail handler. If not, click Make Default.
3. Click OK.

Reading and Sending Mail from Internet Explorer

In Internet Explorer, you can access Outlook Express by clicking the Mail button on the Standard Buttons toolbar, or by choosing Mail And News from the Tools menu. Either way, you see the following options:

- **Read Mail** starts Outlook Express and displays your Inbox.
- **New Message** displays a message-composition window so you can send an e-mail message to someone.
- **Send A Link** displays a message-composition window so you can send an e-mail message to someone. It also includes the text of the current page's URL.
- **Send Page** displays a message-composition window so you can send an e-mail message to someone. It also includes the entire Web page, including graphics. To use this option, your recipient must be able to receive richly formatted (HTML) e-mail.

You can also reply to *mailto URLs,* which are hyperlinks that contain e-mail addresses. When you click a mailto URL, you see a message-composition window. Outlook Express enters the recipient's e-mail address.

Mailing Lists

Mailing lists are one of the most rewarding aspects of the Internet. Imagine being able to find a few dozen or a few hundred people who all share your interest—whether it's collecting Barbie dolls or analyzing the human genome—and entering into daily discussion and resource-sharing with those people. There are thousands of mailing lists on every conceivable subject; many of them are publicly accessible, which means you can join, even if you aren't an expert in a field.

Understanding Mailing Lists

Before joining a mailing list, you should know what to expect. It isn't all sweetness and light.

- Every once in a while, somebody posts a message that really pushes people's buttons, and you get a regrettable phenomenon called a *flame war*—lots of public name-calling and unpleasantness. Until cooler heads prevail, the mailing list will generate more heat than you might be comfortable with.
- People forget how to unsubscribe—there's a procedure you're supposed to follow—so they post pathetic messages with subjects such as, "Will somebody PLEASE tell me how to get off this list?" Your mailbox is cluttered enough without this.
- Personal and important messages to you alone can get lost amid the dozens or hundreds of messages from lists. Join one mailing list, or maybe two, but take care not to join too many.

Finding a Mailing List in Your Area of Interest

Thanks to the volunteer efforts of Stephanie da Silva, you can access a fantastic index of Internet mailing lists on the World Wide Web. The address is www.neosoft.com/internet/paml/. You'll see the Publicly Accessible Mailing Lists page. If you click the Index link, you'll find that you can browse by name or by subject.

TIP

So that mailing-list messages don't get in the way of your personal mail, create a folder for the mailing list and write rules to divert messages from the list to this folder. By all means, write a rule that sends messages containing *unsubscribe* to the Deleted Items folder; you'll find it's common for people to forget how to unsubscribe to the list, and you'll get lots of these very annoying messages.

Mailing lists generate a lot of low priority mail, which can clutter up your Inbox and disguise important messages. Before signing up for a mailing list, learn how to create folders, and learn how to write rules that automatically route incoming messages to folders. For more information, see "Organizing Your Mail Into Folders," page 435.

Subscribing to a Mailing List

After you locate information about a mailing list that looks good, try subscribing to it. Please be sure to follow the directions carefully.

You'll soon receive a confirmation plus information about the mailing list. This information includes directions for unsubscribing to the list. *Create a folder named Unsubscribe Info, and save this message—then you can retrieve it if you decide to unsubscribe.*

Replying to Mailing-List Messages

Messages from the mailing list appear like any other e-mail messages; they simply show up in your Inbox. When you reply to a specific message, it goes to the person who created it—not to the list. That's as it should be, because you don't want to post something to the entire list unless you really have something worth saying.

Please don't post *me too* messages or anything else that you'd find irritating if it showed up in your own mailbox.

Unsubscribing to a Mailing List

There's a procedure for unsubscribing to a mailing list, similar to the one you used to subscribe in the first place. After you subscribe, you'll receive an automatic message from the server detailing how to unsubscribe. *Create a folder named Unsubscribe Info, and save this message; that way you'll know how to get off the mailing list later.*

Unfortunately, it seems that few people save unsubscribe information, so they try to post the unsubscribe message to the mailing list itself. But the unsubscribe message needs to be sent to the server, not to the mailing list, and the server has a different address. The messages these people send don't work, their mailboxes continue to be flooded with unwanted messages, and their messages get increasingly anxious and pathetic-sounding. I know I've said it before, but *please* don't do this. It's really irritating and unfair to people using the mailing list.

Using Outlook Express's Keyboard Shortcuts

To	Press
Delete a mail message	Del or Ctrl+D
Download news for offline reading	Ctrl+Shift+M
Forward a message	Ctrl+F
Go to next unread mail message	Ctrl+U
Go to the next message in the list	Ctrl+> or Ctrl+Shift+> or Alt + Right arrow
Go to the previous message in the list	Ctrl+< or Ctrl+Shift+< or Alt + Left arrow
Go to your Inbox	Ctrl+I
Mark a message as read	Ctrl+Enter or Ctrl+Q
Move between the message list, folder list, and preview pane	Tab
Open a selected message	Ctrl+O or Enter
Create a new message	Ctrl+N
Print the selected message	Ctrl+P
Reply to all	Ctrl+Shift+R
Reply to the message author	Ctrl+R
Send and receive mail	Ctrl+M
Show or hide the folder list	Ctrl+L
View properties of a selected message	Alt+Enter

CHAPTER 13

Personalizing and Maintaining Outlook Express

Many people use Outlook Express as a simple, easy-to-use mail utility, and that's fine. If you're willing to explore some of the program's advanced features, you will discover many more ways to use Outlook Express for your communication needs. By adding contacts to Address Book, you can make use of a feature-rich contact manager that can place all your contact information at your fingertips. As you explore the program's options, you will find many ways to make the program more useful for you. And as you learn how to create folders and write rules to route incoming mail to these folders, you'll discover how to cut down on e-mail-induced "information overload."

This chapter discusses all the ways you can personalize Outlook Express, including how to create a signature that's inserted into your outgoing mail, and even a business card that updates your correspondent's address books. You'll also learn how to manage your e-mail accounts, create additional e-mail accounts, and customize the Outlook Express toolbars.

Using Address Book

Address Book in Outlook Express version 5 is an exceptionally useful utility, and it's easy to use. At its simplest, Address Book is a nifty way of storing names and e-mail addresses and then entering them correctly into the To, Cc, and Bcc fields of the messages you send. (As you'll see, you can set up Address Book so that it adds the names and e-mail addresses of everyone to whom you send e-mail.) But Address Book can do much more. Available at the Windows level to other applications, it's an excellent contact manager for all your communication needs.

With Address Book, you can:

- Import contact information from other applications.
- Store all necessary information about your contacts, including phone numbers, e-mail addresses, business and home information, fax numbers, and even pager information.
- Make this information available to other compatible applications, including Microsoft NetMeeting, Office 2000, Microsoft Phone, and handheld computers that run Windows CE.
- View a summary of your Address Book on the screen when you're using Outlook Express (it's in the Contacts pane).
- Search for information using Internet white-pages services, and add the retrieved information to your contact list.
- Create groups of contacts for do-it-yourself mailing lists. Once you've created the group, you can send mail to everyone on the list just by sending mail to the group's name.
- Send and receive Business Cards. These are electronic versions of the cards people exchange in business contexts. You can create a Business Card that is included with your outgoing messages. If your recipient is using a compatible program, your card is read by the recipient's e-mail program and included in your recipient's Address Book.
- Print your Address Book so that the information is available in your personal planner.

If you create separate identities, each identity has its own Address Book. For an introduction to identities, see "Setting Up Identities," page 328. For information on sharing one person's Address Book with other identities, see "Sharing Address Book Information Across Identities," page 416.

Opening Address Book

To open Address Book, do one of the following:

- On the Outlook Express toolbar, click Addresses.

  or

- From the Tools menu, click Address Book.

  or

- Press Ctrl + Shift + B.

You'll see the Address Book window, shown in Figure 13-1. This figure shows one (fictitious) contact; your Address Book might be blank.

FIGURE 13-1.
Address Book enables you to store names, e-mail addresses, and contact information.

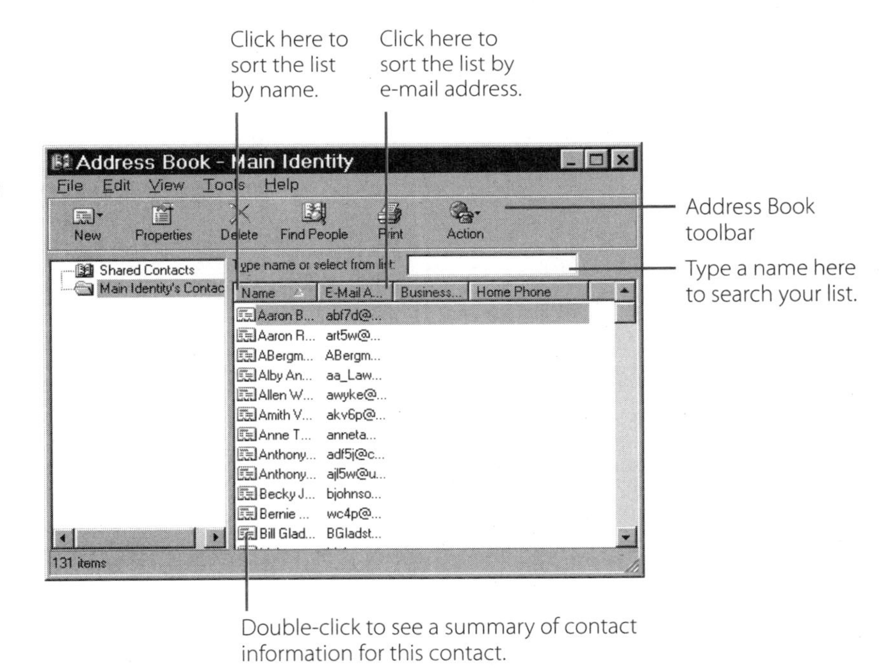

Click here to sort the list by name.
Click here to sort the list by e-mail address.
Address Book toolbar
Type a name here to search your list.
Double-click to see a summary of contact information for this contact.
Address Book - Main Identity
File Edit View Tools Help
New Properties Delete Find People Print Action
Shared Contacts
Main Identity's Contac
Type name or select from list:
Name E-Mail A... Business... Home Phone
131 items

Understanding the Address Book Toolbar

The Address Book window has its own toolbar. Table 13-1 introduces the buttons you'll find on this toolbar; subsequent sections discuss what these buttons do.

TABLE 13-1. Toolbar Buttons (Address Book).

Button name	What it does
New	Enables you to create a new contact, a new folder, or a new group.
Properties	Displays summary information about the selected contact. This button is dimmed if no contact is selected.
Delete	Deletes the selected contact. This button is dimmed if no contact is selected.
Find People	Enables you to search for contact information within Address Book or Internet-based white-pages services.
Print	Prints contact information.
Action	Enables you to initiate actions for the selected contact. You can send mail to the contact, dial the contact's phone number, or place an Internet call via Microsoft NetMeeting.

Making the Microsoft Phone Connection

Imagine yourself waiting for a plane at a distant airport. You don't have a notebook computer with you, and you don't have a secretary back at the office. But you can easily check your e-mail messages just by placing a telephone call, and a pleasant-sounding voice reads your new messages to you! It's made possible by Microsoft Phone, a 900 MHz portable phone and voice-mail system that has several attractive features for Outlook Express users.

Microsoft Phone provides an easy-to-use but powerful voice-mail solution for home and office computer users. The system's base unit connects to your PC by means of a serial port, enabling calls to be intercepted by Microsoft Call Manager, the application that comes with Microsoft Phone. You can create one or more voice-mail boxes, each with a distinctive message. Of course, if you're in your office, you can answer incoming calls by picking up the portable phone, which is packed with nifty features, including voice-command features that enable you to initiate calls by speaking a number or nickname.

For e-mail users, it's the Outlook Express integration that's sure to appeal. After you establish a security code (a four-digit PIN number) for remote access, you can call your number, press an access key, and choose from a menu of options. These include listening to new voice messages—and here's the kicker—listening to new e-mail messages. Microsoft Phone uses advanced voice-mail synthesis to read your messages to you. The application is smart enough to skip a lot of the garbage that often appears in e-mail messages. If you run into spam (unwanted e-mail), you can delete the message right on the spot, and skip to the next one. In order to take advantage of Microsoft Phone's remote e-mail access features, you must leave Outlook Express running on your computer, and you must set up the program to check your e-mail automatically.

Once you've installed both Outlook Express and Microsoft Phone, you'll find that the two get along quite nicely. Outlook Express stores your voice-mail messages in an automatically created My Messages folder, which is stored in your Inbox. If you're writing e-mail to someone, you can send voice-mail messages by forwarding the message as an attachment. (To do this, select the voice-mail message, click Compose on the menu bar, and choose Forward As An Attachment.) Also, the two applications share the same Address Book. When you click the Address Book icon in Microsoft Call Manager, you see the same Address Book information that you've stored in Outlook Express, except that the names and phone numbers are lined up in an easy-to-read, organized list. You can initiate a call just by right-clicking the contact's name. If your phone line has Caller ID, you can even record custom messages for individual contacts—or block their calls entirely.

Importing Contact List Information

If you have created extensive contact list information with another program, you don't have to perform this work again. You can import contact information from the following programs:

- Eudora Pro or Eudora Light (through version 3.0)
- Microsoft Exchange Personal Address Book
- Microsoft Internet Mail for Windows 3.1 Address Book
- Netscape Address Book (version 2 or 3)
- Netscape Communicator Address Book (version 4)

SEE ALSO

For information on exporting Address Book information to a comma separated value (CSV) file, see "Exporting Address Book Information," page 417.

You can also import contact information from *any* program that can export this information in the form of a comma separated values (CSV) text file. Most applications can do this. You an also import contact information that has been written to an LDIF (LDAP Directory Interchange Format) file.

To import Windows Address Book contact information, follow these steps:

1. From the Address Book menu bar, click File, and choose Import.
2. From the submenu, choose Address Book (WAB). ("WAB" stands for Windows Address Book.) You'll see the Select Address Book File To Import From dialog box, shown here:

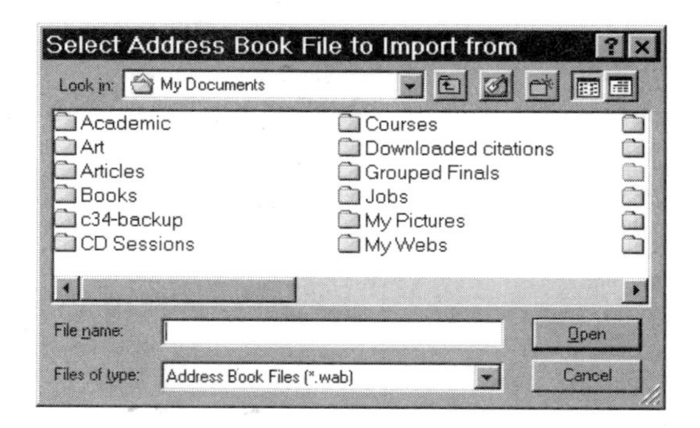

3. Use the Select Address Book dialog box to locate the Windows Address Book file you want to import.

   To find the file, look in the Windows folder, and open the Profiles folder. If more than one user has established profiles for this computer, you'll see two or more folders. Open a profile folder, and select the Windows Address Book file that you want to import. (This file has the .wab extension.)
4. Click OK.

To import contact information from another program, do the following:

1. From the Address Book menu bar, click File, choose Import, and click Other Address Book. You'll see the Address Book Import Tool, shown here:

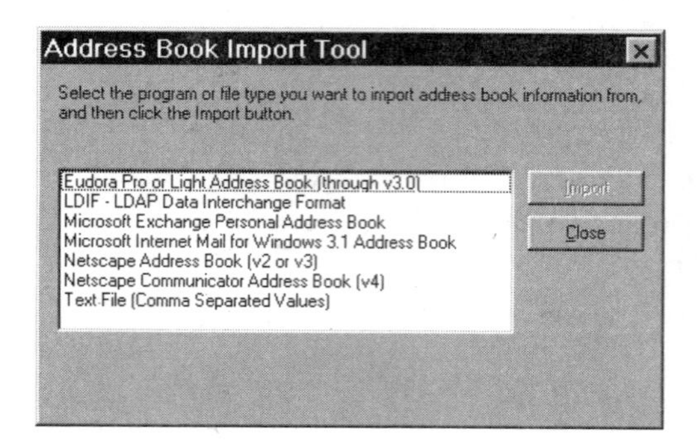

2 Select the program from which you want to import addresses, and click Import. Follow the instructions on the screen to complete importing your addresses.

Automatically Storing Contact Information in Your Address Book

To make Address Book useful, you must add information to it. To do so with very little effort, you can take advantage of features that automatically add names and e-mail addresses to your Address Book. You can also supply contact information manually.

Adding a Correspondent's Information Automatically

You can set up Outlook Express so that the program creates Address Book entries for all the people to whom you send e-mail. This is a fast way to build up the essentials of your Address Book; you can later supply additional information manually, including numbers and addresses.

To add recipients' names and e-mail addresses to your Address Book, do the following:

1 From Outlook Express's Tools menu, choose Options.

2 Click the Send tab. You'll see the page shown here:

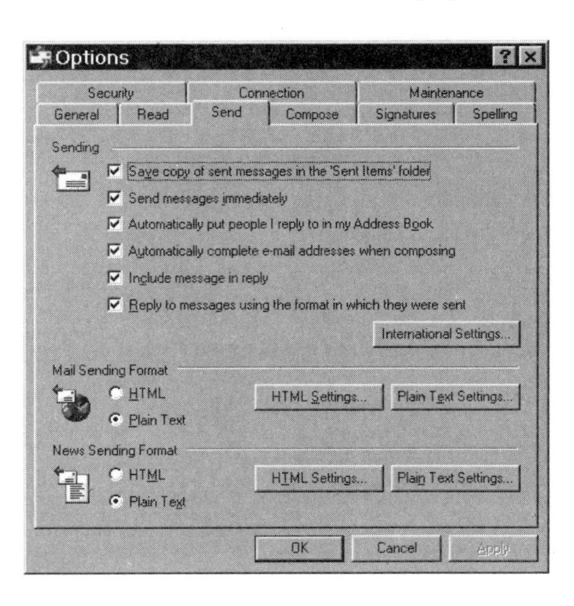

3. Activate the option Automatically Put People I Reply To In My Address Book.

4. Click OK.

Selectively Storing Contact Information

If you don't want to store the names and e-mail addresses of everyone to whom you sent mail, you can take advantage of the following technique. This technique enables you to select the names of people to add to Address Book.

To add a person's e-mail address to your Address Book, follow these steps:

1. In the message list, select a message that contains the address you want to add.

2. Do one of the following:

   - From the Tools menu, choose Add Sender To Address Book.

   or

   - Right-click the message title, and choose Add Sender To Address Book from the pop-up menu. You'll see this person's name or e-mail address in the Contact list.

   Outlook Express adds the sender's e-mail address to your Address Book.

Although Outlook Express tries to interpret the person's first and last names from the From field's information, it might not succeed, so you might need to edit this information. For more information, see "Adding Contact Information Manually," page 403.

Searching for Contact Information

Here's another way to add contact information to your Address Book: Initiate a search of the Web's white-pages directory services, which make contact information available via the Internet. If you find contact information, you can click a button that creates an Address Book entry and records the information. Before typing in a lot of contact information manually, as explained in the next section, try this technique.

To search for contact information, follow these steps:

1 Do one of the following:

- From Outlook Express, click Edit on the menu bar, click Find, and choose People. Alternatively, press Ctrl + E.

  or

- From Address Book, click Find People on the toolbar. You can also click Edit on the menu bar, and choose Find People. Alternatively, press Ctrl + F.

You see the Find People dialog box, shown here:

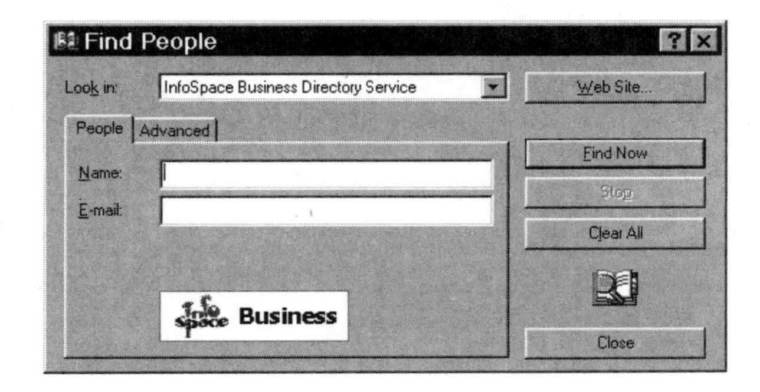

2 From the Look In drop-down list, select the directory you want to search.

About White-Pages Directory Services

Directory services enable Internet users to search for people and businesses throughout the world. Leading directory services include InfoSpace (www.infospace.com), Switchboard (www.switchboard.com), WhoWhere (www.whowhere.lycos.com), and Yahoo! People Search (people.yahoo.com). You can search for information by accessing these sites with Internet Explorer, but there's a better way: You can search from Outlook Express directly, thanks to the Lightweight Directory Access Protocol (LDAP). This protocol defines a standard that enables programs to obtain contact information from LDAP-compatible servers.

For use on an internal network, organizations can set up their own contact servers. If your organization maintains a directory service, you can add the server's address to the list of servers that Outlook Express searches. For more information, see "Managing Accounts" on page 451.

3. Click the People tab, if necessary, and type the name or e-mail address of the person you want to look for.

4. Click Find Now.

   Outlook Express initiates a search of the selected directory service. If matches are found, the Find People dialog box expands. You see a list of matching names and e-mail addresses, such as the one shown here:

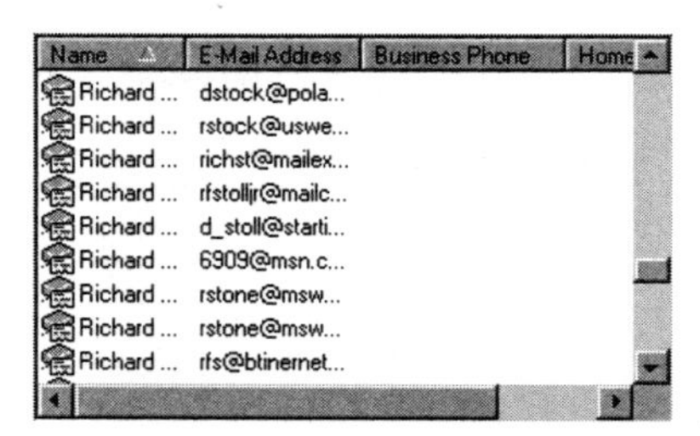

   The list includes close matches as well as exact ones. If the search service doesn't contain any information about this person, you'll see an alert box informing you that the search failed.

5. To see more information about a retrieved contact, select the contact, and click Properties.

6. If your contact appears, select the contact, and click Add To Address Book.

7. If you would like to perform another search without closing the Find People dialog box, click Clear All to clear the retrieved information list.

If your search didn't work, try a different directory service; each has its own, proprietary database of names and e-mail addresses.

Performing an Advanced Search

If your search failed to find information about the contact, you may wish to try an advanced search. This search enables you to specify search information more precisely, and may produce better results.

To perform an advanced search, follow these steps:

1. In the Find People dialog box, click the Advanced Tab. You'll see the Advanced page, shown here:

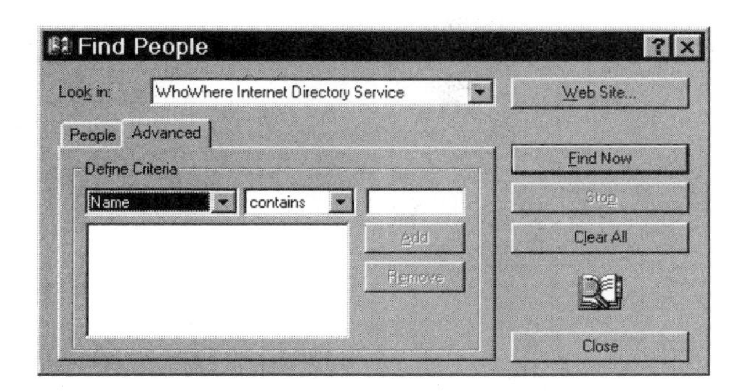

2. In the Define Criteria area, select search criteria by filling in the top three boxes. For example, in the first box, you can choose Name, E-mail, First Name, Last Name, or Organization. In the second box, you can choose Contains, Is, Starts With, Ends With, or Sounds Like. In the third box, type the text you want to match.
3. Click Add to add this criterion to the search.
4. Repeat steps 2 and 3 to add more search criteria if you wish. To remove a criterion, select the criterion, and click Remove.
5. To start the search, click Find Now.
6. To see more information about a retrieved contact, select the contact, and click Properties.
7. If your contact appears, select the contact, and click Add To Address Book.
8. If you would like to perform another search without closing the Find People dialog box, click Clear All to clear the retrieved information list.

Adding Contact Information Manually

The automated technique just discussed adds names and e-mail addresses, but it doesn't add telephone numbers and other information. If you would like to use Outlook Express to store all contact information, not just names and e-mail addresses, you need to add this information manually.

As you'll learn in this section, you can add an amazing amount of information about a contact, including the contact's spouse's and children's names, date of birth, Web-site address, and much more. However, don't let Address Book's capabilities scare you off: you don't need to obtain all of this information in order to use Address Book. You can enter the e-mail address, business address, and telephone numbers, and leave the rest of the fields blank.

To add an entry to Address Book manually, do the following:

1. Display Address Book, if necessary, by clicking Addresses on the Outlook Express toolbar.
2. Click New. From the pop-up menu, choose New Contact. You'll see the Properties dialog box for this contact (see Figure 13-2).

To display last names first, choose a display option here.

Type a nickname if you wish.

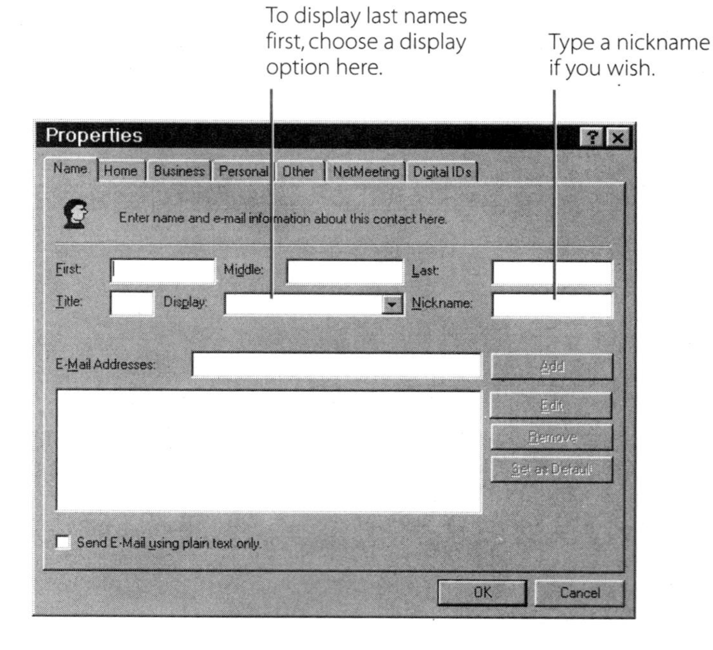

FIGURE 13-2.
Use this page to add your contact's name and e-mail address.

3. Type the person's name and the title.

You can set up Outlook Express so that your mail is sent in HTML (rich formatting), by default. (For information, see "Choosing Mail Composition Options" on page 427.) If this correspondent cannot receive HTML mail, click Send E-mail Using Plain Text Only, in the Name page of the contact's properties.

4. In the Display box, choose the way you want the name displayed. Address Book shows three options: first name, middle name, and last name; last name, first name, and middle name; and last name followed by first name and middle name separated by a comma.
5. If you would like to type a nickname for this person, type it in the Nickname box. You can add this person's e-mail address to an e-mail message quickly by just typing the nickname.
6. In the E-mail address box, type the contact's e-mail address, and click Add.

   You can add additional e-mail addresses for this contact if you wish. Just repeat step 6. If you supply more than one e-mail address, select the main address, and click Set As Default.
7. If this contact cannot receive HTML-formatted e-mail, click Send E-mail Using Plain Text Only.
8. Click Home. You'll see the Home page, shown in Figure 13-3.

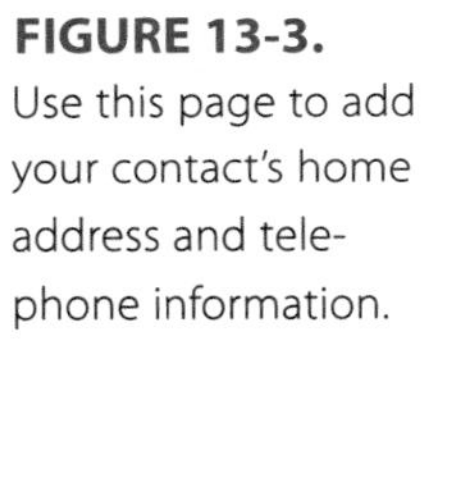

FIGURE 13-3.
Use this page to add your contact's home address and telephone information.

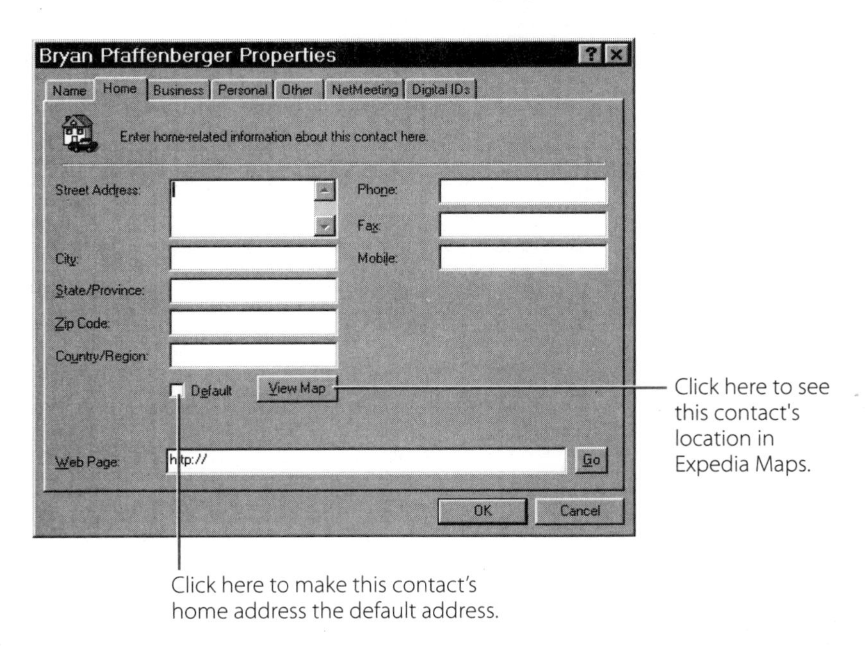

9. Type your contact's home address and phone information.
10. To see a map showing this contact's business location, click View Map. Outlook Express starts Internet Explorer, and displays Expedia Maps (for an example, see Figure 13-4).

FIGURE 13-4.
With Expedia Maps, you can see a map to your contact's location.

TIP

> To get driving directions to your contact's location, click Driving Directions in the Expedia page, and follow the instructions.

11 If your contact has a personal Web page, type the URL in the Web Page box.

12 Click Business to continue. You'll see the Business page, shown in Figure 13-5.

13 Type your contact's business address and phone information.

14 To see a map showing this contact's business location, click View Map. Outlook Express starts Internet Explorer, and displays Expedia Maps (for an example, see Figure 13-4).

15 If your contact has a business Web page, type the URL in the Web Page box.

16 Click Personal. You'll see the Personal page, shown in Figure 13-6.

17 If you'd like to add personal information, do the following:

- In the Spouse box, type your contact's spouse's name.
- To add your contact's children's names, click Add. You'll see New Child in the Children box. Type the child's name. To add another child, click Add. To change a child's information, select a child's name, and click Edit. To delete a child's name, select the name, and click Remove.

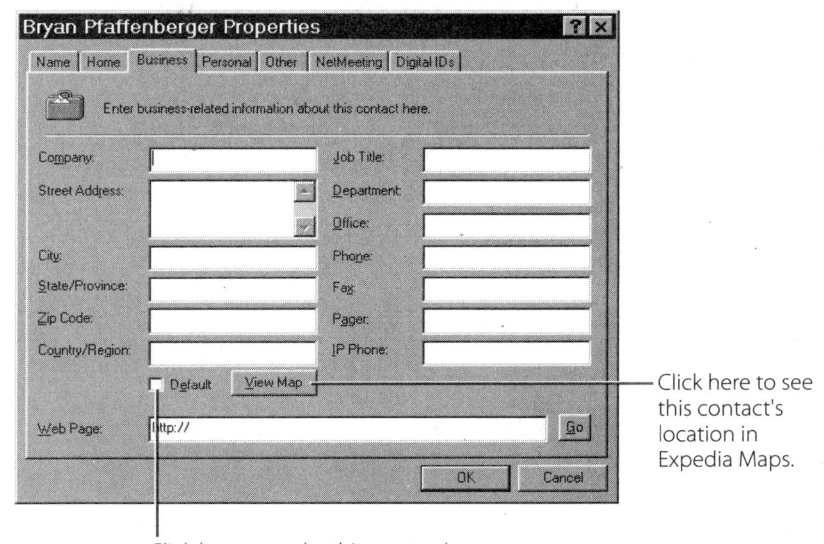

Click here to make this contact's business address the default address.

FIGURE 13-5. Use this page to add your contact's business address and telephone information.

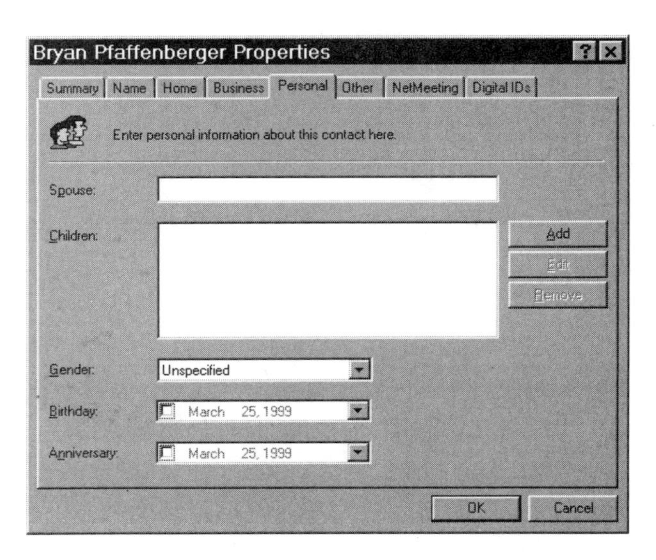

FIGURE 13-6. Here, you can add personal information about your contact.

- To specify your contact's gender, make a choice in the Gender box.

- To indicate your contact's birthday, click the arrow next to the Birthday box. You'll see a calendar, such as the following:

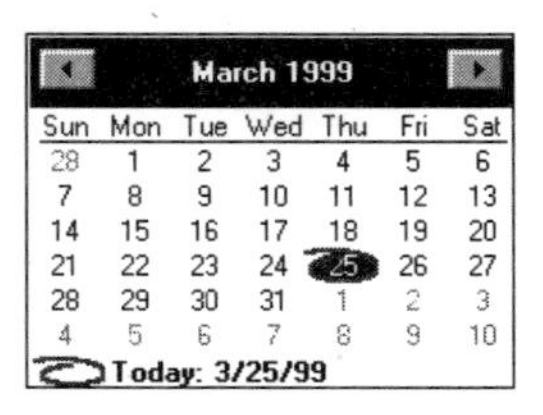

- To change the year, click the year, and use the spinner controls. To change the month, click the left or right arrows. To choose a day, click the day within the calendar. To confirm the birthday, click outside the calendar.

To indicate your contact's anniversary, click the arrow next to the Anniversary box, and use the calendar pop-up, as described above.

18 Click Other. You'll see the Other page, shown in Figure 13-7.

19 In the Notes area, type notes about your contact.

The Group Membership and Folder Location information become relevant if you include this contact in a group, as explained in the next section.

20 Click NetMeeting. You'll see the NetMeeting page, shown in Figure 13-8. In this page, you can add your contact's NetMeeting information.

21 In the Conferencing Server box, type the address of the Conferencing server that your contact uses.

22 In the Conferencing Address box, type your contact's conferencing address. This address may be your contact's e-mail address, but it may be different.

23 Click Add to add this contact's conferencing information to the list box.

SEE ALSO

For information on NetMeeting, see Chapter 18, "Collaborating Online with Microsoft NetMeeting." In this chapter, you'll learn how to obtain the information that's needed to fill out the various areas of the NetMeeting page.

FIGURE 13-7.
In this page, there's room for notes about your contact.

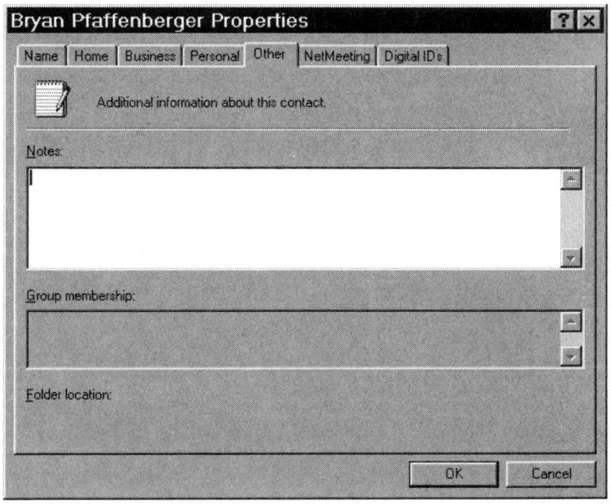

FIGURE 13-8.
This page enables you to record Internet telephone information about your contact.

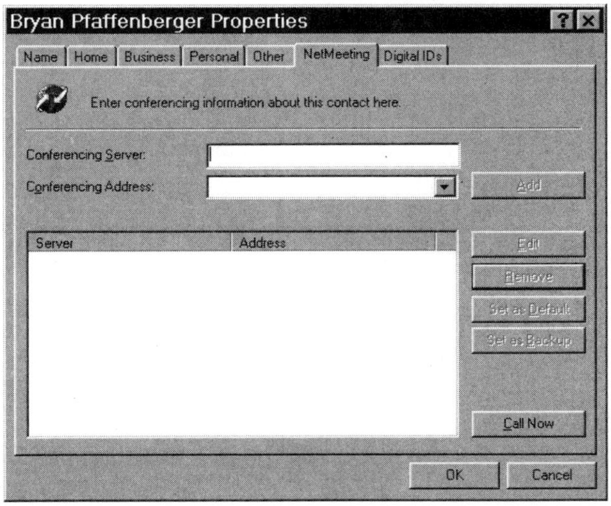

Should you need to edit this contact's conferencing information, select the address, and click Edit. To remove conferencing information, select the address, and click Remove. If you supplied more than one conference address, choose one to serve as the default by selecting the address and clicking Set As Default. To identify an address as a backup in case the main address doesn't work, select the address, and click Set As Backup.

To test the information you've supplied, select an address, and click Call Now.

SEE ALSO
For information on Digital IDs, see Chapter 14, "Using Secure E-Mail."

24 Click Digital IDs. You'll see the Digital IDs page, shown in Figure 13-9. Here, you can manage your contact's digital IDs. If you have not received any digital IDs from this contact, this page will be blank.

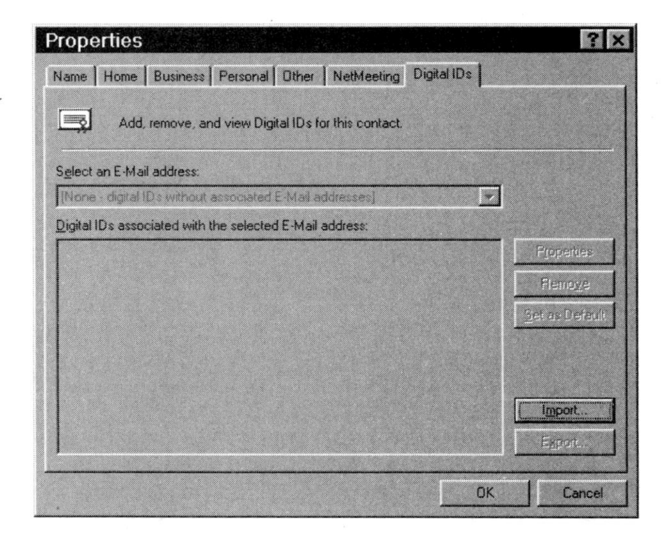

FIGURE 13-9.

In this page, you can store and manage your contact's digital IDs.

25 Select an e-mail address. In the Digital IDs list, you'll see the digital IDs, if any, associated with this digital ID. To view the ID's properties, select the ID, and click Properties. Should you wish to delete a digital ID, select the ID, and click Remove. To set a digital ID as the default, select the ID, and click Set As Default.

If you received a digital ID from this contact on another computer, you can export the digital ID, and then import it. To export an ID, click Export, and specify a location to store the exported ID. To import an ID, click Import, and locate the ID you want to import.

26 Click OK to save this contact's information.

Creating a Business Card

Outlook Express enables you to attach a business card to your outgoing messages. A *business card* contains personal information about you and conforms to an unofficial Internet standard called *vCard*. Some other mail programs can read the vCard format, including Netscape Messenger.

To create a business card, just create an Address Book entry for yourself. You can send the business card in two ways:

- **Selectively.** To include your business card in an outgoing message, click Insert in the composition window menu bar, and choose My Business Card. (This option is dimmed if you haven't created an Address Book entry for yourself.)
- **Automatically.** To include your business card automatically in all outgoing messages, click Tools on the Outlook Express menu bar, and choose Options. Click Compose. In the Business Cards area, activate Mail, and choose your Address Book entry in the list box.

Managing and Organizing Your Address Book

Once you have added many contacts to your Address Book, you may need to edit or delete some of the information you've stored. In addition, you can sort and organize the contact list so that it's easier to use.

Managing Address Book Information

If you need to change a contact's information, display Address Book, and double-click the contact. You'll see the contact's properties. Make your changes, and click OK.

To delete a contact, select the contact, and click Delete on the Address Book toolbar.

Organizing Address Book Information

You can sort the contact list by name, e-mail address, business phone, or home phone number. To do so, just click the button at the top of the column. To change the sort order from ascending to descending, or from descending to ascending, just click the column-header button again.

To change the order in which columns are displayed, point to the column you want to move. Hold down the right mouse button, and drag the column to the position you want.

Creating a Group

Once you've entered two or more names in Address Book, you can create a group. For example, you could create a group consisting of all the people working with you on a project, or all the people with whom you share an interest in a professional sports team.

After you've created the group, you can send a message to the whole group by using the group address instead of individual e-mail addresses.

To create a group, do the following:

1 In Address Book, click View on the menu bar, and choose Folders And Groups, if necessary, so that you can see the Folders And Groups window, shown here:

If you have created more than one identity, you'll see a folder for each identity. You can create the group list in the Shared Contacts folder so that your group will be available to all users, or you can create the group list in one of the user folders.

2 In the Folders And Groups window, select the folder in which you want to create a group.

3 Click the New button on the toolbar, and then click New Group. You'll see the Properties dialog box for your new group, shown in Figure 13-10.

SEE ALSO
For information on setting up identities with Outlook Express, see "Setting Up Identities," page 328.

4 In the Group Name box, type the name of the group.

5 To add contacts to your group, click Select Members. You'll see the Select Group Members dialog box, shown in Figure 13-11.

6 In the contact list, select one or more contacts, and click Select. To select two or more contacts, hold down the Ctrl key and click as many contacts as you like.

7 Click OK to return to the Group Properties dialog box.

8 To add names and addresses manually, type the name and e-mail address in the boxes at the bottom of the dialog box, and click Add. You can also click New Contact to add complete contact information manually.

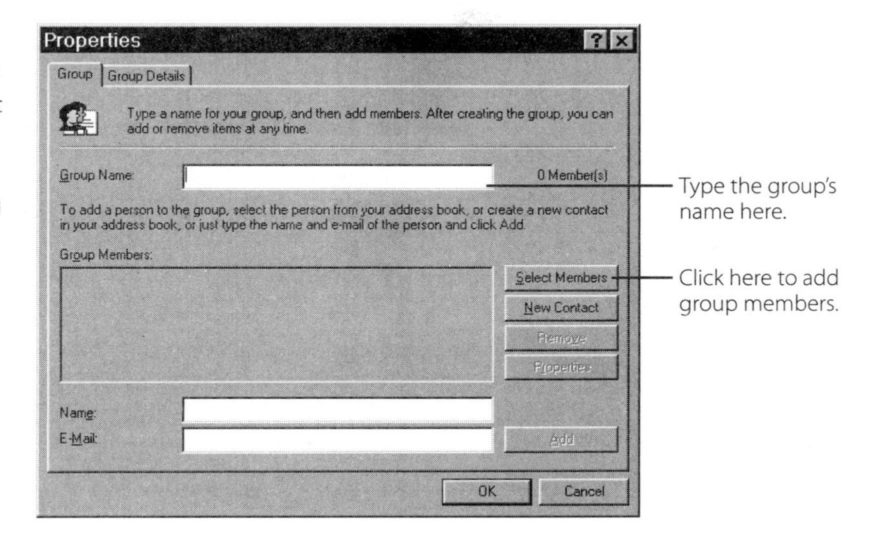

FIGURE 13-10.
In this dialog box, you can create a group list that enables you to send e-mail to two or more people by using just one address.

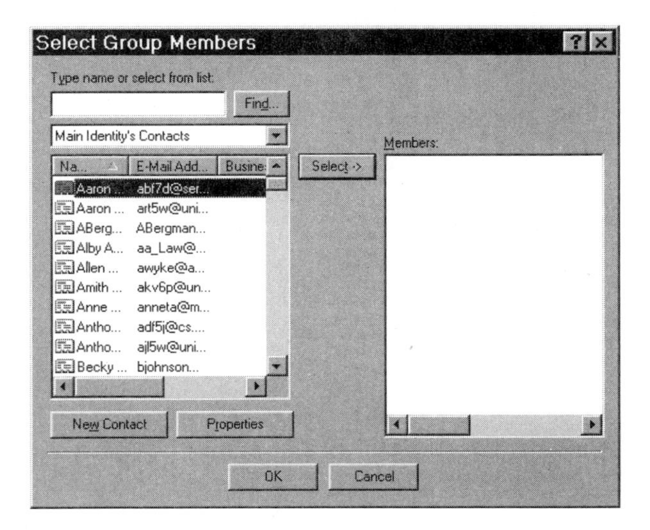

FIGURE 13-11.
To add contacts to your group list, click Select.

9 If the group has a physical location and phone number, click Group Details so that you can add this information. You'll see the Group Details page, shown in Figure 13-12.

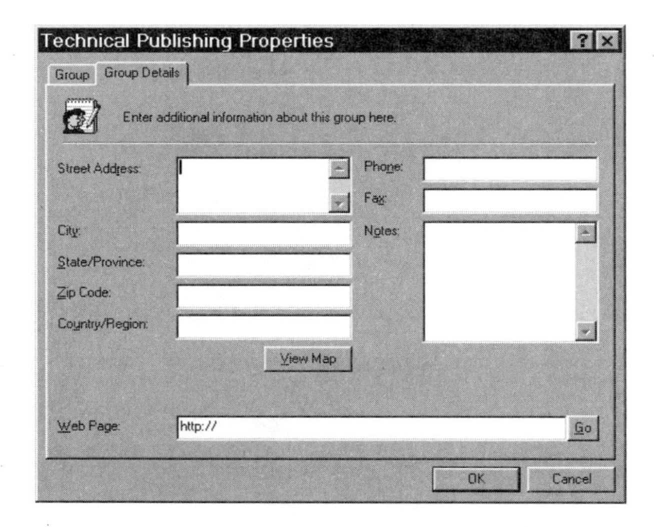

FIGURE 13-12.
If the group has a physical location and phone number, you can add this information in the Group Details page.

10 Add the group's address and additional information.

11 Click OK to complete the group.

After you create the group, you see a group icon in the Folders And Groups window, as shown here:

To send e-mail to the group, click New Mail on the Outlook Express toolbar, and type the group name in the To box. You can also click the Address Book icon next to the To box, and choose your group name from the contact list.

Using Address Book Information in Outlook Express

Once you've created your contact list, you can easily insert e-mail addresses in your messages. Here's how:

1. In Outlook Express, click New Mail to create a new message.
2. Click To. You'll see the Select Recipients dialog box, shown in Figure 13-13.

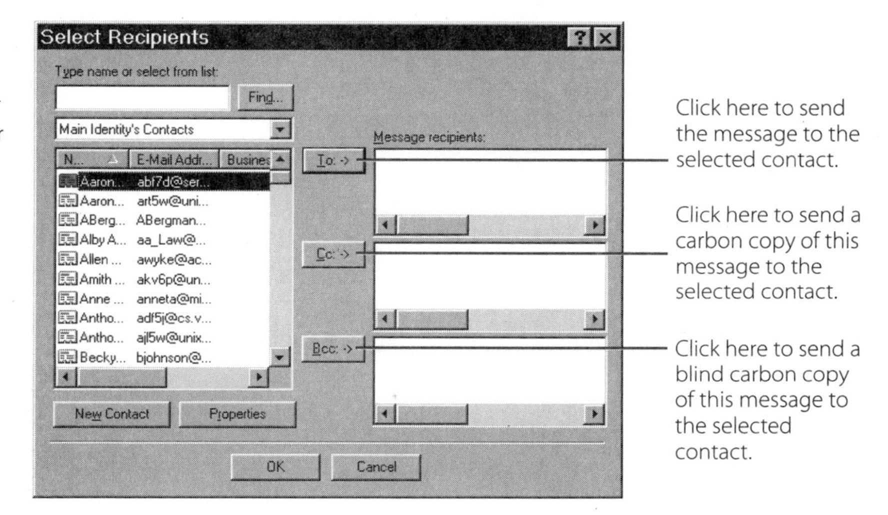
Select Recipients
Type name or select from list:
Find...
Main Identity's Contacts
Message recipients:
To: ->
Cc: ->
Bcc: ->
New Contact
Properties
OK
Cancel
Click here to send the message to the selected contact.
Click here to send a carbon copy of this message to the selected contact.
Click here to send a blind carbon copy of this message to the selected contact.

FIGURE 13-13.
To choose a message recipient, select a contact, and click To, Cc, or Bcc.

3. Select a contact. To search for a contact, type the contact's name in the text box, and click Find.
4. Do one of the following:
   - To send the message to the selected contact, click To.

     or

   - To send a carbon copy of this message to the selected contact, click Cc.

     or

   - To send a blind carbon copy of this message to the selected contact, click Bcc.
5. Click OK to confirm the addresses.

Sharing Address Book Information across Identities

If you've set up identities, you can share contacts across identities, or make your contacts available to all identities.

To share contacts, follow these steps:

1. In Address Book, click View on the menu bar, and choose Folders And Groups, if necessary, to display the Folders And Groups window. In this window, you see the Shared Contacts icon, and the folders of all the identities you've created.
2. In the contact list, select the contact you want to share. To select more than one contact, hold down the Ctrl key, and select as many contacts as you like.
3. Point to the selection, hold down the right mouse button, and drag the selection to the destination folder. To share the contacts with all identities, drag the selection to the Shared Contacts folder.

Printing Your Address Book

You can print your Address Book information in any of the following formats:

- **Memo** prints all of the Address Book information.
- **Business Card** prints contact information in a business-card format.
- **Phone List** prints contact information in a phone-list format.

To print your Address Book information, follow these steps:

1. If you want to print just one record, or selected records, select the records in the contact list.
2. On the Address Book toolbar, click Print. You'll see the Print dialog box, shown in Figure 13-14.
3. Do one of the following:
    - To print all of the items in your Address Book, click All in the Print Range area.

      or

- To print only the selected records, click Selection.

4 In the Print Style area, choose the print style that you want.

5 In the Copies area, choose the number of copies you want to print.

6 Click OK to start printing.

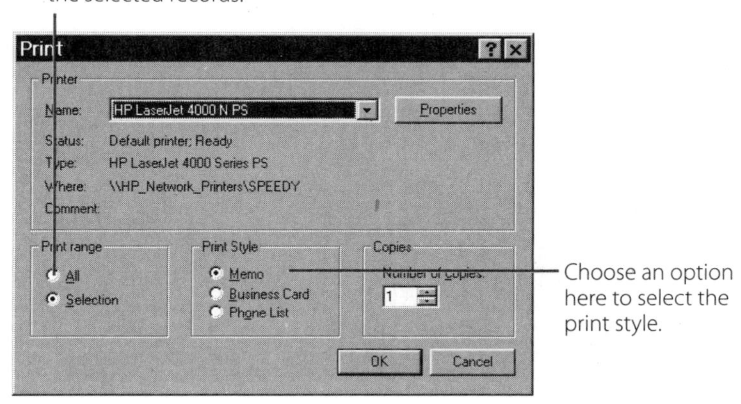

FIGURE 13-14.
When you print Address Book information, you can print all the records or just selected records.

Exporting Address Book Information

If you would like to share your Address Book information with other applications, you can export this information to the following:

- **Windows Address Book.** Choose this export option to export Address Book information to another copy of Internet Explorer, or any other application that can use Windows Address Book (WAB) information.
- **Microsoft Exchange Personal Address Book.** Choose this export option to export Address Book information to the Microsoft Exchange Personal Address Book format.
- **Comma-separated value (CSV).** Choose this export option to export Address Book information to a text file in which the various data fields are separated by commas. Many applications can import data in this format.

To export Address Book information to the Windows Address Book (WAB) format, follow these steps:

1. In Address Book, click the File menu, point to Export, and then click Address Book (WAB).
2. Enter the name of the Windows Address Book file you want to export to, and then click Save.

To export to the Comma-separated value (CSV) format, follow these steps:

1. In Address Book, click the File menu, point to Export, and click Other Address Book.

   You'll see the Address Book Export Tool, shown here:

   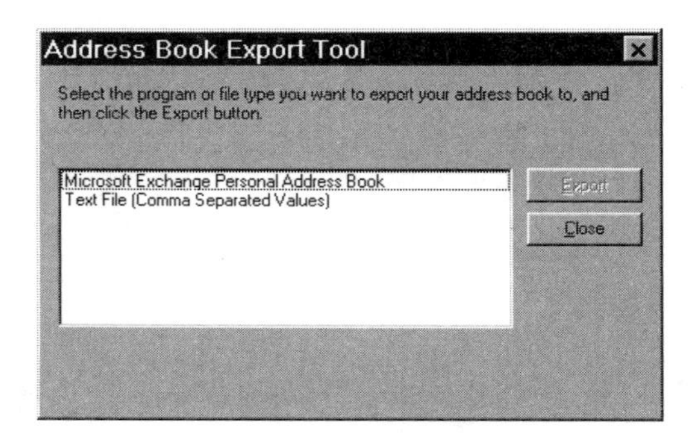

2. Click the address book or file type you want to export to, and then click Export.

   You'll see the next page of the export tool, which asks you to specify a file name and location for the exported data. Click Browse to choose a location other than the default.

3. After specifying the file name and location, click Next. You'll see the next page of the export tool, shown on the next page:

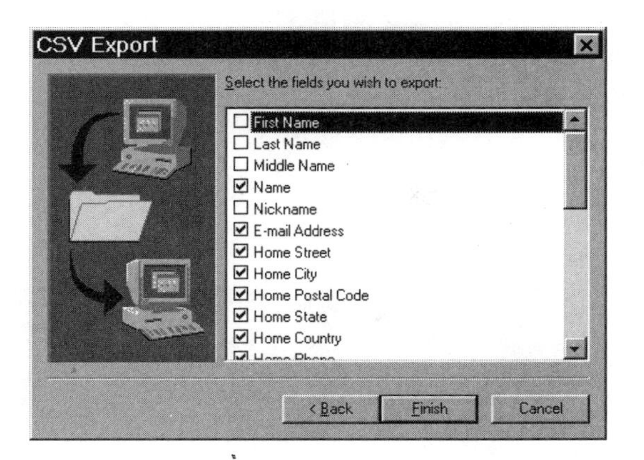

4 Select the fields you want to export, and click Finish.

To export to the Microsoft Exchange Personal Address Book format, you must have installed Microsoft Outlook on your system, and you must also have configured Outlook to be your default client for mail and contacts. This means, essentially, that you'll be switching to Microsoft Outlook for your e-mail, and you're exporting your Outlook Express contacts so that they'll be available in Outlook. To export the contacts, follow these steps:

1 In Address Book, click the File menu, point to Export, and click Other Address Book.

   You'll see the Address Book Export Tool.

2 Select Microsoft Exchange Personal Address Book, and click Export.

   You'll see the Choose Profile dialog box. Choose the Microsoft Outlook profile to which you want to export, and click OK.

Choosing Outlook Express Options

Choosing General Options

In the General page of the Options dialog box, you can choose general options for e-mail and news, including several important options concerning how and when Outlook Express checks for new messages.

To choose general options, follow these steps:

1 On the Outlook Express menu bar, click Tools, and choose Options.

2 If necessary, click the General tab. You'll see the General options, shown in Figure 13-15.

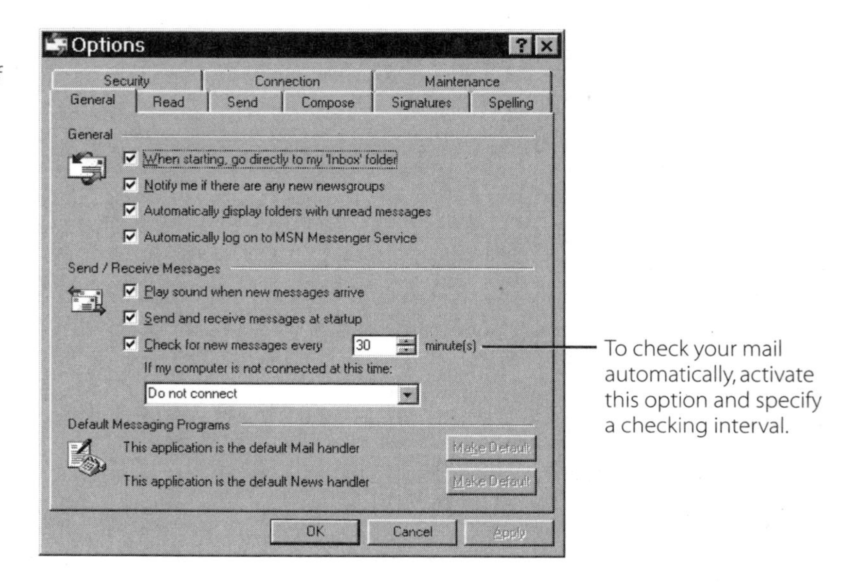

FIGURE 13-15.
In the General page of the Options dialog box, you can set up Outlook Express to check your mail at intervals you specify.

3 In the General area, make choices for the following e-mail options:

- **When Starting, Go Directly To My 'Inbox' Folder.** Activate this option to skip the Starting Outlook Express page.
- **Automatically Display Folders With Unread Messages.** Activate this option to show folders that contain unread messages.

4 In the Send/Receive area, make choices for the following e-mail options:

- **Play Sound When New Messages Arrive.** If you don't want to be bothered by the sound, turn this option off.
- **Send And Receive Messages At Startup.** Leave this option selected if you want Outlook Express to check for messages, and send messages when you log on to the mail server.

- **Check For New Messages Every....** To configure Outlook Express to check for new messages automatically, activate this option, and specify a mail-check interval. In the list box, choose an option to tell Outlook Express what to do if your computer is not connected to the Internet when an update is scheduled. You can choose Do Not Connect (the default), Connect Only When Not Working Offline, or Connect Even While Working Offline. Don't choose the last option if you connect via a modem and use the same line for a telephone; if you do choose the last option, Outlook Express may interrupt your telephone call.

5. In the Default Messaging area, you can see whether Outlook Express is currently configured as the default mail and news handler. If the Make Default button for each option is dimmed, then Outlook Express is the default handler. If one or both of the buttons aren't dimmed, click them to make Outlook Express the default mail and news handler.

Choosing Read Options

In the Read page of the Options dialog box, you can define a default font for viewing the messages you've received. You can also choose a few additional options for displaying the messages you're reading.

To choose mail-reading options, follow these steps:

1. On the Outlook Express menu bar, click Tools, and choose Options.
2. Click the Read tab. You'll see the Read options, shown in Figure 13-16.
3. In the Reading Messages area, choose settings for the following e-mail options:

   - **Mark Message Read After Displaying For....** To mark a message as read after it has been open for a specified number of seconds, activate this option. (A read message no longer appears in boldface.) Specify the number of seconds (the default is 5 seconds).
   - **Show ToolTips In The Message List For Clipped Items.** In the Outlook Express message lists, some information might not be fully visible if there's not enough room. Activate this option to see a tooltip that shows all of the text.

FIGURE 13-16.
You can choose options that can make your messages easier to read.

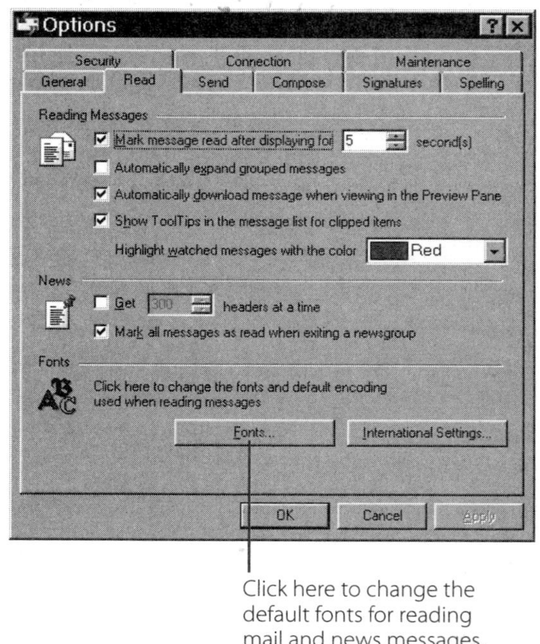

4 In the Fonts area, click Fonts to change the default fonts used for viewing messages. You'll see the Fonts dialog box, shown here:

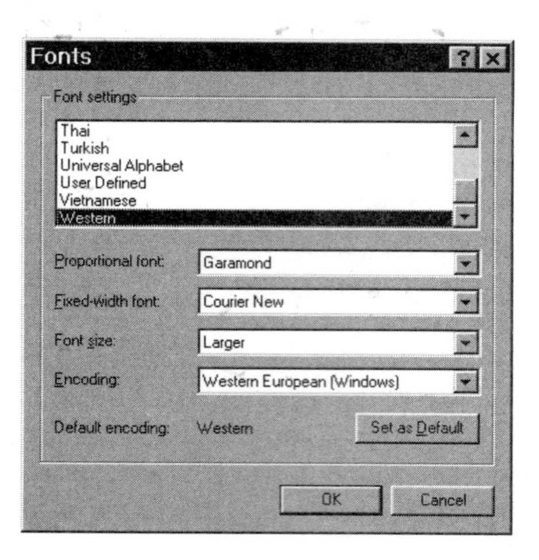

5 In the Font settings area, choose the default character set in the list of character sets. The default is Western European.

6 In the Proportional Font area, choose the font that you want to use for HTML-formatted messages that include text formatted to appear as a generic proportional font.

7 In the Fixed-Width font area, choose the font that you want to use for plain text messages. It's best to use a monospace font such as Courier, in case you receive messages that contain text aligned with manual spacing.

8 In the Font Size area, choose a default font size (you can choose from Smallest, Smaller, Medium, Larger, or Largest).

9 In the Encoding area, choose an encoding scheme. To make a new selection the default, click Set As Default.

10 Click OK to confirm your font options.

11 If you would like to use the default encoding for all incoming messages, even if they are encoded using a different encoding method, click International Settings, and activate Use Default Encoding For All Incoming Messages.

12 Click OK to confirm your mail-reading options.

Choosing Send Options

In the Send page of the Options dialog box, you can define the default settings that Outlook Express uses when sending mail. The most important of these concerns the mail-sending format.

With Outlook Express, you can send and receive richly formatted e-mail that can contain fonts and font sizes, centered text, graphics, and more. Outlook Express can format your mail using HTML, the markup language that underlies the appearance of Web pages. However, people can't read richly formatted mail unless they're using an e-mail program capable of reading HTML. Many people don't use such e-mail programs, and they may not receive your messages correctly unless you switch to the plain-text format for sending messages. However, Outlook Express sends HTML-formatted mail by default if this option is selected in the program's options settings. You may wish to check this setting before sending mail.

TIP

If you want to send HTML-formatted mail, you can still do so, even if you choose Plain Text as the default format. You can choose this option manually for each message you send. To do so, click Format on the Outlook Express menu bar, and click Rich Text (HTML).

To choose mail-reading options, follow these steps:

1 On the Outlook Express menu bar, click Tools, and choose Options.

2 Click the Send tab. You'll see the Send options, shown in Figure 13-17.

If you plan to send and receive e-mail via the Internet, choose this option.

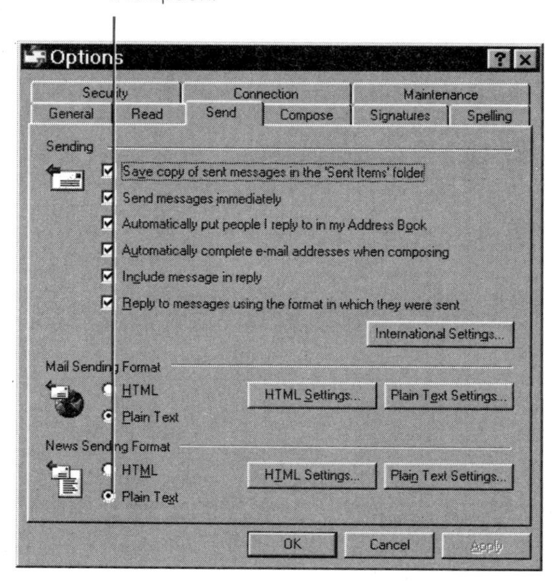

FIGURE 13-17.
In the Send page of the Options dialog box, you can choose mail-sending options.

3 In the Sending area, choose settings for the following e-mail options:

- **Save Copy Of Sent Messages In The 'Sent Items' Folder.** If you want to save copies of your outgoing messages, be sure to activate this option.
- **Send Messages Immediately.** If this option isn't activated, Outlook Express doesn't send messages until you click the Send/Receive button.
- **Automatically Put People I Reply To In My Address Book.** This is a convenient option for automatically recording e-mail addresses, but it adds a lot of addresses to your contact list that you might not use again.

- **Automatically Complete E-mail Addresses When Composing.** This nifty feature saves some keystrokes should you decide to enter your contacts' e-mail addresses manually (instead of choosing them from the Address Book).

- **Include Messages In Reply.** With this option, Outlook Express quotes the original message when you send a reply.

- **Reply To Messages Using The Format In Which They Were Sent.** If you reply to a richly formatted (HTML) message with this option activated, the reply is also sent in HTML. Your replies to plain-text messages will be sent in plain text. Uncheck this option if you want Outlook Express to always use your default mail-sending format (see below).

4 If you would like to change the encoding used for outgoing mail, click International Settings, and choose an encoding.

5 In the Mail Sending Format area, choose a default mail-sending format:

   - **HTML.** Choose this option to send all outgoing mail in HTML by default. This option is not recommended unless you are using Outlook Express on a corporate intranet in which all users are known to have HTML-capable mail programs. Do not choose this option if you plan to send and receive mail on the Internet.

   - **Plain Text.** Choose this option (recommended) to send mail in plain text by default (you can still selectively send messages in HTML format).

6 To choose additional plain-text mail formats, click Plain Text Settings. You'll see the Plain Text Settings dialog box, shown here:

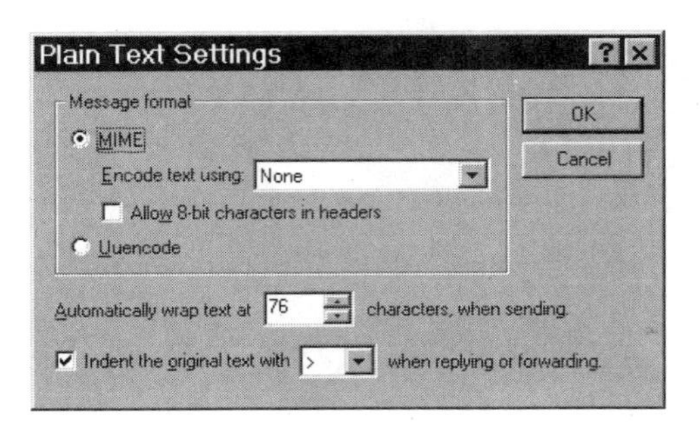

7. For Internet use, you shouldn't change the default settings. Here's what they do:

   - **Message Format.** In this area, you choose the encoding method Outlook Express uses to encode binary files (programs, graphics, sounds, and data files) so that they can be sent via the Internet. The MIME format is fine for Internet use.

   - **Encode Text Using.** This should be set to None; if you encode the text, it will probably look like gibberish when your recipient gets it.

   - **Allow 8-bit Characters In Headers.** To make sure your mail can be read on legacy systems, keep this option unchecked. With this setting, foreign language and other special characters are encoded rather than displayed directly. They can still be displayed by programs that know how to decode the characters.

   - **Automatic Text Wrapping.** Many older e-mail programs cannot wrap text automatically, so it's a good idea to wrap the text at a few characters less than a standard screen width (80 characters). This ensures that your message can be read on legacy systems. The default setting is 76 characters, which is a good choice.

   - **Indentation Character.** The default Internet character is a greater-than bracket (>). This is a good choice for your Internet mail use.

8. Click OK to confirm the plain-text options.

9. To choose HTML mail-sending options, click HTML Settings. You'll see the HTML Settings dialog box:

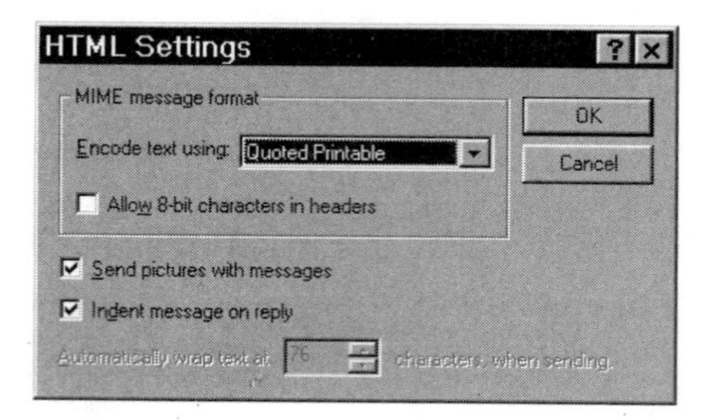

   There's no need to change these settings, but here's what they do:

- **Encode Text Using....** This option specifies the MIME encoding format. Choose None to make sure that your message can be read by people using non-MIME compatible e-mail programs.
- **Allow 8-bit Characters In Headers.** This option enables foreign-language headers, but it may prevent your messages' headers from being legible with older e-mail programs.
- **Send Pictures With Messages.** Activate this option to send the pictures you include with your messages.
- **Indent Messages On Reply.** Activate this option to indent quoted text in replies.

10. Click OK to confirm the HTML options.
11. Click OK to confirm your mail-sending options.

Choosing Mail-Composition Options

In the Compose page of the Options dialog box, you can choose fonts for composing mail, a default Stationery for richly formatted (HTML) mail, and a default Business card to send with all outgoing messages.

To change the default formatting settings for composing mail:

1. From the Tools menu, choose Options. You'll see the Options dialog box.
2. Click the Compose tab. You'll see the Compose options, shown in Figure 13-18.

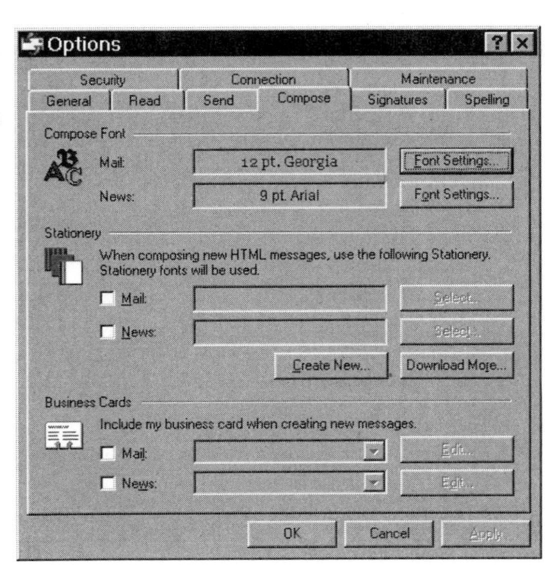

FIGURE 13-18.
In this dialog box, you can choose default fonts for displaying text in the message composition window. You can also choose stationery and create a business card.

SEE ALSO
You can define default mail sending formats for each user in your contact list. If you prefer to use HTML for your mail, but sometimes send mail to users who do not have HTML-capable e-mail programs, you can set up contacts for these users that switch to the plain-text format when you send mail to them. For more information, see "Using the Address Book," page 394.

3 In the Compose Font area, click the Font Settings button next to the Mail font setting to choose default fonts for composing e-mail. You'll see the Font dialog box, shown here:

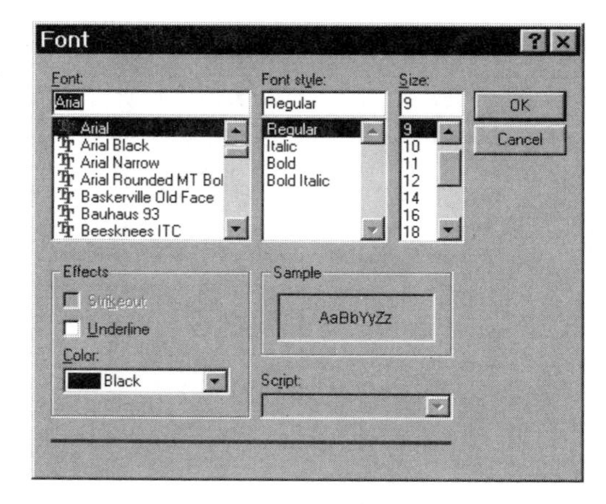

Choose the default font, font style, and font size. You can also choose a default effect and font color.

NOTE

The mail composition font doesn't necessarily affect how your message appears to recipients. If you send plain text e-mail by default, your compose font choices will be lost when you send the message. However, you may still wish to choose a default compose font in order to make the composition window easier to read.

4 Click OK to confirm your font choice.

SEE ALSO
For an introduction to Stationery, see "Using Stationery," page 379. For more information on Business Cards, see "Creating a Business Card," page 411.

5 In the Stationery area, you can define a default Stationery for richly formatted (HTML) messages. To define default Stationery for outgoing e-mail, check the Mail option, and click Select. You'll see the Select Stationery dialog box, shown here:

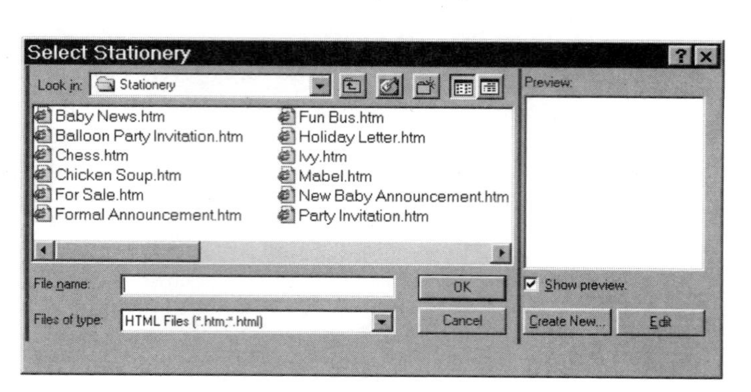

To preview a stationery file, select the file name, and check Show Preview. Click Edit to start FrontPage Express, which enables you to edit the stationery.

6 Click OK to confirm your default mail-sending stationery for richly formatted (HTML) messages.

7 If you would like to send your business card with all outgoing messages, click Mail in the Business Cards area, and choose your Address Book entry in the list box.

8 Click OK to confirm your choices.

Creating a Signature

A signature ("sig," for short) adds a nice touch to your e-mail, as long as it isn't too lengthy. By convention, it's thought best to keep your sig to no more than four lines. That's enough for whatever identifying information you feel comfortable sending.

With Outlook Express, you can create your signature by typing the text in the Signatures page of the Options dialog box. If you wish, you can create the text separately, and save it to a text file.

TIP

There's no need to include your e-mail address in your sig; people get that automatically. But you might want to include your full name, your work number, and your work address. Think long and hard before including personal information such as your home telephone number and address. If you really want to send this information to someone, you can do so in the body of the message.

To create your sig, follow these steps:

1 From the Tools menu, click Options, and click the Signatures tab. You'll see the Signatures page, shown in Figure 13-19.

2 In the Signatures area, choose your preference for the following:

- **Add This Signature To All Outgoing Messages.** When you open the New Message window to start a new message, Mail adds your sig automatically.
- **Don't Add Signature To Replies And Forwards.** This is a nice touch since replies and forwards can get excessively lengthy with all those repeated sigs.

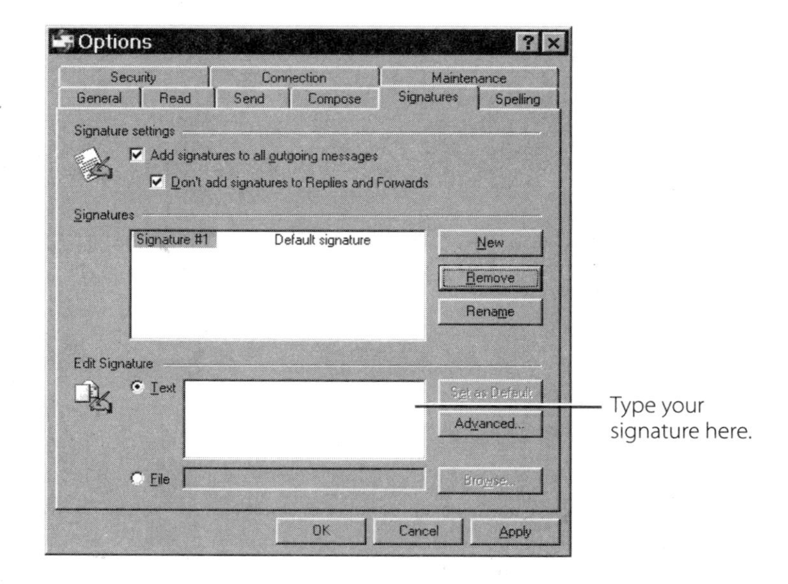

FIGURE 13-19. From the Signature dialog box, you can create an identifying signature for your e-mail.

3 Click New to add a signature. You'll see Signature #1 in the Signatures list box. With this text selected, do one of the following:

- In the Edit Signature area, click Text, and type the signature text.

  or

- Click File, and locate the file that you'd like to use for your signature text.

4 If you would like to create more than one signature, repeat step 3. Then select the signature that you want to use as your default, and click Set As Default.

5 To rename a signature, select the signature, and click Rename. Type a new name, and click OK.

6 Click OK to confirm your signature choices.

TIP

If you send mail from more than one account, you can define a different signature for each account. To do so, create signatures for each account, and then select one of the signatures. Click Advanced, and then click the accounts that will use this signature as the default signature for sending mail.

If you decide against including the sig in all your outgoing messages automatically, you can still include it selectively by clicking Insert on the New Message window's toolbar, and choosing Insert Signature.

A cute trick, in which too many Internet users (including myself) indulge themselves, is to include a little ASCII art picture in their signatures. (Mine used to have a sailboat.) As cunning as these works of art might appear to the eyes of those who create them, they come across as gibberish to anyone who's chosen a proportional font to read mail messages. Since that's increasingly common, it's time to bid a fond farewell to these artistic efforts.

Choosing Spelling Options

Outlook Express can check your spelling for you. In the Spelling page of the Options menu, you can choose settings that affect how the program checks your spelling.

To check for new messages automatically, do the following:

1. On the Tools menu of Outlook Express, click Options. You'll see the Options dialog box.
2. Click the Spelling tab. You'll see the Spelling page (shown in Figure 13-20).
3. Choose settings for the following:
   - **Always Check Spelling Before Sending.** This option checks your spelling before the message is sent. Leave this option on to make sure that your outgoing mail does not contain spelling mistakes.
   - **Suggest Replacements For Misspelled Words.** Leave this option on unless you're using a slow system.
4. The next area enables you to select text to ignore when checking spelling. Since much of the header and other technical information in an e-mail message contains uppercase letters, numbers, or Internet addresses, it's best to leave these options checked (so that this text is skipped). If you uncheck these options, you will spend a lot more time checking spelling because the spell check will flag many of the words in headers. You should change these options only if you frequently send messages containing uppercase words or words containing numbers, and you need these to be checked for errors.
5. In the Language area, choose a default language for spell checking.
6. If you've added words to your Custom dictionary when you checked spelling, you can edit these words. This is useful if you inadvertently added a misspelled word to the custom dictionary.

To edit the custom dictionary, click Edit Custom Dictionary. Outlook Express starts your default-text file editor (Notepad, unless you've installed a different text editor program). Correct and save the entries.

7 Click OK to save your options.

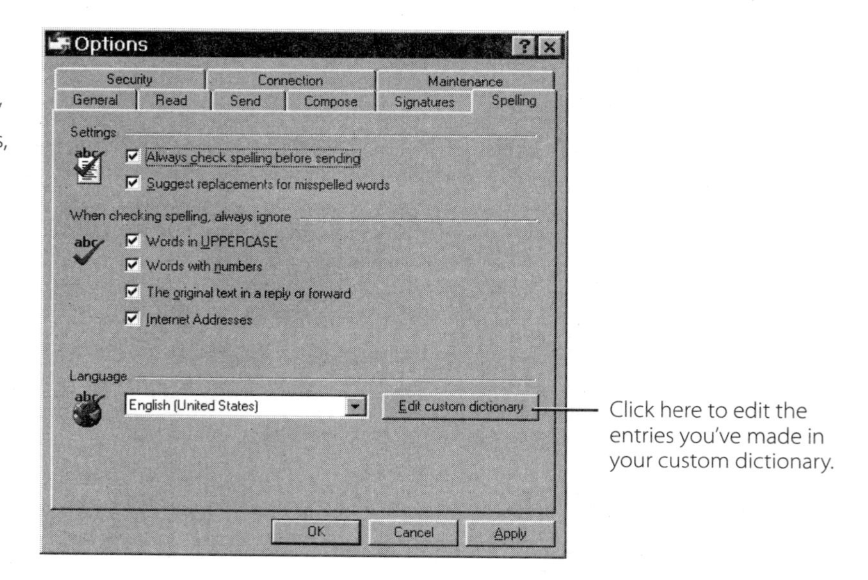

FIGURE 13-20.
The Spelling page enables you to specify spell-checking options, but the defaults are fine for most users.

Choosing Connection Settings

Since Outlook Express shares connection settings with Internet Explorer, you define these settings when you run the Connection Wizard (for more information, see Chapter 4, "Running the Connection Wizard"). However, there are a couple of dial-up settings that you may wish to change.

To choose connection settings, follow these steps:

1 On the Tools menu of Outlook Express, click Options. You'll see the Options dialog box.

2 Click the Connection tab. You'll see the Connection page (shown in Figure 13-21).

3 Choose settings for the following options:

- **Ask Before Switching Dial-Up Connections.** If you have defined more than one dial-up connection, you can activate this option to have Outlook Express ask for confirmation.

before switching to the next available connection. If you don't enable this option, Outlook Express will try the next available dial-up connection automatically. Activate this option if one of the connections involves a long-distance call.

- **Hang Up After Sending And Receiving.** If your Internet service provider bills you by the minute, or if you need to call long-distance to access the Internet, choose this option to minimize the amount of time you spend online. Be aware that this option, if activated, will terminate your Internet connection without asking for confirmation, which can be frustrating if you're using other Internet applications.

4 Click OK to confirm your connection settings.

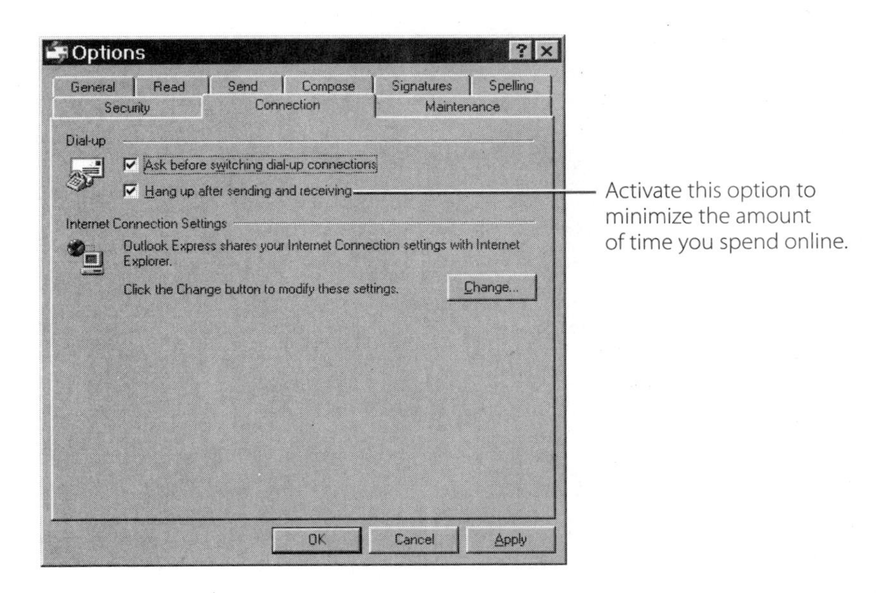

FIGURE 13-21.
In the Connection page, you can choose options for dial-up connections.

Choosing Maintenance Options

The Maintenance page of the Options dialog box contains several settings that pertain to Usenet messages, but there are some important options for e-mail, as well. In particular, you'll need to consider whether you want to erase deleted messages when you exit the program. By default, Outlook Express moves deleted messages to the Deleted Messages folder, and there they stay until you erase them. (To erase the deleted items, point to Deleted Items in the folder list, click the right mouse button, and choose Empty 'Deleted Items' Folder.) If you activate automatic erasing, your Deleted Items folder is emptied when you quit the program, but this setting may permanently erase an inadvertently deleted message.

To choose maintenance options:

1. On the Tools menu of Outlook Express, click Options. You'll see the Options dialog box.
2. Click the Maintenance tab. You'll see the Maintenance page (shown in Figure 13-22).

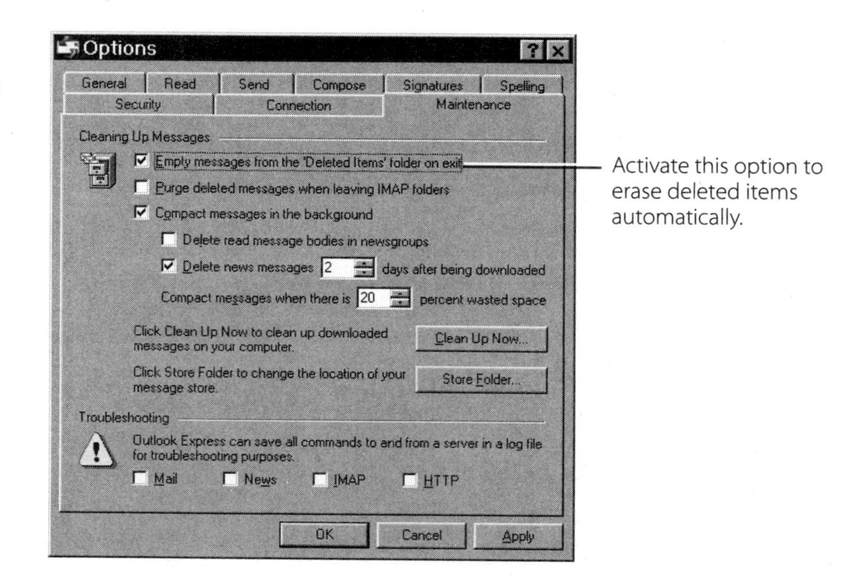

FIGURE 13-22. On the Maintenance page of the Options dialog box, you can choose options for maintaining your messages.

3. Choose settings for the following e-mail options:
   - **Empty Messages From The 'Deleted Items' Folder On Exit.** When you activate this option, Outlook Express permanently erases all the messages you've deleted during the current session. This is somewhat dangerous. If you inadvertently deleted a message, you won't be able to retrieve it after you quit the program.
   - **Purge Deleted Messages When Leaving IMAP Folders.** If you connect using an IMAP server, this option erases deleted messages when you leave the message's folder. Like the above option, this one could destroy a deleted message that you later decide you wanted to keep.

- **Compact Messages In The Background.** To maintain your mail messages, Outlook Express needs to perform a maintenance operation periodically. This operation is called *compacting*, and it eliminates wasted space. If you activate this option, the program lets you continue working while compacting is in progress. Uncheck this option if you're using a slow computer.
- **Compact Messages When There Is....** Here, you specify when compacting kicks in. By default, Outlook Express starts compacting when there is 20 percent wasted space in your message databases.

4. If you would like to change the location where Outlook Express stores your mail messages, click Store Folder. You'll see the Store Location dialog box, shown here:

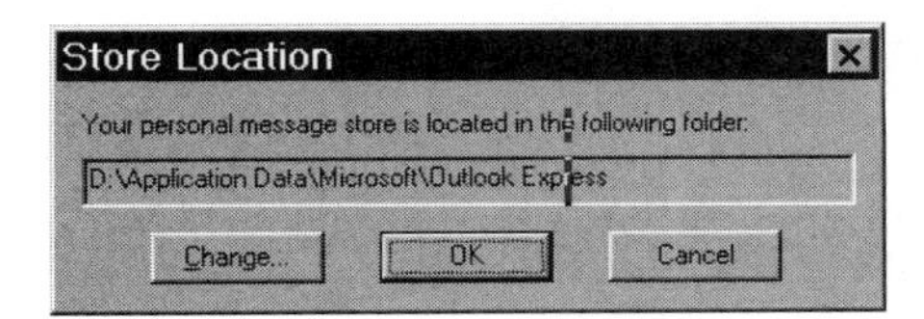

This dialog box shows the store's current location.

5. To change the location, click Change, and select the new storage folder in the Browse For Folder dialog box. Click OK to confirm, and click OK again to return to the Maintenance page.

> If you're having trouble connecting to your server, activate the Mail option in the Troubleshooting area. This will create a text file that saves all the commands going to and from the server. Your ISP may need this information to resolve your connection problems.

Organizing Your Mail into Folders

Once you've started getting mail, you'll find that it's more convenient to store your messages in named folders than to keep everything in your Inbox. For example, suppose you create a folder for all the mail you have received from a certain co-worker. Periodically, you can sort your message list by name so that all this person's messages are grouped together. You can then select them and move them into the folder for permanent storage.

Folders really shine once you've created rules, as explained in the following section. Rules can route incoming mail into folders, so that these messages do not appear in your Inbox. Although you shouldn't write such rules for high-priority items, this is an excellent way to cope with low-priority messages, such as routine memos circulated by your organization, or messages you receive from an Internet mailing list.

Creating a New Folder

To create a new mail folder, follow these steps:

1. In Outlook Express, do one of the following:

   - Click File on the menu bar, point to New, and choose Folder from the pop-up menu.

     or

   - Press Ctrl + Shift + E.

   You'll see the Create Folder dialog box, shown here:

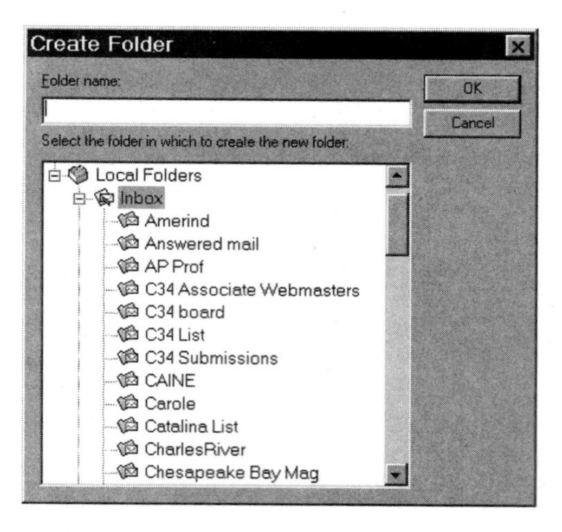

2. In the folder list, select the folder in which you want to create the new folder.

3. In the Folder Name box, type the name of your new folder.

4 Click OK to create the new folder.

5 Repeat steps 1 through 4 to create all the folders you need.

If you display the Outlook Bar, you can add folders to the bar. To add a folder to the bar, right-click the bar background, and choose New Outlook Bar Shortcut. You'll see the Folder List dialog box. Select a folder, and click OK.

Adding Messages to Your New Folder

After you've created a new folder, you can easily add a message to it by selecting the message in the message list and doing one of the following:

- From the Edit menu, select either Move To Folder or Copy To Folder. Select the folder to which you'd like to move the message, and click OK.
- Right-click the message, choose Move To Folder or Copy To Folder, and select the folder to which you'd like to move the message.
- Drag the message to the folder's name in the folder list or to the folder's icon in the Outlook Bar.

Viewing Your Folders

To view the contents of one of the folders you've created, click the folder name in the folder list. To return to the Inbox, choose Inbox from the folder list or just click the Inbox icon on the Outlook Bar.

Creating Rules for Mail Messages

E-mail seems like lots of fun at first—and then you start getting deluged with mail, some of it unimportant or unwanted. For example, many organizations are using e-mail instead of paper for routine memos and notices. By doing so, they're saving money and helping the environment, but they're also overloading employees with a great deal of low priority mail.

Rules won't work for IMAP accounts. You can create rules only if you're using a POP server.

If you start feeling overwhelmed by the amount of mail you're getting, learn how to create rules for mail messages. Rules tell Outlook Express to examine incoming messages for conditions you specify, such as messages from a certain correspondent. For matching messages, you can specify actions, such as moving the matching messages to a mail folder or deleting them entirely. After you write rules for all low-priority or unwanted mail, your Inbox will contain only those messages that you really want to see.

The following section introduces rules, and shows you how to create and manage them. You'll also learn how to block mail from unwanted senders, and how to turn on Outlook Express's junk mail detection, which can detect a high percentage of incoming junk mail.

SEE ALSO

To take full advantage of rules, you need to create folders to store incoming messages. For more information, see "Organizing Your Mail into Folders," page 435.

Understanding Rules

To create a rule, you specify a *condition*. The condition tells Outlook Express what to look for as the program examines incoming messages. For example, you can tell the program to examine each message's From line to see whether it contains a certain e-mail address. Table 13-2 lists the rule conditions you can use.

For messages that meet the condition you specify, you can choose an *action*, such as moving the message to a folder or deleting the message. Table 13-3 lists the actions you can use.

TIP

Plan your rules before trying to create them. You can create rules that can match any text in the To, Cc, From, or Subject lines, or even in the message body. So think of how you will instruct the program to recognize the correct incoming messages. Browse through your Inbox and display messages that you wish had been diverted. For example, suppose you have subscribed to the Holt stock report, which sends a free daily e-mail newsletter containing stock-market results. You want to divert the incoming messages to the Holt Report folder. As you examine the Holt messages, you see that every one contains *GEOHOLT <Geoholt@cris.com>* in the From line. This is good text to use for writing your rule.

Example Rules

Here are some examples of rules as they appear after they're created with Outlook Express.

Most of your rules will look like the following one. It checks the From line for mail from a certain e-mail address, and routes matching messages to a folder:

> Apply this rule after the message arrives
>
> Where the From line contains ERLINK mailto:jimb@bogus.com"
>
> Move it to the Jimmy-Bob folder

TABLE 13-2. Rule Conditions.

Condition	Description
Where the From line contains people	Looks for a specified e-mail address in the From line of incoming messages.
Where the Subject line contains specified words	Looks for the specified text in the Subject line of incoming messages.
Where the message body contains specified words	Looks for the specified text in the body of the incoming message.
Where the To line contains people	Looks for a specified e-mail address in the To line of incoming messages.
Where the CC line contains people	Looks for a specified e-mail address in the CC line of incoming messages.
Where the To or CC line contains people	Looks for a specified e-mail address in the To line or the CC line of incoming messages
Where the message is marked for priority	Checks to see whether incoming messages are marked for a specified priority level (high, normal, or low).
Where the message is from the specified account	Looks for a specified account name in the header information of incoming messages.
Where the message size is more than size	Looks for incoming messages that exceed a specified size in bytes.
Where the message has an attachment	Checks to see whether incoming messages have an attachment.
Where the message is secure	Checks to see whether incoming messages have been encrypted.
For all messages	Applies to all incoming messages.

If you subscribe to an Internet mailing list, examine one of the messages to find out how to route the messages to a folder. Many mailing lists contain the list address in the To line. The following rule routes mail from the Catalina 34 mailing list to a folder:

Apply this rule after the message arrives

Where the To line contains c34@bpmac.seas.virginia.edu

Move it to the C34 folder

TABLE 13-3. Rule Actions.

Condition	Description
Move it to the specified folder	Messages that meet the condition you specify are moved to a folder other than the Inbox.
Copy it to the specified folder	Messages that meet the condition you specify are copied to a folder other than the Inbox (the original is left in the Inbox).
Delete it	Messages that meet the condition you specify are moved to the Deleted Items folder.
Forward it to people	Messages that meet the condition you specified are forwarded to an e-mail address that you specify.
Highlight it with color	Messages that meet the condition you specified are highlighted with a color of your choice.
Flag it	Messages that meet the condition you specified are flagged (a flag appears in the flag column).
Mark it as read	Messages that meet the condition you specified are marked as read (no boldface in the message list).
Mark the message as watched or ignored	This option is designed for use with incoming Usenet messages. For more information, see "Writing Rules for News Messages," page 539.
Reply with message	Automatically replies, with a message you specify, to incoming messages that meet the condition you specified.
Stop processing more rules	If a message meeting the conditions you specified is detected, rule processing stops.
Do not download it from the server	Messages that meet the condition you specified are not downloaded from the server.
Delete it from the server	Messages that meet the condition you specified are deleted from the server without downloading.

I find the following rule very effective for eliminating junk mail. The authors of junk-mail messages have trouble refraining from the use of the exclamation point (for example, "MAKE MONEY FAST!"). This rule is rather drastic and might catch some legitimate messages, so you should check your junk mail folder periodically to make sure that it contains no important messages.

> Apply this rule after the message arrives
>
> Where the Subject line contains "!"
>
> Move it to the Junk Mail folder

Apply this rule after the message arrives.

Some very persistent junk mail senders originate their messages using a variety of servers and subject lines. The following message looks for the company's name within the body of the message:

> Apply this rule after the message arrives
>
> Where the message body contains "Crooked Marketing, Inc."
>
> Move it to the Junk Mail folder

Here's a rule that looks for the tell-tale signs of unwanted adult mail, and zaps it at the server:

> Apply this rule after the message arrives
>
> Where the Subject line contains "XXX"
>
> Delete it from the server

Many of the messages you receive are not exclusively addressed to you. This rule matches messages sent exclusively to me, and highlights them in red:

> Apply this rule after the message arrives
>
> Where the To line contains bp@virginia.edu
>
> Highlight it with Red

The following rule highlights carbon-copy messages in gray:

> Apply this rule after the message arrives
>
> Where the CC line contains bp@virginia.edu
>
> Highlight it with Gray

TIP

It's a great idea to create rules to deal with unwanted mail. However, there's a risk that your rule will route a valid message to your junk mail or Deleted Items folder. To avoid accidentally deleting important mail, you can create an exception list, which consists of your important correspondents' e-mail addresses. For more information, see "Creating Exceptions," page 448.

Creating a Rule for Mail Messages

To create a rule for incoming mail messages, follow these steps:

1. On the Tools menu, point to Message Rules, and then click Mail. You'll see the Message Rules dialog box, shown in Figure 13-23.

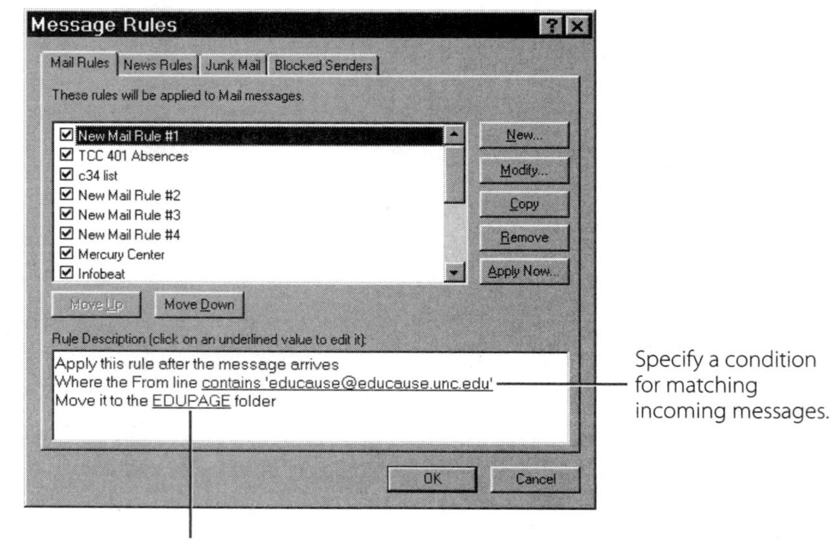

FIGURE 13-23. In this dialog box, you can write rules that route incoming mail to folders.

2. Click the Mail Rules tab if necessary.
3. Click the New button. You'll see the New Mail Rule dialog box, shown in 13-24.
4. In the Select The Conditions For Your Rule list, check the rule you want to use. In the Rule Description area, you'll see the first, generic version of your rule, such as the one shown here:

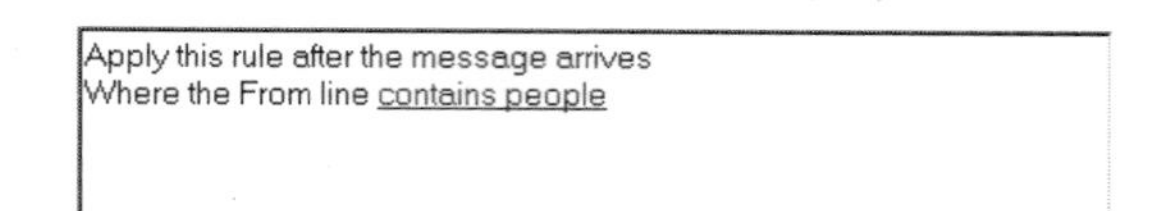

5. In the Rule Description area, click the highlighted text so that you can finish specifying the condition. For example, if you're creating a condition that looks for certain people in a From line, click Contains People. You'll see a dialog box that helps you supply the needed information, such as the following:

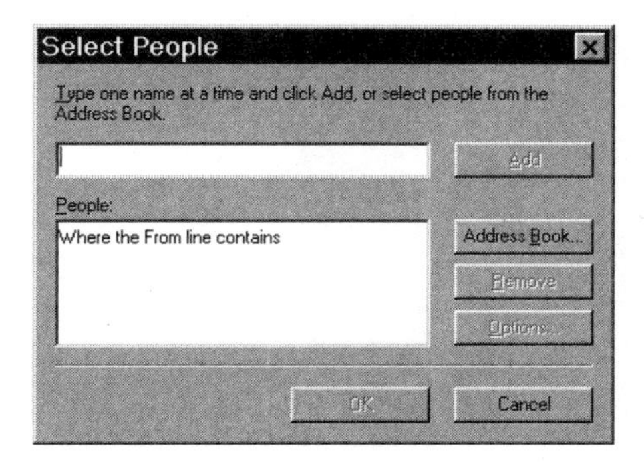

6. In the Select The Action For Your Rule list, check the action you want to use. In the Rule Description area, you'll see an addition to your rule, such as the one shown here:

Apply this rule after the message arrives
Where the From line contains people
Move it to the specified folder

7. Click the highlighted text, if any appears, to supply the information needed to complete the action. For example, if you're writing a rule that routes messages to a folder, click Specified. You'll see the Move dialog box, which enables you to choose the folder to which you want to move the mail.

FIGURE 13-24.

It's easy to create mail rules: first choose a condition, and then choose an action.

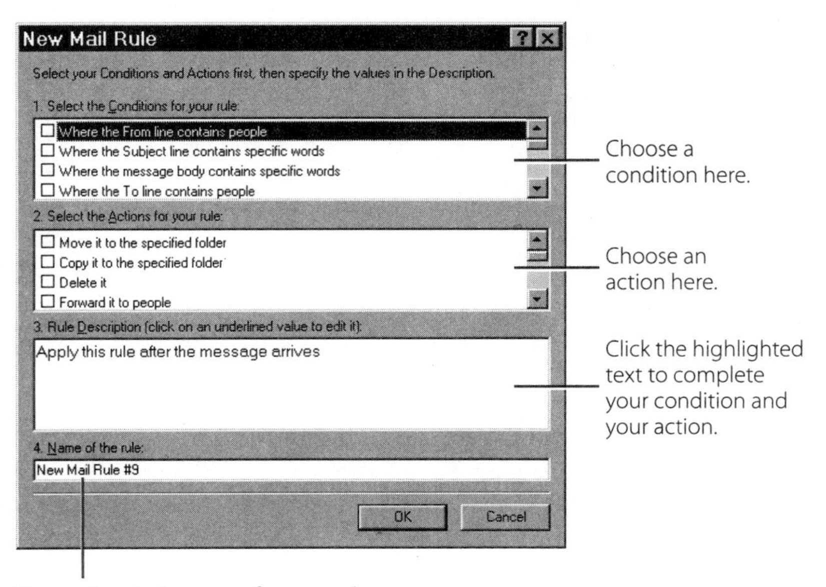

8 In the Name Of The Rule box, type a descriptive name for your rule.

9 Click OK to confirm your rule.

To create a rule with a From condition quickly, point to any message from a certain correspondent in the Outlook Express message list. From the Message menu, choose Create Rule From Message. This command starts a rule with a From condition that contains this correspondent's e-mail address.

Creating Rules with Multiple Conditions

The previous section described how to create a simple rule with one condition and one action. However, you can create complex rules, which contain more than one condition or action. For example, you can create the following rule:

Apply this rule after the message arrives

Where the From line contains fran@bogus.net
and the Subject line contains "Proposal"

Move it to the NSF Proposal folder
and forward it to johnc@bogus.net
and forward it to kyungl@bogus.net

To create a rule with multiple conditions or actions, just select more than one condition or action. If you select more than one condition, Outlook Express automatically inserts the word "and," but this word is highlighted. If you click it, you see the following dialog box:

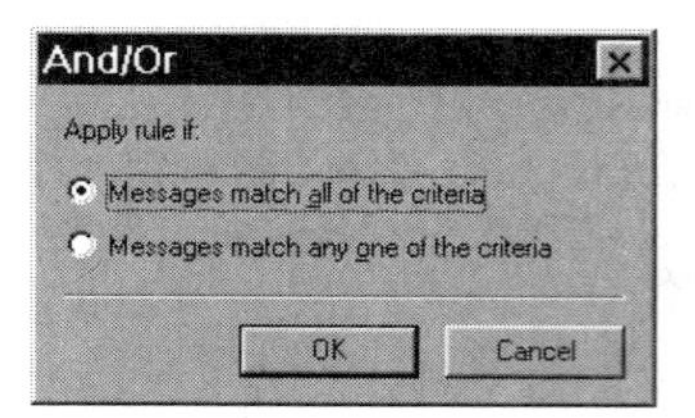

The default option, Messages Match All Of The Criteria, keeps the word "and" in the condition list. If you select Messages Match Any One Of The Criteria, the program changes "and" to "or."

By linking conditions with "or," you can create rules that look for many different conditions in incoming messages. The program takes action if any of the conditions are met. Examine the following example:

Apply this rule after the message arrives

Where the From line contains fran@bogus.net
or the From line contains K "mailto:johnc@bogus.net"
or the From line contains kyungl@bogus.net
Move it to the NSF Proposal folder

The above rule looks for messages from any of the three correspondents, and routes them to the NSF Proposal folder.

To create a new rule quickly, locate an existing rule that uses the same condition and action that the new rule will use, and select this rule. Click Copy, and click the highlighted items to define the new rule.

Dealing with Unwanted Mail

You can write rules to deal with unwanted mail, including unsolicited adult mail and junk-mail advertising, but you could write rules all day and still fail to catch them all. For this reason, Outlook Express provides two additional tools. The first enables you to block all messages from a certain sender. The second, junk-mail detection, uses sophisticated message-analysis techniques to detect unwanted junk mail.

Blocking Senders

You can block messages from a certain e-mail address or an entire domain (the domain is the portion of the e-mail address that comes after the @ sign). After you block an e-mail address or domain, the blocked messages don't appear in your Inbox; the messages are routed immediately to the Delete folder.

To block messages from a certain e-mail address, follow these steps:

1. Select a message from the sender you want to block.
2. From the Message menu, choose Block Sender.

   You'll see a dialog box informing you that mail from this sender will be blocked, and you're asked whether you'd like to remove all mail from that sender from the current mailbox.
3. Click Yes to remove all messages from this sender in the current folder.

You can also block all the messages originating from a certain domain. This is a drastic action, and could block many valid messages. You should use it only if you're convinced that all the mail from this domain is unwanted. For example, a few rogue ISPs actively solicit business from senders of unwanted e-mail.

You'll find numerous lists of what some term "rogue" Internet Service Providers (ISPs) on the Web. These service providers are alleged to tolerate the actions of firms that originate unsolicited commercial e-mail. For an example, see "Promote Responsible Net Commerce: Fight Spam!" (http://www.firstbase.com/spam.htm). Should you discover that you're receiving numerous unwanted messages from a "rogue" ISP, you may wish to block that ISP's domain—but be aware that, by doing so, you may lose legitimate mail sent to you by someone with an account with the same ISP.

To block all incoming messages from an entire domain, follow these steps:

1 Click Tools on the Outlook Express menu bar, point to Message Rules, and choose Blocked Senders List. You'll see the Blocked Senders page of the Message Rules dialog box, shown in Figure 13-25. In this dialog box, you see a list of the e-mail addresses you have already blocked.

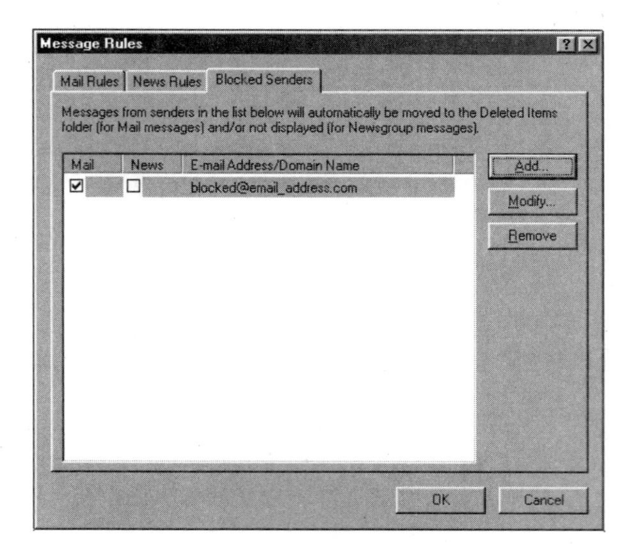

FIGURE 13-25.
In this dialog box, you can create new block-sender rules that can stop unsolicited mail from rogue domains.

2 Click Add. You'll see the Add Sender dialog box, shown on the next page:

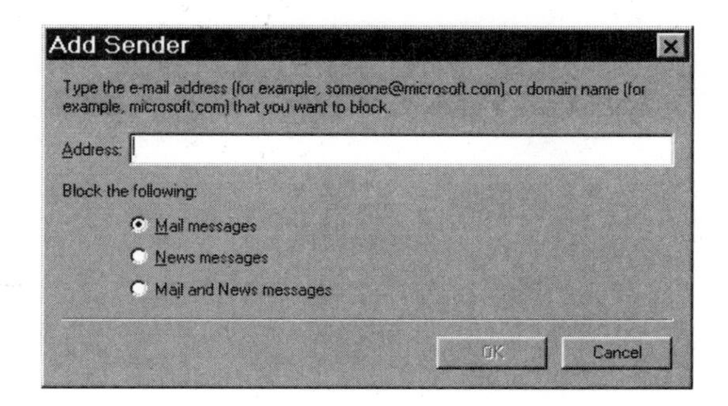

3. In the Address box, type the domain name that you want to block.
4. In the Block The Following list, choose Mail Messages, News Messages, or Mail And News Messages. (If you plan to participate in Usenet, you might as well block news as well as mail messages.)
5. Click OK to confirm.

Applying Rules to Mail Messages

After you create rules, they'll be applied to incoming messages. But that still leaves a lot of mail in your Inbox. To apply your rules to messages you have already received, you can apply the rules to existing messages. Here's how:

1. In the Folder list, click Inbox to open the Inbox folder if necessary. (If you don't see the folder list, choose Inbox from the Folder bar or Outlook bar.)
2. Click Tools on the Outlook Express menu bar, point to Message Rules, and choose Mail from the pop-up menu. You'll see the Message Rules dialog box, with the Mail tab displayed.
3. Click Apply Now. You'll see the Apply Rules Now dialog box, shown in Figure 13-26.
4. Do one of the following:
   - Select the rules you want to apply. To select more than one rule, hold down the Ctrl key and click two or more rules.

     or

   - Click Select All.

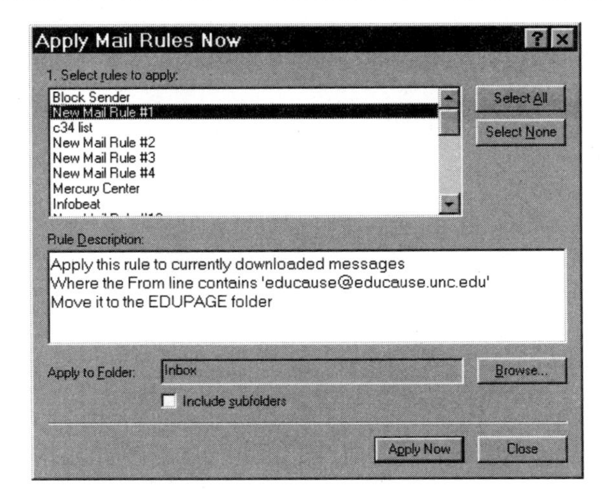

FIGURE 13-26.
In this dialog box, you can apply your rules to existing messages.

5 Click Apply Now.

6 When Outlook Express has finished applying your rules, click OK.

Managing Rules

If a rule does not work as intended, you may need to edit it. You can also delete rules that are no longer needed.

After you create rules that route incoming messages to folders, do not rename or delete the folders. If you do, the rules involving these folders will no longer function.

Editing Rules

To edit a rule, follow these steps:

1 On the Tools menu, point to Message Rules, and choose Mail.

2 Select the rule you want to change, and click Modify.

3 In the Edit Rule dialog box, make the needed changes.

4 Click OK to confirm your changes.

Deleting Rules

To delete an unwanted rule, follow these steps:

1 On the Tools menu, point to Message Rules, and choose Mail.

2 Select the rule you want to delete.

3 Click Remove.

Prioritizing Rules

If you write several rules, it's possible that more than one will apply to a given incoming message. For this reason, you can prioritize your rules. To change a rule's priority, highlight the rule in the Mail Rules page of the Message Rules dialog box, and click Move Up or Move Down to move the rule in the list. The higher the rule in the list, the greater the priority given to the rule.

To illustrate how prioritization solves problems for you, consider this example. Suppose your friend Marvin likes to kid around with silly subject lines such as "Get a life," or "Make money fast." You like Marvin's messages, but you can do without the other "Make money fast" messages, a common type of junk mail. So you write a rule that sends Marvin's letters to the Marvin folder, and another rule that sends any message with "Make money fast" to the Deleted Items folder. To make sure Marvin's messages don't get trashed, even if they contain "Make money fast," you place the Marvin rule higher in the priority list.

Managing Accounts

Many Internet users have more than one e-mail account. For example, it's common to have an e-mail account at work, which is properly used only for legitimate business purposes. For personal messaging, many people have an additional account with an Internet service provider (ISP), which they access from a home computer. A nifty feature of Outlook Express is the program's ability to work with two or more e-mail accounts simultaneously. For example, you can set up your home computer copy of Outlook Express to access your business and your personal e-mail accounts. You see messages from both accounts in your Inbox.

SEE ALSO
For information on setting up your default e-mail account, see Chapter 4, "Running the Connection Wizard."

When you ran the Internet Connection Wizard, as described in Chapter 4, you set up your default e-mail account. To set up one or more additional accounts, use the Internet Accounts dialog box within Outlook Express, as described in this section.

If you switch to a new ISP, you will need to edit your e-mail account settings, as described in this section. You also need to edit these settings if any of the underlying information changes, such as your user name, password, or the address of your ISP's mail servers.

POP accounts can prove very frustrating if you access your mail from more than one computer, but there's a solution. First, here's the problem. Suppose you're reading your mail on Sunday night from your home computer. By default, Outlook Express downloads all new messages, and then removes these messages from the server. On Monday morning, you access your mail from work, but the server no longer contains the messages you downloaded on Sunday. There's an important message to which you need to reply, but it's stored on your home computer! To prevent this problem, click Tools on the Outlook Express menu bar, and choose Accounts. Click the Mail tab, if necessary, and select your e-mail account. Click Properties, and then click the Advanced tab. In the Delivery area, click Leave A Copy Of Messages On Server. To make sure your mailbox does not grow too large, click Remove From Server, and specify 3 days (that's long enough to keep your messages over the weekend). Also click Remove From Server When Deleted From 'Deleted Items.'

Adding a New Account

To configure your new account, you'll need to obtain the required information from your Internet service provider or network administrator. To see a list of what's required, see "Getting the Information You Need for a Dial-Up Account" on page 67.

If you've already set up an e-mail account for Microsoft Outlook, Microsoft Exchange, or Microsoft Windows Messaging clients, you can import the account settings into Outlook Express. To do so, click File on the Outlook Express menu bar, point to Import, and choose Mail Account Settings. Select the account settings you want to import, and click Next to start the import wizard.

SEE ALSO
For information on setting up your e-mail account with the Internet Connection Wizard, see "Setting Up Your E-mail Connection," page 72.

To add an account, follow these steps:

1. On the Tools menu, click Accounts.
2. In the Internet Accounts dialog box, click the Add button, and choose Mail from the pop-up menu. You'll see the portion of the Internet Connection Wizard that enables you to set up your e-mail account. Use the wizard to define your e-mail settings.

Editing Mail-Account Settings

Should you need to change mail-account settings, such as your password or any other supporting information, you can display the properties dialog box for an account.

To change mail-account settings, follow these steps:

1. From the Outlook Express Tools menu, choose Accounts.
2. Click the Mail tab, if necessary.
3. Select the account you want to modify.
4. Click Properties, and click the General tab if necessary. You'll see the General properties, shown here:

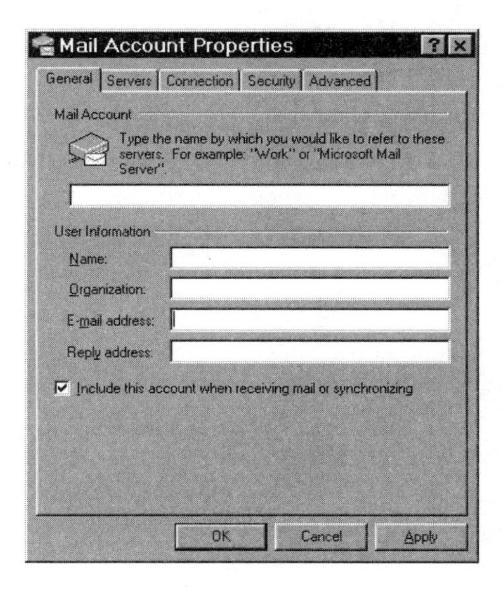

   Here, you can change the mail account name, your name (as it will appear to your e-mail correspondents), your organization's name (this is optional), and your e-mail address. Leave the Reply address box blank unless you want replies to go to a different e-mail address.

5. Click the Servers tab. You'll see the server's properties, shown on the next page:

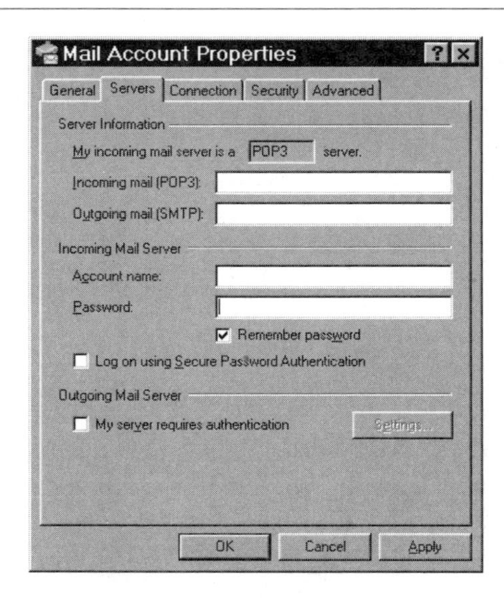

Here, you can change the Internet addresses of your mail servers, as well as your login name and password. You can also activate Secure Password Authentication (SPA).

Your ISP may require you to use a different account name and password for your outgoing mail. To set up authentication for your outgoing mail, click My Server Requires Authentication, in the Outgoing Mail Server area. Then click Settings. You'll see the Outgoing Mail Server dialog box, shown here:

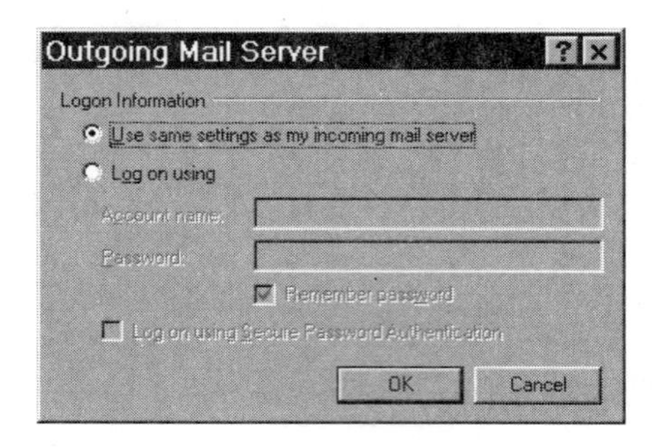

Click Log On Using, and supply the account name and password. Activate the Remember Password option only if you are sure no untrustworthy person will use your computer. If your ISP tells you that Secure Password Authentication is required for the outgoing mail server, check this option. Click OK to confirm these settings and return to the server's properties page.

6 Click the Connection tab. You'll see the Connection properties, shown here:

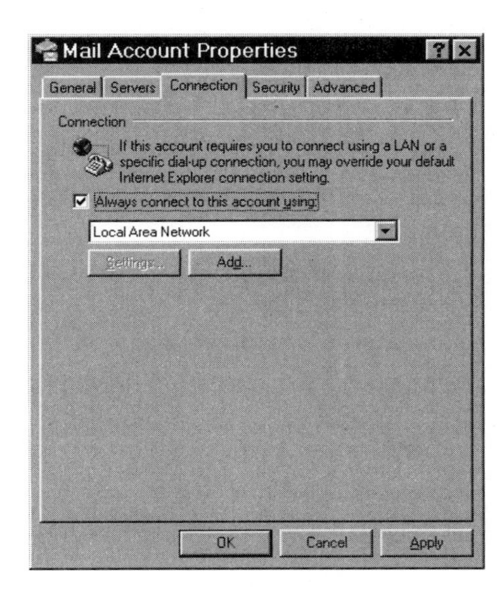

In this dialog box, you can override the default connection that Internet Explorer uses if you wish. To connect using a different method for e-mail, activate Always Connect To This Account Using, and select a connection in the drop-down list box. If you select a dial-up connection, you can click Settings to change any of the dial-up connection settings, including the phone number, modem setting, and connection options. To create a new dial-up connection, click Add, and follow the wizard's instructions.

You'll learn about the Security properties in the next chapter.

7 Click Advanced. You'll see the Advanced properties, shown on the next page:

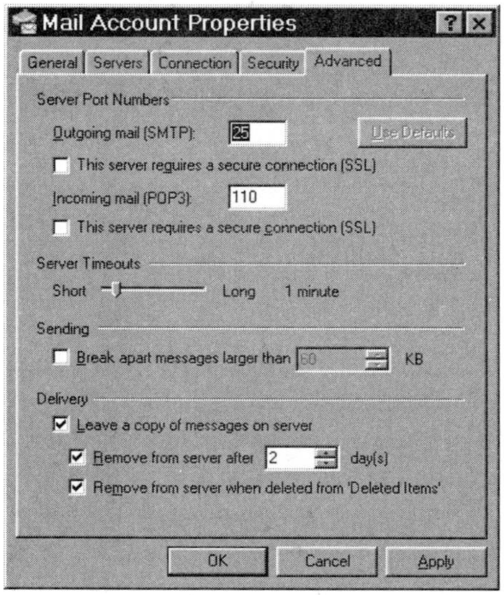

You can adjust the following settings:

- **Server Port Numbers.** Don't change these unless you're directed to do so by your network administrator or service provider. If you're informed that you need to connect via a secure connection, check This Server Requires A Secure Connection (SSL).
- **Server Timeouts.** If you find that Outlook Express sometimes displays an error message informing you that the server did not respond within a certain time, you may wish to increase the length of server timeouts. The default is 1 minute. Try increasing the amount by one-minute increments until you no longer see the error message.
- **Sending.** If you try to send large attachments to users of some older computer systems, your mail may not get through. Should this happen, ask whether you need to break up lengthy messages. If so, activate Break Apart Messages Larger Than 60 KB. You can increase or decrease this message size (60 KB), but try it initially. Don't activate this option unless you've been requested to do so.
- **Delivery.** If you access your mail from more than one computer, activate Leave A Copy Of Messages On Server. So

that your mailbox does not grow too large, activate the option that removes messages from the server after a specified number of days (try 2 or 3, initially). Make the period long enough so that you can access your mail with the other computers you use. In this way, you will have a complete set of messages on all your computers. To reduce the amount of server storage space you consume, be sure to activate Remove From Server When Deleted From 'Deleted Items.'

8 Click OK to confirm the new settings.

Deleting an Account

To delete an account:

1 From the Tools menu, choose Accounts.

2 Click the Mail tab.

3 Select the account.

4 Click Remove.

Customizing the Outlook Express Toolbars

SEE ALSO

For information on displaying, moving, and sizing any of the Internet Explorer toolbars, see "Introducing the Toolbars," page 98.

You can customize the toolbar in Outlook Express's main window, and in the New Message window as well. In both windows, you can decide which buttons you want to display, how they're sized, and whether they contain explanatory text. In this section, you learn how to customize either of the toolbars so that they look the way you want.

Customizing the Toolbar in the Main Outlook Express Window

To customize the Outlook Express toolbar, right-click the toolbar background, and choose Customize from the pop-up menu. You'll see the Customize Toolbar dialog box, shown in figure 13-27.

In the Customize Toolbar dialog box, you can delete existing buttons, add buttons to the toolbar, organize buttons by placing separators between buttons, and change the button order. Table 13-4 explains which buttons are available in the main Outlook Express window, and what they do. Table 13-5 lists the available buttons for the New message window. The same buttons also appear in the composition windows used for replying to messages and forwarding messages.

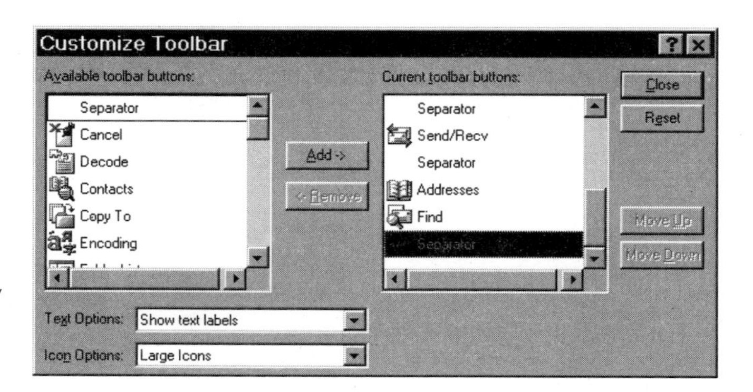

FIGURE 13-27. In this dialog box, you can customize the Outlook Express toolbar by adding or removing icons. You can also choose select options for text display and icon size.

When you access a Usenet account, Outlook Express's toolbar changes to show the buttons you need. So there's no need to customize the e-mail toolbar by adding news-related buttons. For more information on Usenet and the tools that appear when you access a news account, see Chapter 15, "Joining Newsgroups."

Choosing Button-Display Options

You can choose the following options for the buttons on the Outlook Express toolbar:

- **Show Text Labels** displays text labels within the buttons.
- **Selective Text On Right** displays text labels on the Explorer buttons, but not the standard navigation buttons.
- **No Text Labels** hides text labels on all buttons.

TABLE 13-4. Available Toolbar Buttons (Outlook Express Main Window).

Button name	Purpose
Default buttons	
New Mail	Displays the New Message window.
Reply	Initiates a reply to the message currently selected in the message list.
Reply All	Initiates a reply to the message currently selected in the message list, and sends a copy to every address in the original message's header.
Forward	Forwards the message currently selected in the message list.
Print	Prints the message currently selected in the message list.
Delete	Deletes the message currently selected in the message list.
Send/Recv	Contacts the mail server, sends outgoing mail, and receives incoming mail.
Addresses	Displays Address Book.
Find	Displays the Find Message dialog box.
Buttons you can add	
Cancel	In Usenet discussions, enables you to cancel a post you have already sent.
Copy To	Copies the select message or messages to a folder that you specify.
Decode	Decodes a multi-part message.
Contacts	Displays or hides the Contacts pane.
Encoding	Enables you to choose the type of character encoding used for the message text.
Folder List	Displays or hides the Folder list.
Headers	In Usenet discussions, gets new headers from the news server.
Inbox	Displays the Inbox.
Outbox	Displays the Outbox.
Sent Items	Displays the Sent Items folder.

(continued)

TABLE 13-4. *continued*

Button name	Purpose
Buttons you can add	
Help	Accesses Outlook Express help.
IMAP Folders	Accesses your IMAP folders.
Mark All	Marks all the messages in the current folder as read.
Mark Offline	In Usenet discussions, marks articles for offline reading.
Mark Read	Marks the currently selected message as read.
Mark Conversation	In Usenet discussions, marks a conversation as read.
Move To	Moves the selected message or messages to a folder you specify.
New Post	In Usenet discussions, starts a new post (article).
Newsgroups	In Usenet discussions, displays the newsgroup list.
Next Unread	Selects the next unread message in the current folder.
Next Folder	Selects the first unread message in the next folder.
Next Conversation	In Usenet discussions, selects the next conversation with unread messages.
Preview	Displays or hides the preview pane.
Purge	Removes deleted messages from an IMAP server.
Refresh	In Usenet discussions, downloads the message again.
Reply Group	In Usenet discussions, begins a reply that will be accessible to everyone who reads the newsgroup.
Save As	Saves the currently selected message.
Stop	In Usenet discussions, stops downloading headers or messages.
Sync All	In Usenet discussions, begins synchronizing messages according to your synchronization settings.
Undelete	Reverses the last deletion.
Unscramble	In Usenet discussions, unscrambles a message posted with ROT-13 coding.
Offline	Switches between online and offline reading modes.

TABLE 13-5. Available Toolbar Buttons (New Message Window).

Button name	Purpose
Default buttons	
Send	Sends the message.
Cut	Cuts the selection to the Clipboard.
Copy	Copies the selection to the Clipboard.
Paste	Pastes the current Clipboard contents at the cursor's location.
Undo	Undoes the last editing change.
Check	Checks e-mail addresses to make sure they are correct.
Spelling	Starts spell-checking the message.
Attach	Inserts an attachment.
Priority	Enables you to change the message's priority.
Sign	Digitally signs the message.
Encrypt	Encrypts the message for secure transfer.
Offline	Switches between online and offline use.
Buttons you can add	
Encoding	Changes the message's encoding.
Recipients	Displays the Select Recipients dialog box.
Insert Signature	Inserts the current default signature in the document.

You can also choose the icon size:

- **Large icons.** The large buttons look like the ones used in previous versions of Internet Explorer.
- **Small icons.** The small icons are designed to look like the ones you see in Microsoft Office.You can combine text display and button-size options; for example, you can display small icons with selective text.

To change button-display options, follow these steps:

1. In the Customize Toolbar dialog box, click the down arrow next to the Text Options list box, and choose the text option you want.
2. Click the down arrow next to the Icon Options list box, and choose the icon option you want.
3. Click Close to confirm your options.

Removing Unwanted Buttons

Chances are you're happy with most of the default buttons, but perhaps you could do without one or two that you never use. If you later decide you would like to have these buttons on the toolbar again, you can add them by following the procedure in the next section.

To remove unwanted buttons from the toolbar, follow these steps:

1. In the Customize Toolbar dialog box, locate and select the button from the Current Toolbar Buttons list.
2. Click Remove. Outlook Express moves the button to the Available Toolbar Buttons list.
3. Click Close.

Adding Buttons

To add buttons to the toolbar, follow these steps:

1. In the Customize Toolbar dialog box, locate and select the button from the Available Toolbar Buttons list. Click Add. Outlook Express moves the button to the Current Toolbar Buttons list.
2. To change the location of the newly added button, click Move Up or Move Down.
3. To add a separator between buttons, click Separator in the Available Toolbar Buttons list, and click Add. Click Move Up or Move Down to move the separator to the location you want.
4. Click OK to confirm your toolbar choices.

CHAPTER 14

Using Secure E-Mail

If you're sending an e-mail message, there's something you should know: that message is about as confidential as an advertisement pasted to the interior wall of a New York City subway. That's right—anyone can read it. It is disturbing that our legal system hasn't kept pace with technology. The privacy protections for first-class correspondence that we've enjoyed for hundreds of years aren't being extended to electronic communication, despite the fact that an estimated 100 million people now prefer to send e-mail messages rather than traditional letters. If you're using the Internet for any sort of personal or business correspondence that you'd prefer to keep away from prying eyes, you'll be wise to explore the powerful new tools, available in Microsoft Outlook Express, for ensuring the confidentiality of your correspondence.

Outlook Express includes the security features that e-mail users need: digital IDs and encryption. Using a digital ID, you can sign your message so that recipients will be able to verify that it's really from you. Using encryption, you can scramble your message so that nobody except the intended recipient can read it. Taken together, these two measures provide the privacy and confidentiality that e-mail needs to succeed as a public communications medium. You can't do business over the Internet if confidential messages can be intercepted and read by anyone along the way.

Until recently, secure e-mail was very difficult to use; in practice, its use was restricted to the hacker community. Even worse, there were no security standards, which meant that you couldn't exchange secure e-mail with somebody unless that person was using the same e-mail program you were using. Thanks to the new S/MIME protocol, the standards are now in place for the rapid development of secure e-mail. Outlook Express supports this protocol, which means you can exchange secure e-mail with anyone who uses an S/MIME-compatible e-mail program. And as you'll learn in this chapter, Outlook Express has made secure e-mail easy to use.

You don't have to be involved in a multimillion dollar deal for a Bermuda property or be an inventor with a hot new product to have good reasons to keep your e-mail secret. No matter what you're talking about, the simple fact of the matter is that it's nobody's business except the person to whom you're sending your message. How would you like it if, late at night, the staff at your friendly local Internet service provider displayed your e-mail messages and read them out loud, just for a laugh? Technically, it's possible. And from what I've heard from friends who have worked at ISPs, it happens all the time. The answer's simple: seal the envelope.

Introducing Secure E-Mail

In order for electronic mail security to function on the Internet, a standard is needed so that users of different e-mail programs can communicate with each other. In 1996, the Internet Engineering Task Force (IETF) created the S/MIME standard, which defines a comprehensive system for e-mail security. (S/MIME is short for Secure Multipurpose Internet Mail Extensions.)

Advantages of Secure E-Mail

As long as you're using an e-mail program that conforms to the S/MIME protocol, you can send and receive secure e-mail. You have the following capabilities:

- You can attach a digital signature (also called a *digital ID*) to your outgoing messages, so the recipient can verify that the message is really from you and not a forgery. The digital ID also enables the recipient to verify whether the message was tampered with while it was en route.

- You can receive mail with digital signatures, so you can verify that the message you've received is really from the person who ostensibly sent it and not an imposter or a forger. You can also check to see whether the message was tampered with.
- You can send encrypted e-mail that no one can read except the intended recipient.
- You can decode and read encrypted messages sent to you.

What Secure E-Mail Can't Do

Secure e-mail protects your messages from the illegal actions of others who attempt to snoop into your mail, but you shouldn't imagine that encryption can shield you from a legal investigation. U.S. courts have consistently held that, if investigators can subpoena a document, they can also subpoena the encryption key used to encrypt it. Some attorneys believe that a person might be able to cite the U.S. Fifth Amendment (protection against self-incrimination) to avoid divulging an encryption key that was held only in his or her memory, but no such protection is given to encryption keys that are written down or stored in a computer. If you think that secure e-mail can cover up illegal activities, you've a false impression.

What You Need for Secure E-Mail

To use secure e-mail, you need a digital ID, a public key, and a private key. The following sections explain how these components work together to ensure your privacy when corresponding via the Internet.

Your Digital ID

To get going with secure e-mail, you need to obtain a digital ID that supports S/MIME. (Digital IDs are also known as *certificates*.) A digital ID is something like a driver's license or identification card like the ones you show at a supermarket.

You must obtain your digital ID from a *certificate authority* (CA), such as VeriSign (www.verisign.com); once you've obtained this, Outlook Express will generate your public key and private key.

When you send e-mail, you can use your digital ID to "sign" your outgoing message. Because digital signatures are designed to reveal evidence of tampering, your recipient knows two facts when your message arrives:

- First, that the message really came from you (authentication). Digital IDs cannot be forged without the tell-tale signs of tampering. And if someone has tried to tamper with the digital ID or the message to which it is attached, the receiving e-mail program will detect this and display a warning.
- Second, that the message itself has not been altered during transmission (integrity). The digital signature contains information about the message itself, and if any tampering has occurred, the receiving e-mail program will display a warning message.

When somebody receives a message with your digital signature attached, they know that the message is really from you and that it hasn't been tampered with while en route.

Understanding Digital ID Classes

When you obtain a driver's license for the first time you are asked to show some positive identification, such as a birth certificate. Only in this way can the driver's license bureau be confident that you are the person you claim you are, and not some imposter.

Most digital IDs are issued without such stringent identification checks, so you should think twice about trusting them as much as you'd trust a driver's license. Digital IDs designed for individuals' use are divided into three classes; the most common, Class 1, requires very little identification for issuance.

- **Class 1** digital IDs are issued with just one check: the validity of the applicant's e-mail address. To avoid forgery, you cannot complete the installation of a Class 1 digital ID without receiving vital information that is sent back to your e-mail address. This procedure is designed to prevent imposters from obtaining digital IDs for your e-mail address.
- **Class 2** digital IDs provide identity assurance by requiring third-party verification of your personal information (including your name and address). To verify your identity, the issuer checks your application against information in a consumer database.
- **Class 3** digital IDs are the only ones that require individuals to appear before an actual person to verify their identity. A Class 3 digital ID requires you to appear before a notary and prove your identity.

Your Public Key

When you add your digital signature to an e-mail message, you are including your public key. Your public key is an encryption formula that people can use to scramble the messages they send you; in other words, it's an encoding key. Once the message has been encrypted with your public key, no one can read it unless he or she holds the private key—and that's something only you possess.

It's to your advantage to make your public key as widely available as possible. That's why you should always digitally sign your outgoing messages (even if you don't encrypt them). Having received your message with your digital key attached, recipients will also possess your public key, and they will be able to use this key to send encrypted mail to you.

Your Private Key

Your private key resides on your computer, where you keep it safe by means of password protection. This key enables you to unscramble messages that people have sent to you. Obviously, you don't want to make your private key available to anyone else. If you do, your mail is no longer secure.

Using Digital IDs

In order to sign your messages, you need to obtain a digital ID. You then configure Outlook Express to use your digital ID, and you can then add your digital ID to outgoing messages.

If you want to send encrypted mail, you will also want to collect the digital IDs of others. That's because the digital ID contains the sender's public key. When you have someone's public key, you can send them an encrypted message, as explained in a subsequent section of this chapter. Here, you learn how to obtain, configure, and use digital IDs.

Obtaining a Digital ID from a Certificate Authority

Currently, Verisign (www.verisign.com) offers a Class 1 digital ID for a fee of $9.95 per year, which includes the following:

- Authentication of your e-mail address to prevent imposters from taking out a digital certificate in your name.

- Automatic listing in Verisign's public directory, and search capabilities for other Verisign customers' digital IDs.
- $1,000 of NetSure protection against costs caused by corruption, loss, or misuse of your digital ID.
- Free revocation and replacement of your digital ID should the original become corrupted or lost.

At this writing, you could obtain a free 60-day trial version of the Class 1 certificate.

To obtain a digital ID for your use, do the following:

1. From the Tools menu in Outlook Express, choose Accounts.
2. Click the Mail tab.
3. Click your e-mail account.
4. Click Properties. You'll see the properties page for your mail account.
5. Click Security. You'll see the Security page.
6. Click Get Digital ID. Internet Explorer displays a page explaining how to get your digital ID. Look for the link to Verisign's "Get Your ID Now."

Once you've completed the enrollment, VeriSign will send an e-mail message to the address you supplied. In a few minutes, check the Inbox folder in Outlook Express.

1. When the VeriSign message arrives, open it and look for the Continue button. Click the button to connect to VeriSign again. You'll see your new digital ID.
2. Below the digital ID, click the Install button. You'll see a confirmation message once the digital ID has been successfully installed.
3. Click OK to close the message box.

Configuring Outlook Express to Use Your Digital ID

Once you've obtained your digital ID and installed it on your system, you need to configure Outlook Express to use this digital ID for outgoing secure messages. To do so, follow these steps:

1. From the Tools menu in Outlook Express, choose Accounts.
2. Click the Mail tab.
3. Click your e-mail account.
4. Click Properties. You'll see the Properties page for your mail account.
5. Click Security. You'll see the Security page (Figure 14-1).

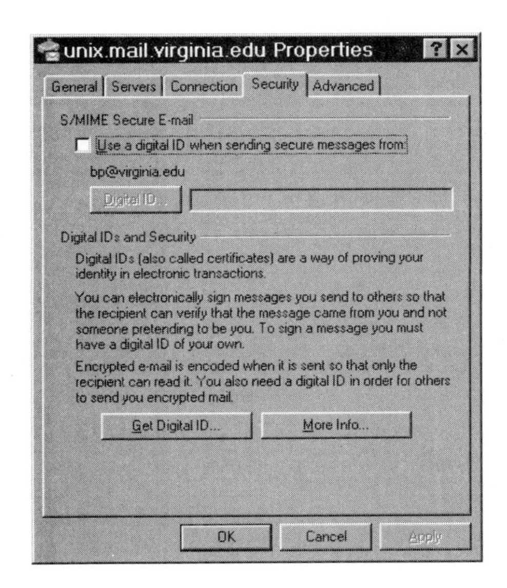

FIGURE 14-1.
On the Security page, you instruct Outlook Express to use your digital ID.

6. Click Use A Digital ID When Sending Secure Messages From.
7. Click the Digital ID button. You'll see the Select Certificate dialog box, shown here:

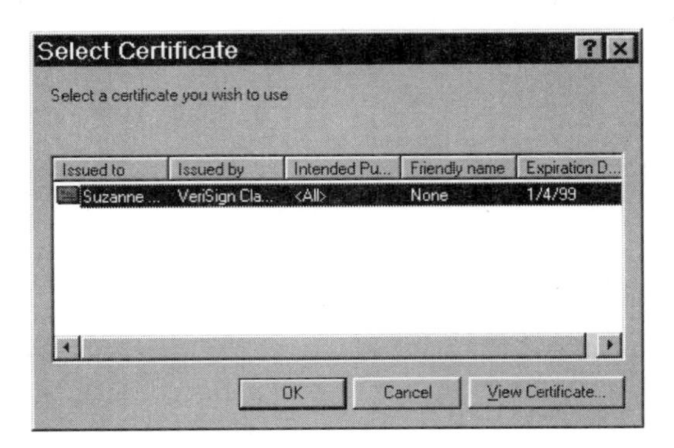

8 Choose your digital ID from the list, and click OK.

9 Click OK, and then click Close.

Now you can send digitally signed and encrypted messages with Outlook Express.

Sending a Digitally Signed Message

After you've obtained the digital ID, it's simple to add it to your messages.

1 Compose your message with Outlook Express.

2 On the toolbar, click Sign. (Or you can choose Tools on the menu bar, and select Digitally Sign.) You'll see a digital ID icon in the message header area (see Figure 14-2).

3 Click Send to send your message.

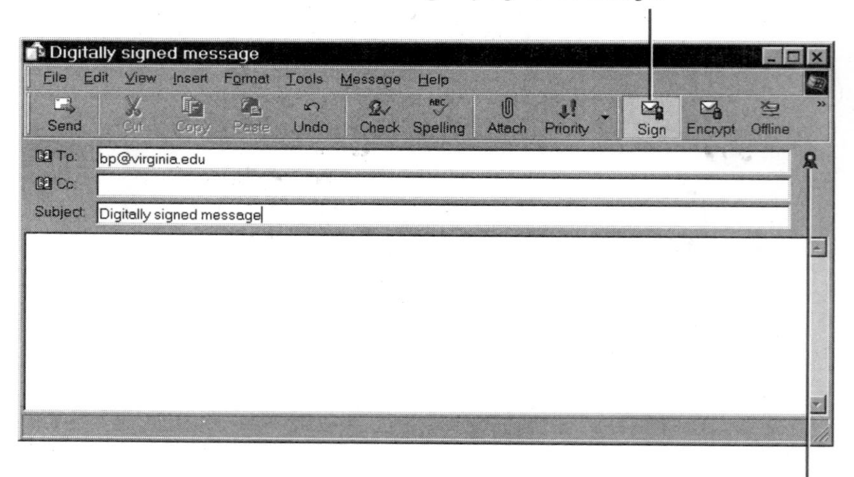

FIGURE 14-2. After you add a digital ID to your message, you see a digital ID icon.

To send a message with a digital signature, you must use the same e-mail account for which the digital ID was issued. If you send mail from more than one e-mail account, you must obtain separate digital IDs for each account.

If you would like to digitally sign all outgoing messages, do the following:

1. Click Tools on the menu bar, and choose Options.
2. Click the Security tab. In the Security page, locate the Secure Mail area and enable Digitally Sign All Outgoing Messages.
3. Click OK to confirm your choice.

Receiving a Digitally Signed Message

The first time somebody sends a digitally signed message to you, you'll see a Security Help message instead of the message text (see Figure 14-3). To prevent Security Help from appearing again, check Don't Show Me This Help Screen Again. Click Continue to view the message.

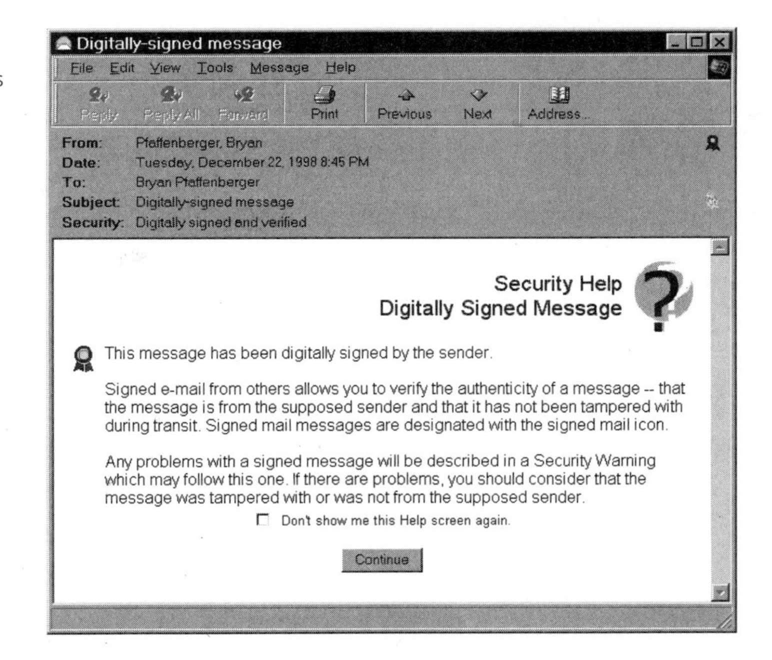

FIGURE 14-3.
Security Help appears the first time you receive a digitally signed message.

To view the digital ID, click the digital ID icon, and choose View Signing Digital ID. You'll see the Signing Digital ID Properties dialog box, shown on the next page:

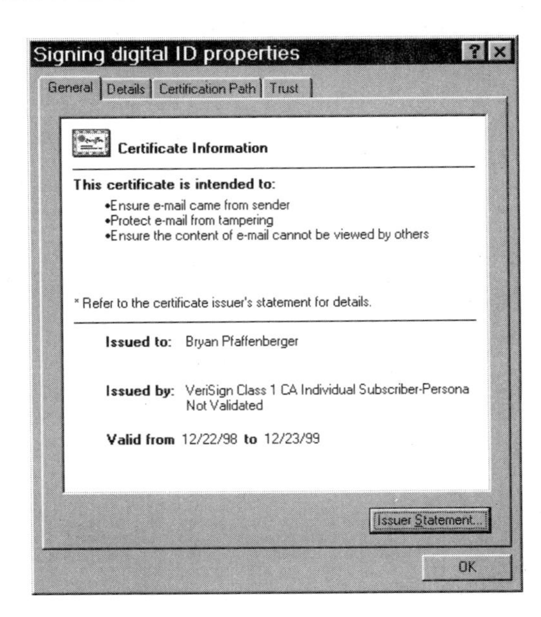

Click the Details tab to see more details about the digital ID.

To see more security information, click the digital ID icon, and choose View Security Properties. You'll see a message properties dialog box, with the Security page displayed:

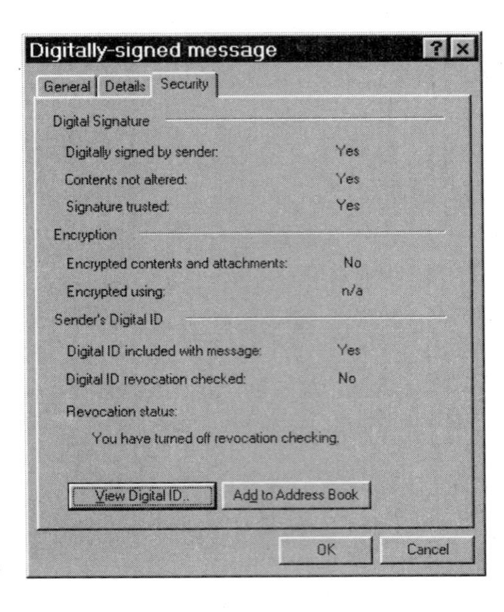

TIP

> By default, Outlook Express assigns trust to certificates issued by recognized certificate authorities. However, you can decide to mistrust a specific certificate should you have any doubts about its authenticity. To do so, display the digital ID's properties, and click the Trust tab. In the Edit Trust area, click Explicitly Don't Trust This Certificate.

This page includes helpful information, including whether the message was altered while en route and whether the signature is trusted.

Obtaining Sender's Digital IDs

To send an encrypted message, you need your correspondent's digital ID. What's more, the digital ID must be present in your correspondent's Address Book entry. For this reason, Outlook Express adds senders' digital IDs to their Address Book entries. The program does this when it receives a message with a digital ID.

NOTE

> If Outlook Express does not add digital IDs to Address Book entries automatically, check the security settings. To do so, click Tools on the Outlook Express menu bar, choose Options, and click the Security tab. Click Advanced, and check Add Senders' Certificates To My Address Book. Click OK to confirm.

After Outlook Express adds a digital ID to a correspondent's Address Book properties, the correspondent's contact-list icon displays a tiny red ribbon. This icon, shown here, indicates that a digital ID has been attached to the entry:

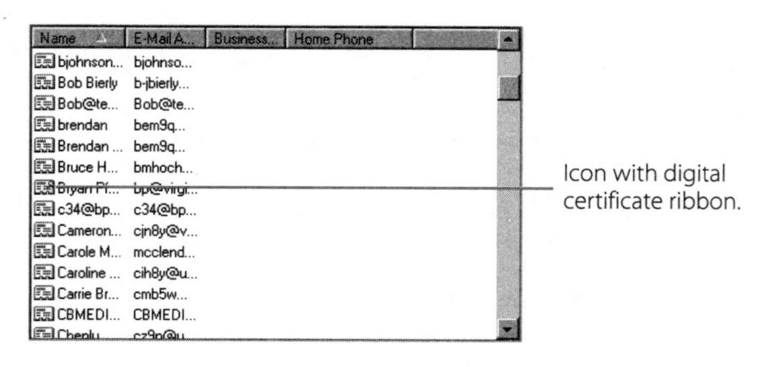

Icon with digital certificate ribbon.

Adding a Digital ID Manually

If no Address Book entry existed for a sender when a digitally signed message arrived, do the following:

SEE ALSO
For information on creating an Address Book entry, see "Adding Contact Information Manually," page 403.

1. Create an Address Book entry for your correspondent.
2. In the Outlook Express message list, select the message you received from this correspondent.
3. From the File menu, choose Properties.
4. Click the Security tab.
5. Click Add To Address Book.
6. Click OK.

Obtaining a Digital ID from the Internet

If you would like to obtain the digital ID of a person who hasn't sent you a message, you can try searching for it on the Internet. To search Verisign's database of digital IDs, access https://digitalid.verisign.com/services/client/index.htm. You can search by e-mail address or name. Once you've located the person's certificate, you can download it to your computer—and then you can send encrypted e-mail to this person.

Checking the Certificate Authority

Is every digital ID trustworthy? In general, yes, as long as the ID has been signed by a recognized certificate authority. But there are other types of digital IDs that are issued by individuals themselves. If you receive a message with such an ID, you'll know that the message hasn't been tampered with, but you won't know whether the message is really from the individual who claims to have sent it. That's the role that's performed by the CA. If there's no CA, then there's no independent corroboration of the individual's identity.

To find out whether an individual's digital ID was issued by a CA, select the individual's Address Book entry. From the File menu, choose Properties. Click the Digital IDs tab. In the Digital IDs area, select the individual's e-mail address, and then select the digital ID that you're curious about. Choose Properties. You'll see the Certificate Properties dialog box for this digital ID (Figure 14-4). Click the General tab if necessary. If the digital ID was signed by a CA, you'll see the CA's name.

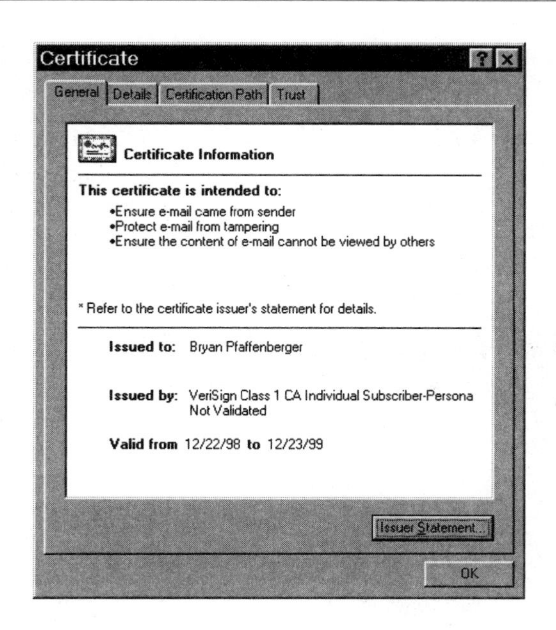

FIGURE 14-4.
You can determine who signed a digital ID by looking at its properties.

If you're displaying a digitally signed message, you can view the signature properties by clicking the digital signature icon (the ribbon symbol) and choosing View Signing Digital ID from the menu that appears.

Changing the Trust Level

By default, Outlook Express trusts a digital ID if it's been signed by an issuer, which might be a problem if the issuer isn't trustworthy. For digital IDs that individuals issue to themselves, you might want to change the trust level. This way, you'll see a warning whenever you use this digital ID.

1. In the Address Book, select the individual's Address Book entry.
2. From the File menu, choose Properties.
3. Select Digital IDs, and choose the digital ID whose trust level you want to change. Click Properties.
4. Click the Trust tab, and then select one of the following options:
   - **Inherit Trust From Issuer.** This is the default option. It trusts any signed ID, even if the sender signed it.

- **Explicitly Trust This Certificate.** For digital IDs from people you know very well, you can choose this option.
- **Explicitly Don't Trust This Certificate.** Choose this option when you do not trust the digital ID for some reason. This option is better than deleting the ID, because you'll see a warning message when you use it to remind yourself that you have previously expressed misgivings about the ID.

Using Revocation Checking

If a digital ID is misused, the certificate authority can revoke it. Outlook Express can check to see whether a given certificate has been revoked. To turn on revocation checking, do the following:

1. In the Outlook Express Tools menu, choose Options.
2. Click the Security tab.
3. Click Advanced.
4. In the Revocation area, click Only When Online. You can use this feature only when you're online.

Sending and Receiving Encrypted Messages

With Outlook Express, sending encrypted messages is all but automatic. However, you cannot send an encrypted message unless you have a copy of your correspondent's digital ID (see "Obtaining Sender's Digital IDs," page 473).

Sending an Encrypted Message

To send an encrypted message, do the following:

1. Click New Mail, and create your message.
2. Click Sign to digitally sign your message. (You can send an encrypted message without a signature, but this would prevent your correspondent from replying to you with an encrypted reply.)
3. Click the Encrypt button on the New Message window's toolbar (see Figure 14-5).
4. Click Send.

FIGURE 14-5.
To encrypt a message, click the Encrypt button.

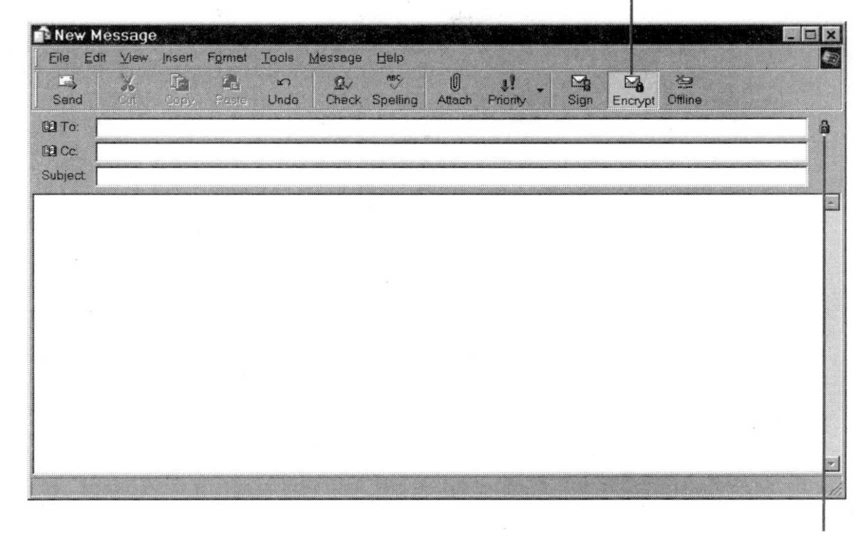

Receiving an Encrypted Message

When you receive an encrypted message, you see a distinctive icon in the message list (see Table 14-1), telling you just what's included—a digital signature, encryption, or both. When you open the message, you see the Private Key Container dialog box, which informs you that the program is using your private key to decrypt the message; click OK to continue. The first time you receive an encrypted message, you'll see Security Help (see Figure 14-6). Click Continue to see the message text.

FIGURE 14-6.
This Security Help message appears the first time you receive an encrypted message.

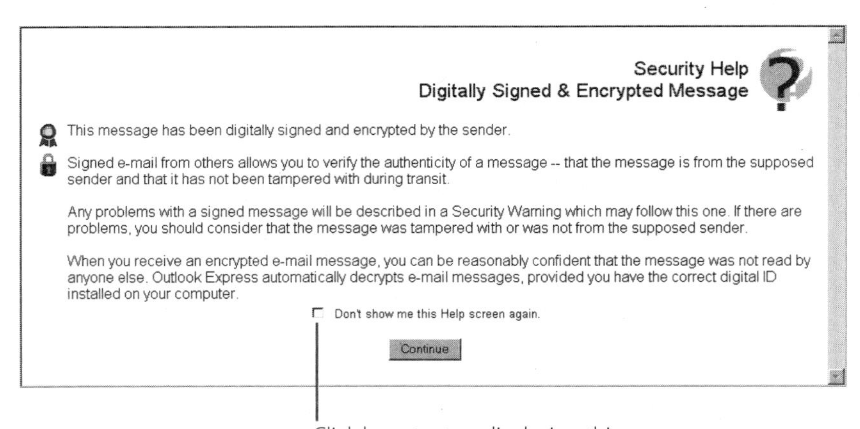

CAUTION
If one of your messages has an icon with a warning signal, that's not a good sign. If the message was digitally signed, the warning signal probably indicates that the message was altered in some way while it was en route. If the message was encrypted, the warning signal similarly indicates that the message isn't quite right and might have been damaged or altered.

TABLE 14-1. Message List Icons for Digitally Signed and Encrypted Messages.

Icon	Meaning
	This message is digitally signed, and you haven't read it.
	This message is encrypted, and you haven't read it.
	This message is signed and encrypted, and you haven't read it.
	This message is digitally signed, and you've read it.
	This message is encrypted, and you've read it.
	This message is encrypted and signed, and you've read it.

Choosing Security Options

CAUTION
If you see a warning signal of any kind, send a message back to the message's sender, requesting that it be sent again. Most likely, the problem is due to some kind of transmission glitch and won't recur.

You can choose options for secure e-mail. To do so, follow these instructions:

1 Click Tools on the menu bar, and choose Options.

2 Click the Security tab. You'll see the Security page, shown here:

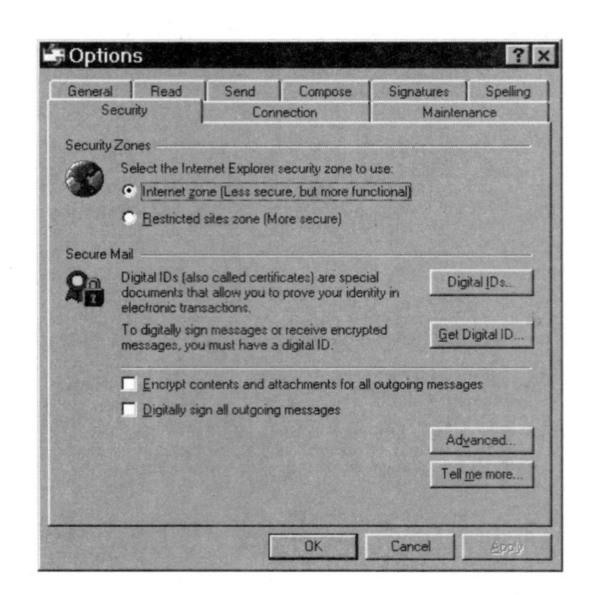

3 In the Secure Mail area, you can choose two options:

- **Encrypt Contents And Attachments For All Outgoing Messages.** This option isn't recommended, since your correspondents probably include many people using e-mail programs that don't support S/MIME.
- **Digitally Sign All Outgoing Messages.** Although this option doesn't prevent most e-mail users from reading your messages, e-mail packages that don't support S/MIME will show a lot of garbage characters at the bottom of your message. This option isn't recommended.

4 Click Advanced. You'll see the Advanced Security Settings dialog box, shown here:

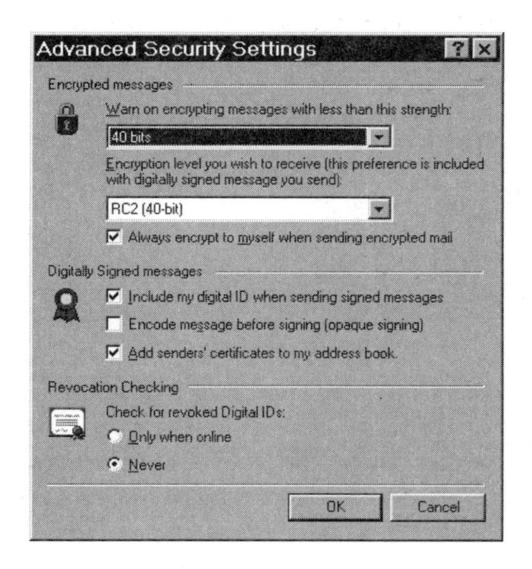

5 In this dialog box, you can choose the following options:

- **Warn On Encrypting Messages With Less Than This Strength.** If you have obtained the secure (128-bit) version of Internet Explorer, you can choose minimum encryption strengths of greater than 40 bits.
- **Encryption Level You Wish To Receive.** If you have obtained the secure (128-bit) version of Internet Explorer, you can choose minimum encryption strengths of greater than 40 bits.

- **Always Encrypt To Myself When Sending Encrypted Messages.** This option encrypts the local copies of your messages stored in the Sent Items folder.
- **Include My Digital ID When Sending Signed Messages.** You must activate this option in order to send digitally signed messages.
- **Encode Messages Before Signing.** This option prevents the recipient from reading the digital ID prior to decrypting the message, adding an extra measure of security.
- **Add Senders' Certificates To My Address Book.** Make sure this option is checked so that Outlook Express will automatically add digital IDs to your Address Book.

6 Click OK to confirm your choices.

CHAPTER 15

Using Hotmail

Hotmail is a free Web-based e-mail service that's exceptionally easy to use. You're probably wondering, though, why you'd have any interest in Hotmail when you have the best available e-mail software, Outlook Express. The answer is neatly summed up in one word: accessibility. Because you use the Web to access your Hotmail account, you can read your mail anywhere you can get access to a Web browser. These days that means you can get your mail from just about any computer, including rental systems at airports, PCs in colleagues' offices, or a computer at the home of a friend you're visiting. Hotmail adds a needed dimension of accessibility to your e-mail usage.

This chapter introduces Hotmail, and surveys its surprisingly lengthy list of features, which include an Address Book, custom folders, rules (called filters) that route incoming mail to custom folders, and even access to your POP3 mail.

Introducing Hotmail

SEE ALSO
Before using Hotmail, review the essentials of e-mail etiquette. See "Learning E-Mail Etiquette," page 342.

With over 15 million subscribers, Hotmail is one of the most popular services on the Web. Once you've looked at Hotmail's advantages, you'll understand why.

What Features Does Hotmail Offer?

Here's a list of some of Hotmail's many positive features:

- Accessible from anywhere you can run a Web browser.
- Displays richly formatted (HTML) messages including fonts and images.
- Displays active hyperlinks in HTML-formatted messages.
- Includes an Address Book for storing frequently used e-mail addresses.
- Ensures flawless messages with spell checking and offers an online dictionary and thesaurus.
- Enables you to create custom folders for categorizing and storing your mail.
- Includes rules (filters) for routing messages to folders and block unwanted mail.
- Enables you to access up to four POP3 e-mail accounts.

Why Is Hotmail Free?

Hotmail is an advertiser-supported service. You'll see banner ads on the pages that show your messages. What's more, they're customized, based on the demographic information you supply when you sign up for Hotmail. You can ignore the advertisements if you wish. They don't take up too much screen room.

What About Privacy?

Hotmail's privacy policy expressly states that the information you supply will not be sold or rented to a third party. In addition, Hotmail promises to respect the privacy of your e-mail. However, you should understand that Hotmail, like any Internet service provider, would have to divulge the contents of your e-mail if presented with a valid court order.

Who Should Use Hotmail?

Just about everyone can benefit from a Hotmail account. Hotmail is especially suitable for any of the following:

- Beginners who need an introduction to basic e-mail concepts
- E-mail users who travel
- Students
- People who don't own computers
- Employees who want a personal e-mail account
- Family members who must share a home e-mail account

What Uses Are Prohibited?

Hotmail's policies prohibit certain uses, including the following:

- Businesses can't use Hotmail to provide e-mail accounts for their employees. However, employees can get Hotmail accounts to avoid sending personal mail via their employers' accounts.
- Hotmail accounts can't be used to send unsolicited, threatening, or harassing mail to others.

TIP

> Before you sign up for a Hotmail account, be sure to read the policies carefully. You'll have an opportunity to do so when you obtain your account, as described in the following section.

What Are the Usage Limits?

Currently, Hotmail limits each account to a maximum of 2 MB of online storage space. (You can see how much storage you're using by scrolling to the bottom of your In-Box.) For this reason, Hotmail isn't a good place to store archival copies of your mail, especially mail containing large attachments. Also, it's not a good idea to subscribe to mailing lists using your Hotmail account. A mailing list could quickly fill up your In-Box and could lead to your account's cancellation.

TIP

> After you've obtained and configured your account, you can find out how much storage space you're using. On the Navigation bar, click Folders. Under the Size column, you'll see the total amount of storage you've used.

Obtaining a Hotmail Account

To obtain a Hotmail account, do the following:

1 On the Links toolbar in Internet Explorer, click Free Hotmail. You'll see the Hotmail home page, shown in Figure 15-1. (If you don't see the Links toolbar, or if you've removed the Hotmail link button, type www.hotmail.com in the Address box, and click the Go button.)

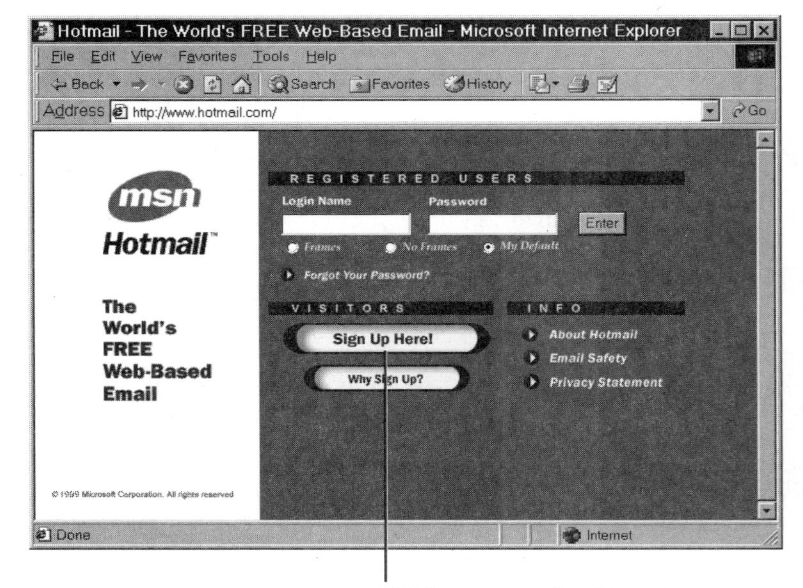

FIGURE 15-1. On Hotmail's home page (www.hotmail.com), you can sign up for an account. You can access your mail if you already have an account.

2 Click Sign Up Here! You'll see the Terms Of Service page. Take a minute to read this page, and make sure you understand the restrictions before proceeding.

3 Scroll to the bottom of the page, and click I Accept. You'll see the Hotmail Registration page.

You'll be asked to supply a lot of personal information (see Figure 15-2), but remember that Hotmail has a good privacy policy. (See "What About Privacy," in the preceding section of this chapter.)

4 Supply the following information:

- **Login name.** You can use letters (a-z), numbers (0-9), and an underscore character. The login name must begin with a letter.

- **Password.** The password must be at least four characters long. Be sure to write it down somewhere so you'll remember it.

- **Personal data.** The requested data includes your state and zip code (for U.S. residents; international users are asked to supply their country, state or province, and postal code), gender (male or female), year of birth, and occupation. Remember, this information is not sold or given to any third party.

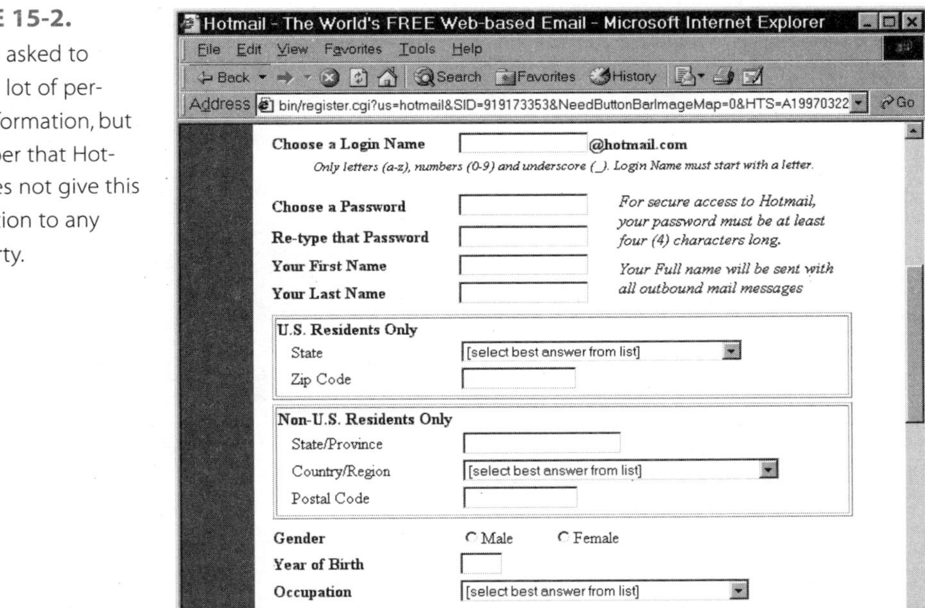

FIGURE 15-2. You'll be asked to supply a lot of personal information, but remember that Hotmail does not give this information to any third party.

5 Decide whether you want to be listed in the Hotmail directory. If you would like to make it easy for people to locate you, click Please List My Name And Location. If you prefer to keep your name and Hotmail address out of the Hotmail directory, click Please Do Not List Me At All.

6 Decide whether you would like to be listed in Internet white pages directories. If you would like to be listed, click Yes, Please Register Me. If you would prefer that your Hotmail address does not appear in white pages directories, click No, Do Not Register Me.

7 Click Submit Registration. If your submission was complete, you'll see a confirmation after a minute or two. Be sure to fill out the hint information, which you can use in case you forget your password.

If you see a page asking you to submit missing information, follow the instructions on the screen to complete your registration.

If your login name has already been taken, you'll be asked to choose a new one.

CAUTION
Always exit Hotmail by clicking Log Out on the Navigation bar. If you leave Hotmail in an open-browser window, somebody else could sit down at your computer and send prank messages in your name.

8 Click OK to continue. You'll see a page welcoming you to Hotmail and offering various promotions. To continue, scroll down to the bottom of the page and click the Continue button.

9 You'll see your In-Box (Figure 15-3), with a welcoming message from the Hotmail staff. You're ready to start using Hotmail!

10 For now, click Log Out.

FIGURE 15-3.
Your Hotmail In-Box enables you to read your e-mail using the Web.

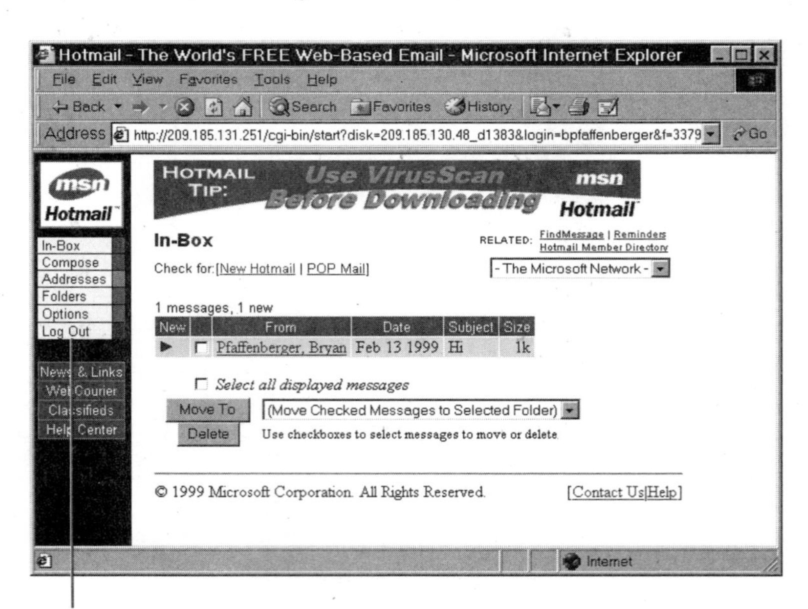

Always log out when you finish using Hotmail.

Logging On to Hotmail

To log on to Hotmail, do any of the following:

- From the MSN home page (www.msn.com), locate the e-mail area. Type your login name and password, and click Enter.

  or

- Go to www.hotmail.com (see Figure 15-1). In the Registered Users area, type your login name and your password, and click Enter.

When you log on by accessing www.hotmail.com, you can choose between the frames and no-frames versions of Hotmail.

Understanding the Hotmail Window

The default frames version of the In-Box window (see Figure 15-4) consists of three panels:

- **Navigation bar.** By clicking the navigation buttons in the Navigation bar, you can access all of Hotmail's pages: In-Box (the page you're currently viewing), Compose (for creating new messages), Addresses (for storing names and e-mail addresses), Folders (for organizing your mail), Options (for choosing Hotmail options), and Log Out (for exiting Hotmail). The Navigation bar stays put, so you can always find your way around Hotmail.
- **Sponsor's Frame.** Here, you'll see advertisements from the companies that help make Hotmail a free service.
- **Media Frame.** Here, you can read and compose your e-mail.

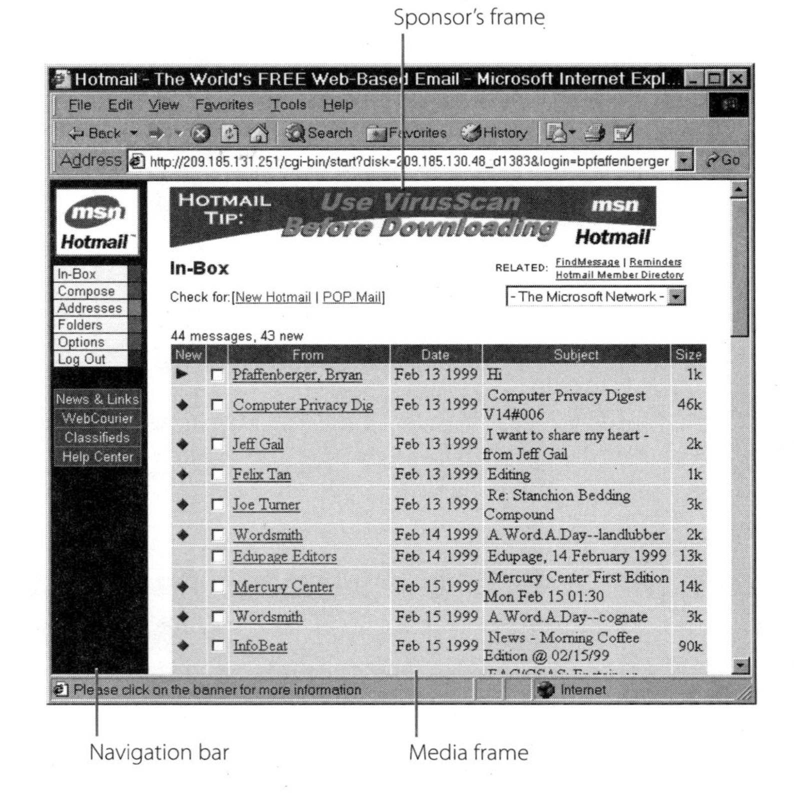

FIGURE 15-4.
In the default, frames version of Hotmail, you see three frames. Use the Navigation bar to access Hotmail's features.

Reading Your Mail

When you open your In-Box, you see your messages. New messages are flagged with an arrow, as shown here:

1 messages, 1 new

New		From	Date	Subject	Size
►	☐	Pfaffenberger, Bryan	Feb 13 1999	Hi	1k

If you have been working with Hotmail for a while, you may wish to see whether you have received any new messages. On the In-Box page, click New Hotmail to update your message list.

Displaying Mail Messages

To read your mail, follow these steps:

1 To open a message, click the hyperlink for that message. By default, the hyperlink is the sender's name.

After you click the message's hyperlink, you'll see the Read Message page (Figure 15-5).

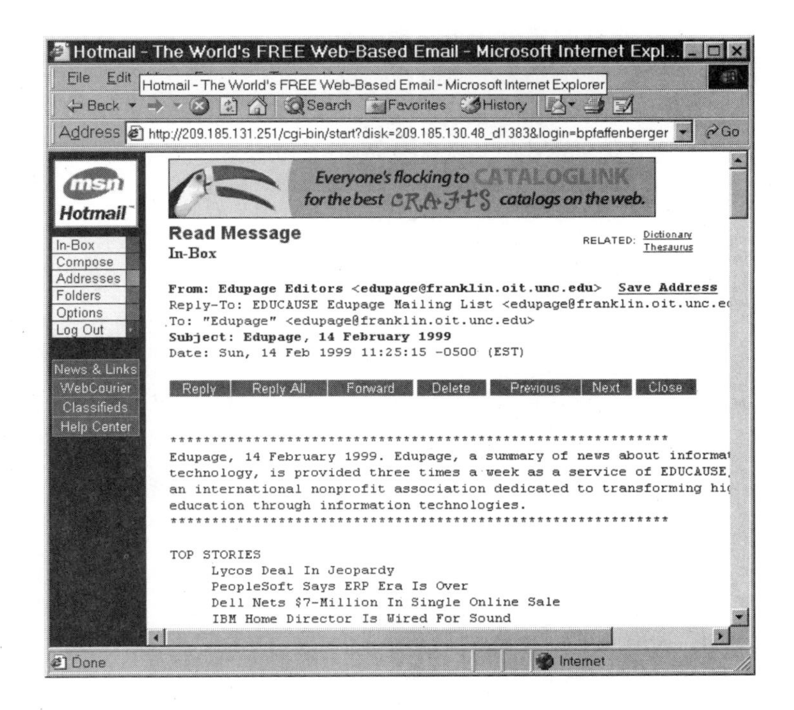

FIGURE 15-5. In the Read Message page, you'll see the message you've received.

If the message contains an attachment, you'll see a paperclip icon. You can download the attachment with or without virus scanning.

Attachment:
Chris_Brooks_recommendation.doc **Download without Scan** **Scan with McAfee**

2 When you finish reading a message, you can click any of the following buttons:

- **Reply** replies to this message's author.
- **Reply All** replies to all the e-mail addresses included in the message's header.

- **Forward** forwards the message to a third party.
- **Delete** deletes the current message.
- **Previous** displays the previous message in the current folder.
- **Next** displays the next message in the current folder.
- **Close** closes the Read Message window and returns to the In-Box.

Finding a Message

If you've received a lot of messages, you may have trouble finding a message you've received. However, you can search for a message. To do so, follow these instructions:

1. Click Find Messages (a link at the top of the In-Box page). You'll see the Find Messages page.
2. Enter the word or phrase you want to electronically search for.
3. Choose the type of search (From/To and Subject fields only, or entire message).
4. Check the folders you want to search.
5. Click Search. You'll see a page showing the messages that match the word or phrase you typed, if any. Click the message hyperlink to open and read a message.

Cleaning Your In-Box

Avoid keeping a lot of messages in your In-Box. Periodically go through and delete the messages you don't want to keep. By checking unwanted messages and clicking the Delete button at the bottom of the In-Box window, you can delete more than one message at a time.

TIP

To delete all of your messages, check Select All Displayed Messages, and click Delete.

Sorting Your Mail

You can sort your mail by clicking any of the buttons at the top of the message list (New, From, Date, Subject, or Size). To sort your messages in reverse order, click the button again.

TIP

To see your most recent messages at the top of the list, sort by Date, and click again, if necessary, to sort the list so that the oldest messages are at the bottom of the list.

Dealing with Unwanted Mail

If you receive an unwanted e-mail message, you can block the sender. To do so, follow these steps:

1. In the Read Message window, click Block Sender.

   You'll see a page explaining that you're about to add the specified e-mail address to your Blocked Senders list. In the future, all mail from this address will go directly to the Trash Can.

2. Click OK to block this sender.

If you later decide to un-block this sender, you can edit your Blocked Senders List. To do so, click Options. On the Options page, click Filters. At the top of the Filters page, you'll see your current Blocked Senders List. To reinstate an address, select the address, press the Delete key, and click OK at the bottom of the page.

Accessing Your POP3 Mail

To configure Hotmail to access your POP3 Mail, do the following:

1. In the In-Box, click POP Mail. You'll see the In-Box POP Server Settings page, shown in Figure 15-6.

FIGURE 15-6. In this Hotmail page, you can configure Hotmail to access your POP3 e-mail accounts.

In-Box
POP Server Settings

Use this form if you have one or more Post Office Protocol (POP) accounts with an existing Internet Service Provider or with your company. If you are unclear about these fields, click the **Help** link for more information. When you are finished filling in the fields, click **OK**.

1st POP Account:
POP Server Name:
POP User Name:
POP User Password:
Server Timeout (seconds): 90
Port Number: 110 *(Standard is 110)*
Leave messages on POP server

New Mail Indicator

2nd POP Account:

New Mail

2 In the 1st POP Account area, type the following:

- **POP Server Name.** This is the name of the e-mail server that receives your incoming mail.
- **POP User Name.** This is your login name or account name. (Usually it's the same as the part of your e-mail address that comes before the @ sign.)
- **POP User Password.** This is the password that you use to access your mail on the POP3 server.

3 Check Leave Messages On POP Server, so that you can access your POP3 mail at work.

4 In the New Mail Indicator area, choose a distinctive new mail icon.

5 If you would like to configure additional POP3 accounts, repeat steps 2 through 4, using the additional areas provided on the on-screen form.

6 Click OK to finish configuring your POP connection.

After you click OK, Hotmail attempts to contact your POP3 server. If there's a problem, you see an error message. Check your typing carefully, and try again.

Hotmail does not automatically download your POP3 mail. To see your POP3 mail, go to the In-Box page if necessary. In the Check For area, click POP Mail.

Composing Messages

To compose messages, you use Hotmail's Compose window, shown in Figure 15-7. As the following sections explain, you can also send messages by replying to existing messages, or forwarding them.

Sending a New Message

To send a new message, follow these steps:

1 In the Navigation bar, click Compose. You'll see the Compose window, shown in Figure 15-7.

2 In the To box, type the recipient's e-mail address.

If you would like to type more than one address, separate the addresses with semicolons, commas, or spaces.

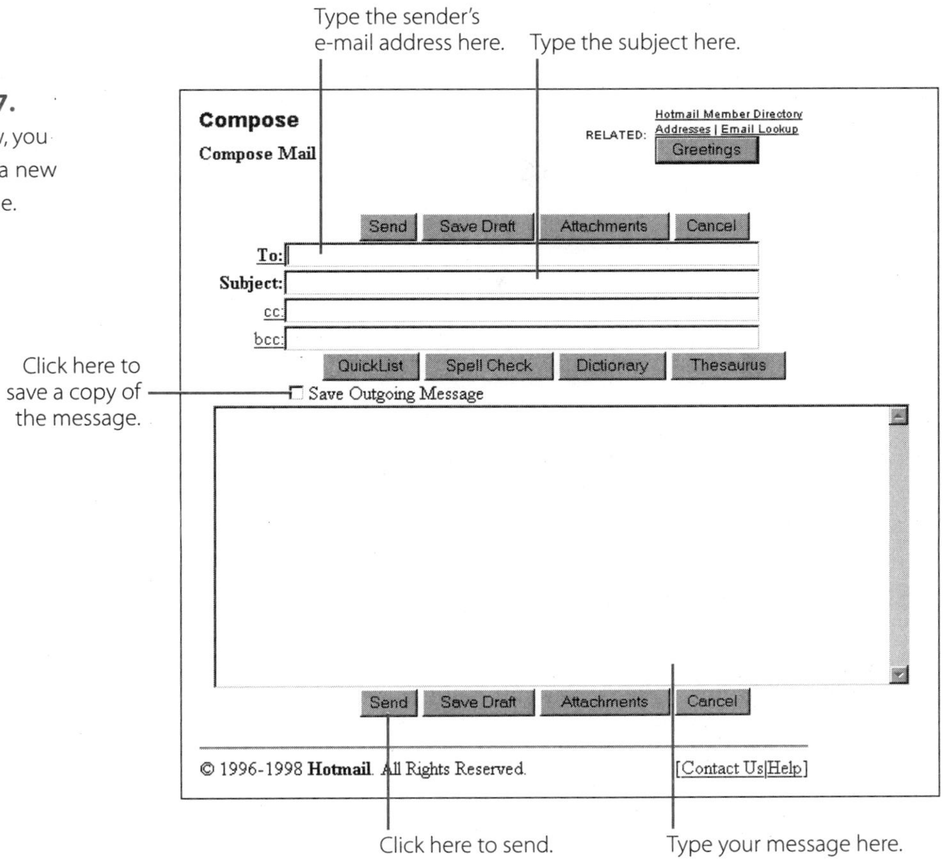

FIGURE 15-7.
In this window, you can compose a new e-mail message.

Type the sender's e-mail address here.
Type the subject here.
Click here to save a copy of the message.
Click here to send.
Type your message here.

Compose
Compose Mail
RELATED: Hotmail Member Directory Addresses | Email Lookup
Greetings
Send | Save Draft | Attachments | Cancel
To:
Subject:
cc:
bcc:
QuickList | Spell Check | Dictionary | Thesaurus
Save Outgoing Message
Send | Save Draft | Attachments | Cancel
© 1996-1998 **Hotmail**. All Rights Reserved.
[Contact Us|Help]

3 In the Subject box, type the message's subject.

4 If you wish, you can type an address in the Cc (carbon copy) or Bcc (blind carbon copy) boxes.

5 If you would like to save a copy of this outgoing message, check Save Outgoing Message.

6 In the message text box, type your message.

7 To help you prepare a flawless message, you can take advantage of a dictionary, thesaurus, and spelling checker.

- To look up a word in the dictionary, click Dictionary, and type the word you want to look up in the text box. Click Search to see the results. You can search again, if you wish. When you're finished, click Done.
- To search for synonyms, click Thesaurus, and type the word you want to look up in the text box. Click Search to see the results. You can search again, if you wish. When you're finished, click Done.
- To check your spelling, click Spell Check. You'll see the Spelling Check page, shown in Figure 15-8. For the highlighted misspelling, enter a new spelling, and click Change. (If the Suggestions list contains the correct spelling, just click the correct spelling to add the word to the Enter New Spelling box.) If the word is spelled correctly, click Add To Dictionary. To ignore this instance of the word, click Ignore. To ignore every instance of this word in the rest of the letter, click Ignore All. When you're finished checking spelling, you see the Compose window again, with the message "Spelling Check Complete."

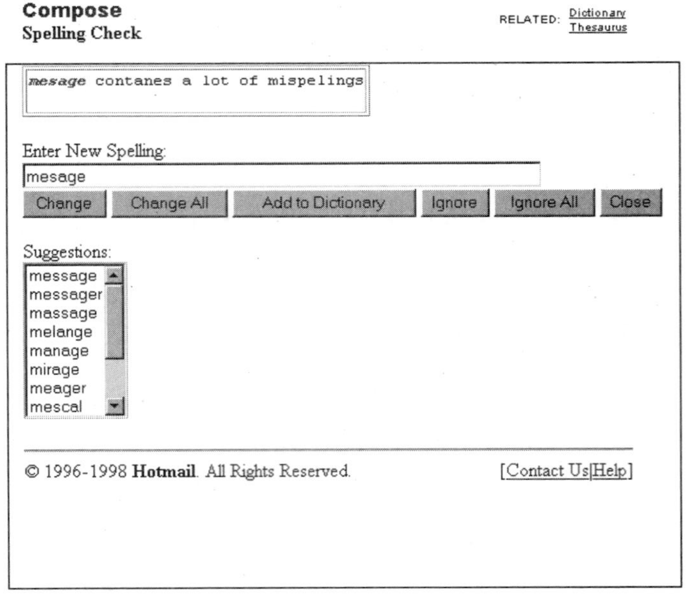

FIGURE 15-8.
Be sure to check your spelling before sending your message.

8 Do one of the following:

- Click Send to send your completed message.

or

- Click Cancel to abandon this message without sending.

If you send your message, you'll see a confirmation. Click OK to confirm.

If you don't have time to finish your letter, click Save Draft. To finish your letter in a subsequent session, click Folders, and click Drafts. Click your message to re-open the Compose window.

Including an Attachment

If you would like to include an attachment in any message you're composing, click the Attachments button in the Compose window. You'll see the Attachments page. Click the Browse button to locate the file, and click Attach To Message. Your computer uploads the file to Hotmail, which might take a few minutes. Click the Done button when you're finished attaching files.

Attachments cannot exceed 1000K.

Replying to a Message

To reply to a message, follow these steps:

1. Click the message hyperlink if necessary to display the message.
2. Click Reply. Hotmail displays the Compose window, as shown in Figure 15-9. Note that Hotmail has inserted the recipient's e-mail address, added Re: to the subject, and quoted the message text.

When Hotmail quotes the original message text, it copies the message header information as well as the message. Unless you have some reason for forwarding the header information, edit this information out, so that your recipient can see what the original message text is about without having to scroll down past the header information.

3. Type your message above the quoted message.
4. Check your spelling if you wish.

5 Click Send or Cancel.

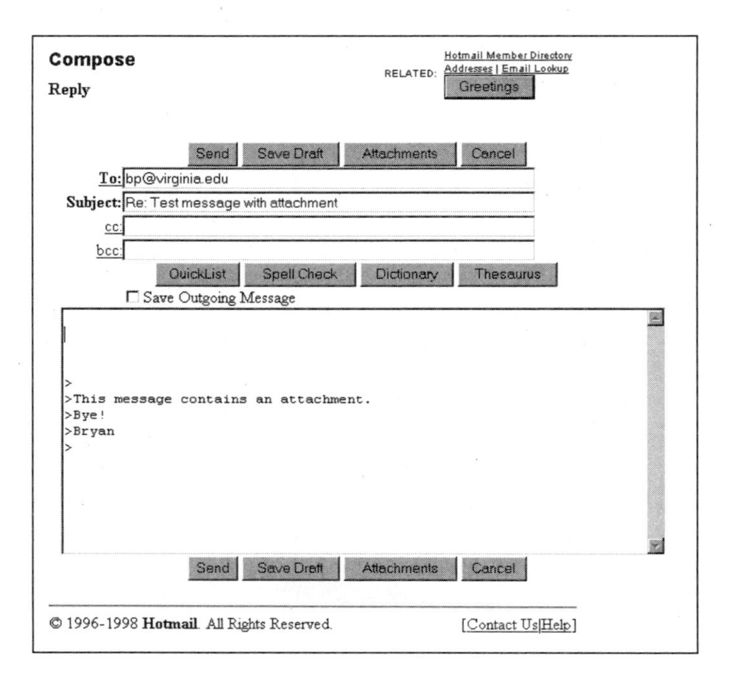

FIGURE 15-9. When you forward a message, Hotmail inserts the recipient's address and adds Re: to the subject line.

Forwarding a Message

To forward a message, follow these steps:

1 Click the message hyperlink if necessary to display the message.

2 Click Forward. Hotmail displays the Compose window. Note that Hotmail has automatically quoted the message text, and added Fwd: to the subject.

3 In the To box, type the recipient's e-mail address.

4 Type your message above the quoted message.

5 Check your spelling if you wish.

6 Click Send or Cancel.

Printing a Message

To print a message, use your browser's print capabilities, as follows:

1. Click within the Media Frame.
2. From the File menu, choose Print. You'll see the Print dialog box.
3. In the Print Frames area, click Only The Selected Frame.
4. Click OK.

Hotmail's reminders are a handy way to remind yourself of important dates. You can set up reminders for a specific day of each year, month, or week. On that date, you'll receive e-mail containing your reminder. To create a reminder, do the following: on the In-Box page, click Reminders. You'll see the Reminders page. Click Create to create a reminder. In the Occasion field, type a name for the reminder, and use the schedule options to define the schedule. In the Additional Details box, type some text for your reminder, and click OK.

Using the Address Book

Hotmail includes an Address Book, which resembles the Address Book you can create with Outlook Express. It's best used to create nicknames for frequently used e-mail addresses. After you create the nickname, you can type the nickname instead of the e-mail address, or choose the nickname from a list. As the following sections explain, you can create individual nicknames (one name for one e-mail address) or group nicknames (one name for two or more addresses).

Creating an Individual Nickname

To avoid typing e-mail addresses incorrectly, you should create nicknames for the e-mail addresses you commonly use. To create an individual nickname, follow these steps:

1. Do one of the following:
   - Display one of this individual's messages. In the Read Message window, click Save Address.

     or

   - In the Navigator bar, click Addresses. You'll see the Addresses window, shown in Figure 15-10. In the Individuals area, click Create.

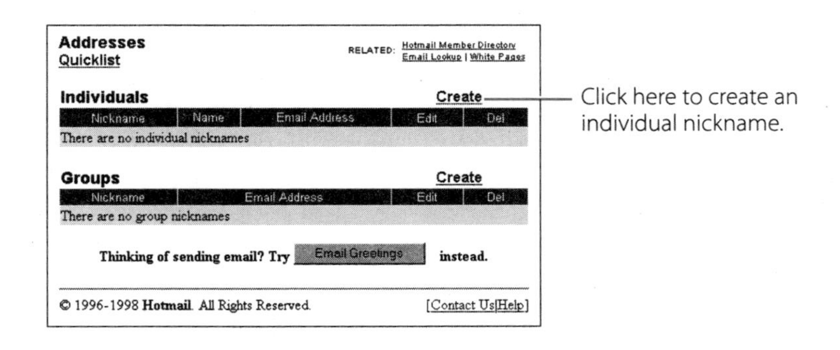

FIGURE 15-10.
You can create nicknames for individuals or groups.

You'll see the Create Individual Nickname window, shown in Figure 15-11.

2 In the Nickname box, type a short nickname. Try using the person's first name and the first letter of the last name (such as judym).

3 In the Email Address box, carefully type this person's e-mail address.

4 Fill out additional contact information if you wish.

5 Click OK. You'll see the nickname entry in the Addresses window.

Should you need to edit a nickname, display the Addresses folder, and click the Edit link that appears on the same line as the nickname. To delete a nickname, click the Delete link on the nickname's line.

Creating a Group Nickname

A group nickname enables you to type or select just one nickname, and send a message to two or more people. To create a group nickname, follow these steps:

1 In the Navigator bar, click Addresses. You'll see the Addresses window, shown in Figure 15-10.

2 In the Groups area, click Create. You'll see the Create Group Nickname window, shown in Figure 15-12.

3 In the Nickname box, type a nickname for the group.

Type a nickname here.
Type the e-mail address here.
Addresses
Create Individual Nickname
Nickname:
Required
Email Address:
First Name:
Last Name:
Street Address:
City:
State/Province:
Zip/Postal Code:
Country:
Company Name:
Home Phone:
Work Phone:
Pager:
Cellular:
Fax:
Other:
Birthday:
Month
Day
Year
OK
Cancel
© 1999 Microsoft Corporation. All Rights Reserved.
[Contact Us|Help]

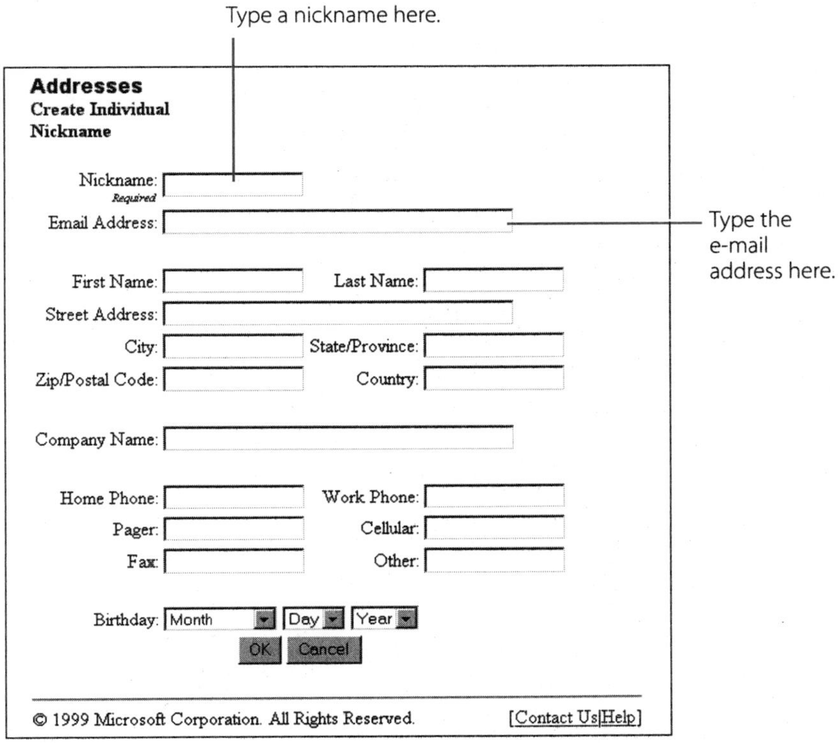

FIGURE 15-11.
In this window, you can create a nickname for an individual e-mail address.

Type the group nickname here.
List the e-mail addresses to be associated with this group.
Addresses
Create Group Nickname
Nickname:
Required
Email addresses to associate with this group:
OK
Cancel
© 1996-1998 Hotmail. All Rights Reserved.
[Contact Us|Help]

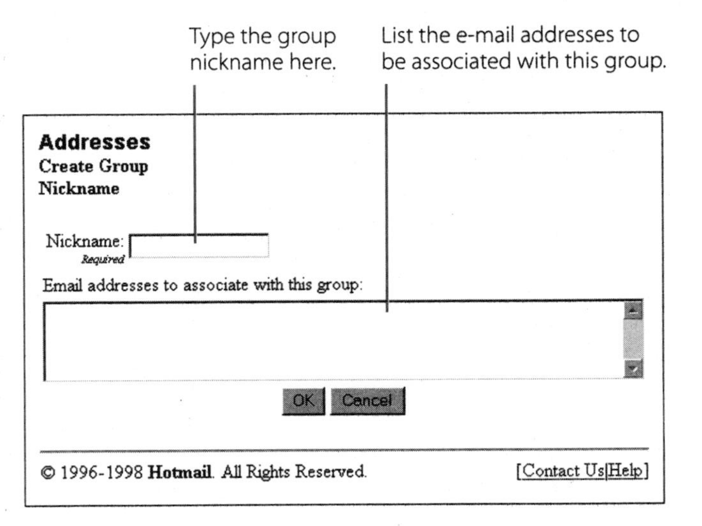

FIGURE 15-12.
In this window, you can create a nickname for a group of e-mail addresses.

4. In the text box, carefully type each group member's e-mail address, followed by a comma and a space, as in the following example:

   johnb@provider.net, megan448@university.edu,
   michaela_s@forest.org

5. Click OK. You'll see the nickname entry in the Addresses window.

Composing a Message with a Nickname

In the Compose window, you can use your nicknames in the following ways:

- To send a message to a single recipient, click Addresses on the Navigation bar, and click the nickname. You'll see a Compose window with the recipient's e-mail address already added.
- In the Compose window, click To. You'll see a pop-up window with your nicknames. Click the check box next to one or more nicknames, and click Mail To. You'll see the nickname's addresses in the To box.
- In the Compose window, type the nickname in the To box.

Using Custom Folders

By default, Hotmail uses the following folders:

- **In-Box** shows your current incoming messages.
- **Sent Messages** stores copies of your sent messages, but only if you clicked Save Outgoing Message when you composed the message.
- **Drafts** stores drafts of your messages.
- **Trash Can** stores deleted messages.

You can create custom folders to organize and store your mail. If you create filters, as described in the following section, Hotmail can automatically route incoming mail to your custom folders.

Creating a Custom Folder

To create a custom folder, do the following:

1. In the Navigation bar, click Folders. You'll see the Folders page, shown in Figure 15-13.

Click here to create a custom folder.

Folders RELATED: FindMessage Filters

Folders **Create**

Folder	Messages	New	Size	Edit	Del
In-Box	102	99	1333k		
Sent Messages	0	0	0k		
Drafts	1	0	1k		
Trash Can	0	0	0k		
Total	103	99	1334k		

 [Contact Us|Help]

FIGURE 15-13.
You can create custom folders to store your messages.

2 Click Create. You'll see the Create Folder page. In the New Folder Name text box, type a name for the new folder, and click OK.

You'll see the new folder in the list on the Folders page.

Moving Your Mail to a Custom Folder

You can move your mail to a custom folder in two ways:

- Manually, following the instructions in this section.
- Automatically, using filters (described in the next section).

TIP

To group your messages for ease in moving them, click the From column-header button. This button sorts your messages in alphabetical order based on the text in the From field.

To move your mail to a custom folder manually, do the following:

1 In the In-Box list, check the messages you want to move.

2 Scroll down to the bottom of the page. In the folders list box, choose the folder to which you would like to move the messages.

3 Click Move To.

Editing and Deleting Folders

CAUTION
When you delete a folder, you also delete all the messages the folder contains. To save these messages, move them to a different folder (or back to the In-Box) before deleting the folder.

If you would like to change a folder's name, do the following:

1 In the Navigation bar, click Folders.

2 In the Folders list, find the line containing the folder you want to edit, and click Edit on that same line. You'll see the Edit Folder page.

3 In the New Folder Name box, type a new name for the folder.

4 Click OK.

To delete a folder, click Delete on the Folders page.

Filtering Mail

If you feel overwhelmed with the volume of low-priority or junk mail you are receiving, create custom folders, as described in the previous section. Then create filters that automatically route this mail to custom folders. The filtered messages won't appear in your In-Box, so you'll be able to see your important personal messages more easily.

To create a filter, do the following:

1 In the Navigation bar, click Options. You'll see the Options page.

2 Click Filters. You'll see the Filters page, with the Blocked Senders List at the top.

3 Scroll down to the Incoming Mail Filters area, shown in Figure 15-14.

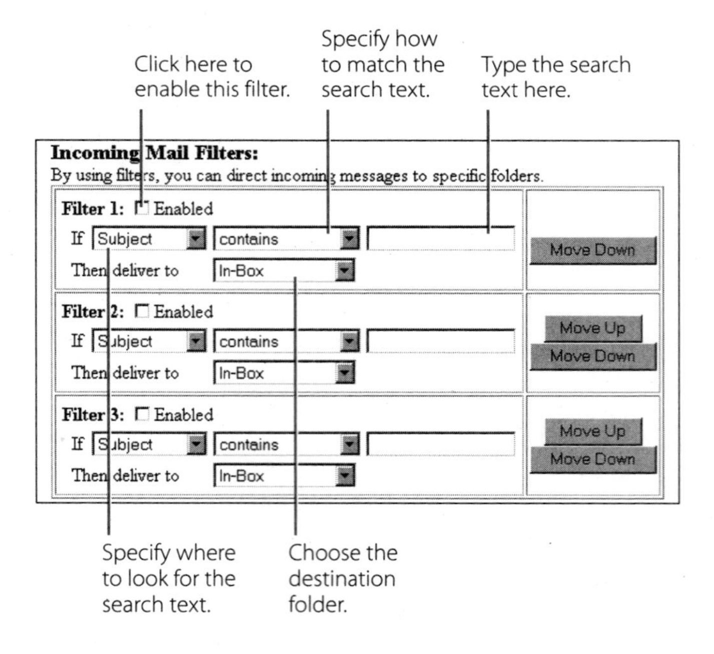

FIGURE 15-14. You can write filters that automatically route incoming mail to custom folders.

4 In the first blank filter box, click Enabled.

5 In the list box that shows the word "Subject," specify where to look for the search text. You can choose Subject, From Name, or From Addr.

6 In the next list box, specify how to match the search text. You can choose from the following options: contains, does not contain, contains word, starts with, ends with, and equals.

7 In the blank text box, type the text you want to match, such as a word, a phrase, a name, or an e-mail address.

8 In the the Deliver To box, choose the folder to which you would like to route the incoming mail.

9 Scroll down to the bottom of the page.

10 To apply the filters to all the messages in your In-Box, click Apply Filters Now.

TIP

If your filters don't work as expected, you may need to change their order. For example, suppose you've written a message that looks for messages from a co-worker, and you want these messages grouped correctly. But you've also written a filter that looks for the word "Hi" in the subject line (this is a favorite junk-mail trick). The "Hi" filter comes before the co-worker filter. What happens if your co-worker sends a message that contains "Hi"? You're right—the message goes to the junk-mail folder. To prevent this, move the co-worker filter up. To do so, display the Filters page, locate the co-worker rule, and move it above the "Hi" rule.

Personalizing Your Hotmail Account

You can personalize your Hotmail account in the following ways:

- **Update your personal information.** To update your personal information, click Options on the Navigation bar, and click Personal. You'll see the Personal page, containing the information you supplied when you created your Hotmail account. Edit this information, and click OK.

- **Change your password.** You should change your password periodically. To do so, click Options on the Navigation bar, and click Password. Type the current and new passwords. You can also type a hint question and answer. Click OK.

- **Create a signature.** To create a signature to be added to all outgoing messages, click Options on the Navigation bar, and click Signature. Type your signature in the text box, and click OK.

You can also choose the following preferences:

- **Appearance.** You can customize the navigation button style and the background style. The default option detects the type of browser you are using and chooses the best appearance.
- **Viewing Style.** The default option, Detect, detects the type of browser you are using, and displays a framed or non-frames version of Hotmail accordingly. You can override the default option by choosing Frames or No Frames.
- **Messages Per Page.** The default setting is 100; you can choose 10, 20, or 50. Your In-Box loads faster with fewer messages displayed.
- **Line Width.** The default setting is 80 characters; you can also choose 64, 72, 96, or 132.
- **AutoJump (Folders).** With this option turned on, selected messages are automatically moved when you choose a folder name in the folder list box (you don't have to click Move To).
- **Message Headers.** The default option, Basic, shows minimum header information. You can also choose Full, None, or Advanced.
- **Replying To Messages.** By default, Hotmail quotes the original message's text by placing a ">" symbol before each line. You can also choose a separator line or no marking of quoted text.
- **Including Original Text (Replying).** By default, Hotmail automatically includes quoted text when you reply to a message. If you click Manual, Hotmail lets you choose whether to include the quoted text.
- **Confirm Sent Messages.** By default, Hotmail displays a confirmation page to show that your message has been sent. To stop displaying this page, click No.
- **Cookies Only Authentication.** Choose this option if you are accessing Hotmail from a network that uses a firewall.

To choose preferences, click Options on the Navigation bar, and click Preferences. Choose the options you want, and scroll to the bottom of the page. Click OK to confirm your choices.

What to Do If You Forget Your Password

If you forget your password, do the following:

1. Go to the Hotmail Login Page at http://www.hotmail.com.
2. Click the "Forgot Your Password?" link.
3. In the Forgot Your Password pop-up window, type your Login Name. (Type your login name only, not "@hotmail.com".)
4. Click Submit. You'll see a page asking your hint question.
5. Type an answer to your hint, and click Show My Password.
6. You'll see your password on the next page.
7. For security reasons, you should now clear your browser's cache. To do so, click Tools on the Internet Explorer menu bar, click Internet Options, and click Delete Files.

CHAPTER 16

Joining Newsgroups

Microsoft Outlook Express isn't just an e-mail program. It also enables you to access newsgroups using the Outlook Express skills you've already learned. Outlook Express handles your mail and news messages using the same consistent user interface; for instance, the newsgroups to which you've subscribed appear as folders, exactly like your mail folders. Since you've already learned Outlook Express, you'll be able to send and receive Usenet messages in short order.

This chapter explains how Outlook Express enables you to use the newsgroups that may be available on your organization's computer system, as well as the tens of thousands of newsgroups available on Usenet, a massive public newsgroup network. (Chances are that your Internet subscription includes Usenet access).

This chapter assumes that you've already learned the fundamentals of Outlook Express. For an overview of Outlook Express, see Chapter 11, "Introducing Outlook Express."

Introducing Newsgroups

A *newsgroup* is a computer-based discussion group in which people can contribute original messages (called *posts* or *articles*), as well as replies to these messages (called *follow-up posts*).

When people think of newsgroups, they are usually thinking of Usenet, a world-wide system of public newsgroups. But many organizations run their own, private newsgroup servers, so the term *newsgroups* isn't exactly synonymous with Usenet. On the Internet, what enables newsgroup discussions is the Network News Transport Protocol (NNTP), discussed in the next section.

Understanding NNTP

On any network that uses the TCP/IP (Internet) protocols, newsgroups can be made available by means of the Network News Transport Protocol (NNTP).

Like other Internet services, Usenet consists of two types of NNTP-aware programs, *NNTP servers* and *NNTP clients*. An NNTP server makes messages available, while NNTP clients enable Internet users to access newsgroups and participate in newsgroup conversations. Outlook Express is a full-featured NNTP client.

Here's how NNTP works, in a nutshell. When somebody contributes a post to an NNTP server, the server broadcasts the message so that, within a few minutes to a few hours, every affiliated server contains a copy of the message.

What Is Usenet?

In brief, Usenet is a huge, public newsgroup service. On the Internet, Usenet messages are conveyed via the NNTP protocol, but other protocols are used to convey Usenet traffic over dial-up connections. With over 50,000 newsgroups available on many servers, Usenet is the largest computer-based discussion system in existence, and it generates an unbelievable volume of data—according to some estimates, as much as 100 GB per day. Admittedly, much of the bulk of this data consists of binary files, such as program and graphic files. Still, you'll find tens of thousands of topically focused newsgroups, many of which typically generate hundreds of messages per day.

Usenet generates a lot of discussion. But is it worth reading? For some, Usenet is a complete waste of time, an undisciplined playground for juveniles, egotists, pranksters, and bigots, all eager to push their uninformed opinions on others. Many people come to this conclusion after a brief Usenet session. There's a lot of hot air on Usenet to be sure. What's more, the network is susceptible to *spamming*—a practice in which inappropriate messages, including self-serving advertisements, are posted to hundreds or even thousands of newsgroups that have nothing to do with the messages' content.

TIP

If you see a message that's so unbelievably stupid that you feel forced to write a correcting response, you may have fallen for an old Usenet prank. To unmask the self-righteous, some people post *trolls*, which are obviously false statements that are planted in the hope that people will rise to the bait, making fools of themselves in the trollers' eyes. (An example: "Everyone knows *Star Wars* was directed by Francis Ford Coppola.") Another trick: posting *flame bait* (deliberately provocative messages that are posted in the hope of starting a *flame war*).

Spams, scams, trolls, and just plain nonsense aside, there are Usenet jewels too. The trick is to stay away from anything that sounds controversial; today's Usenet just doesn't handle controversy well. But if there's a Usenet newsgroup that's topically related to a hobby or professional interest of yours, chances are that you'll find Usenet close to indispensable. Particularly valuable are the many newsgroups that provide support and networking for people trying to deal with disease and death.

In general, the technically oriented newsgroups (especially those in the *comp* hierarchy discussed below) are of the greatest value; there's a genuine spirit of information exchange and resource sharing. Also of generally high quality are the *moderated newsgroups* in which every message is submitted to a human moderator who inspects each one to make sure that it's related to the newsgroup's topic.

NOTE

Please do not post messages to any Usenet newsgroup until you have fully understood the basics of Usenet *netiquette,* discussed later in this chapter. Netiquette isn't mysterious; it's just good manners. Be polite, think of other people's feelings, give credit where credit is due, and don't post anything when you're in the heat of anger. In particular, do not post requests for information that is already in the group's Frequently Asked Questions (FAQ) document.

How Are Newsgroups Organized?

With as many as 80,000 newsgroups available on Usenet servers, it's obvious that some kind of organization is needed to make all this material accessible. This organization is provided by the hierarchical system of newsgroup names.

Here's how this system works. Every newsgroup is part of a *top-level hierarchy,* such as *sci, soc,* or *talk.* The top-level hierarchy indicates the overall topic of the newsgroup; for example, *soc* newsgroups cover the social sciences, social issues, and socializing. Top-level hierarchies fall into three general categories.

- **The standard newsgroups.** Every Usenet server is expected to carry these newsgroups. Examples include comp, misc, news, rec, sci, and soc. In the standard newsgroup hierarchy, newsgroup creation requires a voting procedure, which controls (but does not completely eliminate) the creation of prank newsgroups.
- **The alternative newsgroups.** Anyone who knows the needed NNTP commands can create an alternative newsgroup (such as the thousands of newsgroups in the alt hierarchy). However, Usenet servers are not expected to carry all of these newsgroups.
- **Local newsgroups.** These nÑhìgroups are set up to benefit a local community, a state, a country, a university, a company, or an organization, and they are sometimes available to outsiders.

Table 16-1 provides an overview of the general subject matter of the most common newsgroup hierarchies.

NOTE

Your server may not carry all of the top-level newsgroup hierarchies listed in Table 16-1.

Every newsgroup has at least one other part to its name besides the top-level hierarchy, with the parts separated by dots: *misc.test, comp.risks.* This begins the process of narrowing group content.

Many newsgroups have additional parts to their names, which enable an even finer-grained topical focus: *alt.fan.tolkien, alt.fan.woody-allen.* There are dozens of alt.fan newsgroups. Here are some examples of newsgroups in the rec.photo hierarchy:

- **rec.photo.** General discussion of photography (unmoderated).

- **rec.photo.darkroom.** Discussion of photographic darkroom techniques and equipment.
- **rec.photo.equipment.35mm.** Discussion of 35mm cameras and lenses.
- **rec.photo.equipment.large-format.** Discussion of view cameras and lenses.
- **rec.photo.equipment.medium-format.** Discussion of medium format cameras and lenses.
- **rec.photo.moderated.** Moderated discussion of photography.

TABLE 16-1. Major Top-Level Newsgroup Hierarchies.

Name	Subject area
alt	Alternative newsgroups
bionet	Biology and biomedicine
bit	Discussions from BITNET, an academic network
biz	Business news, marketing, advertising
clari	Commercial, read-only newsgroups containing news and trade reports from wire services
Comp	Computers and computer applications
k12	K–12 education
Misc	Stuff that doesn't fit in the other categories
News	Usenet itself
Rec	Hobbies and sports
Sci	The sciences
Soc	Social issues and socializing
Talk	Discussion of social issues

What Is in a Newsgroup?

When you select a newsgroup to read, you'll see a list of the messages and follow-up messages that people have contributed to that newsgroup. Here's what these terms mean:

- **Message.** Also called a *post,* this is a *message* on a new subject.

- **Follow-up message.** Also called a *follow-up post,* this is a message that someone has contributed in response to someone else's message. Some messages never receive any commentary; others receive many follow-up messages. When there are many follow-up messages on a particular subject, a *thread* of discussion emerges, rather like a conversation. A good newsgroup reader program enables you to follow such a thread.
- **Binaries.** You can find graphics, videos, sounds, and computer programs on Usenet. Because Usenet can handle only ASCII text, they're coded in a special way that eliminates all but the standard ASCII characters. The resulting files are so large that they're often split into multipart posts. To download and use these files, called *binaries,* your newsreader must decode them. Outlook Express can decode both single- and multipart binaries, as you'll learn later in this chapter.

Although you'll find computer programs on Usenet, it's not a good idea to download and run one—at least, not without checking it thoroughly for viruses. It's safe to download graphics and videos (your computer can't get a virus from these), but note that more than a few newsgroups contain pornography, including illegal child pornography and other material that might not be legal in your area.

Introducing Outlook Express's News Features

This section introduces Outlook Express's Usenet capabilities, beginning with an explanation of how to configure the program. You'll also learn how to download the current newsgroup list from the news server and what the news-specific toolbar buttons do.

Getting the Information You Need

To configure Outlook Express to access your news server, you'll need the following information from your Internet service provider:

- **The name of the computer that runs the news server.** This server uses Network News Transport Protocol (NNTP), which is analogous to HyperText Transfer Protocol (HTTP).

- **Whether or not you need to log on to gain access to the news server.** If so, you'll need to know the user name and password you should use.

Configuring Outlook Express to Access Newsgroups

To configure Outlook Express to access your ISP's news server, do the following:

1 From the Outlook Express Tools menu, choose Accounts.

2 Click Add, and choose News. You'll see the first page of the Internet Connection Wizard, shown here:

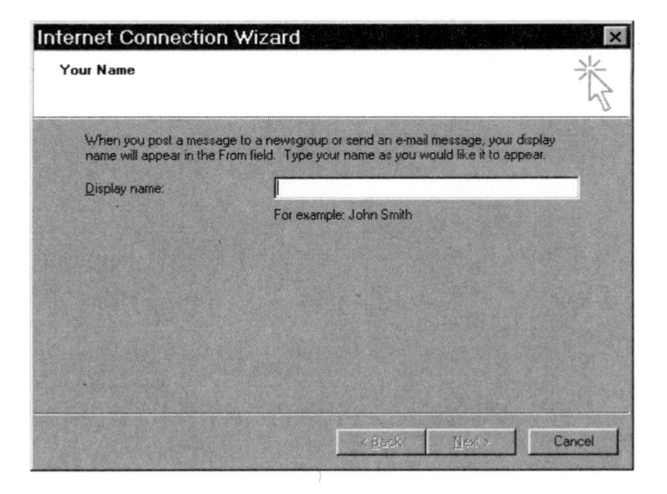

To avoid harassment, consider using a nickname instead of your real name. If you're female and you'd like to minimize unwanted advances, consider using a nickname that doesn't have an obvious gender, such as "Carter," "JB," or "Breeze."

3 Type the name that you want to appear in the From field of your messages, and click Next. You'll see the next page of the wizard, shown on the next page:

Internet Connection Wizard
Internet News E-mail Address
People can reply to your news messages by sending you an e-mail message at the address below--or they may post another news message.
E-mail address:
For example: someone@microsoft.com
< Back
Next >
Cancel

Consider whether you really want to put your real e-mail address here. Although doing so will enable people to send responses to you directly, you may also receive unwanted messages and junk mail. Spammers use automated programs that scan Usenet for e-mail addresses, which they then package and sell. If you do wish to use your real e-mail address, consider adding some junk characters and the words "NOSPAM" in the midst of your address (such as judyp@bog###NOSPAM###us.net), and add a note in your signature telling people to remove these characters if they wish to send you e-mail.

4 In the E-mail Address box, type the e-mail address that you want to appear in your Usenet messages, and click Next. You'll see the next page of the wizard, shown here:

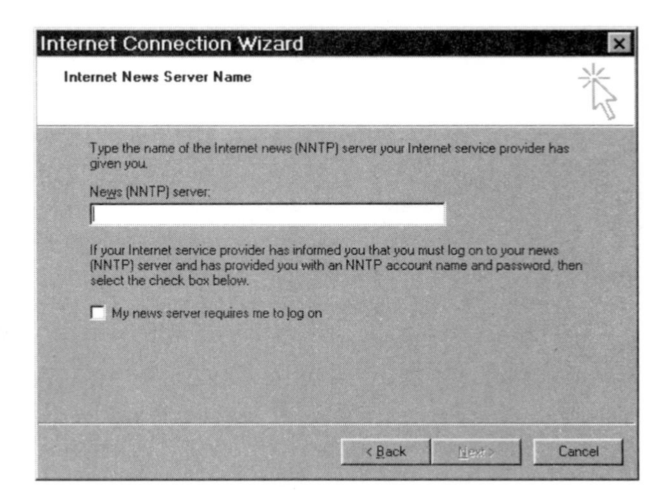

5 Type the name of your news (NNTP) server, and click Next.

If your news server requires you to log on, check My News Server Requires Me To Log On. After you click Next, you'll be asked to type the account name (login name) and password. If you would like Outlook Express to remember your password, check Remember Password. If your server requires Secure Password Authentication (SPA), check Log On Using Secure Password Authentication (SPA).

6 Click Finish.

Downloading the Newsgroup List

After you finish creating your account, you'll see a dialog box asking whether you would like to download the newsgroup list, as shown here:

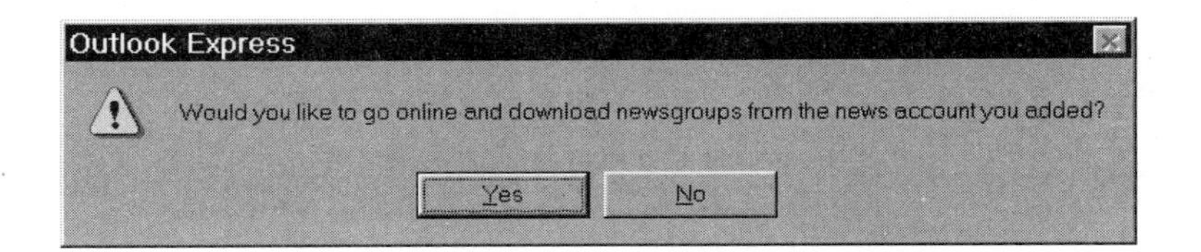

Click Yes. This could take a few minutes. When it's done, you'll see the Newsgroups Subscriptions dialog box. Keep this window on the screen; you'll use it to subscribe to newsgroups, discussed in the next section.

Creating Additional News Accounts

You can create two or more news accounts. Just repeat the procedure just described.

Subscribing and Unsubscribing

After you've created a news account, you should *subscribe* to one or more newsgroups. After you subscribe to a newsgroup, the folder list shows the newsgroup's name and indicates the number of unread messages available on the server. You can then easily read the newsgroup just by clicking its name in the folder list.

When you subscribe to a newsgroup, the settings you are making are purely local ones, involving only the NNTP client that's running on your computer. However, some people don't realize this and post messages begging to be unsubscribed from a newsgroup—which makes them look very foolish. You'll learn how to unsubscribe a newsgroup in this section.

Subscribing to a Newsgroup

Chances are you'll want to read anywhere from a couple to a couple of dozen newsgroups regularly. By subscribing, you create a list of interesting newsgroups that's a lot easier to manage than the entire newsgroup list (with more than 50,000 newsgroups available on many servers).

To subscribe to one or more newsgroups, follow these steps:

1. If necessary, display the Newsgroups Subscriptions dialog box. To do so, select a news server in the folder list, and click the Newsgroups button on the toolbar. You'll see the Newsgroups Subscriptions dialog box, shown in Figure 16-1.
2. In the Accounts area, select the news account you created.
3. Do either of the following:
   - To search for a newsgroup on a topic that interests you, click Also Search Descriptions, and start typing a word (such as "photography") in the text box titled Display Newsgroups Which Contain. Don't type the word quickly; just type one letter at a time, and watch the newsgroup list reset to list just those newsgroups that have names or descriptions containing the characters you've typed.

   or

   - To see all the newsgroups within a hierarchy, type one or more hierarchy names (such as alt.fan or rec.photo).
4. To subscribe to a newsgroup, select it and click Subscribe. You'll see an icon next to the names of newsgroups to which you've subscribed.
5. To see a list of your subscribed newsgroups, click the Subscribed tab.
6. Click OK to exit the Newsgroups Subscription dialog box without displaying a newsgroup.

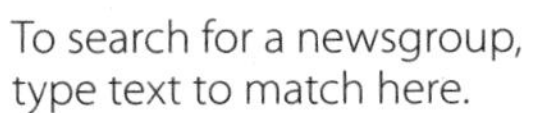

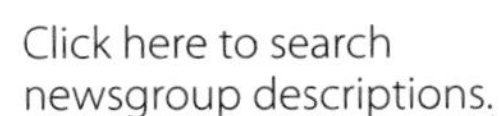

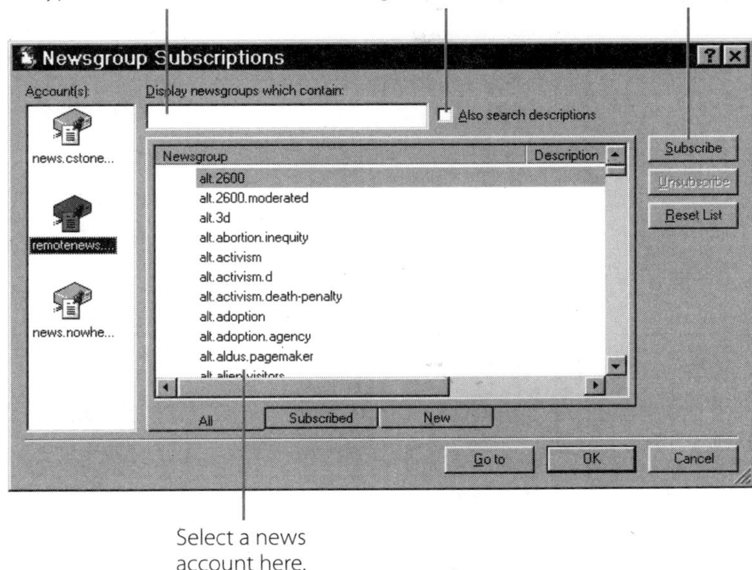

FIGURE 16-1. After you download the newsgroup list, you'll see the newsgroups in this dialog box.

> **NOTE**
>
> Please don't post any messages, original or follow-up, to any newsgroup until you have read the newsgroup for a couple of weeks and understand what type of message is appropriate.

Understanding What's on the Screen

When you access a news account with Outlook Express, you see special features that are designed to enhance newsgroup usage. The following sections explain the Outlook Express features that appear when you've connected to a news account.

Switching from Mail to News

If you've been using Outlook Express to read your mail, you can do either of the following to switch to the program's newsgroup mode:

- In the folder list, click a news account name.
- In the Outlook Express start-up pane, click Read News.

You'll see an Outlook Express window similar to the one shown in Figure 16-2.

FIGURE 16-2.
When you select a news account, Outlook Express changes to display news-related components.

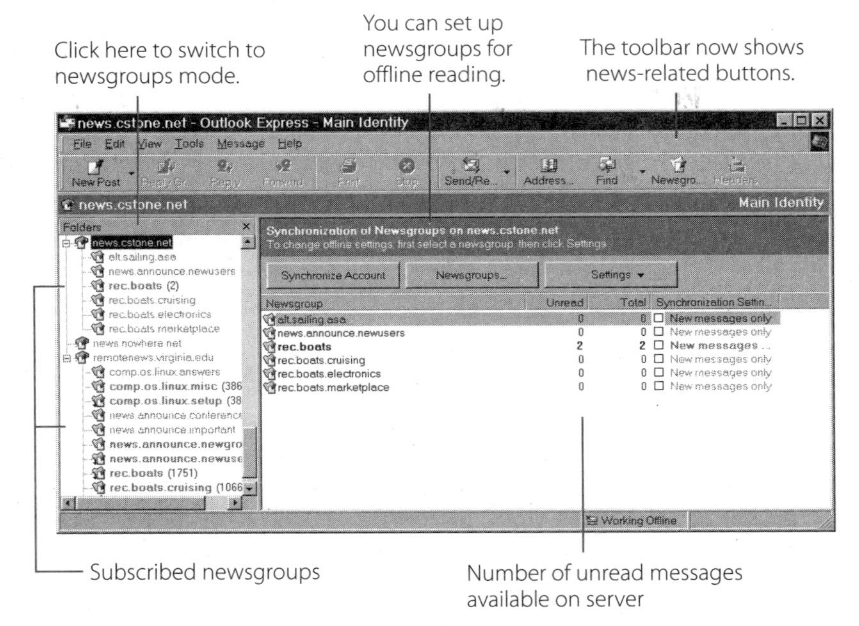

Examining the News-Related Components

In addition to the usual Outlook Express components, you see the following (see Figure 16-2):

- **Newsgroup toolbar.** The toolbar automatically changes to provide the most commonly used newsgroup buttons.
- **Folder list.** The folder list now includes the name of your news accounts. Beneath the news account name, you see your subscribed newsgroups, if any.
- **Synchronization Settings.** In this area, you can set up newsgroups for offline reading, which is discussed later in this chapter.

Using the News Toolbar

The News toolbar contains the commands you'll frequently use when you're exploring newsgroups (see Table 16-2).

SEE ALSO
You can customize the News toolbar. For more information, see "Customizing the News Toolbar," page 544.

TABLE 16-2. Toolbar Buttons (news account selected).

Tool	Action
New Post	Displays a blank New Message window, enabling you to write a new message and post it to the newsgroup.
Reply Group	Creates a reply to the selected message, which you can then post to the currently selected newsgroup.
Reply	Replies to the currently selected message by sending e-mail to the author (does not post a copy to the newsgroup).
Forward Message	Forwards a copy of this message to somebody's e-mail address.
Print	Prints the currently selected message.
Stop	Stops downloading the current message or messages.
Send/Receive	Sends your messages and checks the newsgroup for new messages.
Addresses	Displays your Address Book.
Find	Finds a message in the currently selected folder.
Newsgroups	Displays the Newsgroup window, enabling you to subscribe to newsgroups.
Headers	Gets new headers (message authors and titles) from the current newsgroup.

Reading the News

CAUTION
The header contains information that could enable a knowledgeable investigator to trace your posts back to you—and that's true even if you configured Outlook Express to use a pseudonym and a fake e-mail address. Don't try to use Usenet's apparent anonymity to express opinions for which you do not wish to accept responsibility.

Like e-mail messages, newsgroup messages consist of two parts, a *header* and a *message body*. The header information indicates the message's author, subject, reply address, and additional information.

Downloading Headers

To view the currently available message headers in a newsgroup, click the newsgroup name in the folder list. Outlook Express downloads the first 300 headers currently found on the server. To download additional headers, click Headers on the toolbar, or click Tools on the menu bar, and choose Get Next 300 Headers.

You can configure Outlook Express to download all the available headers. From the Tools menu, choose Options. Click the Read tab. In the News area, uncheck Get 300 Headers At A Time, and click OK.

Understanding How Outlook Express Displays News Messages

When you select a newsgroup, the Outlook Express window displays a message header list and preview pane, as shown in Figure 16-3.

The message list shows the headers currently available on the server.

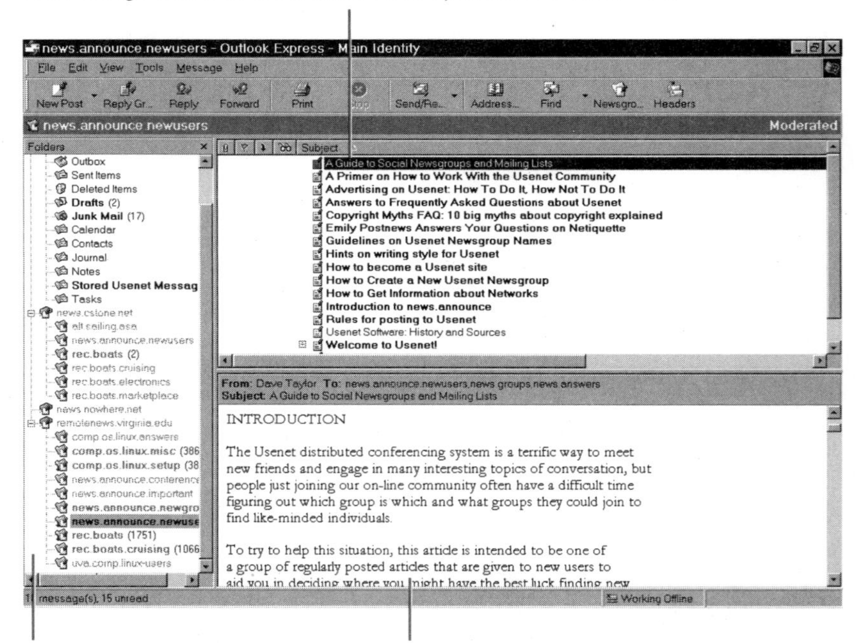

FIGURE 16-3. When you select a newsgroup name, you see a message list and preview pane.

To read a subscribed newsgroup, select its name in the Folders list.

The preview pane shows the body of the selected message.

When you select a message in the message list, you'll see the text of the message in the preview pane (see Figure 16-3). At the top of the preview pane, you see basic information about the message, such as who it's from and the subject.

Using the Message List

By default, Outlook Express organizes news messages in alphabetical order, sorted by the message's subject. The message list looks like a list of e-mail messages, but there's an important difference: messages with the same subject are grouped together. These groups are called *threads* or *conversations*, and they enable you to follow the discussion on a particular topic.

Examining a Conversation

Many posts receive no replies. If one or more people replied to the post, you'll see a plus sign next to the post's title, as shown here:

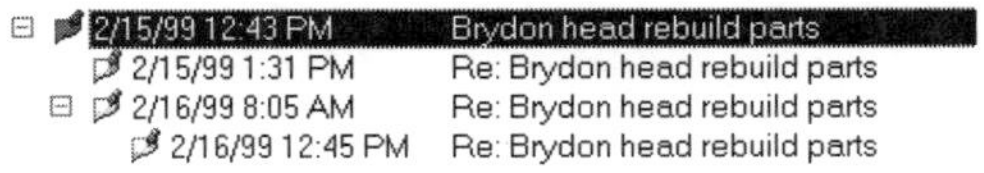

2/15/99 12:43 PM	Brydon head rebuild parts
2/15/99 1:31 PM	Re: Brydon head rebuild parts
2/16/99 8:05 AM	Re: Brydon head rebuild parts
2/16/99 12:45 PM	Re: Brydon head rebuild parts

Note that conversations can be nested, as the above example illustrates. The original post received two replies, and then somebody posted a follow-up post to the second reply.

Expanding and Collapsing Conversations

Conversations are collapsed by default. If you click the plus sign, all the messages that pertain to this subject will appear. The plus sign changes to a minus sign, indicating that all the messages are displayed. To collapse a conversation, click the minus sign. The messages are hidden again, and the plus sign reappears.

By default, threads are collapsed. If you would like Outlook Express to expand threads automatically, go to the Tools menu, select Options, click Read, and select Automatically Expand Grouped Messages.

Understanding Message List Icons

Table 16-3 lists the message-list icons you'll see when you're reading the news online (you'll learn about additional icons later in this chapter).

Navigating the Message List

When you're reading a newsgroup, you can use the same message-list navigation commands that you use when you're reading mail. In addition, you can use some commands that are specific to the special characteristics of newsgroups.

To view the next message down in the list, do one of the following:

- Press Ctrl + > (same as the period key).

  or

- Click View on the menu bar, click Next, and choose Next Message from the submenu.

To view the previous message (going up in the list), press Ctrl + < (same as the comma key).

To skip directly to the next unread message, do one of the following:

- Press Ctrl + U.

  or

- Click View on the menu bar, click Next, and choose Next Unread Message from the submenu.

To skip to the next unread conversation, do one of the following:

- Press Ctrl + Shift + U.

  or

- Click View on the menu bar, click Next, and choose Next Unread Conversation.

TABLE 16-3. Message-List Icons (online newsreading).

Icon	Description
	Collapsed conversation. Click this icon to expand the conversation.
	Expanded conversation. Click this icon to collapse the conversation.
	Unopened message. The message header appears in bold.
	Read message. The header appears in normal style (non-bold).
	Deleted message. This message has been deleted from the server and is no longer accessible.

To skip to the next newsgroup with unread messages:

- Press Ctrl + J.

  or

- Click View on the menu bar, click Next, and choose Next Unread Folder.

SEE ALSO

You can flag news messages, just as you can flag e-mail messages. To learn how to flag a message, see "Flagging Messages," page 354.

Sorting Messages

Like the e-mail message list, newsgroup messages are organized into columns, each of which has a header button. If you click the header button, you can change the order in which messages are sorted. Table 16-5 explains the column-header buttons that appear in the news window, and explains what happens when you click the buttons.

By default, the message list is sorted by the date received, with the most recently dated message at the top.

TABLE 16-5. Column-Header Buttons.

Button name	What it does
Attachment (paper-clip icon)	Sorts messages by whether they contain an attached file; these files are shown first. Same as clicking View, clicking Sort By, and choosing Attachment from the submenu.
Mark for Offline	Sorts message according to priority, with urgent messages first. Same as clicking View, clicking Sort By, and choosing Mark For Offline from the submenu.
Watch/Ignore	Sorts messages according to whether they have been marked for watching or ignoring. Same as clicking View, clicking Sort By, and choosing Watch/ Ignore from the submenu.
Subject	Sorts messages in alphabetical order by the message's subject. Same as clicking View, clicking Sort By, and choosing Subject from the submenu.
From	Sorts messages in alphabetical order by the sender's name. Same as clicking View, clicking Sort By, and choosing From from the submenu.
Sent	Sorts messages by the date received. Same as clicking View, clicking Sort By, and choosing Received from the submenu.
Size	Sorts messages by size. Same as clicking View, clicking Sort By, and choosing Size from the submenu.

TIP

To change the sort order from ascending to descending, or from descending to ascending, just click the column header button again.

Marking and Hiding Read Messages

As you'll quickly discover, a major problem with most newsgroups is the sheer volume of uninteresting posts. To use newsgroups productively, you'll want to learn how to reduce the volume of messages so that you see just the ones pertaining to topics of interest to you. In this section, you learn how to mark messages, conversations, and entire newsgroups as read, and how to use the View menu commands to hide read messages so that you're not assaulted with unwanted information.

Marking Read Messages

Just as when you're viewing an e-mail message list, unread messages appear in bold. When you select a message so that its text appears in the preview pane, or if you double-click a message so that its text appears in the message window, Outlook Express marks the message as read. The message no longer appears in bold and the icon changes. To mark a read message as unread, click Edit on the menu bar, and choose Mark As Unread.

If a conversation proves uninteresting, you can mark it as read. To do so, press Ctrl + T, or click Edit on the menu bar, and choose Mark Conversation As Read.

If you've scanned the latest crop of newsgroup messages and find all the new conversations uninteresting, press Ctrl + T, or click Edit on the menu bar, and choose Mark All Read.

If there's a huge backlog of unread messages that you haven't yet downloaded from the server, and you don't want to go through them, you can mark all of these messages as read (even if you haven't yet downloaded them). To do so, click Edit on the menu bar, and choose Catch Up.

You can automatically mark all messages as read when you exit a newsgroup. To do so, click View on the menu bar, choose Options, and click the Read tab. Check Mark All Messages As Read When Exiting A Newsgroup.

Hiding Read Messages

To cut down the number of messages you see, you can hide read messages. To do so, click View on the menu bar, point to Current View, and choose Hide Read Messages.

TIP

If you're looking for a message you previously read and can't find it, you may have chosen Hide Read Messages. To see your read messages, click View on the menu bar, point to Current View, and choose Show All Messages. To make the View options more accessible, consider displaying the Views toolbar. To do so, right-click the toolbar, and choose Views Bar. The Views bar contains a list box that enables you to show or hide read or ignored messages.

SEE ALSO

To gain more control over how Outlook Express shows or hides messages, see "Customizing Views," page 540.

Hiding Read or Ignored Messages

Another message-viewing option enables you to hide any message that has been read or marked as ignored. To choose this option, click View on the menu bar, point to Current View, and choose Hide Read Or Ignored Messages.

Watching and Ignoring Conversations

As you read a newsgroup, you'll find that some conversations are particularly interesting, while others are equally uninteresting. You can flag interesting messages by choosing Flag Message from the Message menu, but flagging only applies to the selected message. (Note: When you choose Flag Message, you'll see a dialog box asking whether you'd like to add the Flag column to the message pane. So that you can sort messages by whether they're flagged, click OK.) By marking conversations to watch or ignore, you tell Outlook Express to mark all the messages in an entire conversation (including messages you haven't yet downloaded) as messages to watch (interesting messages) or messages to ignore (uninteresting messages).

To mark a thread as watched, do the following:

1. Select the conversation.
2. Click Message on the menu bar, and choose Watch Conversation. You'll see an eyeglass icon in the Watch/Ignore column, as shown in Table 16-6.

To mark a thread as ignored, do the following:

1. Select the conversation.
2. Click Message on the menu bar, and choose Ignore Conversation. You'll see the ignore icon in the Watch/Ignore column, as shown in Table 16-6.

If you've marked one or more threads as Ignored, you can automatically hide them (along with read messages). To do so, click View on the menu bar, point to Current View, and choose Hide Read Or Ignored Messages.

TABLE 16-6. Message-List Icons for Flagging, Watching, and Ignoring Message.

Icon	Description
	The message is flagged.
	The conversation is watched.
	The conversation is ignored.

You can customize the color of your watched messages to make them stand out better. Click the Tools menu, and then click Options. On the Read tab, locate the option called Highlight Watched Messages With The Color. Select a color, and click OK.

SEE ALSO

You print news messages the same way you print e-mail messages. For more information, see "Printing a Message," page 351.

Using the Message Window

As with e-mail, you can read messages by selecting a message and reading the message in the preview pane. You can also read messages in the message window simply by double-clicking the message; you'll see the read-message window with the current message displayed (Figure 16-4).

Reading Coded Messages

If you encounter a message that seems to be complete gibberish, it's possible that it has been encrypted using the simple ROT-13 scheme, which rotates all characters 13 letters forward in the alphabet. In a more genteel day (that is, five years ago), Usenet posters would sometimes employ this simple encryption technique to prevent innocent minds from coming face-to-face with something outrageous. Should you encounter a ROT-13 encoded message, you can decode it promptly by clicking Message on the menu bar and choosing Unscramble (ROT 13).

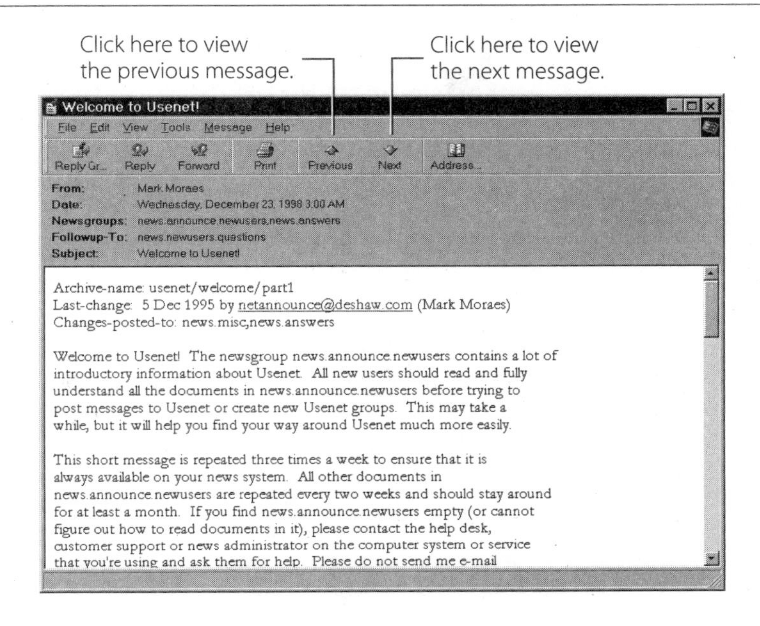

FIGURE 16-4.
You can read messages in the message window.

Adding Your Two Cents' Worth

After reading a Usenet newsgroup for a while, you will doubtless feel the urge to post something. You can send a message in three ways:

- **By replying via e-mail to the message's author.** This is the best way to respond if you have a specific comment or an answer to the author's question, and this information wouldn't be of interest to many people.
- **By posting a reply to the newsgroup.** Do this only if you think that what you have to say would be of interest to many people, not just the author of the message to which you're replying.
- **By posting a new message.** Although valid reasons exist to post messages on a new subject, you should do so only after you fully understand the mission of the newsgroup to which you're posting.

Understanding Netiquette

Before you post a message to Usenet, learn proper *netiquette*—Internet etiquette. Seasoned Usenet users expect everyone, including *newbies* (beginners), to follow some basic rules. If you break these rules, you could find yourself on the wrong end of a barrage of irate e-mail.

 **CAUTION**

Usenet posts don't remain on servers for long, but several companies, such as Deja News, archive Usenet posts and enable Internet users to compile a profile of all the posts you've made. A prospective employer might search your posts to learn more about you. So be aware: when you post a message to Usenet, you're *publishing* your words and whatever else you include in your post—you're making it *public*. Does this mean you shouldn't speak your mind? No, but it does mean that you should speak as if your audience potentially included every significant person in your life—your boss, a prospective spouse, your minister or rabbi, and your friends.

- Be sure to follow a newsgroup's discussion for at least a few days before you post a message. By doing so, you'll learn the types of topics that are appropriate for discussion. You'll also learn what's on peoples' minds, how you can contribute meaningfully, and how to avoid repeating discussions that have been exhausted.
- If the group has a FAQ (list of answers to frequently asked questions), by all means obtain it and read it. You'll find answers to the questions that newbies typically ask, and you're expected to know them. Newsgroup veterans will be annoyed if you ask the same question by posting a message to the group.
- Before posting a reply message to the newsgroup, consider carefully whether your response is really of interest to everyone. If a person asked a question for specific information, chances are that the reply would interest that person and few others. In such a situation, it's best to reply by e-mail. Your reply goes to the person who posted the original message, not to the group.
- When you post a new message, type a descriptive subject line. Don't simply say, "Help needed"—you won't get any. Be specific (for example: "Red Hat Linux 5.2 SCSI Install Problem—Help?").
- Don't post messages that extensively quote somebody's opinion or request, adding only the words "Me too."
- You can post messages to more than one newsgroup; this is called *crossposting*. Crossposting is legitimate when your message is genuinely relevant to more than one newsgroup; for example, suppose you're posting an article on the standard electronic equipment supplied with a certain brand of cruising yacht. Your post would be appropriate in rec.boats.cruising and rec.boats.electronics. Do not crosspost to newsgroups that deal with topics unrelated to your post.
- Never post in anger. If you read a message that bothers you, sleep on it. Chances are, the next day, you'll wonder why such a silly thing got to you.
- Don't criticize someone's spelling and grammar. Usenet is international in scope, and many Usenet posts originate from people who are still learning your language.

TIP

You can post news messages in richly formatted text (HTML) as well as plain text. However, you should not post HTML messages to Usenet since many people are not using HTML-capable newsreaders. By default, Outlook Express posts newsgroup messages in plain text. To make sure this setting is current, click Tools on the Outlook Express menu bar, click Options, and click the Send tab. In the News Sending Format area, make sure Plain Text is selected, and click OK.

Using a Signature

A signature—a necessity for e-mail—is something of a liability on Usenet. Do you really want your home telephone number to be published in a wide-open public forum, where it could be misused? (You can see for yourself how risky this is. Log on to *misc.invest;* often you'll see posts from people saying, "I just inherited $350,000. Can anyone tell me where I should invest it?" A con artist's dream come true!)

Still, you may want to include some information in a sig. If you're posting professionally to special-interest groups, such as those in the *comp* or *rec* hierarchy, chances are your message is less likely to be scrutinized by crooks or pranksters. You might want to risk including your full name and institutional affiliation.

There's also an old Usenet tradition of including a pithy (and preferably enigmatic or caustic) quote in your sig. One of my favorites, especially after considering recent Congressional legislation concerning the Internet, is from Mark Twain: "Suppose you were an idiot. And suppose you were a member of Congress. But I repeat myself."

To create a signature, see "Creating a Signature," page 429.

Posting a Message on a New Subject

To post a message on a new subject, follow these steps:

1 Display the newsgroup to which you want to post.

2 Do one of the following:

- Click New Post on the toolbar.

  or

- Click File on the menu bar, point to New, and choose New Message.

You'll see the New Message window, which closely resembles the New Message window that appears when you create a new mail message (see Figure 16-5).

3 If you have created more than one news account, you'll see a News Server list box. To send your message from a different server, choose the server in this list box.

4 In the Newsgroups box, you'll see the newsgroup that was selected when you clicked New Post. To select additional newsgroups for crossposting, click the Newsgroups button (this is the word "Newsgroups" next to the text box). You'll see the Pick Newsgroups dialog box, shown here:

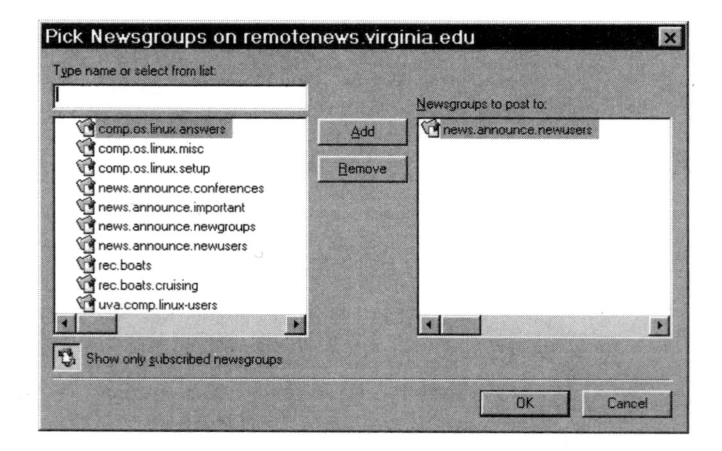

To show all newsgroups, not just the subscribed newsgroups, uncheck the Show Only Subscribed Newsgroups button. To add a newsgroup to the newsgroup posting list, select the newsgroup, and click Add. To remove a newsgroup from the list of newsgroups to post to, select the newsgroup, and click Remove. Then click OK.

5 To send a carbon copy of your message via e-mail, type the recipient's address in the Cc box, or click Cc and choose the recipient's address from your Address Book.

6 In the Subject box, type a short but descriptive subject for your message.

7 In the text area, type your message text. Be brief and to the point.

8 To include a binary file as an attachment to your message, click Attach, and locate the file you want to include.

9 Click Spelling to check your message's spelling.

10 To post your message, click Send.

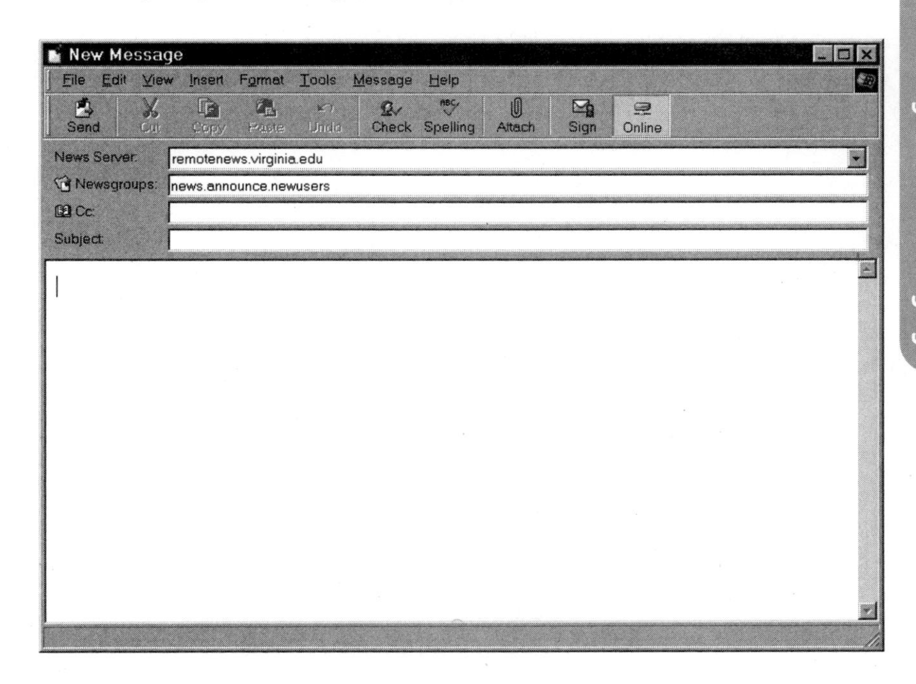

FIGURE 16-5. The New Message window enables you to create a Usenet message.

You may not see your post right away. Most Usenet servers process new messages during idle periods. Try waiting a half hour. Then click Headers and look for your post.

Replying by E-Mail

If your reply would be of interest mainly to the author of the original message, reply by e-mail instead of posting a follow-up message. To reply via e-mail, follow these steps:

1 Select the message to which you want to reply.

2 Do one of the following:

- On the toolbar, click Reply.

  or

- Press Ctrl + R.

  or

For more information on the New Message window, see "Understanding the New Message Window," page 365.

- From the Message menu, click Reply To Sender.

You'll see a reply window, which is identical to the one you see when you reply to an e-mail message. Outlook Express supplies the recipient's e-mail address and places "Re:" before the message subject.

3. Type your reply.
4. Click Send.

Creating a Follow-Up Message

You can usefully contribute to Usenet by sending a follow-up message if both of the following are true:

1. You actually possess some experience, facts, or ideas that meaningfully contribute to the topic under discussion; *and*
2. What you have to say will prove of interest not just to the original author but to many others who read the newsgroup.

If you're satisfied that your prospective follow-up post passes both of these tests, do the following:

1. Select the message to which you want to post a follow-up message.
2. Do one of the following:
   - On the toolbar, click Reply Group.

     or

   - Press Ctrl + G.

     or

   - From the Message menu, click Reply To Group.

   You'll see a reply window, which is identical to the one you see when you reply to an e-mail message. Outlook Express automatically supplies the recipient's e-mail address and places "Re:" before the message subject.
3. Type your reply.
4. Click Send.

TIP

> To reply to the group and send e-mail to the original message's author, and to do so simultaneously, choose Reply All from the Message menu, or press Ctrl + Shift + R.

Forwarding a Message

To forward a message to somebody via e-mail, follow these steps:

1. Select the message.
2. Do one of the following:
   - Click the Forward button.

     or
   - Press Ctrl + F.

     or
   - Click Message on the menu bar, and choose Forward.
3. In the To box, type the recipient's e-mail address, or click To to choose the recipient from your Address Book.
4. Type a brief message explaining why you are forwarding the message.
5. Click Send.

If you wish, you can forward the message as an attachment. An attachment is a separate, closed file added to the message you send. As long as your recipient's e-mail program can handle attachments, this file can be opened, read, saved, printed, or stored. This option is best if you're forwarding something really lengthy.

To forward a message as an attachment, do the following:

1. Select the message.
2. Click Message on the menu bar, and choose Forward As Attachment.
3. Type an address and add explanatory text if you like.
4. Click Send to send your message.

Understanding Message List Icons for Replies and Forwarded Messages

After you've replied to a message, Outlook Express uses message list icons to show you which action you've taken. These icons are shown in Table 16-7.

TABLE 16-7. Message List Icons for Replies and Forwarded Messages

Icon	Description
	The news message has been replied to.
	The news message has been forwarded.

Working Offline

If you must limit the time you spend online, you can take advantage of Outlook Express's extensive features for offline news usage. You can selectively download messages for later, offline reading, or you can create synchronization settings that automatically download message headers and bodies for selected newsgroups.

Downloading Messages Selectively

To mark messages for selective downloading, do the following:

1. If you would like to select certain messages or conversations for downloading, select one or more. (To select two or more messages or conversations, hold down the Ctrl key and click the messages you want to download.)
2. Click Tools on the menu bar, point to Mark For Offline, and select one of the following:
   - To download selected messages, choose Download Message Later.
   - To download selected conversations, choose Download Conversation Later.

- To download all the current messages, choose Download All Messages Later.

After you mark messages for downloading, you'll see a download icon in the Download column. See Table 16-8 for an explanation of these icons.

3 To download the messages to your computer, click Tools on the menu bar, and click Synchronize Newsgroup.

TABLE 16-8. Message Lists Icons for Messages and Conversations Marked to be Downloaded.

Icon	Description
[download icon]	Message marked to be downloaded.
[+ download icon]	Conversation marked to be downloaded.
[− download icon]	Original post in a conversation is marked to be downloaded, but the rest of the conversation is not marked to be downloaded.

Using Synchronization

With synchronization, you create downloading settings for each of your subscribed newsgroups.

Understanding Synchronization Options

You can choose from the following synchronization options:

- **All Messages** downloads all the message headers and bodies.
- **New Messages** downloads only the new message headers and bodies (since the last time you synchronized this newsgroup).
- **Headers Only** downloads only the message headers.

Choosing Synchronization Options

To set up newsgroups for synchronization, do the following:

1 In the folder list, select a news account. You'll see your list of subscribed newsgroups and current synchronizations, such as the illustration shown on the next page:

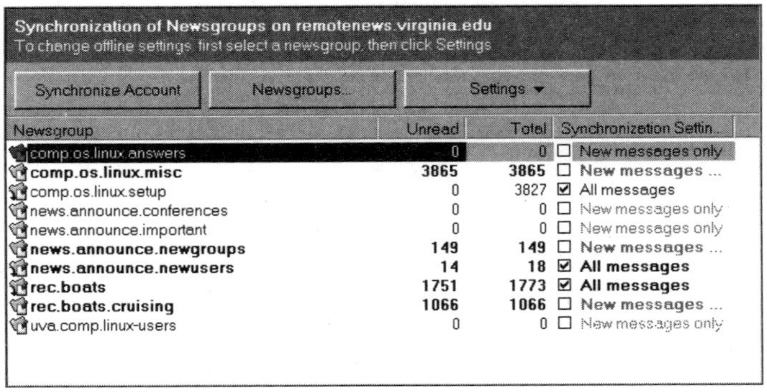

Synchronization of Newsgroups on remotenews.virginia.edu
To change offline settings, first select a newsgroup, then click Settings

Synchronize Account | Newsgroups... | Settings ▾

Newsgroup	Unread	Total	Synchronization Settin...
comp.os.linux.answers	0	0	☐ New messages only
comp.os.linux.misc	3865	3865	☐ New messages ...
comp.os.linux.setup	0	3827	☑ All messages
news.announce.conferences	0	0	☐ New messages only
news.announce.important	0	0	☐ New messages only
news.announce.newgroups	149	149	☐ New messages ...
news.announce.newusers	14	18	☑ All messages
rec.boats	1751	1773	☑ All messages
rec.boats.cruising	1066	1066	☐ New messages ...
uva.comp.linux-users	0	0	☐ New messages only

2 Select the newsgroup you want to synchronize.

3 Click the Settings button, and choose a synchronization option.

After you choose the option, you'll see a check mark in the Synchronization column, and you'll also see your synchronization choice.

4 If you would like to synchronize additional newsgroups, repeat steps 2 and 3.

Synchronizing Newsgroups

Once you've chosen synchronization options for subscribed newsgroups, click Synchronize Account to begin downloading messages.

After you've synchronized your newsgroups, you'll see special message-list icons that indicate that a message has been downloaded (see Table 16-9).

Viewing Downloaded Messages

If you would like to see the message headers for only those messages you have downloaded, click View on the menu bar, point to Current View, and choose Show Downloaded Messages.

TABLE 16-9. Message List Icons for Downloaded Messages.

Icon	Description
	The message has been marked read, and is stored in a message file on your computer.
	The message has not been marked as read, and the header and body are stored in a message file on your computer.

Decoding Binaries

With Outlook Express, you can download and decode binary files, including graphics, sounds, videos, and programs. What's more, you can do so even if they're split up into multiple parts, which is often necessary given the message-length limitations imposed by some portions of the Usenet network.

CAUTION
Bear in mind that binary files, including program files and Office documents, may contain viruses. If you download a file from Usenet, run a virus checker on the file before using it.

Downloading and Viewing an Attachment

To decode a binary file that's contained in a message, simply select the message. Outlook Express will download and decode the message, and it will appear as an attachment in the Attach box. This box shows the name and size of the files, and uses application icons to indicate which application will open this file, as shown in the following illustration:

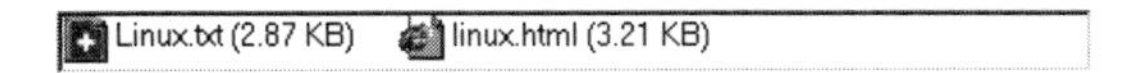

To open the attachment, do the following:

1 In the Attach box, double-click the attachment icon.

   You'll see the Open Attachment Warning dialog box, shown here:

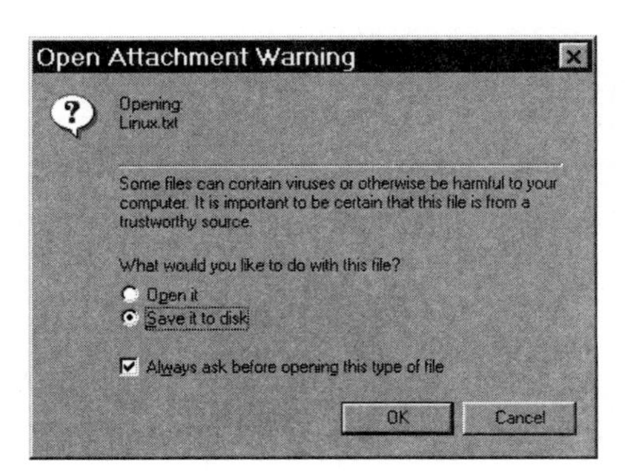

2 Do one of the following:

   - To open the attachment, click Open It.

   or

   - To save the attachment to disk, click Save It To Disk.

3. If you would like to skip this warning and open all attachments without seeing this warning, uncheck Always Ask Before Opening This Type Of File.
4. Click OK.

Decoding Multi-Part Binary Files

People who post multi-part binary files generally indicate the total number of files in the post, and each message indicates which part of the binary the message contains. Note the following example:

Picture of Yosemite valley (1/3)
Picture of Yosemite valley (2/3)
Picture of Yosemite valley (3/3)

To decode a multi-part binary file, do the following:

1. Select all the message parts.

   If you can't find all the message parts, you can't download the file.

2. From the Message menu, choose Combine And Decode.

   You'll see the Combine And Decode dialog box.

3. Make sure the message parts are in the correct order. To move a message part up or down, select the message part, and click Move Up or Move Down. When you are sure the message parts are in the correct order, click OK.

   Outlook Express decodes the message. You'll see the finished message in a message window; the binary file appears as an attachment, which you can open or save (as explained in the previous section).

Writing Rules for News Messages

Chapter 13 shows you how to write rules that examine incoming e-mail messages and performs certain actions based on conditions you specify. For example, you could write a rule that looks for the word "Suzanne" in the From field, and routes Suzanne's messages to the Suzanne folder.

You can also write rules for incoming news messages. For example, you can do the following:

- Automatically delete any Usenet message from an unwanted sender or server.
- Examine all the messages in all your subscribed newsgroups in search of subject words you specify, and flag these messages as important.
- Mark as watched any conversation whose subject contains words you specify.

To learn how to create rules, see "Creating Rules for Mail Messages," page 437. The procedure you follow to create rules for news is almost exactly the same, except for the following:

- When you see the Message Rules dialog box, click the News tab.
- For news rules, you use different conditions and actions, which are listed in Tables 16-10 and 16-11.

TABLE 16-10. Conditions for News Rules.

Condition	Description
Where the message is on the specified newsgroup	Looks for messages in the newsgroup you specify.
Where the From line contains people	Looks for a specified e-mail address in the From line of incoming messages.
Where the Subject line contains specific words	Looks for the specified text in the Subject line of incoming messages.
Where the message is from the specified account	Looks for messages among all the subscribed newsgroups in a news account that you specify.
Where the message was sent more than *x* days ago	Selects messages sent more than a specified number of days ago.
Where the number of lines in the message is more than *x* lines	Selects messages whose attachments exceed a specified number of lines.
For all messages	Applies to all incoming messages.

TABLE 16-11. Actions for News Rules.

Action	Description
Delete it	Messages that meet the condition you specify are moved to the Deleted Items folder.
Highlight it with color	Messages that meet the condition you specified are highlighted with a color of your choice.
Flag it	Messages that meet the condition you specified are flagged (a flag appears in the flag column).
Mark it as read	Messages that meet the condition you specified are marked as read (no boldface in the message list).
Mark the message as watched or ignored	Messages that meet the condition you specified are marked as watched or ignored.
Mark it for download	Messages that meet the condition you specified are marked for downloading.
Stop processing more rules	If a message meeting the conditions you specified is detected, rule processing stops.

Customizing Views

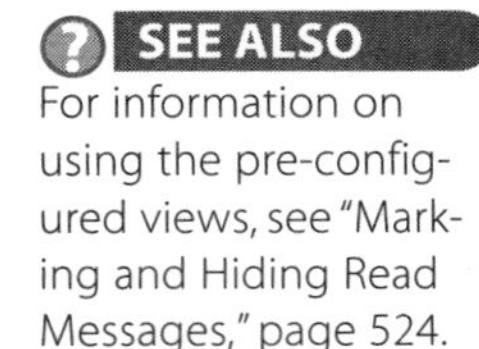

SEE ALSO
For information on using the pre-configured views, see "Marking and Hiding Read Messages," page 524.

To gain more control over how Outlook Express shows or hides news messages, you can create new, customized views. A view is a type of rule that checks messages to see whether they meet a certain condition, and then hides or displays the messages. Outlook Express comes with four pre-configured views (Show All Messages, Hide Read Messages, Hide Read Or Ignored Messages, and Show Downloaded Messages).

Understanding Views

Like rules, views enable you to specify conditions (see Table 16-12 for a list of conditions relevant to views). For example, you can ask Outlook Express to check messages to see whether they have been marked as ignored. For messages that meet the specified condition, you can choose to show or hide the messages.

What can you do with views? Here are some suggestions:

- Create a view that shows only the conversations that you've chosen to watch.

- Create a view to show only those messages that contain a certain word in the subject line.
- Create a view to show only those messages that have attachments.

TABLE 16-12. Conditions for Views.

Condition	Description
Where the From line contains people	Looks for a specified e-mail address in the From line of incoming messages.
Where the Subject line contains specific words	Looks for the specified text in the Subject line of incoming messages.
Where the message is from the specified account	Looks for messages among all the subscribed newsgroups in a news account that you specify.
Where the message was sent more than *x* days ago	Selects messages sent more than a specified number of days ago.
Where the number of lines in the message is more than *x* lines	Selects messages whose attachments exceed a specified number of lines.
Where the message has an attachment	Selects messages that contain an attachment.
Where the message has been read	Selects messages that have been marked as read.
Where the message body has been downloaded	Selects messages that have been downloaded for offline reading.
Where the message is flagged	Selects messages that have been flagged.
Where the message is watched or ignored	Selects messages that have been either watched or ignored or both.
Where the message is marked as priority	Selects messages that have been marked for low or high priority.
Where the message is secure	Selects digitally signed or encrypted messages.
For all messages	Applies to all incoming messages.

Customizing the Current View

To customize the current view, follow these steps:

1 Click View on the menu bar, point to Current View, and choose Customize Current View. You'll see the Customize Current View dialog box, shown here:

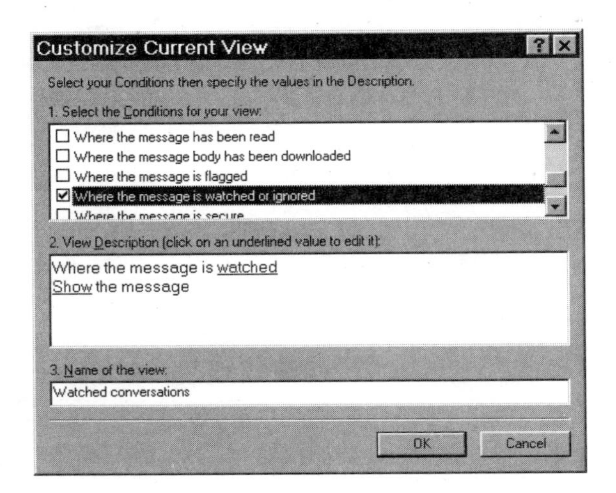

2 In the condition list, click the condition you want to use.

3 In the description list, click on underlined values to change them.

4 In the name area, type a descriptive name for your view.

5 Click OK.

Creating a New View

You can create a new view from scratch if you wish. To create a customized view, follow these steps:

1 Click View on the menu bar, point to Current View, and choose Define Views. You'll see the Define Views dialog box, shown on the next page:

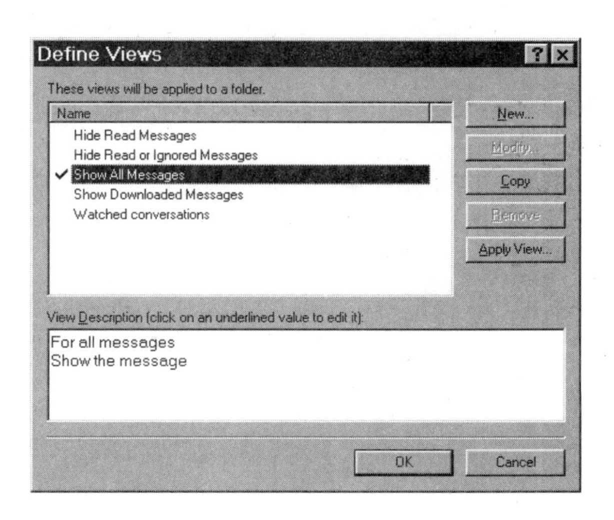

This dialog box shows all the currently defined views, including any you've created.

2 To create a new view, click New. You'll see the New View dialog box, shown here:

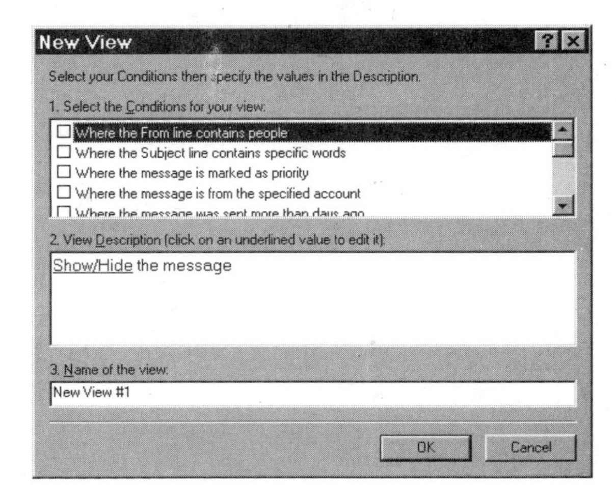

3 In the condition list, click the condition you want to use.

4 In the description list, click on underlined values to change them.

5 In the name area, type a descriptive name for your view.

6 Click OK.

Managing Views

Once you've created custom views, you can use the Define Views dialog box to manage them. To display the Define Views dialog box, click View on the menu bar, point to Current View, and choose Define Views.

To edit a view, select the view and click Modify. Change the condition and description, and click OK.

To delete a view, select the view, and click Remove.

To apply a view, do the following:

1. In the Define Rules dialog box, select the rule you want to apply.
2. Click Apply View. You'll see the Apply View dialog box, shown here:

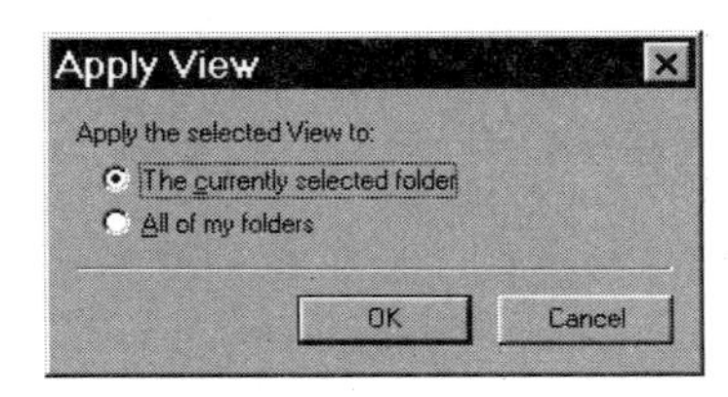

3. Choose one of the following:
   - The option The Currently Selected Folder applies the rule to the selected newsgroup only.

   or

   - The option All Of My Folders, be aware, applies the rule to all your mail and news folders!
4. Click OK.

Customizing the News Toolbar

For information on using the Customize Toolbar dialog box, see "Customizing the Outlook Express Toolbars," page 457.

To customize the Outlook Express toolbar for newsreading, right-click the toolbar background, and choose Customize from the pop-up menu. You'll see the Customize Toolbar dialog box, shown in Figure 16-6.

Chapter 13 discusses the Customize Toolbar dialog box in detail. Here, you'll find information on the available buttons for the main news window (Table 16-13), the news reading window (Table 16-14), and the New Message window for news posting (Table 16-15).

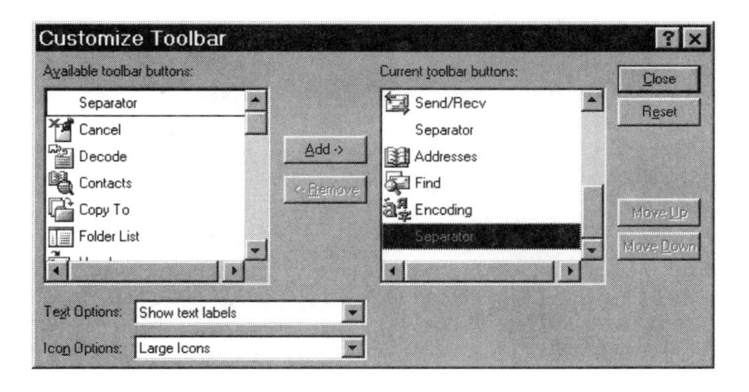

FIGURE 16-6. Using this dialog box, you can customize the toolbars that appear for reading and composing news messages.

TABLE 16-13. Available Toolbar Buttons (main news window).

Button name	Purpose
Default buttons	
New Post	Displays the New Message window.
Reply Group	Posts a follow-up message to the newsgroup.
Reply	Sends a reply to the message's author via e-mail.
Forward	Forwards the message currently selected in the message list.
Print	Prints the message currently selected in the message list.
Stop	Stops downloading headers and messages.
Send/Recv	Contacts the mail server, sends outgoing mail, and receives incoming mail.
Addresses	Displays the Address Book.
Find	Displays the Find Message dialog box.
Newsgroups	Displays the Newsgroups dialog box.
Headers	Gets new headers from the server.
Buttons you can add	
Cancel	In Usenet discussions, enables you to cancel a post you have already sent.
Decode	Decodes a multi-part message.
Contacts	Displays or hides the Contacts pane.

(continued)

TABLE 16-13. *continued*

Button name	Purpose
Copy To	Enables you to copy selected items to another mail or news folder.
Delete	Deletes the selected message.
Encoding	Enables you to change the encoding method.
Folder List	Shows or hides the folder list.
Inbox	Shows or hides the e-mail inbox.
Outbox	Shows or hides the e-mail outbox.
Sent Items	Shows or hides the sent items folder.
Help	Accesses Outlook Express help.
IMAP Folders	Accesses your IMAP folders.
Mark All	Marks all the messages in the current folder as read.
Mark Offline	In Usenet discussions, marks articles for offline reading.
Mark Read	Marks the currently selected message as read.
Mark Conversation	In Usenet discussions, marks a conversation as read.
Mark Unread	Marks the selected message as unread.
Move To	Moves the selected message or messages to a folder you specify.
New Mail	Displays the New Message window.
Newsgroups	In Usenet discussions, displays the newsgroup list.
Next Unread	Selects the next unread message in the current folder.
Next Folder	Selects the first unread message in the next folder.
Next Conversation	In Usenet discussions, selects the next conversation with unread messages.
Preview	Displays or hides the preview pane.
Purge	Removes deleted messages from an IMAP server.
Refresh	In Usenet discussions, downloads the message again.
Reply All	In Usenet discussions, begins a reply that will be accessible to everyone who reads the newsgroup.
Save As	Saves the currently selected message.

(continued)

TABLE 16-13. *continued*

Button name	Purpose
Sync All	In Usenet discussions, begins synchronizing messages according to your synchronization settings.
Undelete	Reverses the last deletion.
Unscramble	In Usenet discussions, unscrambles a message posted with ROT-13 coding.
Offline	Switches between online and offline reading modes.

TABLE 16-14. Available Toolbar Buttons (message window).

Button name	Purpose
Default buttons	
Reply Group	Posts a follow-up message to the newsgroup.
Reply	Sends a reply to the message's author via e-mail.
Forward	Forwards the message currently selected in the message list.
Print	Prints the message currently selected in the message list.
Previous	Displays the previous message in the message list.
Next	Displays the next message in the message list.
Addresses	Displays the Address Book.
Buttons you can add	
Copy To	Enables you to copy selected items to another mail or news folder.
Delete	Deletes the selected message.
Encoding	Enables you to change the encoding method.
Help	Accesses Outlook Express help.
Mark Conversation	In Usenet discussions, marks a conversation as read.
Move To	Moves the selected message or messages to a folder you specify.
Next Conversation	In Usenet discussions, selects the next conversation with unread messages.

(continued)

TABLE 16-14. *continued*

Button name	Purpose
Next Unread	Selects the next unread message in the current folder.
Reply All	Replies to the newsgroup and sends an e-mail copy to the message's author.
Save As	Saves the currently selected message.
Unscramble	In Usenet discussions, unscrambles a message posted with ROT-13 coding.

TABLE 16-15. Available Toolbar Buttons (new message window).

Button name	Purpose
Default buttons	
Send	Sends the message.
Cut	Cuts the selection to the Clipboard.
Copy	Copies the selection to the Clipboard.
Paste	Pastes the current Clipboard content at the cursor's location.
Undo	Undoes the last editing change.
Check	Checks e-mail addresses to make sure they are correct.
Spelling	Starts spell-checking the message.
Attach	Inserts an attachment.
Sign	Digitally signs the message.
Offline	Switches between online and offline use.
Buttons you can add	
Encoding	Changes the message's encoding.
Encrypt	Encrypts the message. This option shouldn't be used for news messages.
Recipients	Displays the Select Recipients dialog box.
Priority	Sets the message priority. This option shouldn't be used for news messages.
Insert Signature	Inserts the current default signature in the document.

Customizing Outlook Express's News Features

To choose options for news, click Tools on the menu bar, and choose Options. You'll see the Options dialog box. Chapter 13 discusses the many e-mail options you'll find in this dialog box; this section focuses on the news-related options.

Choosing General Options

To choose general options, follow these steps:

1 On the Outlook Express menu bar, click Tools, and choose Options.

2 If necessary, click the General tab. You'll see the General options.

3 Make a choice for the following news option:

- **Notify Me If There Are Any New Newsgroups.** Activate this option to see a message if Outlook Express detects new newsgroups on your news server. You may wish to turn this feature off if you're not interested in being notified about new newsgroups.

In the Default Messaging Programs area, you can see whether Outlook Express is currently configured as the default news handler. If the Make Default button for the news handler option is dimmed, then Outlook Express is the default handler. If the Make Default button isn't dimmed, click it to make Outlook Express the default-news handler.

SEE ALSO
This section discusses only those options that are specific to news reading. Many of the options discussed in Chapter 13 pertain both to e-mail and news, such as display fonts, signatures, and more. For more information, see "Choosing Outlook Express Options," page 419.

Choosing News-Reading Options

In the Read page of the Options dialog box, you can define a default font for viewing the messages you've received. You can also choose a few additional options for displaying the messages you're reading.

To choose news-reading options, follow these steps:

1 On the Outlook Express menu bar, click Tools, and choose Options.

2 Click the Read tab. You'll see the Read options.

3 In the Reading Messages area, choose a setting for the following news option:

- **Automatically Expand Grouped Messages.** This option automatically expands conversations.

4 In the News area, choose a setting for the following news options:

- **Get 300 Headers At A Time.** To change the number of headers that are downloaded when you enter a newsgroup, increase or decrease the number. To download all available headers automatically, uncheck this option.

- **Mark All Messages As Read When Exiting A Newsgroup.** This option marks all the current messages as read when you leave the newsgroup. When you next visit the newsgroup and download new headers, you will be able to see which messages are new.

Choosing Send Options

In the Send page of the Options dialog box, you can define the default settings that Outlook Express uses when posting your messages to newsgroups. If you post to Usenet, make sure the default is set to Plain Text rather than HTML.

To choose send options, follow these steps:

1 On the Outlook Express menu bar, click Tools, and choose Options.

2 Click the Send tab. You'll see the Send options.

3 In the News-Sending Format area, choose a default mail-sending format:

- **HTML.** Choose this option to send all outgoing posts in HTML by default. This option is not recommended unless you are using Outlook Express on a corporate intranet in which all users are known to have HTML-capable news programs. Do not choose this option if you plan to send and receive news posts on the Internet.

- **Plain Text.** Choose this option (recommended) to send posts in plain text by default (you can still selectively send posts in HTML format).

Choosing Maintenance Options

The Maintenance page of the Options dialog box contains several important news-related options. They can help you cut down the volume of stored headers and messages on your computer.

To choose maintenance options:

1. On the Tools menu of Outlook Express, click Options. You'll see the Options dialog box.
2. Click the Maintenance tab. You'll see the Maintenance page (shown in Figure 13-22 on page 434).
3. Choose settings for the following news options:
   - **Compact Messages In The Background.** Activate this option if you wish to choose any of the options indented beneath it.
   - **Delete Read Message Bodies In Newsgroups.** When you check this option, Outlook Express deletes the message bodies of read messages when the program performs the compacting operation. This greatly reduces the amount of disk space required for news storage. Don't check this option if you would like to keep message bodies indefinitely.
   - **Delete News Messages 5 Days After Being Downloaded.** When you check this option, Outlook Express deletes message bodies more than 5 days old when it performs the compacting operation. You can increase or decrease the number of days. This option also reduces the amount of disk space required for news storage. Don't check this option if you would like to keep message headers and message bodies indefinitely.

CHAPTER 17

Talking It Up with Microsoft Chat

Imagine getting together regularly with a group of friends. You share mutual interests, and you've gotten to know and like each other. The conversation is rewarding, and the friendship is real. But you're not meeting at the local pub. Instead, you're meeting in a real-time, text-chatting "channel," made possible by Internet Relay Chat (IRC). There's no other way you could meet, really, since one of your friends lives in Helsinki, Finland, another in Colombo, Sri Lanka, and a third in Kyoto, Japan. If this scenario sounds like fun, you'll want to try running Microsoft Chat, the full-featured IRC client that's included in the Internet Explorer software suite.

You can use Microsoft Chat for text chatting, but the program has an unusual twist. When you access Microsoft's chat servers, the program enables you to engage in graphics-based chatting, in which all participants—including you—are represented on the screen by means of comic characters. When you're using comic chatting, you can supplement your messages by choosing a range of differing emotions, including surprise, anger, pleasure, or boredom. Given that one of the limitations of text chatting is the difficulty of conveying contextual emotion, you'll find this innovation to be loads of fun.

This chapter focuses on Chat's comic chatting capabilities; however, Chat fully supports all IRC commands, which are discussed at the end of the chapter.

Introducing Internet Relay Chat (IRC)

Like all Internet services, IRC requires two types of software: *servers* and *clients*. Public IRC servers are maintained voluntarily by Internet service providers, software companies, freenets, and a few universities. Many organizations also run private IRC servers; for example, corporations use them to enable employee communication. In education, teachers use them to enrich discussion outside the classroom. Whether you're accessing private or public IRC server, you need an IRC client such as Microsoft Chat. On a single IRC server, you can join a conversation channel and get involved in a text-based give-and-take with as many as a dozen or more people at a time. Because public IRC servers can link with international IRC networks, you may be chatting with people who are physically separated by thousands of miles.

TIP

> For an introduction to IRC, try http://www. newircusers. com. You'll find plenty of information, tips, and strategies for successful IRC use.

IRC isn't like Usenet in the sense that it's a single, massive network, in which every server has an up-to-the-minute copy of the standard newsgroups. Rather, you'll find several different IRC networks, each of which has its own, unique characteristics (see Table 17-1). These networks are totally separate; if you're on UnderNet, you can't chat with somebody who's connected to DALNet.

Participating in public IRC networks can be fun, but it has a well-deserved bad reputation. For one thing, it's a hangout for some of the most malicious and antisocial hackers you'll ever run across, whose common aim is to ruin everyone's fun. In addition, there's a lot of illegal activity on IRC; many channels exist for the sole purpose of exchanging pornography (including child pornography) and illegal copies of commercial software (called *warez*). If you can manage to steer clear of the misfits and criminals, though, IRC provides an interesting diversion to the everyday grind. It's a fun way to spend a lunch break. If you're lucky enough to find a channel visited by like-minded people, and you return regularly, you can form lasting relationships that might migrate to other media, including e-mail and real life.

TABLE 17-1. IRC Networks.

Network name	Description	Home page
EFNet	One of the original IRC networks. Few safeguards against antisocial activity; not for beginners. Frequented by hackers who love to play tricks on newbies.	None
UnderNet	A friendlier version of EFnet with built-in safeguards against various antisocial tricks used to suppress discussion on EFnet.	www.undernet.org
DALnet	Specifically designed to provide a friendly environment with built-in safeguards against antisocial activity.	www.dal.net
IRCNet	A European branch of EFnet. Not for beginners.	None
ChatNet	One of the newer IRC networks; like UnderNet and DALNet, it's designed to provide a friendly chatting environment.	www.chatnet.org
Microsoft Chat Servers	Designed for use with Microsoft Chat; supports comic chatting.	http://www.microsoft.com/ie/chat

The Finnish Factor

Finland is a small Scandinavian country, but Finns are making a big impact on computing and the Internet. With a national population of less than most major American cities, Finland is nevertheless responsible for an impressive series of technical innovations, including the Linux operating system (widely used to run Web servers) and Internet Relay Chat (IRC).

Created by Jarkko Oikarinen in 1988, IRC went on to play a role in the demise of the Soviet Union. Linked by IRC, Soviet students and dissidents learned the truth that the state-controlled media wouldn't admit: the democracy movement was succeeding in its quest to break the Communist Party's control. Today, IRC has grown into a series of globe-spanning networks with an unknown—but huge—number of daily users. In recognition of Oikarinen's contribution to the Internet, the University of Oulu network administrator was the recipient of the 1997 Dvorak Award for personal achievement in global computer-based communications.

What's the reason for Finland's disproportionate contribution to Internet technical innovation? Finns say that the country's sparse population is a factor, and perhaps a major one. In remote areas, with only a few houses within hundreds of square miles, there's a thirst for human contact. That's one reason for the Finnish mania for cellular phones; 1 out of every 2 Finns has one. And 2 out of 5 are connected to the Internet!

In a text-based IRC client, the conversation runs like this:

> [Joe-Bob] Where are you from?
>
> [Nikkie] Belgium.
>
> [Joe-Bob] What part?

You can describe actions as well as type text:

> [Joe-Bob opens the bar and pours everyone a longneck.]

Getting Started with Microsoft Chat

Microsoft Chat is a graphics-based IRC client that links the give-and-take of IRC chat with a real-time comic strip. You choose one of several characters, and you see your character on the screen, interacting with others, as if you were living out a cartoon (Figure 17-1). The words you type appear in your character's word balloons in the frames of a comic strip. Microsoft Chat automatically inserts other characters in each cartoon panel and creates new panels as needed. Before long, you'll find yourself in a story. You can even give emotions to your character and choose to "say," "think," or "whisper" words to other characters.

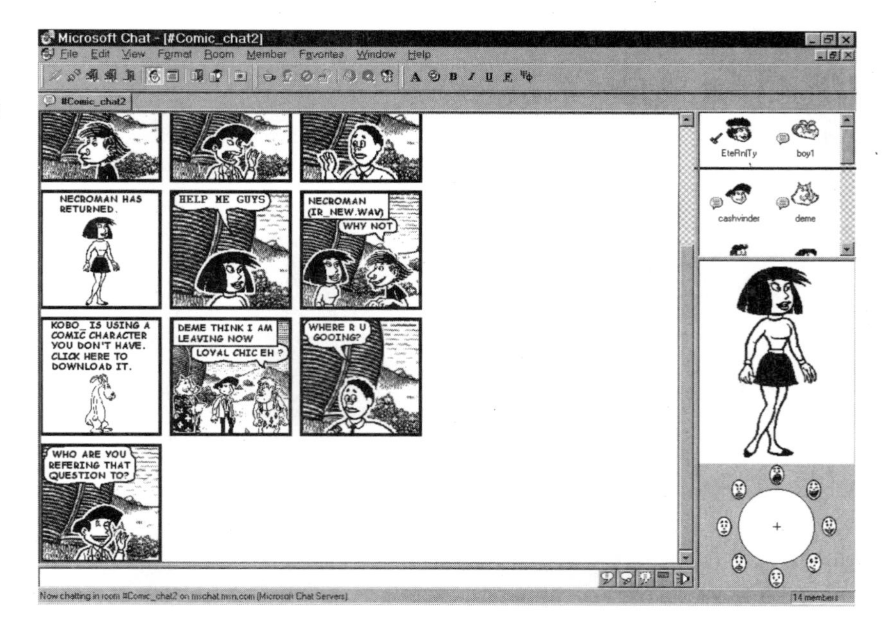

FIGURE 17-1.
Microsoft Chat makes you part of a real-time comic strip.

> **NOTE** Don't think that the use of comic characters in Microsoft Chat means that this application is for kids—it isn't. IRC discussion groups, called *channels*, often involve flirting, profanity, sexual situations, and aggressive behavior. It's strictly an adult playground.

Installing Chat

If you didn't install Chat when you installed Internet Explorer, do the following:

1. Start Internet Explorer.
2. From the Tools menu, choose Windows Update.
3. Follow the instructions on the screen to select and install Microsoft Chat.

Starting Chat

To start Microsoft Chat, follow these steps:

1. On the taskbar, click Start.
2. Point to Programs.
3. Point to Accessories.
4. Point to Internet Tools.
5. Choose Microsoft Chat.

   You'll see the Chat Connection dialog box, shown here:

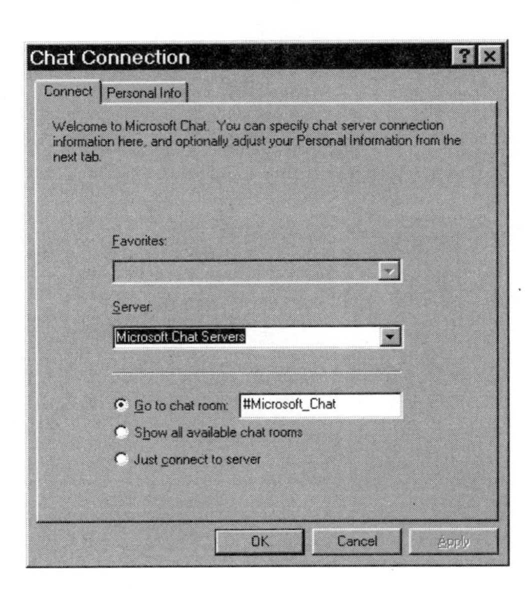

In subsequent Chat sessions, you can use this dialog box to connect to an IRC server. For now, you should choose a persona and supply needed configuration information before you connect. See the next section for information on configuring Chat.

6 Leave the Chat Connection dialog box on the screen, and proceed to the next section ("Configuring Your Personal Information").

A Microsoft Chat Romance (A Story from Cyberspace)

"Cleopatra, are you here?" I saw her name on the member list pane. Sure enough, she popped up.

"Hi," she said. But then Brutus walked in, and the rest is Microsoft Chat history.

It was supposed to be a discussion group for pet owners. After the usual round of introductions, we learned that Cleopatra, a nurse, lived in Australia, while Brutus, a musician, lived on the outskirts of London.

Cleopatra asked brightly whether we ought to talk about pets, but I pointed out that we really didn't have to, and Cleopatra beamed. It wasn't long before Cleopatra and Brutus fell to talking; it turned out that he works in an advertising firm during the day but plays bass guitar for a funk band in London at night.

As Brutus beguiled the lovely Cleopatra with compliment after compliment, she paused to ask herself, "Is he coming on to me?"

Seeing her train of thought, I whispered, "Yes, he is."

Cleopatra was thrilled. Not one to ignore a cue, I slipped aside and put some romantic music on the CD player.

In further conversation, Brutus and Cleopatra discovered that they had both visited Bangkok. They discussed the shows, the pollution, the traffic.

Smiling warmly, Brutus said, "I like you, Cleopatra." The happy couple exchanged their real names—and whispered more, but I couldn't quite catch what they said. I think they might have exchanged e-mail addresses.

At that very moment, though, the captivating Latoya arrived. Cleopatra exclaimed furiously, "Another woman!" Ever the gentleman, Brutus invited Latoya to stay, leading to a jealous tirade on Cleopatra's part. Latoya, feeling unwanted and unwelcome, left the room in a huff.

I was starting to feel the way Latoya did, but I thought I still had a role to play. I was right, too.

"I apologize for getting jealous," Cleopatra said, adding, "She is attractive, though," in a none-too-subtle test.

"Not as attractive as you, though," Brutus replied, adroitly.

Cleopatra thought to herself, "He's so sweet."

Brutus chose that very moment to pop the question, "Will you marry me, Cleopatra?"

A Microsoft Chat Romance ***continued***

"Well...," Cleopatra replied.

I whispered to Cleopatra, "You hardly know him."

Cleopatra played for time. "Should I or shouldn't I?" she mused. "He is attractive."

Brutus urged her on, a bit too aggressively, I thought, so I whispered to him, "Don't pressure her! Give her time and be supportive!"

"Thanks," Brutus whispered back.

But Brutus had won me over, too. I found myself whispering to Cleopatra, "Actually he is a very nice guy."

This did the trick. "Well, OK Brutus, let's get married."

I congratulated the happy couple.

Cleopatra turned to me, radiant. "If it wasn't for you convincing me.... Thanks."

The couple agreed to live in Bangkok. Brutus asked me to be the best man. Just then Jetboy happened by, and after a quick, whispered exchange, he agreed to perform the nuptials. Just as Brutus slipped the ring on Cleopatra's finger, though, she said, "But...," leading Jetboy to say, a tad testily, "It's a little late now, isn't it?" Cleopatra relaxed and beamed, and before any of us knew what had happened, Brutus and Cleopatra had slipped away.

Configuring Your Personal Information

To configure your personal information, do the following:

1 In the Chat Connection dialog box, click the Personal Info tab. You'll see the Personal Info page, as shown here:

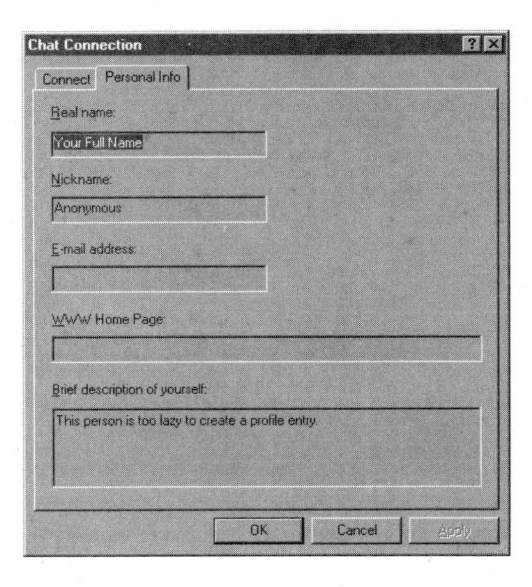

2. In the Real Name box, type your real name if you wish. This is strictly optional, and it's not recommended if you're planning to chat on the public IRC.
3. In the Nickname box, type a nickname. This is the name IRC users will see.
4. In the E-mail Address box, type your e-mail address if you wish. Again, this is strictly optional; it's not recommended if you're planning to chat on the public IRC. You can supply your e-mail address to individuals whom you have reason to trust.
5. In the WWW Home Page box, type the address of your personal home page, if any. Again, this isn't recommended if you're planning to chat on the public IRC.
6. In the Brief Description Of Yourself box, type a brief personal description. IRC users can access and read this information to learn more about you.
7. Click Apply to save this information.
8. Click Cancel to close the Chat Connection dialog box without connecting, and proceed to the next section.

   You'll see a dialog box informing you that you're working offline now.
9. Click OK.

Choosing a Character

If you're planning to try comic chatting, you need to choose a character for yourself. To do so, follow these steps:

1. From the View menu, choose Comic Strip.
2. From the View menu, choose Options. You'll see the Microsoft Chat Options dialog box.
3. Click the Character tab. You'll see the list of characters, shown in Figure 17-2.
4. Below the preview pane, drag within the emotion wheel to choose a default emotion for your character.
5. Click Comics View. The important option here is Page Layout. Choose a panel width (1, 2, 3, or 4 panels) that doesn't cause your screen to scroll horizontally. (If you later find that the screen

scrolls, choose this command again and reduce the number of displayed panels.) Try 2 to start.

6 Click the Background tab and choose the background you prefer.

7 Click OK.

If you don't see the Character tab in the Options dialog box, click OK, and choose Comic Strip from the View menu. When you choose Options from the View menu, you'll see the Character tab.

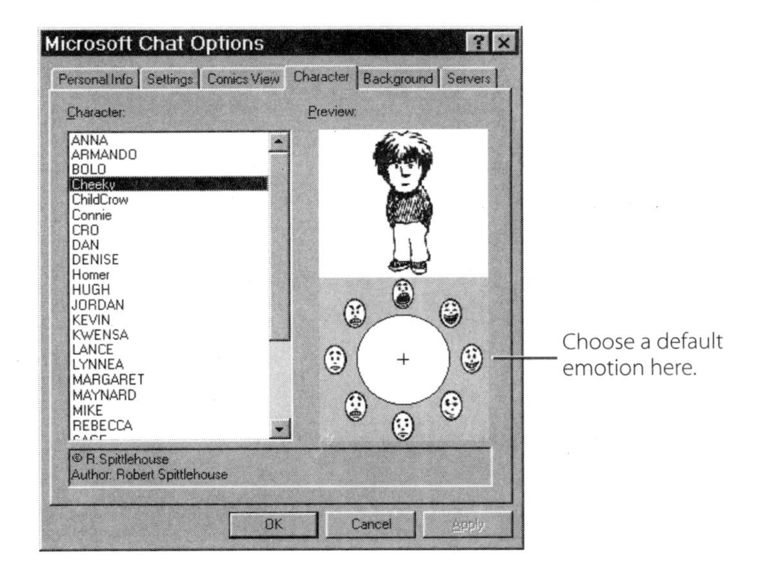

FIGURE 17-2. For comic chatting, choose a character.

Understanding the Chat Window

The Chat window (Figure 17-3) has four panes:

- **Self-View Pane.** Here's your character. To choose emotions, drag around the black dot in the emotion wheel. At the edges, you find the eight extreme emotions: Shout, Angry, Happy, Bored, Sad, Laugh, Scared, Coy. As you drag the dot from the edge toward the center, the emotion is less extreme. Take some time to experiment with the emotion wheel. To adopt a neutral pose, drag the dot to the center. (If you access an IRC server in the plain-text mode, you don't see the self-view pane.)

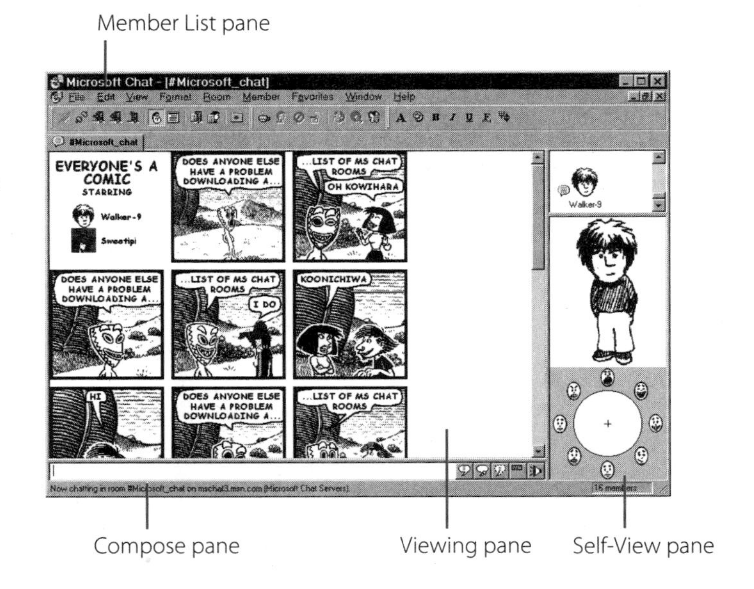

FIGURE 17-3.
When you're using comic chatting, you use these parts of the Chat window.

- **Member List Pane.** This pane lists the current characters. You can view the member list as text names or icons. To select one of these options, go to the View menu, select Member List, and then choose List or Icon. You can also click the right mouse button within the member list pane and choose List or Icon.
- **Viewing Pane.** Here you see the underlying IRC conversation as a comic strip. If you'd like to see just the text, go to the View menu and select Plain Text. To restore the comic strip, choose Comic Strip.
- **Compose Pane.** In this pane, you type the words that you want to appear in your character's word balloon. You can choose Say (words everyone can read), Think (thoughts everyone can read), Whisper (words only one person can read), and Action (words, prefaced by your nickname, that appear at the top of the cartoon panel). You can also click Play Sound to play a .wav file that others will hear (if their computers support .wav sounds).

NOTE

> You can view more than one chat room at a time. Each room is tabbed (note #Microsoft_chat tab at the top of the viewing pane in Figure 17-3). To switch to a different room, click the room's tab.

Using the Chat Toolbar

As with most Internet Explorer modules, you'll find that the most frequently used commands are found on the toolbar. Table 17-2 explains the buttons on the Chat toolbar from left to right.

TABLE 17-2. Chat Toolbar Buttons.

Tool	Action
Connect	Opens the Chat Connection dialog box and enables you to connect to a chat server.
Disconnect	Breaks the current connection with the chat server.
Enter Room	Displays the Enter Room dialog box, which enables you to type the name of an existing or new room to enter.
Leave Room	Leaves the room you're currently in.
Create Room	Creates a new chat room.
Comics View	View the comic characters.
Text View	Chat using text only.
Chat Room List	View the current list of chat groups.
User List	View the current list of users online. (You can also search for a specific user.)
Open Favorites	Opens your Favorites folder and enables you to add a conversation to your favorites list.
Away From Keyboard	Advises chat room members that you're away from the keyboard.
Get Identity	Get the selected person's identity.
Ignore	Ignore the selected person.
Whisper Box	Lets you carry on more than one whispered conversation at a time.
Send Email	Sends e-mail to the selected user.
Visit HomePage	Opens the Web page of the selected user.
MSN Community Center	Accesses the MSN Community Center for Web-based chatting.
Set Font	Changes the font used.
Set Font Color	Changes the font color of the outgoing text.

(continued)

TABLE 17-2. *continued*

Tool	Action
Set/Reset Bold	Boldfaces the outgoing text.
Set/Reset Italic	Italicizes the outgoing text.
Set/Reset Underline	Underlines the outgoing text.
Set/Reset Fixed Pitch Font	Sets the pitch of the outgoing text.
Set/Reset Symbol Font	Sets the symbol attribute of the outgoing text.

Action Buttons

When you're chatting in comic mode, you can use the action buttons that appear to the right of the compose pane. These buttons are shown below. Table 17-3 explains what these buttons do.

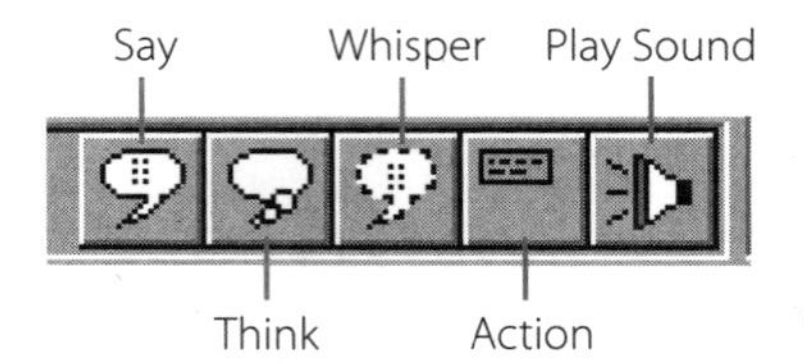

TABLE 17-3. Action Buttons (comic chat).

Tool	Action
Say	Makes a statement that appears inside a word balloon.
Think	Shows a word balloon with "thought" bubbles around it (you're thinking something to yourself but others can see it).
Whisper	Sends a word balloon that is visible only to the people you have selected in the member list. The word "balloon" is surrounded by a dotted line to indicate that it's a whisper.
Action	Describes an action you are undertaking. The description appears in a box across the top of the comic-strip pane. Your nickname is indicated as the source of the action.
Play Sound	Plays a sound, but only if other chat room members have the sound installed on their computers. The sound is indicated in a box at the top of the comic-strip pane. Your nickname is indicated as the source of the sound.

Connecting to an IRC Server

Now that you've configured Chat, try connecting to a chat server and joining a chat channel. You can connect using the predefined networks and servers. In addition, you can configure Chat with information that will enable you to access networks and servers not included in the predefined lists.

Connecting to a Predefined Network and Server

Chat contains predefined connection information for a number of popular IRC networks, including the Microsoft Chat Servers (which enable you to use comic chatting).

To connect to an IRC server:

1. From the View menu, choose one of the following:

   - **Comic Strip.** Choose this option if you're planning to access one of the Microsoft Chat Servers and plan to use the comic chatting mode. After choosing this option, you'll see the self-view pane.

   - **Plain Text.** Choose this option if you're planning to access any other IRC server. After choosing this option, the self-view pane is hidden.

2. Do one of the following:

   - On the toolbar, click Connect.

     or

   - From the File menu, choose New Connection.

     or

   - Press Ctrl + N.

   You'll see the Chat Connection dialog box, with the Connect page displayed.

3. In the Server list box, choose an IRC network. You can choose from Microsoft Chat Servers, as well as several established IRC networks (including EFNet, DALNet, Undernet, IRCNet, and ChatNet).

If you would like to try one of the IRC networks, remember that DALNet, Undernet, and ChatNet are likely to provide the friendliest experience for newcomers.

4 Choose one of the following:

- **Go To Chat Room.** By default, this option is configured to take you to a beginner's chat room on the Microsoft Chat Server.
- **Show All Available Chat Rooms.** This option displays a list of chat rooms so you can choose which room to enter.
- **Just Connect To The Server.** This option establishes a connection with the server; you can choose a chat room later.

5 Click OK.

Chat attempts to connect to a chat server. If the connection is successful, you'll see a dialog box containing a message from the server, such as the following:

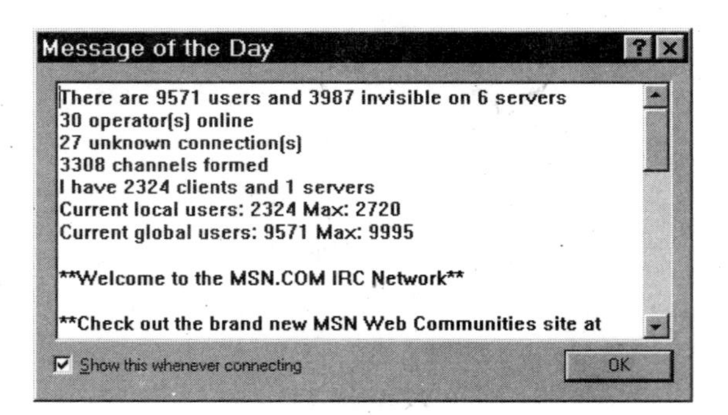

Depending on which server you access, you may see information on how many users are online. You may also see the server's usage policy.

6 Click OK.

Adding and Removing Servers and Networks

Microsoft Chat comes with a good selection of servers for several networks. However, there are many additional networks. What's more, on each network, servers come and go. By following the instructions in this section, you can add or remove networks and servers.

TIP

> On IRC, small is beautiful. The larger the network, the more likely it is that network administrators will have lost the ability to cope with hackers. The newer, smaller networks, such as those discussed in Table 17-4, offer a much more congenial chatting environment.

Adding a Network

To add a network, follow these steps:

1. On the View menu, click Options. You'll see the Microsoft Chat Options dialog box.
2. Click Servers. You'll see the Servers page, shown here:

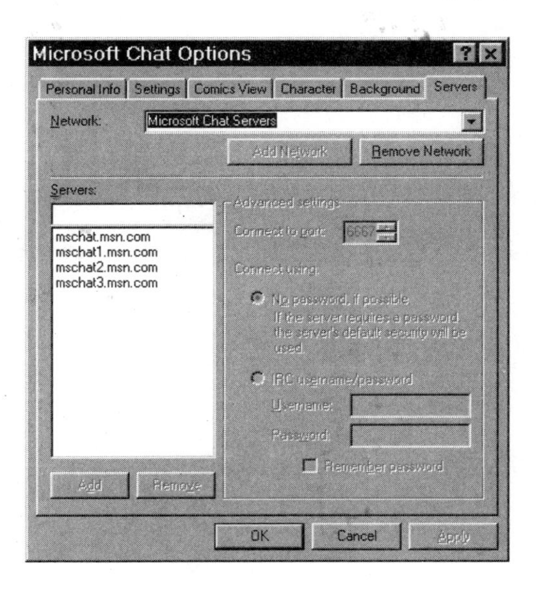

3. In the Network box, type the network's name.
4. Click Add Network.

   Chat adds the network's name to the network list.

   Before you can use this network, you must add servers, as described in the following section.

Adding a Server

You can add two types of servers:

- **Random server connection.** Some servers provide addresses that enable you to connect automatically to any available server. If you're adding a network that makes a random server connection available, be sure to add this server address. It's convenient to use because Chat will keep trying until it finds an available server.
- **Specific server address.** You can specify server addresses. You will also need to specify the port number, so be sure to obtain this information.

To add a server, follow these steps:

1. On the View menu, click Options. You'll see the Microsoft Chat Options dialog box.
2. Click Servers. You'll see the Servers page.
3. In the Network box, choose the network that the server uses.
4. In the Servers box, type the server address then click Add.

TABLE 17-4. Additional IRC Networks.

Network	Description	Random server address	Web page
BeyondIRC	A new, small network stressing friendly chatting in a supportive atmosphere.	irc. snowhill. com	http://www. beyondirc. net
Mystical. Net	A new, small network with an emphasis on magic, mysticism, and hassle-free chatting.	irc. mystical. net	http://www. mystical. net
StarChat	Emphasizes science-fiction and role playing.	See the list of servers at http://www. starchat. net/ servers. html	http://www. starchat. net.
WonkNet	New, small network with an emphasis on reliable inter-server connectivity.	See the list of servers at http://www. wonk. net/ servers/	http://www. wonk.net
Xworld	New, small network with an emphasis on hassle-free, high-speed chatting.	See the list of servers at http://www. xworld. org/ servers/	http://www. xworld. org

5. In the Connect To Port box, change the port number, if necessary. The default port number for IRC is 6667, but some servers use different port numbers.

6 Under Connect Using, you can set up password authentication. Click IRC Username/Password, and type your user name and password. If you would like Chat to remember the password so that you do not have to type it every time you access this server, click Remember Password. (Do not choose this option if your computer is used by others.)

7 Click OK to confirm your server options.

Choosing a Channel

Unless you specified a channel when you connected to the server, you must choose a chatting channel in order to join a conversation. If you know the name of the channel, you can join it directly. Alternatively, you can display a list of all available channels, and choose one from the list. You can also search the channel list.

Going to a Channel Directly

To go to a channel when you know its exact name, follow these steps:

1 Do one of the following:

- On the toolbar, click Enter Room.

  or

- From the Room menu, choose Enter Room.

You'll see the Enter Room dialog box, shown here:

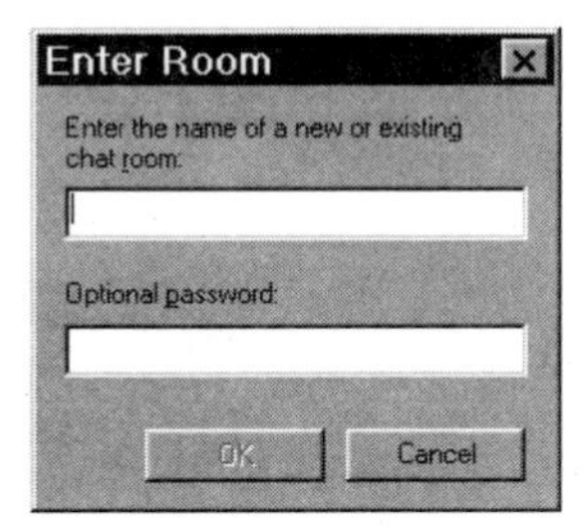

2 Type the name of the room.

3 If necessary, type the password.

4 Click OK.

Displaying the Room List

To display a list of all available rooms, follow these steps:

1. Do one of the following:

   - On the toolbar, click Chat Room List.

     or

   - From the Room menu, choose Room List.

   You'll see the Chat Room List dialog box, shown in Figure 17-4.

2. To search for a room manually, scroll down the list of available chat rooms. To re-sort the list, click any of the column-header buttons (Room, Members, or Topic). To change the sort order from ascending to descending, or vice versa, click the button again.

3. To display only those chat rooms whose names contain characters you specify, type the characters in the text box at the top of the dialog box. To search room topics too, check Also Search In Room Topics.

4. To show only those rooms that contain a specified minimum number of members, select a number in the Min box. To show only those rooms that contain less than a specified maximum number of members, select a number in the Max box.

5. To show only those rooms that have been officially registered on the server, click Show Only Registered Rooms. These chat rooms are likely to meet the server's acceptable use guidelines.

6. To see a list of the people currently chatting in a room, select the room, and click List Members. You'll see the User List dialog box, shown here:

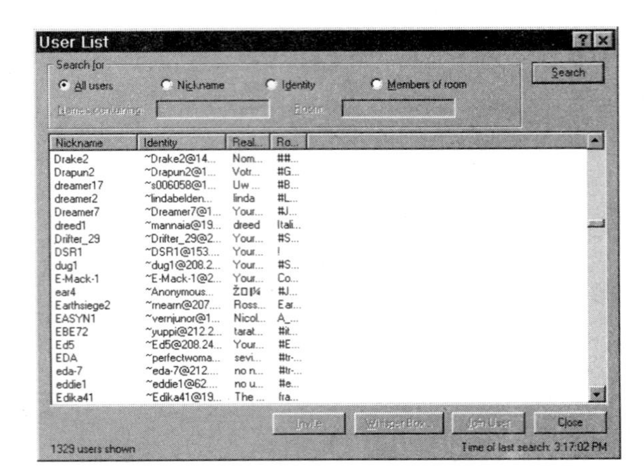

Click Close.

7. To see the latest list of chat rooms, click Update List.

8. To join a chat room, select the room, and click Join Room.

> To search for only those chat rooms in which there's probably some active chatting, but not too many members, set Min to 3 and Max to 12.

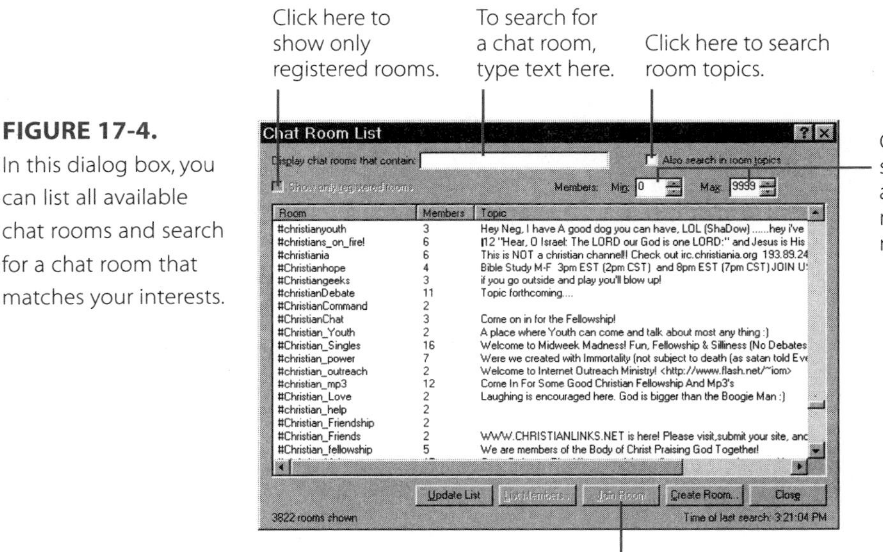

FIGURE 17-4.
In this dialog box, you can list all available chat rooms and search for a chat room that matches your interests.

Searching for a Channel

If you didn't find the chat room you're looking for in the Chat Room list, you may want to search for a channel of interest using Liszt, located at http://www.liszt.bluemarble.net/chat. This service currently enables you to search a list of nearly 40,000 IRC channels on more than two dozen IRC networks.

Established channels

#50plus (Undernet) For those of us who have had our Black Birthdays. Strives to be the friendliest channel on UnderNet (http://INK "http://www.netten.net/50plus/" www. netten. net/50plus/).
#Beethoven (DALnet) For fans of the classical composer (http://www.geocities.com/Vienna/3948/).
#Mystery (BeyondIRC.) For fans of detective novels (http://www2. ari. net/saunderf/mystery/mystery. html).

Jumping into the Conversation

You've joined a chat room. Chances are, you've arrived in the midst of an on-going conversation. You don't have to announce your arrival, since your name now appears in the message list. Chances are, somebody will say hello to you. If not, you can introduce yourself. In the following sections, you'll learn how to perform all the basic chatting actions in the comic chat environment (see Figure 17-5).

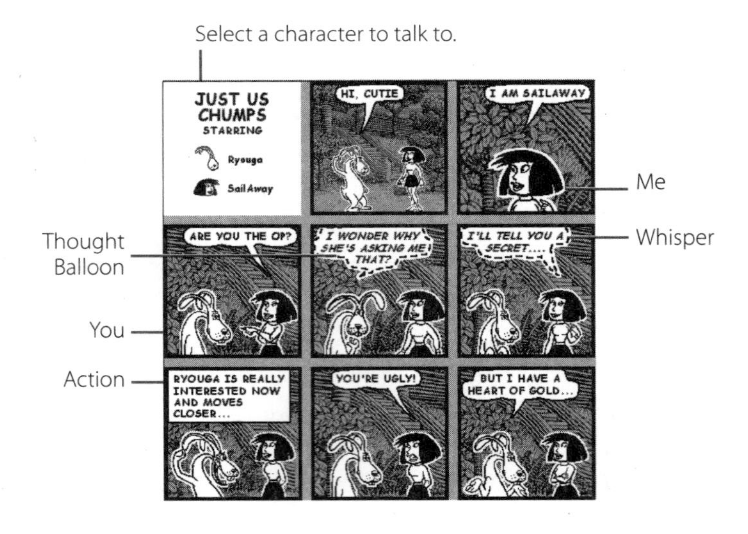

FIGURE 17-5. In comic chatting mode, you can talk, think aloud, whisper, and describe actions.

Understanding Character Gestures

When you type certain words or characters, Microsoft Chat automatically alters your character's gestures. Table 17-5 on page 574 lists the text that changes your character's appearance on the screen.

TIP

If you do not want your character's appearance to be altered based on what you type, you can freeze your character. To do so, point to your character in the self-view pane, right click, and select Frozen. Your character's emotion will stay the same until you unselect Frozen or choose a new emotion in the emotion wheel.

IRC Lingo for Newbies

addy. Slang for e-mail address.
DCC. Acronym for Direct Client to Client. With a DCC connection, two computers are directly connected via the Internet and do not require the server's interconnection. Do not configure your client to enable DCC without confirmation because hackers may try to use DCC to erase data on your computer.
bot. A script that initiates a series of actions. For example, you can obtain a bot that serves a drink to everyone in the room. Unfortunately, some bots are malicious; for example, war bots are designed to prevent others from being able to chat. Due to the prevalence of malicious bots, some servers prohibit bots entirely or require you to register them before use.
IRCop. A network administrator who can be contacted for assistance with problems such as harassment, password problems, ban/ignore evasion, or unwanted advertising.
lag. The time it takes for a user's message to appear on the displays of other chat-room members. Typically, expect a lag of one or two seconds. Network congestion can increase lag.
lamer. Derogatory term for an inept newcomer.
nickname (abbreviated nick). A pseudonym that you choose; this name appears in other users' member lists and identifies your contributions. On some IRC networks, you can register your nickname so that no one else may use it.
op. Abbreviation for Operator Status. A user with this status can alter a channel's mode, ban unwanted users, and assign op status to others.
split (also called netsplit). A breakdown in server-to-server communication. This may result in the sudden departure of many or most members of a chat channel. If their departure was caused by a split, they will probably return soon once the servers have re-established communication.

TABLE 17-5. Words and Characters That Alter Your Character's Appearance.

When you type:	Your character:
I	Points to himself or herself.
You	Points to the other person.
Hello or Hi	Waves.
Bye	Waves.
Welcome	Waves.
Howdy	Waves.
are you	Points to the other person.
will you	Points to the other person.
did you	Points to the other person.
aren't you	Points to the other person.
don't you	Points to the other person.
I'm	Points to himself or herself.
I will	Points to himself or herself.
I'll	Points to himself or herself.
I am	Points to himself or herself.
All capitals	Shouts.
!!!	Shouts.
ROTFL ("roll on the floor laughing")	Laughs.
LOL ("laugh out loud")	Laughs.
:) or :-)	Is happy.
:(or :-(	Is sad.
;-)	Is coy.

Talking to Someone

To say something to another character, follow these steps:

1. In the member list, select the person you want to talk to.
2. In the self-view pane, choose an emotion from the emotion wheel.
3. In the compose pane, type the text you want to appear.

If you would like to format the text, select your text and click one of the formatting buttons (Font, Color, Bold, Italic, or Underline). Please use these options in moderation.

4 To send the text you've typed, press Enter or click Say.

Thinking Aloud

A thought shows others what you're thinking and can add a fun dimension to your conversation. Others can see what you're thinking.

To think aloud, follow these steps:

1 In the self-view pane, choose an emotion from the emotion wheel.

2 In the compose pane, type the text you want to appear in the thought balloon.

3 To send the text you've typed, click Think or use the Ctrl + T shortcut.

Whispering to Someone

When you whisper to someone, only the characters you select can see what you said. Other participants are unaware of the exchange.

To whisper to someone:

1 In the member list, select the characters to which you would like to whisper.

2 In the self-view pane, choose an emotion from the emotion wheel.

3 In the compose pane, type the text you want to appear.

4 To send the text you've typed, click Whisper or use the Ctrl + W shortcut.

To open a whisper box, where you can carry out a text-only whispered conversation, do the following:

1 Right-click a character, and select Whisper Box.

You'll see a text-chatting window.

2 Type text in the message pane, and click Whisper. You can also whisper an action (click Whisper Action) or whisper a sound (click Whisper Sound).

If a member is using a comic character you don't have, you'll see a message informing you that you can download it by clicking the word "here." Click this word to download the comic character automatically.

Performing an Action

You can describe an action you perform. The action begins with your name, and it appears in a panel at the top of the cartoon frame. Type the text that describes your action. Remember that Microsoft Chat will automatically insert your name at the beginning of the action, so plan your text accordingly. If your name is SusieQ, when you type "sidles up to the bar" and click the Action button, others will see "SusieQ sidles up to the bar."

To describe an action:

1. In the self-view pane, choose an emotion from the emotion wheel.
2. In the Compose pane, type the text you want to appear. Remember that your name will appear at the beginning of the text you type.
3. Click Action, or use the Ctrl + J shortcut.

Playing a Sound

You can select a sound to play, but bear in mind that others will not hear the sound unless their systems have the sound installed.

To send a sound:

1. Click Play Sound. You'll see the Play Sound dialog box, shown here:

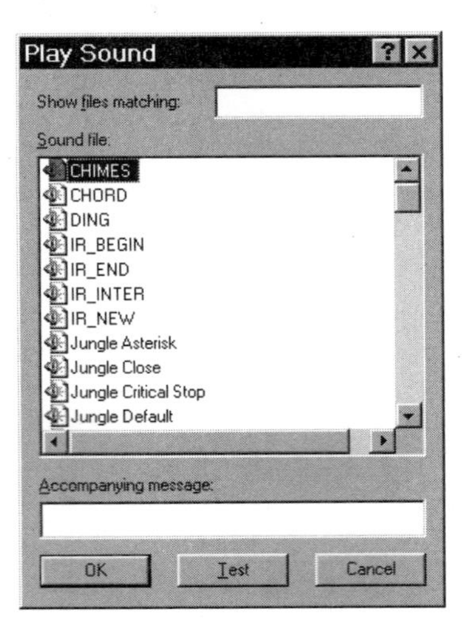

2 In the Sound File list, select a sound to play.

3 In the Accompanying Message box, type a message to send with the sound.

4 Click OK.

Viewing a User's Profile

Did you fill out your profile? No? Maybe somebody else filled out theirs. To find out, click a character's name or icon in the member list pane and click the right mouse button. Choose Get Profile from the pop-up menu. You'll see the character's profile, if any, in a special frame inserted within the comic. (Only you see this frame.)

Viewing a User's Identity

Every user has an identity, which is composed of the user's nickname, an "at" (@) sign, and part of the Internet address of the computer from which the person is accessing IRC. To view a character's identity, do the following:

1 In the member list, select the user.

2 From the Member menu, choose Get Identity.

Sending E-Mail to a User

If a user supplied a valid e-mail address when filling out the personal profile, you can send e-mail to the user.

To send e-mail to a user, do the following:

1 In the member list, select the person to whom you would like to send a message.

2 From the Member menu, choose Send E-Mail. If an e-mail address is found, Outlook Express starts and displays a New Message window with the user's e-mail address already entered.

Viewing a User's Home Page

If a user has a personal home page, and supplied the URL when filling out the personal profile, you can view the page.

To view a user's personal home page, do the following:

1 In the member list, select the person whose homepage you want to view.

2 From the Member menu, choose Visit Home Page. If a URL is found, Internet Explorer starts and displays the home page.

Sending a File

To send a file from your computer to another user, do the following:

1 In the member list, select the person to whom you would like to send the file.

2 From the Member menu, choose Send File. You'll see an Open dialog box.

3 Locate the file you want to send, and click OK. You'll see a dialog box informing you that Chat is waiting for confirmation before sending the file.

What to do about antisocial behavior on IRC

Sooner or later, you'll run into one or more of the following antisocial behaviors on IRC. Here's what to do:

- **Channel takeover.** A con game that begins with an attempt to gain op status from the legitimate channel operator; subsequently the attacker denies op status and destroys the channel. To avoid this, never give op status to a person you don't know.
- **Flooding.** Uploading a huge amount of text in such a way that other channel members cannot communicate. You can suppress flooding by ignoring the user who originates the flood.
- **Harassment.** Persistent, even relentless harassment that follows the targeted user from channel to channel and is designed to drive the user off the server. You can ignore the user, but you should also report the user's actions to the server's IRCops.
- **Nuking.** Attacking the targeted user's computer by originating repeated TCP/IP messages, thus slowing down the user's computer or even causing it to crash. If you believe you have been the target of nuking, notify the server's administrators.
- **Trolling.** Making exaggerated, inflammatory statements for the sole purpose of tricking others into responding emotionally. Ignore this user.
- **Preaching.** Disregarding the channel's topic and attempting to convert others to your point of view. Ignore this user.

The person to whom you're sending the file will see a dialog box warning about the possibilities of viruses, and asking for confirmation before accepting the file. If the selected user clicks Yes, file transfer begins.

Ignoring a User

If another user is bothering you, you can ignore this person. After ignoring the person, you will no longer see the ignored person's messages (although other members will, unless they also choose to ignore him or her).

To ignore a person, right-click the person's character in the member list, and click Ignore. You'll see a comic pane reminding you that you've ignored this person.

Informing Users You're Away from the Keyboard

To tell members you're away from the keyboard, do the following:

1. Click Member on the menu bar, and choose away from keyboard. You'll see the Away From Keyboard dialog box, shown here:

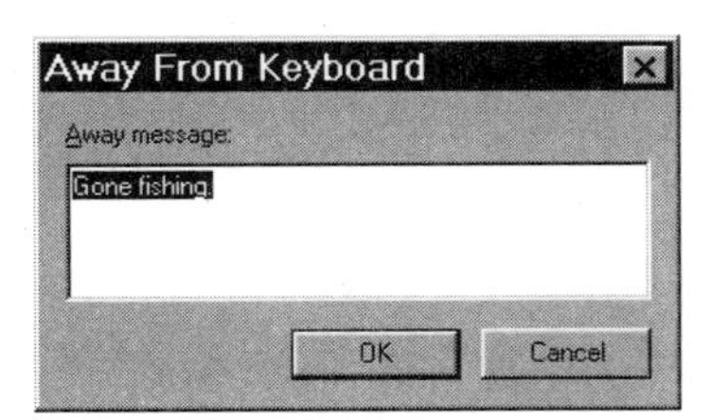

2. In the dialog box, type the message you want to send to other room members.

3. Click OK.

Adding Favorites List

Found a great chat room? Add it to your Favorites by choosing the Favorites menu and selecting Add To Favorites. To return to your favorite chat rooms later, choose Open Favorites, select the favorite from the dialog box, and click Open.

Saving and Printing

If you've had a great session, you might want to save it and print it.

Saving a Chat Session

To save the chat session, do the following:

1. From the File menu, choose Save.
2. In the Save dialog box, type a file name, and click OK.

Printing a Chat Session

To print the chat session, do the following:

1. From the File menu, choose Print. You'll see the Print dialog box, shown here:

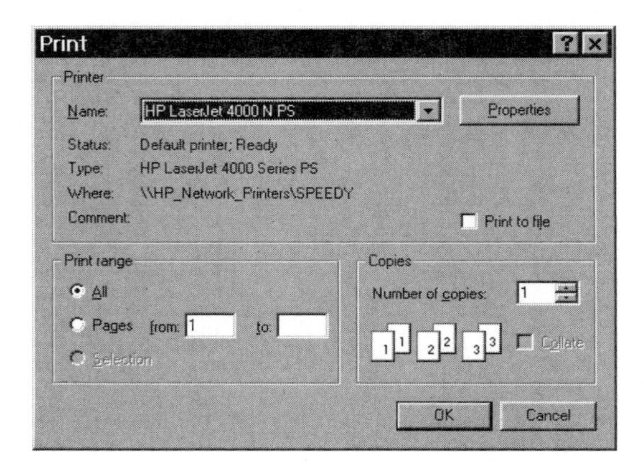

2. Choose the printing options you want, and click OK.

Exiting a Channel

To exit a channel, do one of the following:

- Click Leave Room on the toolbar.

  or

- From the Room menu, choose Leave Room.

Contacting Users

If you've made some friends on the Chat server and would like to locate them, you can search for them or invite them to join your chat room.

Searching for Users by Nickname

If you've met somebody on the server that you'd like to talk to again, you can search for users by following these steps:

1. From the Member menu, choose User List. You'll see the User List dialog box, shown in Figure 17-6.

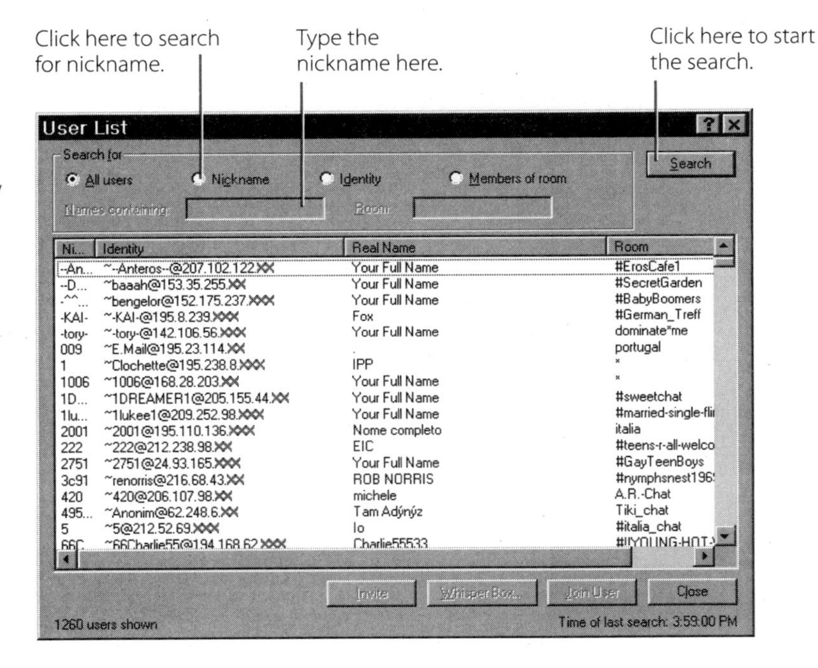

FIGURE 17-6.
In this dialog box, you can search for users by their nicknames.

2. Click Nickname.
3. In the Names Containing box, type all or part of the user's nickname.
4. Click Search. If Chat can find the user, you'll see the user's name in the user list. You'll also see the name of the room where the user is chatting.

5 To join the user in the room that the user is currently in, select the user's nickname, and click Join User.

6 To invite the user to join you in the chat room you're currently in, select the user's nickname, and click Invite. The user will see a dialog box such as the following:

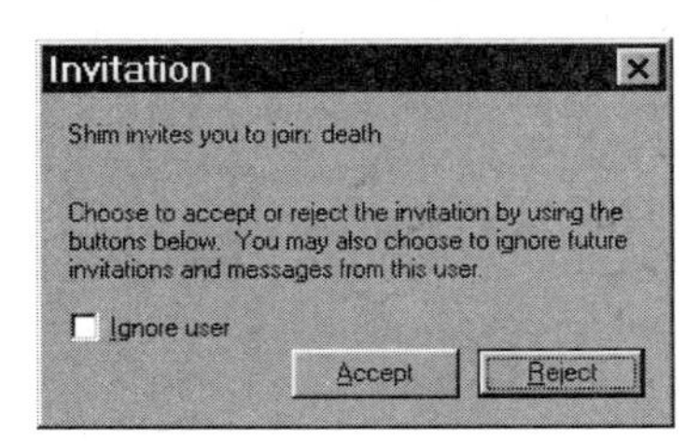

7 To open a whisper box to converse with this person by means of text chatting, select the person's nickname and click Whisper Box. When the whisper box appears, type a message, and click Whisper.

Inviting Users to Join a Room

You can invite people to join a chat room even if you haven't searched for them. To do so, follow these steps:

1 From the Member menu, choose Invite. You'll see the Invite dialog box, shown here:

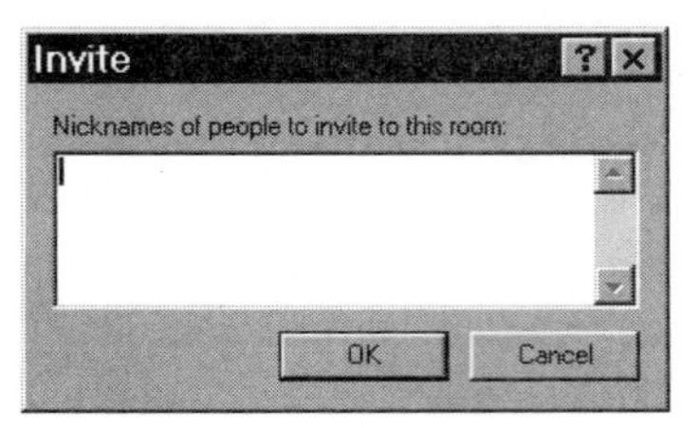

2 Type one or more nicknames, and click OK. If one or more of the users isn't connected, you'll see a message informing you that they're not online.

Dealing with Unwanted Invitations

If you receive invitations that you don't want, just click Ignore User when the Invitation dialog box appears.

Creating a New Chat Room

A very cool thing about IRC is the ability to create your own chat room. You can create a new chat room, define the topic, and wait for interested users to appear. Alternatively, you can create a hidden chat room, which doesn't appear on the chat-room list. To enter the chat room, users must know the chat room's name. This is a great way to get a group of friends or family members together for a previously arranged discussion (you can make the arrangements on e-mail). To ensure privacy, you can define a password for the room and hide group members' nicknames from the user list.

When you create a room, you become the chat-room host (the channel operator, or op, in IRC terminology). As host, you possess many privileges. If a problem user enters your room, you can kick the user out temporarily; the user will see a message explaining why you've done this. If the user comes back and repeats the behavior, you can permanently ban the user from the chat room. In addition, you can change chat-room settings at any time.

Understanding Chat-Room Attributes

When you create a channel, you become the room host (the channel op, in IRC-talk); you're in control. You, and you only, can give the room the following attributes:

- **Moderated** limits the right to talk to the room host and designated speakers. Everyone else is a spectator.
- **Set Topic Anyone** specifies whether anyone can set the room topic.
- **Invite Only** specifies whether an invitation is the only way to enter the room.
- **Hidden** hides the room name so that it does not appear in the Chat Room list. Users have to know the name in order to gain entry.
- **Private** specifies whether information about room members is accessible to others.
- **Set Maximum Users** determines the maximum number of users.
- **Optional Password** defines a password that is needed to gain entrance to the room.

Creating a Room

To create a room, follow these steps:

1 Do one of the following:

- Click Create Room on the toolbar.

  or

- From the Room menu, choose Create Room.

You'll see the Create Chat Room dialog box, shown here:

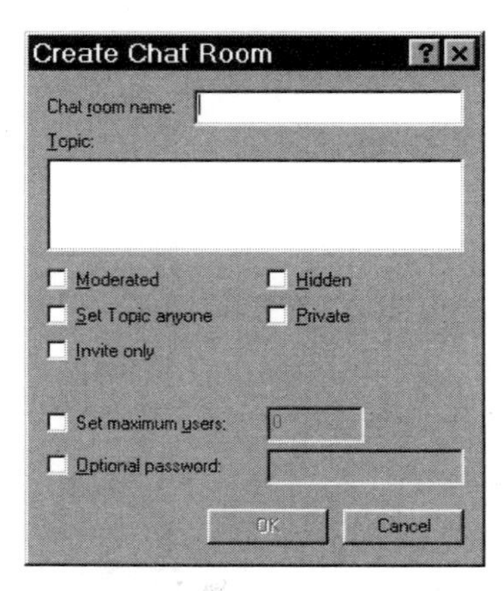

2 In the Chat Room Name box, type a name for your chat room.

3 In the Topic box, type a brief but descriptive topic.

4 Choose the room options you want.

5 Click OK to create the room. You'll see the new room. In the member list, you see your character with a gavel icon, as shown here:

This icon indicates that you are the room host.

Kicking and Banning Users

As the room host, you possess the power to deal with troublesome users. You can kick a problem user out of the room temporarily or ban them permanently.

Kicking a User Out of a Chat Room

If your chat room is being harassed by a problem user, you can kick the user out of the room temporarily. You can explain the reason for the kick.

To kick somebody out of your room temporarily, do the following:

1 In the member list, right-click the person's character, and choose Kick.

You'll see the following dialog box:

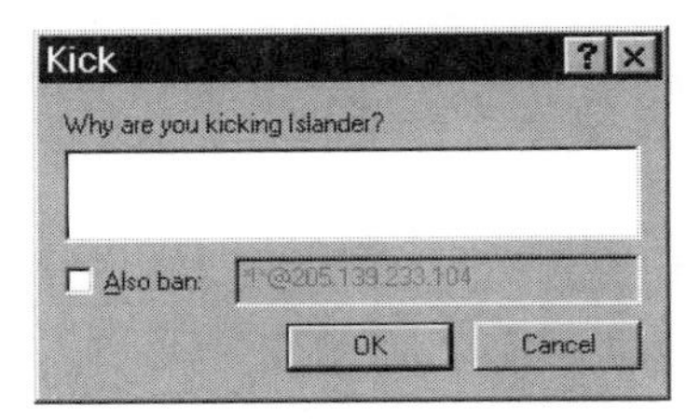

2 Type a reason, and click OK.

The kickee sees a dialog box such as this one:

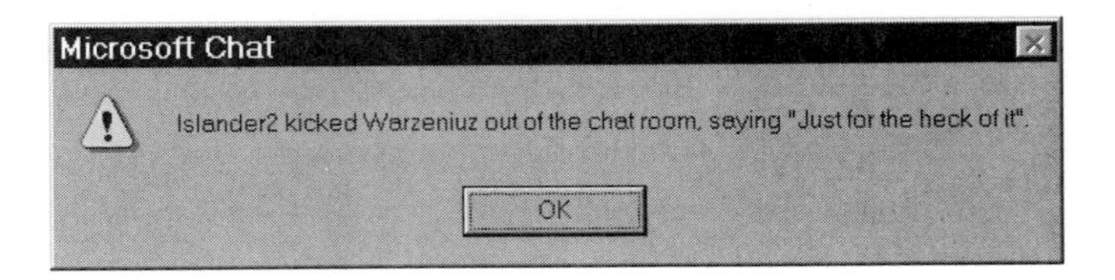

Banning a User Permanently

If the problem user returns and continues to misbehave, you can permanently ban the user from the room. The ban remains in effect until you unban the user.

To ban a user permanently:

1 In the member list, right-click the person's name, and choose Ban/UnBan. You'll see the following dialog box:

2 Click OK to ban the user.

To unban the user:

3 In the member list, right-click the person's name, and choose Ban/UnBan.

4 Select the user, and click Unban.

5 Click OK.

Giving Speaking Rights

If you've set up a moderated chat room, only those members who possess speaking privileges may participate in the conversation. To bestow speaking rights on a member, right-click the member's name, and choose Speaker. To take speaking rights away, right-click the member's name, and choose Spectator.

Sending Automatic Greetings

You can automatically send a greeting to every newcomer to your room. To do so, follow these steps:

1 Do one of the following:

- From the View menu, choose Automation.

or

- Press Ctrl + L.

You'll see the Microsoft Chat Automations dialog box, shown here:

2 In the Automatic Greeting area, choose the method of sending the message. The best choice is Whisper It, since this will not interrupt others' conversations.

3 In the text area, edit the text. The wildcards %Nickname% and %Room% are automatically changed to the user's nickname and the current room's name.

4 Click OK.

Changing Chat-Room Settings

The chat room's host can change the channel properties at any time. To change these properties, do the following:

1 From the Room menu, choose Room Properties.

You'll see the Room Properties dialog box, which enables you to adjust any of the room's settings.

2 Make the changes you want, and click OK.

Creating Macros

A *macro* is a brief message that you can send by pressing a key combination. You can choose from ten keys (Alt + 0 through Alt + 9).

Defining the Macro

To create a macro, follow these steps:

1. Do one of the following:
    - From the View menu, choose Automation.

      or
    - Press Ctrl + L.

      or
    - From the View menu, point to Macros, and choose Define Macros.

   You'll see the Microsoft Chat Automations dialog box.
2. Click General if necessary.
3. In the Key combination area, select a key combination.
4. In the Name area, type a name for the macro.
5. In the text area, type the text you want to send when you press this key combination.
6. Click Add Macro.

Using the Macro

To use the macro, just press the key combination you defined. Alternatively, click View on the menu bar, point to Macros, and choose the macro from the pop-up menu.

Creating Logon Notifications

If you'd like to be notified when an IRC friend logs on, you can create automatic logon notifications.

Defining Logon Notifications

To define a logon notification, follow these steps:

1 Do one of the following:

- From the View menu, choose Automation.

  or

- Press Ctrl + L.

You'll see the Microsoft Chat Automations dialog box.

2 Click Logon Notifications. You'll see the Logon Notifications page, shown here:

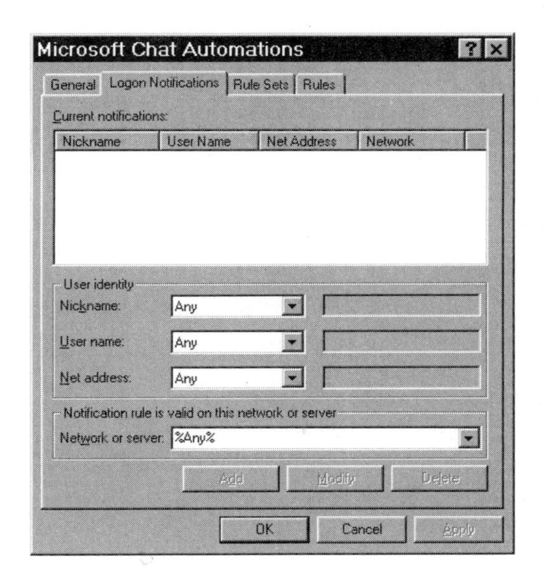

3 In the User Identity area, click a match method other than Any (you can choose from Equals, Contains, Starts With, or Ends With). Use Equals.

4 In the text box on the same line, type the nickname.

5 If desired, enter the User Name and Net Address to match. These are optional.

6 In the last text box, choose a network or server, or just leave the default setting (%Any%).

7 Click Add.

8 To define additional logon notifications, repeat steps 3 through 7.

9 Click OK.

Viewing Logon Notifications

To see whether you have received a logon notification, do the following:

1. From the View menu, choose Logon Notifications. You'll see the Logon Notifications dialog box.
2. If the user is present, you can do any of the following:
    - **Whisper Box.** Click this button to create a whisper box to chat with this person in a text-only mode.
    - **Invite.** Click this button to invite the user to join the room you're in.
    - **Join User.** Click this button to go to the room the user is in.

Creating Rules

In Microsoft Chat, a *rule* goes beyond a macro, in that it *automatically* initiates an action when a specified event occurs. For example, if a user other than yourself is kicked from a room, you can automatically send a thought to everyone in the room, such as "Good riddance."

Rules may seem complex at first glance, but it's actually quite easy to create a rule, once you've grasped the basic concept.

Events and Actions

To create a rule, you specify an event that kicks the rule into operation, and also an action for the rule to perform:

- **Event.** Examples of events are a user inviting you to a room or a user being kicked from a room. For a complete list of events, see Table 17-5.
- **Actions.** Examples of actions are displaying a message window or executing a macro. Actions are triggered by specific events. For a complete list of actions, see Table 17-6.

Here are some examples of rules you can create by specifying an event and choosing an action:

- When someone invites you to a room, you respond by sending the whispered message, "Thank you for the invitation."

- If someone sends you a message in a chat room that isn't in the active chat room window, your computer beeps to alert you that someone's trying to talk to you.
- If your friend Bloogie logs on to the server, you send Bloogie an invitation to join you in whatever room is currently displayed as your active chat-room window.

Event Parameters

When you choose an event, you also select a *parameter*, an additional condition that specifies further information about the event. For example, suppose you choose the event "A user in your room sends a message to you." You can choose from the following nickname parameters:

- **A specific nickname** (such as SailAway). The event occurs only if SailAway sends a message to you.
- **A nickname with wildcards** (such as Sail*). The event occurs only if someone with a name beginning with Sail sends a message to you.
- **A keyword** (such as %Anyone%). The event occurs if anyone sends a message to you.

TABLE 17-6. Events.

Events
A new room is created.
A user becomes a host in a room.
A user connects to your chat server or network.
A user disconnects from your chat server or network.
A user in your room sends a whisper to you.
A user invites you to a room.
A user is kicked from a room.
A user joins a room.
A user leaves a room.
A user outside your room sends a whisper to you.
A user sends a message to a room.

TABLE 17-7. Actions.

Activate or deactivate a rule set.
Ban the event's user from the room.
Disconnect from the current chat server or network.
Display a message window.
Don't display the event in the history window.
Execute a macro.
Get the identity of the event's user.
Get the lag time of the event's user.
Get the local time of a user.
Get the profile of the event's user.
Get the version information of the event's user.
Highlight the message associated with the event.
Invite the event's user to a room.
Join a room.
Kick the event's user from the room.
Leave the event's room.
Make the event's user a host of the room.
Make the machine beep.
Play a sound on your machine.
Replace a part of an incoming message.
Send a line of a file to a room.
Send a message to a room.
Send a sound to a room.
Send a thought to a room.
Send a whisper to a user in your room.
Send a whisper to a user outside your room.
Send an action to a room.
Start ignoring the event's user.
Whisper a line of a file to a user.

Wildcard Symbols

If you're typing a nickname or room name with wildcards, you can use the following wildcard symbols:

- * Matches any number of characters (Sail* matches SailAway, Sailor, Sailing).
- ? Matches a single character (Sail? matches Sails).

Types of Event Parameters

Event parameters fall into four categories:

- **Nickname.** You can supply a specific nickname, use wildcards, or choose from nickname keywords (constants), such as %Any-one% or %AnyoneButMe%.
- **Message.** You can type a specific message, or use the %Any% keyword.
- **Room.** You can supply the name of a specific chat room, use wildcards, or choose from room keywords, such as %AnyOfMyRooms%.
- **Network.** You can name the network, or use the keyword %Any%.

Nickname Keywords

For nicknames, you can use the following keywords:

- **%AnyoneButMe%.** The event will be triggered for all users except yourself.
- **%AnyOne%.** The event will be triggered for all users including yourself.
- **%Me%.** The event will be triggered only by yourself.

Message Keywords

For messages, you can use the %Any% keyword to match any message sent to you.

Room Keywords

For rooms, you can use the following keywords:

- **%AnyOfMyRooms%.** The event will be triggered in all the rooms that you are in.

- **%MyActivatedRoom%.** The event will be triggered only in the room that is in the active window.
- **%MyInactivatedRooms%.** The event will be triggered in all rooms *other* than the one that's displayed in the active window.

Network Keywords

For networks, you can use the %Any% keyword, which matches any IRC network.

Action Parameters

In addition to event parameters, you can also specify action parameters. For example, if you choose the action Display A Message Window, you define the parameter message. To define the parameter, you type the message text.

Here are some of the keywords you can use in action parameters:

- **%EventNickname%.** The nickname of the user who triggered the rule replaces %EventNickname%.
- **%EventServer%.** The server of the user who triggered the rule replaces %EventServer%.
- **%EventMessage%.** The message that triggered the rule replaces %EventMessage%.
- **%EventRoom%.** The room name of the event that triggered the rule replaces %EventRoom%.

Creating a Rule Set

To begin creating your own rules, you start by creating a rule set. You can call your first rule set something like "MyRules."

To create a rule set:

1. From the View menu, click Automation.

   You'll see the Microsoft Chat Automations dialog box.

2. Click Rule Sets. You'll see the Rule Sets page, shown on the next page:

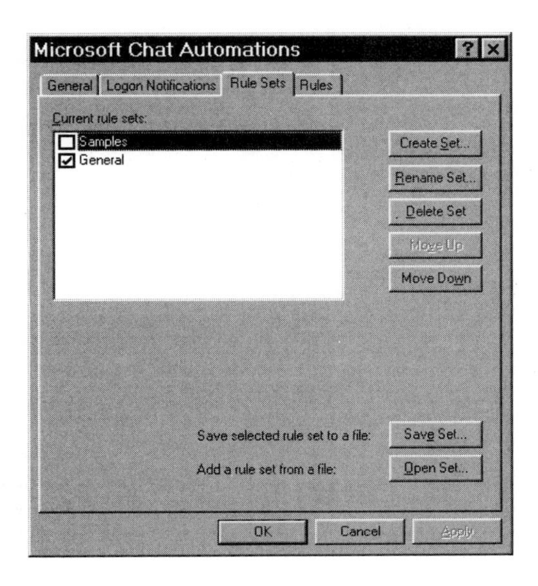

3. Click Create Set. You'll see the Creating Rule Set dialog box.
4. In the Creating Rule Set dialog box, type the rule set name.
5. Click OK.

Creating and Managing Rules

Now that you've created a rule set, you can create your rules. You can edit rules, activate or deactivate rules, delete rules, add rules to rule sets, and change the order in which rules execute.

Creating a Rule

To create a rule, follow these steps:

1. From the View menu, click Automation.

   You'll see the Microsoft Chat Automations dialog box.

2. Click Rules. You'll see the Rules page, shown on the next page:

3 In the Current rules set list, choose the rule set you just created if necessary.

4 If you would like to modify an existing rule instead of creating one from scratch, select the copy that appears in the rule list box, and click Duplicate Rule. (This option isn't available if the rule list is empty.)

5 Click Add Rule. You'll see the Edit Rule dialog box, shown here:

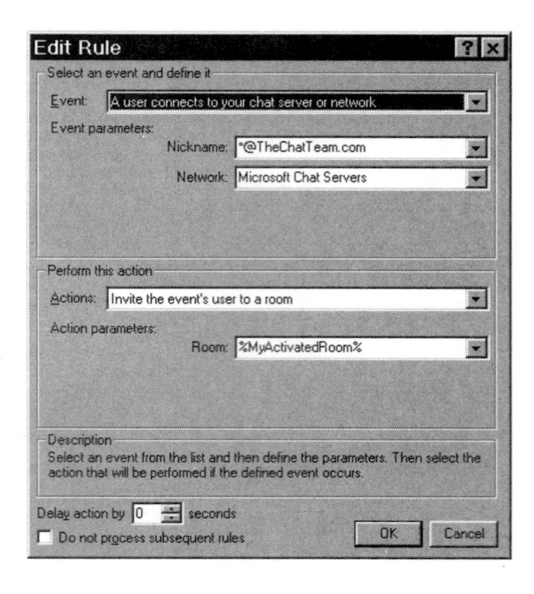

6. In the Event box, choose an event.
7. In the Event Parameters area, type text to match, or click the down arrow to see available keywords.
8. In the Perform This Action area, choose an action to perform when this event is triggered.
9. In the Action Parameters area, type text to match, or click the down arrow to see available keywords.
10. To delay the rule's action, type a number in the Delay Action By 0 Seconds box.
11. If you would like this rule to prevent subsequent rules from executing, click Do Not Process Subsequent Rules.
12. Click OK.

Editing a Rule

To edit an existing rule, do the following:

1. From the View menu, click Automation.

   You'll see the Microsoft Chat Automations dialog box.
2. Click Rules. You'll see the Rules page.
3. In the Current Rule Sets list, select the rule set that contains the rule you want to edit.
4. In the Rules Of Selected Set list, select the rule.
5. Click Edit Rule. You'll see the Edit Rule dialog box with the rule's current settings displayed.
6. Change the rule's settings.
7. Click OK.

Deactivating and Activating a Rule

To activate or deactivate an existing rule, do the following:

1. From the View menu, click Automation.

   You'll see the Microsoft Chat Automations dialog box.
2. Click Rules. You'll see the Rules page.
3. In the Current Rule Sets list, select the rule set that contains the rule you want to delete.

4 In the Rules Of Selected Set list, select the rule.

5 Do one of the following:

- To activate the rule, make sure there is a check mark in the check box at the beginning of the rule.
- To deactivate the rule, uncheck the rule.

6 Click OK.

Deleting a Rule

To delete an existing rule, do the following:

1 From the View menu, click Automation.

   You'll see the Microsoft Chat Automations dialog box.

2 Click Rules. You'll see the Rules page.

3 In the Current Rule Sets list, select the rule set that contains the rule you want to delete.

4 In the Rules Of Selected Set list, select the rule you want to delete.

5 Click Delete Rule.

Adding a Rule to a Rule Set

You can copy a rule from one rule set to another. This is much easier than creating a rule from scratch.

To copy an existing rule to a different rule set, do the following:

1 From the View menu, click Automation.

   You'll see the Microsoft Chat Automations dialog box.

2 Click Rules. You'll see the Rules page.

3 In the Current Rule Sets list, select the rule set that contains the rule you want to copy.

4 In the Rules Of Selected Set list, select the rule you want to copy.

5 Click Add To Sets. You'll see the Add To Rule Sets dialog box, shown on the next page:

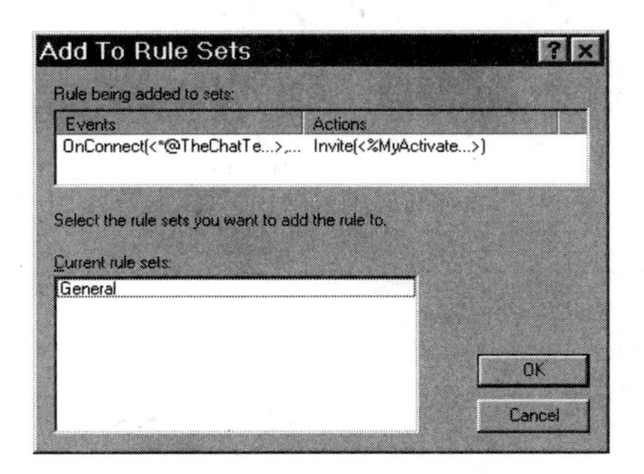

6 In the Current Rule Sets list, select the rule set to which you would like to copy the rule.

7 Click OK.

Changing the Order in which Rules Execute

You may wish to change the order in which rules execute. For example, suppose you write a rule that sounds a beep when SailAway logs on to the server, and another one that sends SailAway an invitation. If the logon rule comes before the invitation rule, you'll know that SailAway is connected before the invitation is sent.

To change the order of rules in a rule set, do the following:

1 From the View menu, click Automation.

   You'll see the Microsoft Chat Automations dialog box.

2 Click Rules. You'll see the Rules page.

3 In the Current Rule Sets list, select the rule set that contains the rule you want to move up or down.

4 Select the rule.

5 Click Move Up or Move Down.

6 To change the position of other rules, repeat steps 4 and 5.

7 Click OK.

Managing Rule Sets

Once you've created a rule set, you can manage the sets. You can rename sets, activate or deactivate sets, delete sets, or change the order in which sets execute. You can also save selected rules to a file, so that you can use the rules with a copy of Microsoft Chat on another computer. Once you've saved this file, you can import it.

Rename a Rule Set

To rename a rule, follow these steps:

1. From the View menu, click Automation.

   You'll see the Microsoft Chat Automations dialog box.

2. Click Rule Sets.
3. Select the rule set you want to rename.
4. Click Rename Set.
5. Type the new rule-set name.
6. Click OK.

Deactivating and Activating a Rule Set

To activate or deactivate a rule set, do the following:

1. From the View menu, click Automation.
2. Click Rule Sets. You'll see the Rule Sets page.
3. In the Current Rule Sets list, select the rule set that you want to activate or deactivate.
4. Do one of the following:
   - To activate the rule set, make sure there is a check mark in the check box at the beginning of the rule set.
   - To deactivate the rule set, uncheck the rule set.
5. Click OK.

Deleting a Rule Set

To delete a rule set, do the following:

1. From the View menu, click Automation.

   You'll see the Microsoft Chat Automations dialog box.

2. Click Rule Sets. You'll see the Rule Sets page.
3. In the Current Rule Sets list, select the rule set that that you want to delete.
4. Click Delete Set.

Changing the Order in which Rule Sets Execute

To change the order in which rule sets execute, do the following:

1. From the View menu, click Automation.

   You'll see the Microsoft Chat Automations dialog box.

2. Click Rule Sets. You'll see the Rule Sets page.
3. In the Current Rule Sets list, select the rule set that you want to move up or down.
4. Click Move Up or Move Down.
5. To change the position of other rules, repeat steps 3 and 4.
6. Click OK.

Exporting and Importing Rule Sets

If you use Microsoft Chat on another computer, you'll be glad to know that you don't have to re-create all your rules. You can save a rule set to a file. You can then transfer this file to a second machine and import the rule set using the copy of Microsoft Chat running on that machine.

To export a rule set to a file:

1. From the View menu, click Automation.

   You'll see the Microsoft Chat Automations dialog box.

2. Click Rule Sets. You'll see the Rule Sets page.
3. In the Current Rule Sets list, select the rule set that you want to export.
4. Click Save Set. You'll see a Save As dialog box.
5. Choose a location to save the file, and click OK.

After you've saved a rule set to a file, you can import the file using another copy of Microsoft Chat. To get the file to another computer, you could send it as an attachment to an e-mail message, transfer it via a local area network, or save the file to a floppy disk that you can insert in the second machine.

To import a rule set:

1. From the View menu, click Automation.

   You'll see the Microsoft Chat Automations dialog box.

2. Click Rule Sets. You'll see the Rule Sets page.
3. Click Open Set. You'll see an Open dialog box.
4. Locate and select the file, and click OK.

Using Chat with IRC Servers

Microsoft Chat is a full-featured IRC client that you can use with any standards-conformant IRC server. When you access a server other than a Microsoft Chat server, you'll chat in plain text. However, you can continue to use the Chat interface for all of the purposes discussed in this chapter. Should you wish to use the manually typed IRC commands, you can do so. These commands are summarized in Tables 17-8 and 17-9.

To read the reference information in these tables, keep the following symbols in mind:

- **Angle brackets** (<>) surround a word signifying the type of information you supply (for example, if you see <nickname>, you type a user's nickname).
- A **bar symbol** (|) means "or. "
- **Square brackets** ([]) indicate something optional.
- **Curly brackets** ({}) indicate that you can type two or more entries here.

Here's an example of an IRC command that uses some of these symbols:

```
/Ison {<nickname> <space><nickname>}
```

The curly brackets indicate that you can type more than one nickname, and <space> indicates that you should do so by typing a space between each nickname. You could type any of the following:

```
/Ison SailAway
/Ison SailAway Bloogie
/Ison SailAway Bloogie Catafegon
```

NOTE

You can use IRCX commands only on IRC servers that support the extended IRC command set. To find out whether a server supports these commands, type /IRCX and press Enter.

TABLE 17-8. Basic Commands for Chatting.

Command	Syntax	Example	Description
/Action	/Action <text>	/Action gives J-bird a big hug.	Displays your nickname followed by the specified text.
/Away	/Away <reason>	/Away phone call; be right back.	Changes your setting to "Away" and displays your reason.
/Away	/Away	/Away	Notifies members of your return to the chat room after being "Away."
/Invite	/Invite <nickname>	/Invite Sailaway	Invites the user to join the group you are currently in, or to open a whisper box.
/Ison	/Ison {<nickname> <space><nickname>}	/Ison Sailaway Bloogie Ryouga	Verifies whether one or more specific users are on the server.
/Join	/Join <room_name>	/Join #southflorida	Joins the specified channel.
/List	/List [<room_name>]	/List #south*,sail*,backpack*	Opens the Room List dialog box. To check for specific rooms, specify their names separated by commas, but not spaces. Wild cards allowed.
/Listx	/Listx [<room_name>]	/Listx #southflorida	Returns a list of all the rooms and their topics in the Status window. To check for specific rooms, specify their names separated by commas, but not spaces. Wild cards allowed.
/Me	/Me <message>	/Me gives J-bird a big hug	Displays your nickname followed by the specified text. (Same as /Action.)

(continued)

TABLE 17-8. *continued*

Command	Syntax	Example	Description
/Msg	/Msg <nickname|room_name> <message>	/Msg Sailaway Hey, let's talk privately for a while	Sends a message as a whisper to one or more users (if you use nicknames) or as a regular message to everyone in the room you are in (if you specify a room name).
/Names	/Names	/Names	Displays a list of other users connected to your server in the Status window.
/Nick	/Nick <nickname>	/Nick Bloogie	Changes your nickname.
/Notice	/Notice <nickname> <message>	/Notice SailAway Sure, let's talk.	Opens the recipient's Whisper Box with your message.
/Part	/Part	/Part	Used by you to leave the current room.
/Privmsg	/Privmsg <nickname|room_name> <message>	/Privmsg Sailaway Hey, let's talk privately for a while	Sends a message as a whisper to one or more users (if you use nicknames) or as a regular message to everyone in the room you are in (if you specify a room name).
/Quit	/Quit	/Quit	Closes your connection to the server.
/Sound	/Sound <nickname|room_name> <"sound_file"> [<message>] wav	/Sound SailAway ocean. See if this brings back memories...	Sends a sound file to the selected user or room.
/Sound off	/Sound off	/Sound off	Stops the playing of any sound file on your computer.
/Think	/Think <message>	/Think Wonder what she's thinking...	Displays a message as a thought.
/Time	/Time	/Time	Returns the server name, as well as the local date and time of the server.
/Topic: (All users)	/Topic <room_name>	/Topic #southflorida	Displays the room topic in the Status window.
/Userhost	/Userhost <nickname> {<space><nickname>}	/Userhost SailAway Bloogie	Verifies whether selected users are signed on to the server.

(continued)

TABLE 17-8. *continued*

Command	Syntax	Example	Description
/Who	/Who [<nickname>]	/Who SailAway	Displays users who match the query, if there are any, in the User List dialog box. Wildcards allowed.
/Whois	/Whois <nickname> {,<nickname>}	/Whois SailAway	Displays information on selected user(s) in the Status window.
/Whisper	/Whisper <room_name> <nickname> <message>	/Whisper SailAway Let's talk privately.	Sends a whisper to the selected user (but without opening a whisper box).

TABLE 17-9. Commands for Creating and Hosting Chat Rooms.

Command	Syntax	Description
/Access (IRCX only)	/Access <room_name> ADD|DELETE <entry_type> <entry_type> <nick!user@host. domain> <time> :[reason]	Used by owners and hosts to specify the type of access to a room that users are permitted. Provides five types of access: GRANT, DENY, VOICE, HOST, and OWNER.
/Access (IRCX only)	/access <room_name> LIST	This parameter lists all access entries currently defined for a room.
/Access (IRCX only)	/access <room_name> CLEAR [entry_type] access <room_name>	This parameter clears out either the entire access list for a room or a specific type of entry in it. If [entry_type] is omitted, all entries will be cleared. Note: Only a room owner can use /CLEAR on OWNER entries.
/Admin	/Admin	Used to find the name of the administrator of the server.
/Create	/create<room_name> <modes> <mode arguments>	Makes a new room and sets its properties. See the /Mode command below for possible arguments.
/Info	/Info	Queries the server for information.
/IRCX (IRCX only)	/IRCX or /ISIRCX	Queries the server for IRCX compatibility.
/Kick	/Kick<room_name> <nickname>[<reason>]	Used by room hosts to kick out users from the specified room.
/Links	/Links	Returns a list of all servers known by the server queried.

(continued)

TABLE 17-9. *continued*

Command	Syntax	Description
/Mode (Nickname)	/Mode <nickname> <user_modes>	Changes the user mode of the specified nickname. The plus sign (+) before the <user_modes> changes the user's mode as described below; the minus sign (-) removes the mode from the user. <user_modes> are as follows: i Marks the user as invisible. o Marks the user as an operator. q Allows a room owner to give owner status to another user. (IRCX only)
/Mode (Room_Name)	/Mode <room_name> [<room_modes>] [<max_member>] [<nickname>] [<nickname_mask>] [<password>]	Sets the mode of the chat room. <room_modes> are as follows: a Sets the room mode so that only authenticated users can join the room. Only system administrators can use this argument. (IRCX only) b Sets a ban to keep users out. d Sets a room mode so that when a room is full, another room is created. Only system administrators can use this argument. (IRCX only) h Sets hidden room mode. (IRCX only) i Sets invitation-only room mode. k Sets a room password. l Sets the user limit in the room. m Sets moderated room mode. n Marks the room so no messages can be sent from outside the room. o Gives operator privileges to a user for a specified room. p Sets private room mode. r Sets registered room mode. (IRCX only) s Sets secret room mode. t Sets room mode so that hosts and owners are the only ones who can change the room topic. u Sets room mode so that messages are sent to hosts if the user cannot enter the room. (IRCX only) v Sets the room mode so that the user can speak on a moderated room. w Sets the room mode so that nobody can whisper in the room. (IRCX only) x Sets auditorium room mode. This argument can be used only with /Create. (IRCX only) z Sets room mode so users can see whether a service on the server is monitoring the room. This mode is set by the server. (IRCX only)

(continued)

TABLE 17-9. *continued*

Command	Syntax	Description
/MOTD	/MOTD	Displays the server's message of the day in the Status window.
/Oper (IRCX only)	/Oper <user_name> <password>	Changes user status to operator status.
/Prop	/Prop <room_name> <property_name> <parameters>	Allows room owners to modify extended room properties that are available on IRCX servers. <room_name> is the room where the settings should be applied. <property_name> is the property of the room to modify. The available properties are:
	OwnerKey <OwnerKey>	Sets a room password that will grant owner status to anyone who joins that room using the owner key.
	HostKey <HostKey>	Sets a room password that will grant host status to anyone who joins that room using the host key.
	MemberKey <MemberKey>	Sets a room password that all users must use to join the room.
	OnJoin:<message>	Sets a message to be sent to anyone who joins the room. If <message> is omitted, the current OnJoin message will be cleared.
	OnPart:<message>	Sets a message to be sent to anyone who leaves the room. If <message> is omitted, the current OnPart message will be cleared.
/Quote	/Quote <command> (same as /Raw)	Allows you to send commands to the server unprocessed. For example, for commands that Microsoft Chat doesn't support, you can use /raw to send the command to the server.
/Raw	/Raw <command>	Allows you to send commands to the server unprocessed. For example, for commands that Microsoft Chat doesn't support, you can use /raw to send the command to the server.
/Server	/Server <server[port]network>	Connects you to a server or network.
/Topic	/Topic<room_name> <topic> (Room host)	Used by room host to set a topic for the current room.
/Version	/Version	Queries the server and returns its version to the Status window.

CHAPTER 18

Collaborating Online with Microsoft NetMeeting

The Internet will change the way we work—that's certain. E-mail already has become close to indispensable, both for internal communication within companies and with co-workers and colleagues around the world. With Microsoft NetMeeting, there's a new way to collaborate using the Internet as a communications medium.

Microsoft NetMeeting is a real-time Internet communication tool that enables you to converse with other Internet users as if you were using a telephone. But it's far more than an Internet telephone. NetMeeting includes the following advanced features:

- **Point-to-point audio and video communication via the Internet.** Think of it as a free long-distance phone call. The audio quality isn't fantastic, and often there's a delay of a second or two—but hey, it's free! If your computer is equipped with a digital video camera, you can also send real-time video images along with your voice. And if you're conversing with somebody who also has a digital video camera, you can see each other while you're talking.

- **A shared whiteboard space.** Everyone participating in the meeting, whether it's just 2 of you or 25, can collaborate within this graphic space. Anyone can draw and type, and everyone sees the results as they're created.
- **A chat area.** Users can type and send text-based messages, which everyone who's connected can see.
- **File transfer.** While you're in a meeting with one other person or more, you can send a file, and everyone will receive a copy. Others can send files to you, too.
- **Application sharing.** You can start any Microsoft Windows application on your system, and others can see what you're doing. For example, you can start Excel and show everyone your worksheet. You can even select an option that enables collaborators to make changes to your document.
- **Multipoint communication.** Most other Internet telephony standards support only point-to-point (two people) communications for whiteboarding. With NetMeeting, you can involve three or more people in the shared whiteboard space, the chat area, and application sharing.
- **Standards-based.** Unlike many Internet telephony programs, NetMeeting is based on open standards, which are currently supported by more than two dozen companies. This is very important since the reason Internet telephony hasn't taken off is that the various programs won't work with each other. With NetMeeting, you'll be able to talk with people who use other standards-based programs, including a recent offering from Intel.

Whether or not you've ever tried an Internet audio/video-conferencing application, you'll soon be chatting away happily and collaborating over the Internet with this chapter as your guide.

Introducing NetMeeting

NetMeeting, part of the Internet Explorer software suite, is consistently rated as the best available audio/video-conferencing software. Because NetMeeting conforms to established Internet audio/video conferencing standards, you can use NetMeeting to communicate with people who are using programs made by other software publishers.

NetMeeting is an excellent program, and thousands of people use it every day. Still, it's important that you understand the limitations of Internet-based audio/video conferencing: for example, you may need to upgrade your multimedia hardware and Internet connection to get acceptable results. Worse, you can't just "dial" another Internet user, thanks to the fact that most Internet users connect via dial-up accounts. In dial-up accounts, Internet service providers (ISPs) assign each caller a temporary Internet address (also called an IP address). You need to know this address to call someone, but it may change every time an Internet connection is made. Imagine the difficulties you'd have using an ordinary telephone if all of your contacts' phone numbers changed one or more times per day.

This section provides additional detail about NetMeeting's strengths and limitations, and points out ways to solve the inherent problems of Internet audio/video conferencing.

Understanding Internet Telephony Standards

NetMeeting conforms to a suite of international audio and video teleconferencing standards, including the H.323 standard, regulated by the International Telecommunications Union (ITU). This means that you can use NetMeeting to communicate with Internet users who are running H.323-compatible programs other than NetMeeting. Some programs are listed in Table 18-1.

TIP

If you're having trouble connecting with somebody using an Internet audio/video-conferencing program other than NetMeeting, try adjusting Net-Meeting's default network bandwidth so that the program assumes you're using an ISDN connection. (For instructions, see "Choosing General Options," page 643.) With this setting, NetMeeting uses the G.711 codec, which is part of the H.323 standard.

NetMeeting also supports the Lightweight Directory Access Protocol (LDAP), an Internet Engineering Task Force (IETF) standard that defines how applications can query "white pages" information located on directory servers. Microsoft's Internet Locator Service (ILS) directory servers, discussed below, make use of this standard.

TABLE 18-1. H.323-Compatible Audio/Video-Conferencing Programs (selected).

Program	Manufacturer
Enhanced CU-SeeMe	(White Pine Software)
Internet Comm Suite	(SmithMicro)
Internet Phone	(VocalTec)
Intel Video Phone	(Intel)
Net2Phone	(IDT)
VDOPhone	(VDOnet)

By means of an H.323 gateway, NetMeeting can place a call to a conventional telephone. Internet LineJACK (Quicknet Technologies) is a H.323 gateway card for Windows 95/98/2000 or NT. The card enables you to place any of the following types of calls: PC-to-PC via the Internet, PC-to-phone, and phone-to-PC.

Looking at What You'll Need

NetMeeting is free, but you'll need a fast Internet connection and a good multimedia PC to get acceptable results. Here's what you need:

- **A fast Internet connection.** Although NetMeeting will work with a 14,400 bps modem, you should use at least a 28,800 bps modem. NetMeeting works best over ISDN and local area network (LAN) connections.
- **Sound card, speakers, and microphone.** To use NetMeeting, you need to equip your computer with these accessories. For NetMeeting, the best sound card will have *full duplex* capabilities, which means you can talk and listen at the same time. You'll get the best results when all callers are using full-duplex sound cards. Because it's very inconvenient to talk to people using a microphone and your computer speakers, you may wish to purchase a headset, such as Andrea Electronics Corporation's PC Headset (http://www.andreaelectronics.com).
- **Video equipment.** If you want to use NetMeeting's video capabilities, you need either a video-capture card and camera, or a video camera that connects through your computer's parallel port or USB port. If you use a video camera that connects through the parallel port, you'll get much better performance if the port

is a bi-directional (ECP or EPP) port rather than a standard uni-directional port. You get the best performance with a video-capture board since this board includes its own processing capabilities and takes the load off your computer's processor. To use video, you need a computer with a Pentium or Celeron processor.

TIP

Even if you do not have a video capture card or video camera, you can still receive video images that other users send.

NetMeeting Solutions in Computer-Based Training

Suppose you're a manager, and you're deploying a new, complex software system in your company, designed to optimize resource planning in regional distribution centers. You need to train users how to use the new software. But here's the rub. The people that need the training are located in nearly two dozen widely dispersed offices. To send your instructor to all of those offices would be both expensive and time consuming.

That's where NetMeeting comes in. Instead of hiring a bevy of trainers, you equip each office with a dedicated PC that's configured to run NetMeeting optimally; each is equipped with a high-quality sound system and cordless headset. At headquarters, a private Internet locator server (ILS) provides links between all of the branch offices and the one instructor you've hired, who's working out of the main office. At prearranged times, students log on to receive training.

To train users how to use the new software, the trainer takes advantage of NetMeeting's amazing ability to enable conference participants to share an application. The instructor and student are looking at exactly the same thing on the screen, so that students can ask questions as they come up.

What's the result? A leading retailer recently implemented a NetMeeting solution along precisely these lines. Benefits include significantly reduced training costs, simplified scheduling, and instructors who are devoting their time to training rather than traveling.

TIP

Internet Phone Jack (Quicknet Technologies) is a full-duplex sound card that enables you to use an analog telephone to work with NetMeeting. The most recent version seamlessly integrates with the Internet "buddy list" program ICQ, enabling you to call other Internet users by dialing their ICQ number (your contacts can call you the same way). For more information, see http://www.quicknet.net.

Determining Whether Your Sound Card Is Full-Duplex

You can perform this simple test to determine whether your sound card is capable of full-duplex audio:

1. Click Start, point to Programs, point to Accessories, point to Entertainment, and choose Sound Recorder.
2. Repeat step 1 to start a second Sound Recorder session.
3. In the first Sound Recorder session, play a sound (.wav) file that is at least 30 seconds long. To do this, follow these steps:

   On the File menu, click Open. In the Open dialog box, locate and select an appropriate .wav file. Click Open.
4. While the first session of Sound Recorder plays the .wav file, switch to the second session of Sound Recorder and record a .wav file. To do this, click the Record button at the bottom of the Sound Recorder window (the rightmost button with the red circle).

If you can record a .wav file while the other .wav file continues to play, your sound card and the sound card drivers support full-duplex audio.

TIP

> Did your sound card fail the test? It might be capable of full-duplex audio if you install the latest drivers. To see a list of links to audio- and video-equipment suppliers, where you can obtain the latest drivers, access http://www.microsoft.com/netmeeting/?/netmeeting/urltable. htm.

Understanding NetMeeting's Limitations

Before you start dreaming about eliminating long-distance telephone charges, bear the following in mind:

- For best results, everyone connected to a call needs a fast Internet connection and a full-duplex sound card.
- The Internet wasn't designed to deliver real-time audio and video. You'll hear a lot of noise, including delays, echoes, and garbled sound. Sometimes you'll lose the connection.
- For acceptable audio quality, conversational privacy, and convenient use, you may need to equip your computer with a headset.
- You can't make or receive a call unless you're sitting in front of a computer that's running NetMeeting and connected to the Internet.

More Than a "Telephone"

Although you can place free computer-to-computer calls using NetMeeting, the program is at its best as a means of long-distance collaboration. What makes this possible is NetMeeting's amazing ability to enable users to share Windows applications. Here's an example of what you can do with NetMeeting's application-sharing capabilities:

- **Go over a proposal with a client.** As you work on the figures and agree on the terms, you can make the changes. When you're done, you can send your client the completed file for further review and printing.
- **Write a document collaboratively.** You and your collaborators can jointly compose a Microsoft Word document on the screen.
- **Make a presentation.** Using NetMeeting's application-sharing capabilities, you can share a PowerPoint presentation in a meeting involving two or more participants—even if they're scattered all over the world. You can even give them control of the application so they can navigate through the slides as they please.
- **Develop a Web-page design.** Work interactively with your Webmaster to develop your home page. As you express your preferences, your Webmaster composes the code. With a click of the mouse, you can see the results in Internet Explorer.

These are only some of the potential application-sharing possibilities of NetMeeting. You can share any Microsoft Windows application using NetMeeting!

Understanding Directory (ILS) Servers

To establish a direct connection with your contact, NetMeeting must have your contact's Internet address, also called IP number. However, most people connect to the Internet by means of dial-up connections.

To solve this problem, NetMeeting's designers created *directory servers* (also called *Internet Locator Servers,* or ILS servers for short). (In previous versions of NetMeeting, these servers were called ULS servers.) When you start NetMeeting, the program sends your e-mail address and your current Internet address to the server. By accessing your name or e-mail address through the directory server, people can call you even though your Internet address has changed.

Not all directory servers are public. If you're using NetMeeting from within an organization, you might be given the address of an organizational directory server. (An organization can set up a directory server using Microsoft Internet Information Server and Microsoft Windows NT.) To specify a default directory server other than Microsoft's, start NetMeeting, go to the Tools menu, select Options, click Calling, and type a new address in the Server Name box.

Although directory servers get around the problem of temporarily assigned IP addresses, they aren't a satisfactory solution. ILS servers aren't sufficiently *scalable* to handle thousands, let alone millions, of users. (The term *scalability* refers to a technology's ability to cope with growing numbers of users.) Your correspondents are listed on the directory server only if they've logged on. However, because directory servers can handle only so many listings at a time, people may experience difficulty logging on, especially at times of peak usage. You may find that the best way to connect with your correspondents is to send e-mail that asks them to find out their current Internet address (also called IP address) so you can call them directly. For more information, see "Placing a Call with an Internet Address" on page 626.

The Buddy-List Solution

"Buddy-list" programs, such as ICQ, AOL Instant Messenger, and the soon-to-appear MSN Messenger service, provide the best solution to the problem of keeping track of your Internet "phone numbers." In brief, a buddy-list program gives you a universal Internet identification number, one that's unique to you. The software runs on your computer in the background; when you log on to the Internet, the program contacts the buddy-list server, and registers your current IP address. You can set up buddy-list programs so that you are notified when your friends are online; they can set up their lists so that they know when *you're* online. With ICQ, you can send an Internet Telephony request to any of the callers on your list. When someone sends a request to you, you can accept the call request if you wish, and NetMeeting starts automatically.

Why is the buddy-list solution better? Buddy-list technology is much more scalable than ILS directory servers. Buddy-list servers can handle millions of users. Reportedly, ICQ has 20 million registered users. Already announced (but not ready for initial testing at the time of this book's publication) is Microsoft's version of buddy-list software, called MSN Messenger Service, which will work with your Hotmail e-mail account. For more information on MSN Messenger Service, check out the Hotmail home page (http://www.hotmail.com).

Getting Started with NetMeeting

Now that you know what NetMeeting's capabilities are, you're ready to try them yourself. Get started by configuring your audio system and understanding NetMeeting's window.

Installing NetMeeting

If you didn't install NetMeeting when you installed Internet Explorer, do the following:

1. From Internet Explorer's Tools menu, choose Windows Update.
2. Follow the instructions on the screen to locate and install the latest version of NetMeeting.

NetMeeting automatically installs the Intel Connection Advisor, a utility that runs in the background and enables you to check your audio and video data-transfer rates.

Running NetMeeting for the First Time

To use NetMeeting for real-time audio communication, you'll need a sound card, speakers or headphones, and a microphone. The first time you run Microsoft NetMeeting, the Audio Tuning Wizard will appear, and you'll be asked to test your microphone. Be sure it's connected and ready to go.

To run NetMeeting for the first time, do the following:

1. From the Start menu, point to Programs, point to Internet Explorer, and choose NetMeeting. You'll see the Microsoft NetMeeting configuration wizard.
2. Click Next. You'll see the next page of the wizard, which asks you to select a directory server, as shown here:

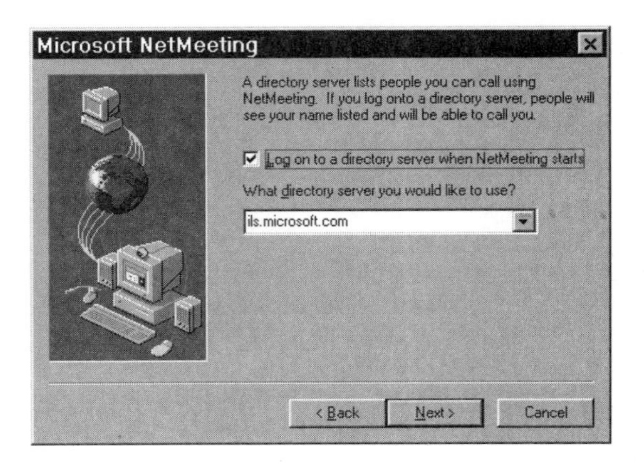

Do one of the following:

- If your network administrator gave you the address of a directory server, type it in the list box.

  or

- Choose a directory server from the list box. You can use Microsoft's directory servers, or directory servers run by Four11.com.

3 Click Next. You'll see a page asking for information, as shown here:

SEE ALSO
If you would like to change your connection information, you can use the Options dialog box. For more information, see "Specifying Your Information" on page 644.

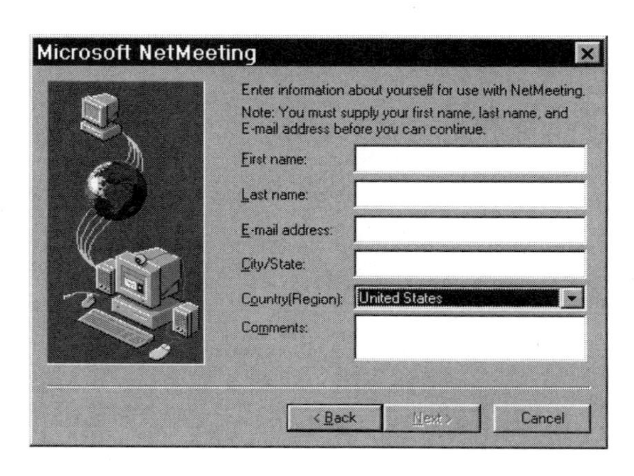

4 Do one of the following:

- For personal use, consider supplying a nickname instead of your real name. You must supply your real e-mail address, or the directory service will not work.

  or

- For business use, type your real name.

The additional fields (City/State, Country, and Comments) are optional.

5 Click Next. You'll see a page asking whether you would like to categorize the information you've supplied as intended for personal use, business use, or adults-only use. Choose one of these options.

6 Click Next. You'll see a page asking what type of connection you are using (14440 bps Modem, 28800 bps Or Faster Modem, ISDN, or Local Area Network). Choose an option.

7. Click Next. You'll see the first page of the Audio Tuning Wizard. Close all other programs that play or record sound.

8. Click Next. You'll see a page indicating which wave devices NetMeeting proposes to use for recording and playing back audio. To change these settings, choose another installed wave device in the list boxes.

9. Click Next. Make sure your microphone and speakers are connected. Click Test to hear a sample sound.

10. Click Next. You'll see the microphone test. Read the text into the microphone as directed. NetMeeting will adjust the audio level automatically.

11. Click Next, and click Finish to complete configuring NetMeeting. You'll see the Microsoft NetMeeting window, discussed in the following section.

TIP

If people have trouble hearing your audio, you can run the audio tuning portion of the setup wizard again. To do so, click Tools on the NetMeeting menu bar, and choose Audio Tuning Wizard.

Looking at NetMeeting

After you've finished running the NetMeeting configuration wizard, you'll see NetMeeting on the screen (Figure 18-1). In addition, you'll see the NetMeeting icon on the taskbar.

The following sections appear in NetMeeting's window.

- **Title Bar.** To reposition the NetMeeting window, drag the title bar. To maximize the window quickly, double-click the title bar. Double-click again to restore the previous size.

- **Menu Bar.** Here you'll find all the NetMeeting commands, but the most frequently used commands are found on the toolbar.

- **Toolbar.** The toolbar contains the following buttons: Call, Hang Up, Stop, Refresh, Properties, SpeedDial, and Send Mail. To display or hide the Toolbar, select Toolbar from the View menu.

- **Audio Controls.** From here you can adjust the microphone and speaker volume.

- **Navigation Icons.** In this area, you can view one of four different lists. The Directory, SpeedDial, Current Call, and History lists are all accessible via a set of four tabs that run vertically along the left side of the window.

- **Status Bar.** In this area, NetMeeting displays messages and information about its status and what it's doing. You can hide the status bar by selecting Status Bar from the View menu, but it's worth keeping it visible because some of the messages are useful or important.

Adjust microphone volume here.

Adjust speaker volume here.

Click here to view the directory-server list.

Click here to open the speed dial window.

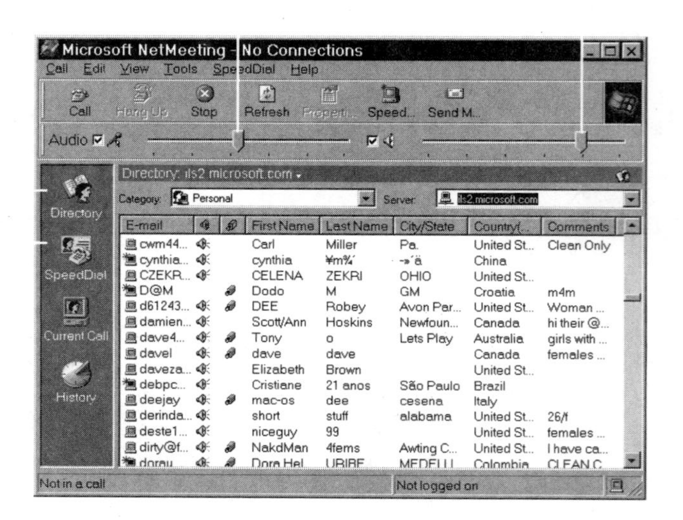

FIGURE 18-1. With Microsoft NetMeeting, you can talk anywhere the Internet reaches.

With the Current Call tab, you can view information about the people connected to you. You'll see the person's name, information about whether sharing is enabled and the type of connection that's been achieved (voice or no voice), and any other information that the person has elected to make public by means of the Directory server. When you initially make your connection, the first thing you'll want to know is whether audio is enabled, so it's nice to see this information automatically.

Navigating in NetMeeting

What you see in NetMeeting's workspace depends on which navigation icon you've clicked. When you click the Directory icon, you see the current directory server's list of people you can call (see Figure 18-1). If you click SpeedDial, you see the current list of calling shortcuts you've created. (Since you've just started with NetMeeting, you don't have any SpeedDial shortcuts yet.) Clicking Current Call displays the current call, if any. (This workspace appears automatically when a call is in progress.) If you click History, you'll see a list of calls you've previously made.

The NetMeeting Toolbar

NetMeeting's toolbar contains the most frequently chosen commands. Table 18-2 provides a quick overview of what these tools do.

TABLE 18-2. Buttons on the NetMeeting Toolbar.

Tool	Action
Call	Initiates a call.
Hang Up	Hangs up the connection.
Stop	Stops the current download.
Refresh	Refreshes the current window.
Properties	Displays properties for the currently selected item.
SpeedDial	Opens the SpeedDial window.
Send Mail	Opens the New Message window in Outlook Express.

Using the List Area

NetMeeting displays four different lists in the list area. To see a list, click the appropriate tab in the tab bar running down the left side of the window.

- **Directory.** Once you've logged on to a directory server, you'll see the current list of users in the directory list. To call one of these users, select the user's entry and click Call.
- **SpeedDial.** In the SpeedDial list, you'll see the names of people you've put on your SpeedDial list. (If you haven't added any, this list is blank.)
- **Current Call.** This list shows information about the current call. This window also contains the Remote Video window. (If you prefer, you can detach this window by choosing Detach Remote Video from the View menu.)
- **History.** This window shows calls you've placed previously.

Do you have a video camera mounted on your computer, ready to go? From the Tools menu, select Options, and click the Video tab. Enable the option Automatically Send Video At The Start Of Each Call to automatically start sending video. Note that you can send video even if the person you're talking to doesn't have a camera. If you'd like to receive video automatically, enable the option Automatically Receive Video At The Start Of Each Call.

Finding People and Initiating Calls

To find someone to call, you can use the following strategies, which are explained in more detail in this section:

- **NetMeeting's Directory window.** To view the list of available callers, click Directory on the navigation bar.
- **Microsoft Web Directory.** Microsoft maintains a Web-based directory of people currently accessible via its directory server. The Web-based directory offers enhanced search capabilities. To access the Web directory, click Call on the menu bar, and choose Web Directory.
- **Additional Web directories.** You can find additional directories of Internet telephone numbers on the Web.
- **Making arrangements via e-mail or buddy lists.** If you can't find the person you want to call in the directory, you can send e-mail to the person requesting a response that includes connection information (specifically, the Internet address of the computer this person is using). An increasingly popular way to make such arrangements involves the use of buddy-list software (such as the popular ICQ), which alerts you when your contacts are online. ICQ can work directly with NetMeeting; you can send a request for a phone call, and if the caller accepts, NetMeeting starts automatically.

If NetMeeting cannot access the Microsoft directory server for some reason, use the Web directory; it's not as up-to-the-minute accurate as the NetMeeting directory, but most of the links will work.

Finding People with NetMeeting's Directory Window

To place a call using the directory window you see within NetMeeting, follow these steps:

1. Click the Directory icon. You'll see the Directory list.
2. In the Category list box, choose the category of user that you want to call. Categories include business or personal users, users who have video cameras, users in your country, and others. To see the largest possible list, choose All.
3. In the Server list box, choose the server you want to use.

You'll find more than one server available at most times. If you don't find the user you're looking for on the first server, try another. Note that you stay logged on to the same server even if you access another server's directory list.

4. To search for a user, click on the header of the column you would like to search and scroll through the list.

TABLE 18-3. Icons in the Directory and Current Call Windows.

Icon	Description
	Person is in a call.
	Person has a microphone and speakers.
	Person has a video camera.
	Person can share applications, run Whiteboard and Chat, and send files.

If you close NetMeeting, wait a few minutes before you start the program again. Without the wait, you may have problems connecting to the directory server.

Finding People with Microsoft's Web Directory

The Web directory parallels the information shown in the NetMeeting directory window, except that it's delayed by a few minutes. (For this reason, some of the people listed might have logged off, while others are online but don't yet appear in the list.) It's best to use the Directory window to locate callers. However, sometimes the Directory window isn't available due to the heavy loads placed on Microsoft's directory servers. In such cases, use the Web directory instead.

To place a call using the Web directory, follow these steps:

1 From the Call menu, choose Web Directory.

Internet Explorer starts, and displays the Web Directory page, shown in Figure 18-2.

2 Do one of the following:

- To view the current directory listings, click Look at User Directory.

or

- To search for a user, click Search. You'll see the Search page, shown here:

Microsoft® NetMeeting™ Complete Internet Conferencing

ils4 Search

To find a particular NetMeeting user, enter the search criteria below, and press the Submit button:

First Name: City/State:
Last Name: Country: < All >
Email: Comments:

Submit Reset

Type information in one or more fields, and click Submit.

3 When you've located the link to the person you want to call, click on the link to switch back to NetMeeting and initiate the call. (If NetMeeting isn't running when you click the link, the program will start automatically.)

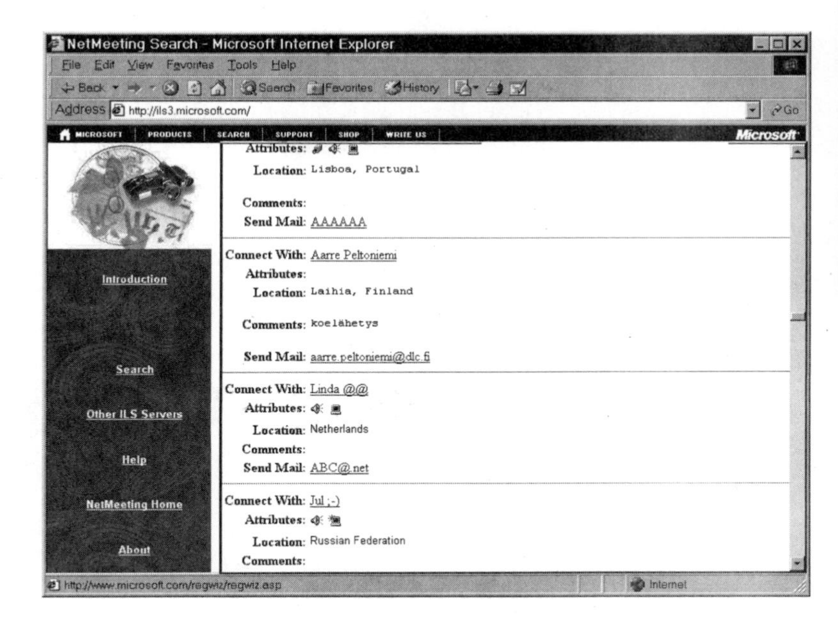

FIGURE 18-2.
Microsoft's Web directory comes in handy when NetMeeting's directory isn't working.

Locating Additional ILS Servers

SEE ALSO
To change the default directory server, see "Choosing Calling Options," page 645.

Dozens of organizations run ILS servers and make their directory lists available on the public Internet. To see the most comprehensive available list of such servers, visit NetMeeting Place, located at http://www.netmeet.net. Not affiliated with Microsoft, the site is devoted to promoting the use of NetMeeting for online conferencing.

TIP

NetMeeting Super Enhancer (NMSE) enables you to add ILS server names to NetMeeting's directory-server list, a capability that isn't built into NetMeeting. This free (copyrighted) program is available from NetMeeting Place (http://www.netmeet.net/nmse. htm).

Making Call Arrangements via E-Mail or Buddy Lists

Most NetMeeting users agree that the best way to contact callers involves exchanging Internet addresses (also called IP addresses). Once

SEE ALSO

For more information on ICQ, see the ICQ home page at http://www.icq.com.

you've done this, you can place a NetMeeting call directly, without the intervention of a directory server. You can exchange current Internet addresses by e-mail, but by far, the most convenient way lies in using buddy-list software (such as ICQ, AOL Instant Messenger, or Microsoft's forthcoming MSN Messenger Service). These programs give each subscriber a unique Internet identification number. You can add people to your "buddy list," and the server software informs you when they're online. If you would like to place a call to one of your contacts who's online, you simply send a text message that includes your current IP address. With ICQ, you can initiate a call request automatically; if the caller accepts the call, ICQ starts NetMeeting automatically.

TIP

Quicknet Technologies' Internet SwitchBoard, designed to work with its Internet PhoneJACK and Internet LineJACK products, enables you to use your ICQ number as a universal contact number. Either of these products enables you to use a conventional analog phone to work with NetMeeting. When you call a contact, you use your contact's ICQ number as the "telephone number." The software first attempts the call via a PC-to-PC NetMeeting connection. If the called person isn't online, the call is routed by Net2Phone, a leading PC-to-phone service provider.

Placing a Call with an Internet Address

If you know somebody's Internet address (four numbers separated by dots, with no spaces), you can place a call to this person without going through the Directory server. Users of corporate LANs often have permanent Internet addresses. You can also obtain the Internet addresses (also called IP addresses) of people who access the Internet via dial-up connections; although these people are connecting using a temporarily assigned Internet address, you can still call them if you know the address that their computer is using during the current online session.

TIP

Remember, if your correspondents are using Windows 98, they can find out which IP address they're using by clicking Start, choosing Run, typing winipcfg, and pressing Enter.

To place a call with an Internet address,

1 From the Call menu, choose New Call.

   You'll see the New Call dialog box, shown on the next page:

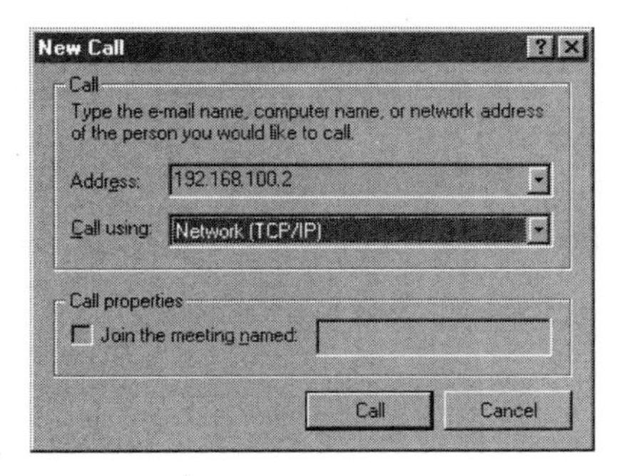

2. In the Address box, type the person's Internet address. The address will consist of four numbers separated by dots, with no spaces.
3. In the Call Using box, choose Network (TCP/IP).
4. If you've been notified that there is a meeting taking place, enable Join The Meeting Named and type in the name of the meeting you want to join.
5. Click the Call button.

After you've placed a few calls, you can see a list of the most recently used numbers by clicking the History tab. You can also place a call to one of these numbers simply by choosing it and clicking the Call button.

Troubleshooting Call Problems

When you try to call somebody listed on the directory server, you may get the message, "User is unable to accept Microsoft NetMeeting calls." Possible reasons include:

- The user refused your call.
- The user is no longer connected to the Internet, even though the link still appears in the directory.
- The user might not have NetMeeting running.

NOTE

If you save connection information and re-use it later, NetMeeting may fail to connect, or it might connect you to a different person. That's because the saved information includes the caller's Internet address. If the caller is using a dial-up connection, this address may change the next time the user logs on. In addition, some other user might be assigned the Internet address that NetMeeting stored. To solve this problem, always call this person by clicking an entry in the directory server, or use e-mail or a buddy-list program to exchange current Internet addresses each time you call.

If you experience an audio or video problem, look at the Intel Connection Advisor icon on the taskbar. If it's showing a caution symbol (a yellow triangle with an exclamation point), click the icon to see what's wrong and how to solve the problem.

Managing Calls

When you establish a call, you'll see the Current Call window, shown in Figure 18-3. The list box shows the names of all of the callers in the current conference. To the right, you see windows for videoconferencing. If neither caller has video capabilities, these windows are inactive, as they are in Figure 18-3.

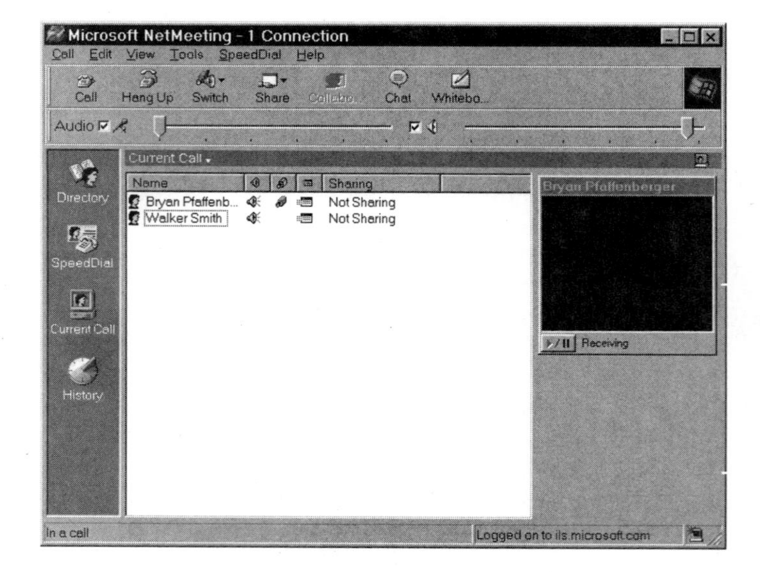

FIGURE 18-3. When you're in a call, you see the Current Call window.

Don't be surprised if you can't say "Hello" right away. NetMeeting needs a little time to determine what type of connection is possible.

The icons placed next to each caller's name indicate the type of connection that's possible with this person. In Figure 18-3, for example, both callers have audio capabilities, but one of them lacks video capabilities.

If the person you're talking to can't hear you very well, try increasing the microphone volume by moving the slider control. Also, try speaking more directly into the microphone. To adjust the speaker volume, move the slider control next to the speaker icon.

TIP

To see information about the person you're talking to, right-click the person's name and choose Properties. You'll see a Properties dialog box, which lists the information that this person has made available to the Directory server.

Sending E-Mail If Your Call Does Not Go Through

If the person you called rejects the call, you'll see the following dialog box:

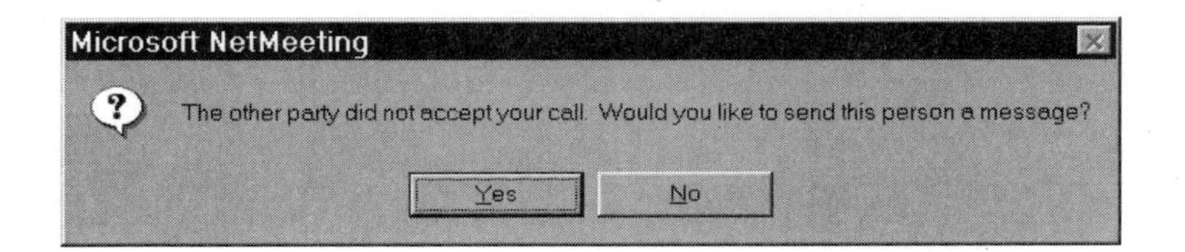

To send an e-mail message to this person, click Yes. NetMeeting starts Outlook Express. You'll see the New Message window, with a message addressed to the caller. Included as an attachment is a SpeedDial shortcut, which this person could click to return your call. Add a short message, and click OK.

If you connect to the Internet via a dial-up connection, your Internet address will likely change the next time you log on. If so, the SpeedDial shortcut you sent may not work. If you're on a buddy-list network such as ICQ, you may wish to include your membership number so that the caller can track you down that way.

Receiving a Call

When a call comes in, you'll hear a ringing sound and see the dialog box shown here: asking whether or not you want to accept the call.

Do one of the following:

- Click Accept to accept the call.

or

- Click Ignore to reject the call.

Adjusting Video

If your computer is equipped with a digital video camera, you can send video to the people you call. They can receive the video even if they don't have a video camera. Likewise, you can receive video sent by others, even if your system isn't equipped with a video camera.

To send and receive video, you must first turn video on, as explained in these steps:

1. From the Tools menu, point to Video.
2. Do one of the following:
   - Choose Send to send video from your computer. (If you don't have a digital video camera, this option is dimmed.)
   - Choose Receive to receive video sent by others.

TIP

If you're viewing video over a slow connection, you may find that the video interferes with audio reception. To turn video off, click Tools on the menu bar, point to Video, and choose Send so that the check mark disappears.

If you wish, you can detach the video from the NetMeeting window so that it appears in its own window. To detach the window, click Tools on the menu bar, point to Video, and choose Detach My Video or Detach Remote Video. To place the video windows back in the NetMeeting window, choose one or both of these options again.

Refusing All Calls

SEE ALSO

You can turn video on or off permanently in the Options dialog box. You can also set the image size, choose video quality, and select video camera properties. For more information, see "Choosing Video Options," page 646.

If you do not want to be disturbed while you're working, you can refuse all calls. To do so, follow these steps:

1. From the Call menu, choose Do Not Disturb.

   You'll see a dialog box warning you that you won't be able to receive calls until you turn off Do Not Disturb.

   To suppress this message in the future, click Don't Show Me This Message Again.

2. Click OK.

After you choose Do Not Disturb, you'll see an "X" on the NetMeeting taskbar icon, indicating that you're refusing all calls.

To accept calls again, click Call on the menu bar, and choose Do Not Disturb again so that the check mark disappears.

Hanging Up

To terminate a call, do one of the following:

- On the toolbar, click Hang Up.

  or

- From the Call menu, choose Hang Up.

Other callers will see a message that you've left the conference.

Creating and Using SpeedDial Shortcuts

SpeedDial shortcuts enable you to establish a call quickly. You can easily create a SpeedDial shortcut during a call, but you can also create a shortcut when no call is in progress. Once you've created a shortcut, you can use it to place calls. The following sections explain these procedures.

Creating a SpeedDial Shortcut During a Call

The easiest way to create one is to do so while you're conferencing with someone. To create the SpeedDial shortcut, do the following:

1. Click the Current Call icon, if necessary, to display the caller list.
2. Point to the caller, and click the right-mouse button.
3. From the pop-up menu, choose Add SpeedDial.

   The caller is added to your SpeedDial list.

Creating a SpeedDial When You're Not in a Call

To create a SpeedDial when you're not connected with someone, do the following:

1. From the SpeedDial menu, choose Add SpeedDial. You'll see the Add SpeedDial dialog box, shown here:

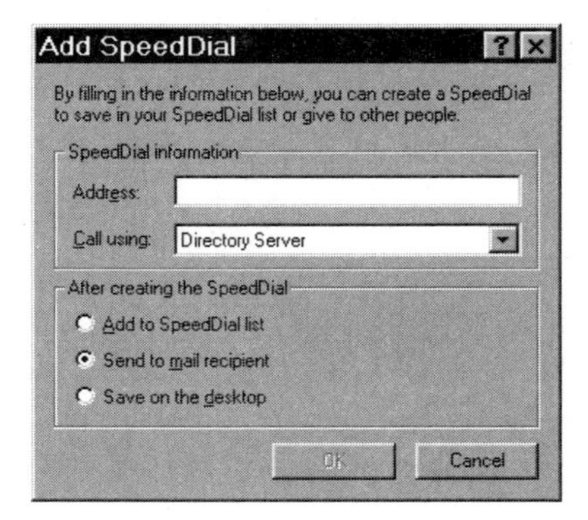

SEE ALSO

To specify SpeedDial defaults, see "Choosing Calling Options," on pages 645.

2 In the SpeedDial information area, type the one of the following:

- For a caller who registers on a directory server, type the directory server name, followed by a slash and the e-mail name (for example, ils.Microsoft.com/sallym).
- If you're calling a person who has a permanent Internet (IP) address, type the address.

3 In the Call Using area, choose one of the following:

- For callers on directory servers, choose Directory Server.
- For callers using Internet addresses, choose Network (TCP/IP).

4 In the After Creating The SpeedDial area, choose an option. You can Add To SpeedDial List, Send To Mail Recipient, or Save On The Desktop.

5 Click OK.

To have NetMeeting make SpeedDial entries for the people you call and for those who call you, click Tools on the menu bar and choose Options. You'll see the Options dialog box. Click the Calling tab. Check Always in the box called Automatically Add SpeedDials For People I Call And People Who Call Me.

Placing a Call with SpeedDial

To place a call with SpeedDial, you must first create a SpeedDial entry, as described later in this chapter. When that is done, follow these steps to place your call.

1. Click the SpeedDial tab. NetMeeting will display all the names you have entered into the SpeedDial list.
2. Choose the person you want to call from the SpeedDial list.
3. Click the Call button in the toolbar; NetMeeting will display a New Call dialog box with the address already in place.
4. Choose the type of connection appropriate for the person you're calling. If this person is registered on a Directory Server, select Call Using Directory Server. If you know this person's permanent IP address, select Network (TCP/IP). If you aren't sure and want NetMeeting to decide, select Automatic.
5. If there is a meeting taking place, enable Join The Meeting Named and type in the name of the meeting you want to join.

Starting a Meeting

When you start a meeting, you don't need to actually place a call. Rather, the people who call you can join or leave, much as they would in a chat room on Microsoft Chat. You can choose to accept callers automatically or to screen them.

Although you can set up a meeting for more than two people, only two people can communicate via audio and video at a time. For this reason, you'll probably want to set up a text-chat session, as described in the next section.

> To set up the meeting, contact people via e-mail and set up a time.

To start a meeting, do the following:

1. From the Call menu, choose Host Meeting. You'll see a dialog box explaining how a meeting works. To suppress this message, check Don't Show Me This Message Again, and click OK.

   You'll see a Current Call window with your name added.
2. When callers arrive, you'll see requests to join the meeting. You can approve or reject these requests.
3. To switch audio and video to another user, click Switch on the toolbar, and select a caller's name.

4 To eject someone from the meeting, right-click the caller's name, and choose Remove From Meeting.

5 To stop your participation in the meeting, click Hang Up or go to the Call menu and select Hang Up. If you're the host of the meeting, all parties will lose their connections when you hang up.

Conferencing with Text Chatting

If you're hosting a meeting, or if network performance degrades so that you can't understand the audio, you will need to communicate using the Chat window.

Opening the Chat Window

To open the Chat window, follow these steps:

1 Do one of the following:

- In the Current Call window, click Chat on the toolbar.

  or

- From the Tools menu, choose Chat.

  or

- Press Ctrl + T shortcut.

You'll see the Chat window, shown in Figure 18-4.

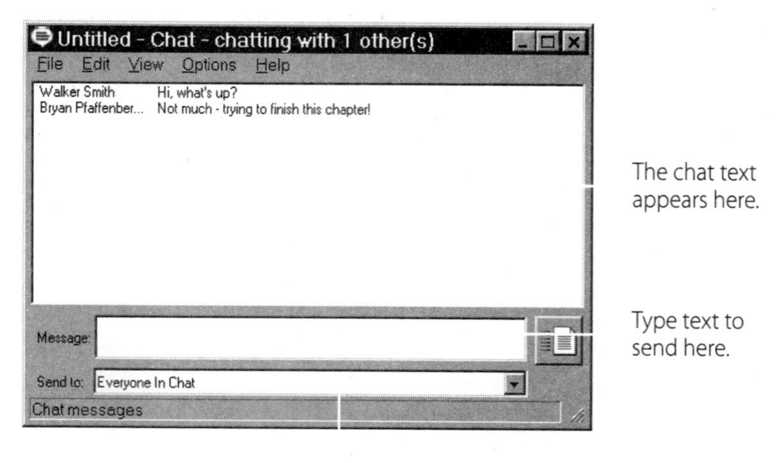

FIGURE 18-4.
You can communicate via text chatting with the Chat window.

2 To send text, choose a recipient in the Send To area (you can choose a single caller, or Everyone In Chat). Type the text in the Message area, and press Enter.

Choosing the Chat Format

By default, NetMeeting places the person's name at the beginning of each line the person types and wraps lengthy lines so that the line starts next to the person's information. You can choose additional chat formats. You can display or hide the person's name, as well as the date and time, in the information automatically inserted with each line of text. You can also format the entire message to be placed on one line instead of wrapping the text. Or you can choose a formatting option that places the information display on the line preceding the text the person types.

To choose chat formats, follow these steps:

1 From the Chat window's Options menu, choose Chat Format.

You'll see the Chat Format dialog box, shown here:

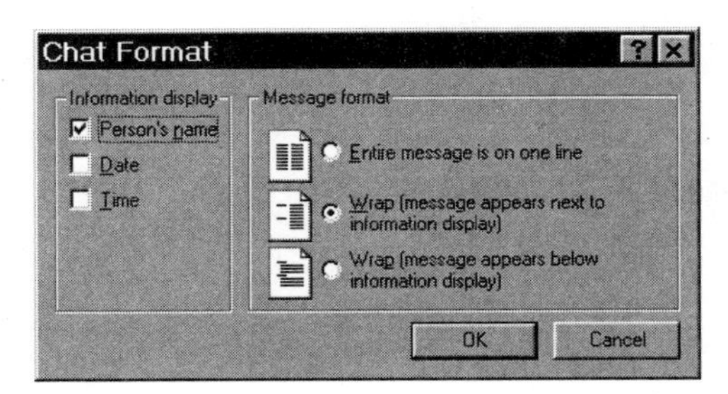

2 In the Information Display area, check the items you want to display.

3 In the Message Format area, choose the text wrapping method.

4 Click OK to confirm your choices.

Saving and Printing Chat Files

If you wish, you can save and print a chat conversation the same way you save any text document.

To save the conversation, follow these steps:

1 From the Chat window's File menu, choose Save.

2 In the Save dialog box, type a file name, choose a location, and click Save.

To print the conversation, follow these steps:

1 From the Chat window's File menu, choose Print.

2 In the Print dialog box, choose the printing options you want, and click OK.

If you haven't saved a conversation, you'll see an alert box when you exit the conversation that asks you whether you want to save it. To save it, click Yes. To abandon the conversation, click No. To return to Chat, click Cancel.

Using Whiteboard

Whiteboard provides a shared graphical workspace for generating and sharing ideas. Although Whiteboard appears to resemble the simple Windows Paint accessory, it's a full-featured accessory that offers multiple pages, a yellow highlighter for emphasizing text or graphics, and screen-capture capabilities that enable you to take a "snapshot" of a window and show it to others in the meeting.

Starting Whiteboard

To start Whiteboard, follow these steps:

Do one of the following:

- In the Current Call window, click Whiteboard on the toolbar.

  or

- From the Tools menu, choose Whiteboard.

  or

- Press Ctr + W.

You'll see the Whiteboard window (Figure 18-5).

After you start Whiteboard, all other meeting participants will also see their Whiteboards. Collaboration is enabled so that a change made by any participant will be seen by everyone.

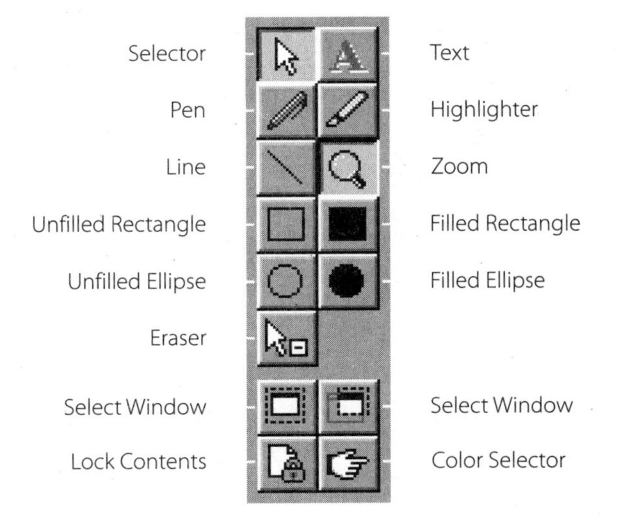

FIGURE 18-5. The Whiteboard offers tools callers can use in a shared graphical workspace.

Understanding the Whiteboard Window

The Whiteboard window has the usual window features, including the title bar and menu bar. In addition, you'll find the following:

- **Toolbar.** Click here to use the various tools. To hide or display the toolbar, go to the View menu and select Tool Bar.
- **Color Selector.** Click here to select a color when you're typing or drawing.
- **Page Selector.** These tools are useful when Whiteboard contains more than one page.
- **Status Bar.** The status bar displays Whiteboard's messages. To hide or display the status bar, choose Status Bar from the View menu.

When you're working in the Whiteboard window, you can zoom in for a closer look. Simply go to the View menu and select Zoom, or click the Zoom tool. To restore the window to the default magnification, select or click Zoom again.

You will see your own pointer in the window, but others can't see your pointer. If you would like to point at something in your window, select Remote Pointer from the Tools menu, or click the Remote Pointer On tool. A hand symbol appears in everyone's Whiteboard windows, which you can then move by dragging it with your mouse pointer.

Although Whiteboard superficially resembles the Paint accessory, it is far superior. Each addition you make can be individually selected, edited, or moved.

Using the Tools

On the toolbar, you'll find the tools that enable you to create text and drawings, highlight text or graphics on the screen, and paste windows into Whiteboard. Here's a quick overview of the tools you can use to add content to the window.

Choosing a Color and Line Width

For each drawing object you create, you can choose a color and line width. To change the object's color, choose a color from the color selector, or go to the Options menu, select Colors, click a color in the Color dialog box, and click OK. To change the object's line width, click a line width in the toolbar, or go to the Options menu, select Line Width, and choose a line thickness from the submenu.

Editing and Highlighting

After you create an object with the text or drawing tools, you can move the object by selecting it with the Selector tool and dragging it to its new position. You can send the object to the background—select Send To Back from the Edit menu—or bring the object to the foreground—select Bring To Front from the Edit menu. Use the Delete key to delete a selected object.

A nifty feature of Whiteboard is the Highlighter. To highlight text or graphics within the Whiteboard window, click the Highlighter tool. If necessary, click the yellow color in the color selector.

Pasting a Window into Whiteboard

You can show meeting participants a selected part of your screen or all of another window by pasting a graphic "snapshot" of the selected screen area or window into Whiteboard.

To prepare for pasting, minimize Whiteboard and arrange the screen so that the material you want to paste is visible. Then restore Whiteboard.

To paste a portion of the screen into Whiteboard, click Select Area (or go to the Tools menu and choose Select Area). Whiteboard disappears, enabling you to select a screen area by dragging. When you release the mouse button, you see your selection within Whiteboard. Click the Selector tool, and drag the window to position it.

TABLE 18-4. Whiteboard Tools.

Selector	Description
Text	Click here to add text to Whiteboard. After clicking the tool, click the pointer where you want to start entering text. To change the font, font size, or font effects (strike-out or underline), click the Font Options button or go to the Options menu and select Font. Make the choices you want in the Font dialog box, and click OK.
Pen	Click here to draw a freehand line. After clicking the tool, drag within the window to draw shapes.
Highlighter	Click this tool to mark the window with a yellow highlighter.
Line	Click here to draw a straight line. After clicking the tool, hold down the mouse button and drag within the window to draw a straight line. Release the mouse button where you want the line to end.
Zoom	Click to zoom the window to a higher magnification; click again to restore the previous magnification.
Unfilled Rectangle	Click here to create a rectangle that doesn't have a background color.
Filled Rectangle	Click here to create a rectangle that's automatically filled with the background color currently selected in the color selector.
Unfilled Ellipse	Click here to create an ellipse that doesn't have a background color.
Filled Ellipse	Click here to create an ellipse that's filled with the background color currently selected in the color selector.
Eraser	Click here to switch to the eraser; you can erase something by clicking it.
Select Window	Click here to select another window on your screen; this will be pasted into Whiteboard as a graphic.
Select Area	Click here to select an area of another window on your screen; it will be pasted into Whiteboard as a graphic.
Lock contents	Click here to freeze the window contents so that other users cannot modify the Whiteboard.
Remove pointer	Click here to insert a pointer that all users can see.

To paste a window into Whiteboard, click Select Window (or go to the Tools menu and choose Select Window). Whiteboard disappears, enabling you to click the window you want to paste into Whiteboard. After you click this window, Whiteboard reappears and you see the window within Whiteboard. Click the Selector tool, and drag the window to position it.

> **NOTE**
>
> Unlike a shared application, a window pasted into Whiteboard isn't live. Participants won't see any changes you subsequently make in the original window. However, pasting a window into Whiteboard consumes much less Internet bandwidth than running a live demonstration. If there is no need to show conferees a running application, use the Whiteboard.

Paging Through Whiteboard

You can add more than one page to Whiteboard using the page selector tools (see Figure 18-5): First Page, Previous Page, Page, Next Page, Last Page, and Insert New Page.

To add an additional page to Whiteboard, click Insert New Page. The number in the Last Page box increases to show the total number of pages.

To move to a page, click the Next Page or Previous Page buttons, or type a page number in the Page box and press Enter. You can go to the beginning by clicking First Page or to the end by clicking Last Page.

Sharing Applications

The most advanced feature of NetMeeting is the program's ability to display a shared application on the screens of everyone participating in a meeting. You also have the option of enabling others in a meeting to control the program and work with the data you're displaying.

To share an application, follow these steps:

1 Start the application you want to share.

On the toolbar, click Share. You'll see the following message:

At this point, other callers will see your application, but they won't be able to work with it or modify it. In order to share control of the application, you and all other callers must chose Collaborate from the toolbar.

2 If you would like to make the application available for modification and control by other users, click Collaborate.

   In order to collaborate, others in the conference must also click Collaborate.

If you're sharing an application, clicking on its window will bring it to the foreground not only in your computer but in the computers of everyone in the meeting. If someone else is sharing a program with you, the program starts automatically and you see the application on the screen. To take control of the program, double-click the program window. (You can do this only if the person sharing the program has enabled collaboration.) To stop collaborating, go to the Tools menu and click Stop Collaborating (or click the Collaborate button again).

Sending and Receiving Files

One of NetMeeting's most useful features is file transfer, which enables you to send and receive files while you're connected with others. (If more than one person is in a meeting with you, you can send the file to everyone in the meeting or choose the person to whom you'd like to send the file.) The file transfer is efficient and relatively quick, depending on the quality of your Internet connection. Best of all, the person receiving the file can verify whether it arrived intact and confirm via audio or the Chat window.

Sending a File to Everyone in the Meeting

To send a file to everyone in the meeting,

1 Do one of the following:

   - Press Ctrl + F.

   or

   - From the Tools menu, point to File Transfer, and choose Send File.

   You'll see the Select A File To Send dialog box.

2 Locate and select the file you want to send, and click Send.

You'll see a progress indicator as the file as sent.

When the file transfer is complete, you'll see a dialog box confirming the transfer.

Sending a File to One Person

To send a file to just one person in a meeting, right-click the person's name and click Send File. You'll see a dialog box that enables you to select the file you want to send. When you've selected the file, click OK.

Receiving a File

If a caller sends you a file, you'll see the dialog box shown here:

Do one of the following:

- To save the file, click Close.

  or

- To view the file, click Open.

  or

- To delete the file without saving it, click Delete.

Viewing the Received Files Folder

To view the folder where your received files are stored, do the following:

1 From the Tools menu, point to File Transfer, and click Open Received Files Folder.

2 In this folder, you can open, rename, or delete the files you've received.

Customizing Microsoft NetMeeting

To choose custom options for NetMeeting, click Tools on the menu bar, and choose Options. You'll see the Options dialog box; the following sections discuss the options available on each page.

Choosing General Options

In the General page of the Options dialog box, shown in the following illustration, you can choose general NetMeeting options, select a default bandwidth, and determine where received files are stored.

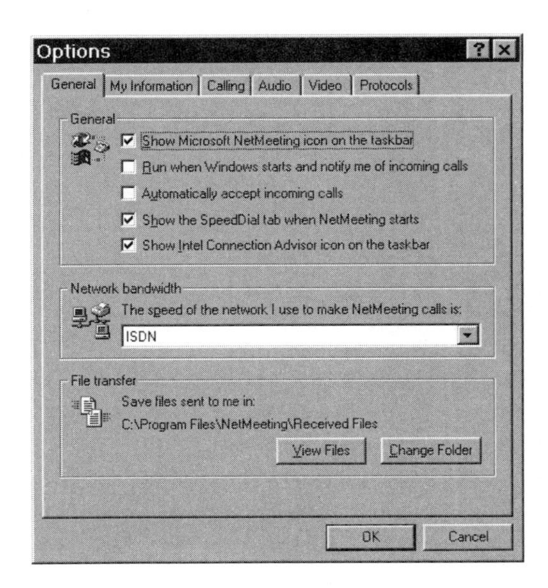

You may wish to adjust the following:

- **Show Microsoft NetMeeting Icon On The Taskbar.** This option displays a convenient icon on the taskbar. If NetMeeting is running in the background, this icon enables you to open NetMeeting and answer calls conveniently.
- **Run When Windows Starts And Notify Me Of Incoming Calls.** Enable this option if you would like to have Windows start NetMeeting at the beginning of each session. With this option checked, you can make sure you won't miss calls.

- **Automatically Accept Incoming Calls.** This option isn't recommended if you make your name available on public ILS servers.
- **Show The SpeedDial Tab When NetMeeting Starts.** This option is checked by default, but you can turn it off if you don't want to use SpeedDial shortcuts.
- **Show Intel Connection Advisor Icon On The Taskbar.** You can uncheck this option if your connections are good and you don't need to troubleshoot your audio.

If you plan to use NetMeeting regularly for business purposes, be sure to check the options that start the program when Windows starts and that accept incoming calls. In this way you can be sure you won't miss callers.

Specifying Your Information

In the My Information page, shown here, you can change your personal information:

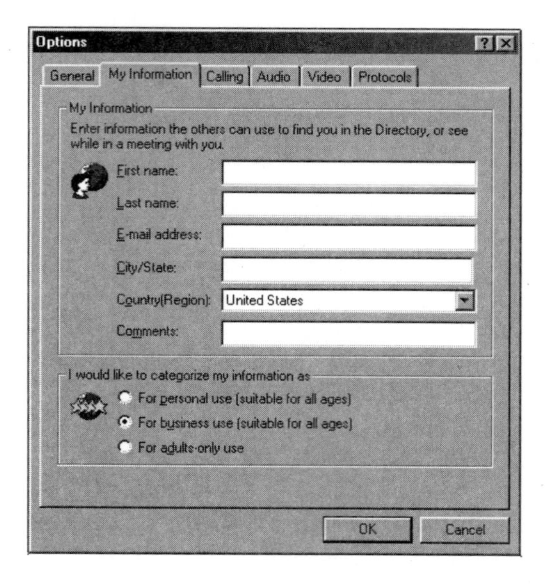

This is the information you supplied when you installed NetMeeting.

Choosing Calling Options

In the Calling page, shown here, you can specify a default directory server, set up automatic SpeedDial shortcuts, and specify SpeedDial defaults:

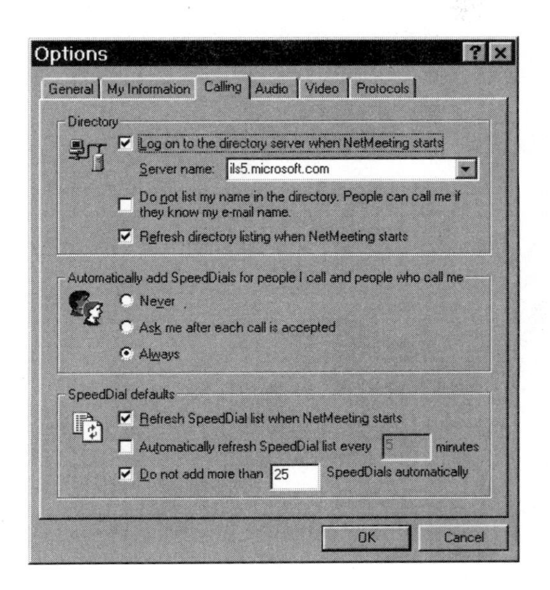

You may wish to change some of these options:

- **Log On To The Directory Server When NetMeeting Starts.** In the Server Name box, specify the server that you want NetMeeting to use. If you don't want to log on to a server, uncheck this option.
- **Do Not List My Name In The Directory.** Choose this option if you would like people to call you only if they know your e-mail address.
- **Refresh Directory Listing When NetMeeting Starts.** This is the default option, and it's a good one; people come and go from directories, so you want to use an up-to-date list.

Choosing Audio Options

In the Audio page, shown here, you can choose audio options.

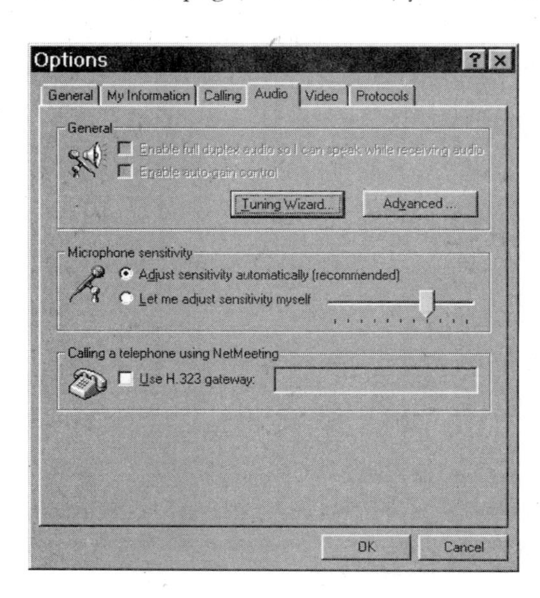

You may wish to adjust these settings:

- **Enable Full-Duplex Audio So I Can Speak While Receiving Audio.** Check this option if you have a full-duplex sound card. It's dimmed if your sound card can't handle full-duplex audio.
- **Enable Auto-Gain Control.** This option adjusts the volume based on how loud your voice is. Uncheck this option if you're working in a setting with a lot of background noise.

Choosing Video Options

In the Video page, shown on the next page, you can choose options for sending and receiving video.

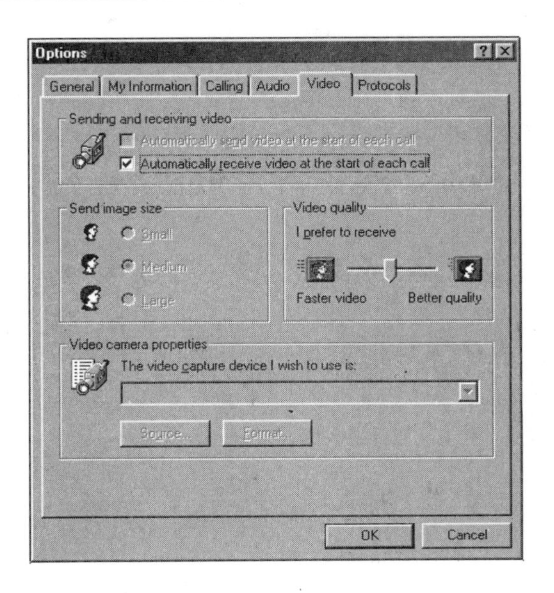

You may wish to adjust the following:

- **Automatically Send Video At The Start Of Each Call.** Check this option if you have a digital video camera mounted on your computer and ready to use for video conferencing purposes. This option is dimmed if you don't have video hardware.
- **Automatically Receive Video At The Start Of Each Call.** This option is checked by default, and this setting is a good one. If you uncheck it, you might not realize that a caller is trying to send video.
- **Video Quality.** Quality is set to medium by default; choose Better Quality if you have a fast system, or Faster Video if you have a slow system.

TIP

NetMeeting configures video-camera properties when you install the program. If you upgrade your video hardware after installing NetMeeting, use the Video Camera Properties area to select your new video equipment.

Choosing Protocols

The Protocols page enables you to check the Null Modem protocol, which you can use to connect two computers by means of their serial ports. Don't uncheck Network (TCP/IP); this protocol is needed to send audio and video over the Internet.

PART V

Publishing Your Own Content

CHAPTER 19

Learning Web Publishing Essentials

The Web isn't strictly a couch potato's medium; you can create content as well as sit back and groove on it. That's exactly what makes the Web so vibrant and exciting. Sure, it's fun to browse the big commercial sites. But you'll really understand the Web when you find that little page somewhere—a page that few others would find interesting—that contains exactly the information you need. The Web grows richer every time a user decides, "Hey, what I've got to say just might be useful to somebody else."

This chapter introduces Microsoft FrontPage Express, the Internet Explorer module that enables anyone to create compelling Web content. You don't need to learn HTML to create exciting Web pages with FrontPage Express; it's as easy as using a word processing program. In this chapter, you'll learn how to use the Home Page Wizard to create a personal or business home page quickly. You'll also learn how to edit the page you've created. In the next chapter, you'll learn how to add all kinds of cool features to your pages, including background sounds, background graphics, ActiveX controls, and much more.

NOTE

Microsoft FrontPage Express is a simplified version of Microsoft FrontPage, but don't let the word *simplified* fool you. FrontPage Express may seem simple on the surface, but there's a world of HTML functions beneath. Three chapters certainly can't cover every feature and capability of FrontPage Express, especially for anyone who knows a little HTML. So this chapter and the next one are designed to serve as an introduction to FrontPage Express, highlighting the features that Web authors use most often—as well as the ones that are the most fun.

Introducing Web Publishing

The Web becomes richer every time a new page appears. Until recently, though, the difficulty of learning HTML posed a roadblock to widespread Web publishing. HTML, short for HyperText Markup Language, enables Web authors to prepare documents for publication on the Web.

Understanding HTML

HTML is a *markup language*. Unlike a word processing program, which inserts formatting codes that tell a printer how to print a document, a markup language is used (at least ideally) to do no more than identify the parts of a document. Formatting is—ideally—left up to the browser.

When you use a markup language, you insert codes, called *tags*, that identify a certain document component, such as a title or heading. These components are called *elements*.

Looking at HTML Tags

Most HTML elements require you to supply a start tag and an end tag; both are needed so that the program reading the file can tell where the document element begins. For example, the following examples show how to mark a level 1 (major) heading, a paragraph of document text, and a bulleted list:

```
<H1>This is a Major Heading.</H1>
<P>Here is the text of a text paragraph. Most
browsers display a text paragraph with flush left
alignment, single line spacing, and a blank line
before the paragraph.</P>
<UL>
 <LI>This is the first line of a bulleted list.</LI>
 <LI>This is the second line of a bulleted list.</LI>
 <LI>This is the third line of a bulleted list.</LI>
</UL>
```

Browsers are programmed to detect HTML markup, and they display documents according to the underlying HTML. You don't normally see the HTML in your browser; if you want to see it, go to the View menu and select Source. Figure 19-1 shows some of the HTML code that underlies a popular Web page.

FIGURE 19-1.
It's a tough job to edit HTML documents directly because the HTML instructions, or tags, get in the way.

View or Edit HTML

```
<html>

<head>
<meta http-equiv="Content-Type"
content="text/html; charset=iso-8859-1">
<meta name="created by" content="Tim Radcliffe">
<meta name="GENERATOR" content="Microsoft FrontPage Express 2.0">
<title>TCC Home</title>
</head>

<body bgcolor="#FFFFFF" link="#745D27">

<table border="0" cellpadding="0" cellspacing="0" width="808"
height="455">
    <tr>
        <td valign="top" width="100%"><div align="center"><center><table
        border="0" cellpadding="0" cellspacing="0" width="789">
            <tr>
                <td valign="bottom" width="36%"><img
                src="LOGO.JPG" width="266" height="151"
                naturalsizeflag="3"> </td>
                <td width="64%"><img src="TITLE.JPG" width="491"
                height="138" naturalsizeflag="0"> </td>
            </tr>
        </table>
        </center></div><div align="center"><center><table
        border="0" cellpadding="0" width="795" height="41">
            <tr>
                <td width="100%" height="36"><!--webbot
                bot="ImageMap" startspan
                rectangle=" (535,5) (682, 21)  http://repo-nt.tcc.virgin
                rectangle=" (444,6) (524, 20)  CLASSWEB/classweb.html"
                rectangle=" (326,5) (433, 21)  FACSTAFF/facstaff.html"
                rectangle=" (212,5) (314, 23)  MEDIA/media.html"
                rectangle=" (96,6) (198, 20)  THESIS/thesis.html"
                rectangle=" (2,7) (88, 22)  ABOUT/about.html"
                rectangle=" (0,0) (700, 22)  ABOUT/about.html"
                src="navbarl.gif" border="0" width="789"
                height="22" naturalsizeflag="3" ismap --><MAP NAME="Fron
                bot="ImageMap" i-checksum="50112" endspan --> </td>
            </tr>
        </table>
```

Original   Current   Show Color Coding   OK   Cancel   Help

View or edit the current HTML

Grasping the Problems of HTML

As the above example suggests, HTML isn't all that difficult to learn, but it does require a few days or a couple of weeks of study and experimentation. But HTML isn't sufficient for most Web-publishing purposes. The strict "no formatting" rule doesn't cut it with most Web authors, who want to control their Web page's appearance, for example, by choosing fonts, colors, and layout options. And that's where the problems started.

In order to create a market, browser publishers added tags that enabled HTML authors to add rich formatting to their documents. The result? An uneditable, error-prone mess, such as the following:

```
<H1><FONT face="Helvetica"><B>This is a Major
Heading.</B></FONT></H1>
<P align="justify"><FONT face="Times Roman">Here is
the text of a text paragraph. Most browsers display
```

```
a text paragraph with flush-left alignment, single-
line spacing, and a blank line before the
paragraph.</FONT></P>
```

Like other Web authors, you'll want to add formatting to your pages. But doing so creates an editing nightmare. For example, suppose you want to change some text. Finding it, and making the changes without disturbing the HTML code, is quite a trick. That's why WYSIWYG (what you see is what you get) editors were created.

WYSIWYG Editors

Thanks to a new generation of WYSIWYG HTML editors, the tedium's gone. (WYSIWYG, by the way, is pronounced wiss-see-wig.) With a WYSIWYG editor, you create a Web page much the way you'd create a word processing document. You type text and choose formatting commands that affect the text's appearance. A good WYSIWYG editor creates all the HTML code for you. You can also add graphics and other multimedia resources. And all the while, the program shows your document the way it will look when it's displayed by a Web browser. Any changes you make are instantly reflected on the screen. You don't have to switch to your browser to see what your document looks like; you see your document's appearance while you're editing.

You'll find quite a few WYSIWYG editors in today's market, but one of the most impressive is included with the Microsoft Internet Explorer Suite: FrontPage Express. Figure 19-2 shows how FrontPage Express displays HTML files in a WYSIWYG environment, enabling you to create and edit Web pages as easily as you would write or modify a word processing document. (This is the same document shown in Figure 19-1.) You can even create and edit tables, as Figure 19-2 shows.

Why FrontPage Express?

FrontPage Express is easy to use, and it's included with the Microsoft Internet Explorer Suite. It is essentially a simplified version of FrontPage Editor, the WYSIWYG editor that's included in Microsoft FrontPage. FrontPage is a professional Web-publishing program—and it isn't free. So it's a genuine bargain to get so much of FrontPage Editor's power in this simplified version.

But don't let *simplified* fool you into thinking that FrontPage Express is useful only for simplistic Web pages. FrontPage Express offers more than enough features to help you create highly effective and complex

Web pages. To make your page as appealing as possible, you can add fonts, tables, sounds, ActiveX controls, Java applets, and much more.

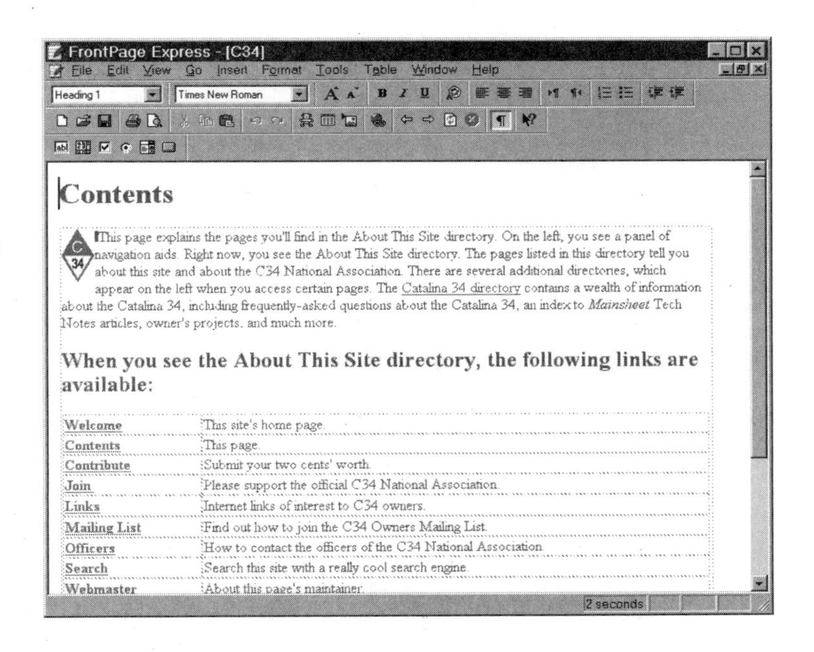

FIGURE 19-2.
FrontPage Express displays HTML files in a what-you-see-is-what-you-get (WYSIWYG) environment, enabling you to create and edit Web pages easily.

Moving Up to Microsoft FrontPage

So if FrontPage Express contains virtually all of the tools you need to create and edit high-quality Web pages, why would anyone need the full FrontPage package?

FrontPage Express is designed for individuals who prepare their own pages and upload these pages to Web servers that somebody else maintains. Microsoft FrontPage, in contrast, is designed for Web professionals who not only prepare Web content but also administer complex Web sites. Site administrators appreciate the organization and administration features of FrontPage, such as an automatic utility that checks all of a site's hyperlinks to see if any of them are broken (that is, refer to documents that have been moved or deleted).

Although FrontPage is a powerful program, it is still very easy to use, and that's especially true if you've learned FrontPage Express. Closely resembling FrontPage Express are the tools FrontPage provides for Web-page creation, editing, and formatting. Once you've learned the fundamentals of FrontPage Express, as presented in this and the next chapter, you'll have an excellent start in Web publishing.

For information on publishing your Web pages, see Chapter 21, "Publishing Your Pages on the Internet."

Understanding the Web-Publishing Process

To make your completed Web pages available for others to see, you need to place them on a computer that's running a Web server. (Remember, a Web server is a program that runs on an Internet-connected computer.) This program waits in the background until someone clicks a hyperlink that's pointed at one of the Web pages stored on the server's computer. The server processes this request and sends out a copy of the desired document, along with any associated graphics, multimedia resources, controls, or applets that the page contains. Since publishing your page will involve uploading it to a computer that's running a Web server, this section briefly describes the Web-publishing process.

Introducing Web Publishing Wizard

Running a Web server requires a computer with a permanent Internet connection—something most people don't have. Most Internet users access the Internet by means of a dial-up connection and a modem, but this type of connection isn't sufficient for running a Web server. For this reason, most Web authors prefer to *upload* (send) their pages to their Internet service provider's Web server. When the Web pages are placed in an ISP's Web storage space, they become accessible to other Internet users.

When you're ready to publish your page, you can use Web Publishing Wizard, one of the options you can download along with Internet Explorer. You'll learn how to use the wizard in Chapter 21.

Introducing Personal Web Server

If you access the Internet by means of a dial-up connection, you can't make your Web pages available through a Web server running on your own computer. However, many people use Windows computers connected to corporate local area networks (LANs), and LANs are often hooked up to the Internet. If you access the Internet by means of a LAN, it's possible that your computer has a permanent Internet connection. If so, you can use Personal Web Server to make your Web pages available to other users on your network.

Personal Web Server is extremely easy to use. Even if you have no previous experience running a server of any kind, you can set up a Web server easily with this program. You'll learn how to use Personal Web Server in Chapter 21.

Publishing with Microsoft Internet Information Server (IIS)

If the server you're planning to use is running Windows NT Server Microsoft Internet Information Server (IIS), you're in luck. You can take advantage of several advanced FrontPage Express features, including these:

- **Page templates and wizards.** FrontPage Express enables you to create Web pages with forms that collect user input, send the user a page acknowledging this input, and store the input in a separate file.
- **WebBots.** Without any programming, you can create *WebBots,* which are hidden scripts you place in your Web page. Included with FrontPage Express are scripts that include another Web page at the script's location, a Search utility that enables users to search all the documents in your site, and a time stamp that displays the day's date and time.

Note that these features work only if you publish your page using Microsoft Internet Information Server (IIS), or the FrontPage extensions, software that Microsoft makes available so that users of other servers can take advantage of FrontPage features. What's terrific about these features is that they automate tasks that formerly could be accomplished only by means of tedious server-side programming using the Common Gateway Interface (CGI) and other programming tools. If you plan to publish using IIS, and you like the page templates, wizards, and WebBots, you've yet another reason to investigate Microsoft FrontPage because it includes many more of these.

If you're planning to publish your Web pages on your Internet service provider's computers, find out whether your ISP is running Microsoft Internet Information Server, or the FrontPage extensions. If so, you can use the special features of FrontPage Express, such as themes and WebBots.

Introducing FrontPage Express

FrontPage Express is an easy-to-use WYSIWYG program for creating and editing Web documents. In the following sections, you'll learn how to install and start the program, and you'll explore the toolbars, which contain almost all the commands you'll use.

Installing and Starting FrontPage Express

If you didn't install FrontPage Express when you installed Internet Explorer, start Internet Explorer, click Tools on the menu bar, and choose Windows Update. Follow the on-screen instructions to install FrontPage Express.

To start FrontPage Express, click Start on the taskbar, point to Programs, point to Accessories, point to Internet Tools, and choose FrontPage Express.

Exploring the FrontPage Express Window

FrontPage Express opens in its own window and has its own unique toolbars. Take a couple of minutes to familiarize yourself with the toolbars; they hold the key to many of the neat things that FrontPage Express can do.

If you don't see one or more of the toolbars explained on the following pages, click View on the menu bar and choose the toolbar's name.

The Standard Toolbar

The standard toolbar is shown in the following illustration:

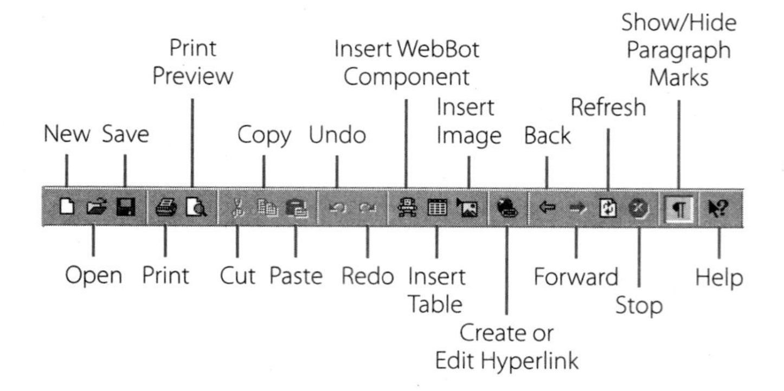

Like the toolbars in Internet Explorer, the FrontPage Express toolbars can be dragged to new locations. Unlike Internet Explorer's toolbars, though, these toolbars can be repositioned anywhere on the screen. (In this way, they're like Microsoft Office toolbars.) You can detach the toolbar from the FrontPage Express window completely so that the toolbar becomes a separate window that you can drag anywhere on the screen.

This toolbar provides basic commands for creating, opening, saving, and printing files, as well as editing and navigation functions. It also enables you to enter some of FrontPage Express's functions, such as WebBots. Table 19-1 connects specific buttons with their functions.

TABLE 19-1. Tools on the Standard Toolbar.

Name	Action
New	Creates a new file.
Open	Opens a page from your local drive or from the network.
Save	Saves the current page.
Print	Prints the current page.
Print Preview	Displays a Print Preview window showing the page's appearance as it will print on your printer.
Cut	Cuts the selection to the Clipboard.
Copy	Copies the selection to the Clipboard.
Paste	Inserts the Clipboard's contents at the cursor's location.
Undo	Cancels the last editing action.
Redo	Repeats an editing action or restores the last action canceled by Undo.
Insert WebBot Component	Inserts a WebBot component at the cursor's location.
Insert Table	Inserts a table at the cursor's location.
Insert Image	Inserts an inline image at the cursor's location.
Create or Edit Hyperlink	Inserts a hyperlink or edits an existing hyperlink at the cursor's location.
Back	Moves to the previous document.
Forward	Moves to the next document.
Refresh	Retrieves a new copy of the page from the network.
Stop	Stops downloading the current page.
Show/Hide	Displays or hides paragraph marks and table boundaries. paragraph marks
Help	Displays help for the feature you click after pressing this button.

The Format Toolbar

The format toolbar is shown here:

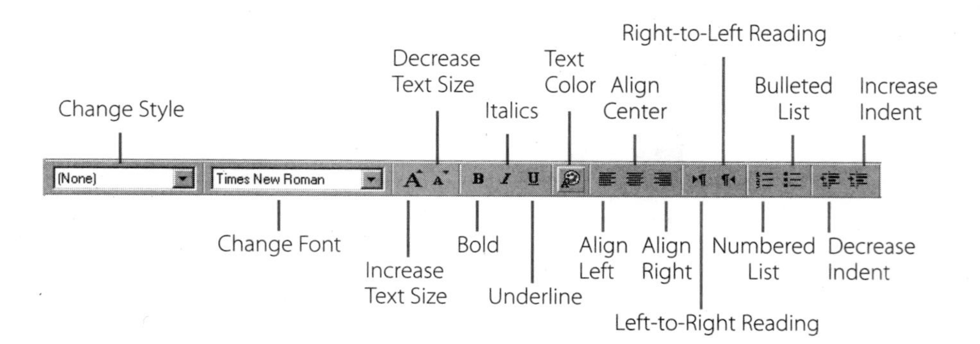

This toolbar enables you to choose paragraph styles, fonts, font sizes, character emphases, character colors, alignments, and indents. You can access these tools in two ways. One way is to click the button and start typing. The text you type will take on the format you've chosen. The second way is to select some text and then click the button. The format you choose will be applied only to the text you've selected. Table 19-2 details your options in the format toolbar.

The Forms Toolbar

You can use the forms toolbar to enter interactive features, such as text boxes, drop-down list boxes, check boxes, and radio buttons. That sounds nice, but bear in mind that these features by themselves won't do anything. In order to accomplish a meaningful task, the output of these interactive features must be linked with a server-side script or program. Most Web authors don't have the necessary technical skills to add these features. They require custom programming on the server side, and the price can be high.

If you're planning to publish your pages with Microsoft Internet Information Server, you can take advantage of the Form Page Wizard, which enables you to create a form—complete with all the programming necessary to work with IIS. The wizard guides you through the process of creating a form and enables you to choose from a number of options. For example, you can choose whether you want to save the results to a Web page or a text file. As you produce the form page, you create each input field by choosing options from the wizard. The result is a form page that's designed to solicit precisely the information you need.

You can then modify this page with FrontPage Express by adding backgrounds, graphics, fonts, other formatting, and hyperlinks.

Since forms, the forms toolbar, and the Form Page Wizard require IIS or custom programming, they're beyond the scope of this book. Even so, you can still create Web pages that include interactive features. Later in this chapter, for example, you'll learn how to create mailto links, which bring up a mail composition window for feedback. If you're planning to give your page to a service provider who will provide the scripting and programming necessary to get the forms to work, you can go ahead and create a page with form features such as drop-down list boxes and radio buttons. Just keep in mind that these features won't work unless they're linked to a script. (Forms will be discussed further in Chapter 19.)

TABLE 19-2. Tools on the Format Toolbar.

Name	Action
Change Style	Assigns a paragraph style for headings and lists.
Change Font	Assigns a font.
Increase Text Size	Increases the font size.
Decrease Text Size	Decreases the font size.
Bold	Creates bold-character emphasis.
Italic	Creates italic-character emphasis.
Underline	Creates underlining.
Text Color	Chooses a text color.
Align Left	Aligns text flush left.
Center	Centers the text.
Align Right	Aligns text flush right.
Left-to-Right Reading	Formats the document for left-to-right reading.
Right-to-Left Reading	Formats the document for right-to-left reading, which is required for certain foreign languages.
Numbered List	Creates a numbered list.
Bulleted List	Creates a bulleted list.
Decrease Indent	Decreases the paragraph indent.
Increase Indent	Increases the paragraph indent.

The forms toolbar is shown here:

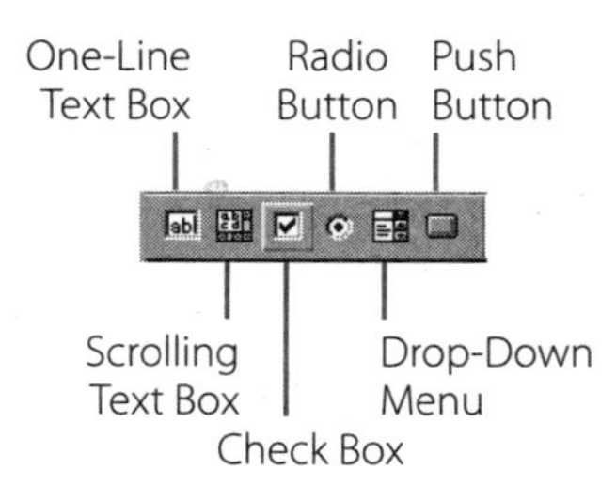

This toolbar enables you to enter interactive form features by clicking one of the buttons. Table 19-3 explains what they do.

TABLE 19-3. Tools on the Forms Toolbar.

Name	Action
One-Line Text Box	Enters a one-line text box (no scrolling).
Scrolling Text Box	Enters a text box that enables the user to enter more than one line of text, with scrolling.
Check Box	Enters a check box.
Radio Button	Enters a radio button.
Drop-Down Menu	Enters a drop-down menu.
Push Button	Enters a push button.

FrontPage Express uses pop-up menus that change depending on their context. To see a pop-up menu, point to something on-screen, and click the right-mouse button. You'll see options pertinent to what you've clicked.

Creating a Web Page with FrontPage Express

Using the tools in FrontPage Express, you can create or modify a Web page in the following ways:

- **Use the page wizards.** FrontPage Express comes with several page wizards, including the Personal Home Page Wizard, the New Web View Folder (for customizing your Windows folders), and several wizards for creating pages designed to work with Internet Information Server. To use a page wizard, choose New from the File menu and select a wizard from the New Page dialog box.
- **Create a page from scratch.** When you start FrontPage Express, the program displays a new, blank page. You can use this to create a new Web page. Another way to begin is to click the New button on the standard toolbar or select New from the File menu, and then choose Normal Page from the New Page dialog box.
- **Edit a page on the Web.** You can open any Web page in FrontPage Express by displaying the page in Internet Explorer and then clicking the Edit button or choosing Edit With Microsoft FrontPage Editor from the File menu. Any changes you make won't affect the Web page you've downloaded, unless you possess the password that would enable you to upload these changes to the Web server's computer.

In the following section, you'll learn how to create a home page using the Personal Home Page Wizard. In the sections to come, you'll try creating a page from scratch. You'll also learn how to edit an existing page.

Creating a Home Page Using Personal Home Page Wizard

What's the first Web page you're likely to publish? I'll bet it's a personal home page, a page that contains information about you, such as contact details, biographical material, current projects, and special interests. In a company, such a page provides other employees with a means of contacting you. More broadly, a personal home page provides a way for people to find out more about you and to get in touch with you. The benefits of having a home page range from opening exciting new career possibilities to getting in touch with friends from long ago.

Creating Your Home Page

To create a home page with the Personal Home Page Wizard, follow these steps:

1. From the File menu, choose the New command or press Ctrl + N. You'll see the New Page dialog box, shown here:

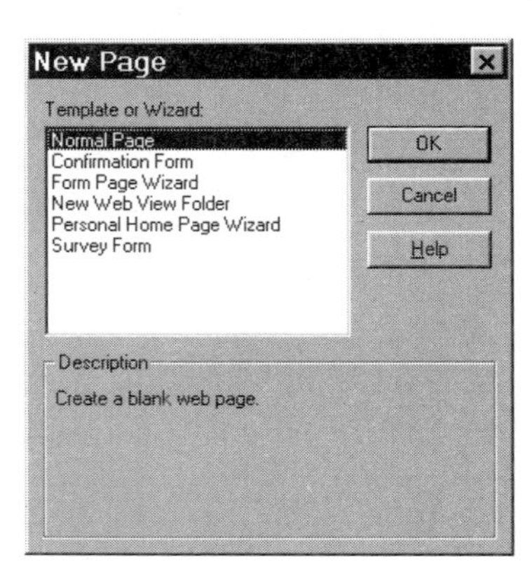

2. Choose Personal Home Page Wizard to see the Personal Home Page Wizard dialog box, shown here:

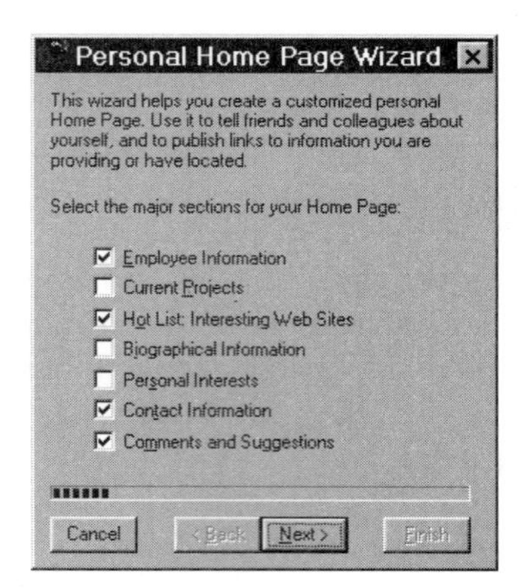

3. Select the types of information you want to include, and click Next. You'll see a page asking you to specify the Page URL and the Page Title, shown on the next page:

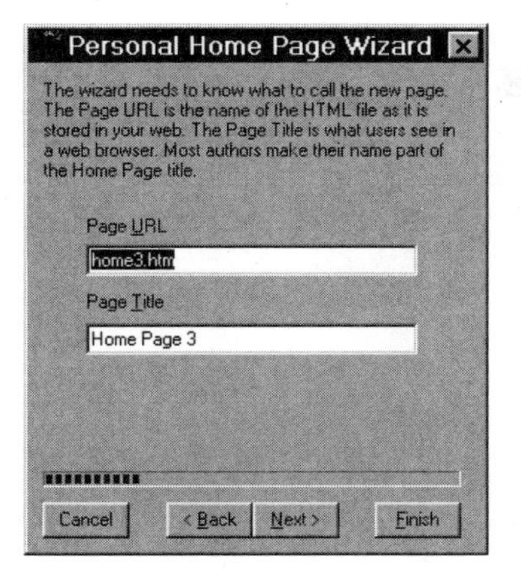

4 In the Page URL box, type a name for your file. On many servers, a file with the name *index.html* is displayed whenever anyone accesses your public Web directory. For now, name your file *home1.html*. You can always rename the file later.

5 In the Page Title box, type a title for your page. The page title is displayed on the browser's title bar, not on the page itself. Still, it's important. Many of the Web's search engines give priority to words found within the title. You should certainly include your name to make it easier for people to find you.

6 Click Next to go to the next page of the wizard. You'll see the page shown here:

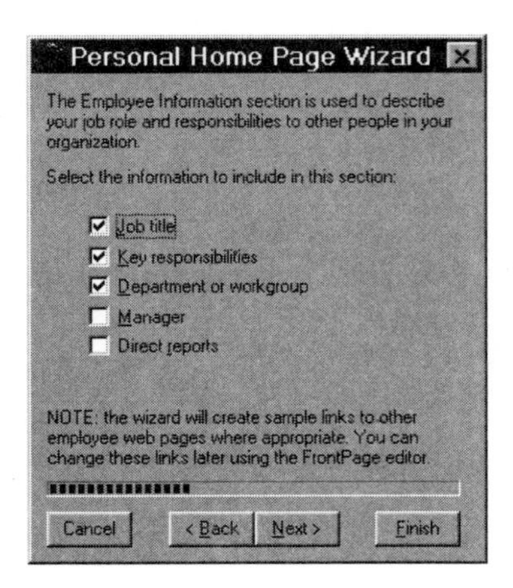

If you're creating a page to display on your company's Web server, these options are important. Select the ones that you'd like to include, and click Next.

7 If you selected Current Projects among the items to include, you'll see the projects page, shown here:

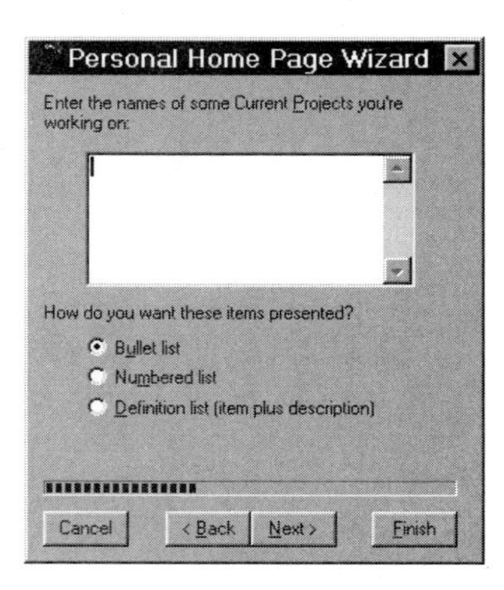

Type the names of your current projects, and then select a list option (bulleted list, numbered list, or definition list). Click Next to go to the next page.

8 If you selected Hot List Of Interesting Web Sites among the items to include, you'll see the page shown here:

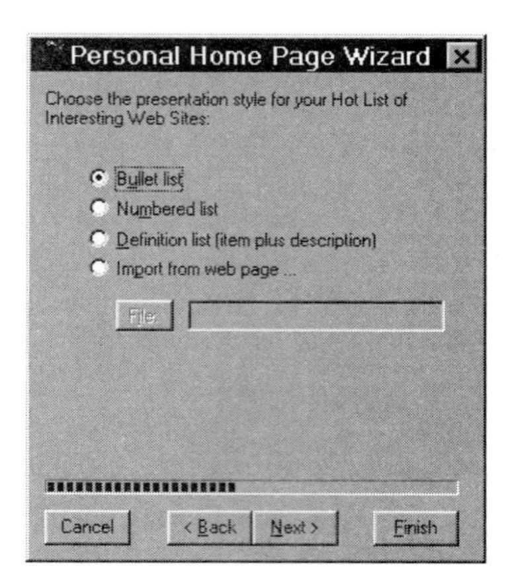

This page asks you how you want your Web sites listed. You can choose from a bulleted list, numbered list, or definition list. You can also import all the links from a specified page if you wish.

When you're finished making your selection, click Next.

9 If you selected Biography among the items to include, you'll see the following page:

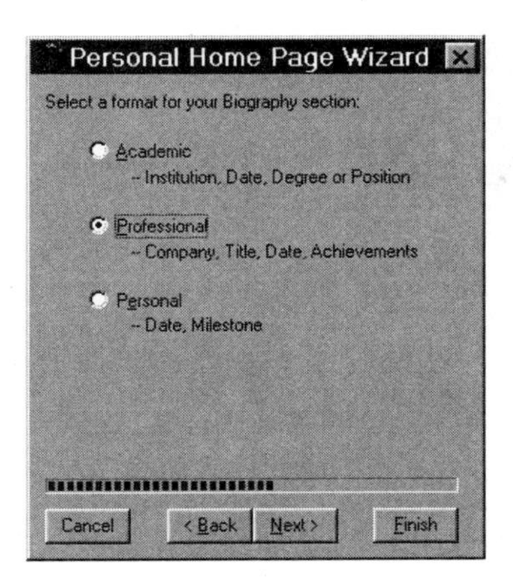

This page asks you to specify the format for your biography section. You can choose from academic, professional, or personal. Choose one of these, and click Next.

10 If you selected Personal Interests among the items to include, you'll see the following page:

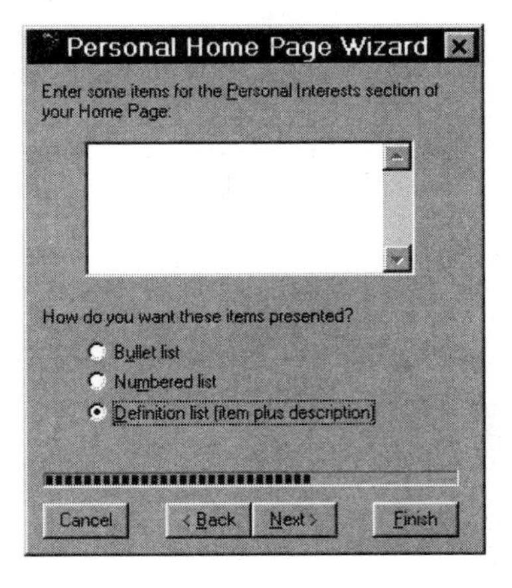

This page asks you to type a list of your personal interests. Type an interest, and press Enter. When you're done, click Next.

11 If you selected Contact Information among the items to include, you'll see the page shown here:

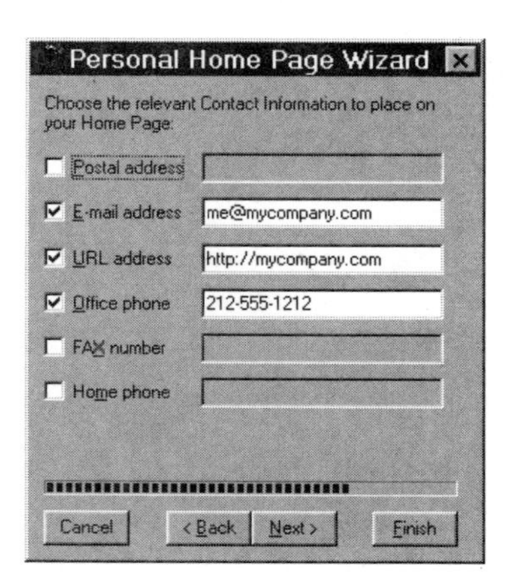

Add the contact information that you'd like to include, and click Next.

12 If you selected Comments And Suggestions among the items to include, you'll see the following page:

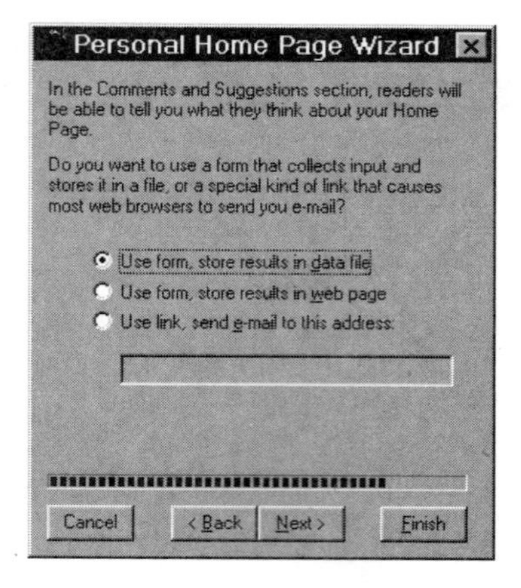

This page asks how you'd like your comments and suggestions to be solicited and stored. Unless you're publishing your page with Microsoft Internet Information Server, choose Use Link and type your e-mail address in the text box. Click Next to continue.

13 You now see a dialog box showing the items on your home page and asking how you'd like them organized, as shown on the next page:

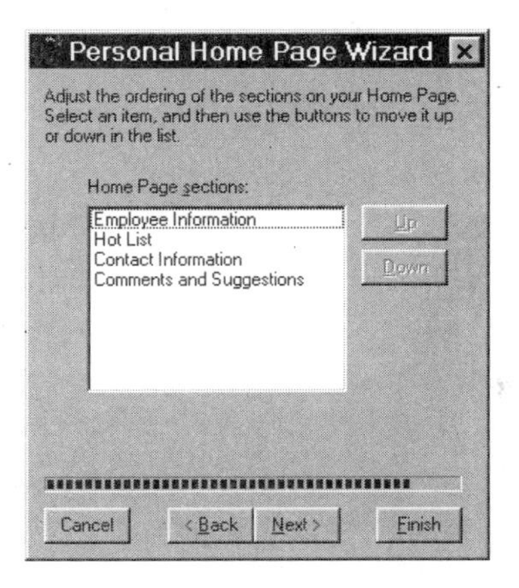

To move an item, select it and click Up or Down. When you're done, click Next.

14 You'll see a page informing you that you're finished. Click Finish to create your page, which you'll see on-screen (Figure 19-3).

As you can see from Figure 19-3, your home page isn't done. You have the outlines of your Web page, but you need to add personalized text and finishing touches. You'll learn how in the next section, titled "Learning the Basics of Web-Page Editing."

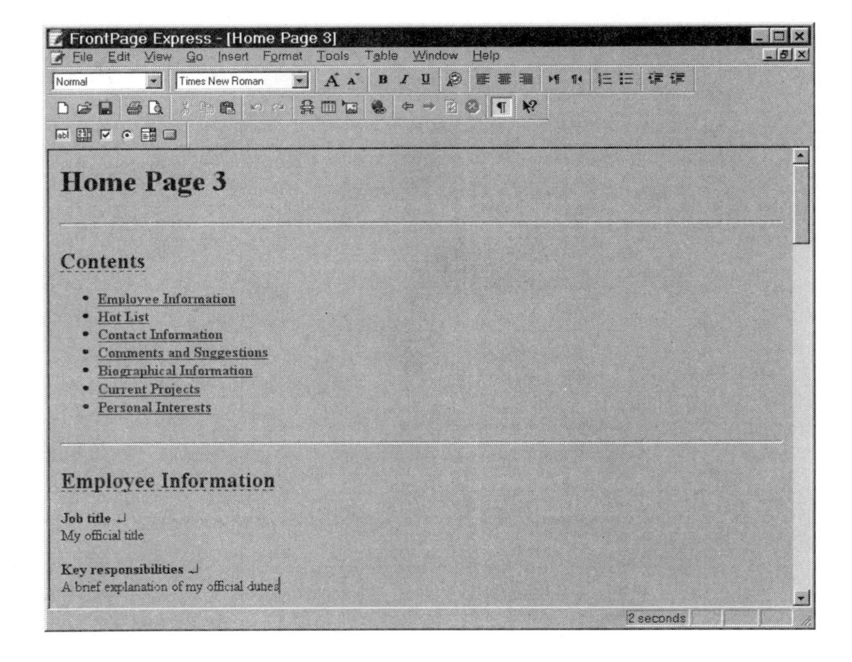

FIGURE 19-3.
Personal Home Page Wizard creates a draft of your home page based on your input.

Navigating Documents within FrontPage Express

The Home Page Wizard creates hyperlinks within your document. Under Contents, for example, you'll find a list of links to locations further down the page. To navigate the links you see within a FrontPage Express document, do the following:

1. Hold down the Ctrl key, and point to the link. You'll see the pointer change to an arrow.
2. Click the left mouse button. FrontPage Express displays the link you clicked.

Once you've navigated links with FrontPage Express, you can use the program's Back and Forward buttons, located on the Standard toolbar, to navigate among the pages you're editing.

If you would like to see hidden documents that you've already opened, you can use the Window menu to bring a hidden document to the foreground. Click Window on the menu bar, and choose the name of the document you want to see.

Learning the Basics of Web-Page Editing

Editing Web documents with FrontPage Express is very much like editing a document in a word processing program. For the most part, you can use the skills you've already learned in word processing to create and edit Web documents.

There are a couple of differences between word processing and Web authoring that you should bear in mind. Web browsers ignore any additional spaces or blank lines that you enter. If you try to space text by adding extra spaces or lines, browsers will ignore them, and your text won't look the way you intended. (As you'll learn later in this chapter, there is an HTML tag that tells browsers to follow your spacing, but this tag is the exception.) Also, there's no such thing as a tab in HTML.

Typing and Editing Text

You can easily add text to your document. Simply place the cursor where you want the text to appear, and start typing. You can use any of the usual Windows editing commands to make corrections or insertions while you're typing.

By default, FrontPage Express enters all your text in the Normal style. (To see the current style, look at the Change Style box in the Format Toolbar.) This style corresponds to the text paragraph tag (<P>) in HTML: your text is formatted with flush-left alignment, single-line spacing, and a blank line before the paragraph. In addition, the program defaults to the Times New Roman font. Actually, the font you're using is a generic proportionally spaced font; people can customize their browsers to display any proportionally spaced font for this text. You'll learn more about formatting later in this chapter and in Chapter 20.

TIP

> If you're editing your personal home page, created with the Personal Home Page Wizard, you'll find that the program has inserted numerous comments that tell you what to insert. These comments won't print. If you would prefer to delete them, click within the comment to select the entire comment, and press Delete.

Controlling Line and Paragraph Breaks

You can enter two kinds of line breaks with FrontPage Express:

- **Shift + Enter.** When you press the Shift + Enter combination, the program starts a new line without adding a blank line.
- **Enter.** When you press Enter, the program starts a new paragraph with a blank line in front of it. You can create additional blank lines by pressing Shift + Enter or Enter more than once.

If you need to see where you've pressed Shift + Enter, click Show/Hide Paragraph Marks on the format toolbar. You'll see a bent arrow showing where you've started a new line with this command. To remove a line break, delete the bent arrow symbol.

Finding and Replacing

If you're editing a lengthy document, you can use the Find command to locate specific text in your document.

To find text in your document, follow these steps:

1. Do one of the following:
   - From the Edit menu, choose Find.

     or
   - Press Ctrl + F.

You'll see the Find dialog box, shown here:

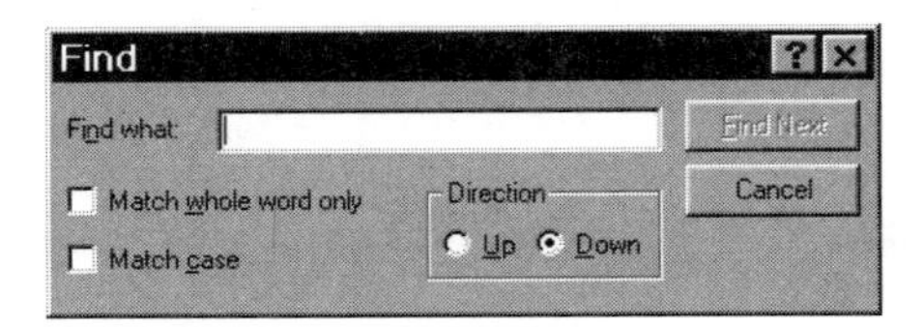

2. In the Find What box, type the text you want to match.
3. To match a word, check Match Whole Word Only.
4. To match the capitalization pattern you typed, check Match Case.
5. To choose a direction, click Up or Down.
6. Click Find Next.

You can replace text one item at a time or automatically throughout your document.

To replace text,

1. Do one of the following:
   - From the Edit menu, choose Replace.

     or

   - Press Ctrl + H.

   You'll see the Replace dialog box, shown here:

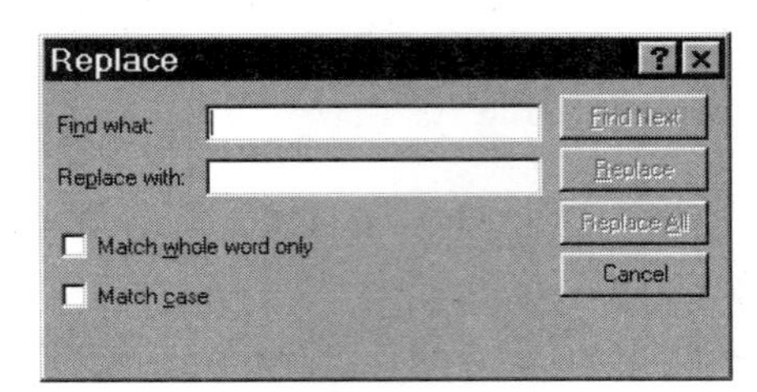

2. In the Find What box, type the text you want to match.
3. In the Replace With box, type the text to insert.
4. To match a word, check Match Whole Word Only.
5. To match the capitalization pattern you typed, check Match Case.

6. Do one of the following:

   - To search for the next instance of the text, click Find Next.
   - To replace text that FrontPage Express has matched and selected, click Replace.
   - To replace all of the instances of the search text without confirmation, click Replace All.

Learning the Basics of Web-Page Formatting

In word processing, you can use basic paragraph styles, such as text paragraphs, bulleted lists, and numbered lists. The same goes with Web publishing. In this section, you'll learn about the basic paragraph styles you can use in your Web page. You can also add character styles, such as bold and italic.

Using Paragraph Styles

Whenever you enter text, you're using one of several paragraph styles. To choose a style, select the text and click on a style from the Choose Style list box (in the Format toolbar). Another alternative is to press Enter, choose a style from the Choose Style list box, and start typing.

The following list provides an overview of the styles you can use:

- **Normal.** You should use normal style for entering ordinary text, the kind you place in paragraphs.
- **Address.** Address style is typically used to type the page creator's name and e-mail address, which appear at the bottom of the page.
- **Bulleted List.** Use this style to create a bulleted list. To add another item to the list, just press Enter. You can also create a bulleted list by clicking the Bulleted List button in the Format toolbar.
- **Defined Term.** This style positions the text flush left. To add a definition, just press Enter. FrontPage Express then moves to a definition style for the next line.
- **Definition.** Used with the Defined Term style, this style formats the selected text with an indent. When you're finished typing the definition, press Enter. FrontPage Express creates a Defined Term style for the next line.

- **Directory List.** In FrontPage Express, this style creates a bulleted list that's indistinguishable from the Bulleted List style. However, some browsers will format this list differently. Use the Bulleted List style instead.
- **Formatted.** This style enables you to format your text using the spacebar; the browser will recognize additional spaces and display your text the way you've typed it.
- **Headings 1 through 6.** To enable you to create headings and subheadings with distinctive formats, FrontPage Express offers six formatted levels. Very few Web authors use more than two headings.
- **Menu List.** In FrontPage Express, this style creates a bulleted list that's indistinguishable from the Bulleted List style. However, some browsers will format this list differently. Use the Bulleted List style instead.
- **Numbered List.** Use this style to create a numbered list. To add another item to the list, just press Enter. You can also create a numbered list by clicking the Numbered List button in the Format toolbar.

Figure 19-4 shows the appearance of most of these styles. Note, though, that most Web authors use only a few of them: normal, bulleted list, numbered list, and two heading styles.

To stop typing text in a particular style and return to normal paragraph text, press Enter and choose Normal from the Change Styles list box.

To change a style or select additional options for styles other than lists, select the text that you've formatted with the style, click the right mouse button, and choose Paragraph Properties from the pop-up menu. In the Paragraph Properties dialog box, you can select a different style, and you can also choose alignments for styles (Left, Center, and Right).

If you would like to choose options for lists, right-click the list and choose List Properties; you'll see a dialog box that enables you to choose bullet shapes, number formats, and numbering options. You can also use the List Properties dialog box to set the starting number of a numbered list to something other than one.

FIGURE 19-4.
You can use any of these styles to enter or format text.

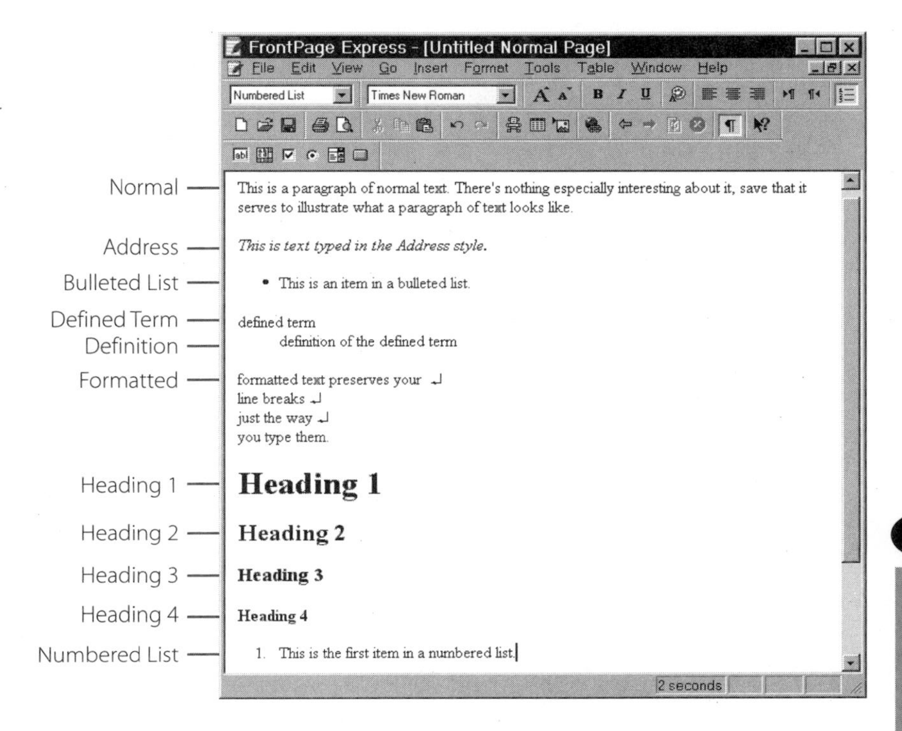

Understanding Character Styles

You can add the following emphases to the text you type. Either type the text and then select the style, or choose the command and then type the text. To remove formatting from characters, either repeat the formatting command or go to the Format menu and select Remove Formatting.

- **Bold.** Click the Bold button on the Format toolbar, or press Ctrl + B.
- **Italic.** Click the Italic button on the Format toolbar, or press Ctrl + I.
- **Bold Italic.** Choose Font from the Format menu. You'll see the Font dialog box. In the Font Style list, choose Bold Italic and click OK.
- **Underline.** Click the Underline button on the Format toolbar, or press Ctrl + U.

- **Strikethrough.** Choose Font from the Format menu. In the Font dialog box, click Strikethrough and click OK.
- **Typewriter.** Choose Font from the Format menu. In the Font dialog box, click Typewriter and click OK.

Creating Hyperlinks

Most Web pages contain one or more hyperlinks, which users can click to display other pages. FrontPage Express makes it easy to add hyperlinks to your document.

Understanding Hyperlinks

A hyperlink has two parts. The *link text* is the text that appears in your Web page. Given distinctive formatting (usually colored and underlined), the link text is clicked to display a different page. The URL is the address of the Internet resource to be retrieved when the user clicks the hyperlink. It doesn't have to be a Web page; you can also create links to Usenet newsgroups, files in FTP archives, and many other types of Internet resources.

There's an ultra-cool, ultra-easy way to create hyperlinks quickly. Use Internet Explorer to display a Web page that contains hyperlinks that you'd like to add to your page. Click the mouse button on one of the hyperlinks, and drag it into the FrontPage Express window. When you reach the place you want the hyperlink to appear, release the mouse button. The hyperlink appears in your document, along with the anchor. You can use this quick method to create a lengthy list of hyperlinks.

You can create three types of hyperlinks:

- **Links to other Web sites.** These links, called *absolute links*, specify the full and exact location of a Web page on another server. To create this type of link, you must know the exact URL.
- **Links to bookmarks within the current document.** You can create links that scroll the window to a bookmark's location within the same document. To do so, you must first create bookmarks in your document, as explained later in this section.
- **Links to other Web documents in the same or nearby directories on your server.** These links, called *relative links*, enable you to specify links to other documents on your site.

Inserting a Hyperlink to Another Web Site (Absolute Links)

To create a hyperlink to a page somewhere on the World Wide Web, note the URL and follow these steps:

1. Position the cursor where you want the hyperlink to appear.
2. Type the text that you want to appear as link text (the colored and underlined text that the user clicks). Select the text.
3. Do one of the following:
   - Click the Create Or Edit Hyperlink button on the Format toolbar.
     or
   - From the Insert menu, choose Hyperlink.
     or
   - Press Ctrl + K.

   You'll see the Create Hyperlink dialog box, shown here:

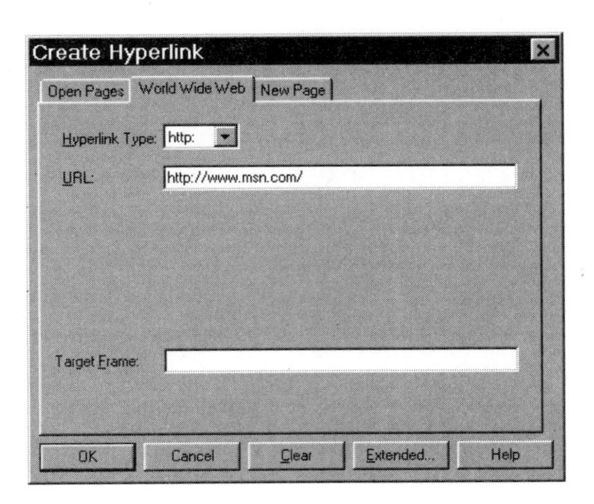

4. Click the World Wide Web tab.
5. Click the Hyperlink Type box, and choose the protocol of the link you're creating.

   Remember, protocol refers to the type of Internet service that's involved in retrieving the desired information. You can create links using the following protocols: *file* (a file on your local system), *ftp* (a File Transfer Protocol file), *gopher* (a Gopher document), *http* (a page on the World Wide Web), *https* (a secure Web site using Secure Sockets Layer [SSL] security), *mailto* (a mail-response link), *news* (a link to a Usenet newsgroup), *telnet* (a link to a telnet [mainframe computer] site), and *wais* (a link to a WAIS—Wide Area Information Server—database).

6 In the URL box, type the rest of the URL.

7 If you're linking to a frame document and you know the name of the frame that you want to link to, type the frame's name in the Target Frame box. Otherwise, just leave this box blank.

8 Click OK to create the hyperlink.

Inserting a Hyperlink to Another Location in the Same Document (Links to Bookmarks)

You can create links to specified locations in the same document. In order to create such links, you must first create *bookmarks*, which are named locations within your document. When users click the link you create, the window scrolls to the bookmark, and places the bookmark at the top of the window.

To create bookmarks, follow these steps:

1 Place the cursor where you want the bookmark to appear.

2 From the Edit menu, choose Bookmarks. You'll see the Bookmark dialog box, shown here:

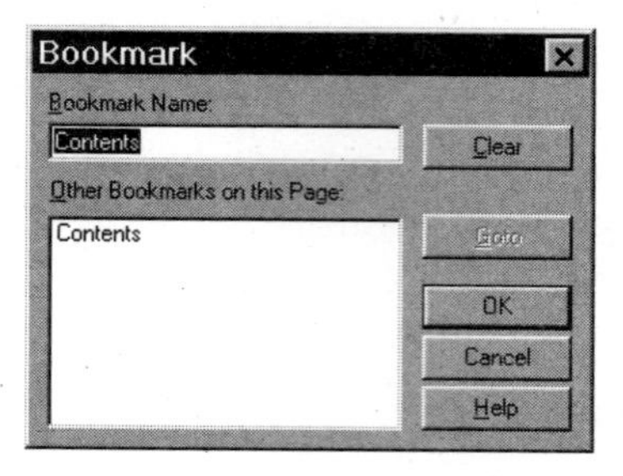

3 In the Bookmark Name box, type the name of the bookmark. The name should be all one word.

4 Click OK.

To create a link to the bookmark, do the following:

1 Position the cursor where you want the hyperlink to appear.

2 Type the text that you want to appear as link text (the colored and underlined text that the user clicks). Select the text.

3 Click the Create Or Edit Hyperlink button on the Format toolbar.

or

- From the Insert menu, choose Hyperlink.

or

- Press Ctrl + K.

You'll see the Create Hyperlink dialog box.

4 Click Open Pages. You'll see the Open Pages page, shown here:

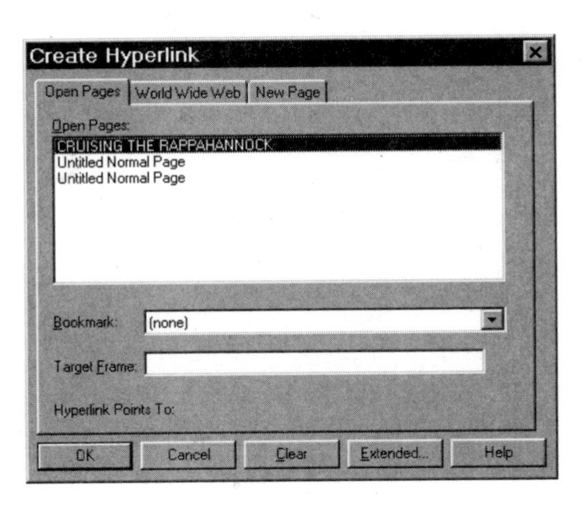

5 In the Open Pages list, select the document you are currently editing.

6 In the Bookmark list, select the bookmark to which you would like this text to link.

7 Click OK.

Inserting a Hyperlink to Another Document on Your Server (Relative Links)

If you are creating a Web presentation that involves more than one page, you can create *relative links* that jump to these documents. Unlike an absolute link, a relative link doesn't include a fully specified URL. Instead, it contains only the name of the document to which you're linking, and optionally some directory information.

Here's an example of a relative link (minus the HTML):

```
cruising.htm
```

If I create a link to this document, without specifying a full URL, browsers assume that the document is located *in the same directory* as the document containing the link.

You can add directory information. For example, consider the following relative link (again, minus the HTML):

```
/images/sailing.jpg
```

The browser will assume that this document is located in the /images directory, which is a subdirectory of the directory that contains the current document.

You can refer to directories *above* the one in which the document is stored. Here's an example:

```
../../marinas/marinaguide.htm
```

The browser will go up two directories, locate the /marina directory, and find marinaguide.htm.

TIP

Unless you're creating a huge site with hundreds of Web pages, you will be wise to keep all of your HTML documents in the *same directory*. Doing so minimizes the chance that you'll make a mistake somehow, ranging from typing the directory symbols wrong or unthinkingly rearranging the server's directory structure. One exception: many Web authors like to keep all their graphics in a subdirectory called /images.

Why use relative links? There's a huge advantage. When you're creating a multi-page presentation, you will probably want to store the pages temporarily on your computer. With relative links, the links will work fine, so you can test your work. The links work fine because they say, in effect, "Look for this document in the same directory that the current document is in." Later, you will probably upload your pages to a Web server, as described in Chapter 21. The links still work fine there, because they still say, "Look for this document in the same directory that the current document is in." If you had used absolute (fully specified) URLs for links to other documents in your presentation, you'd have to retype every one of them!

TIP

> The rule is very simple. When you're creating links to other pages that you'll create and store in the same server-storage space, *use relative links.* Never use absolute links!

To create a relative link, do the following:

1. Open the document in which you want to insert the link.
2. Position the cursor where you want the hyperlink to appear.
3. Type the text that you want to appear as link text (the colored and underlined text that the user clicks). Select the text.
4. Click the Create Or Edit Hyperlink button on the Format toolbar.

   or

   - From the Insert menu, choose Hyperlink.

   or

   - Press Ctrl + K.

   You'll see the Create Hyperlink dialog box.
5. Click the World Wide Web tab if necessary.
6. In the URL box, erase http://. The box should be blank.
7. Type the name of the document to which you are linking, such as cruising.htm. You can add directory information if you wish, but it's best to keep all your HTML documents in the same directory.
8. Click OK.

> If you move your pages, or upload them to a server, *make sure they stay together in the same directory.*

Editing Hyperlinks

If a hyperlink isn't working properly, you might have typed the URL incorrectly. To edit the hyperlink, place the cursor on it and click Create Or Edit Hyperlink on the Format toolbar. You'll see the Edit Hyperlink dialog box, with the current hyperlink information displayed. Check the URL carefully for errors. If you find an error, correct it and click OK.

Be sure to test your hyperlinks. You can do so from within FrontPage Express. Connect to the Internet, if necessary. Hold down the Ctrl key, and click the link you created. FrontPage Express displays the page for editing in a new window. If you see an error message, something's wrong with the URL. If the page displays, everything's OK. Click the Back button on the Standard toolbar to return to your page.

Soliciting Feedback with a Mailto Hyperlink

Here's a neat trick. Using a *mailto hyperlink* enables you to place a hyperlink in your document that, when clicked, displays an e-mail composition window with your e-mail address already entered. Note that this works only if the person clicking this link is using a mail-capable browser—but these days, almost everyone does. To create a mailto hyperlink, follow these steps:

1 Type and select the anchor text that you want to appear in your Web page. (You might want to type your e-mail address so it's visible to people who don't have mail-capable browsers.)

2 Click the Create Or Edit Hyperlink button on the Format toolbar, or press Ctrl + K. You'll see the Create Hyperlink dialog box, shown here:

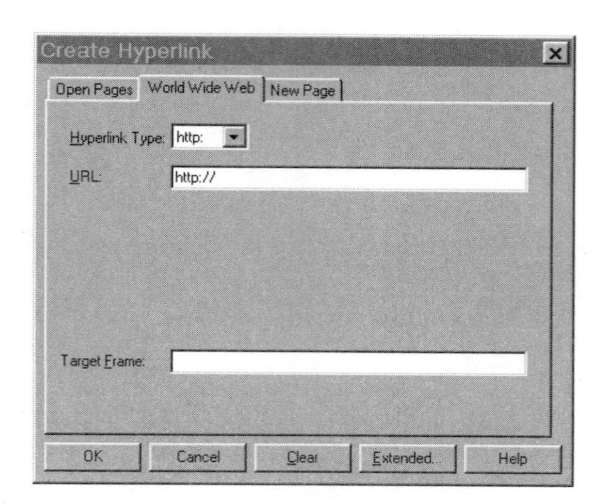

3 In the Hyperlink Type box, choose Mailto.

4 In the URL area, carefully type your e-mail address after Mailto.

   Don't add any spaces.

5 Click OK.

Creating a Page from Scratch

If you want to create a page from scratch instead of using the Personal Home Page Wizard, open a new document by clicking the New button on the Standard toolbar. You can also select New from the File menu, and choose Normal Page from the New Page dialog box.

Once you've started a new Web page, you need to give it a title. To do so, follow these steps:

1 From the File menu, choose Page Properties. You'll see the Page Properties dialog box, shown here:

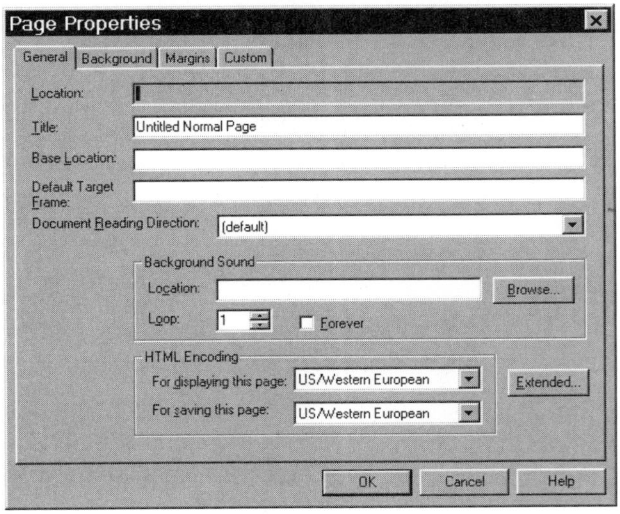

2 In the Title box, type your page's title. This title will appear on the title bar of a browser displaying your page.

3 Click OK.

Saving Your Page

If your page isn't finished, you can save it locally until you're ready to publish it. To do so, follow these steps:

1 Click Save on the Standard toolbar.

or

- From the File menu, choose Save.

or

- Press Ctrl + S.

You'll see the Save As dialog box, shown here:

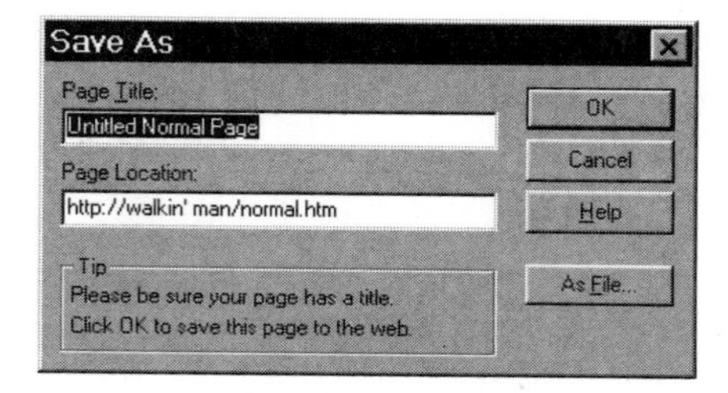

2 Click As File, you'll see the Save As File dialog box.

3 In the Save As File dialog box, type a file name and choose a storage location.

4 Click Save.

CHAPTER 20

Adding Visual Excitement and Interactivity

In the previous chapter, you learned how to sketch out a Web page, whether you use the Personal Home Page Wizard or create the page from scratch. Either way, with what you've learned so far, your page is basically Early Mosaic, a noted art epoch characterized by plain backgrounds, lots of text, default fonts, no graphics, and precious little zing, unless you're a darned good writer. (Mosaic was the first popular Web browser, and most of the pages available during Mosaic's heyday weren't exactly thrilling from a visual standpoint.) In this chapter, you'll transcend the humdrum by adding all kinds of visual, auditory, and computational excitement to your page, including sounds, videos, animations, WebBot components, ActiveX controls, Java applets, JavaScript scripts, and more.

Opening Your Page

Let's begin by opening the very ordinary page that you created in the last chapter. If you published the page following the instructions in Chapter 21, you can open it from the Web. If you saved the file to your disk, you can open it from there, too.

To open your document the easiest way, click File on the menu bar and choose the document's name from the File menu. The File menu stores the names of the last four documents you opened. You can open documents this way wherever you saved them, either from the Web or from your hard disk.

Opening Your Web Page from the Web

To open your published file from the Web, follow these steps:

1 Do one of the following:

- From the File menu, choose Open.

  or

- Click Open on the Standard Toolbar.

  or

- Press Ctrl + O. You'll see the Open File dialog box, shown here:

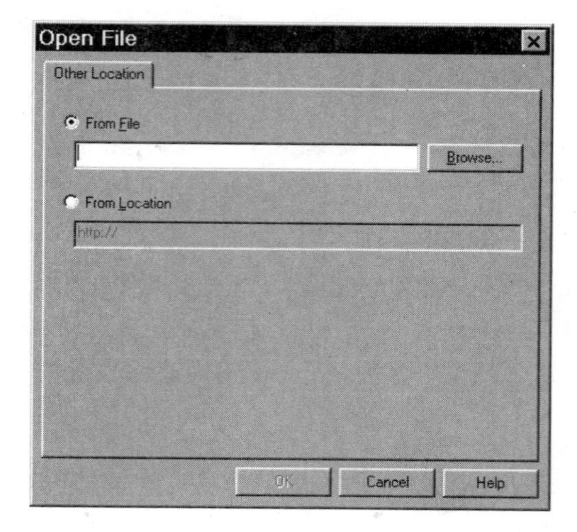

2. Click From Location, and type the URL of the Web page you published.
3. Click OK.

Opening a Local Copy of Your Web Page

If you didn't publish your Web page, you can open it from your hard disk. To do so, follow these instructions:

1. Do one of the following:
   - From the File menu, choose Open.

     or
   - Click Open on the Standard Toolbar.

     or
   - Press Ctrl + O. You'll see the Open File dialog box.
2. Click From File, and click Browse.
3. Locate the file you want to open, and click Open.

Enhancing Your Document's Background

Now that you've displayed your document, it's time to dispense with the ordinary. By the time you're finished with this section, your Early Mosaic document will start showing signs of life. Here's the menu: choose background colors, background graphics, or a background watermark. And how about a background sound that plays when users open your page? If this sounds super-advanced, read on—it's easy with FrontPage Express.

Choosing a Default Color Scheme for Your Document

You can choose a default color scheme for your document. When you do so, you select colors for the following elements:

- **Background.** Your choice of a background color affects the browser window background.
- **Text.** This color choice affects all the text you enter, with the exception of hyperlinks.

- **Hyperlink.** This selection affects hyperlinks that have not yet been visited. (The user's history list keeps track of which sites have been visited.)
- **Visited hyperlink.** This selection affects hyperlinks that have been visited.
- **Active hyperlink.** This selection affects a hyperlink only when the user has positioned the mouse pointer over the hyperlink text.

By now, you've browsed the Web enough that you've probably encountered a page that hits you with some unbelievably ugly and unreadable combination of background and text colors. Please avoid falling into this trap, and remember that legibility is your main goal. You can assign default colors to text as well as to backgrounds and make the two work together, but bear in mind that contrast is critical. If your background is very dark, your text should be very light—and vice versa. And don't forget the small matter of taste. You get shock value out of purple text on a green background, but not repeat visitors.

To choose a default color scheme for your page, follow these steps:

1. From the Format menu, choose Background. You'll see the Page Properties dialog box, thoughtfully opened to the Background page (Figure 19-1).
2. In the Background area, select a color for your document's background.
3. In the Text area, select a color for the non-hyperlink text in your document.
4. In the Hyperlink area, select a color for the unvisited-hyperlink text.
5. In the Visited Hyperlink area, select a color for visited-hyperlink text. This should be duller than the hyperlink text color.
6. In the Active Hyperlink area, select a color that appears briefly when the user clicks a hyperlink. This should be brighter than the other two hyperlink colors.
7. To confirm your color choices, click OK.

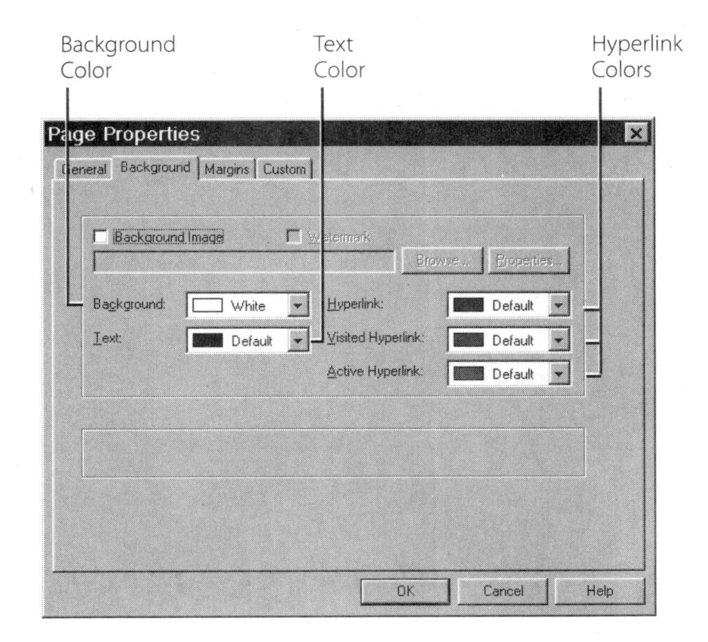

FIGURE 20-1.
In this dialog box, you can choose a background color and default text colors for your document.

Choosing Background Graphics

If a background color doesn't add the zing you're looking for, you can substitute a background graphic. *Background graphics* are relatively small GIF or JPEG files that are tiled so that they fill the entire browser's window, even if the user enlarges the window. But please, don't use a graphic that's too busy. The best background graphics are those that have a consistent, overall tone, like the texture graphic shown in Figure 20-2.

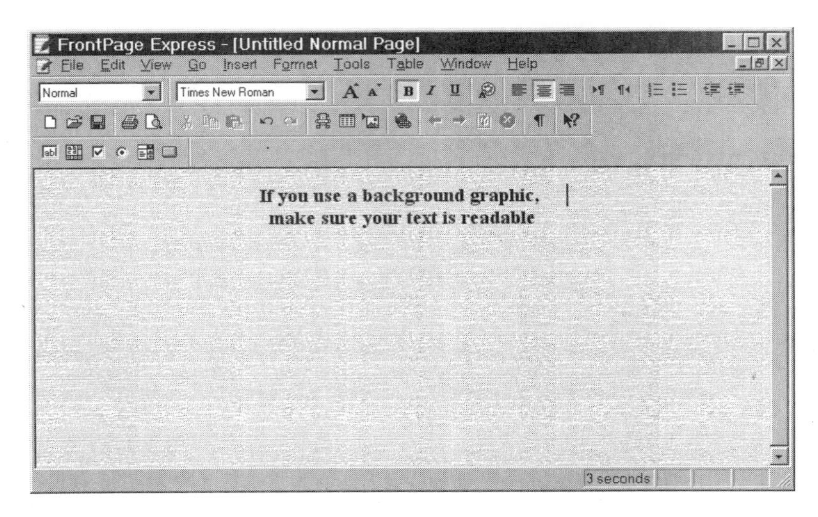

FIGURE 20-2.
Good background graphics enhance your pages; bad ones make them hard to read.

TIP

Where can you find background graphics? You'll find many freebie background graphics on the Web. Try an AltaVista search for *"background graphics."* In Internet Explorer, you can also save any background graphic to your system by right-clicking the page background and choosing Save Background As. Please note, though, that the technical ability to do this does not necessarily mean that it's ethical. If you would like to use somebody else's background graphic, ask for permission by e-mailing the page creator. Most people are actually quite happy to grant permission if you only ask. If you don't ask, and you're creating your page for profit-seeking purposes, you're exposing yourself and your company to risk. In other words, don't do it.

To add a background graphic to your page, do the following:

1. From the Format menu, choose Background. You'll see the Page Properties dialog box, opened to the Background page.
2. Click Background Image.
3. Click the Browse button to locate the graphic you want to use. Click OK to confirm.

Although the Page Properties dialog box enables you to specify the URL for a background graphic, please don't use this feature to link your page's background to a graphic that's stored elsewhere on the Web. This is murder on other people's servers, and it needlessly multiplies the amount of data that has to get shuffled back and forth in order to display your page. If you want to use somebody else's background graphic, get permission to do so and use a copy that's stored on your own Web server.

Adding a Background Watermark

What's a watermark? In brief, it's a background graphic that doesn't scroll along with the text. The effect is cool for just about any background graphic—the text seems to float over the graphic—but it's almost essential for large, complex background graphics with abrupt borders. These look terrible if the user sees the tile boundary separating two copies of the graphic. By defining the background graphic as a watermark, you can effectively prevent the tile boundary from coming into view.

Watermarks don't conform to HTML standards, and they appear only if your page is viewed with Microsoft Internet Explorer. If you want your Web pages to look the same for users of other browsers, don't use watermarks.

To create a watermark, simply click the Watermark check box when you create your background graphic. Note that the Watermark option doesn't become available until you've clicked Background Image. A watermark is a background, after all, and until you've added a background graphic, you can't have a watermark.

Adding a Background Sound

A background sound begins to play when somebody opens a page to which a sound has been attached. With FrontPage Express, you can easily add sounds to your pages, and you can choose options that affect how the sounds are played.

You can add many different kinds of sounds as a background sound, including the following:

- **WAV (Windows sounds).** This is the default Windows sound format. Quality is good, but your sound might not play on Unix or Macintosh systems.
- **AU (Sun/NeXT sounds).** This is a mono-only, low-quality sound format, but almost any browser can play it.
- **AIFF (Apple/Silicon Graphics sounds).** This format is also widely supported by browsers.
- **MIDI (Musical Instrument Digital Interface files).** These are text files containing instructions to a synthesizer. Any computer equipped with a MIDI-capable sound card can play MIDI sounds.

To add a background sound to your page, follow these steps:

1. From the File menu, choose Page Properties.
2. Click the General tab, if necessary, to display the General options, shown on the next page:

3 Next to the Location box in the Background Sound area, click Browse to locate, select, and open the sound. (You can use a sound that's on your system or one located on the Web.)

4 In the Loop box, choose the number of times you want the sound to repeat; click Forever to repeat the sound until the user leaves the page.

5 Click OK to confirm.

Not all browsers are configured to play background sounds, and a few older browsers can't play them at all. If your page is accessed by somebody using a browser that can't play the sound, the user won't hear it. However, your page will still display.

Adding Visual Interest to the Text

You can jazz up your text in a number of ways, including adding colors and emphases, changing fonts and font sizes, varying alignments and indents—even using scrolling text (marquees).

Adding Character Emphasis and Color

You can add character emphases to your text by selecting the text and clicking Bold, Italic, or Underline.

Because most browsers underline hyperlink text, the use of underlining isn't recommended. Users might confuse underlined text with a hyperlink, and get frustrated because nothing happens when they click it.

To add color, do the following:

1. Select the text.
2. Click the Text Color button on the toolbar. You'll see the Color dialog box, shown here:

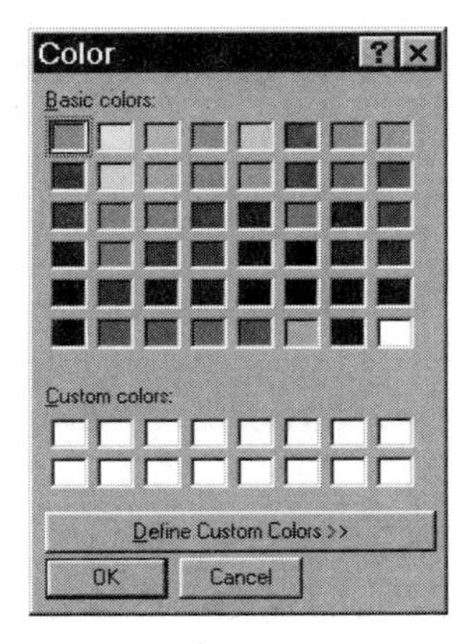

3. Click the color you want to use.
4. Click OK.

Although you can use the Color dialog box to define custom colors, it's best to use the basic colors. Some browsers may display custom colors in a way that differs slightly—and sometimes significantly—from the way the color looks on your screen.

Changing the Font Size

On the Web, font sizes are defined in two different ways: relative and points. You can specify *relative font sizes* using numbers from 1 (smallest) to 7 (largest). The default is size 3. Just what this means in terms of point size depends on the browser. With Microsoft Internet Explorer, size 3 type looks like normal-sized text (about 12 points). Almost all browsers support this means of specifying font size. Also, new HTML standards enable Web authors to specify sizes in *printer's points* (72 points equal 1 inch). However, some older browsers do not support this.

FrontPage Express uses a combination of relative sizes and points, as shown in the following table. This correlation allows you to specify font size in relative terms and still ensure that your choice will appear correctly, even if someone's using an older browser.

TABLE 20-1. Relative Font Sizes: Equivalent in Printer's Points.

Relative font size	Equivalent in points
1	8 pt
2	10 pt
3	12 pt
4	14 pt
5	18 pt
6	24 pt
7	36 pt

There are two ways to change the size of text in your page: with the Format Toolbar and with the Fonts dialog box.

To change font size with the Format Toolbar, follow these steps:

1 Select the text.

2 Do one of the following:

- Click the Increase Text Size button (the large "A").

  or

- Click the Decrease Text Size button (the small "A").

To change font size with the Font dialog box, follow these steps:

1 Select the text.

2 Do one of the following:

- Point to the selection, and press Alt + Enter.

  or

- Right-click the selection, and choose Font Properties.

  or

- From the Format menu, choose Font.

You'll see the Font dialog box, shown here:

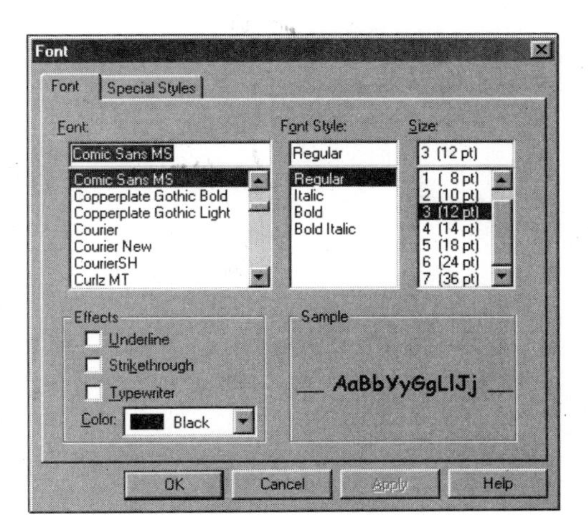

3 Choose the font size you want.

4 Click Enter.

Using Special Character Styles

In addition to the character formats already discussed, you can choose from the following:

- **Strikethrough.** This format is sometimes used in legal documents to show text that has been deleted.
- **Typewriter.** This format simulates a fixed-width (monospace) typewriter font.
- **Blink.** The formatted text blinks. Please use this format sparingly; readers find it very annoying.
- **Superscript.** The formatted character is positioned above the line.
- **Subscript.** The formatted character is positioned below the line.

NOTE

You can choose additional character styles, called Citation, Sample, Definition, Code, Variable, and Keyboard. However, these styles are very seldom used in Web documents, and some aren't supported in the latest versions of HTML. It's best to avoid their use.

To choose the strikethrough or character styles:

1 Select the text.

2 Point to the selection, and press Alt + Enter.

or

- Right-click the selection, and choose Font Properties.

or

- From the Format menu, choose Font.

3 In the Effects area, choose the font effect you want.

4 Click OK.

To choose other styles:

1 Select the text.

2 Point to the selection, and press Alt + Enter.

or

- Right-click the selection, and choose Font Properties.

or

- From the Format menu, choose Font.

3 Click the Special Styles tab. You'll see the Special Styles dialog box, shown here:

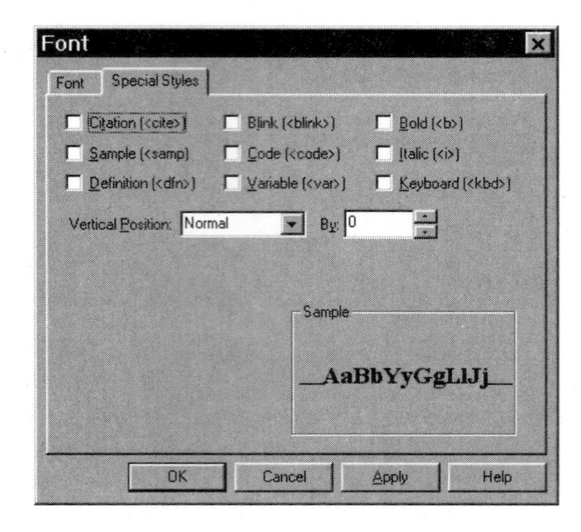

4 Check the style or styles you want. To use subscript or superscript, choose Subscript or Superscript in the Vertical Position list box, and choose a line offset.

5 Click OK.

Adding Special Characters and Symbols

To facilitate the exchange of HTML documents over the Internet, HTML was initially designed so that all HTML documents would include nothing but the standard ASCII characters. This is obviously insufficient for U.S. domestic as well as international use, because this limited character set does not include many symbols needed for everyday use (such as a copyright or registered trademark symbol). To supplement HTML, a means of coding special characters was developed. For example, a copyright symbol is coded as follows:

```
&copy;
```

Thanks to FrontPage Express, you don't have to memorize such codes. You can choose them from a menu. To do so, follow these steps:

1 From the Insert menu, choose Symbol.

   You'll see the Symbol dialog box, shown here:

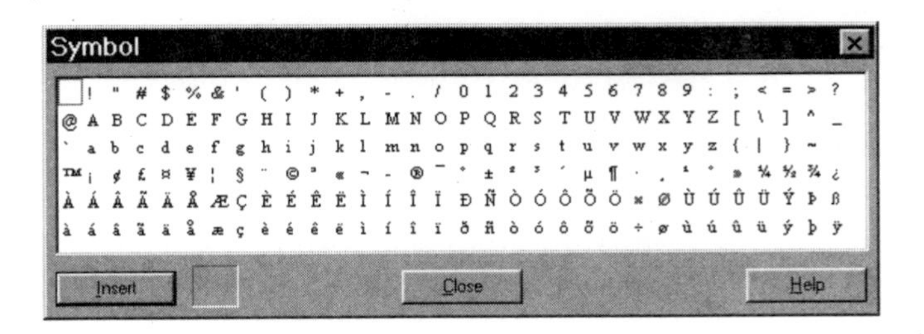

2 Click the symbol you want to insert.

   You'll see an enlarged version of the symbol in the preview box.

3 Click Insert to insert the symbol.

Choosing Fonts

By default, you work with two fonts in Web documents:

- **Proportionally spaced font.** This is the font used for most elements, including headings, lists, and text paragraphs.

- **Monospace (typewriter) font.** This font is associated with a few special-purpose elements, such as Code and Keyboard. You can also assign this font as a character style.

FrontPage Express enables you to choose specific fonts, such as the ones installed on your system, but there's a hitch: the people reading your page may not see your font choices. The fonts you've chosen will show up *only* if the people accessing your page have exactly the same fonts installed on their computer systems. If they don't, their browsers will display the page using the default proportionally spaced and monospace fonts.

To help improve the font situation, Microsoft designed several exceptionally attractive TrueType fonts and made them available to the public for free (see Figure 20-3). Available for Windows and Macintosh systems, these fonts include Trebuchet MS, Georgia, Verdana, Comic Sans MS, Times New Roman, Courier New, Arial Black, and Impact, as well as a font containing cool symbols called Webdings. These fonts are specifically designed to look good on the relatively low-resolution display technology that characterizes the Web. (But frankly, they're so nice that you can use them for almost any purpose.) To obtain these fonts, download them from www.microsoft.com/typography.

You probably already have these fonts installed on your system; they're included with Internet Explorer. To find out, click Start on the taskbar, point to Settings, and choose Control Panel. Double-click Fonts, and see whether these fonts are already installed.

If you would like to use these TrueType fonts on your Web pages, include a link to Microsoft's site so that users can download them, if they haven't already done so.

Should you use these fonts? They've been widely distributed, so there's a good chance they'll show up when somebody views your page. However, they're more likely to be found on Microsoft Windows systems.

To choose fonts for your text, follow these steps:

1. Select the text.
2. Do one of the following:
   - On the Format Toolbar, choose the font you want from the font list box.

   or

- Select the text, and press Alt + Enter. You'll see the Font dialog box. In the font list, choose a font, and click OK.

  or

- From the Format menu, choose Font. You'll see the Font dialog box. In the font list, choose a font, and click OK.

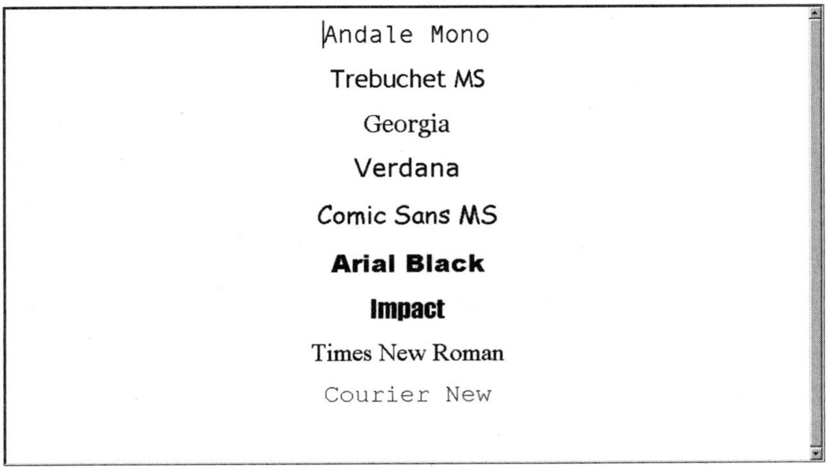

FIGURE 20-3.
Microsoft's Core Web Fonts are freely available and widely installed on Microsoft Windows systems.

Andale Mono
Trebuchet MS
Georgia
Verdana
Comic Sans MS
Arial Black
Impact
Times New Roman
Courier New

Aligning and Indenting Text

As the previous chapter explained, you build your document using the basic, built-in styles, such as those for various lists and normal paragraphs. However, you can align and indent text in any style. (Almost all of the newer browsers support these alignment and indentation options, although a few older browsers might not.) Figure 20-4 shows your alignment choices; the figure also demonstrates the effect you get when you use white text against a black background. The font is Trebuchet MS.

Choosing Paragraph Alignments

To align text, do the following:

1. Select the entire paragraph you want to align.
2. Do one of the following:
   - On the Format Toolbar, click an alignment button.

     or

- Right-click the selection, and choose Paragraph Properties from the pop-up menu. In the Paragraph Alignment box, choose an alignment. Click OK to confirm.

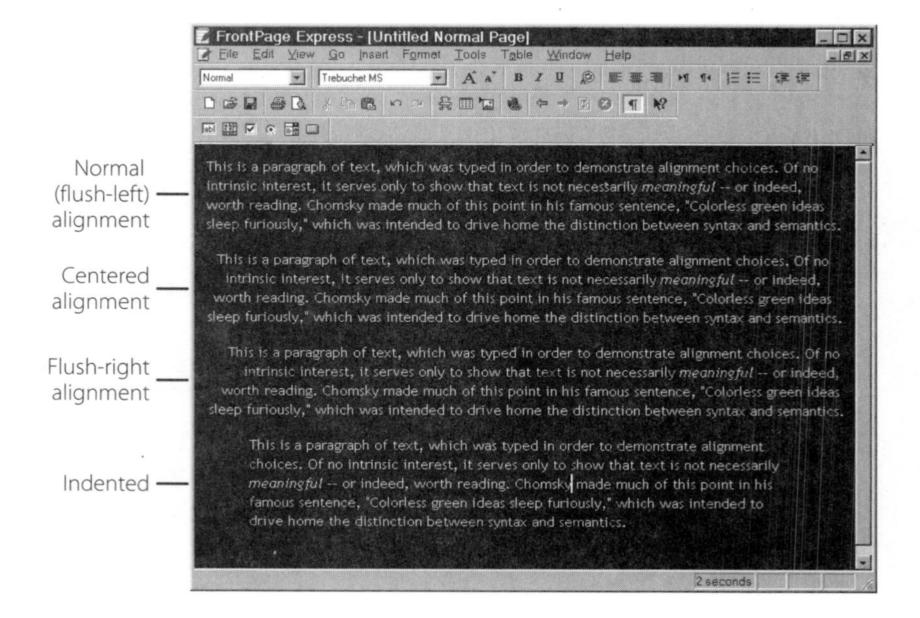

FIGURE 20-4. You can align and indent your text using the choices shown here.

Choosing Paragraph Alignments

To align text, do the following:

1. Select the entire paragraph you want to align.
2. Do one of the following:
   - On the Format Toolbar, click an alignment button.

     or

   - Right-click the selection, and choose Paragraph Properties from the pop-up menu. In the Paragraph Alignment box, choose an alignment. Click OK to confirm.

Indenting Text

To indent text, do the following:

1. Select the entire paragraph you want to indent.
2. On the Format Toolbar, click Increase Indent. You can click this button more than once to increase the indentation.

Cancelling Text Indentation

To cancel an indentation, do the following:

1. Select the entire paragraph you want to indent.
2. On the Format Toolbar, click Decrease Indent. You can keep clicking this button until the text moves flush to the left margin.

Adding a Marquee

Here's a quick way to add some visual spice to your page: add a marquee, or scrolling text. A *marquee* consists of a line of text that moves across your page. You can control the direction (left or right), speed of movement, behavior (scrolling, sliding, or bouncing back and forth), alignment with text (top, middle, or bottom), text size, repetition, and color. To insert a marquee, follow these steps:

1. Place the insertion point where you want to add a marquee, and then from the Insert menu, choose Marquee. You'll see the Marquee Properties dialog box, shown here:

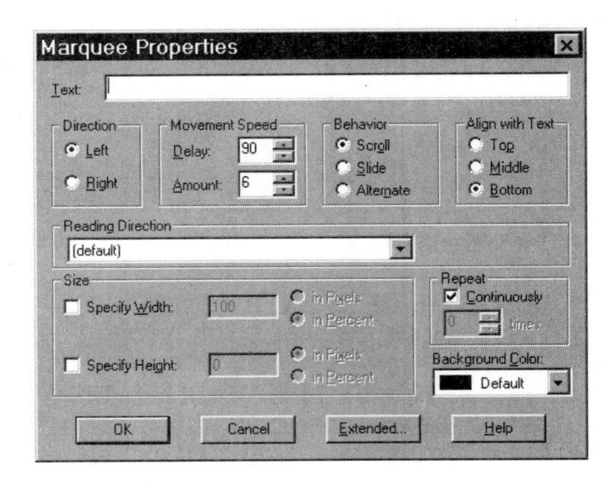

2. In the Text box, type the text you want to appear in the marquee.
3. For the other settings, try using the defaults for now. Later you can go back and change these until you get the effect you want.
4. Click OK. You'll see the marquee in your page, but FrontPage Express doesn't show how it scrolls. (To check the results, access your Web page through Internet Explorer.)

> **NOTE**
>
> At this time, marquees aren't supported by browsers other than Microsoft Internet Explorer. If you add a marquee to your page and someone using another browser accesses it, the marquee text will appear, but it won't scroll.

Inserting Graphics

You can add any JPEG or GIF graphic to your Web page, taking full advantage of the advanced features of these graphics formats that smooth the downloading process. You can also control the graphic's alignment, spacing, and size.

Understanding Graphics File Formats

You can include two types of graphics in your Web page.

- **JPEG** is short for Joint Photographic Experts Group. This graphics format uses *lossy compression,* in which some of the original information is discarded in order to reduce the size of the file. This loss isn't apparent to the eye unless the compression ratio is pushed too far. JPEG graphics are used for complex visual images with many colors, such as photographs. Some JPEG graphics, called *progressive JPEG graphics,* are designed to download so that a quick, rough version of the image appears, then gradually takes on more definition. This feature enables viewers to get an idea of how the page will look without having to wait for the whole download.
- **GIF** stands for Graphics Interchange Format, a graphic format originally developed by CompuServe. Although GIF graphics cannot store as many colors as JPEG graphics, they compress large single-color areas more efficiently. GIF graphics are a great choice if your graphic contains areas of solid color. There are two GIF standards, called GIF 87 and GIF 89a. The GIF 89a standard enables a single GIF file to contain more than one image, which makes it possible to create animations quickly and inexpensively. Another very cool feature of the GIF 89a format is *transparency,* the ability to define the background color so that it blends with the color of your Web page's background. To create GIF animations and transparent GIFs, you need a graphics editor such as Paint Shop Pro.

Inserting Graphics

To incorporate a graphic into your page, follow these steps:

1. Position the cursor where you want the graphic to appear.
2. Do one of the following:
   - On the Standard Toolbar, click Insert Image.

     or

   - From the Insert menu, choose Image.

   You'll see the Image dialog box, shown here:

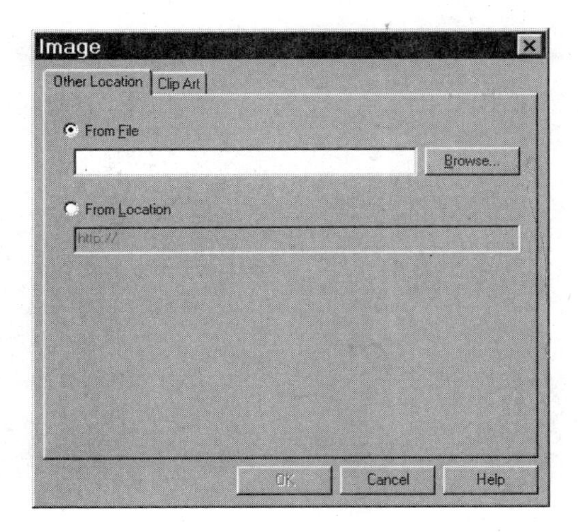

3. Click From File, and click the Browse button to locate, select, and open the graphics file.
4. Click OK to insert the image.

NOTE

Although FrontPage Express allows you to insert a graphic from the Web, you should not do so without first asking permission—not only for copyright purposes, but also because inserting a graphic in this way places an additional load on the server where the graphic is stored.

You'll see the graphic in your document, positioned using the default layout and size options—which you probably won't find satisfactory (see Figure 20-5 on page 704).

Choosing Graphics Options

By default, FrontPage Express positions graphics flush-left and aligns text to the right of the graphic; the text is aligned with the graphic's baseline. You can change these options, and you can specify the graphic's size and make other choices.

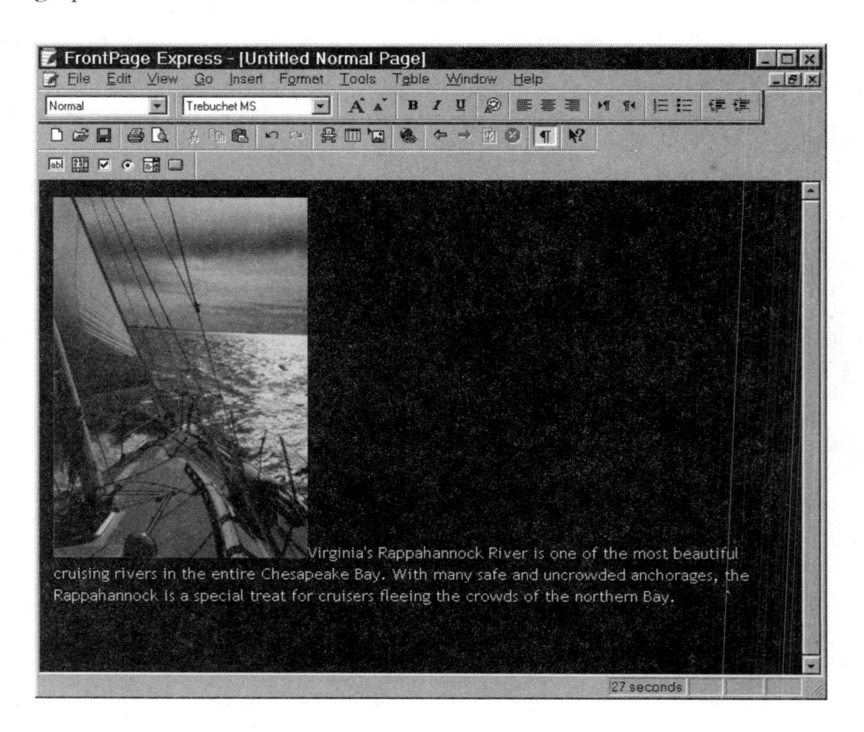

FIGURE 20-5. Adding graphics to your Web pages is easy, but you probably won't be happy with the way the graphic is initially situated.

The following list explains the options you can choose:

- **Alignment.** This option controls the position of the graphic in relation to surrounding text. You can align the text at the top, center, or bottom of the graphic, and you can also choose to position the graphic to the right or left of the text. You'll find some other options here, but they aren't supported by most browsers.
- **Border Thickness.** Here, you specify the width of the border surrounding the graphic. By default, this is zero (no border).
- **Horizontal Spacing.** This choice controls the amount of space between the graphic and surrounding text (to the left or right). By default, this is zero, but it's a good idea to change this to one or two so that there's a little blank space around the graphic.
- **Vertical Spacing.** With this option, you can add some space above and below the graphic. You may want to do this if the graphic looks crowded next to other graphics or text.

- **Size.** If you would like to change the size of the graphic, click Specify Size and choose a width and height. (You can enter these in pixels or a percentage of screen width.) Note, though, that FrontPage Express doesn't automatically preserve the graphic's *aspect ratio* (the relation between the width and height), so making changes here might introduce unwanted distortions.

To choose graphic options, including alignment, follow these steps:

1. Select the graphic.
2. Do one of the following:
   - Press Alt + Enter.

     or

   - Right-click the graphic, and choose Image Properties.

   You'll see the Image Properties dialog box, shown here:

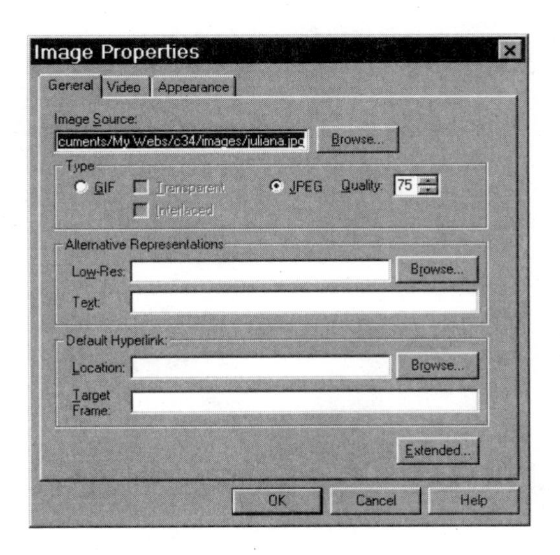

3. In the Type box, you can choose the following options:
   - **GIF** If you've added a GIF graphic, you can choose Transparent (choose this option for GIFs with a transparent background) or Interlaced (a low-resolution version of the entire picture downloads, and then becomes sharper).
   - **JPEG** You can adjust the quality. The higher the quality, the less compression is used, so the file size is larger, and downloads take longer.

4 In the Alternative Representation area, identify the location of a low-resolution version of this graphic if you have one. In the Text box, type text to display if the user has switched off graphics or is using a non-graphics browser.

5 If you would like this graphic to contain a hyperlink, type the URL in the Location box.

6 Click the Appearance tab. You'll see the Appearance options, shown here:

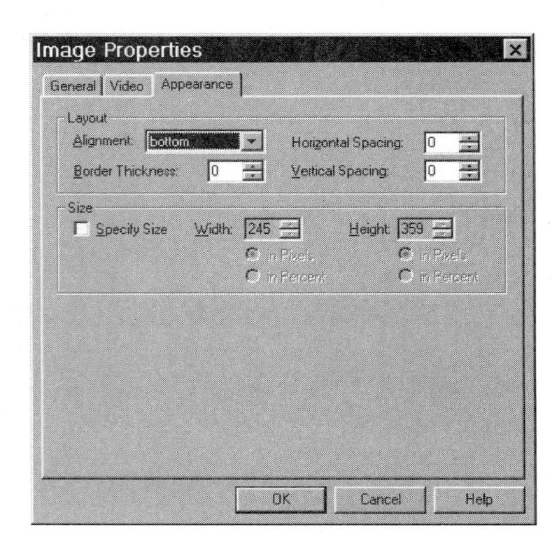

7 In the Alignment box, choose an alignment. The best options are Left and Right because these options enable the text to flow around the graphic (see Figure 20-6).

8 To add space between the graphic and surrounding text, increase the values in the Horizontal Spacing and Vertical Spacing boxes. The measurements are in screen pixels.

9 To add a border to your graphic, increase the value in the Border Thickness box. Adding borders isn't recommended.

10 If you would like to change the size of your graphic, click Specify Size, and adjust the Width and Height values. It isn't a good idea to use these controls because FrontPage Express does not automatically maintain the *aspect ratio* of your picture (the term aspect ratio refers to the ratio between the picture's horizontal and vertical dimensions). If you change the aspect ratio, the picture will look distorted.

11 Click OK to confirm your options.

FIGURE 20-6.
If you choose Left alignment for your graphic, the text is positioned to the right of the graphic, as shown here. You can choose Right alignment to position the text to the left of the graphic.

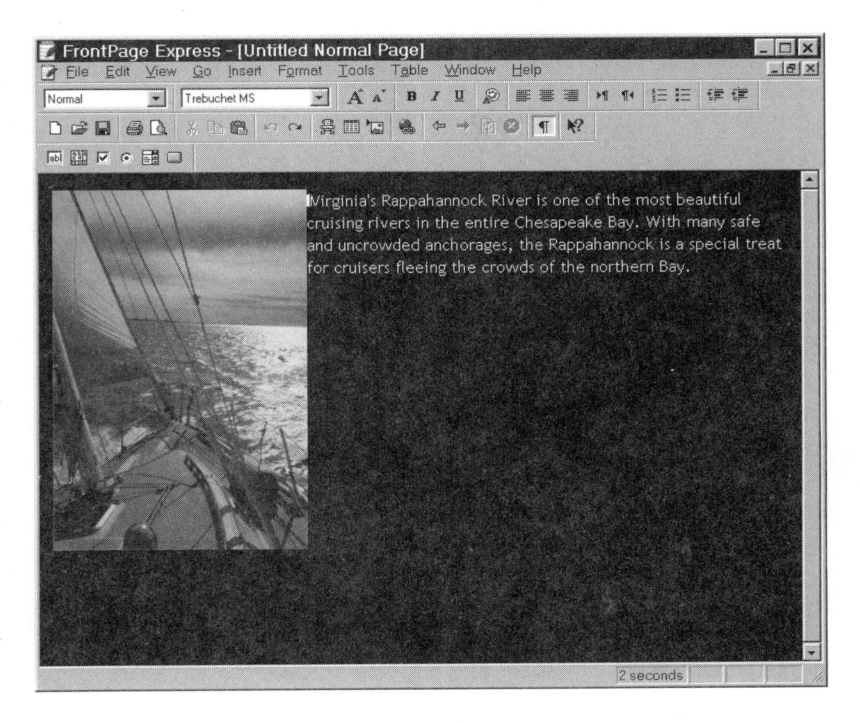

Inserting Videos

You can insert a video into your document just as easily as you can insert a graphic. Here's how:

1 Position the cursor where you want the video to be inserted within your document.

2 From the Insert menu, choose Video. You'll see the Other Location dialog box.

3 In the From File area, click Browse to locate, select, and open the video file you want to use. (You can also choose From Location, and type a Web address. However, you shouldn't do this without first asking permission of the site's owner.)

After you insert the video, you'll see a placeholder indicating the graphic's location. To choose options for displaying the video, see the next section.

Choosing Video Options

To display the properties dialog box, do one of the following:

1 To choose options for the video, do one of the following:

- Right-click the video placeholder, and choose Image Properties.

  or

- From the Edit menu, choose Image Properties.

  or

- Select the placeholder, and press Alt + Enter.

You'll see the Image Properties dialog box, with the Video tab displayed, as shown here:

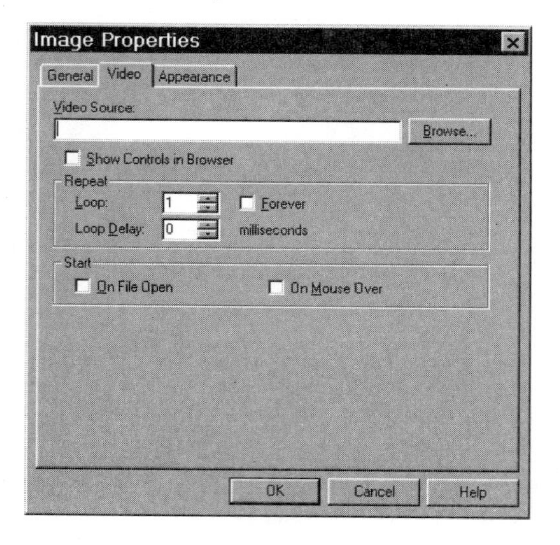

2 If you would like to include video controls within the browser, click Show Controls In Browser. If you leave this box unchecked, the browser will show the video in an external-helper program, such as Windows Media Player.

3 In the Repeat area, choose the number of times to loop (the default is 1 play only), or click Forever. If you wish, enter a loop delay in milliseconds.

4 In the Start area, indicate when you want the video to start.

Check one of the following: On File Open (starts playing the video when the file opens) or On Mouse Over (starts playing when the user moves the mouse over the video).

5 Click OK to confirm.

After you insert the video, you'll see a still version of the video, or an outline shape, depending on which type of video you inserted.

If you would like to delete the video, simply select it and press Delete.

Understanding Video-File Formats

You can insert the following types of videos into your FrontPage Express document:

- **AVI.** This is the default Microsoft Windows video format. Although quality is good and the video can include sound, AVI files take up a lot of disk space and download time. In addition, people who are using Macintosh or Unix machines may not have the software needed to play AVI videos.
- **MOV (QuickTime).** This is Apple's video format. Quality and compression are good, but people using Windows or Unix computers may not have the software needed to play MOV videos.
- **MPEG.** This is the best all-around choice for Web videos. Compression and quality are good, and MPEG videos can include sound. The format is well supported on most types of computers.

Creating Tables

If you've ever created tables with a word-processing program, you know how easy and useful they are. You define the number of rows and columns you want, and you get a matrix of *cells,* areas in which you can type text. Within each cell, you can type as much as you want, and the program adjusts the table dimensions and boundaries. With FrontPage Express, it's just as easy to create and edit tables.

NOTE

Tables aren't just for entering tabular data. They're the key to effective Web-page design. Short of using frames, which many users dislike, there's no other way to position text in two or more columns. You should learn how to create tables, even if you don't plan to publish tabular data. Using a simple, two-cell table, you can create a very cool Web page.

Inserting a Table

To add a table to your document, follow these steps:

1 Position the cursor where you want the table to appear.

2 From the Table menu, choose Insert Table. You'll see the Insert Table dialog box, shown here:

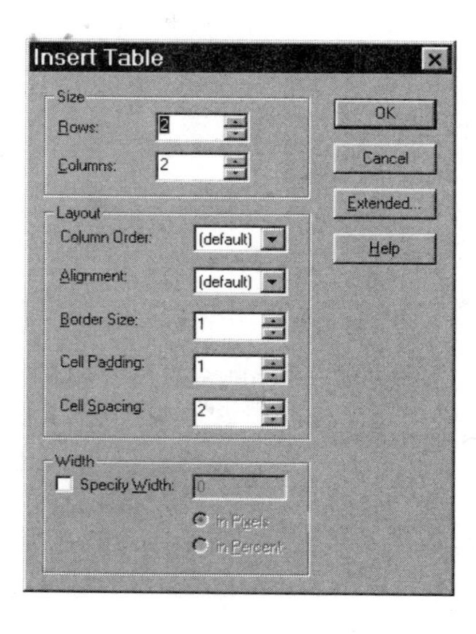

3 In the Size area, choose the number of rows and columns you want the table to have.

4 In the Layout area, you can choose the following options:

- **Column Order.** This option is included for international use. You can choose LTR (left to right) or RTL (right to left).
- **Alignment.** Choose a default alignment for all the cells in the table. You can override this for individual cells.
- **Border Size.** Choose a border width in pixels. To hide the border, enter 0 (zero).
- **Cell Padding.** To add some space between the table-cell border and the cell text, increase this number.
- **Cell Spacing.** To add some space between cells, increase this number.

5 In the Width area, you can set the table's width if you wish. (By default, the table expands or contracts depending on the amount

of window width). To choose a width, click Specify Width, and type a width. You can specify the width in pixels or a percentage of available screen space.

6 Click OK to confirm your options. You'll see your table in your document (see Figure 20-7).

Typing Text in Table Cells

By default, FrontPage Express creates a table with invisible borders and dynamically sized cells. To create your table, simply start typing in one of the cells. FrontPage will expand the cell as needed to accommodate as much text as you type. If you run out of room, the program starts a new line; you don't have to press Enter.

Within a table, the Tab key—useless elsewhere in an HTML document—finally takes on a meaningful function: You press it to move to the next cell. If you're at the end of the table, pressing Tab creates a new row.

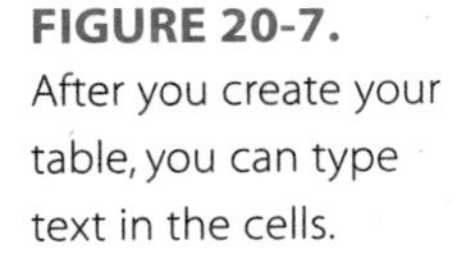

FIGURE 20-7.
After you create your table, you can type text in the cells.

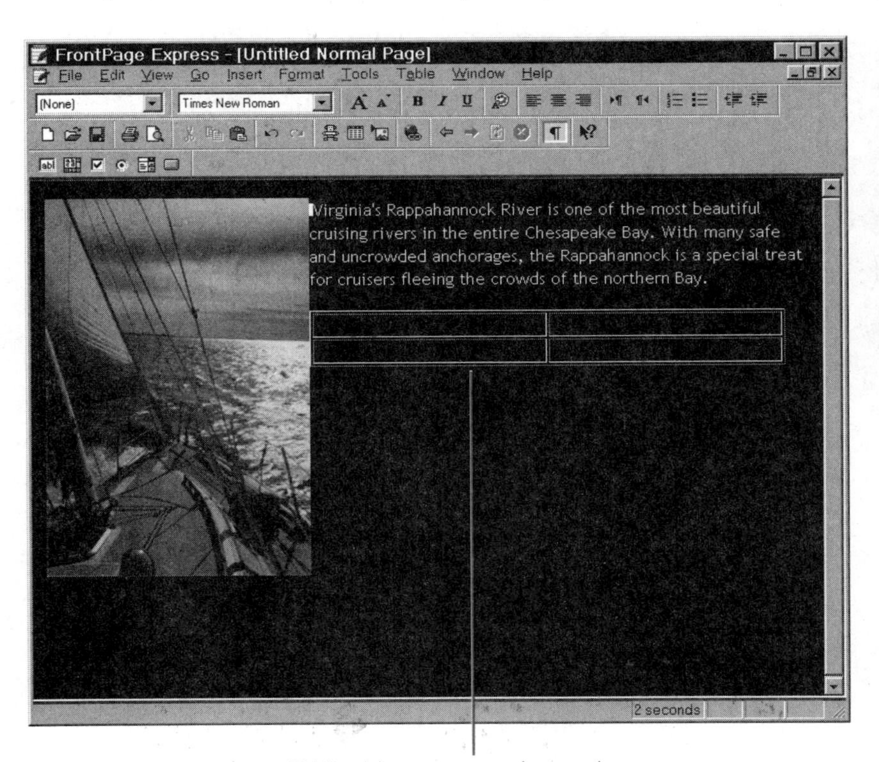

Editing the Table Structure

When you created your table, you chose the number of rows and columns you wanted. But you're not stuck with this. You can add rows and columns, or you can delete them if you add too many. In addition, you can add cells anywhere you like, even if a given column has more or fewer cells than another. You can also split cells and merge cells. You'll quickly learn the steps you take to perform these table-editing tasks.

Adding Rows, Columns, or Cells

To add a cell, position the cursor where you want the new cell to appear and choose Insert Cell from the Table menu.

If you want to add a new row at the end of your table, position the cursor in the last cell and press Tab. To insert a row or column within the table, position the cursor where you'd like the new one to appear, go to the Table menu, and select Insert Rows Or Columns. You'll see the Insert Rows Or Columns dialog box, shown here:

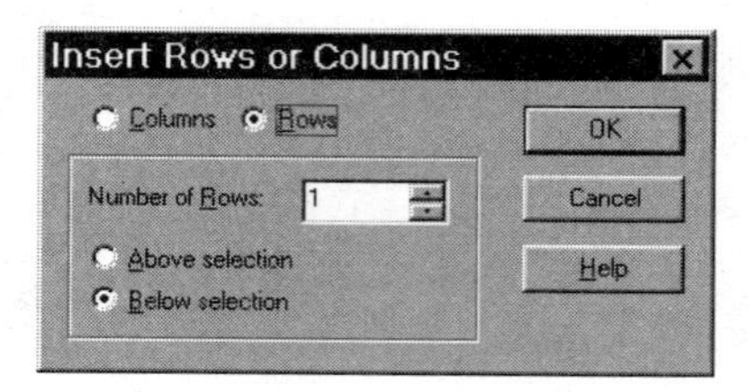

Choose Columns or Rows, and do one of the following:

- If you chose Columns, indicate the number of columns you want to add, and choose where you'd like the new columns inserted (left or right of the selection). Click OK.
- If you chose Rows, indicate the number of rows you want to add, and choose where you'd like the new rows inserted (above or below the selection). Click OK.

Deleting Rows, Columns, or Cells

To delete rows, columns, or cells, you must first select them. Use the selection commands on the Table menu—ordinary selection techniques won't work.

To select a cell, place the cursor in the cell and choose Select Cell from the Table menu. To delete the cell, press the Delete key.

To select a row or column, place the cursor anywhere in the row or column, go to the Table menu, and choose either Select Row or Select Column. Press Delete to remove the row or column.

You can also select rows and columns with the mouse, thanks to an invisible selection area positioned just outside the table area. To select a column, move the mouse to the white space just above the top of the column. When you see a down arrow, click the left-mouse button. To select a row, move the mouse to the white space just to the left of the row until you see a right arrow. Then click the left-mouse button.

Splitting a Cell

You can split a cell into two or more rows or two or more columns. Place the cursor in the cell, go to the Table menu, and choose Split Cells. You'll see the Split Cells dialog box, shown here:

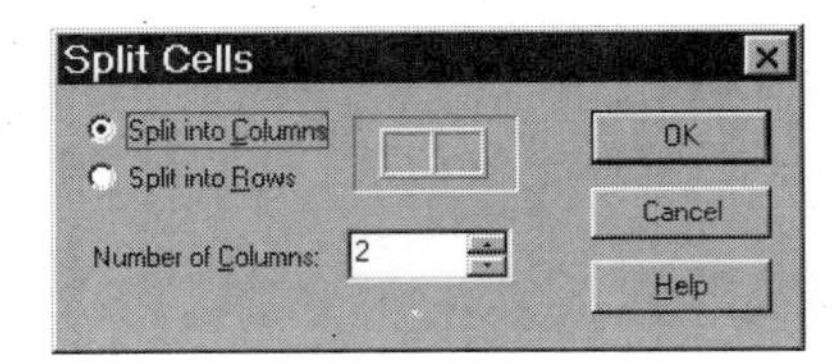

Choose Split Into Columns or Split Into Rows, and specify the number. Click OK when you're done.

Merging Cells

You can also merge two cells into one. Select the cells by dragging across them, and choose Merge Cells from the Table menu.

Choosing Table and Cell Properties

You can choose a variety of properties for the entire table or for individual cells. These properties include alignments, border size, extra space, absolute widths, and more. You can even add a background graphic or color to the whole table or to a particular cell.

Looking at Common Properties

You can choose many of the same properties for tables and individual cells. The following options are common to both:

- **Horizontal Alignment.** This option formats text as flush-left, center, or flush-right. The default setting leaves this up to the browser, which usually formats table text flush-left.

- **Custom Background.** You can use a background graphic or choose a background color.
- **Custom Colors.** If your table has a border width greater than 1 pixel, you can create a three-dimensional border effect by specifying the color to use for the light border (the top and left borders for the table, bottom and right for cells) and the dark border (bottom and right for the table, top and left for cells).

If you choose alignment, background, or color options for an individual cell, your choice overrides the current table properties. For example, suppose you've chosen a blue background for your whole table, but you select a red background for one of the cells within the table. Only that cell appears red.

Choosing Table Properties

To choose properties for your whole table, choose Table Properties from the Table menu or right-click the table and choose from the pop-up menu. You'll see the Table Properties dialog box, shown here:

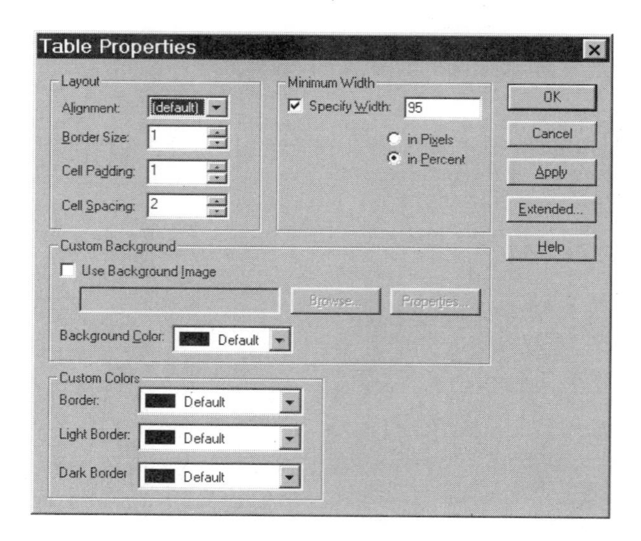

In addition to the properties shared with cells, tables use the following options:

- **Border Size.** By default, FrontPage Express omits the border. If you add a border, you can choose custom colors, including a light and dark border for three-dimensional effects.

- **Cell Padding.** The cell padding setting enables you to offset the text from the table border. By default, the program inserts 1 pixel of padding, which is enough to separate the text from the border. You can "open up" the table by increasing this measurement. (Don't make it smaller than 1.)
- **Cell Spacing.** The cell spacing setting enables you to add additional space between cells. If you add a border, this option splits the border, producing an effect in which each cell appears to be surrounded by a frame.
- **Minimum Width.** You can specify the minimum width of your table in pixels or as a percentage of the window width. To make sure your table always spans the browser's window, specify a width of 100 and click In Percent.

To see how the borders, cell padding, and cell spacing work together, create a small table and try varying the options. Create the table, and then choose Table Properties from the Table menu. Select an option, and click Apply to see the results without leaving the Table Properties dialog box. (Move the dialog box to one side so you can see your table).

Choosing Cell Properties

Once you've chosen properties for the whole table, you can choose properties for individual cells. To do so, place the cursor in a cell and choose Cell Properties from the Table menu. (You can also point to the cell, click the right-mouse button, and choose Cell Properties from the pop-up menu.) You'll see the Cell Properties dialog box, shown here:

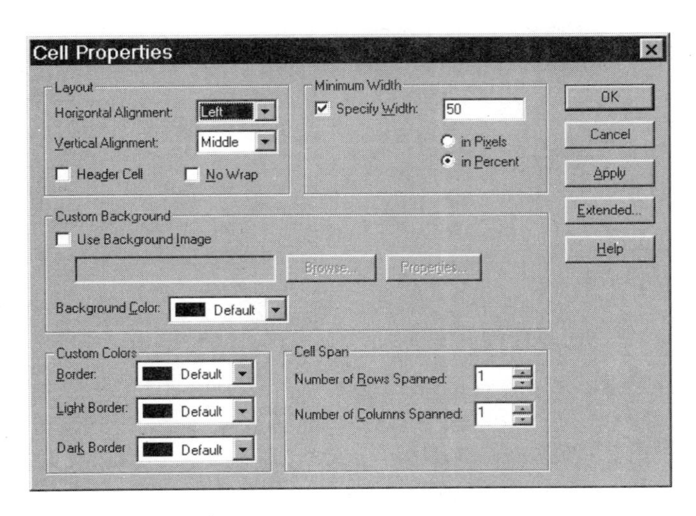

A number of the same properties appear in the Table Properties dialog box, including horizontal alignment, minimum width, custom background, and custom colors. In addition, you'll find these properties:

- **Vertical Alignment.** The default is Middle, but you can choose Top or Bottom.
- **Header Cell.** Click this option to format this cell's text in bold.
- **No Wrap.** Click this option to prevent text-wrapping in this cell.
- **Cell Span.** You can enlarge a cell so that it spans a specified number of rows or columns. To make a cell span rows, columns, or both, increase the settings in the Cell Span area. After you span rows or columns, you'll have some extra cells, since the program pushes them aside to make room for the cell that spans two or more rows or columns. Simply delete these extra cells.

Adding a Table Caption

To add a caption to your table, go to the Table menu and choose Insert Caption. FrontPage Express positions the cursor at the top of the table and enables you to type a centered caption. If you'd prefer to place the caption at the bottom of the table, go to the Table menu, choose Caption Properties, and select Bottom Of Table.

Using Table Layout Tricks

Tables aren't just for tabular data, as the previous section stressed. Professional Web designers use them to control document layout, and so can you. To see how Web authors use tables, find any non-framed page that appears to have a multiple-column layout, click the Edit button on the Standard buttons toolbar, and take a look at the page in FrontPage Express. Microsoft's own Start Page turns out to be a table made up of cells that span rows and columns as needed. Cool trick, isn't it?

If Internet Explorer opens Windows Notepad instead of FrontPage Express, you can change the default HTML editor. To do so, click Tools on the Internet Explorer menu bar, choose Options, and click the Programs tab. in the HTML Editor list box, choose FrontPage Express, and click OK.

A two-column, one-row table at the beginning of your document gives you control over the placement of a graphic next to text. The page shown in Figure 20-8 uses this technique.

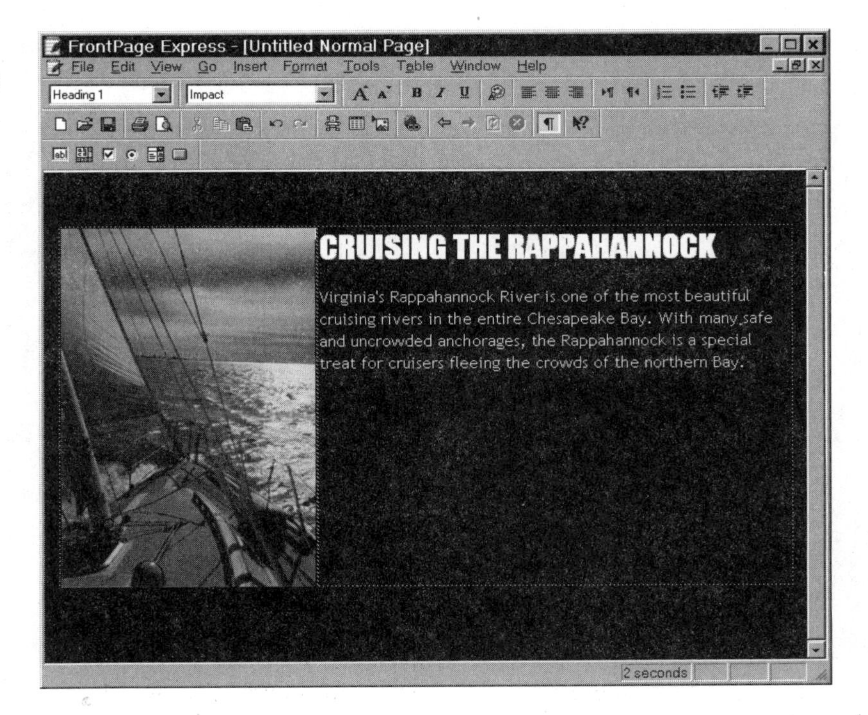

FIGURE 20-8.
This page was laid out with a two-column, one-row table. The dotted lines show where the table borders are located, but this page won't show borders when viewed by a browser because they're set to 0 (zero).

Creating Forms with the Form Page Wizard

You've surely filled out forms on Web sites many times. With FrontPage Express, you can create your own forms. But there's a catch. Forms don't do anything unless you direct the form's output to a program that's capable of decoding the output and acting on it. In most cases, this means that you'll need a programmer to handle the interface between the form output and the server.

That's where WebBots come in. If you can publish your pages on a server that supports the FrontPage extensions, you don't have to do any programming to create a form that solicits information from users and saves the output of a form in a file that you can later open and read. The file can be saved in a variety of formats, including a Web page with each entry in a bulleted list, or a text database using commas, tabs, or spaces as separators for each item. When users fill out the form and click the Submit button, they see a confirmation page.

Introducing the Forms Page Wizard

Is creating the form difficult? No, thanks to the Form Page Wizard, described first in this section. Subsequently, you'll learn how to create your own form components, but you'll need your ISP's assistance to get your own forms to work.

The Save Results WebBot is only one of several available with FrontPage 2000. When you move up to FrontPage 2000, you get wizards or templates to create forms for feedback submission, a guest book, a search page, and a Web-site registration form that requires people to establish a username and password before they can access the site.

With the Form Page Wizard, you can easily create a form that solicits information from people, and then saves the results in a file. Bear in mind that the form will work only on servers running Microsoft Internet Information Server (IIS) or the Microsoft FrontPage extensions. The Form Page Wizard makes use of the Save Results WebBot, one of three WebBots that you'll find in FrontPage Express

If you're not sure whether your server can handle the form output from the Save Results WebBot, ask your ISP before creating the form.

Running the Form Page Wizard

To create a form with the Form Page Wizard, follow these steps:

1 From the File menu, choose New. You'll see the New Page dialog box, shown here:

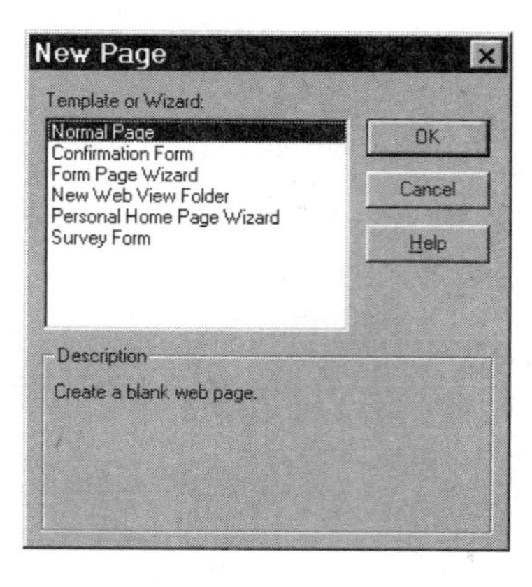

2 Select Form Page Wizard, and click OK. You'll see the first page of the Form Page Wizard, which explains what the wizard does.

3 Click Next to continue. You'll see a page requesting the Page URL and title, shown here:

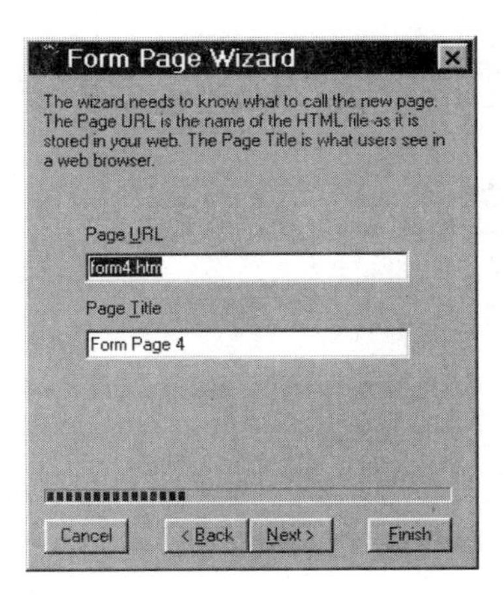

4 Type a relative URL (file name) for the Page URL, and type a descriptive page title.

5 Click Next to continue. You'll see the next page, which enables you to add questions.

6 Click Add. You'll see a page that enables you to choose the type of information you want to include, shown here:

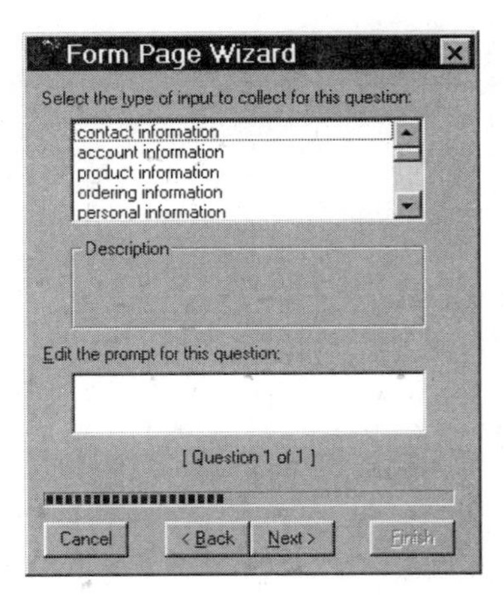

You can choose from the following:

Contact Information creates a form section that solicits name, title, organization, address, work phone, home phone, fax, e-mail address, and URL; you can select the questions to include.

Account Information creates a form section that solicits a user name and password if your site is password-protected.

Product Information creates a form section that enables users to request information about a product, model, platform and version, product code, and serial number (you can choose which items to include).

Ordering Information creates a form section that solicits order information, including a list of products and services, billing information, and shipping information.

Personal Information creates a form section that solicits name, age, sex, height weight, id number, hair color, and eye color (you can choose which items to include).

One Of Several Options creates a form section in which the user can choose one item from options you specify; you choose from Radio Buttons, Drop-Down Menu, or List formats. This is a "generic" option that lets you specify what types of options are being solicited.

Any Of Several Options creates a form section in which the user can choose any number of items.

Boolean (yes/no) creates a form section in which the user can answer by means of a Check Box, Yes/No Radio Buttons, or True/False Radio Buttons.

Date creates a form section in which the user can supply the date.

Time creates a form section in which the user can supply the time.

Range creates a form section in which the user can give responses to a survey question, such as On A Scale Of 1 To 5, "Bad, Poor, Average, Fair, Good," or "From Disagree Strongly To Agree Strongly."

Number creates a form section that solicits a numerical response, and enables you to specify the maximum length and currency prefix, if any.

String creates a form section that includes a one-line text box for user-text input; you can specify the maximum length.

Paragraph creates a scrolling text box in which the user can type more than one line of text.

7 Select an input type.

8 In Edit The Prompt For This Question, type the question that you want your user to see in this section.

9 Click Next. You'll see a page that asks you to select the specific type of information you want to include. For example, shown here is the page that appears when you choose Contact Information:

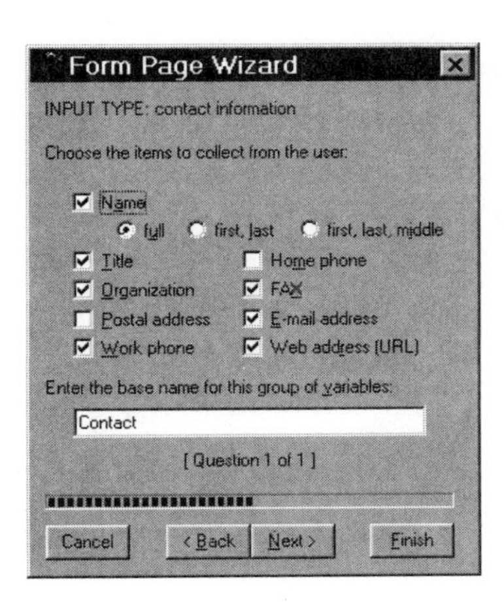

10 Click Next to confirm your choices. You'll see the wizard's question management page, shown here:

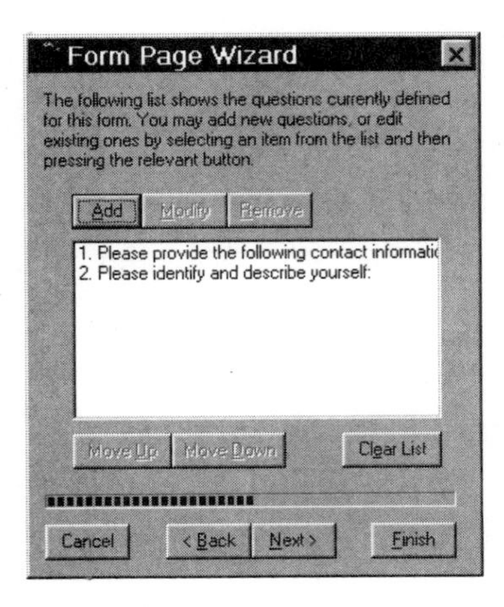

This page shows the input item you just added.

11 To add additional input items, click Add, and repeat steps 7 through 10.

12 When you're finished adding input items, you'll see the list of items in the question management page, as shown here:

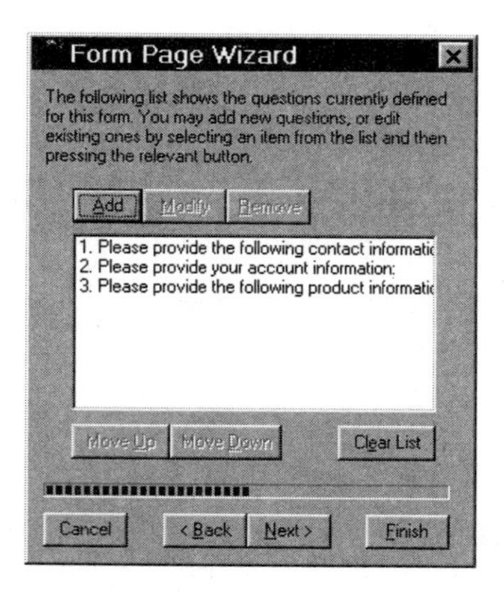

You can do the following:

Add. Insert more items, if you wish.

Modify. To edit an item, select it, and click Modify.

Remove. To remove an item, select it, and click Remove.

Move Up. To move an item up in the list, so that it appears higher on the Web page, select the item, and click Move Up.

Move Down. To move an item down in the list, so that it appears lower on the Web page, select the item, and click Move Down.

Clear List. To clear the entire list and start over, click Clear List.

13 When you're finished adding and managing items, click Next. You'll see the Presentation Options page, shown on the next page:

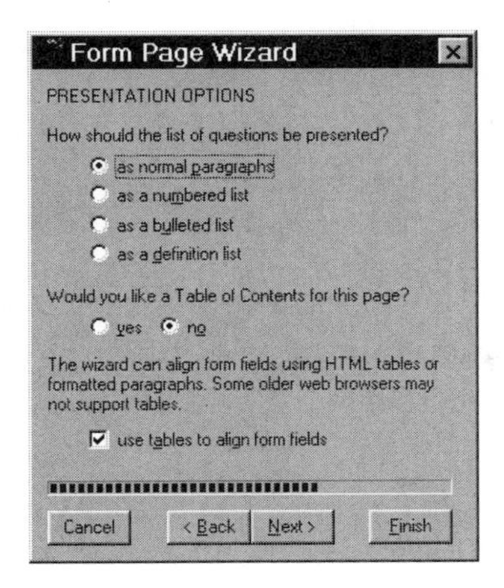

14 Choose the presentation options you want, and click Next. You'll see the Output Options page, shown here:

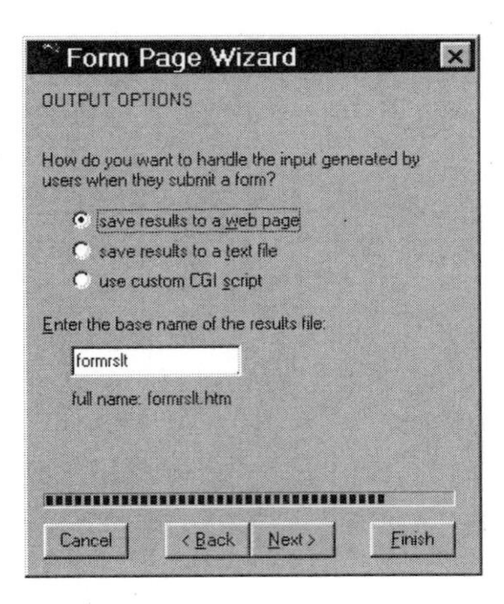

Choose the output option you want, click Next, and click Finish.

The result won't win prizes in a Web beauty contest, but it features the essentials of a solid Web form—and what's more, all the programming has been added to make this form work with Microsoft servers (or servers running the Microsoft FrontPage Extensions). You can now modify the form with color and formatting to suit your style.

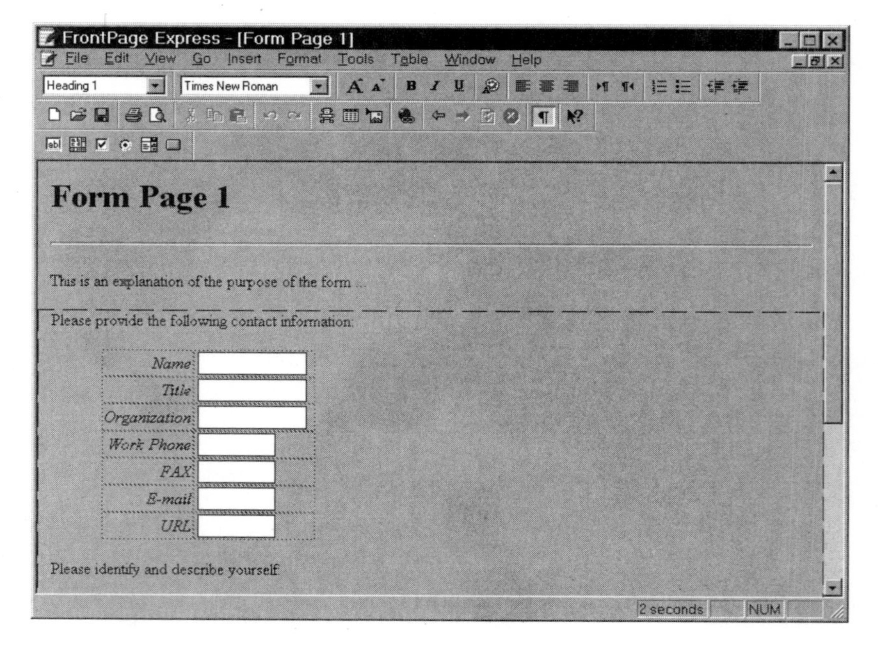

FIGURE 20-9.
This form was automatically generated by the Form Page Wizard. The dotted black line shows the form area.

Creating Custom Forms

If you would like to create your own forms, remember that custom programming is needed to deal with the output of the forms. Check with your ISP to find out what's involved. Even if you can't do the programming yourself, you can still create the form page. Your ISP will tell you how to modify the page so that the form output will be directed to the available forms-processing software.

Understanding Form Output

When a user fills out a form and clicks the Submit button, the browser sends information to the server. This information is formatted as a series of *name-value pairs*. This isn't as complex as it sounds. Each input control, such as a text box, has a unique *name*, which you give to the control when you create the control. After the user fills out the form (for example, by typing text in a text box), the user's responses give each control an associated *value*. (For example, the response to the "First Name" question will be a name, such as "Susan" or "Frank.") The form output consists of a list containing each of the form's control names followed by the values that the user chose.

Form output is in plain text, but it's not very readable. That's why software is needed to decode the form output. However, you can have form output sent to your e-mail address, and you can get shareware programs that strip the output of all the funny characters, leaving just the field names and values. This is a low-tech way of implementing forms-based interactivity, but it's feasible only if you expect a few responses since you must deal with each submission manually.

TIP

Several shareware programs are available that can decode forms output routed to your e-mail account; an example is WebForms (http://www.q-d.com/wf.htm); the publisher claims compatibility with Internet Explorer mailto forms. (Please note that I haven't tested this program.)

More than likely, your ISP has already created programs that can deal with forms output. If such programs exist, implementing your form may be as simple as getting the program's name and adding it to the Forms Properties dialog box, as described later in this section. Once again, call your ISP!

Before creating input controls, sketch out the way you want your form to appear. Think about the type of information you're soliciting. With some planning, you'll do a much better job designing your form.

Looking at Input Controls

With FrontPage Express, you can create the following form input controls, illustrated in Figure 20-10:

- **One-Line Text Box** accepts text input on one line only. You can specify the size of the box and the maximum number of characters that can be typed.
- **Scrolling Text Box** accepts more than one line of text input. You can specify the box's size.
- **Check Box** creates a check box; you can specify whether it's checked or not. You can group check boxes so that a user can choose zero to all of the options in an area.
- **Radio Button** creates a radio button; you can specify whether it's selected or not. You can group radio buttons so that a user must choose one of the options in an area.
- **Drop-Down Menu** creates a drop-down list box; you can add as many options as you choose. You can also specify whether one of the options is displayed by default.

- **Push Button** creates a push button; you must create a Submit push button, and you can also add a Reset button.

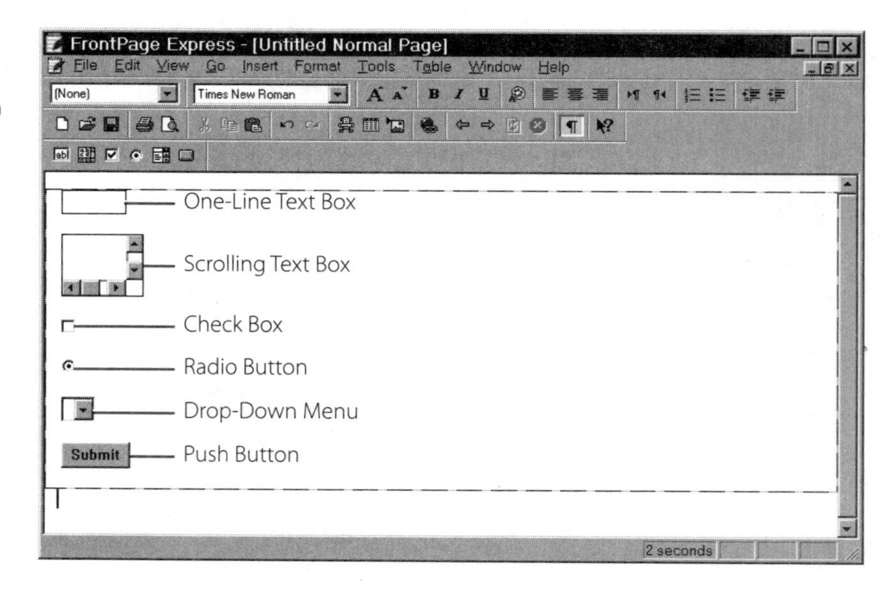

FIGURE 20-10. You can add the following controls within a form area.

Beginning the Form

To begin the form, do the following:

1. Place the cursor where you want the form to appear.
2. Insert an input control, as described in the following sections. Inserting the control creates the form area, signified by a rectangular box around the input control you added (see Figure 20-10).

Make sure that all the controls you add are within the form area, outlined by the dashed lines.

Consider creating a two-column table for your form. In the left column, you place explanatory and prompt text, such as "Please type your name." In the right column, you place the controls, such as text boxes. To insert check-box and radio-button areas, you can merge the cells in a row. The result will look very neat.

Inserting a One-Line Text Box

One-line text boxes enable the user to type a short response. For longer responses, use scrolling text boxes.

To insert a one-line text box, follow these steps:

1. Place the cursor where you want the control to appear.
2. Do one of the following:
   - From the Forms Toolbar, click the One-Line Text Box button.

     or
   - From the Insert menu, point to Form Field, and choose One-Line Text Box.

   FrontPage Express inserts the text box.
3. To choose properties for this control, do one of the following:
   - Double-click the control.

     or
   - Select the control, and press Alt + Enter.

     or
   - Right-click the control, and choose Form Field Properties.

   You'll see the Text Box Properties dialog box, shown here:

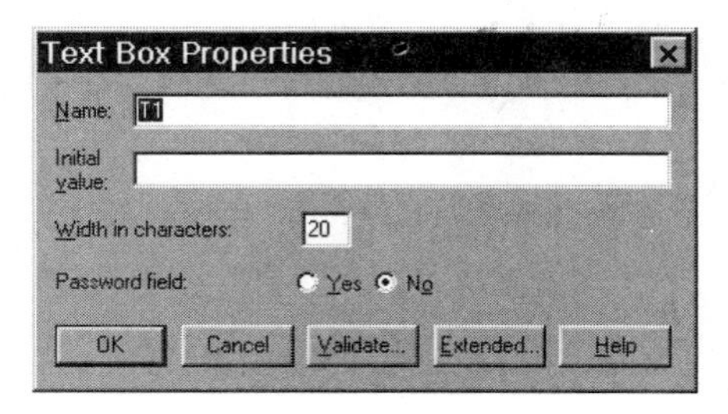

4. In the Name box, type a name to identify the field (one word only, no spaces).

   In the Initial Value area, type the text that you want to appear in this text box, if any. The user can edit this text.

   In the Width In Characters box, type the width of the box. Make sure it's long enough to fit the text you're requesting.

5 In the Password Field area, click Yes if you would like to make the entered text appear in asterisks. (This is the best option since it prevents onlookers from seeing the password that the user types.)

6 Click OK to confirm the control's properties.

After you've inserted a one-line or scrolling text box, you can size the box by selecting it and dragging the handles.

Inserting a Scrolling Text Box

A scrolling text box enables the user to type more than one line of text. If you're soliciting a short response, use a one-line text box instead.

To insert a scrolling text box, follow these steps:

1 Place the cursor where you want the control to appear.

2 Do one of the following:

- From the Forms Toolbar, click the Scrolling Text Box button.

  or

- From the Insert menu, point to Form Field, and choose Scrolling Text Box.

FrontPage Express creates the control.

3 To choose properties for this control, do one of the following:

- Double-click the control.

  or

- Select the control, and press Alt + Enter.

  or

- Right-click the control, and choose Form Field Properties.

You'll see the Scrolling Text Box Properties dialog box, shown on the next page:

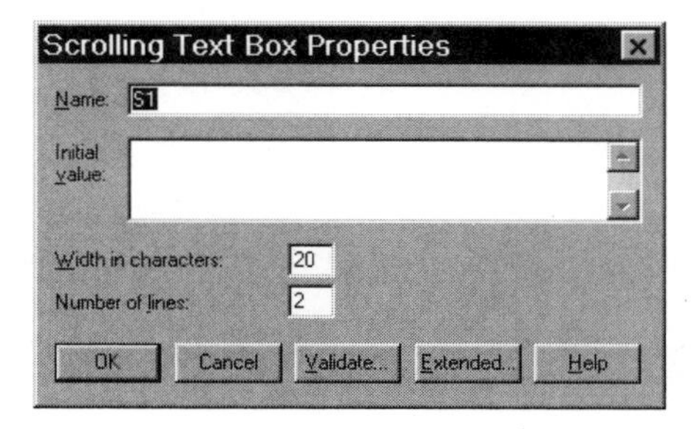

4 In the Name area, type a name for this field.

5 In the Initial Value area, type the text, if any, that you want to appear by default. The user can edit this text.

6 In the Width In Characters box, choose a width.

7 In the Number Of Lines box, choose the number of lines you want to display.

8 Click OK to confirm the control's properties.

Inserting a Check Box

A check box can be used singly, or in groups to allow users to choose any of the items they want (or none). If you want to restrict the user's choice to one item only, use radio buttons.

To insert a check box, follow these steps:

1 Place the cursor where you want the control to appear.

2 Do one of the following:

- From the Forms Toolbar, click the Check Box button.

  or

- From the Insert menu, point to Form Field, and choose Check Box

FrontPage Express inserts the control in your document.

3 To choose properties for this control, do one of the following:

- Double-click the control.

  or

- Select the control, and press Alt + Enter.

  or

- Right-click the control, and choose Form Field Properties.

You'll see the Check Box Properties dialog box, shown here:

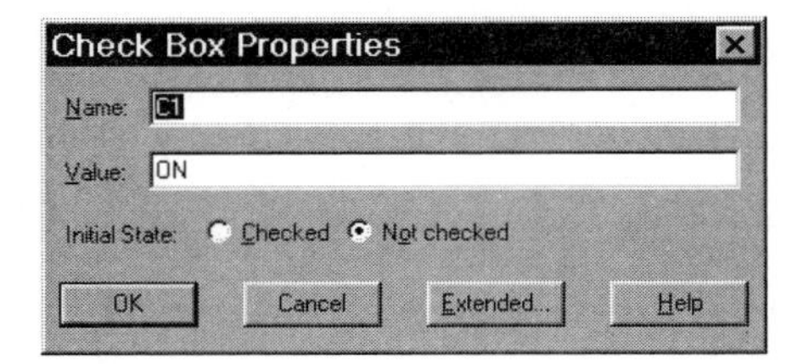

4 In the Name area, type a name for this field.

5 In the Value area, type the value to associate with this field if the check box is checked. This value will be shown in the form output. If the check box asks users to indicate whether they'd like to receive e-mail, type YES.

6 In the Initial State area, click Checked or Unchecked.

7 Click OK to confirm the control's properties.

Inserting a Radio Button

When you create radio buttons, you group them so that the user selects one out of the available options. To group the buttons, you give all of them the same group name. You can create additional groups by creating radio buttons with different group names.

To insert a group of radio buttons, follow these steps:

1 Place the cursor where you want the control to appear.

2 Do one of the following:

- From the Forms Toolbar, click the Radio Button tool.

  or

- From the Insert menu, point to Form Field, and choose Radio Button.

FrontPage Express inserts the radio button in your document.

3 To choose properties for this control, do one of the following:

- Double-click the control.

  or

- Select the control, and press Alt + Enter.

  or

- Right-click the control, and choose Form Field Properties.

You'll see the Radio Button Properties dialog box, shown here:

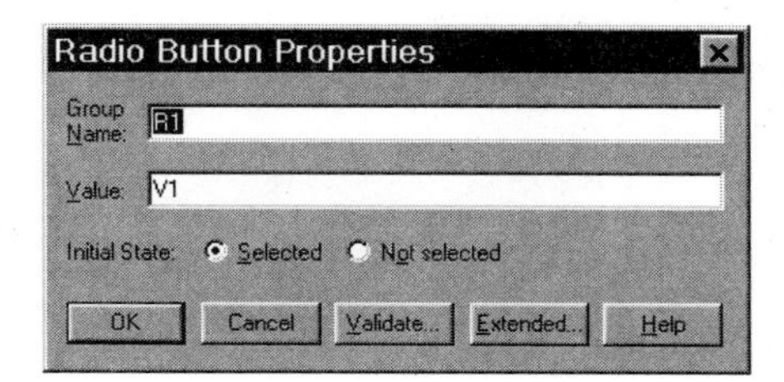

4 In the Group Name area, type a group name for this group of radio buttons.

5 In the Value area, type the value to associate with this field if the option is checked. Type a descriptive value so you know how to interpret the form results. For example, if you have a group of radio buttons that asks the user to specify a preference for a return contact, with the options E-mail, Telephone, or Letter, you can use these words as the values for each radio button.

6 In the Initial State area, click Selected or Unselected.

7 Click OK to confirm the control's properties.

Inserting a Drop-Down Menu

To insert a drop-down menu, follow these steps:

1 Place the cursor where you want the control to appear.

2 Do one of the following:

- From the Forms Toolbar, click the Drop-Down Menu button.

  or

- From the Insert menu, point to Form Field, and choose Drop-Down Menu.

FrontPage Express inserts the control in your document.

3 To choose properties for this control, do one of the following:

- Double-click the control.

  or

- Select the control, and press Alt + Enter.

  or

- Right-click the control, and choose Form Field Properties.

You'll see the Drop-Down Menu Properties dialog box, shown here:

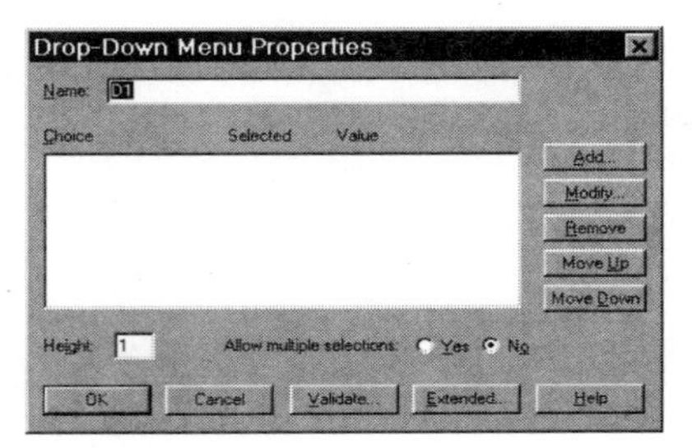

4 In the Name area, type a name for this field.

5 If you would like the user to be able to select more than one option, click Yes next to Allow Multiple Selections. If you click No, the user can make only one selection.

6 In the Height area, type the number of lines of text that you want to appear in the menu box. The default is one.

7 To add a line to the menu, click Add. You'll see the Add Choice dialog box, shown here:

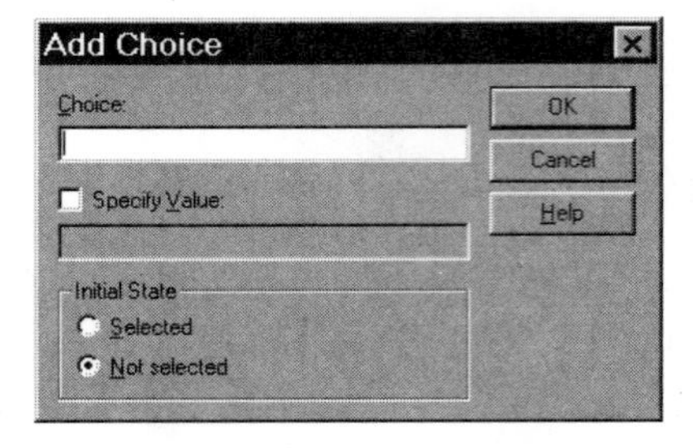

8 In the Choice area, type the text you want to appear in the menu.

9 If you want the value for this choice to be different from the text in the Choice box, click Specify Value, and type the value in the text box.

10 In the Initial State area, determine whether you want this choice to be selected or not. The selected choice appears in the list box.

11 Click OK to add the choice. You'll see the option in the Drop-Down Menu Properties dialog box.

12 To add additional options, repeat steps 7 through 11.

13 Once you've finished adding options, you can do the following:

Modify. To modify an option, select the option and click Modify.

Remove. To delete an option, select the option, and click Remove.

Move Up. To move an option up in the menu, select the option, and click Move Up.

Move Down. To move an option down in the menu, select the option, and click Move Down.

14 Click OK to confirm the control's properties.

Inserting a Push Button

To complete your form, you must insert a Submit button, preferably at the bottom of the form. You may also want to insert a Reset button, which enables the user to clear the form.

NOTE

You can create buttons for purposes other than submitting form data or clearing the form, but these buttons require custom programming.

To insert a Submit or Reset button, follow these steps:

1 Place the cursor where you want the control to appear.

2 Do one of the following:

- From the Forms Toolbar, click the Push Button tool.

or

- From the Insert menu, point to Form Field, and choose Push Button.

FrontPage Express inserts the control in your document.

3 To choose properties for this control, do one of the following:

- Double-click the control.

  or

- Select the control, and press Alt + Enter.

  or

- Right-click the control, and choose Form Field Properties.

You'll see the Push Button Properties dialog box, shown here:

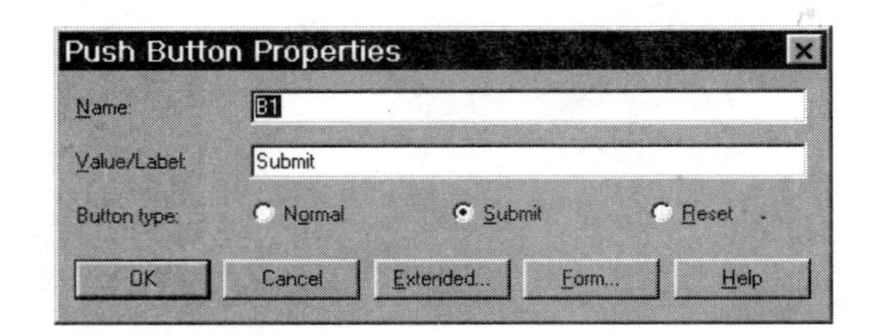

4 In the Name area, type a name for this field.

5 In the Value/Label area, type the text that you want to appear on the button's face.

6 In the Button Type area, select Submit or Reset.

7 Click OK to confirm the control's properties.

Inserting Active Content

You can add the following types of active content to your FrontPage Express document:

- **WebBot Components.** You can choose from Include (automatically includes a specified file at the component's location), Search (creates a search page for your site), and Timestamp (automatically inserts the time and date of the file's last location).

- **ActiveX Control.** These are mini-programs that add interactivity to your site. If you're not a programmer, you can download public-domain ActiveX controls and add them to your page. Note that ActiveX controls are natively supported only by Internet Explorer; people who use other browsers must obtain a plug-in program in order to view ActiveX content.

- **Java Applet.** Java Applets are mini-programs that you can embed on your page. If you're not a programmer, you can download public domain Java applets and add them to your page. To use Java applets, users must have browsers that can work with Java; most browsers in common use today do support Java.
- **Plug-in.** Plug-ins are programs that can be added to a browser. If you insert data designed to be used with a plug-in, the browser looks for and starts the plug-in automatically.
- **PowerPoint Animation.** You can insert an animation prepared with Microsoft PowerPoint, and determine whether the animation is inserted as an ActiveX control or as a plug-in.
- **Script.** Scripts are mini-programs that you insert right in your Web page. If you're not a programmer, you can download public domain scripts and use them. You can insert VBScript or JavaScript scripts.

Inserting a WebBot Component

It's easy to include WebBot components, but bear in mind that these components won't work unless your Web server supports the Microsoft FrontPage Extensions (check with your ISP to make sure).

Inserting the Include Component

The Include component automatically inserts a separate Web page at the cursor's location. The insertion occurs when the user accesses the page. With this component, you can create what appears to be a single page, but in fact it's made up of two or more separate pages. You could use the Include component to include form output that has been saved in a Web-page format.

To insert an Include component, follow these steps:

1. From the Insert menu, choose WebBot Component.

   You'll see the Insert WebBot Component dialog box.

2. Select Include, and click OK. You'll see the WebBot Include Component Properties dialog box.
3. Type the page's location.
4. Click OK.

FrontPage Express inserts the WebBot component; you'll see the file name. If you point to the component, you'll see the WebBot cursor, indicating that a WebBot has been inserted. To modify the WebBot, double-click the file name.

Inserting the Search Component

This nifty component enables you to set up a search page for your site. If you include this component, the server automatically generates a file containing all the words that appear in all the pages of your site. The search component enables users to search for pages containing specified keywords, and generates a new page containing links to the pages that contain these words.

To insert a Search component, follow these steps:

1. From the Insert menu, choose WebBot Component.

   You'll see the Insert WebBot Component dialog box.

2. Select Search, and click OK. You'll see the WebBot Search Component Properties dialog box, shown here:

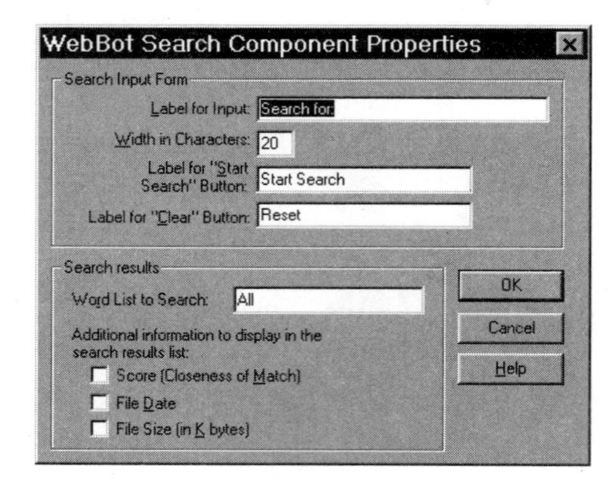

3. It's best to use the default settings. However, in the Search Results area, you can check options to display additional information to display in the results list.

4. Click OK to insert the component.

FrontPage Express inserts a form that includes a text box to type search questions, as well as a Start Search and Reset button. Add explanatory text to tell users how to use the search form.

Inserting a TimeStamp Component

This component automates a very tedious task: specifying the date that the page was last edited. Web authors normally include such a date at the bottom of the page; this enables users to judge whether the page is up to date.

To insert a TimeStamp component, follow these steps:

1. From the Insert menu, choose WebBot Component.

   You'll see the Insert WebBot Component dialog box.

2. Select Timestamp, and click OK. You'll see the WebBot Timestamp Component Properties dialog box, shown here:

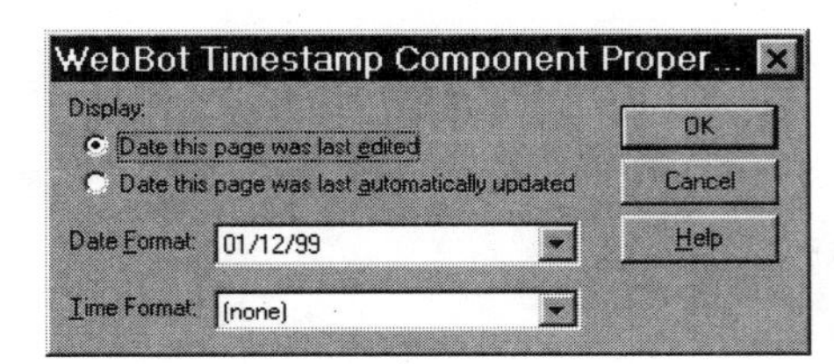

3. In the Display area, choose a date option. If you manually update the page, choose Date This Page Was Last Edited. If the page is automatically updated by forms output, choose Date This Page Was Last Automatically Updated.
4. In the Date Format box, choose a date format.
5. In the Time Format box, choose a time format. Choose None to hide the time.
6. Click OK.

Adding an ActiveX Control

FrontPage Express provides great tools for including ActiveX controls on your Web page. You can use ActiveX controls for a number of cool things, including three-dimensional buttons, animations, and pull-down menus. Bear in mind, though, that users won't be able to view the page unless they're using a browser capable of running ActiveX.

TIP

> Microsoft's Site Builder Network offers a number of free ActiveX controls that you can include on your Web pages. Visit the Tools and Samples page at http://www.microsoft.com/gallery/default.asp.

In order to insert ActiveX controls on your page, you must first obtain and install the control on your computer (if you don't, FrontPage Express can't access it). Be sure to read the control's documentation thoroughly.

Once you've installed the control on your system, you can add it to your page by following these steps:

1. Place the cursor where you want the ActiveX control to appear.
2. From the Insert menu, choose Other Components, and then select ActiveX Control. You'll see the ActiveX Control Properties dialog box, shown here:

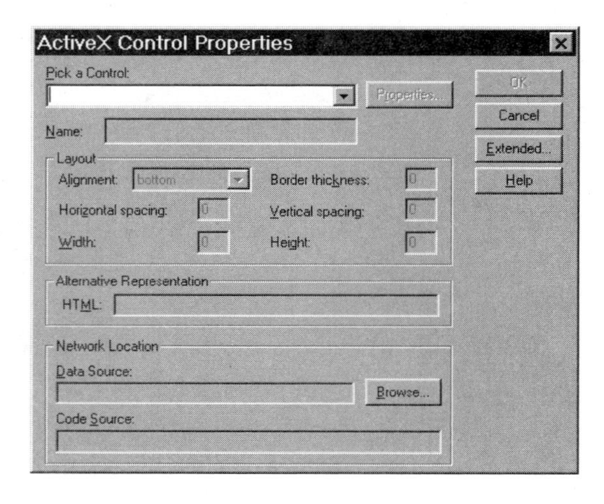

3. In the Pick A Control box, click the down arrow to see a list of the ActiveX controls installed on your system and choose the control you want to add.
4. Accept the default layout settings for now. (If you'd like to adjust the alignment and other position settings later, select the control and press Alt + Enter.)
5. Click OK to add the control to your page.

To modify the control in any way, just double-click the icon. To delete the control, delete the icon.

Including a Java Applet

If you've found a Java Applet that you want to include on your page, find and read the applet's documentation. You'll need to know the applet's *parameters*, which are aspects of the applet that you can adjust. You also need to know the *value* you should specify for each parameter. Once again, you'll need the documentation in order to find out which parameters and values to specify.

To insert a Java applet on your page, follow these steps:

1. Place the cursor where you want the Java applet to appear.
2. From the Insert menu, choose Other Components, and then select Java Applet. You'll see the Java Applet Properties dialog box, shown here:

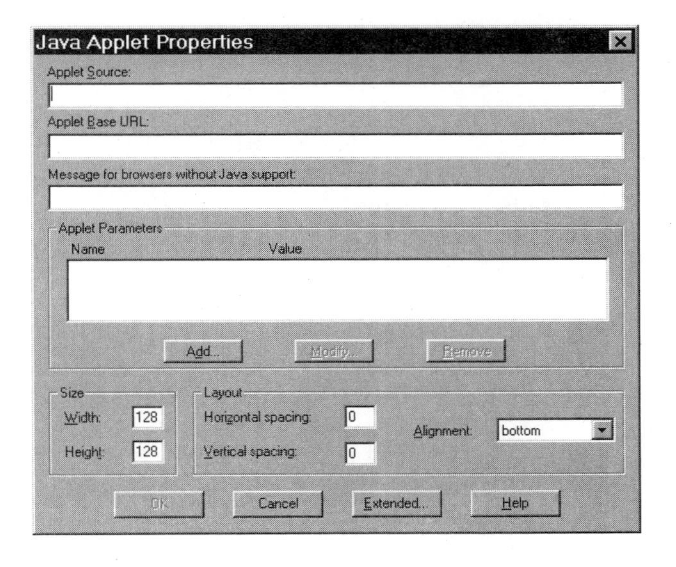

3. In the Applet Source box, type the location of the applet (applets are files with the .class extension). You should store the applet in the same directory as the referring page, or in a /java directory below the directory in which the referring page is stored.
4. Type a message for browsers that do not have browser support, such as "This applet requires Java, but your browser isn't configured to work with or does not support Java."
5. In the Applet Parameters area, click Add. You'll see the Set Attribute Value dialog box.
6. In the Name box, carefully type the parameter's exact name. You must type this exactly the way it's spelled in the documentation.
7. If the parameter requires a value, check Specify Value, and type the value in the Value box.

8. Click OK.
9. To configure additional applet parameters, repeat steps 6 through 9.
10. In the Size and Layout areas, choose sizes and formats for the applet. Check the applet's documentation for suggestions.
11. Click OK to insert the applet.

After you insert the applet, you'll see a big "J" icon in your document. To modify the applet in any way, just double-click this icon. To delete the applet, delete the icon.

Including Plug-In Data

Plug-ins work with data sources that couldn't otherwise be displayed within Web pages, but they require that users download and install plug-in software.

If you insert a plug-in in your Web page, be sure to include a link to the plug-in program's Web site so that users can download and install the plug-in software.

To insert a plug-in into your document, follow these steps:

1. Place the cursor where you want the plug-in to appear.
2. From the Insert menu, choose Other Components, and then select Plug-In. You'll see the Plug-In Properties dialog box, shown here:

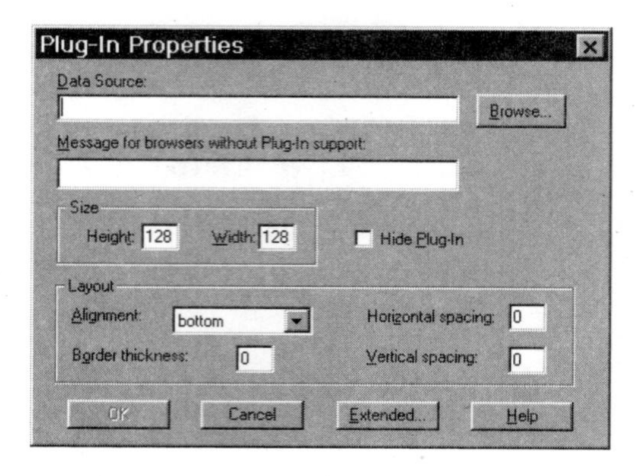

3. In the Data Source box, type the URL of the plug-in program.
4. For browsers without plug-in support, type a message explaining which plug-in you have embedded and where it can be downloaded.
5. In the Size and Layout areas, type a size, and choose layout options for the plug-in display area. (Note that these options affect only those plug-ins designed to appear inline, that is, within a Web page instead of opening a new window.) Consult the plug-in software's documentation for suggestions.

After you insert the plug-in, you'll see a big plug icon in your document. To modify the plug-in in any way, just double-click this icon. To delete the plug-in, delete the icon.

Including a PowerPoint Animation

You can insert a PowerPoint animation into your page. To do so, follow these instructions:

1. Place the cursor where you want the PowerPoint animation to appear.
2. From the Insert menu, choose Other Components, and then select PowerPoint Animation. You'll see the PowerPoint Animation dialog box.
3. Type the location of the animation file.
4. In the Insert As area, choose one of the following:

   ActiveX Control. If you choose this option, users won't have to have the PowerPoint viewer to view the animation, but you restrict your audience to users of Microsoft Internet Explorer.

   Plug-In. If you choose this option, users will need to download and install the PowerPoint viewer in order to see the animation.
5. Click OK.

After you insert the animation, you'll see a plug-in icon or an ActiveX icon, depending on which option you chose. To modify the plug-in in any way, just double-click this icon. To delete the plug-in, delete the icon.

Including a Script

JavaScript is a scripting language for the Web. Originally developed by Netscape Communications and recently standardized, JavaScript is loosely based on Java, but it's much easier to use. Unlike Java applets, which aren't readable on screen, JavaScript scripts can be typed directly into a Web document. On the Web, you'll find hundreds of free JavaScript scripts, which you can add to your document using FrontPage Express's nifty drag-and-drop capabilities.

You can also include VBScript scripts, but bear in mind that the scripts won't work unless your page is accessed by Microsoft Internet Explorer.

TIP

> Look for JavaScript scripts that you can use on your page without modifying the underlying code. For example, there are a number of freebie JavaScript scripts that display the current date and time. These need no modification to be used on your page.

Adding the JavaScript with Drag and Drop

You can easily include a JavaScript in your Web page using these steps:

1. Using Internet Explorer, display the page that contains the JavaScript.
2. Click Edit. You'll see the page in FrontPage Express. The JavaScript appears as a small J in a box with a yellow background.
3. From the Window menu, choose Tile so that you can see your page as well as the page containing the JavaScript.
4. Drag the JavaScript to your page, and release the mouse button.

Viewing the script's properties

After you've added a JavaScript to your page, you'll want to view the script. Select the script's icon, and press Alt + Enter. You can also point to the script's icon and click the right-mouse button, or choose WebBot Component Properties from the Edit menu. You'll see the Script dialog box, with the JavaScript shown in plain text. If you know a little JavaScript language, you can modify the code.

Inserting a script by typing it

You may run across scripts in books or magazines. If so, you can type them into the Script dialog box and add them to your pages. Just be sure to copy the script exactly. All the funny-looking symbols are important!

1. From the Insert menu, choose Script. You'll see a blank Script dialog box.
2. In the Language area, choose the script language.
3. In the Script area, type your script.
4. Proofread your typing carefully.
5. Click OK.

CHAPTER 21

Publishing Your Pages on the Internet

Once you've created a Web page, you need to publish it—and in the Web world, publishing means placing a copy of your page on a computer that's running a Web server. Unless you're lucky enough to have a computer with a permanent Internet address, that means uploading the file to your Internet service provider (ISP) and placing it within a directory that makes your page available on the Internet.

You can transfer your pages to a Web server in two ways:

- **Web Publishing Wizard.** This is the best solution if you're uploading your page to a server that supports the Microsoft FrontPage Extensions. (Call your ISP to find out.) You can also use the Web Publishing Wizard to upload your files to other types of servers, but it's easier to use Internet Explorer's built-in FTP upload and download capabilities.

- **Internet Explorer FTP Support.** Internet Explorer can upload and download files to FTP servers. To upload files to an FTP server, you must have a user name and password. Once you've supplied these to Internet Explorer, you can work with the FTP server to transfer your files to your Web publishing directory.

Publishing with the Web Publishing Wizard

If you're publishing your pages to a server that's running the Microsoft FrontPage Extensions, you'll find the Web Publishing Wizard to be exceptionally easy to use. Once you've set up the program with your server's information, you can quickly publish your Web pages. How quick? Simply drag them to an icon on your desktop, and they're published. You'll learn how to create such an icon later in this section, which begins with a discussion of gathering needed information and running the Web Publishing Wizard for the first time.

Getting the Information You Need

To run the Web Publishing Wizard, you will need the following information:

- **Connection method.** Ask your ISP which type of connection method you need to use to upload your pages for Web publishing. The Web Publishing Wizard can upload files by means of FTP, HTTP Post, or Secure Site Content Development (SS CD).
- **Server or FTP address.** You'll need the URL of the server.
- **Directory location or folder.** This is the actual subdirectory or folder name where your files are stored.

Running the Wizard

Once you've obtained the information you need, you can run the wizard; you'll upload your first files, and you'll also save server information so that uploading is easier in the future.

To run the Web Publishing Wizard, follow these steps:

1. On the Start menu, click Start, point to Programs, point to Accessories, point to Internet Tools, and click Web Publishing Wizard.

   You'll see the first page of the Web Publishing Wizard.

2 Click Next. You'll see the Web Publishing Wizard, shown here:

3 You can publish any of the following:

- **A Folder.** This option enables you to select an entire folder. You can publish subfolders too if you wish.

  To publish a folder, click Browse Folders, locate the folder you want to publish, and click OK. To include subfolders, check Include Subfolders.

- **A File.** This option enables you to publish just one file.

To publish a file, click Browse Files, locate and select the file you want to publish, and click OK.

4 Click Next. You'll see the next page, where you choose a Web server.

5 Click New. You'll see a page where you name the Web server.

6 In the Descriptive Name box, type a descriptive name for the server (one that will remind you which server you're using, like Server At Work).

7 Click Next. You'll see a page where you can type the URL and local directory.

8 In the URL or Internet address box, type the URL that your ISP gave you.

9 In the Local Directory box, type the local directory on your computer where you store the file or folder to be uploaded.

10 Click Next. The Web Publishing Wizard will attempt to connect to your server.

   You'll see the Network Password dialog box.

11 Type your user name and password, and click OK.

   You'll see a page informing you that the wizard is ready to start publishing your files.

12 Click Finish.

   You'll see a message confirming that the wizard has successfully uploaded your files.

NOTE

> If you see a message informing you that the Web Publishing Wizard needs more information in order to publish your file, call your ISP and ask for specific instructions on how to upload files to your server. (Chances are your ISP's server does not support the FrontPage Extensions.) Alternatively, try uploading your files via FTP, as described on the next page.

Publishing from Windows Explorer

You can publish your files quickly by using Windows Explorer, the file-management utility provided with Microsoft Windows 98.

To publish a file using Windows Explorer:

1 In Windows Explorer, select one or more files to upload.

2 Right-click the selection, point to Send To, and choose Web Publishing Wizard.

   You'll see the first page of the Web Publishing Wizard.

3 Click Next. You'll see the page where you select a Web server.

4 Choose the server you previously defined, and click Next.

   If you would like to define a new server, click Add, and follow the instructions to confirm the server information.

5 Click Next and Finish to publish your files.

Publishing Using Drag and Drop

To publish a folder or file using drag and drop:

1. Create a desktop shortcut to Web Publishing Wizard.
2. In Windows Explorer, select the folder or file you want to publish. Make sure the wizard shortcut is visible in the background.
3. Click the folder or file, and drag it to the shortcut.
4. You'll see the first page of the Web Publishing Wizard.
5. Click Next. You'll see the page where you select a Web server.
6. Choose the server you previously defined, and click Next.

   If you would like to define a new server, click Add, and follow the instructions to confirm the server information.
7. Click Next and Finish to publish your files.

Uploading Your Pages Using FTP

Like previous versions of Internet Explorer, Internet Explorer 5 can download files from public (anonymous) FTP servers. What's new with Internet Explorer 5 is the ability to *upload* files to FTP servers. When you log on to a remote FTP server, you can use your user name and password to access the remote computer's directories and files, which you can navigate using the familiar tools of Windows Explorer. With Internet Explorer 5, using FTP is as easy as using your own computer.

Accessing an FTP Server

To access an FTP server with Internet Explorer, do the following:

1. In the Address bar, type the following: ftp:// followed by your login name, a colon, your password, an "at" (@) sign, and the name of the server, as in the following example:

   ```
   ftp://myname:mypassword@ftp.myserver.net
   ```
2. Press Enter or click Go. You'll see the remote server's directories and files. Figure 21-1 shows an example.

TIP

Once you've accessed an FTP server using the procedure just described, save the site as a favorite. You can then choose the favorite instead of typing the FTP server's address. (You'll still have to type the password, though; it's not saved due to the security risks involved.)

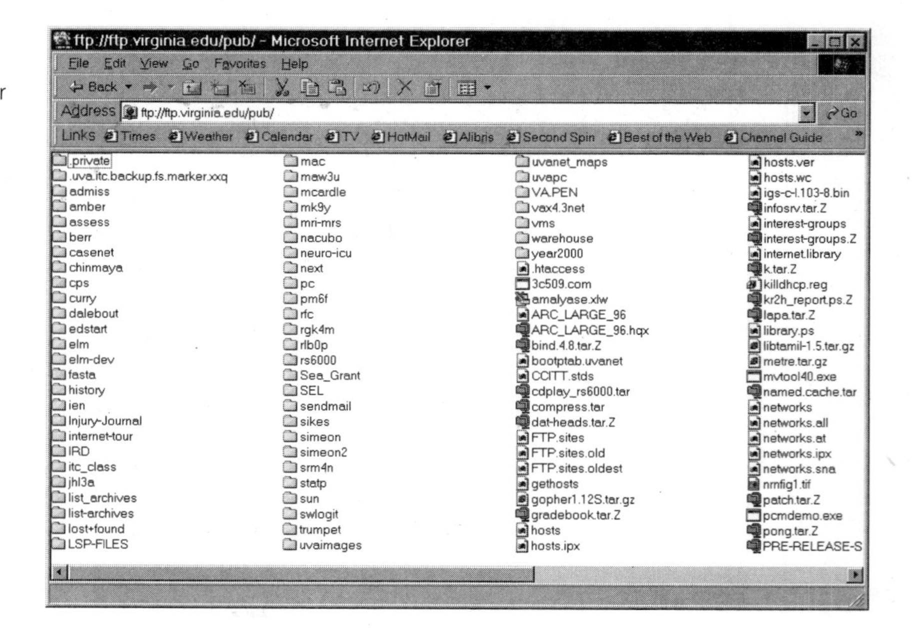

FIGURE 21-1.
With Internet Explorer 5, you can work with FTP files and folders the same way you work with files and folders on your own system.

Try accessing your FTP server this way. Type ftp:// followed by the server's Internet address (such as ftp://ftp.myserver.net), and click Go or press Enter. If the server requires a login name and password, you'll see an error message informing you that anonymous access isn't allowed. (Internet Explorer attempts to log in using anonymous access by default.) With many servers, you can supply the login name and password at this point by clicking File on the menu bar, and choosing Login As. You'll see a dialog box that prompts you for your user name and password. Supply this information, and click OK. Note that this technique won't work with certain types of FTP servers.

APPENDIX A

Installing Internet Explorer 5

When you install Internet Explorer 5, you can choose among two pre-configured sets of components: Minimal or Typical. You can also create a custom installation using the Minimal Install, which lets you select Internet Explorer 5 components. The next section, "Understanding What's Included," lists all the available components.

To install Internet Explorer 5, you can run the Setup program included on this book's CD-ROM, as explained in the section titled "Running Setup." After you've installed the software, you can install additional components in two ways:

- **Install on Demand.** If you access a Web page that requires an Internet Explorer component that you don't have installed, you'll see a dialog box asking whether you'd like to install the component. Click OK to install the needed component automatically.
- **Windows Update.** To install additional Internet Explorer components, you can use Windows Update, as explained in the section titled "Installing Components with Windows Update."

Understanding What's Included

Internet Explorer 5 consists of the Web browser, Internet Explorer, and many additional components, including communication tools, multimedia software, Web authoring components, support for multiple languages, and more. Table A-1 lists the available components.

When you install Internet Explorer, you can choose from the Minimal or Typical installation. Table A-2 indicates which components are included in each configuration.

If you plan to work with all or most of the applications discussed in this book, choose the Custom installation and select the full complement of options.

TABLE A-1. Components of Internet Explorer 5.

Component	Description
Internet Explorer 5 Components	
Internet Explorer 5 Web Browser	Installs just the browser; does not include offline browsing, help, Java, the Connection Wizard, or any other additional features.
Offline Browsing Pack	Enables you to save Web pages with all associated content (including graphics and scripts) for offline viewing.
Internet Explorer Help	Installs Help files for Internet Explorer 5.
Microsoft virtual machine	Enables you to display Java applets.
Internet Connection Wizard	Provides an easy way to connect to the Internet.
Internet Explorer Core Fonts	Installs a collection of TrueType fonts that are often used by Web authors. With these fonts installed, you can see the fonts in Web pages that have used them.
Dynamic HTML Data Binding	Enables Internet Explorer 5 to get information from databases and display this information within Web pages.
Internet Explorer Browsing Enhancements	Installs graphical FTP helper and activates font embedding support.

(continued)

TABLE A-1. *continued*

Component	Description
Communication Components	
NetMeeting	Enables you to participate in audio/video teleconferencing via the Internet.
Outlook Express	Installs a full-featured e-mail and news client.
Chat 2.5	Enables you to participate in text- or graphics-based chatting via Internet Relay Chat (IRC).
Multimedia Components	
Windows Media Player	Plays a wide variety of sound and video files that you can download from the Internet.
Windows Media Player Codecs	Windows Media Player support files for audio and video playback.
Media Player RealNetwork Support	Plays Real Audio and Real Video sounds and videos.
DirectAnimation	Enables you to display animations within Internet Explorer.
Vector Graphics Rendering (VML)	Enables you to view vector graphics embedded within Web pages.
AOL ART Image Format Support	For AOL users; provides support for the AOL ART format so that graphics using this format can be displayed within Internet Explorer.
Macromedia Shockwave	Installs support for high-quality multimedia presentations that are displayed within Internet Explorer.
Macromedia Flash Player	Installs support for high-quality animations that are displayed within Internet Explorer.
Web Authoring Components	
FrontPage Express	Enables you to create and edit Web pages without knowing HTML.
Web Publishing Wizard	Provides an easy-to-use means of uploading Web pages to your ISP's Web server.
Web Folders	Enables you to manage FrontPage servers the same way you manage files on your computer.
Visual Basic Scripting Support	Enables you to run VBScripts that some Web authors embed in their Web pages.
Additional Web Fonts	Installs additional TrueType fonts so that you can view these fonts within Web pages that use them.

(continued)

TABLE A-1. *continued*

Component	Description
Additional Components	
Wallet	Enables you to store your personal and credit-card information securely and to upload this information to secure Web shopping sites.
Multi-Language Support	
Language Auto-Selection	Enables Internet Explorer to detect a Web page's language automatically.
Japanese Text Display Support	Enables Internet Explorer to display Japanese text.
Japanese Text Input Support	Enables you to type Japanese text in forms input boxes within Internet Explorer.
Korean Text Display Support	Enables Internet Explorer to display Korean text.
Korean Text Input Support	Enables you to type Korean text in forms input boxes within Internet Explorer.
Pan-European Text Display Support	Enables Internet Explorer to display Central European languages, as well as Cyrillic, Greek, Turkish, and Baltic languages.
Chinese (Traditional) Text Display Support	Enables Internet Explorer to display Chinese text.
Chinese (Traditional) Text Input Support	Enables you to type Chinese text in forms input boxes within Internet Explorer.
Chinese (Simplified) Text Display Support	Enables Internet Explorer to display Chinese text.
Chinese (Simplified) Text Input Support	Enables you to type Chinese text in forms input boxes within Internet Explorer.
Vietnamese Text Display Support	Enables Internet Explorer to display Vietnamese text.
Hebrew Text Display Support	Enables Internet Explorer to display Hebrew text.
Arabic Text Display Support	Enables Internet Explorer to display Arabic text.
Thai Text Display Support	Enables Internet Explorer to display Thai text.

TABLE A-2. Components Installed with the Typical and Minimal Packages, and Custom Install Options.

Installation Package	Included Components
Minimal	Internet Explorer 5 Web browser Offline Browsing Pack Internet Connection Wizard Internet Explorer Help Visual Basic Scripting Support
Typical	Internet Explorer 5 Web browser Offline Browsing Pack Internet Explorer Help Internet Connection Wizard Internet Explorer Browsing Enhancement Outlook Express AOL ART Image Format Support Visual Basic Scripting Support Language Auto-Selection
Custom options	Internet Explorer 5 Web Browser Offline Browsing Pack Internet Explorer Help Microsoft virtual machine Internet Connection Wizard Internet Explorer Core Fonts Dynamic HTML Data Binding Internet Explorer Browsing Enhancements NetMeeting Outlook Express Chat 2.5 Windows Media Player Windows Media Player Codecs Media Player RealNetwork Support DirectAnimation Vector Graphics Rendering (VML) AOL ART Image Format Support Macromedia Shockwave Macromedia Flash Player FrontPage Express Web Publishing Wizard Web Folders Visual Basic Scripting Support Additional Web Fonts Wallet Language Auto-Selection

Running Setup

You can install Internet Explorer 5 and all the software in the Internet Explorer suite by running the CD-ROM included with this book.

To install Internet Explorer 5 on your computer, do the following:

1. **Important:** Close all the programs you're using.
2. Insert the CD packaged with this book in your CD-ROM drive. The Setup program will start automatically.
3. Select Install Internet Explorer 5 And Internet Tools.
4. The End User License dialog box appears. After reviewing the license, select the I Accept The Agreement option and click Next.
5. Follow the on-screen instructions until you see the following:

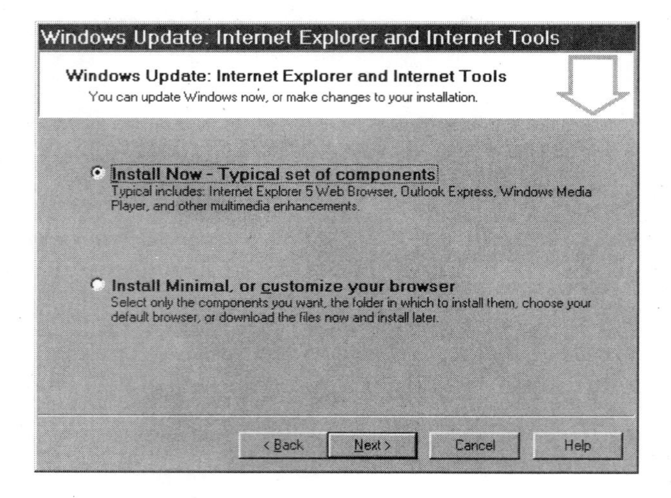

6. Do one of the following:
   - To install the Typical component set, click Install Now—Typical set of components, and skip to step 9.

     or

   - To install the Minimal set of components, or to select components yourself, click Install Minimal, Or Customize Your Browser, and go to the next step.
7. Click Next. You'll see the Component Options page, shown on the next page:

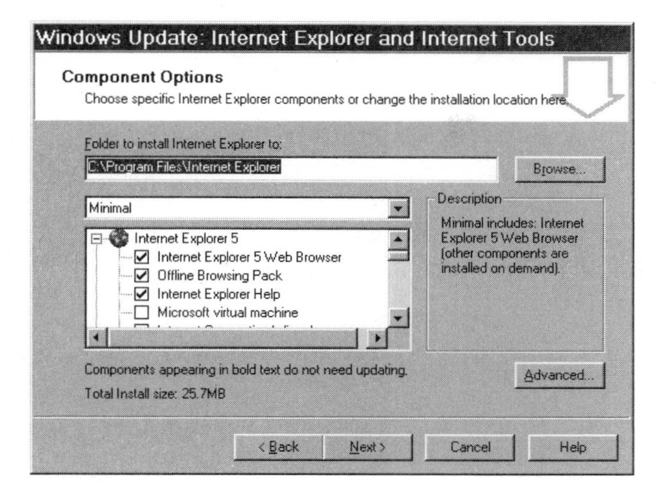

8 Select individual components from the component list.

9 To choose advanced options, click the Advanced button. You'll see the dialog box shown here:

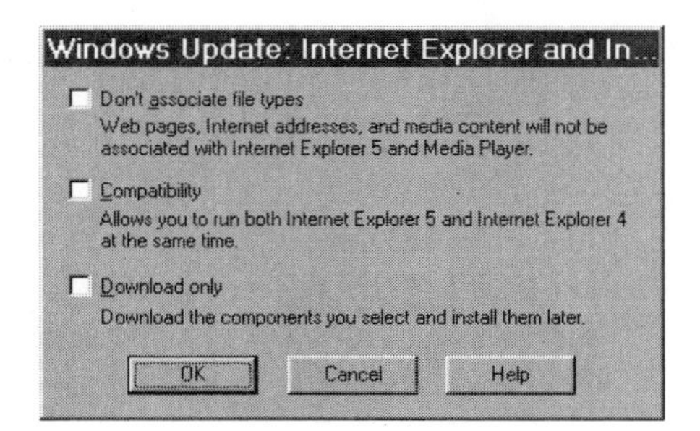

10 Choose any of the following:

Don't Associate File Types. Check this option only if you routinely use another browser and wish to continue doing so.

Compatibility. Check this option if you would like to run Internet Explorer 4 as well as Internet Explorer 5, or use applications that require Internet Explorer 4 to be installed.

Download Only. Check this option to download the selected components and install them later, instead of installing them immediately upon download.

11 Click Next, and follow the on-screen instructions to complete the installation of Internet Explorer 5.

Installing Components with Windows Update

Windows Update is a Web-accessible service that can check your Windows and Internet Explorer installation. It informs you which components you can add to your system and enables you to download these components from the Internet.

It's an excellent idea to visit Windows Update periodically. From time to time, Microsoft uses this service to distribute Critical Updates (updated software that resolves problems discovered in Windows or Internet Explorer).

To install additional components after running the Internet Explorer 5 Setup program, do the following:

1. Start Internet Explorer.
2. From the Tools menu, choose Windows Update. You'll see a dialog box asking you to install and run "Microsoft Windows Update Active Setup." Click Yes. Then you'll see a dialog box asking whether you would like Windows Update to determine which components have been installed on your system.
3. Click Yes. You'll see a Web page showing you updates that are available for your Windows system.
4. Scroll down to the area where Internet Explorer 5 and related tools are listed. If you don't see this area, you have installed all available Internet Explorer components.
5. Check the components you want to install.
6. Click Download.
7. Follow the on-screen instructions to download the components you selected.

Index

B

C

D

F

J

O

W

X

Y

Z

About the Author

Bryan Pfaffenberger, Ph.D., is a bestselling author of dozens of books on computer and Internet subjects, including Microsoft Internet Explorer (all the way back to the pre-frame version 1.0). He is a recognized expert on Web searching, Web page design, and Internet security and privacy issues. Reviewers and readers alike praise his works for explaining complex technical subjects with clarity, accessibility, and wit. He is currently Associate Professor of Technology, Culture, and Communication at the University of Virginia, where he has taught technical writing and the history of technology since 1985. When not involved in such serious activities, Pfaffenberger enjoys sailing his Catalina sailboat, Juliana, on Virginia's beautiful Rappahannock River and Chesapeake Bay. He lives in the countryside of Albemarle County, Virginia, with his family and a very spoiled cat.

Colophon

The manuscript for this book was prepared and submitted to Microsoft Press in electronic form. Text files were prepared using Microsoft Word 2000. Pages were composed using Adobe PageMaker 6.5 for the Macintosh, with text in Garamond and display type in Myriad. Composed pages were sent to the printer as electronic prepress files.

Production Services

Robert Kern,
Technical Publishing

Cover Designer

Tim Girvin Design, Inc.

Interior Graphic Designers

Kim Eggleston
Amy Peppler Adams,
designLab

Copy Editor

Ellen Fussell

Compositor

Lorraine B. Elder

Technical Editor

R. Allen Wyke

Proofreader

Jessica Ryan

Indexer

Timothy Griffin

MICROSOFT LICENSE AGREEMENT

Book Companion CD

IMPORTANT—READ CAREFULLY: This Microsoft End-User License Agreement ("EULA") is a legal agreement between you (either an individual or an entity) and Microsoft Corporation for the Microsoft product identified above, which includes computer software and may include associated media, printed materials, and "online" or electronic documentation ("SOFTWARE PRODUCT"). Any component included within the SOFTWARE PRODUCT that is accompanied by a separate End-User License Agreement shall be governed by such agreement and not the terms set forth below. By installing, copying, or otherwise using the SOFTWARE PRODUCT, you agree to be bound by the terms of this EULA. If you do not agree to the terms of this EULA, you are not authorized to install, copy, or otherwise use the SOFTWARE PRODUCT; you may, however, return the SOFTWARE PRODUCT, along with all printed materials and other items that form a part of the Microsoft product that includes the SOFTWARE PRODUCT, to the place you obtained them for a full refund.

SOFTWARE PRODUCT LICENSE

The SOFTWARE PRODUCT is protected by United States copyright laws and international copyright treaties, as well as other intellectual property laws and treaties. The SOFTWARE PRODUCT is licensed, not sold.

1. **GRANT OF LICENSE.** This EULA grants you the following rights:

   a. **Software Product.** You may install and use one copy of the SOFTWARE PRODUCT on a single computer. The primary user of the computer on which the SOFTWARE PRODUCT is installed may make a second copy for his or her exclusive use on a portable computer.

   b. **Storage/Network Use.** You may also store or install a copy of the SOFTWARE PRODUCT on a storage device, such as a network server, used only to install or run the SOFTWARE PRODUCT on your other computers over an internal network; however, you must acquire and dedicate a license for each separate computer on which the SOFTWARE PRODUCT is installed or run from the storage device. A license for the SOFTWARE PRODUCT may not be shared or used concurrently on different computers.

   c. **License Pak.** If you have acquired this EULA in a Microsoft License Pak, you may make the number of additional copies of the computer software portion of the SOFTWARE PRODUCT authorized on the printed copy of this EULA, and you may use each copy in the manner specified above. You are also entitled to make a corresponding number of secondary copies for portable computer use as specified above.

   d. **Sample Code.** Solely with respect to portions, if any, of the SOFTWARE PRODUCT that are identified within the SOFTWARE PRODUCT as sample code (the "SAMPLE CODE"):

      i. **Use and Modification.** Microsoft grants you the right to use and modify the source code version of the SAMPLE CODE, *provided* you comply with subsection (d)(iii) below. You may not distribute the SAMPLE CODE, or any modified version of the SAMPLE CODE, in source code form.

      ii. **Redistributable Files.** Provided you comply with subsection (d)(iii) below, Microsoft grants you a nonexclusive, royalty-free right to reproduce and distribute the object code version of the SAMPLE CODE and of any modified SAMPLE CODE, other than SAMPLE CODE, or any modified version thereof, designated as not redistributable in the Readme file that forms a part of the SOFTWARE PRODUCT (the "Non-Redistributable Sample Code"). All SAMPLE CODE other than the Non-Redistributable Sample Code is collectively referred to as the "REDISTRIBUTABLES."

      iii. **Redistribution Requirements.** If you redistribute the REDISTRIBUTABLES, you agree to: (i) distribute the REDISTRIBUTABLES in object code form only in conjunction with and as a part of your software application product; (ii) not use Microsoft's name, logo, or trademarks to market your software application product; (iii) include a valid copyright notice on your software application product; (iv) indemnify, hold harmless, and defend Microsoft from and against any claims or lawsuits, including attorney's fees, that arise or result from the use or distribution of your software application product; and (v) not permit further distribution of the REDISTRIBUTABLES by your end user. Contact Microsoft for the applicable royalties due and other licensing terms for all other uses and/or distribution of the REDISTRIBUTABLES.

2. **DESCRIPTION OF OTHER RIGHTS AND LIMITATIONS.**

   - **Limitations on Reverse Engineering, Decompilation, and Disassembly.** You may not reverse engineer, decompile, or disassemble the SOFTWARE PRODUCT, except and only to the extent that such activity is expressly permitted by applicable law notwithstanding this limitation.
   - **Separation of Components.** The SOFTWARE PRODUCT is licensed as a single product. Its component parts may not be separated for use on more than one computer.
   - **Rental.** You may not rent, lease, or lend the SOFTWARE PRODUCT.
   - **Support Services.** Microsoft may, but is not obligated to, provide you with support services related to the SOFTWARE PRODUCT ("Support Services"). Use of Support Services is governed by the Microsoft policies and programs described in the

user manual, in "online" documentation, and/or in other Microsoft-provided materials. Any supplemental software code provided to you as part of the Support Services shall be considered part of the SOFTWARE PRODUCT and subject to the terms and conditions of this EULA. With respect to technical information you provide to Microsoft as part of the Support Services, Microsoft may use such information for its business purposes, including for product support and development. Microsoft will not utilize such technical information in a form that personally identifies you.

- **Software Transfer.** You may permanently transfer all of your rights under this EULA, provided you retain no copies, you transfer all of the SOFTWARE PRODUCT (including all component parts, the media and printed materials, any upgrades, this EULA, and, if applicable, the Certificate of Authenticity), **and** the recipient agrees to the terms of this EULA.
- **Termination.** Without prejudice to any other rights, Microsoft may terminate this EULA if you fail to comply with the terms and conditions of this EULA. In such event, you must destroy all copies of the SOFTWARE PRODUCT and all of its component parts.

3. **COPYRIGHT.** All title and copyrights in and to the SOFTWARE PRODUCT (including but not limited to any images, photographs, animations, video, audio, music, text, SAMPLE CODE, REDISTRIBUTABLES, and "applets" incorporated into the SOFTWARE PRODUCT) and any copies of the SOFTWARE PRODUCT are owned by Microsoft or its suppliers. The SOFTWARE PRODUCT is protected by copyright laws and international treaty provisions. Therefore, you must treat the SOFTWARE PRODUCT like any other copyrighted material **except** that you may install the SOFTWARE PRODUCT on a single computer provided you keep the original solely for backup or archival purposes. You may not copy the printed materials accompanying the SOFTWARE PRODUCT.

4. **U.S. GOVERNMENT RESTRICTED RIGHTS.** The SOFTWARE PRODUCT and documentation are provided with RESTRICTED RIGHTS. Use, duplication, or disclosure by the Government is subject to restrictions as set forth in subparagraph (c)(1)(ii) of the Rights in Technical Data and Computer Software clause at DFARS 252.227-7013 or subparagraphs (c)(1) and (2) of the Commercial Computer Software—Restricted Rights at 48 CFR 52.227-19, as applicable. Manufacturer is Microsoft Corporation/One Microsoft Way/Redmond, WA 98052-6399.

5. **EXPORT RESTRICTIONS.** You agree that you will not export or re-export the SOFTWARE PRODUCT, any part thereof, or any process or service that is the direct product of the SOFTWARE PRODUCT (the foregoing collectively referred to as the "Restricted Components"), to any country, person, entity, or end user subject to U.S. export restrictions. You specifically agree not to export or re-export any of the Restricted Components (i) to any country to which the U.S. has embargoed or restricted the export of goods or services, which currently include, but are not necessarily limited to, Cuba, Iran, Iraq, Libya, North Korea, Sudan, and Syria, or to any national of any such country, wherever located, who intends to transmit or transport the Restricted Components back to such country; (ii) to any end user who you know or have reason to know will utilize the Restricted Components in the design, development, or production of nuclear, chemical, or biological weapons; or (iii) to any end user who has been prohibited from participating in U.S. export transactions by any federal agency of the U.S. government. You warrant and represent that neither the BXA nor any other U.S. federal agency has suspended, revoked, or denied your export privileges.

DISCLAIMER OF WARRANTY

NO WARRANTIES OR CONDITIONS. MICROSOFT EXPRESSLY DISCLAIMS ANY WARRANTY OR CONDITION FOR THE SOFTWARE PRODUCT. THE SOFTWARE PRODUCT AND ANY RELATED DOCUMENTATION ARE PROVIDED "AS IS" WITHOUT WARRANTY OR CONDITION OF ANY KIND, EITHER EXPRESS OR IMPLIED, INCLUDING, WITHOUT LIMITATION, THE IMPLIED WARRANTIES OF MERCHANTABILITY, FITNESS FOR A PARTICULAR PURPOSE, OR NONINFRINGEMENT. THE ENTIRE RISK ARISING OUT OF USE OR PERFORMANCE OF THE SOFTWARE PRODUCT REMAINS WITH YOU.

LIMITATION OF LIABILITY. TO THE MAXIMUM EXTENT PERMITTED BY APPLICABLE LAW, IN NO EVENT SHALL MICROSOFT OR ITS SUPPLIERS BE LIABLE FOR ANY SPECIAL, INCIDENTAL, INDIRECT, OR CONSEQUENTIAL DAMAGES WHATSOEVER (INCLUDING, WITHOUT LIMITATION, DAMAGES FOR LOSS OF BUSINESS PROFITS, BUSINESS INTERRUPTION, LOSS OF BUSINESS INFORMATION, OR ANY OTHER PECUNIARY LOSS) ARISING OUT OF THE USE OF OR INABILITY TO USE THE SOFTWARE PRODUCT OR THE PROVISION OF OR FAILURE TO PROVIDE SUPPORT SERVICES, EVEN IF MICROSOFT HAS BEEN ADVISED OF THE POSSIBILITY OF SUCH DAMAGES. IN ANY CASE, MICROSOFT'S ENTIRE LIABILITY UNDER ANY PROVISION OF THIS EULA SHALL BE LIMITED TO THE GREATER OF THE AMOUNT ACTUALLY PAID BY YOU FOR THE SOFTWARE PRODUCT OR US$5.00; PROVIDED, HOWEVER, IF YOU HAVE ENTERED INTO A MICROSOFT SUPPORT SERVICES AGREEMENT, MICROSOFT'S ENTIRE LIABILITY REGARDING SUPPORT SERVICES SHALL BE GOVERNED BY THE TERMS OF THAT AGREEMENT. BECAUSE SOME STATES AND JURISDICTIONS DO NOT ALLOW THE EXCLUSION OR LIMITATION OF LIABILITY, THE ABOVE LIMITATION MAY NOT APPLY TO YOU.

MISCELLANEOUS

This EULA is governed by the laws of the State of Washington USA, except and only to the extent that applicable law mandates governing law of a different jurisdiction.

Should you have any questions concerning this EULA, or if you desire to contact Microsoft for any reason, please contact the Microsoft subsidiary serving your country, or write: Microsoft Sales Information Center/One Microsoft Way/Redmond, WA 98052-6399.

PN 097-0002296

Register Today!

Return this
Running Microsoft® Internet Explorer 5
registration card today

OWNER REGISTRATION CARD **1-57231-949-6**

Running Microsoft® Internet Explorer 5

FIRST NAME MIDDLE INITIAL LAST NAME

INSTITUTION OR COMPANY NAME

ADDRESS

CITY STATE ZIP

( )

E-MAIL ADDRESS PHONE NUMBER

U.S. and Canada addresses only. Fill in information above and mail postage-free.
Please mail only the bottom half of this page.

start
faster
go
farther